SHAKESPEARE SURVEY
75

Othello

SHAKESPEARE SURVEY
ADVISORY BOARD

JONATHAN BATE
DAVID STERLING BROWN
MARK THORNTON BURNETT
MARGRETA DE GRAZIA
CARLA DELLA GATTA
MICHAEL DOBSON
TON HOENSELAARS
PETER HOLLAND
JOHN JOWETT

HESTER LEES-JEFFRIES
VANESSA LIM
HARRY R. MCCARTHY
LUCY MUNRO
CLAUDIA OLK
LENA COWEN ORLIN
REIKO OYA
SIMON PALFREY
AYANNA THOMPSON

Assistant to the Editor KATIE MENNIS

(1) *Shakespeare and his Stage*
(2) *Shakespearian Production*
(3) *The Man and the Writer*
(4) *Interpretation*
(5) *Textual Criticism*
(6) *The Histories*
(7) *Style and Language*
(8) *The Comedies*
(9) *Hamlet*
(10) *The Roman Plays*
(11) *The Last Plays (with an index to Surveys 1–10)*
(12) *The Elizabethan Theatre*
(13) *King Lear*
(14) *Shakespeare and his Contemporaries*
(15) *The Poems and Music*
(16) *Shakespeare in the Modern World*
(17) *Shakespeare in his Own Age*
(18) *Shakespeare Then Till Now*
(19) *Macbeth*
(20) *Shakespearian and Other Tragedy*
(21) *Othello (with an index to Surveys 11–20)*
(22) *Aspects of Shakespearian Comedy*
(23) *Shakespeare's Language*
(24) *Shakespeare: Theatre Poet*
(25) *Shakespeare's Problem Plays*
(26) *Shakespeare's Jacobean Tragedies*
(27) *Shakespeare's Early Tragedies*
(28) *Shakespeare and the Ideas of his Time*
(29) *Shakespeare's Last Plays*
(30) *Henry IV to Hamlet*
(31) *Shakespeare and the Classical World (with an index to Surveys 21–30)*
(32) *The Middle Comedies*
(33) *King Lear*
(34) *Characterization in Shakespeare*
(35) *Shakespeare in the Nineteenth Century*
(36) *Shakespeare in the Twentieth Century*
(37) *Shakespeare's Earlier Comedies*
(38) *Shakespeare and History*
(39) *Shakespeare on Film and Television*
(40) *Current Approaches to Shakespeare through Language, Text and Theatre*
(41) *Shakespearian Stages and Staging (with an index to Surveys 31–40)*
(42) *Shakespeare and the Elizabethans*
(43) *The Tempest and After*
(44) *Shakespeare and Politics*
(45) *Hamlet and its Afterlife*
(46) *Shakespeare and Sexuality*
(47) *Playing Places for Shakespeare*
(48) *Shakespeare and Cultural Exchange*
(49) *Romeo and Juliet and its Afterlife*
(50) *Shakespeare and Language*
(51) *Shakespeare in the Eighteenth Century (with an index to Surveys 41–50)*
(52) *Shakespeare and the Globe*
(53) *Shakespeare and Narrative*
(54) *Shakespeare and Religions*
(55) *King Lear and its Afterlife*
(56) *Shakespeare and Comedy*
(57) *Macbeth and its Afterlife*
(58) *Writing About Shakespeare*
(59) *Editing Shakespeare*
(60) *Theatres for Shakespeare*
(61) *Shakespeare, Sound and Screen*
(62) *Close Encounters with Shakespeare's Text*
(63) *Shakespeare's English Histories and their Afterlives*
(64) *Shakespeare as Cultural Catalyst*
(65) *A Midsummer Night's Dream*
(66) *Working with Shakespeare*
(67) *Shakespeare's Collaborative Work*
(68) *Shakespeare, Origins and Originality*
(69) *Shakespeare and Rome*
(70) *Creating Shakespeare*
(71) *Re-Creating Shakespeare*
(72) *Shakespeare and War*
(73) *Shakespeare and the City*
(74) *Shakespeare and Education*
(75) *Othello*

Shakespeare Survey: A Sixty-Year Cumulative Index
Aspects of Macbeth
Aspects of Othello
Aspects of Hamlet
Aspects of King Lear
Aspects of Shakespeare's 'Problem Plays'

SHAKESPEARE SURVEY

75

Othello

EDITED BY

EMMA SMITH

CAMBRIDGE
UNIVERSITY PRESS

Shaftesbury Road, Cambridge CB2 8EA, United Kingdom

One Liberty Plaza, 20th Floor, New York, NY 10006, USA

477 Williamstown Road, Port Melbourne, VIC 3207, Australia

314–321, 3rd Floor, Plot 3, Splendor Forum, Jasola District Centre,
New Delhi – 110025, India

103 Penang Road, #05–06/07, Visioncrest Commercial, Singapore 238467

Cambridge University Press is part of the University of Cambridge.

It furthers the University's mission by disseminating knowledge in the pursuit of
education, learning and research at the highest international levels of excellence.

www.cambridge.org
Information on this title: www.cambridge.org/9781009245821
DOI: 10.1017/9781009245845

© Cambridge University Press 2022

This publication is in copyright. Subject to statutory exception
and to the provisions of relevant collective licensing agreements,
no reproduction of any part may take place without the written
permission of Cambridge University Press.

First published 2022

Printed in the United Kingdom by TJ Books Limited, Padstow Cornwall

A catalogue record for this publication is available from the British Library.

ISBN 978-1-009-24582-1 Hardback

Cambridge University Press has no responsibility for the persistence or accuracy of
URLs for external or third-party internet websites referred to in this publication
and does not guarantee that any content on such websites is, or will remain,
accurate or appropriate.

EDITOR'S NOTE

Shakespeare Survey 75 has as its theme '*Othello*'. Volume 76 will take up the theme of the International Shakespeare Conference, to be held in Stratford-upon-Avon in 2022, 'Shakespeare, the Virtual and the Digital': submissions on this topic are warmly encouraged and should be sent as email attachments to the editor at emma.smith@hertford.ox.ac.uk. The deadline is 1 September 2022. The following issue, 77, will be on Shakespeare's poetry, with a deadline of 1 September 2023. There is also limited space in each issue for articles not on the theme. The Advisory Board is particularly keen to encourage proposals for small clusters of 3–5 articles on a Shakespearian theme, topic or approach. These can be submitted to the editor at any time in the year. All submissions are read by the editor and by at least one member of the Advisory Board. We warmly welcome both early-career and more established scholars to consider *Survey* as a venue for their work.

Part of *Survey*'s distinctiveness is its reviews. Review copies, including article offprints, should be addressed to the editor at Hertford College, Oxford OX1 3BW: our reviewers inevitably have to exercise some selection about what they cover. On that note, I am most grateful to Russell Jackson and Jane Kingsley-Smith, who step down as *Survey* reviewers with their contributions to the current issue.

EMMA SMITH

CONTRIBUTORS

RICHARD ASHBY, *King's College London*
LISA M. BARKSDALE-SHAW, *Arizona State University*
MARK THORNTON BURNETT, *Queen's University Belfast*
PATRICIA A. CAHILL, *Emory University*
ZAINAB S. CHEEMA, *Florida Gulf Coast University*
MOLLY CLARK, *Merton College, Oxford*
EMMA DEPLEDGE, *University of Neuchâtel*
JENNIFER J. EDWARDS, *The Queen's College, Oxford*
JOSHUA R. HELD, *Trinity International University*
JONATHAN Y. H. HUI, *Nanyang Technological University Singapore*
RUSSELL JACKSON, *University of Birmingham*
MARGARET JANE KIDNIE, *University of Western Ontario*
JANE KINGSLEY-SMITH, *University of Roehampton*
PETER KIRWAN, *University of Nottingham*
JEREMY LOPEZ, *University of Toronto*
ABHIRUP MASCHARAK, *Jadavpur University Kolkata*
RICHARD MEEK, *University of Hull*
KATIE MENNIS, *Somerville College, Oxford*
JOHN-MARK PHILO, *The University of East Anglia*
ROBERT B. PIERCE, *Oberlin College*
LOIS POTTER, *University of Delaware*
JAMES SHAW, *Bodleian Library Oxford*
IMAN SHEEHA, *Brunel University London*
NICOLE SHERIKO, *Christ's College, University of Cambridge*
BAILEY SINCOX, *Harvard University*
ANDREA SMITH, *University of East Anglia*
YIK LING YONG, *Nanyang Technological University Singapore*
AGNIESZKA ŻUKOWSKA, *University of Gdańsk*

CONTENTS

List of Illustrations *page* ix

MARK THORNTON BURNETT	Understanding *Iago*, an Italian Film Adaptation of *Othello*: Clientelism, Corruption, Politics	1
ABHIRUP MASCHARAK	Circumventing Marginality: The Curious Case of India's *Othello* Screen Adaptations	15
PATRICIA A. CAHILL	Othello's Kin: Legacy, Belonging and *The Fortunes of the Moor*	32
ANDREA SMITH	'More Fair than Black': Othellos on British Radio	49
AGNIESZKA ŻUKOWSKA	'This Fair Paper': *Othello* and the Artists' Book	60
YIK LING YONG	*Othello*: A Dialogue with the Built Environment	73
IMAN SHEEHA	'[A] Maid Called Barbary': *Othello*, Moorish Maidservants and the Black Presence in Early Modern England	89
LISA M. BARKSDALE-SHAW	'The Moor's Abused by Some Most Villainous Knave, Some Base Notorious Knave, Some Scurvy Fellow': Legal Spaces, Racial Trauma and Shakespeare's *The Tragedy of Othello, the Moor of Venice*	103
JOHN-MARK PHILO	Ben Jonson's *Sejanus* and Shakespeare's *Othello*: Two Plays Performed by the King's Men in 1603	122
NICOLE SHERIKO	Iago and the Clown: Disassembling the Vice in *Othello*	137
JOSHUA R. HELD	Pitying Desdemona in Folio *Othello*: Race, Gender and the Willow Song	148
JEREMY LOPEZ	Desdemona's Honest Friend	166
JENNIFER J. EDWARDS	Suffering Ecstasy: *Othello* and the Drama of Displacement	180
RICHARD MEEK	Othello's Sympathies: Emotion, Agency and Identification	194
MARGARET JANE KIDNIE	Warning the Stage: Shakespeare's Mid-Scene Entrance Conventions	208
BAILEY SINCOX	Looking for Perdita in Ali Smith's *Summer*	229
ZAINAB S. CHEEMA	Grafted to the Moor: Anglo-Spanish Dynastic Marriage and Miscegenated Whiteness in *The Winter's Tale*	240
MOLLY CLARK	Rhyme, History and Memory in *A Mirror for Magistrates* and *Henry VI*	256

CONTENTS

KATIE MENNIS	'Bad' Love Lyrics and Poetic Hypocrisy from Gascoigne to Benson's Shakespeare	265
ROBERT B. PIERCE	Viola's Telemachy	281
JONATHAN Y. H. HUI	New Analogical Evidence for *Cymbeline*'s Folkloric Composition in the Medieval Icelandic *Ála flekks saga*	287
RICHARD ASHBY	'But When Extremities Speak': Harley Granville-Barker, *Coriolanus*, the World Wars and the State of Exception	313
	Shakespeare Performances in England, 2021	
LOIS POTTER	London Productions	
PETER KIRWAN	Productions Outside London	342
JAMES SHAW	Professional Shakespeare Productions in the British Isles, January-December 2020	357

The Year's Contribution to Shakespeare Studies   361
  1 Critical Studies *reviewed by* JANE KINGSLEY-SMITH   361
  2 Performance *reviewed by* RUSSELL JACKSON   375
  3 Editions and Textual Studies *reviewed by* EMMA DEPLEDGE   384

Abstracts of Articles in *Shakespeare Survey* 75   399
Index   403

ILLUSTRATIONS

1. Postcard invitation, accompanying the DVD release of *Iago* (dir. Volfango di Biasi, 2009), to enter a competition to win a romantic break for two in Venice. Medusa Film / author collection. *page* 4
2. The DVD cover of *Iago* (dir. Volfango di Biasi, 2009) shows Iago (Nicolas Vaporidis) and Desdemona (Laura Chiatti) locked in an exploratory embrace. Medusa Film / author collection. 13
3. Kate Cronin, *A Jealousy So Strong, That Judgement Cannot Cure*. Image courtesy of the artist. 61
4. Kate Cronin, *A Jealousy So Strong, That Judgement Cannot Cure*. Image courtesy of the artist. 65
5. Borbonesa, *Othello: A Bestiary – With Floral Additions*, I.3. Image courtesy of the artists; photo by Lee Shearman. 65
6. Borbonesa, *Othello: A Bestiary – With Floral Additions*, III.4–IV.1. Image courtesy of the artists; photo by Lee Shearman. 67
7. Emily Martin, *Desdemona, In Her Own Words*, act 3: Why. Image courtesy of the artist. 71
8. Emily Martin, *Desdemona, In Her Own Words*, detail of the word magnets. Image courtesy of the artist. 72
9. Detail from Q2 *Hamlet* (1604–5), sig. N2. STC 22276, Folger Shakespeare Library. Used by permission of the Folger Shakespeare Library under a Creative Commons Attribution – ShareAlike 4.0 International Licence. 209
10. Detail from Q2 *Hamlet* (1604–5), sig. L3 v. STC 22276, Folger Shakespeare Library. Used by permission of the Folger Shakespeare Library under a Creative Commons Attribution – ShareAlike 4.0 International Licence. 209
11. Detail from F *Hamlet* (1623), sig. pp6 r, TLN 3566–87. STC 22273 F.1 no. 68, Folger Shakespeare Library. Used by permission of the Folger Shakespeare Library under a Creative Commons Attribution – ShareAlike 4.0 International Licence. 210
12. Detail from Nathan Field, John Fletcher and Philip Massinger, with Robert Daborne, *The Honest Man's Fortune* (8 February 1624), MS Dyce 25.F.9, fol. 14b, © Victoria and Albert Museum, London. 216
13. Barker cites the strike on Pearl Harbor in *Coriolanus* 1.2. © Image courtesy of Senate House Library, University of London. 317
14. Barker calls Cominius an appeaser in *Coriolanus* 3.1. © Image courtesy of Senate House Library, University of London. 325
15. *Romeo and Juliet*, Shakespeare's Globe. Alfred Enoch as Romeo. © Marc Brenner. 335
16. *Twelfth Night*, Shakespeare's Globe. Michelle Terry as Viola and Ciarán O'Brien as Sebastian. © Marc Brenner. 336
17. Hattie Ladbury as the Duke, in *Measure for Measure*, Sam Wanamaker Playhouse. © Helen Murray. 340

LIST OF ILLUSTRATIONS

18. The Handlebards, *Romeo and Juliet*, publicity art. Photograph by Rah Petherbridge.   343
19. Hermione (Kemi-Bo Jacobs) on trial in *The Winter's Tale*, dir. Erica Whyman. Photograph by Topher McGrillis, © RSC.   347
20. The Lydia & Manfred Gorvy Garden Theatre. Photograph by Pete Le May, © RSC.   349
21. Adrianna (Hedydd Dylan) in *The Comedy of Errors*, dir. Phillip Breen. Photograph by Pete Le May, © RSC.   350
22. The ensemble in *Henry VI, Part One Open Rehearsal Project*, dir. Gregory Doran and Owen Horsley. Photograph by Ellie Kurtz, © RSC.   353
23. Talbot and his men capture the Countess of Auvergne in *Henry VI, Part One Open Rehearsal Project*, dir. Gregory Doran and Owen Horsley. Photograph by Ellie Kurtz, © RSC.   355

UNDERSTANDING *IAGO*, AN ITALIAN FILM ADAPTATION OF *OTHELLO*: CLIENTELISM, CORRUPTION, POLITICS

MARK THORNTON BURNETT

'Liberamente inspirati dell' "OTELLO" di WILLIAM SHAKESPEARE' ('loosely based on William Shakespeare's *Othello*'), according to the closing credits, *Iago* (dir. Volfango di Biasi, 2009) was released on 27 February 2009 (in Italy only). While the film takes *Othello* as its source of stimulation, it reimagines the play in several key respects. It features a lengthy 'preface', taking some considerable time (over half of the film's length) to set up the drama of act 1. Approximating iambic pentameter with a demotic Italian vernacular, *Iago* then proceeds to follow the plot and structure of *Othello* quite closely. But completing the film's adaptive excess is an 'additional act': this 'extra' screen time shifts the anticipated ending of *Othello* and delivers a narrative attendant upon, and emerging from, the Shakespearian conclusions of act 5.

Perhaps most distinctively, *Iago* offers us Iago's backstory rather than Othello's, envisioning the lieutenant 'of exceeding honesty' as the wronged hero of the piece (*Othello*, 3.3.262). In a symptomatic scene, Brabanzio (Gabriele Lavia), the Rector of the Faculty of Architecture at the University of Venice (and father to the beautiful Desdemona (Laura Chiatti)), luxuriates in his impeccably appointed office. Velvet-suited, and sporting a gold earring and dark cravat, he simultaneously suggests a Doge, a headmaster and a supercilious *paterfamilias*. As befits his high-ranking position, the gorgeous office overlooks a sun-dappled courtyard in which manicured hedges frame marble statuary, a fountain spurts from a grotto and trimmed trees sway gently in the breeze. Here to protest is Iago (Nicolas Vaporidis), the Faculty's most brilliant – but impoverished – student. Thanks to a backroom deal dreamed up by Brabanzio and world-renowned architect Philippe Moreau (Mamadou Dioume), Otello (Aurélien Gaya), Moreau's son, Black and hailing from Paris, has been parachuted in to lead the Faculty's entry to the city's Biennale event. Even though Iago is doing all the work, he remains an uncredited assistant. 'Otello ... hasn't got a grasp ... I've had to do everything', Iago complains. Brabanzio's reply highlights his own imbrication in nepotism and corruption: 'I value your discretion ... the university senate made the ... choice ... we'd have to make a big fuss ... Our profession is complicated ... it's politics.' His unwillingness to countenance Iago's complaint, and the obvious cultivation of clientelism, speak to what historian Paul Ginsborg identifies in contemporary Italy as a 'patrimonialism' undergirded by 'fierce acquisitive instincts ... family ambitions and clan loyalties'.[1] Disillusioned at the revelation of a 'politics' that is denying him his due, Iago leaves the Venetian office with an even greater sense of embitterment.

Iago joins a long list of Shakespeare-inspired Italian films, including *Che cosa sonole le nuvole?* ('What are Clouds For?', dir. Pier Paulo Pasolini, 1967), *Un Ameleto di meno* ('One Hamlet More',

---

[1] Paul Ginsborg, *Silvio Berlusconi: Television, Power and Patrimony* (London and New York, 2004), p. 6.

dir. Carmelo Bene, 1972), *Sud side stori* ('South Side Story', dir. Roberta Torre, 2000), *Cesare deve morire* ('Caesar Must Die', dir. Paolo and Vittoria Taviani, 2012) and *La stoffa dei sogni* ('The Stuff of Dreams', dir. Gianfranco Cabiddu, 2016) – adaptations of *Othello*, *Hamlet*, *Romeo and Juliet*, *Julius Caesar* and *The Tempest*, respectively.[2] To this list must be added *The Taming of the Shrew* (dir. Franco Zeffirelli, 1967) and *Romeo and Juliet* (dir. Franco Zeffirelli, 1968), which are forever associated with Italy thanks to ravishing cinematography and the *auteur* status of their director, and which, in their day, set new standards in terms of orientation, casting and aesthetics.[3] Generalizations in such a wide-ranging generic sample are hazardous, but it is possible to maintain that the Italian Shakespeare film is marked by a suggestive deployment of natural and urban locations, a critical privileging of regional and class rivalries and an absorption in political legacies. In this sense, *Iago* is true to form. At the same time, *Iago* follows in the footsteps of, and takes some of its energy from, its immediate 'Venice-set film' forebears, including *Othello* (dir. Oliver Parker, 1995) and *William Shakespeare's 'The Merchant of Venice'* (dir. Michael Radford, 2004), imitating the studied use of setting but moving away from the early modern period by situating the story firmly in the contemporary. The alliance with the contemporary – action in the here and now unfolds against the period backdrop of Venice – signals one of the ways in which, while linked to other films, *Iago* is simultaneously something of a curiosity in the history of Italian cinema's engagement with Shakespeare. In a singular combination, the film endorses a variety of genres and influences (it functions as both 'teen film' and 'Venice-set film'), looking outwards and inwards in its discovery of disappointment, excess and post-millennial Italian angst. Operating thus, it brings into play some of the themes and trends of what has been termed the 'Berlusconi era' (named after the politician and media baron Silvio Berlusconi, prime minister of Italy in a series of four governments during 1994–1995, 2001–2006 and 2008–2011).[4] *Iago* takes on additional complexions of meaning, this article argues, in the light of accusations surrounding Berlusconi during his tenure in power, including collusion, conflict of interest, fraud and abuse of power.[5]

The film's Italian identifiers are easy to spot. As a 'Venice-set film', understood by film critics Michael Pigott and Anna Sloan as a genre that prioritizes an 'urban-marine playground' of 'picturesque beauty' and 'moral depravity', *Iago* announces a subscription to authentic settings (apart from some sequences in Castelfranco Veneto, the film was shot entirely in Venice itself) and a *mise en scène* comprised of murky waterways, shimmering palazzos, sun-baked squares and ornately arched bridges.[6] As a 'teen film' conceptualized around architecture students, *Iago* makes of

---

[2] For discussion of these adaptations, see Mark Thornton Burnett, *'Hamlet' and World Cinema* (Cambridge, 2019), pp. 41–4; Martin Butler, 'A *Tempest* between Naples and Sardinia: Gianfranco Cabiddu's *La stoffa dei sogni*', *Shakespeare Bulletin* 37 (2019), 209–340; Maurizio Calbi, *Spectral Shakespeares: Media Adaptations in the Twenty-First Century* (New York, 2013), pp. 81–98; Sonia Massai, 'Subjection and redemption in Pasolini's *Othello*', in *Worldwide Shakespeares: Local Appropriations in Film and Performance*, ed. Sonia Massai (New York and London, 2005), pp. 95–103; Mariangela Tempera, 'Shakespeare behind Italian bars: the Rebibbia Project, *The Tempest*, and *Caesar Must Die*', in *Shakespeare, Italy, and Transnational Exchange: Early Modern to Present*, ed. Enza De Francisci and Chris Stamatakis (New York and London, 2017), pp. 265–76.

[3] See Mark Thornton Burnett, Courtney Lehmann, Marguerite Rippy and Ramona Wray, *Great Shakespeareans: Welles, Kurosawa, Kozintsev, Zeffirelli* (London and New York, 2013), pp. 141–86.

[4] John Foot, *Modern Italy*, 2nd ed. (Basingstoke and New York, 2014), p. 15.

[5] Daniele Albertazzi and Nina Rothenburg, 'Introduction: this tide is not for turning', in *Resisting the Tide: Cultures of Opposition under Berlusconi (2001–06)*, ed. Daniele Albertazzi, Clodagh Brook, Charlotte Ross and Nina Rothenburg (New York and London, 2009), pp. 1–16, esp. p. 2; Maria Elisa Montironi, 'Narrating and unravelling Italian crises through Shakespeare (2000–2016)', in *Shakespeare and Crisis: One Hundred Years of Italian Narratives*, ed. Silvia Bigliazzi (Amsterdam and Philadelphia, 2020), pp. 245–75, esp. p. 260.

[6] Michael Pigott, 'Introduction', in *World Film Locations: Venice*, ed. Michael Pigott (Bristol, 2013), p. 5; Anna Sloan, 'The tourist gaze', in *World Film Locations: Venice*, ed. Pigott, pp. 8–9.

Venice a campus. It takes the imprint of *William Shakespeare's 'Romeo + Juliet'* (dir. Baz Luhrmann, 1996) and related high-school Shakespeare films such as *'O'* (dir. Tim Blake Nelson, 2001), detailing the intrigues and passions of its quintessentially youthful cast. In this way, it makes youthful the archetypal 'Venice-set film' while prioritizing the city's association with romance.[7] (The DVD version of the film released in Italy included a postcard invitation to enter a competition – 'Venice in Love' – to win a romantic weekend for two at the Palazzo Priuli, San Marco; see Figure 1).

In keeping with a film aesthetic that makes much of appearances and possessions – costume credits for *Iago* reference Bulgari, Chanel, Dolce & Gabbana and Gucci – the adaptation spotlights the trappings of wealth and entitlement as part of its rationale. The fashion-shoot elements of this *Othello* thus serve both market-driven and narrative-centred purposes. Venice, as *Iago* represents it, as well as signifying a wonderfully evocative series of period structures and places, is something of a catwalk – a luxury location populated by equally luxurious people and consumables. Except for Iago, who, in a sartorial illustration of his downtrodden position and as an index of his distance from haute couture, is shot throughout in shabby dark jacket and trousers, most of the film's players are photographed to show off in a manner akin to a *Vogue* editorial. Furthermore, as part of a repurposing of the play's characters and relationships, the lovelorn longings of Roderigo (Lorenzo Gleijeses) in *Othello* are displaced in the film on to Iago, while the homoeroticism of the Iago–Othello relationship is freshly located in the Roderigo character. Roderigo, brother in the film to Bianca (Luana Rossetti), is played as gay and camp and dressed in open shirt, necklace, outrageous collars, sequins, and puce coloured jackets. In *Iago*, Iago and Emilia (Giulia Steigerwalt) are friends rather than husband and wife, with Emilia's concomitantly extended role registered in her dominatrix-style black leather outfit, furs, studded bodice and chains (fashion as bondage). Perhaps, most strikingly, Otello and Cassio (Fabio Ghidoni) in *Iago* are cousins: their new relation both underscores the praxes of nepotism that the film makes its partial subject (one leads, and the other is second assistant on, the team entering the Biennale event) and points up defining monetary accoutrements. As Drake Stutesman notes, in what could be a summation of the film's fashion-aware preferences, 'fashion is the sweep of a Look (a lifestyle)' or 'a message'.[8] While Cassio is arresting in his casually draped and costly long scarves, Otello makes for a socially dominant impression with a gym-toned physique accentuated by tight-fitting cashmere top and polo shirts and accessorized by a crucial property – a pristine white handkerchief.

As Shakespeare adaptation, *Iago* has only been occasionally considered in Shakespeare on film criticism, possibly because it was not internationally distributed and fared unimpressively at the Italian box-office.[9] Yet recent developments in adaptation studies and discussion in critical race theory make the film ripe for analysis. In what follows, I argue for a reading of the film that explores representations of race and difference inside intersecting representations of corruption, clientelism and class. The article takes *Iago*'s three engagements with *Othello* – labelled here as *Preface*, *Play* and *Additional Act* – and looks at each in turn to identify the ways in which this Shakespearian adaptation functions to mediate a contemporary Italian crisis.

---

[7] Jeff Cotton, 'Venice: city of the imagination', in *World Film Locations: Venice*, ed. Pigott, pp. 6–7, esp. p. 6.

[8] Drake Stutesman, 'Costume design, or, what is fashion in film?', in *Fashion in Film*, ed. Adrienne Munich (Bloomington and Indianapolis, 2011), pp. 17–39; pp. 20–1, p. 18.

[9] Sujata Iyengar, 'Beds, handkerchiefs, and moving objects in *Othello*', in *Variable Objects: Shakespeare and Speculative Appropriation*, ed. Valerie M. Fazel and Louise Geddes (Edinburgh, 2021), pp. 21–36, esp. pp. 27–33; Douglas M. Lanier, 'Vlogging the bard: serialization, social media, Shakespeare', in *Broadcast Your Shakespeare: Continuity and Change across Media*, ed. Stephen O'Neill (London and New York, 2018), pp. 185–206, esp. p. 186; Catherine O'Rawe, *Stars and Masculinities in Contemporary Italian Cinema* (Basingstoke and New York, 2014), p. 175.

MARK THORNTON BURNETT

1 Postcard invitation, accompanying the DVD release of *Iago* (dir. Volfango di Biasi, 2009), to enter a competition to win a romantic break for two in Venice. Medusa Film / author collection.

PREFACE

Kyle Grady writes that Iago's lack of obvious motive allows Shakespeare to develop a 'more mercurial and complicated villain': 'certitude' is replaced 'with loose ends'.[10] In *Iago*, by contrast, the titular character, echoing the phrasing of his Shakespearian counterpart ('People ... care about ... what you seem to be'), is given a history, a backstory that explains his motivations and allows us to see him and them psychologically. At the start of the film, Iago explains how his origins disenfranchise him and prevent advancement: tousle-haired and sombrely dressed, he recounts the story of abandonment by his 'bricklayer' father, his lack of 'luck' and his generally straitened circumstances ('I borrow books'). Akin to the stereotype of the struggling Renaissance scholar, Iago is labelled a 'poor, starving bookworm' by fellow students. The invocation extends

---

[10] Kyle Grady, 'Othello, Colin Powell, and post-racial anachronisms', *Shakespeare Quarterly* 67 (2016), 68–83; p. 68.

hints in *Othello* at the same time as it builds upon the plotlines of plays such as *Macbeth* (the passing over of the 'brave [and] ... valiant ... captain' (1.1.16, 24, 34) for Malcolm) and *The Merchant of Venice*, that other Venice-set play centred on group forms of stigmatization and exclusion. Understanding Iago in this fashion is also contextually resonant. It suggests that, in a 'debt-ridden' climate, and at a time of rising 'unemployment' and 'widening inequality' in Italy, the figure of a working-class student served as a readily recognizable trope.[11] Certainly, as some historians have suggested, Italy during this period was characterized by 'latent rigidities ... Barriers ... blocked career progress', with 'declining prospects for mobility'.[12] To some extent, then, *Iago* executes a socially responsive operation, forming an alliance both with contemporaneous Italian theatre productions of Shakespeare in which 'characters' serve as 'metaphors for [the] ... unemployed and ... artists', and with Italian cinema's predilection for exploring questions of class and privilege.[13]

The fictive biography legitimizes Iago's idealism. Against a backdrop of disadvantage, he expounds in the campus design studio his thesis of meritocracy, a thesis that runs counter to the realities of what Andrea Mammone and Giuseppe A. Veltri term Italy's 'non-meritocratic system'.[14] 'I have a dream', Iago states, elaborating: 'in a faraway kingdom ... is a happy place ... a fair and ordered world where people are free and flourish.' The visual expression of his philosophy is the model city he has built, with its stairwell leading to the heavens (suggestive of disencumbered progress) and a spatial organization that enables 'desire' and 'love'. Repeatedly, Iago is discovered in visionary mode, as when, for example, he holds forth in a Biennale pavilion about his 'city of the future': the camera pans expansively over computer graphics of civic spaces, and soaring buildings, a dreamscape of opportunity fired by a belief in egalitarianism. Later in the film, again in the campus design studio, he is sharply distinguished from Otello who is only interested in market interests and late capitalist initiatives. Here, Otello executively alters the entry, privileging the 'business district' as the only site of 'progress'. Subsequently, in a care-worn square, surrounded by crumbling brick walls and chipped masonry, Iago laments, 'He wants to build a gilded prison where all people do is work ... It's designed to ... turn them into slaves.' Both the faded setting, and the expression of discontent, dramatically mark Iago off from the directions and tendencies of his world.

Inside the film's understanding of Iago as an inventive artist committed to epic and ethical ventures is its discovery of an institutional system averse to mobility and change. Iago's professional ambitions, the film makes clear, are unrealizable. Not only is he passed over as lead on his Faculty's entry to the Biennale event – he is also dictated to, and subordinated by, praxes of privilege that protect the upper echelons. Suggestive in this connection is the way in which, at the public exhibition of their individual projects, the students are rewarded based on familial connections. For example, because she is the Rector's daughter, Desdemona (a student in the Faculty) is given top marks for her 'environmentally friendly' city design: 'excellent work ... 100%', Professor Telli (Pietro De Silva) gushes. His indulgent look, and smiling countenance, are more than enough to demonstrate that the treatment she is accorded is institutionally inflected in her favour.

For his part, Iago's more innovative design, with its emphasis on 'democratic space', access for 'everyone', and 'passageways' linking 'the outskirts to the heart', is questioned and given a mere 'commendation' after qualifying discussion. In fact, in its

---

[11] Bill Emmott, *Good Italy, Bad Italy: Why Italy Must Conquer Its Demons to Face the Future* (New Haven and London, 2012), pp. 6, 17, 90.

[12] Paul Ginsborg, *Italy and Its Discontents: Family, Civil Society, State, 1980–2001* (London and New York, 2001), p. 32.

[13] Montironi, 'Narrating and unravelling', p. 268; Carlo Celli and Marga Cottino-Jones, *A New Guide to Italian Cinema* (New York, 2007), pp. 154–6.

[14] Andrea Mammone and Giuseppe A. Veltri, 'A "sickman" in Europe', in *Italy Today: The Sick Man of Europe*, ed. Andrea Mammone and Giuseppe A. Veltri (London and New York, 2010), pp. 1–15, esp. p. 2.

anatomization of a system that maintains its own interests, *Iago* gestures towards the practices for which the 'Berlusconi era' has become known, including clientelism, a system of social relations which involves, as John Foot notes, 'an exchange of resources between a patron and a client': these resources may not be 'jobs, or even cash, but can be much more ephemeral "goods" such as trust, the promise of a future "recommendation", or even the banking of such resources for future use'.[15] It is precisely such an arrangement that Brabanzio dangles before Iago when, in the office scene, he assures him patronisingly that 'I recognise your worth . . . I will offer you proper work, my friend.' In situations of 'high unemployment and poverty', when 'resources' are in short supply, clientelism thrives, and the system is inextricably associated with illegality.[16] During the 1990s and 2000s, political corruption was linked to all the major parties in Italy, not least after the 'Clean Hands' (*Mani Pulite*) operation of 1992 uncovered widespread bribery and malpractice.[17] And clientelism and corruption are at the heart of one of the preface's core scenes – the backroom deal between Brabanzio and world-renowned architect, and father of Otello, Philippe Moreau. By a cosy fireside, Brabanzio, referencing 'the contract to build the bridge', states: 'just . . . sign the consultation . . . you're not responsible . . . for the . . . outcome . . . We need to make all [our] friends happy . . . there's a lot of politics.' In reply, Moreau accepts the 'favour', including his son's admission to the Faculty, with discourses of unpalatable business establishing Brabanzio and Moreau as equally enmeshed in shady networks of benefit only to those already in power.

Iago derives ideological impact not just from Iago's institutional marginalization but also from the extent to which this is paralleled in a concomitant romantic disappointment. As several episodes make clear, the wronged hero's tribulations in love echo his frustrations at the profession: one is a microcosm of the other, and Iago, it seems, is good enough for neither. As lover, Iago in the film surrogates for Roderigo in the play, taking on a romantic mantle in penning a love letter to Desdemona, casting her in a fairy-tale light ('She's a sad princess, and I'll rescue her from the tower') and informing his friends that they are destined to be together ('she's my pole-star'). Typically, and matching the film's attachment to Venice's fabled reputation as a city of love, this latter scene takes place in St Mark's Square at night, the camera's lingering on St Mark's Clock Tower, with its golden medieval astrological symbols, lending a visual illustration to his conviction. Quintessentially, Iago meets the expectations of a melancholy lover (as indicated in his black attire) battling against the odds, introducing into the reimagined backstory of *Othello* a class-driven plotline more akin to popular versions of *Romeo and Juliet*. World cinema adaptations of *Romeo and Juliet* often understand the play in terms of social divisions that keep the lovers separate, and *Iago* is comparable.[18] The disparity in the worlds that Iago and Desdemona inhabit is self-evident from the start. For instance, with no mother and obliged to live with his aunt, Iago is glimpsed making his way home to a mean apartment in Venice's backstreets: cinematography specifies his route into the 'sestiere de San Paulo' (St Paul district), while establishing shots concentrate on washing hanging between faded buildings, indexes of a working neighbourhood. The apartment itself signals want: the stairwell is dingy, kitschy figurines decorate the walls, and the whole is cramped and constricted. In contradistinction is Desdemona's domestic space. Always in a combination of silky white and sparkly gold, and described by Iago as 'divine' (the soundtrack that introduces her is the song 'So Divine' by Honeybird), Desdemona lives in a lofty, colonnaded palazzo, upward-tilting camerawork indicating her distance from her would-be lover's plebeian circumstances. With its flocked wallpaper, exclusive sidepieces and antique spinning globe, the canal-side palazzo belongs to

---

[15] Foot, *Italy*, p. 188. [16] Foot, *Italy*, p. 190.
[17] Rosalind Galt, *The New European Cinema: Redrawing the Map* (New York, 2006), p. 48.
[18] Mark Thornton Burnett, *Shakespeare and World Cinema* (Cambridge, 2013), pp. 195–231.

a superior universe entirely of its own. Moreover, the fact that the palazzo is accessed via a private gated bridge suggests an enclosed body longed for by, but unavailable to, the love-struck Iago. The two settings could not be more romantically apart. Adding to issues of inaccessibility, and seemingly crystallizing the sense of her remoteness, Desdemona does not respond immediately to Iago's admittedly hesitant approaches, and, when she subsequently falls for Otello's charms, the humiliated student is distraught: 'I'll never love again … I didn't think it would hurt this much … I'm drowning', he states, using an appropriate watery metaphor.

It is because Desdemona and Otello belong to similarly elevated environments that, as the film understands it, they are drawn to each other. *Iago* lenses Otello, Black, Paris-based and connected through family to Venice's nepotism, as arrogant and overweening. 'I've spent my life going between Paris, Tokyo and New York', he brags to Desdemona, adding, 'I've studied design systems that even professors couldn't imagine.' A vernacular version of the play's 'round unvarnished tale … the story of [Othello's] life' (1.3.90, 128), Otello's boasts are delivered against a backdrop of the Rialto Bridge and the Fondaco dei Turchi palazzo, constructs that symbolically affirm the speaker's membership of a modern, mercantile elite. Elsewhere, Otello appears at Roderigo's party as a gladiator (the film's approximation of 'our noble and valiant general' (2.2.1–2)) and in a tailor-made suit sporting a key around his neck (the freedom of the city is his, it is suggested).

In fact, the party concatenates the thematic of an Iago who is overlooked and dispossessed. Nodding to the Capulet ball scene in *William Shakespeare's 'Romeo + Juliet'* (1996) but incorporating more fully *Othello*'s musical militarism ('the shrill trump, / The spirit-stirring drum, th'ear-piercing fife' (3.3.356–7)), *Iago* represents this occasion of excess as the moment at which Iago loses Desdemona to Otello. Taking place in a glittery white palazzo, stocked with ornamental pools, the party, and its masked and costumed partygoers (devils, pirates and emperors), recall Venice's cinematic association with carnival, with a playground of transformation and alternative identities. Yet, for Iago, there is no transformation from his lowly self, the soldierly formations of the dancers drawing attention to his experience of exclusion and loss. The military note is equally emphasized in the ribald remarks of the partygoers ('Bring us the spoils of the enemy') and in the spectacle of a cross-dressed, chain-mailed Roderigo standing in triumph over his male dancer conquest. Contextually, this defining point in Iago's development has its place in the individualistic energies of the era, in what Paul Ginsborg has characterized as contemporary Italy's 'interconnected' imperatives of 'hedonism' and 'consumption'.[19] At the same time, in passages where visuals overtake dialogue, the score approves the direction of travel away from Iago and towards the face-painted warrior Otello as he seduces Desdemona in the library. Hence, the song of inferiority and supplication, 'Beggin'', performed by Madcon, with its haunting complaint, 'I'm on my knees when I'm begging', gives way to the more confidently forthright 'Louxor J'adore', performed by Philippe Katerine, with its motifs of luxury and appeased desire. This is Otello's music, secured through his father's status, and all march to it. With the party, the process of Iago being pushed out, and the filling in of his backstory, are complete. Iago returns home to the depressive notes of Patrick Walton's 'The Great Escape' ('Things are looking down … eat up all the grey', the lyrics sound), and ascends the stairwell to his aunt's apartment, only to fall asleep, the muted colours of the scene gradually fading to black.

PLAY

The shift away from backstory and towards the Shakespearian text is presented as an awakening, as up-tempo plaintive strings and aggressive trumpets indicate the arrival of the play proper. Shaken into consciousness by his aunt, Iago springs into

---

[19] Ginsborg, *Italy*, p. 85.

life, suggesting a complement of motivation is now fully in place. Shortly afterwards, sotto voce, Iago announces the first strand of his plan to destroy Otello, his martial metaphors reinforcing the idea of a war between men: 'Otello ... show me what you're worth on the battlefield.' Visual suggestions – dark bridges and neglected backstreets – are clarified in dialogue, as when Iago confides in Roderigo, 'I won't be honest anymore.' The implication is that Iago now realizes that acting with integrity allows for little movement within a nepotistic network (a change in tactics is demanded). The similarity to the play's opening, and the Shakespearian Iago's confession that 'I know my price ... Whip me such honest knaves' (1.1.11, 49), advertises the engagement with text even as it registers the transition of the character into an alternative mode. In the light of the film's structuring of narrative and motive, we are sensitized with a particular urgency to the processes through which Iago is newly established as dissembler.

More specifically, and introducing into the film what is only a matter of report in the play, the elopement of Desdemona with Otello for a nocturnal assignation is visualized in a sequence that shows them escaping on a gondola together. The chaos of *Othello*'s opening is duly caught in shots of choppy canal water and distorted shadows, the effect of which is to suggest disturbed psychic states and unsettled vision (buildings and objects merge eerily into their reflections). In addition, the green-filtered tinge that overlays the episode hints both at Otello's jealousy-to-be and, because we see through Iago's gaze, the latter's own professional and personal jealousy. The legitimacy of Iago's vengefulness is intimated in the camera's concentration on his pursed lips and downcast eyes. Later, Iago describes the white handkerchief as 'the green-eyed monster coming crawling to my aid', going on, 'Jealousy ... Soon someone else will taste what I have been feeding on.' The consumptive metaphor implies not only how far Iago is himself consumed by jealousy, but also his desire for another to suffer with a similarly debilitating experience.

Martin Orkin and Alexa Alice Joubin note that, in *Othello*, 'modes of racial hatred' are conveyed in 'manifestly offensive utterances [that] ... reiterate ... traditional fears of miscegenation, allegations of sexual excess, perversion, bestiality and imaginings of "black barbarity"'.[20] Such associations are encapsulated in the 'sign' of the 'Sagittary' (1.1.159–60), the fictive inn at which Othello and Desdemona meet – emblazoned, as it is, with the mark of the centaur, a mythological beast suggestive of the 'Barbary horse' (1.1.113–14) and an intermingled racial and sexual history. By contrast, in *Iago*, while echoes of the Shakespearian 'sign' are hinted at in Roderigo's reference to the 'Calle Moro' ('Moor Street'), racist slurs do not otherwise intrude.[21] The adaptive procedure is to replace the play's racial subtexts with terms of sexual shame. 'How does it feel to be a cuckolded father?', Roderigo taunts from the street adjoining Brabanzio's palazzo, adding, 'All Venice is laughing about it ... [Desdemona's] making a spectacle of herself and your good name.' As the dialogue makes clear, the stress here is on social embarrassment. Typical, then, is the way in which Brabanzio chides his daughter when she returns home: 'Think of the neighbours ... the humiliation', he obsesses. As an integral part of its adaptive approach, *Iago* distances itself from the most objectionable elements of its source, playing up the contemporary and ensuring for Iago unambiguous audience engagement. We see the process at work again during the rousing of Brabanzio when a silent Iago watches from the sidelines (he is differentiated here from the verbally abusive 'ensign' (1.1.32) of the play) while a cloaked, bewigged and sunglasses-wearing Roderigo does the necessary work. *Othello*, of course, envisions Roderigo as a duped innocent, but, in a further reorientation of identification, *Iago* represents him as co-conspiring with Iago because he believes in his fellow student's cause. The

---

[20] Martin Orkin with Alexa Alice Joubin, *Race* (London and New York, 2019), pp. 39, 41.
[21] See Susie Boulton and Christopher Catling, *Eyewitness Travel: Venice & the Veneto* (London and New York, 2016), p. 299.

adjustment builds on the premises of the preface and makes clear that Iago's desire for revenge is supported, and is supportable.

If Iago is stripped of racism, he is simultaneously purged of misogyny. The play shows us Iago delighting in riling Cassio via a provocatively sexualized construction of Desdemona ('I'll warrant her full of game' (2.3.199)), but, in *Iago*, Desdemona is removed as the inflammatory reference-point. At a bar in a picturesque night-time square, sexual accusations pass instead between Cassio and Roderigo, the latter, theatrically exploiting his gay persona, having been primed to infuriate the former by challenging his masculinity. Once again, it is noticeable that Iago does not participate in the exchange of homophobic and ego-enraging insults ('a flute to play ... behind us' and 'Cassio-Dick here'). The resulting violence is ramped up by the stomping rhythms of the score ('Ces bottes sont fait pour marcher'), the theme of which is made manifest in the camera's focus on Iago stealing Cassio's compact disc (the only record of his work towards the Biennale event) and replacing it with a broken substitute. As a downward tilt reveals the shattered shards of the disc and a tangle of destructive feet, Cassio's fate, it seems, is sealed. 'You're out', explodes an irate Otello, who has witnessed the event and dispassionately rejects his assistant's excuses.

The compact disc is but one of the film's charged – and jealousy-producing – properties. In one of the few discussions of the film, Sujata Iyengar notes that *Iago* 'distributes the handkerchief's function among several items: a Polaroid snapshot of Desdemona and Cassio kissing, taken by Iago in a ... more innocent time ... a lace handkerchief ... stolen by Emilia and planted in Cassio's bed; and the compact disc'.[22] Circulating and splitting in this manner, *Iago* makes the gulling of Otello/Othello particularly persuasive, removing what is often a credibility sticking-point in production. As the film understands it, Otello is tricked at multiple levels, steered into insecurity by Desdemona's urgings ('Call Cassio'), her intemperance and the sight of her and Cassio together. Among the various properties utilized in his intrigue, Cassio's card-index box of sexual conquests, into which Iago has planted the Polaroid snapshot, looms large. 'Accidentally' coming across the fatal image, but claiming that it amounts to 'nothing', Iago finds his rival more than susceptible to suggestion. 'Nothing? Why were you trying to hide it?' Otello questions. Here, the card-index box works as the filmic equivalent to the play's metaphor of the 'brain' that houses a 'monster' (3.3.118, 111), and the result is an exasperated and disempowered Otello ('What does it mean?' he demands).

Possibly Iyengar underestimates the extent to which the handkerchief in *Iago* remains significant. Notably, Desdemona, lent Othello's words from the play, speaks of 'a family heirloom ... made of silk': in this formulation, she is given the responsibility of explaining the handkerchief, and its history, to the filmic audience. Unlike her more careless dramatic counterpart, *Iago*'s Desdemona is represented as aware of the meanings of the 'present' she has been gifted and conscious of what might be involved in its loss. We, too, are made conscious of the handkerchief's symbolic power and thus of the devastating potential of its going astray. In fact, when we arrive at the anticipated seduction/subordination of Otello by Iago (the structurally linked scenes of 3.3 and 4.1), it is no surprise to see how the world-renowned architect's son is already in his fellow student's thrall. In that it has been well prepared for, the shift in the power balance is psychologically persuasive. Immediately after the gulling of Cassio, Iago is applauded by Roderigo as a 'genio' ('genius'), an appellation that testifies to his growing hold over the action. Revealingly, it is shortly before this accolade that Iago breaks the third wall and stares insolently into camera. Surrogating for the play's soliloquies, the wordless close-up both meta-cinematically announces Iago's mastery and complements the film's meta-theatrical language. Looking through stairwells at the effect of his stratagems, for instance, Iago observes, 'I'm drafting Otello's part as well',

---

[22] Iyengar, 'Beds, handkerchiefs, and moving objects', p. 31.

his disclosure confirming his combined designer and director role.

Indeed, in the representation of Iago's intrigue, the film is able to rehearse the key set-pieces of the play at breakneck speed, including the attempted rehabilitation of Cassio ('He's already caused enough trouble', a piqued Otello notes) and Otello's quizzing Desdemona about her movements. These ensue in such rapid succession that Iago's grasp of the plot's entanglements seems unassailable. Interestingly, via these episodes, we are reminded of how structurally entrenched corruption and clientelism have become in the Venetian university. Thus, in relation to the Faculty entry, Iago assures Otello, 'I'll have a look at your part … then you finish it', an offer that allows him to mimic Brabanzio's earlier advice. 'Make a show of friendship', Iago counsels Otello about Cassio, adding, 'Leaders need to play at politics.' It is as if Iago, now in the position of patron, is turning systems of favouritism and obligation to his own advantage. Typically, the film's realization of the linked scenes of 3.3 and 4.1 is split between two Venetian locales. One moment Otello and Iago look down on Desdemona crossing a bridge from a lofty rooftop with a vista over towers and steeples. In terms of point of view, and aided by blocking that foregrounds his gesturing, it is Iago's narrative perspective that dominates. The next moment, Iago and Otello confer in the latter's apartment, complete with antique prints, leather sofas and fashion-conscious accessories. The sumptuous *Elle Decor Italia* magazine interiors notwithstanding, a sense of Otello's entrapment now obtains, as suggested in the ornate grilles at the windows and the room's rising verticals. Yet, despite the increase in his manipulative stature, Iago remains during these scenes the unhappy outsider. For example, pausing on a romantic bridge that gives onto a Renaissance church's busy façade, Iago informs Desdemona, 'Somebody like me has to work twice as hard to get results', his comment operating to prioritize the continuing realities of class and its excluding effects.

Of course, the issue of who is excluded, and why, is central to *Othello*. Both the dark palette of the play phase of the film, and possibly Iago's apprehension that 'people' in Otello's iteration of the city are akin to 'slaves', invite us to think more about how *Iago* negotiates the play's racial subtexts. Ayanna Thompson reminds us that 'race-making' takes on different forms at 'different historical moments to create structural and material inequalities', and her comment is useful in sensitizing us to specific articulations of race in the Italy of the early twenty-first century.[23] Perhaps because Italy's modern imperial history was relatively brief (constituted by a period of colonial occupation in Eritrea, Ethiopia, Libya and Somalia that came to a close with the fall of Benito Mussolini's fascist rule), debate about categories of Italian citizenship and nationhood have raged in recent decades.[24] In particular, the arrival in Italy of Arab and North African migrants – or *extracomunitari* as they are nicknamed – has been accompanied, as Vanessa Maher explains, by an outburst of 'racist and xenophobic reactions' and anti-immigration legislation.[25] An immigration law was passed in 2002; in 2008, as part of his electoral campaign, Berlusconi addressed issues around Roma and Sinti immigration in terms of national security; and in 2009, the immigration law was reinstated and reinforced.[26] Even if it aims to dissociate itself from such developments, as refracted in its attempted cleansing of the play's racist utterances, *Iago* finds it impossible to escape the pressure of its racist contexts entirely. Crucially, both

---

[23] Ayanna Thompson, 'Did the concept of race exist for Shakespeare and his contemporaries? An introduction', in *The Cambridge Companion to Shakespeare and Race*, ed. Ayanna Thompson (Cambridge, 2021), pp. 1–16, esp. p. 7.

[24] Sante Matteo, 'African Italy, bridging continents and cultures', in *ItaliAfrica: Bridging Continents and Cultures*, ed. Sante Matteo (Stony Brook, 2001), pp. 1–22, esp. p. 6.

[25] Vanessa Maher, 'Immigration and social identities', in *Italian Cultural Studies: An Introduction*, ed. David Forgacs and Robert Lumley (Oxford, 1996), pp. 160–77, esp. p. 163.

[26] Montironi, 'Narrating and unravelling', p. 269; Nando Sigona, '"Gypsies out of Italy!": social exclusion and racial discrimination of Roma and Sinti in Italy', in *Italy Today: The Sick Man of Europe*, ed. Mammone and Veltri, pp. 143–57, esp. p. 150.

ITALIAN FILM ADAPTATION OF OTHELLO

contemporaneous projections, and colonial legacies, find release in Cassio, Otello's cousin, his character functioning as the site where some of the most unpalatable aspects of the 'Berlusconi era' meet. As well as to homophobia, Cassio gives vent to frustrations that cluster around the Otello figure. '[Otello has] put me in a real mess ... My father made it quite clear: no Biennale, no masters in Tokyo ... No Tokyo, no Japanese girls ... Have you ever screwed a J*p? [It's] all thanks to that s****y n****r!', he rages. Delivered in his swanky apartment, Cassio's comments continue the narrative of privilege, linking a conviction of entitlement to sexualized assumptions about Asian women and toxic masculinity. In addition, because Cassio is shot here against a backdrop of a poster of a cartoon character from the 1940s and 1950s, Gim Toro, he is tied to constructs of Italy's regressive attitudes. The poster shows a jungle scene in which the stripy topped hero battles tigers as a young Asian woman looks on admiringly.[27] Such is the effect of the juxtaposition that we are invited to see in Cassio a contemporary – and masculinized – expression of Italy's imperial past. Some of *Iago*'s repurposing manoeuvres are underlined here – for Iago to be empathetic, Cassio must be objectionable. The worse the latter appears, the better the former is presented – Iago appearing through comparison as more future-oriented and progressively attuned.

Yet discourses of toxicity are not easily dislodged. At the close of the play phase of *Iago*, the bloodbath of *Othello* is avoided, and no deaths occur. Aggressivity and upset remain as norms as an enraged Otello assaults a furious Cassio and then tears upstairs to the design studio to strike Desdemona and berate her for her presumed infidelities: 'That bitch!', he exclaims. In this way, the key moments of the intrigue are recalled in violent combinations: Iago's question ('The truth – is that what you want?') brings us back to his earlier renunciation of 'honesty', while Cassio's realization ('Can't you see he's playing us off against each other?') is the tipping-point that precipitates the student's exposure. The spectacle of Otello wrecking the model, and dashing thereby the team's Biennale chances, is a climactic moment. Idealism dissolves as does the construct of a world in which 'people' come together for a common purpose in a level environment. In this concluding scenario, the destructive direction of *Othello* is reconceived, the central players crushed but remaining, and the consequences of Iago's intrigue still to be fully played out.

ADDITIONAL ACT

In contradistinction to the play, the film delivers on the expectation that Iago will explain himself, reversing centuries of performative silence and concatenating the representation of a type whose behaviours have been contextualized from the start. Against the backdrop of the smashed-up studio, Iago makes his frustrations crystal clear. Addressing Otello, he exclaims, 'You ... you're not ... capable of managing a project. Weren't you the first to jump at using my work so you didn't look bad? ... A name's not enough to give you talent!' Turning then to Brabanzio, Iago excoriates the Rector for putting 'friends and ... business' above all else and ignoring 'merit', continuing, 'Without people like you, the world would be a better place and people like me wouldn't have to fight to survive!' Via this rush of eloquence, the film's intersecting motifs of meritocracy, clientelism and corruption, and the compulsion to revenge, are sited at centre stage. In reply, Brabanzio, who has been called on to intervene in the affray, is incredulous, labelling the student a 'terrorist'. The term underlines his perception of an unacceptable 'politics' mobilized in the espousal of a cause, and situates Iago wholly outside the system he has consistently chafed against. Adding salt to the wound, Desdemona slaps Iago and storms out of the studio, the suggestion being that he is now multiply rejected.

However, by elaborating an additional act, *Iago* pushes through and eventually transforms the

---

[27] The poster reproduces the cover of the 12-page issue 63 of *Gim Toro, La divoratrice d'uomini / The Man Eater* (1947).

implications of Desdemona's response. Important here is the provision of a Desdemona–Emilia exchange which complicates the male-on-male dynamic of the adaptation as a whole. True to her Shakespearian counterpart's function as a voice of reprimand and reason in 4.2 and 5.1, Emilia, once the disorder has dissipated, remonstrates with Desdemona in the campus square: 'You knew Iago was dying of love for you ... you humiliated him ... [and] didn't think twice about defending those old school-ties boys ... Come down from your tower', she berates. Picking up on the earlier reference to Desdemona's fairy-tale inaccessibility, Emilia's gendered critique highlights the role of women in a network in which men predominate. Listening to Emilia's words, Desdemona is obliged to confront her own responsibilities. The Rector's daughter, it is implied, is complicit, and in such a way that the nepotism so vital to clientelism and corruption is sustained and enabled.

Reflecting on the end of *Othello* and stage properties, Robert C. Evans notes the 'bed that plays such a prominent role', in a reading that is expanded on by Lynda E. Boose when she singles out 'the imagined chamber ... [the] forbidden space which [the play] has repeatedly eroticised'.[28] In each of its three phases – preface, play, additional act – *Iago* interpolates the wronged hero's bedroom. With preface and play, the bedroom features to signify Iago's removal from a world of privilege. As the high point of the additional act, however, the movement is reversed: Desdemona leaves her world to enter Iago's (see Figure 2). She seeks him out in his own *sestiere*, her displacement rounding off the film's domestic trajectory. The emphasis on Iago's bedroom as the destination-point of the film recalls the ways in which, in *Othello*, 'prurient descriptions' and 'viewer gratification' consort in a form of early modern 'pornography'.[29] 'You're arrogant and conceited ... Destroying everything around you ... You've destroyed my father ... destroyed my relationship ... destroyed Otello', Desdemona upbraids. Yet her condemnation quickly gives way to invitation, as, sitting on the bed and revealing herself to be only partially dressed, she states: 'I want to be with an important man ... Take me, you've won, promise me you'll always love me like this.'

There is much that is unpalatable here, including the representation of Desdemona's submissiveness and the sense of a defeat that amounts to sexual victory. But winning Desdemona means that Iago emerges triumphant, and this is underlined in an interpolated sequence showing Brabanzio much reduced – bumbling and clumsy, he hesitates on his stairwell: 'My God, where am I going?' In losing his way – and his place as a controlling *paterfamilias* – Brabanzio simultaneously rescinds institutional authority. By contrast, the bedroom motif of a cross-class couple underscores the future promise of the meritocratic city; the values to which Iago still subscribes, it is implied, will democratize the older order. As a reflection of the alteration in mood, the episode is overlaid with an upbeat pop soundtrack: the lyrics to 'Love is noise' by The Verve accentuate being 'saved' by 'righteous anger', living in the 'city', and working as 'one'. As the consummation becomes the culmination of *Iago*'s story, the embracing pair is discreetly – theatrically – veiled. The film's ultimate shot – a bright red superimposed curtain being draped over the spectacle of the lovers – self-consciously evokes Lodovico's reference in *Othello* to the 'loading of this bed' (5.2.373) and his demand that the curtains be drawn. At this climactic moment, however, the curtains fall not on tragedy but on a scene of sexual intimacy and romantic commitment which signals a new beginning.

The hopefulness of this ending continues in a series of tongue-in-cheek inserts interspersed over the credits. The final one of these – in a playful nod – returns us to Shakespeare's titular hero. Otello is discovered on a bench looking despairing – for the

---

[28] Robert C. Evans, 'Introduction', in *'Othello': A Critical Reader*, ed. Robert C. Evans (London and New York, 2015), pp. 1–14, esp. p. 9; Lynda E. Boose, '"Let it be hid": the pornographic aesthetic of Shakespeare's *Othello*', in *'Othello': Contemporary Critical Essays*, ed. Lena Cowen Orlin (Basingstoke, 2004), pp. 22–48, esp. p. 22.
[29] Boose, '"Let it be hid"', pp. 26, 27, 35.

ITALIAN FILM ADAPTATION OF *OTHELLO*

2 The DVD cover of *Iago* (dir. Volfango di Biasi, 2009) shows Iago (Nicolas Vaporidis) and Desdemona (Laura Chiatti) locked in an exploratory embrace. Medusa Film / author collection.

first time he is imagined as the archetypally rendered Othello defined by 'fragmented ... orientations' who is 'culturally adrift, alienated and alone'.[30] The inset reminds us that clientelism, and its corruptive consequences, harm even those who benefit materially from it. 'I'm a loser, a failure, a fake', Otello moans, but his depressive introspection is immediately challenged by a passing Roderigo.[31] 'What do you mean?', Roderigo asks him, 'You're a bright guy, full of talent ... You're the best ... Would

[30] Carol Mejia LaPerle, 'Race in Shakespeare's tragedies', in *The Cambridge Companion to Shakespeare and Race*, ed. Ayanna Thompson (Cambridge, 2021), pp. 77–92, esp. p. 89; Ian Smith, 'We are Othello: speaking of race in early modern studies', *Shakespeare Quarterly* 67 (2016), 104–24; p. 112.

[31] His despondency, we realize, is the result of the dressing down he has received earlier at Brabanzio's hands, in a scene that approximates even as it brings forward Othello's being called to account for his actions before the Venetian senators.

you like to come to my place for dinner?' Catherine O'Rawe argues that some recent Italian films examining migration represent 'bonds of affection ... between male migrants and Italians' and 'continue the homosocial thematic' for which 'Italian cinema' is known.[32] Certainly, as Otello eagerly responds to Roderigo's invitation, ideas of connectivity – if not hospitality and welcome – are foregrounded. The positives of such a discovery of the character never prioritized in *Iago* are reflected in the iconic image of Venice which is now introduced. As the camera switches to reveal Otello and Roderigo seated on the bench together, we move into a wide shot of the magnificent façade of the Basilica di Santa Maria della Salute, with its breath-taking vista across the Grand Canal towards St Mark's Square. It is the picture-postcard view of Venice for which we have waited, affirming that, for the reformed Otello, Venice, available and authenticated, now properly opens its doors. Incorporating Shakespeare's tragic hero within a millennial generation defined by same-sex attraction, the film concludes with a fantasy of the possibilities of meritocracy in a contemporary, cosmopolitan and youthful Venice, one that is alive to the prospect of fresh opportunities presenting themselves and further stories evolving.

---

[32] Catherine O'Rawe, 'Contemporary cinema', in *Directory of World Cinema: Italy*, ed. Louis Bayman (Bristol, 2011), pp. 255–6, esp. p. 256. In this connection, *Iago* bears brief comparison with *Sud side stori* ('South Side Story'), the Italian adaptation of *Romeo and Juliet* which, Maurizio Calbi argues, 'brings an allegorical dimension to bear on the issues of migration and hospitality it continually foregrounds' (Calbi, *Spectral Shakespeares*, p. 82).

CIRCUMVENTING MARGINALITY: THE CURIOUS CASE OF INDIA'S *OTHELLO* SCREEN ADAPTATIONS

ABHIRUP MASCHARAK

Nearly an hour into B. R. Chopra's *Hamraaz* ('Confidant', 1967), Kumar, the protagonist, starts suspecting his wife, Meena, of infidelity. That his suspicions are incorrect is something that the film clarifies only later. But it hints at the unjust nature of his misgivings at the very moment that they start taking root in his mind by having him, a theatre actor, perform in the title role of *Othello*. Notably, the scenes we see him act in include those of Iago manipulating Othello with claims of Desdemona's supposed adultery, and Othello's subsequent murder of Desdemona. Kumar, distraught over the possibility of Meena's unfaithfulness, lets his anger seep into his performance, so much so that he almost kills Shabnam, his co-star playing Desdemona, during the enactment of *Othello*'s climax. Later, when he intercepts what he thinks is a love-letter to Meena from her lover, Kumar leaves his residence on the pretext of going to Poona, but actually loiters around the house in disguise, hoping to catch Meena and her paramour in the act. His disguise consists of a false beard and a black coat, which resembles the bearded look he had sported and the dark robes he had worn while playing Othello. As he waits outside his house, an unknown killer shoots Meena dead, and Kumar, upon seeing her corpse, is devastated not only by her death, but also by the realization that, had he remained *in* the house with his wife, he could have protected her. As he weeps and calls himself Meena's 'kaatil' ('murderer'), one is reminded of Othello's lament in the aftermath of his murder of Desdemona: 'Whip me, ye devils, / From the possession of this heavenly sight. / Blow me about in winds, roast me in sulphur, / Wash me in steep-down gulfs of liquid fire! / O, Desdemon! Dead Desdemon! Dead! O! O!' (*Othello*, 5.2.284–8)

A similar invocation of *Othello* occurs in Vinay Shukla's *Mirch* ('Spice', 2010), an anthology film in which an aspiring filmmaker narrates to a potential financier a script that consists of four humorously erotic stories. The third of these stories is about Manjul, a young husband, who grows doubtful of his wife Manjula's loyalty, and approaches a friend for help. This friend, who works in a theatre and thinks Manjul is being unnecessarily paranoid, tries to reason with him, and when Manjul keeps insisting that he needs to know for sure whether his wife has been unfaithful, the friend looks at him and asks, pointedly, 'You have read *Othello*, haven't you?'

Neither of these films is an adaptation of *Othello*, at least not in any traditional sense. *Mirch*'s association with the play is restricted to that one reference, while *Hamraaz* invokes *Othello* only to underscore the extent of Kumar's jealousy; the main plot, which charts Kumar's search for Meena's killer while outrunning the policeman who considers Kumar the murderer, does not have anything to do with Shakespeare's play. Both films, however, are relevant to any study of Indian cinema's treatment of this particular play, as the films' invocation of *Othello* is symptomatic of how Indian filmmakers, across generations, have looked upon it: as just a domestic drama revolving around love, betrayal and jealousy. The issue of

Othello's race and/or the marginality to which it relegates him have rarely found any insightful, sustained exploration in the Indian films which draw upon the play, whether one looks at loose appropriations such as Ajoy Kar's *Saptapadi* ('The Seven Steps', 1961) and T. Prakash Rao's *Izzat* ('Honour', 1968), or more faithful/traditional adaptations such as Jayaraj's *Kaliyattam* ('The Play of God', 1997) and Vishal Bhardwaj's *Omkara* (2006). Even as these films touch upon the topics of the differences of race, religion and caste, they ultimately generate drama not by exploring those differences, but by trying to have the viewers emotionally invested in the outcome of the romance at the centre of these films. The personal in these films, that is to say, never becomes the political.

In this article, I wish to study the *Othello* adaptations mentioned in the previous paragraph in detail, in order to determine the cause behind this persistent avoidance of the issue of marginality that is so central to the play. To do so, I have employed what Karen Kline, in her taxonomy of the paradigms under which screen adaptations may be studied, calls the Materialist paradigm, an approach whereby an adaptation is viewed not in terms of its fidelity (or lack thereof) to its literary source, but vis-à-vis the circumstances under which it was produced. Those adopting this paradigm in their study of a film adaptation consider it, as Kline puts it, a product of both 'cultural-historical processes' (that is, the socio-political zeitgeist of the time and place it was made in) and 'the extratextual forces operating within the production process' of the film (such as what genres of films were in vogue during the particular period and in the particular film industry producing the adaptation, the penchant of its director or screenwriter towards making films of a specific variety, the onscreen persona of its lead actors, and so on).[1] Since these Indian *Othello* adaptations have been made in different languages, by different directors and in different periods, the tendency to sidestep the matter of Othello's marginality, while common to all the films, was likely the outcome of not a single, overarching reason, but of causes specific to each film. The Materialist paradigm, therefore, is best suited to understand those causes, since it allows for a case-by-case study of the conditions – social, cultural and political – under which they were made, and which had likely contributed to the avoidance of the issue of marginality in each of these films.

I begin the study with the Hindi-language *Omkara*, since it is the most well known of the Indian screen adaptations of *Othello*. Set in the hinterlands of Uttar Pradesh, it recasts the Moor of Venice as Omkara Shukla, the right-hand man of Tiwari, a powerful gangster-turned-politician. When Omkara selects his aide Keshav, or Kesu, as his deputy, Omkara's other aide, Ishwar Tyagi (called 'Langda', or 'lame', by others because he walks with a limp), becomes livid, and plots against Omkara by sowing in his mind the suspicion that Kesu and Dolly Mishra, Omkara's paramour, are having a dalliance. Plot-wise, the film is largely faithful to the play, and its dialogues correspond, mostly, to Shakespeare's lines. This fidelity extends, at first glance, to Omkara's characterization. His father, we learn, was a Brahmin, but his mother was a woman from a so-called 'lower caste'. This mixed parentage is obviously part of the endeavour to make Omkara an Other/outsider, as is the casting of Ajay Devgn, an actor with a darker complexion than most leading men in Hindi cinema, as Omkara. The makers even dress Devgn, frequently, in black clothes and make him wear dark sunglasses, as if to make sure he looks 'darker' and stands out among his more light-skinned co-stars, much as Othello stands out as the solitary Black man in the otherwise white Venetian society.

The trouble, however, is that the film shows little of the ramifications of either Omkara's caste or his complexion. Shakespeare never lets us forget Othello's vulnerability as an ethnic Other even as we learn that he is a respected general for the Duke of Venice. When other characters are not speaking

---

[1] Karen Kline, '*The Accidental Tourist* on page and on screen: interrogating normative theories about film adaptation', *Literature/Film Quarterly* 24 (1996), 70–83; p. 74.

of him in a language replete with racial slurs ('Thick-lips' (*Othello*, 1.1.66), 'black ram' (1.1.88), 'Barbary horse' (1.1.113–14), 'sooty bosom' (1.2.71)) or reviling his looks as hideous (as Brabantio does in act 1, scene 2), they refer to him, constantly, as 'the Moor'. While that term is not always uttered pejoratively in the play, its repeated usage does draw our attention to Othello's racial difference from other Venetians. Establishing that difference is important, because that alone explains why Iago is able to manipulate Othello into turning against Desdemona. Othello has had to fight hard to achieve the stature he currently enjoys among Venetians. It is only after enduring enslavement and endangering his life, often in battles for Venice in various parts of the world, that he has gained respect. Yet, while the people around him appreciate the service that Othello has rendered to Venice, they hardly seem to view him as their equal, as Brabantio's outrage over Othello and Desdemona's marriage demonstrates: one would not be wrong in assuming that other white Venetians would have reacted similarly had Othello married any of their daughters. In other words, Othello, despite his respectable standing as a general, is made aware, in the form of Brabantio's prejudiced tirades, that he is not deemed fit to marry into a white Venetian family – that all that he has done for Venice as a military commander is not enough for people to overlook his racial identity. So, when Iago suggests that Desdemona is attracted to Cassio, who is not just white but also younger and conventionally handsome, one understands why Othello would believe this to be true. His insecurities over his race and looks and age, insecurities which the society he inhabits has hammered into him, make him conclude that Desdemona, having got over her initial infatuation with him, has, as Iago puts it, drifted towards a man 'of her own clime, complexion and degree' (*Othello*, 3.3.235). His lament that Desdemona has turned disloyal to him because 'Haply, for I am black / And have not those soft parts of conversation / That chamberers have' serves as evidence of these insecurities (3.3.267–9).

Omkara locates no such insecurity in its titular character, whose position as a powerful, dreaded mobster is threatened in no discernible way by his caste or colour. The film, as a matter of fact, is not even interested in making Omkara as much of an outsider as Othello is. The latter, one must note, is not born of the union between a Black and a white parent; he is, as a Moor, a complete racial Other. Omkara, on the other hand, does not belong fully to the so-called 'lower caste', as one of his parents is Brahmin. Significantly, that parent is his father rather than his mother. Since Indian society decrees that children will carry the surnames, and hence the caste and religious identities, of their fathers, Omkara can successfully downplay his 'half-caste' status, using the surname (Shukla) of his Brahmin father, wearing the so-called 'sacred thread' of the Brahmins around his neck, and performing rituals inside Hindu shrines alongside Brahmins. The other Brahmins around him – Tiwari, Kesu, Dolly, even Tyagi – never seem to view him as inferior to them, and, on the rare occasion when they do refer to his mixed parentage, they call him 'aadha Brahman' ('half Brahmin'), thereby identifying him in terms of his link to the dominant caste rather than the so-called 'lower' one to which his mother belonged. Dolly endorses this perception of Omkara when she says, in reply to Omkara describing himself as partially Brahmin, 'A half-moon is still a moon'; as a Brahmin herself, she believes that being a Brahmin man's son is reason enough to consider Omkara a Brahmin as well. Having a Brahmin father, then, goes a long way in letting Omkara into the upper echelon of the caste hierarchy, and wins him privileges Othello never enjoys. Even the occasional insult Omkara endures for having a so-called 'low-caste' mother serves to show his comparative privilege rather than render him an outsider. Dolly's father, a Brahmin, chastises Omkara for eloping with his daughter by linking his behaviour to his mother: 'I forgot that you are only partly Brahmin; your mother is that bloody low-caste woman.' His choice of words ought to give us pause: how, despite his knowledge of Omkara's parentage, could Dolly's father 'forget' that Omkara is not fully a Brahmin? Similarly, why does he, while enumerating to Tiwari his reasons behind his objection to Omkara and Dolly's relationship, refer first to Omkara being a 'jahil gunda' ('uncouth goon'), then a 'daitya' ('demon') and only then as 'jaat ka aadha' ('half-caste'), indicating that he is repelled more by Omkara's association with the world of crime and murder than by his mixed-caste status? The answer, presumably, is that, as the son of a Shukla, the favoured protégé of a Tiwari – the chief to Brahmins such as Tyagi and Kesu – and now the paramour of a Brahmin girl like Dolly, Omkara is, for all practical purposes, a Brahmin himself, and Dolly's father knows as much. His insulting comment on Omkara's mother is little more than a futile display of anger, caused more by his daughter's disobedience than anything else, which is why Omkara shrugs off the remark with a disdainful smile. As Saksham Sharda says:

The question that we are consequently faced with is whether it is impossible for the director Vishal Bhardwaj even fictionally to construct a credible situation in which a Brahmin woman marries an outcaste in contemporary India. For the tale of *Othello*, it could be argued, is not analogous to 'near-black half-Brahmin' Omkara marrying a 'near-white Brahmin' woman like Dolly. Far from it: the tale of *Othello* is the untold story of Omkara's father (a pure Brahmin) marrying a *kanjar* woman ... a story from which *Omkara* consciously shies away.[2]

His dark complexion similarly poses little challenge to his power. When Indu, the counterpart of Emilia in the film, sees Omkara and Dolly together for the first time, she makes fun of the contrast between his swarthiness and her much lighter skin tone. Her words, however, are part of the good-natured, playful banter between her and Omkara (whom she considers her brother), rather than the equivalent of the racist slurs hurled at Othello by Iago and Brabantio. Indeed, she caps off her jokes by comparing Omkara to Krishna, the dark-skinned Hindu god, and 'Omkara', it may be noted, is one of the many names of Shiva, another Hindu deity. These references to divinity are fitting because, in terms of the power he wields, Omkara may well be regarded as a god vis-à-vis the people he lords it over.

This begs the question: what makes Omkara susceptible to Tyagi's machinations? If he is this powerful, and if his caste or looks pose as little a threat to his authority as the film would have us believe, then what sense of insecurity could possibly have left him vulnerable to the lies Tyagi peddles? The film never quite manages to answer these questions. Poonam Trivedi suggests that differences of class, rather than caste, have contributed to Omkara's suspicions.[3] Unlike him, Dolly and Kesu are college-educated and can speak in English. They belong, or can be seen as belonging, to a more elite, sophisticated section of the society, where Omkara, for all his might, would be a misfit. But even this possibility receives no convincing portrayal in the film. Kesu may have been dubbed 'firangi' (a Hindi term for white foreigners) by some because of his knowledge of the English language, but he is no upper-class man. He belongs, squarely, to the same milieu as Omkara and Tyagi. He is seen, mostly, in the same dusty, quasi-rural settings as them; speaks, mostly, in the same Hindi dialect as they do; and does the same job (henchman for Tiwari). Furthermore, in his exchanges with Kesu, Omkara never shows any hint of feeling intimidated by the latter's 'Englishness'. Indeed, he seems to hold the ability to converse in English in no special regard; when Dolly sings an English song for him, Omkara, far from being awed, bursts out laughing at her off-key rendition. There appears to be no significant age-gap between him and Dolly either, and in those moments when Omkara is shirtless, he displays a muscular, toned, conventionally attractive physique that belies the possibility that he could be regarded as 'ugly' in the way that Othello is. In the light of these facts, the only explanation for Tyagi's success in manipulating Omkara is that the latter is just pathologically jealous by nature.

---

[2] Saksham Sharda, 'Black skin, black castes: overcoming a fidelity discourse in Bhardwaj's *Omkara*', *Shakespeare Bulletin* 35 (2017), 599–626; p. 617.
[3] Poonam Trivedi, 'Remaking Shakespeare in India: Vishal Bhardwaj's films', in *The Cambridge Companion to Shakespeare on Screen*, ed. Russell Jackson (Cambridge, 2020), p. 242.

But should one settle for that explanation – and one probably must, seeing that Bhardwaj himself has said of his film, 'We're focusing on the jealousy more than racism'[4] – then Omkara can hardly be considered a marginal figure, and the mentions in the film of his caste and complexion make him only perfunctorily similar to Othello.

This disinterest on the part of *Omkara* in portraying its central character as marginal in any genuine sense can probably be attributed to Bhardwaj's decision to retell *Othello* as a gangster saga. The film, in fact, may be seen as part of a slew of gangster films birthed by a newfound interest in the genre in the Hindi film industry during the late 1990s, possibly in response to the 1993 bomb blasts in Mumbai (where the industry is located) that turned out to be the handiwork of the gangster Dawood Ibrahim. Dilip Shankar's *Aatank hi Aatank* ('Reign of Terror', 1995) and Sudhir Mishra's *Is Raat Ki Subah Nahin* ('This Endless Night', 1996) are early examples of this interest. But it was with the release of Ram Gopal Varma's *Satya* (1998), considered a landmark in Hindi cinema because of its gritty, realistic portrayal of gangsterism, that underworld sagas became a frequent phenomenon in Hindi films, with Varma's *Company* (2001) and *Sarkar* ('Overlord', 2005), Vishram Sawant's *D* (2005), Vinay Shukla's *Godmother* (1999), Mahesh Manjrekar's *Vaastav* ('The Reality', 1999) and *Hathyar* ('Weapon', 2002) and Anurag Kashyap's *Black Friday* (2004) releasing in quick succession, and swelling the hitherto impoverished ranks of Hindi gangster cinema. This interest in gangster stories remained consistent till about 2012, when Kashyap's *Gangs of Wasseypur*, a sprawling mafia epic, was released; since then, interest in the genre seems to have petered out. Bhardwaj, who had been the music composer for *Satya* and *Godmother*, was evidently influenced by this trend, which explains why *Maqbool* (2003), his adaptation of *Macbeth*, is set in the underworld. The critical acclaim the film received had likely convinced him to retell *Othello* against a similar backdrop. But the decision to turn Shakespeare's characters into gangsters has the unfortunate outcome of robbing his stories of their tragic facet. *Macbeth* and *Othello* are tragedies not just because the protagonists die in the end, but because they are upright, noble individuals who go astray, partly owing to flaws of their own (ambition in the case of Macbeth, a degree of gullibility in the case of Othello), and partly because of others' machinations (Lady Macbeth, Iago). The titular characters in *Maqbool* and *Omkara*, on the other hand, are already criminals, gangsters who kill and coerce others for a living. So, when they commit further murders, it is not a case of good men turning bad, but of bad men turning worse.

In the case of *Omkara*, the gangster story format similarly gets in the way of exploring marginality. Gangster films are essentially stories of the struggle for power, chronicling the lengths to which men in the mob go to gain or keep it by using force, cunning or treachery. Bhardwaj puts the plot of *Othello* to the service of this template. Consequently, where Iago's hostility towards Othello has distinct racial connotations – we see him speak derisively of Othello's Blackness right from the first scene – Tyagi's vendetta against Omkara comes across as nothing more than anger at being passed over in the race to gain a higher position and greater power in Tiwari's gang. Despite the disparity in their castes, one cannot read into Tyagi's motives any trace of casteism, since nothing he says or does indicates that his enmity is rooted in the low regard that the so-called 'upper castes' in India have for the so-called 'lower castes'. Indeed, he is genuinely loyal to Omkara before being denied the promotion: it is he who holds back the wedding procession of Dolly's would-be husband Rajjo and helps Omkara to elope with Dolly, and it is demonstrations of fealty such as this which, one presumes, make Omkara call Tyagi his 'bhai' ('brother'). Tyagi, in other words, seems less the racially prejudiced Iago who goes after a Black man, and more a character along the lines of, say, Carlo Rizzi from Francis Coppola's *The Godfather* (1974), who,

---

[4] Quoted in Stephen Alter, *Fantasies of a Bollywood Love Thief* (New Delhi, 2007), p. 51.

disgruntled at being refused the sort of wealth and power he thought he would enjoy as the son-in-law of the Corleone family, commits acts of betrayal that lead to Sonny Corleone's death. In fact, seeing that *Maqbool* contains an obvious homage to *The Godfather* in the scene where Jahangir Khan, the counterpart of Duncan, refuses a lucrative deal à la Vito Corleone, the idea that Bhardwaj's next Shakespeare adaptation would lend to a Shakespearian character (Iago) the traits of a character from *The Godfather* (Carlo) is not implausible. To put it more succinctly, since *Omkara* is a gangster film, and the lust for power that defines the motivations of many a character in such films is reason enough for Tyagi to turn against Omkara, the film does not bother to impart to Omkara a truly marginalized identity like Othello's, one which would make him the target of the prejudices that the haves typically display towards the have-nots. The aforementioned efforts to portray Omkara, despite his mixed heritage, as more of a powerful figure than a subaltern like Othello may also be attributed to the film's allegiance to the gangster genre, which, though at least nominally opposed to its protagonists' illegal way of life, also aims to fascinate viewers with the power they wield, and making Omkara a genuine subaltern is not conducive to that aim. Bhardwaj's love for gangster films is apparent to anyone familiar with his works. After *Maqbool* and *Omkara*, he directed *Kaminey* ('Scoundrels', 2009), a dark comedy-caper set in the Mumbai underworld, and wrote and produced Abhishek Chaubey's *Ishqiya* ('A Tale of Love', 2010), which portrays the misadventures of a pair of gangsters. He also penned the dialogues for the Iranian director Majid Majidi's Mumbai-based drama *Beyond the Clouds* (2016), which is the story of a young man's struggles to escape the drug mafia he works for. In the case of *Omkara*, this predilection for the gangster genre works against the film, at least as far as its handling of the issue of marginality is concerned.

Bhardwaj had cited *Kaliyattam*, a Malayalam take on *Othello*, as one of his models for making *Omkara*. Since *Kaliyattam* was not just a critically acclaimed work but also the sole instance of a direct adaptation of *Othello* in Indian cinema before *Omkara*, it makes sense that Bhardwaj would take his cues from that film while translocating Shakespeare's tragedy to India. But while *Kaliyattam* might have been helpful to Bhardwaj as a template for how to produce an *Othello* adaptation which keeps the plot unchanged while adding to it the requisite Indianizing touches, it also seems to have bequeathed to *Omkara* the neglectful treatment of the theme of marginality: like Bhardwaj's film, it introduces the topic of caste- and looks-based discrimination, only to sidestep it quickly and give us a depoliticized tale of a marriage turning bad. Perumalayan, the Othello of this film, is the lead dancer in a troupe of *theyyam* performers. *Theyyam* is a folk art form practised in parts of Kerala, in which music, dance and mime are fused into a performance that tells the stories of gods and legendary heroes. The leading dancer in this socio-religious spectacle is believed to become possessed with the divine figure(s) he is playing. Hence, despite hailing mostly from the so-called 'lower castes', these dancers are treated reverentially for the duration of their performances, even by the Brahmins. Retelling *Othello* against the backdrop of *theyyam* is thus a good opportunity to delve into the play's themes of marginality and discrimination.

Like *Omkara*, *Kaliyattam* makes Perumalayan an Other not just in terms of his caste but also his looks, and goes further than *Omkara* in this regard. Suresh Gopi, who plays Perumalayan, does not have Devgn's brawny physique, and Perumalayan not only is dark-skinned, but bears on his face scars caused by smallpox. The contrast that therefore exists between him and his so-called 'upper-caste', fair-skinned, beautiful wife Thamara is evidently meant to convey to viewers the sense of disruption that a marriage like this will create in a society such as Kerala's, a state with a long and complex history of caste-based discrimination. And yet that sense of disruption never really makes itself felt. Thamara's father is outraged when his daughter marries Perumalayan, but that outrage causes no significant hurt to the latter; the denizens of the village he resides in leave him alone once Thamara attests that she has come with Perumalayan willingly, and the father, though still upset by the union, retreats as well. In real life, inter-caste marriages like Perumalayan and Thamara's in the rustic hinterlands of Kerala and other parts of India frequently lead to honour killings of the couple by the so-called 'upper-caste' people.[5] It is not clear why Perumalayan is spared any such horror. His position as the leading dancer of his *theyyam* troupe cannot explain this, for the reverence which dancers like him enjoy while they perform is, as Trisha Mitra says, 'fleeting', and does not extend beyond the sphere of those performances: 'He does represent an incarnation of a god and carries much respect within the performative space but outside it he is as disenfranchised as the rest of his community.'[6] When the Duke of Venice brushes aside Brabantio's complaints upon learning that Desdemona has married Othello voluntarily, he does so not because of his generosity in racial matters, but because of his vested interest in having Othello on his side, for he is faced with an imminent Turkish invasion, and will need Othello's military skills to deal with that crisis. The *naduvazhi* (chieftain) of Perumalayan's village has no such pressing reason to overlook the defying of the caste system which the protagonist's marriage with Thamara represents. It is curious, then, that neither the *naduvazhi* nor the other so-called 'upper-caste' people in the village demonstrate much anger at Perumalayan's relationship with Thamara, and, since we do not see him experience any casteist opprobrium, we cannot, also, read his character as a particularly marginalized one.

What dilutes the theme of marginality further is the film's characterization of Paniyan and Kanthan, the counterparts of Iago and Cassio, respectively. Iago's hostility towards Othello is, as mentioned earlier, tinged palpably with racial prejudice: he rarely speaks of the Moorish general without a disparaging reference to the latter's ethnicity. Consequently, it is both easy and accurate to read Iago's machinations against Othello as not just the misdeeds of an underling who feels slighted by his superior, but also as the violence inflicted by a white man on a Black man whom the white man thinks has gained more power than a non-white individual should. Paniyan's ploys against Perumalayan, however, carry no such connotation, because Paniyan belongs to the same so-called 'lower caste' as Perumalayan, and does not, therefore, belong to a dominant social group in the way Iago, being white, does vis-à-vis the Black Othello. The performer in the lowly role of the clown in Perumalayan's *theyyam* troupe, Paniyan, wants to be chosen as the successor to Perumalayan for the position of the lead dancer. When Perumalayan chooses Kanthan instead as the successor, Paniyan decides to avenge this perceived slight by destroying Perumalayan's marriage. Paniyan's grudge, then, is purely a personal one, and cannot be read as symbolic of the oppression of disenfranchised people by dominant ones in the way Iago's schemes against Othello can be. Kanthan, similarly, comes from the same caste and social status as Perumalayan, which makes the latter's suspicions regarding Kanthan and Thamara less credible. Othello believes Iago's lies regarding Desdemona and Cassio's dalliance because Iago taps, cleverly, into Othello's insecurity that his white wife will gravitate, as per the 'natural' order of things, towards a man of her own race. Since Kanthan is no upper-caste person as Thamara is, Perumalayan has little reason to entertain similar trepidations. It is true that Kanthan does not have the blemished countenance of Perumalayan, but even this cannot fully explain Perumalayan's insecurity. Thamara fell in love with him after seeing his *theyyam* performances. This means that she values his talents over his looks, and is swayed by him rather than the more handsome Kanthan, who performs alongside Perumalayan in those same *theyyam*s. A scene of

---

[5] Two such recent cases of honour killings in Kerala are the murders of Kevin P. Joseph in 2019, and Aneesh in 2020. They were from the so-called 'lower castes' and were killed by the families of the women they were married to.

[6] Trisha Mitra, 'The Othello-figure in three Indian films: *Kaliyattam*, *Omkara* and *Saptapadi*', in *Performing Shakespeare in India: Exploring Indianness, Literatures and Cultures*, ed. Sharmistha Panja and Babli Moitra Saraf (New Delhi, 2016), pp. 95–107; p. 100.

lovemaking between husband and wife further shows that Thamara has no issues with Perumalayan's appearance. Moreover, we learn later that it was Kanthan who acted as the go-between for Perumalayan and Thamara when they began seeing each other, thereby facilitating their romance. Collectively, these details undercut the idea that Perumalayan, like Othello, is a marginal figure whose insecurities are exploited by those who occupy the higher rungs of the society. Rather, like Omkara, he comes across simply as unusually jealous and gullible.

Indeed, scholars, in their analyses of the film, have concurred that it evades the issue of casteism and reduces *Othello* to a generic story of jealousy destroying a relationship. Koel Chatterjee states, 'Through the course of the film, the question of caste difference gives way to the emphasized theme of jealousy, as will be the case in *Omkara*.'[7] C. S. Venkiteswaran notes: '*Othello* is one of the most frequently filmed Shakespearean plays. Many of its cinematic versions have explored the racial difference and the conflicts it engenders. *Kaliyattam*, despite the scope for such explorations in terms of caste divisions and hierarchies ... desists from pushing this too far. Instead it focusses on the emotional conflicts arising out of jealousy, suspicion, ambition and desire.'[8]

Ania Loomba likewise observes:

But although it seems that director Jayaraj wants to use both Shakespeare and Theyyam not to reflect upon either of them so much as upon the question of caste in Kerala, in this respect the film is ultimately disappointing, for it doesn't do anything with its explosive ingredients and with the astute positioning of Othello as the Theyyam 'kolam' [lead dancer]. ... While Theyyam has been the medium of social protest in Kerala, in this film the question of caste difference vanishes, and is not articulated alongside the theme of jealousy.[9]

None of these scholars has, however, written on the possible reasons as to *why* the film thus sidesteps the topic of caste, and therefore the topic of marginality. The answer to that *why* can perhaps be found in Jayaraj's proclivities as a director. His interest in telling stories of conflict and friction within families best explains why *Kaliyattam* is, despite its flirtations with the issues of caste and colour, ultimately just a story of domestic strife culminating in tragedy. *Kudumbasametham* ('With Family', 1992), for instance, charts the tensions between a son who opts for a career in music and a father who vehemently opposes this. *Paithrukam* ('Heritage', 1993) is also centred on a father–son conflict, this time over the question of faith; the father is a devout man while the son is a non-believer. *Thumboli Kadappuram* ('Thumboli Beach', 1995) shows the dilemma of a woman caught between the husband she loves and the father who does not like the husband. *Desadanam* ('Journey to Wisdom', 1996) tells the story of the dispute between three generations in a family when a grandfather decides to induct his grandson, who shows an uncommonly sharp grasp of religious scriptures at an early age, into a monastic order, while the boy's parents refuse to be thus separated from their son. The critical success enjoyed by these films, especially *Paithrukam* and *Desadanam*, is the most likely cause behind Jayaraj's decision to retell *Othello* in the same vein as these earlier films of his – that is, as yet another family drama, this time focused on husband and wife. His own words confirm this; in speaking of what drew him to *Othello*, Jayaraj remarks, 'The tragedy of Othello haunted me for many nights. Why would a man so much in love with his wife, kill her?'[10] He was

---

[7] Koel Chatterjee, 'Bollywood Shakespeares from Gulzar to Bhardwaj: Adapting, assimilating and culturalizing the Bard' (unpublished Ph.D. thesis, Royal Holloway University of London, 2018), p. 192: https://pure.royalholloway.ac.uk/portal/files/29754322/2018ChatterjeeKPhD.pdf.

[8] C. S. Venkiteswaran, 'Shakespeare in Malayalam cinema: cultural and mythic interface, narrative negotiations', in *Shakespeare and Indian Cinemas: 'Local Habitations'*, ed. Paromita Chakravarti and Poonam Trivedi (New York, 2019), pp. 75–92; p. 82.

[9] Ania Loomba, 'Shakespeare and the possibilities of postcolonial performance', in *A Companion to Shakespeare and Performance*, ed. Barbara Hodgdon and W. B. Worthen (Oxford, 2005), pp. 121–37; p. 131.

[10] 'A mix of history, folklore and Shakespeare', *The Hindu*, 31 August 2016, www.google.com/amp/s/www.thehindu.com/features/metroplus/A-mix-of-history-folklore-and-Shakespeare/article14599953.ece/amp.

'haunted', then, not by how Othello's race is weaponized against him by a white society, but by the disintegration of a loving relationship and its culmination in murder. Unsurprisingly, then, that is what his film is preoccupied with, while treating Perumalayan's caste and dark, disfigured looks as superficial counterparts to Othello's Blackness – as features that make him, nominally, an outcast like Othello, even as the film defines him predominantly as a jealous husband. The auteurist approach to studying a filmmaker's works aims at identifying specific features of his films – stylistic touches, thematic concerns, genre preferences – that recur throughout his oeuvre and make it distinctive. If we adopt that approach to studying the two Indian *Othello* films discussed thus far, then it is fair to conclude that – just as Bhardwaj's interest in gangster films, coupled with the interest of the Hindi film industry in the same genre during the late 1990s and 2000s, led to his adapting *Othello* as a gangster drama – Jayaraj, owing to his predisposition towards sombre family dramas, and the success he had enjoyed as the maker of the same, interprets *Othello* as less a story of a marginalized man and more as the saga of a marriage that sours lethally.

Izzat and *Saptapadi*, the films I seek to discuss hereafter, differ from *Omkara* and *Kaliyattam* in two important ways. First, as has been mentioned earlier, *Izzat* and *Saptapadi* do not so much adapt *Othello* as appropriate it. While Bhardwaj and Jayaraj follow the plot of *Othello* faithfully and have characters who are recognizable counterparts to those in Shakespeare's play, *Izzat* and *Saptapadi* have plots and characters that are *not* analogous to those of *Othello*; rather, these latter films use references to *Othello* to address the themes of race and discrimination. Second, *Omkara* and *Kaliyattam* represent a comparatively niche variety of cinema. They may have the star-studded casts and song-and-dance sequences that characterize most mainstream Indian films, but the way they were advertised as Shakespeare adaptations, and (especially in the case of *Omkara*) the way the details of their screenings in national and international film festivals were announced prior to their release, make it clear that they were intended as prestige productions meant for a relatively elite audience, one that would have a more than passing knowledge of *Othello* and would appreciate the films for their links to the Bard. *Izzat* and *Saptapadi*, on the other hand, are, for the want of a better term, more 'massy', aimed not at any specific segment of the population but at all and sundry, and rely not on their references to Shakespeare but on their stars, music and wholesome, wish-fulfilling storylines to draw the viewers. They are, thus, more mainstream than *Omkara* and *Kaliyattam*, and this mainstream nature of the films plays, as we shall see, an important role in shaping their treatment of the theme of marginality.

Shekhar, the protagonist of *Izzat*, is the illegitimate son of a *zamindar* (landlord) and Savli, an *adivasi* (tribal) woman. When he learns, after Savli's death, that his father had cruelly discarded his mother after impregnating her, he vows revenge, and gets a job at the *zamindar*'s mill to get closer to the latter. Before long, he learns that he has a stepbrother, Dilip, who looks just like him, except for the complexion: Dilip has lighter skin, while Shekhar, being the son of an *adivasi* woman, is dark-complexioned. Upon Shekhar's arrival in the mill, a lot of people mistake him for Dilip, and wonder aloud how Dilip has become 'kala' (Black). The romance that develops later between Shekhar and the fair-skinned Deepa can be described as similar to Othello and Desdemona's romance, not just because of the inter-ethnic nature of their relationship, but also because *Othello* is directly invoked during their first meeting. During this meeting, Deepa is holding the book *The Tribal World of Verrier Elwin,* while Shekhar picks up a copy of *Othello*, and their conversation veers towards the injustices meted out to Othello because of his race. The respective books that Shekhar and Deepa hold in this scene clarify that *Izzat* wished to draw parallels between Othello's plight as a Black man in a white society, and the plight, in post-independence India, of the *adivasi*s, who have often found themselves on the receiving end of violence and discrimination by the rich, so-called 'upper-caste' people. The latter are happy to use the *adivasi*s for their own pleasure or needs – seen in the *zamindar*'s liaison with Savli, and the fact that most of the workers in the *zamindar*'s mill are *adivasi*s – but never accord them equal rights, much as Othello, despite his services to the Venetian army, is still considered unfit to marry a white woman. Shekhar's conversation with Deepa on *Othello* shows that he has, like Othello, internalized some of the prejudice he is subjected to. Othello wonders, upon learning of Desdemona's supposed adultery, whether she has chosen Cassio over him because he, Othello, is Black. Shekhar, similarly, wonders if a 'kala' and 'badsurat' ('ugly') person like Othello can really win the love and devotion of a beautiful woman like Desdemona. Later, his sense of insecurity becomes more prominent when Deepa says that she loves him; like Othello, he is unsure if he, who is also 'kala', is deserving of her love. Dilip, meanwhile, is romancing an *adivasi* woman called Jhumki, a relationship which Dilip's father, the *zamindar*, opposes. Shekhar, therefore, decides that he must make sure that Jhumki does not experience the jilting that his mother did, and that having Dilip marry Jhumki would also be the best revenge he can inflict on the *zamindar*. Lots of trials and tribulations ensue, but things turn out well in the end, with Shekhar marrying Deepa and Dilip marrying Jhumki, and the *zamindar* seeing the error of his ways and blessing these inter-ethnic couples.

The film, then, can be described as a positive spin on Shakespeare's play, one in which a marginalized protagonist's life does not end in tragedy. Certain choices made by the filmmakers, though, compromise its handling of marginality. The first and most egregious of these choices is the casting of Dharmendra as Shekhar and Dilip. Hailing from the state of Punjab, Dharmendra has the sort of fair complexion which mainstream Hindi cinema prefers in its leading men and women. That preference, in turn, is reflective of the obsession prevalent in India (and especially northern India, to which the Hindi film industry mainly caters) over fair skin – matrimonial advertisements in Indian newspapers routinely mention fair complexion as a desirable trait in prospective brides and grooms, those with darker complexion are considered less attractive, and beauty products which promise to lighten the skin do roaring business. *Izzat*, in casting Dharmendra as Shekhar, shows just how pervasive this obsession is: even as it aims to tell the story of a dark-skinned, half-*adivasi* man whose complexion is disdainfully commented on by those around him, it casts in that role not a dark-skinned actor, but a fair-skinned one like Dharmendra, who the viewers would know is not really 'kala'. The makers seemed to have wanted it both ways; they included in the film progressive diatribes against colour prejudices, while assuring the viewers, by casting a blackfaced Dharmendra as Shekhar, that they were adhering to the prevalent norms of beauty – that while Shekhar may be dark-skinned, the actor playing him is the usual *gora* (fair) hero of Hindi cinema who is merely wearing a layer of make-up. And even the application of that make-up/blackface on Dharmendra-as-Shekhar was likely deemed permissible by *Izzat*'s makers because the film also has Dharmendra-as-Dilip – that is, Dharmendra as he truly looks, Dharmendra the fair-skinned, handsome actor who had already gained a measure of success with releases such as Ramesh Saigal's *Shola aur Shabnam* ('Fire and Dew', 1961), Bimal Roy's *Bandini* ('The Shackled Woman', 1963), Mohan Kumar's *Ayee Milan Ki Bela* ('The Hour of Union Comes', 1964), Chetan Anand's *Haqeeqat* ('The Real World', 1964), O. P. Ralhan's *Phool aur Paththar* ('Flowers and Stones', 1966) and J. Om's *Aaye Din Bahar Ke* ('Happy Days Have Come', 1966). To sum up, the growing stardom of Dharmendra, whose conventional good looks contributed significantly to his popularity, and the view that fair complexions are more attractive than darker ones, which permeates the Indian society in general, led to the casting of Dharmendra in blackface – rather than an actor who is actually dark-skinned – as the part-*adivasi* man, with the simultaneous presence of the fair Dharmendra in Dilip's role underscoring both the dictate of stardom and the colourism. Jhumki, the tribal woman, is likewise played not by an actress of the character's ethnicity, but by Jayalalitha, who, like Dharmendra, was a fair-skinned rising star (albeit in Tamil and Kannada films rather than Hindi ones) at the time of *Izzat*'s release. One can credibly assume that this practice of casting light-skinned actors adorned with blackface in roles that should have been played by dark-skinned performers was encouraged by similar trends in Hollywood; performers as respected as Orson Welles and Laurence Olivier had donned blackface, for instance, to play Othello. This practice has, rightly, been criticized in recent years for three reasons. Firstly, blackface has its roots in the American minstrel and vaudeville shows of the nineteenth and early twentieth centuries in which white comedians darkened their faces to play Black people in acts that perpetuated harmful stereotypes regarding the Black community. Secondly, while white actors could don make-up to play Blacks and even win praise for that impersonation, the opposite was rarely true. As Ayanna Thompson says:

In Shakespeare's lifetime, blackness was performed in two modes – exhibition (black people on display) and imitation (white men in racial prosthetics). Because in the exhibition mode all the power resided in the viewer (not the one exhibited), and because in the imitation mode all the power resided in the white, blacked up performer, performances of blackness were a white performance property for actors and audiences. In the nineteenth century, blackness and whiteness were performed by black actors for the first time in the United States and the United Kingdom, and their performances challenged the long-standing assumptions that (1) blackness was a white performance property and (2) only white actors could be virtuoso performers. These early nineteenth-century black performers were denigrated by white critics, white audiences, and their fellow white actors for 'aping' white performance modes.[11]

Thirdly, selecting white actors to play non-white characters deprives non-white actors of roles that should rightfully belong to them, creating race-based disparity in income and opportunity in the film industry. By the same token, the casting of a blackfaced Dharmendra, or even Jayalalitha (who was spared the blackface, presumably, because unlike Dharmendra, she did not have another role as a fair-skinned person in the film), as *adivasis* is equally deserving of criticism. After all, when a film professes to making a statement against the marginalization that *adivasi*s are subjected to for (among other things) their skin colour, and invokes *Othello* to make that point, but cannot even bring itself to cast dark-skinned actors for the *adivasi* characters, how sincere, really, is it in its condemnation of racial discrimination, and how well does it understand *Othello*?

Indeed, the aforementioned discussion on *Othello* between Shekhar and Deepa in the film hints at the makers' misunderstanding of the play and, by extension, of the subject of marginality. During that conversation, Deepa opines that Othello himself is responsible for the tragedy that befalls him, since he cannot shake off the chip on his shoulder regarding his race. This is a rather insensitive take on the play, since it is not Othello who cannot get over the fact that he is Black, but the people around him; it is they who view him, despite his accomplishments, as ultimately a racial Other, keep reminding him of the same, and then use his resultant insecurity against him. Deepa's misreading of the play puts the blame for Othello's insecurity on him, rather than on the discriminatory society he inhabits, which is tantamount to telling a marginalized person that his marginality is his own fault – that his anger at his oppressors, rather than the oppressor's crimes, is the reason behind his misery. Her flawed reading of *Othello* is important in the context of this film, for her view that Othello is responsible for his own misfortunes is reflected in the film's characterization of Shekhar. The latter comes to the *zamindar*'s estate with revenge on his mind, even making an unsuccessful attempt on the *zamindar*'s life in an early scene. Whether or not one supports the violence he was planning to inflict, there can be no doubt that Shekhar has good reason to hold the *zamindar*, and the upper-caste/upper-class society he represents, in contempt.

---

[11] Ayanna Thompson, *Blackface* (New York, 2021), p. 68.

Over the course of the film, however, Shekhar loses that sense of indignation and softens towards the *zamindar* family. As he says to the *zamindar* later, he made no further attempts to kill him because the love he had received from his half-siblings Dilip and Neelu (the *zamindar*'s daughter) prevented him from robbing them of their father. This is a curious thing for Shekhar to say, since neither Dilip nor Neelu display any particular affection for him at any point. Neelu treats him lovingly at first only because she mistakes him for Dilip; once she learns the truth, she betrays no fondness for Shekhar anymore. Dilip does treat him with a degree of friendliness, but is not above using Shekhar for his own ends. When the *zamindar* orders Dilip to marry Deepa, and Dilip can neither bring himself to do so nor summon up the courage to tell his father that he loves Jhumki and will marry only her, he asks Shekhar to impersonate him (Dilip) and meet Deepa instead, hoping that Shekhar's dark complexion will cause Deepa to turn him down as a prospective husband. This stratagem, based as it is on the assumption that Shekhar's complexion makes him unattractive, is quite insulting to him. So, when Shekhar speaks of the love he has received from Dilip and Neelu, one must wonder why the filmmakers have given the character such a line. The answer, in the light of Deepa's views on Othello, seems to be that the makers believed that if Shekhar is to avoid Othello's tragic end, he must rid himself of, as Deepa put it, the 'ahsas', or consciousness, of his marginalization. To do so, he must first rid himself of his anger at those who relegated him to his marginal position, and that is why the film posits, however unconvincingly, that Dilip's and Neelu's 'love' has blunted Shekhar's justified grudge against the *zamindar* and the upper strata of the society. As per the worldview propagated in the film, marginalization of the dispossessed is to be solved not by challenging the oppressors who cause the marginalization, but by adopting a conciliatory attitude towards the oppressors so that they treat the marginalized better. To validate this conservative stance, *Izzat* goes so far as to turn the *adivasis*, the marginalized group it had purportedly sought to champion, into the villains in the final segment of the film. The most serious hindrance to Dilip and Jhumki's eventual union comes not from the *zamindar*, but from Dukal, an *adivasi* man who lusts after Jhumki, and who injures Dilip and kidnaps Jhumki when the pair prepare to marry. Meanwhile, Manglu, another *adivasi* man who used to be the *zamindar*'s loyal bodyguard, turns against his employer upon discovering how the *zamindar* had treated Savli, whom Manglu knew and was fond of; he then incites the other *adivasis* to burn down the *zamindar*'s mill. The half-*adivasi* Shekhar, who had started out as a righteous fighter against the oppression of the *zamindar*s, must, by the final reels, battle the other *adivasi*s not just to rescue another *adivasi* (Jhumki), but also to defend the *zamindar* and his scion, Dilip. He even takes a bullet for the *zamindar*, prompting the latter to acknowledge Shekhar as his son. The grudge which the dispossessed and the marginalized hold against the powerful is, according to *Izzat*, the real threat, and they must, the film states, get over that grudge and demonstrate selfless camaraderie towards the powerful (as Shekhar does by protecting the *zamindar*'s mill and endangering his life for the *zamindar*) so as to win over the latter. As a half-*adivasi*, dark-skinned, illegitimate son of an unfeeling landlord, Shekhar is certainly a marginalized figure. But the film does his marginality a disservice by suggesting, via Deepa's opinion that Othello's 'ahsas' of his marginality is the cause of his tragedy, that Shekhar's acute 'ahsas' of his own marginal position at the beginning of the film is the real problem, and that he must dull that 'ahsas' and endear himself to the powerful so as to gain their favour. The message in *Othello* is the exact opposite of this: Shakespeare shows us, realistically, that, even if a Black person serves a white society loyally, there is no guarantee that he will be treated well in return, that his position as a marginalized individual will change for the better. Despite its citation of *Othello*, therefore, *Izzat*'s understanding of the play's treatment of marginality leaves much to be desired.

If one is to understand the reasons why *Izzat* refrains from channelling Shakespeare's uncompromisingly grim portrayal of the tragedy suffered by an ethnically marginalized character, one could start by noting that, despite the recent proliferation in scholarly writings on Shakespeare adaptations in Hindi cinema, the industry's engagement with the Bard has been sporadic. In the thirty years that make up the period of the 1950s to the 1970s, there had been only two Hindi films that count as Shakespeare adaptations: Kishore Sahu's *Hamlet* (1954), and Debu Sen's *Do Dooni Char* ('Two Times Two is Four', 1968), which is based on *The Comedy of Errors*. Neither was a box-office success. It would be fair to say that, during this period, Shakespeare was viewed by most in the Hindi film industry as highbrow and difficult. It was only after the commercial success of the *Romeo and Juliet* adaptations *Ek Duuje Ke Liye* ('Made for Each Other', 1981) and *Qayamat Se Qayamat Tak* ('From Calamity to Calamity', 1988) – directed by K. Balachander and Mansoor Khan, respectively – and Gulzar's *Angoor* ('Grapes', 1982), another adaptation of *The Comedy of Errors*, that Shakespeare came to be regarded as a lucrative source for mainstream Hindi cinema to tap. This paved the way for many other adaptations of *Romeo and Juliet* (which Indian directors seem to adapt frequently because the play, in recounting the story of tragic, star-crossed lovers, echoes many such tales and legends – Laila and Majnu, Mirza and Sahiban, Heer and Ranjha – that already enjoy much popularity in India), Bhardwaj's trilogy (which consists of, alongside *Maqbool* and *Omkara*, the 2014 *Hamlet* adaptation *Haider*), and Sharat Katariya's *10ml Love* (2012), an adaptation of *A Midsummer Night's Dream*. *Izzat*, thus, was made at a time when Shakespeare was hardly staple material for Hindi cinema. Rather, what held sway in the industry at the time was the *masala* format. A colloquial term used, usually, in the context of Hindi cinema, *masala* refers to mainstream potboiler films that combine within themselves scenes of action, romance, comedy and melodrama, as well as songs and dances: a complete 'package' of entertainment. While this mode of filmmaking has been somewhat on the wane in recent years, it dominated Hindi cinema till the early 1990s, and *Izzat*, made during the 1960s – an era that was both the heyday of *masala* cinema and, as stated earlier, a period when adapting Shakespeare was not a common practice among Hindi filmmakers – unsurprisingly swears more of an allegiance to the dictates of *masala* cinema than to *Othello*. It must, hence, make space for multiple musical numbers, a prolonged comedy track, and a fight scene or two, leaving little time for a thorough exploration of marginality. It must make space, also, for a subject that is nearly ubiquitous in mainstream Hindi cinema: the sanctity of the family.

The influence of the two Indian epics, *The Ramayana* and *The Mahabharata*, on Hindi cinema is a well-acknowledged phenomenon, and since these epics often glorify devotion to family over personal interests (such as Rama accepting an unjust exile in deference to his father in *The Ramayana*, or the Pandava brothers marrying Draupadi to obey a command by their mother Kunti, even when that command was issued inadvertently, in *The Mahabharata*), the value of the family is also an oft-repeated theme, where protagonists are not autonomous individuals, but defined by their relationships with the members of their family, be it the one they were born into, or the one they have started with their life-partners. The figure of the loner (someone like Clint Eastwood's 'Man with No Name', for example) is virtually impossible to find in mainstream/*masala* Hindi releases. What is more, any conflict that exists in this cinema between the protagonists and their families usually culminates in a happy resolution. This is not only because mainstream/*masala* films aim chiefly to entertain and happy endings are more conducive to that goal than tragic ones, but also because Indian society is, on the whole, more family-oriented, and concerned less with celebrating individualism than Western ones (again, the glorification of familial obligations in the Indian epics and religious scriptures, and the dominant role they have played in shaping the average Indian mind, are reasons behind this), and films which reflect a pro-family stance have a better chance of receiving the viewers' patronage. This is why *Izzat* must replace Shekhar's anger at the *zamindar* with a growing affection for the latter and his children; no matter how exploitative or unethical the *zamindar* may have been, he is also

Shekhar's father, and sons (even illegitimate ones like Shekhar) in Hindi mainstream/*masala* films cannot go *completely* against their fathers, and an amicable resolution must somehow be worked out. Shekhar's climactic defending of his father against the *adivasi*s with whom he should have found greater common ground is motivated by this principle of Hindi mainstream/*masala* cinema: fidelity to family, that is to say, has to take precedence over the forging of solidarity among the marginalized. Hence, *Othello*, in an out-and-out *masala* production such as *Izzat*, can remain only a point of reference to illustrate what racial prejudice is. It cannot become the film's main constituent element, because the rules of *masala* cinema prevent it from becoming so.

Saptapadi is similarly compromised in its portrayal of marginality owing to its being a particular sort of mainstream film – a Bengali romantic melodrama with Uttam Kumar and Suchitra Sen in the lead roles. This pair, following the success of releases like Agradoot's *Agnipariksha* ('Trial by Fire', 1953) and Sudhir Mukherjee's *Shapmochan* ('The Lifting of the Curse', 1955), quickly came to be regarded as the quintessential romantic couple of Bengali cinema, and many of their subsequent films, even when drawing upon literary sources that are not romantic in nature, mould those literary works into romantic tales to cater to the actors' fan following. One sees this in the films *Sabar Uparey* ('Above All Else', 1955) and *Kuhak* ('The Enchanter', 1960), both directed by Agradoot. These films are adaptations of A. J. Cronin's *Beyond This Place* (1950) and Davis Grubb's *The Night of the Hunter* (1953), respectively. But where both of these novels are works of crime fiction, their Bengali screen adaptations attenuate the crime-and-detection aspects of the novel to play up Kumar's star appeal as the romantic hero. Hence, while *Beyond This Place* is primarily about a son's quest to prove that his father has been unjustly imprisoned for a murder he never committed, *Sabar Uparey* uses the storyline of the father's travails only to facilitate the romance between the characters played by Kumar and Sen, as the latter helps the former to free his father. The focus in the film shifts from the son's detective work to prove his father's innocence to the blossoming love between Kumar's and Sen's characters, and the consolidation of that love into imminent marriage. Such, indeed, was Kumar's stature as a romantic hero that the desire to show him as such often dominated the filmmakers' consciousness even when he was cast opposite heroines other than Sen. In *Kuhak*, for instance, he is paired with Sabitri Chatterjee, but the film still prioritizes romance over everything else. *The Night of the Hunter* has for its protagonist an unrepentantly psychopathic, murderous pastor, who terrorizes a couple of children to learn the location of a hidden pile of money. Kumar plays the counterpart of the pastor in *Kuhak*, but his character is hardly the psychopath from the novel – instead, he is a man torn between his greed for the money and his love for a woman, with the latter impulse ultimately winning. *Saptapadi*, similarly, may adduce *Othello* to endorse the inter-racial, inter-religious love story it narrates, but is more invested in portraying its leads as devoted lovers than as marginal entities.

The *Othello* reference in the film comes in the form of a staging of the play at a medical college in Calcutta, with the protagonists Krishnendu (Kumar) and Rina (Sen) playing Othello and Desdemona, respectively. Krishnendu is an Indian Hindu, and Rina a Christian and the daughter of an Englishman. Their relationship, prior to their participation in the play, is fraught with hostility, especially on the part of Rina, who calls Krishnendu a 'darkie' and a 'heathen'. As the film is set during the early 1940s, when World War II was under way and India was under British rule, the enmity of a white woman like Rina could have had serious repercussions for a colonized subject like Krishnendu. But since the film is conceptualized, more than anything else, as an Uttam–Suchitra romance, Rina never becomes a threat to Krishnendu – the latter, in fact, laughs off her slurs and even plays pranks on her in return. These initial tussles between them take the shape of a popular convention in romantic films, where the hero and the heroine start out on the wrong footing but eventually fall in love. Krishnendu and Rina thus come across in these portions as lovers-to-be, and not as a colonized Indian man who experiences marginalization at the hands of a member of the colonizing British.

The film, as a matter of fact, is eager to ensure that viewers do *not* see Krishnendu as marginalized. Instead, in deference to Kumar's stardom, *Saptapadi* portrays him as someone who stands tall among his peers. An excellent student, a skilled footballer and a gifted actor, he is intellectually, physically and culturally the equal, if not the superior, of the British people around him, and the latter recognize him as such. Clayton, the British student with whom Krishnendu fights during a football match, and whom he replaces in the *Othello* production, congratulates Krishnendu for his impressive performance in the play, and so does Clayton's white fiancée. Rina is won over by his performance as well, and they start a relationship. The film tries, in these scenes, to show not just how a play on interracial love brings together two individuals from different races who were initially at loggerheads, but also how Krishnendu uses a play by Shakespeare, the greatest of British cultural icons, to prove his worth as an Indian to the British, to win their respect and, in Rina's case, love. Since *Saptapadi* is a star-centric production, and since it is Krishnendu's acting (rather than his academic achievements or prowess at football) that ultimately wins Rina's heart (and the admiration of the other British characters), one would not be wrong in reading the rapturous reception of Krishnendu's performance as the film's meta-commentary on Kumar's popularity as an actor. But in choosing to highlight Kumar's stardom and showing Rina's (and, by extension, the other British individuals') prejudices melting away in the face of his thespian abilities, *Saptapadi*, like *Izzat*, misses the point that *Othello* makes regarding marginality: that where there is a fundamental imbalance of power (as there is between the lone Black man Othello and the prejudiced, dominantly white Venetian society, and as there was between the British and the Indians in colonial India), those on the lower end of that imbalance do not cease to be vulnerable just because they have performed a feat which pleases or serves the interests of the powerful. That is why Othello meets a tragic end despite his services as a general of Venice. So the idea that Krishnendu would cease to be a 'darkie' and a 'heathen' to the British just because he has acted splendidly in a Shakespeare production is wishful thinking, and the inclusion of such a development in the film can be explained only by its greater commitment to being a star vehicle for Kumar and Sen than to being a study of marginality.

Tied to this avoidance of the theme of marginality is the film's portrayal of Krishnendu's relationship with Rina as less 'scandalous' than that between Othello and Desdemona. Krishnendu starts out as someone who, as Paromita Chakravarti puts it, has a 'poised balance of modernity and tradition',[12] as a student of medical science who plans to go abroad for higher studies while displaying a 'cheeky resistance against Anglicisation' when confronted with the anti-Indian prejudice of the British.[13] Once he falls in love with Rina, and her father demands that Krishnendu convert to Christianity if he is to marry her, Krishnendu readily agrees. He attributes this readiness to his agnosticism, declaring that he would happily leave Hinduism behind and embrace Christ if this lets him marry the woman he loves. The conversion, however, marks the beginning of what Chakravarti describes as the loss of his 'indigenous identity', for he 'ends up adopting the archetypal role of evangelical colonialism – that of the missionary priest',[14] thereby severing ties with both the Hindu identity he was born into and the agnostic identity he had chosen for himself. It is as if the film, having paired an Indian man and a white woman romantically, decides that such a coupling is excessively disruptive, and must be

---

[12] Paromita Chakravarti, 'Modernity, postcoloniality, and *Othello*: the case of *Saptapadi*', in *Remaking Shakespeare: Performance across Media, Genres and Cultures*, ed. Pascale Aebischer, Nigel Wheale and Edward Esche (London, 2003), pp. 39–55; p. 50.
[13] Chakravarti, 'Modernity, postcoloniality, and *Othello*', p. 50.
[14] Chakravarti, 'Modernity, postcoloniality, and *Othello*', p. 49.

rendered more palatable by reducing the differences between Rina and Krishnendu. Hence, Krishnendu, to quote Chakravarti, undergoes an 'assimilation into the white, Christian society'[15] of Rina through his adoption of Christianity and evangelism, a process that can be said to have reached its completion when he, in the final scene, is seen carrying Rina to a church, to be 'united in the eye of a patently Christian God'.[16] Rina, meanwhile, learns that she is something of a 'darkie' herself, birthed as she was through an illicit liaison between her British father and his Indian servant, which means that her attraction to Krishnendu was not as strange or unusual a development as it seemed. The racial and religious chasm between them thus lessened, the union between them is now more plausible. What is notable here is that both Krishnendu's conversion and the realization on Rina's part that she is not racially 'pure' could have been used to construct for them marginalized identities, but the film does not do so. The unjust nature of the demand by Rina's father that Krishnendu become a Christian, which is essentially a colonizer's attempt to impose part of his identity on a colonized to 'improve' the latter, is barely allowed to register; Krishnendu's aforementioned agnosticism means that he thinks little of changing his religion, which in turn prevents the viewers from seeing it as an example of colonial hegemony at work. Later, when he does become a Christian, his condition could have mirrored that of the Bengali poet Michael Madhusudan Dutt, who converted to Christianity in order to become more 'English' but instead found himself in limbo – disowned, on one hand, by his orthodox religious father, and treated, despite his conversion, as a second-class citizen by the British. But *Saptapadi* shows no such discrimination against Krishnendu by the British post-conversion, and while he does have a conservative Hindu father he grows estranged from, that estrangement turns out to be temporary. The father, having emotionally blackmailed Rina into deserting Krishnendu, eventually grows contrite, and facilitates the lovers' reunion. Krishnendu thus finds a place among the colonizers through his embracing of Christianity, wins his traditionalist father's approval, *and* gets the girl – which is hardly what a marginalized subaltern's life looks like. As for Rina, there is little indication that her true identity – that of a mixed-race woman born out of wedlock – is known to the world at large. No matter how tormented she herself may have grown upon learning this, to others she still occupies the privileged position of a white woman in a colonized land. The only person to whom she confesses her racial identity is the non-judgemental Krishnendu, which means that she is in little danger of becoming a racial Other like Othello. Instead, by integrating Krishnendu among the British via his conversion and the services he renders to the colonizers as a doctor during the war (while also effecting a reconciliation with his Hindu father), and by making Rina a half-Indian (who nonetheless remains a part of the British society owing to her white appearance and the services that *she* renders as a nurse to the British army), *Saptapadi* ensures that its couple find enough middle ground to remain together, rather than splintering apart like the Black Othello and white Desdemona. Uttam's brother, Tarun Kumar, describes in a memoir how Tarun had persuaded Tarashankar Bandopadhyay, on whose novel *Saptapadi* was based, to give the filmmakers the permission to alter the novel's downbeat ending into a happier one, so as to convey to viewers a message on the power of love to overcome all impediments.[17] Such a message was needed because the film had in the lead stars whose success had been built on romantic dramas that usually had a happy ending, and a tragic ending like those of Bandopadhyay's novel or *Othello* was less likely to find favour with the audience. The refusal to make Krishnendu or Rina a marginalized entity aims, one can therefore guess, to reach that desired happy ending more easily.

---

[15] Chakravarti, 'Modernity, postcoloniality, and *Othello*', p. 50.
[16] Chakravarti, 'Modernity, postcoloniality, and *Othello*', p. 50.
[17] Tarun Kumar, *Aamar Dada Uttam Kumar* (Kolkata, 2000), p. 188.

CIRCUMVENTING MARGINALITY

CONCLUSION

Among Shakespeare's plays, *Othello*, with its focus on the themes of race and marginality, should have a particular resonance in India, a formerly colonized nation which has, since independence, witnessed numerous conflicts caused by divisions of religion, caste and ethnicity. Yet, as I have endeavoured to demonstrate in this article, the Indian screen adaptations and appropriations of *Othello*, regardless of the era and the language they were made in, have, despite their surface engagement with it, ultimately circumvented the play's theme of marginality. I have attempted – by following the approach to studying screen adaptations that Karen Kline calls the Materialist paradigm – to understand why each of these films thus avoids the theme of marginality that is so crucial to Shakespeare's play. In the case of *Omkara*, I have discussed how its apparently marginal titular character is anything but, and have explored, further, how its director's love for gangster films, which is reflective of Hindi cinema's turn-of-the-millennium fascination with that genre, led to the film's evasion of the themes of marginality. *Kaliyattam* is equally evasive in that regard, and the reason, I have argued, is, again, its director's penchant for making a particular type of film – namely, the family melodrama – which made him treat *Othello* as just a story of a disintegrating marriage. With *Izzat* and *Saptapadi*, I have tried to show how the onscreen personae of the lead actors in these films, and, in *Izzat*'s case, the dictates of the *masala* cinema format, prevented them from delving meaningfully into Othello's marginalized identity even as they referenced the play.

Interestingly, while these adaptations of *Othello* have consistently sidestepped the subject of marginality, other Indian releases have adapted/appropriated other Shakespeare plays to explore and celebrate marginal identities. Nagraj Manjule's *Sairat* ('Wild', 2016) uses the *Romeo and Juliet* template to tell an inter-caste love story which (unlike *Omkara* and *Kaliyattam*) does not shy away from depicting casteist violence; Kenny Basumatary's *Local Kung Fu 2* (2017), an adaptation of *The Comedy of Errors*, includes a gay character and decries homophobia, and Vandana Kataria's *Noblemen* (2019) is an interesting, if not entirely successful, attempt to draw parallels, via its chronicling of a production of *The Merchant of Venice* in a posh Indian boarding school, between the theme of anti-Semitism in that play and the culture of bullying and homophobia prevalent in such schools. Even Bhardwaj shows greater willingness to tackle marginal identities with his third Shakespeare adaptation, *Haider*, than he did with *Omkara*, using *Hamlet* to depict the human rights violations faced by Kashmiri Muslims. The Materialist paradigm may be employed to determine what factors and circumstances enabled these films, many of which are not even based on an issue-oriented play such as *Othello*, nevertheless to address social issues and examine marginality meaningfully. The merit of the Materialist paradigm is that it forgoes the usual practice of equating fidelity with quality, and concentrates, instead, on the determinants that shape an adaptation into the faithful or non-faithful film that it is, thereby providing us with a more complete understanding of the processes through which a work of literature is turned into a work of cinema. So, just as this paradigm has been used in this article to explain why various Indian screen versions of *Othello* have circumvented the play's theme of marginality, it can be used, also, to understand why the other Indian Shakespeare adaptations/appropriations mentioned in this paragraph incorporate that theme even if it means deviating from their source plays. Through such an exercise, we can gain a greater insight into how Shakespeare has been used to address the less-than-pleasant realities of India.

OTHELLO'S KIN: LEGACY, BELONGING AND *THE FORTUNES OF THE MOOR*

PATRICIA A. CAHILL[1]

Among the countless events commemorating the 400th anniversary of Shakespeare's death in 2016 was a remarkable staged reading at Emory University of the two-act drama *Fortunes of the Moor*, which was written and directed by the late Barbara Molette (1940–2017) and her husband Carlton Molette (born 1939), whose collaborations have earned them many accolades, including the National Black Theatre Festival's 'Living Legend' Award. *Fortunes* takes its title from the last speech in *Othello* when Desdemona's cousin Lodovico urges their uncle Graziano to lay claim to Othello's worldly possessions, to 'seize upon the fortunes of the Moor' (5.2.376).[2] However, the Molettes' play proposes that the 'fortunes' sought by Desdemona's relatives belong to someone else: a son to whom Desdemona had secretly given birth before travelling to Cyprus, and who is being cared for in a Venetian convent. Key to the narrative is a scheme fabricated by Gratiano and for which he employs Lodovico to dispatch the infant secretly to Africa so as to claim his inheritance as their own. The play depicts the events of a single day when Brabantio (here, imagined as alive) learns that he has a grandson; the baby's African relatives – Othello's uncle Hassan, aunt Elissa and sister Somaia – arrive in Venice; and Gratiano, realizing that his plans are going awry, becomes increasingly murderous. As *Fortunes* pointedly explores questions of race and kinship, it invites playgoers to consider to whom the infant and the fortunes rightly belong: Brabantio who seeks 'continuation of [his] blood', or Somaia who speaks of her 'duty and pleasure to raise [her] brother's child as though he were [her] own'.[3]

As I sat in the theatre on 9 November 2016 awaiting the Theatre Emory reading of *Fortunes*, I felt grateful to enter the playwrights' world far from that day's troubling news: the United States presidential election upset that left many people stunned. Almost at once, however, I noticed that *Fortunes* evoked that political moment rather than offering escape from it. Most unsettlingly, I could hear its present-day resonances in the Venetians' racist invective about Africa and Africans, and especially in Gratiano's calm certitude, while arranging for the kidnapping and murder of the baby, that, when this heinous action came to light, the so-called 'Moors' would be blamed. After all, the newly elected president had won followers by promoting 'birtherism' conspiracies that impugned Kenya, the birthplace of his predecessor's father; casting majority-Black cities

---

[1] I dedicate this article to the memory of Barbara Molette, and thank Carlton Molette for his many inspiring conversations. Grateful thanks are also due to Carolyn Betensky, Gabrielle Dudley, Kim Hall, Walter Kalaidjian, the late Pellom McDaniels III and Emma Smith.

[2] On these lines, see Emily C. Bartels, '"Making more of the Moor": Aaron, Othello, and Renaissance refashionings of race', *Shakespeare Quarterly* 41 (1990), 433–54; p. 454; and Emily Weissbourd, '"Search this ulcer soundly": sex as contagion in *The Changeling* and *Othello*', in *Contagion and the Shakespearean Stage*, ed. Darryl Chalk and Mary Floyd-Wilson (Cham, 2019), pp. 105–25; p. 118: https://link.springer.com/chapter/10.1007/978-3-030-14428-9_6.

[3] Barbara Molette and Carlton Molette, *Fortunes of the Moor* (Bloomington, 2016), p. 32 and p. 16 (hereafter cited parenthetically).

as dystopias; re-tweeting the lie that Black Americans were responsible for most murders of whites; and, just a few weeks before the election, reprising his false allegations about the Central Park Five, the Black and Latinx boys wrongly imprisoned for a brutal attack on a white woman in 1989.[4] In short, the language of *Fortunes* – a play about early modern Venice – sounded disturbingly contemporary, attesting to enduring patterns of anti-Black racism. Nevertheless, as I listened to the Theatre Emory actors and to a post-show conversation with the playwrights, what also stood out to me was that this play offers a compelling counternarrative to Shakespeare's tragedy: a profound affirmation of Black ingenuity and survival in a racist world – one that felt especially welcome on such an otherwise bleak day. As a white mother of a Black son, I also found the play's staging of kinship and community particularly appealing. But as a Shakespearian, I had questions: above all, I wondered how *Fortunes* came to be, and how it came to be that *Fortunes* is not widely recognized as part of the *Othello* canon.

In this article, I explore these questions, while considering *Fortunes* in the context of both *Othello* and the Molettes' archive at Emory University. Originally conceived as a straightforward story about a custody battle that begins after Shakespeare's tragedy ends, *Fortunes* exists in two very different versions: the first full draft, which dates from September 1994 and was originally staged in Harlem in the following year, and the version that represents the text as it was revised in 1997 and self-published in 2016.[5] As I discuss, both versions of *Fortunes* are indebted to the tradition of Black radical thought known as Afrocentrism, although they clearly eschew the gender and racial politics for which some Afrocentric texts have rightly been critiqued.[6] As they decentre whiteness, both texts thus foreground Black female voices and explicitly reject ideas of racial purity. Moreover, both texts resonate with the claim put forth by Patricia Hill Collins that '[i]n a climate of institutionalized racism that valorizes Whiteness, Afrocentrism offers an affirmation of Blackness, a love ethic directed toward Black people'.[7] In what follows, I detail how *Fortunes*, even as it responds to *Othello*, performs this love ethic.

As part of my analysis, I trace the play's genesis, evolution and reception, with an eye towards urging upon white Shakespearians a kind of reparations work, for while Black theatre makers have, from the start, championed *Fortunes*, our predominantly white Shakespeare industry has yet to acknowledge this play as *Othello*'s legacy.[8]

SEIZING

Soon after the 1995 premiere of *Fortunes*, *New York Times* theatre critic Mel Gussow described the play as an '*Othello* sequel', and the appellation has stuck.[9] In fact, as I discuss below, the playwrights

---

[4] Andrew Prokop, 'Trump fanned a conspiracy about Obama's birthplace for years. Now he pretends Clinton started it', *Vox*, 16 September 2016: www.vox.com/2016/9/16/12938066/donald-trump-obama-birth-certificate-birther; Richard Fausset, Alan Blinder and John Eligon, 'Donald Trump's description of Black America is offending those living in it', *New York Times*, 24 August 2016: www.nytimes.com/2016/08/25/us/politics/donald-trump-black-voters.html; Philip Bump, 'Donald Trump retweeted a very wrong set of numbers on race and murder', *Washington Post*, 22 November 2015: www.washingtonpost.com/news/the-fix/wp/2015/11/22/trump-retweeted-a-very-wrong-set-of-numbers-on-race-and-murder; Steven A. Holmes, 'Member of "Central Park 5" blasts Trump', *CNN Politics*, 7 October 2016, www.cnn.com/2016/10/06/politics/reality-check-donald-trump-central-park-5/index.html.

[5] '*Fortunes of the Moor* by Barbara and Carlton Molette. First full draft Sept. 17, 1994', Carlton W. and Barbara J. Molette papers, Stuart A. Rose Manuscript, Archives, and Rare Book Library, Emory University (hereafter 'MP'), Box 20, Folder 5.

[6] On the place of Afrocentrism within the Black radical tradition, see Sarah Balakrishnan, 'Afrocentrism revisited: Africa in the philosophy of Black nationalism', *Souls* 22 (2020), 71–88. On overlaps between misogyny, racism and Afrocentrism, see Patricia Hill Collins, *From Black Power to Hip Hop: Racism, Nationalism and Feminism* (Philadelphia, 2006), pp. 95–122.

[7] Collins, *From Black Power*, p. 119. Collins cites Cornel West in her discussion of a 'love ethic'.

[8] An exception is Lena Orlin's enthusiastic support of a panel featuring R. Candy Tate's interview with Carlton Molette at the Shakespeare Association of America 45th meeting in Atlanta in April 2017.

[9] Mel Gussow, 'Enter, spiritedly, the world of Black theater', *New York Times*, 5 August 1995, p. 12.

did initially plan to write a sequel, and the play does contemplate what happens after Shakespeare's play ends; it takes up that disconcerting moment when Shakespeare, having just asked audiences to look at the 'tragic loading of this bed' (5.2.373) – a bed strewn with the corpses of Desdemona, Emilia and Othello – calls attention to the fact that, with Othello dead, his property is available to be claimed. That said, *Fortunes* is a far more complex work than 'sequel' suggests, offering audiences not so much a continuation of Shakespeare's text as a challenge to the certainties of that text – including, of course, Graziano's claim that Desdemona's 'match was mortal' to Brabantio (5.2.212). In other words, *Fortunes* can best be understood as an appropriation, for, as it depicts the Venetian effort to 'seize upon' Othello's possessions, the play takes a form that, as Jean Marsden has influentially observed, itself entails the 'desire for possession' and a 'seizure for one's own uses'.[10]

What are the 'uses' for which the Molettes may have 'seized' Shakespeare's literary property? An answer to this question can be broached by considering the play alongside the playwrights' first literary collaboration, *Rosalee Pritchett*, a play dating from 1970 that epitomizes the kind of formally experimental and politically engaged work that has marked their careers. First professionally staged by New York's Negro Ensemble Company (NEC), a theatre recognized as the 'apogee of the black arts movement', and revived in 2017 for the NEC's 50th Anniversary season, this play – not unlike *Othello* – ponders internalized racism and the vulnerability of Black people to state violence.[11] Focusing on upper-class bridge-playing Black women who are critical of Black protest, it depicts the trauma that follows when white National Guardsmen (played, transgressively, by Black actors in whiteface) stop one of the women for a supposed curfew violation in the wake of an uprising, and then sexually assault her. The play ends without a final curtain because, as the playwrights explain, 'The audience ought to leave this play perturbed [and] dissatisfied.'[12] Reviewing the first NEC performance in the *New York Times*, critic Clayton Riley declared the Molettes to be 'significant new dramatists' and noted that 'their concerns are with the pitch and flavor of contemporary Black life, its ambivalences and contradictions, its emotional peaks and valleys, and the almost illogical beauty attending its rapidly changing days and nights'.[13]

What Riley identified as the Molettes' commitment to capturing the beauty and contradictions of contemporary Black life is visible throughout their subsequent collaborations. Together, over five decades, they wrote more than twenty plays, and individually they wrote, directed, produced and created costumes and set designs for a great many more. Equally significantly, they held teaching and administrative positions at many universities, including seven different historically Black institutions.[14] Through such work, Carlton Molette helped to develop the field of Black theatre studies in the 1970s, and both playwrights variously trained actors, playwrights, directors, designers and theatre technicians. As scholars, they helped to recover the history of Black theatre in America; highlighted the challenges faced by female playwrights such as Alice Childress and Lorraine Hansberry to get their works taken seriously; co-authored the influential textbook *Black Theatre: Premise and Presentation* (1986, 1992), which they revised and expanded as *Afrocentric Theater* (2013); helped to found the American Theatre Association's Black Theatre Program and the Black Theatre Network; and served as presidents of the National Conference

---

[10] Jean I. Marsden, *The Appropriation of Shakespeare: Post-Renaissance Reconstructions of the Works and the Myth* (New York, 1991), p. 1.

[11] Anthony D. Hill and Douglas Q. Barnett, *Historical Dictionary of African American Theater* (Lanham, 2009), p. xliv.

[12] Carlton W. Molette and Barbara J. Molette, *Rosalee Pritchett* (New York, 1972), p. 4.

[13] Clayton Riley, 'My quarrels notwithstanding, I liked them', *New York Times*, 7 February 1971, Section D, p. 3.

[14] Their teaching and administrative careers included the following Historically Black Colleges and Universities (HBCUs): Tuskegee University, Howard University, Florida A & M University, Spelman College, Texas Southern University, Lincoln University of Missouri, and Coppin State University.

on African American Theatre. When looked at in the context of this work, it is easy to see that the Molettes' appropriation of *Othello* should not be understood as a case of two playwrights paying homage to the Bard. Rather, *Fortunes*, like all the Molettes' work, clearly exemplifies activist theatre: an effort to challenge racial injustice and illuminate the richness of Black life even if – or, perhaps, especially if – their vision unsettles some playgoers, leaving them perturbed and dissatisfied.

A more specific context within which to situate the Molettes' appropriation or 'seizing' of *Othello* can be found in a short letter contained in their archive, from C. Bernard Jackson, the Black playwright and director who, after the Watts Riots, founded the Inner City Cultural Center, a Los Angeles institution that became famous for its non-traditional casting and its support of hundreds of theatre artists of colour.[15] In the note, dating from late 1995, Jackson enthusiastically requests a copy of *Fortunes*, which was then having its New York premiere, and he prefaces this request with a question: 'What is this fascination we seem to have with Othello?' This captivation can be seen in the fact that, coincidentally, December 1995 saw the American release of Oliver Parker's film of *Othello* starring Laurence Fishburne, which marked the first time a major film cast a Black actor in the title role. Unsurprisingly, newspaper reviews of the film drew on stereotypes about dangerous Black men, commonly citing Tina Turner's abusive husband – whom Fishburne had played in the 1993 Hollywood biopic *What's Love Got to Do with It* – as well as O. J. Simpson, whose highly publicized criminal murder trial was unfolding in 1995.[16] In fact, even before this trial, news anchor Dan Rather had declared – while reporting on the infamous 1994 Ford Bronco police chase ending with Simpson's arrest – that Simpson reminded him of Othello.[17] For the Molettes to 'seize' Shakespeare's tragedy in this cultural moment, then, was to reject the idea of Othello as a homicidal Black man rightly seized by white authorities – a racist trope that remains a staple of American media.

But Jackson's use of the first-person plural pronoun in his question about 'this fascination we seem to have with Othello' also points in another direction and to a specific experience with Shakespeare's tragedy that the three playwrights shared. In a 2008 interview with the pre-eminent scholar and archivist of Black theatre James Hatch, Barbara Molette mentions that, decades earlier, she and her husband had stayed up all night with Jackson talking about *Othello*.[18] This conversation led not only to *Fortunes*, but also, in 1979, to another appropriation of Shakespeare's tragedy: Jackson's drama *Iago* in which both Emilia and Iago are Black, and Emilia aims to vindicate Iago, explaining that they acted out of fierce loyalty, seeking to protect Othello from white Venetians, especially the villainous Cassio. In the course of the same 2008 interview with Hatch, Carlton Molette remarks that, during this late-night exchange, he had shared a memory from the early 1960s – namely, that, when he directed *Othello* at Tuskegee University 'at the height of the Civil Rights movement', his students had concluded that the most interesting character in the play was Iago. As he explains in the 2008 interview, he was fascinated that Black students who had watched an all-Black production understood that there was something wrong with Shakespeare's most substantial speaking role for a Black character. Further, Molette ventures, *Fortunes* had found success in the theatre precisely because so many Black

---

[15] 'C. Bernard Jackson to Barbara and Carlton Molette' [1995], MP Box 20, Folder 8.

[16] See Philip C. Kolin, 'Blackness made visible: a survey of *Othello* in criticism, on stage, and on screen', in *'Othello': New Critical Essays*, ed. Philip C. Kolin (New York and London, 2002), pp. 1–88; pp. 65–7.

[17] See Barbara Hodgdon, 'Race-ing *Othello*, re-engendering white-out', in *Shakespeare, the Movie: Popularizing the Plays on Film, TV, and Video*, ed. Lynda E. Boose and Richard Burt (London, 1997), pp. 23–44; p. 23.

[18] 'Molette, Carlton and Barbara Molette, interviewed by James Hatch, May 8, 2008', Camille Billops and James V. Hatch archives at Emory University, Stuart A. Rose Manuscript, Archives, and Rare Book Library, Emory University.

theatre artists have felt frustration with *Othello*: 'there is this army of Black actors out there who have all been asked to play the role of Othello and they all run into a set of problems'. Especially challenging, he argues, is that Shakespeare's Iago-centric play 'essentially treats Othello as though his life begins when he becomes Venetian and totally disengages him from his roots', so that 'when you do Shakespeare's *Othello*, the actor is never given a whole person'.[19] Clearly, as such comments underscore, when the Molettes 'seized' *Othello*, it was an assertion of affiliation as much as anything else. To imagine Shakespeare's tragic protagonist as embedded in a community with others like him, as belonging to people of African descent and to a place other than Venice, is of course fundamentally an ethical act: an attempt to conceptualize the personhood of which Shakespeare had deprived him, and to make him whole.

LOCATING

The Molettes' initial efforts to solve the set of problems they identified in *Othello* – problems not unlike those described by many Black actors[20] – can be glimpsed in the earliest archival document relating to *Fortunes*: a brief synopsis, dated May 1994, of a yet-to-be-written five-act play entitled '*Othello*: The Sequel'.[21] The synopsis shows that the Molettes were not interested in reconceiving the role of Shakespeare's villain as Jackson had done; instead, they sought to offer a more pervasive exploration of Venetian treachery. The proposed play would juxtapose a Venetian family riven with disloyalty and a close-knit African family eager to embrace new kin. Act 1 would open with the play's villain – Brabantio's unnamed nephew – conversing with a messenger who has just located Othello's father in Morocco and escorted him to Venice to retrieve the child without Brabantio's knowledge. Act 2 would introduce Othello's two wives and Othello's father, who is referred to as 'the Moor' and who decries Brabantio's lack of hospitality, asking, 'Why has he not come with outstretched arms to encircle me and call me family?'[22] Acts 3 and 4 would showcase the willingness of Emilia and Brabantio to go along with the nephew's plan to kidnap the baby, as well as the nephew's willingness to kill the baby when Brabantio refuses to relinquish him. Finally, act 5 would show Othello's father outwitting the Venetians by getting hold of the baby and sending him safely to Morocco, while Brabantio would speak the play's last words: 'I have no grandson.'[23]

The play the Molettes actually wrote – both their first full draft dating from September 1994 and their revision dating from the summer of 1997 – differs significantly from the play imagined in this synopsis. They dropped the title '*Othello*: The Sequel', and the five-act drama became a two-act work – changes that perhaps intimate their unwillingness to follow in Shakespeare's footsteps. But their most significant change was that the three African characters of the synopsis were transformed into Hassan, Elissa and Somaia and placed at the drama's centre. Such focus clearly signalled the playwrights' embrace of Afrocentrism, the heterogeneous grassroots movement and intellectual tradition that gained traction in the United States in the 1980s as it became associated with a wide range of phenomena, from the wearing of kente cloth and the creation of the Kwanzaa holiday to the scholarly and popular writings of Molefi Kete Asante, who famously urged an African-centred perspective and a reorientation away from the universalizing claims of much Western thought.[24]

---

[19] 'Molette, Carlton and Barbara Molette, interviewed by James Hatch'.
[20] See, for example, Ayanna Thompson's 'Introduction' to William Shakespeare, *Othello*, rev. ed., ed. E. A. J. Honigmann (London, 2016), pp. 87–90. Thompson notes how, in 1998, Hugh Quarshie's public questioning of whether Black actors might take on the role of Othello without legitimizing racial stereotypes paved the way for other Black actors to speak out about their discomfort with the play.
[21] '*Othello*: The Sequel, 14 May 1994', MP Box 20, Folder 5.
[22] '*Othello*: The Sequel', p. 5. [23] '*Othello*: The Sequel', p. 13.
[24] See, for example, Molefi Kete Asante, *Afrocentricity* (Buffalo, NY, 1980).

To be sure, *Fortunes* was not the first play to bring Afrocentrism and *Othello* into close proximity. That distinction might go to the *Othello* directed by the celebrated Black actor/director Harold Scott in 1990, which was the first *Othello* staged at the Folger Shakespeare Theater and likely the first multiracial *Othello* both to cast Black actors in the roles of Iago and Emilia *and* to dress Othello in the turbans and veils associated with the Muslim and semi-nomadic Tuareg community of Mauritania.[25] But for the Molettes, as they argue in an essay accompanying the printed text of *Fortunes*, Afrocentric theatre implies far more than the costuming of Black actors in African attire.[26] Rather, it has to do with the vantage point from which playwrights conceive, and audiences receive, drama. Accordingly, in their commentary on *Fortunes*, they cite Asante's notion of 'location', adding that what most matters is a play's 'conceptual' location: Afrocentric theatre, they conclude, is created by those who situate themselves conceptually within African culture and who envision an audience who may respond to their call.[27] In line with this view, the Molettes explain how their travel to Ghana in 1997 led to their realization that the 'place from which [they] originally envisioned [the play] was more Eurocentric than [they] had realized or intended' (p. 105), an insight to which I will return. What is worth underscoring here is the Molettes' point that, for Black playwrights, this act of self-location – of centring oneself in one's African identity and expecting such imaginative sympathy in one's audience – is both an aesthetic framework and, in our racist society, a matter of arduous work. Indeed, they connect their aspiration to create Afrocentric theatre with W. E. B. Du Bois's 'double consciousness', which they identify as the 'difficulty, maybe even the impossibility, for African Americans to achieve a culturally centered position'.[28]

For all its attention to the struggle of the Africans in Venice, the first version of *Fortunes* affirms both a history of Black survival and a pan-African identity that is emphasized by the play's identification of Othello's relatives with the continent rather than, as in the synopsis, simply with Morocco.

Thus, the African characters celebrate African resources and geographies, from the salt mines of the Sahara to the Ashanti gold of Ghanaian marketplaces, and they accuse Virgil of having slandered the great Carthaginian queen Elissa by portraying her as Dido, the lover forsaken by Aeneas. In a similarly Afrocentric vein, this version emphasizes the strength of the African social fabric, so that Othello's three relatives easily come together around female and matrilineal duties: Somaia speaks of her responsibility, as the older sister of Othello, to raise his child, and Hassan declares that, as the brother of Othello's mother, he 'cannot allow the child ... to be raised apart from his kin'.[29] Significantly, this version of the play juxtaposes this solidarity with the fractured alliances of Desdemona's family: Gratiano and Lodovico, for instance, concoct their plot partly to punish Brabantio for his alleged theft of their paternal inheritance. Most importantly, this version emphasizes that the Africans prevail over the formidable obstacles they encounter in Venice. Indeed, through the scene of their final triumph, the play pointedly recalls Othello's success at winning over the Venetian senate with his rhetorical skill, for, just after Hassan delivers a speech denouncing the Venetian denigration of Africans, deriding the idea of racial purity and averring that he 'will love the child no less because his mother was Venetian', Brabantio relinquishes the infant and declares that

---

[25] On this production, see Angela C. Pao, *No Safe Spaces: Recasting Race, Ethnicity, and Nationality in American Theater* (Ann Arbor, MI, 2010), pp. 91–6.

[26] Barbara Molette and Carlton Molette, 'Overcoming double consciousness: exploring *Fortunes of the Moor*', in Molette and Molette, *Fortunes*, pp. 103–9.

[27] Molette and Molette, 'Overcoming double consciousness', p. 105. See also the essay's expanded version entitled 'What makes Black theatre Black: exploring *Fortunes of the Moor*' dated 1998 in MP Box 17, Folder 7, which states: 'changing one's thinking from Eurocentric to Afrocentric is not as quick or easy as taking off a sport coat and putting on a dashiki'.

[28] Molette and Molette, 'Overcoming double consciousness', p. 103.

[29] '*Fortunes of the Moor* by Barbara and Carlton Molette. First full draft', p. 67 (hereafter cited parenthetically).

'the Moor has spoken eloquently of conditions in Venice from which [he] ha[s] no power to protect [his] heir' (p. 80). In short, by appropriating *Othello*, this version of the play fully imagines the Africans as agential subjects rather than passive objects; not surprisingly, then, it concludes with the relocation of Othello's heir to Africa, where – audiences are told – he will receive a new African name.

This first version of *Fortunes* engages with *Othello* most conspicuously through its depiction of the pervasiveness of Venetian slavery, emphasizing that, as the Africans seek to claim the baby, they face the possibility – named by Hassan, who is a wealthy, cosmopolitan leather merchant – of their being 'shackled and chained and [taken] to a slave market' (p. 42). In many scenes, the African characters explicitly condemn the hypocrisy of the Venetians, reminding audiences that the transatlantic trade entailed a redefinition of Christian principles to support atrocity. But, crucially, it goes well beyond these individual voices of condemnation to imply that Shakespeare's tragedy offers a complete whitewashing of history, for *Fortunes* presents Venice as a place where enslavement simply cannot be avoided. Beginning at daybreak at a pier from which Venetian vessels leave for Africa, the play shows the Africans moving about a city where 'advertisements [are] posted ... listing names and private attributes of persons to be sold at auction to the highest bidder' (p. 60), and it ends that evening in the convent that houses the child whom Lodovico contemplates selling to enslavers before agreeing to have him murdered.

As the play repeatedly alerts audiences to the fact that, historically, the Venetian Republic depended upon the enslavement of Black people from sub-Saharan Africa, it responds directly to the history Othello narrates when he tells the senators that he wooed Desdemona with tales 'Of [his] being taken by the insolent foe / And sold to slavery' and of his 'redemption thence' (1.3.136–7), and to *Othello*'s more allusive references to this larger history, including its several uses of the word 'slave' as a term of abuse. Of course, *Othello* is notoriously oblique on the subject of enslavement, and some scholars have even resisted the idea of reading the play in the context of the European enslavement of sub-Saharan Africans, claiming instead that it should be read only in the context of piracy and privateering in the Islamic Mediterranean.[30] But *Fortunes* insists that, to understand *Othello*, audiences must reckon with chattel slavery. Indeed, a document in the Molettes' archive about their desire to pursue research in Europe suggests that the playwrights were intent on detailing as accurately as possible the historical role of Venice in enabling the global trade in enslaved Africans: the play, so they hoped, would 'expose the historical foundations of racism – the greed that caused the slave trade to emerge and the societal politics and hypocrisies that continue to [have an] impact upon people of African ancestry'.[31] By emphasizing the ongoing potency of this traumatic history, *Fortunes* in fact resembles many Afrocentric texts, which, as Sarah Balakrishnan has pointed out, recognize the 'originary dispossession' of Africans as precisely what precipitates a 'counterinsurgency' in which Black individuals claim their identity as Africans.[32]

The first version of *Fortunes* focuses squarely on African dispossession in its opening scene. With searing irony, the scene reveals that Gratiano, who has just welcomed Lodovico back from Africa, intends to become an arts patron after he invests the infant's inheritance in the booming business of the transatlantic trade – in effect, that he intends to seize Othello's fortune so as to enable others to seize captive Africans. As this

---

[30] On the significance of the Atlantic slave trade for understandings of *Othello*, see Emily Weissbourd, '"I have done the state some service": reading slavery in *Othello* through Juan Latino', *Comparative Drama* 47 (2013), 529–51; on Othello's enslavement as a temporary condition, see Matthieu Chapman, *Anti-Black Racism in Early Modern English Drama: The Other 'Other'* (London, 2017); and on the relative absence of references to slavery and the use of 'slave' as a term of abuse, see Camille Wells Slights, 'Slaves and subjects in *Othello*', *Shakespeare Quarterly* 48 (1997), 377–90.

[31] Barbara J. Molette and Carlton W. Molette, '*Fortunes of the Moor* description of the project', in MP Box 20, Folder 8.

[32] Balakrishnan, 'Afrocentrism revisited', p. 75.

first scene progresses, the play points to the Venetians' refusal to recognize African personhood – so, for instance, a merchant shares with Gratiano an account of what is contained in the ships that arrive from Africa: 'gold, ivory, ebony, turtle shells, ostrich feathers, rhinoceros horns, and slaves' (p. 12). Foregrounding Venetian talk about 'Good business practices', the scene shows the merchant boasting of his fiscal wisdom in selecting a Portuguese captain for his enslaving venture, noting his skill in 'pack[ing] his ships' hold to get the maximum amount of cargo' and commenting that the vessel 'will hold up to 800 slaves, tightly packed' (p. 12). Through this conversation – especially the dehumanizing language of 'yield' and of profits and loss – the play underscores the everyday horror of the transatlantic business established by the Portuguese. Significantly, through such dialogue, this scene also summons up the dense networks of commercial language in *Othello* – from its opening description of Cassio as a 'counter-caster' or accountant (1.1.30) to its extensive wordplay on 'credit' – thereby hinting at the shadowy presence in *Othello* of the transatlantic trade.[33] But, unlike *Othello*, *Fortunes* does not overlook the corporeal impact of enslavement. Rather, this scene emphasizes its brutalities through the merchant's matter-of-fact explanation of his terror tactics – the display of the corpse of anyone caught trying to escape – and his casual reference to mass murder: 'If we deliver 400 or so of the 800 slaves we ship, a handsome profit still awaits us' (p. 13). Equally disturbingly, this scene repeatedly returns to the image of the 'hold' and its contents. Describing the space as filled first with 'tightly packed' persons imagined as 'slave cargo', and then with 'sugar cane and tobacco', *Fortunes* represents the devastating image of enslaved Africans confined in the hold of a ship through the eyes of these would-be profiteers (p. 13). As such, this scene brings to mind Christina Sharpe's recent account of Black 'wakeness' as an awareness arising from chattel slavery, including the way the materiality of the slave ship, such as 'the hold', haunts Black life today, even as such metaphors are a site for artistic production.[34]

What the play ultimately focuses on, however, is not the anti-Blackness embodied by the Venetian investors in chattel slavery, but rather the fact of resistance and resilience in the face of such unfreedom. This emphasis is apparent in the play's second scene – the one that introduces the play's African characters – as the three refer to the family member they grieve and whose child they seek as 'Tarik' rather than 'Othello'. By showing that Othello's very name attests to his captivity, the play seems designed both to startle and to demand recognition of the objectification – the stripping of personhood – that enslavement entails. But, equally strikingly, when Hassan explains to the puzzled Gratiano that this Tarik of whom they speak is Othello by another name, the play insists upon something other than the subjugation of Africans:

The name 'Othello' was given to him when he was captured and sold as a slave. The name given to him by his parents was Tarik. He was named for the African general, who more than 800 years ago, conquered the lands now known as Spain. The mountain that you call Gibraltar was named Gebel Tarik by the African soldiers who conquered Spain under his leadership. In our language that means 'the mountains of Tarik'. The natives of Spain corrupted the original name and called the mountain Gibraltar. General Tarik built a castle on top of Gibraltar that remains there today. (p. 16)

Significantly, the play here does not simply name the fact of Tarik/Othello's enslavement. Rather, it enfolds that history in a counternarrative about the eighth-century Islamic conquest of the Iberian peninsula, which, along with the image of the still-standing mountaintop castle, aligns African culture with endurance rather than subjection, attaching to Hassan's dead nephew an

---

[33] On this network, see Patricia Parker, 'Cassio, cash, and the "infidel o": arithmetic, double-entry bookkeeping, and *Othello*'s unfaithful accounts', in *A Companion to the Global Renaissance: English Literature and Culture in the Era of Expansion*, ed. Jyotsna G. Singh (Chichester, 2009), pp. 223–41.
[34] Christina Sharpe, *In the Wake: On Blackness and Being* (Durham and London, 2016).

African identity that is independent of and prior to European enslavement.

Arguably, then, the radical nature of the Molettes' appropriation of *Othello* has less to do with its making the presence of slavery in Venice unequivocally clear than it has to do with its attention to ongoing legacies, especially as expressed in the affective bonds among the play's African characters. What matters, the play suggests, is that, despite attempts to deny Africans the capacity for filiation, kinship persists. It endures after Tarik/Othello has been 'captured and shipped away in chains', and it endures after his death, just as the castle atop Gibraltar remains long after the death of General Tarik (p. 42). Or, to put it otherwise: what is so powerful about *Fortunes* in relationship to *Othello* is the Molettes' uncompromising insistence on Tarik/Othello as a man beloved. Such affect is on view in the play's second scene, which introduces the African characters and in which Hassan tells Gratiano of his deep love for his nephew. But more powerful still are the subsequent scenes in which audiences eavesdrop on the intimate conversation among Hassan, Elissa and Somaia as they contemplate the precarious status of freedom for Tarik/Othello and as they give voice to their difficult love for him. They ruminate, for example, on why he remained in Venice: Elissa ascribes it to his affection for Desdemona, while Hassan attributes it to his 'every-increasing fortune and celebrity' and suggests with sadness that 'the years Tarik spent in captivity gave him both an unquenchable appetite for adoration and an inability to distinguish friend from enemy when each heaped praise upon him' (p. 18). Somaia speaks of his having been 'deprived of family' in Venice and – in lines that evoke Shakespeare's account of Brabanzio's death – she mentions her parents' devastating grief upon their learning of his marriage to Desdemona (p. 42). Offering perspectives absent from *Othello*, the play also invites scrutiny of this marriage, so that Elissa, for example, proposes that he 'made the only choices available to him', that 'he was very lonely' and 'needed [her] to interpret the ways of these alien Venetians' (p. 42). Importantly, the play also points to Desdemona's ethical obligations to Tarik/Othello. In fact, as Elissa speculates that Desdemona 'was unable or unwilling to believe the magnitude of evil in her kinsmen and in other Venetians she has loved and held in high esteem' (42), the play reframes Shakespeare's tragedy in terms of what Charles W. Mills has influentially described as 'white ignorance', the epistemology of actively not-knowing that underpins systemic racism.[35]

By offering such musings about Tarik/Othello, this version of *Fortunes* refutes the terms *Othello* offers when it first lauds him as a 'noble and valiant general' (2.2.1–2) and then condemns him as the stereotypical 'cruel moor' (5.2.256). Rather, *Fortunes* maintains that enslavement changed Tarik/Othello: indeed, Somaia suggests that his enslaver required him to become violent, offering an account that recalls the fighting matches organized by enslavers in the American South.[36] In addition, the play, as though repairing the harm inflicted upon Othello by his isolation in the Shakespearian text, offers retrospective visions of him in community with others like him. In place of Shakespeare's exotic warrior who woos Desdemona with tales of cannibals and monsters, the play offers Elissa's memory of Tarik/Othello amusing children with stories he learned from 'infidels' about the 'men whose heads grew beneath their shoulders and of the Anthropophagi' (39). In place of Shakespeare's 'rash and most unfortunate man' (5.2.289), the play evokes a young man who spoke to young children of the 'ordeals of his enslavement', so that they would 'stay close to home' and 'never have to suffer as he did' (39). In place of Shakespeare's ruthless murderer (5.2.256), the play describes a boy who 'was always gentle when he played with children' (39). Similarly, when Somaia expresses her eagerness to see '[her] new son' – hoping she will 'see the face of [her] brother' in '[her] brother's child', and

---

[35] Charles W. Mills, *Black Rights / White Wrongs: The Critique of Racial Liberalism* (New York, 2017).
[36] See Sergio Lussana, '"To see who was best on the plantation": enslaved fighting contests and masculinity in the antebellum plantation South', *The Journal of Southern History* 76 (2010), 901–22.

pondering whether 'he smiles like Tarik' (38) – the play substitutes tenderness towards Othello's face for the many moments in which Shakespeare presents Othello's visage as a problem: something that Desdemona must overlook or can see only 'in [the] mind' (1.3.252), and that Othello disparages as 'begrimed and black' (3.3.392). Most movingly, perhaps, when Somaia speaks of her impatience to 'tell [the child] of the ancestors and also of his father's joys and hopes of childhood, before he was captured by the infidels and sold into slavery' (40), the play responds to Othello's famous speech just before his death in which, as Ian Smith has brilliantly discussed, he asks for a narrator of his life: 'Speak of me as I am' (5.2.351).[37]

But to say that *Fortunes*, by envisioning this African woman eager to transmit her brother's legacy, responds to Othello's request to have his humanity recognized – a request that heartbreakingly goes unanswered in Shakespeare's play – is not to diminish the play's status as protest drama. On the contrary, *Fortunes*, by depicting the African visitors and the baby as always in danger, lodges a protest against this Venetian world. Indeed, so fierce is *Fortunes*' protective stance towards the kin of Tarik/Othello that the play turns to white bodies to call attention to Black precarity. More specifically, towards the play's end, harrowing scenes offer something of a Shakespeare remix as they show Gratiano inflaming a mob against the African visitors to Venice after he learns that Lodovico and his accomplice have kidnapped and killed a baby, which they all wrongly believe is the heir to Tarik/Othello. Thus, Gratiano's rabble-rousing rhetoric conflates speeches that Shakespeare assigns to Iago and Desdemona's father, thereby refuting the notion that racism is Iago's singular malignity.[38] Similarly, Gratiano's manufactured outrage inadvertently leads to a scene evoking the blackface history of *Othello*: namely, the onstage slaying of Lodovico, who, unbeknown to Gratiano, has darkened his face and 'disguised [himself] as a Moor' (68). Ultimately, of course, these violent scenes link *Othello* to America's history of racist terror in which the lynching of Black men was regularly framed as a defence of white innocence and white female virtue.[39] When *Fortunes* depicts the killing of the (white) baby followed swiftly by the retributive murder of the disguised Lodovico and his accomplice, the play, with outrage and grief, calls out for recognition of those of African descent whose lives – no matter how young – may be taken without consequence.

***

I turn now to the printed text of *Fortunes* and to the Molettes' aforementioned statement that their 1997 revision resulted in a more fully Afrocentric text. As the playwrights have noted in their account of the revision process, their summer collaboration with some twenty Black professionals – actors, musicians and dancers – who then made up Abibigromma, the National Theatre Company of Ghana, prompted them to think more about the writing and reception of their play.[40] They considered that they wrote *Fortunes*, which has roles for eight white and (only) three Black characters, after they each left careers at HBCUs for predominately white universities, a fact that – they suggested – had perhaps shifted their work in the direction of

---

[37] Ian Smith, 'We are Othello: speaking of race in early modern studies', *Shakespeare Quarterly* 67 (2016), 104–24.
[38] Gratiano's warnings – 'Look to your own children, especially your chaste daughters. Did not one such dusky Moor come to Venice and steal by witchcraft and magic the daughter of my beloved brother who is an honorable Senator?' (58) and 'Look to your wives! These burly creatures through the use of potions will climb between your sheets' (58) – draw on Iago's admonition, 'Look to your house, your daughter, and your bags' (1.1.80); Iago's declaration that Othello has 'robbed' Brabanzio of his daughter (1.1.86); Brabanzio's charge that Othello used 'spells and medicines' and 'witchcraft' to charm Desdemona (1.3.61, 64); Iago's claim that there are rumours that Othello "twixt my sheets / . . . has done my office' (1.3.379–80); and Iago's warning to Othello to 'Look to your wife' (3.3.201).
[39] The lynching parallel is even more obvious in the revised version of *Fortunes* in which the mob yells, 'You'll see Venetian justice. String up the black thieves' (73).
[40] See Molette and Molette, 'What makes Black theatre Black', on which I base this account.

whiteness. They also recalled that some white playgoers had opined to them that the play centred on Gratiano (rather than the three Africans), which made the playwrights wonder whether 'for most white people ... Black people are only interesting when seen through the eyes of a white character', as they so often are seen in Hollywood movies.[41] But the Molettes also recalled that the Black actor David Downing, who had played Gratiano in an early staged reading of *Fortunes* – and who, years earlier, had played a white National Guardsman in *Rosalee Pritchett* – had urged them to produce an all-Black *Fortunes*. Taken together, the Molettes' reflections underscore that the different versions of *Fortunes* cannot be explained solely in terms of the playwrights' changing levels of commitment to Afrocentrism. Rather, to understand the play's evolution, we must also consider that, as Arthur Little has contended, Shakespeare has long been understood as 'white property' and has been geared towards white audiences.[42] Certainly, this history has mitigated against the existence of Black Shakespeare, ensuring that Black theatre artists who engage with Shakespeare need to grapple with distinct pressures around whiteness that, wittingly or unwittingly, shape their work. After all, the Molettes were surely correct when they suggested that *Fortunes* in its first incarnation could be very appealing to predominantly white universities and theatre companies seeking to meet 'diversity goals'.[43]

The Molettes' most significant revision to *Fortunes* – the most telling sign of its 'enhanced' Afrocentrism – is not that Elissa and Somaia speak more, and the Venetians speak less, than they do in the original. Nor is it that Hassan states at the end of the play that he has witnessed Gratiano's execution, an act ordered by Brabantio. Rather, it is that the Molettes – as a result of conversations with Mohamed ben Abdallah, the pioneering Ghanaian playwright who founded the National Theatre while serving as a cultural minister in the revolutionary government in the 1980s and 1990s – abandoned the play's traditional realist aesthetic and adopted a new 'abibigoro' form. Often translated as 'Black theatre' or 'African theatre', abibigoro is a dramatic style developed by Abdallah that entails alternating patterns of narration and action, fusing interactive West African storytelling techniques with drama, music, dance and mime.[44] As the Molettes took up this form, they shifted the play's location to Africa, added a prologue and a brief epilogue, and created new characters: the Griot who transmits the story of what happened in Venice via a point of view that is at once communal (he is a storehouse of ancestral wisdom) and personal (he morphs into and out of the 'Hassan' character), and the unnamed townspeople who variously impersonate Venetians and Africans, dance, beat on African drums, and comment on the action. In other words, through this indigenous African form, the Molettes reshaped the first version of the play so that what happens in Venice is no longer the play proper, but rather has become a story within the play. Moreover, because this story is partly narrated by the Griot / Hassan and partly enacted by the townspeople, the revised play – unlike the first version – is imagined only from the perspective of Africans. In short, *Fortunes* no longer takes the shape of a simple protest against or indictment of *Othello*. Rather than exist in opposition to the Shakespearian tragedy, *Fortunes*, in its revised state, instead represents an enveloping of that play. As the playwrights relocate *Fortunes* to Africa, enclose the Venetian narrative within the African frame, and add West African ritual, masks, textiles, drums and dance, *Othello* becomes contained within – indeed, subordinated to – African and diasporic culture.

Put otherwise, the revised play materializes an African world that is absent from Shakespeare's

---

[41] Molette and Molette, 'What makes Black theatre Black', p. 5.
[42] Arthur L. Little, 'Re-historicizing race, white melancholia, and the Shakespearean property', *Shakespeare Quarterly* 67 (2016), 84–103.
[43] Molette and Molette, 'Overcoming double consciousness', p. 107.
[44] On abibigoro, see Awo Mana Asiedu, 'Abibigoro: the theatre of Mohamed Ben Abdallah', in *Trends in Twenty-First Century African Theatre and Performance*, ed. Kenechukwu Igweonu (Amsterdam, 2011), pp. 367–84.

tragedy, and to which the characters in the first version of *Fortunes* can only gesture. Thus, while the first version of *Fortunes* is set in Venice on a day in 1565, the revised version is set in 'Hassan's village' – which, of course, is also the birthplace of Tarik/Othello – at an unspecified time, possibly many generations after the events in the story. Equally important, the revised play begins with the townspeople and the Griot 'wearing or carrying African masks', speaking directly to the audience, and informing them that they will present a play (1). Effectively, of course, this prologue pushes back on *Othello*'s ending with the prospect of the Venetian seizure of African property, for all the stage properties – as well as costumes and scenery – are visibly African. Moreover, as the stage directions indicate, one prop, 'an empty cradle' that is illuminated during the Prologue, is especially important insofar as it emblematizes the potentiality of a post-*Othello* future (1). In fact, later in the play, two related stage properties that recall Othello's handkerchief – namely, two textiles depicted as possible coverings for the baby – suggest alternative orientations towards this future. One, intended to single out the baby for kidnapping, is a Venetian blanket embroidered with Brabantio's family crest, which evokes patrilineal claims and reproductive futurity. The other is a quilt brought to Venice from Africa about which Elissa says, 'he'll touch [it] and feel its warmth and know his spirit connects to ours and to our ancestors' (60), which suggests a future severed from the Venetian past and a sense of affiliation based on affective 'warmth' rather than lineal bloodlines. At the play's end, when the baby is brought on stage, he is wrapped within this African quilt, a literalization of the kinship within which the play enfolds *Othello*.

Significantly, before *Fortunes* re-makes community in this way, the play suggests that the townspeople may desire a different future for the infant. Specifically, at the play's start, the townspeople – whose seemingly spontaneous verbal and non-verbal interaction evokes African American call-and-response dynamics – seem to be on the side of the African visitors to Venice. They underwrite the power of the Griot / Hassan character as they repeat the names to which he refers, and they imply through their concern for the child that 'family' must be broadly defined and informal adoption of children recognized as a longstanding tradition. Thus, when the townspeople hear the tale of Brabantio's banishment of Desdemona, they assert that it is impossible to disavow a child; they insist that 'there is no wealth where there is no children'; and they express compassionate concern: 'After Desdemona and Tarik are gone, who is responsible for the child? Who will teach him to wash his hands, so he can eat with the elders?' (4). But, as the play progresses, the townspeople interrupt, seeking to change the story's outcome. Most notably, they first demand that Gratiano's treachery be stopped before the infant can be slain and, later, as they accuse Hassan, Elissa and Somaia of selfishness, they order the Griot / Hassan to relinquish the child so that the Venetians will grow to respect Africans, for the child's 'virtue will show them that we are not murderers and savages' (88). In response, the Griot / Hassan pushes back against the townspeople, asking whether 'Venetian approval [is] a reasonable price for your self-respect' (88). Through the staging of this conflict, *Fortunes* not only meditates on internalized anti-Blackness, it also suggests that in a racist world Black self-possession depends on community.

As is clear from this dialogue, the revised *Fortunes* is every bit as attuned to race as was the earlier version. Indeed, insofar as the play includes no 'real' Venetians – only the townspeople's impersonations of them – it depicts racial identities only from African perspectives, thus ensuring that Tarik/Othello can never become what he signifies so tragically in *Othello*: a figure of white fantasy. Moreover, because the revised play allows actors to employ the masks brought onstage in the Prologue to suggest racial difference, the revised play can powerfully disrupt a 'realistic' understanding of race, such as that implied in the play's earlier version. In the Abibigromma production, for example, some actors carried and wore traditional carved wooden masks created in a local village, while others wore white, *commedia dell'arte* style masks. This mask-based racial imaginary has the potential to unsettle audience members who are used to a certain racial equilibrium, as is evident from a reviewer's comment – in an otherwise rave review of a Chicago performance in 1999 – that the all-Black cast was a 'rather controversial choice, given that if the reverse were the case, there would be many outraged cries'.[45] Clearly, through this refusal to simulate embodied race, the revised play effectively inverts *Othello*: it establishes an Afrocentric imaginary as the locus for its racial understanding.

Crucially, because the revised *Fortunes* puts the Griot / Hassan in charge of the Venetian story, it also goes much further than the earlier version in inviting audiences to question the veracity of *Othello*. Thus, while the play's first version hints at the inaccuracy of Lodovico's report of the death of Desdemona's father in *Othello*, the revision indicates through the Griot/Hassan character that much of *Othello* cannot be trusted. Most significantly, perhaps, when the Griot / Hassan tells the tale of Tarik/Othello in the Prologue, he states that 'Tarik's trusted assistant, a soldier named Iago, betrays Tarik and murders both Tarik and Desdemona as they sleep. Iago even murders his own wife when she threatens to reveal his colossal evil' (5). In other words, the revised play here underscores the reality of false allegations, a view that gains particular resonance because the Griot/Hassan character speaks in the present tense. This claim is later affirmed in the story-within-the-play when Hassan tells Somaia that they are powerless against the Venetian determination to blame her brother despite the fact that 'no proof supports the rumor that he murdered Desdemona. And we need no assurance of his innocence' (7). Later, even Lodovico counters Brabantio's claim that 'Othello murdered [his] daughter' by acknowledging that 'persistent rumors' support a version of the story in which Iago is the real murderer (37). In short, through this counterfactual, the play demands a re-thinking of the entire premise upon which Shakespeare's tragedy is based.

Somewhat paradoxically, as the revised *Fortunes* embraces the abibigoro form, it also draws new lines of affiliation with Shakespeare, linking his most renowned teller of tales with the West African tradition of storytelling. Further, in prioritizing the Griot/Hassan character and the action of telling the tale, the play in effect delivers on Somaia's promise in the play's first version to narrate Tarik/Othello's life. The revised *Fortunes* not only enacts that promise by turning the narrative into a collective re-telling via music, dance and call-and-response dialogue, but also indicates that the agreement has been kept for generations. Thus, as the play begins, the townspeople announce that the Griot will perform a ritual pouring of a 'libation' – an offering of drink to ancestral spirits – which emphasizes that the Griot has been taught how to tell the stories that have been preserved by the elders. Moreover, as the Griot speaks to the townspeople, he prefaces his story of the three travellers who 'never lost sight of their mission – to cherish our children as the ancestors have taught us' – with a narrative that he presumes they already know (2):

But first, I shall remind you of our kinsman, Tarik. When he was just a boy, some evil men found him alone, not far from this very place. These men brutally attacked him and took him away before we knew he was in danger. The vicious kidnappers shipped our kinsman to a distant land called Venice and sold him as a slave. In keeping with their custom, his captors refused to call him by the name his family gave him. His captors gave him the name 'Othello'. (3)

Clearly, the Griot's speech offers the same history as does the earlier version of the play. Here, however, everything is different, for as the Griot speaks to the townspeople and the audience, he explicitly gathers the listeners together as a community. That is, he offers a 'remind[er]' of 'our kinsman', and he evokes a shared space: 'this very place'. By evoking the story of Tarik/Othello as a collective memory located in a communal space that is imagined as proximate to the historical site of violence, *Fortunes* demands we recognize landscapes of trauma,

---

[45] Hedy Weiss, 'Review: Fortunes of the Moor', *Chicago Sun Times*, 26 January 1999, p. 27.

where past and present meet, where slavery's after-lives continue to be felt. Significantly, the name 'Othello' is spoken for the first time in this scene, underscoring the fact that the proper noun is inextricably bound to his status as property. But it is also significant that this shared space near – 'not far from' – the space of historical trauma has just been marked as sacred by the Griot's pouring of the libation. To tell this story here, so the play implies, is a reparative gesture, a demonstration that those who have been stolen through slavery have not been forgotten.

Yet the role of the Griot / Hassan is not simply to memorialize. Rather, insofar as the abibigoro form draws on the West African storytelling tradition, the Griot / Hassan is also charged with celebrating the wit and resourcefulness of Tarik/Othello's paternal relatives – just as, say, the teller of the Ananse tales celebrates the cunning of a trickster spider. Or, as Barbara Molette put it in her 2008 interview with Hatch, in taking up this African form, the playwrights reconfigured the play so that what audiences are urged to wonder is not whether Hassan, Elissa and Somaia will retrieve the baby but, rather, *how* they will retrieve him, a question that of course keeps the play's focus on the African visitors instead of on Venetian efforts to seize Othello's property. Because of the abibigoro form, then, audiences are trained to admire the way in which Elissa and Somaia persevere until they locate the baby in one of Venice's many convents, and the way that Hassan, in a debate about the baby's future, throws Brabantio off balance by casually pointing out that he 'could return to Venice with several thousand men whose military skills and valor nearly equal Tarik's' (98). Similarly, audiences are prompted to notice the skill with which the African visitors silence Brabantio with a barrage of questions designed to make him realize the ubiquity of Venetian racism, ranging from Elissa's 'Does your Venetian nobility guarantee the child will not be abducted and sold as a slave?' to Hassan's 'A dimpled infant may amuse your friends, but will they be amused when he's old enough to notice their daughters?' (98). But, most notably, the abibigoro form ensures that audiences appreciate Hassan's sly tactics as he seals a deal in which Brabantio believes that he will get the inheritance and Hassan will get the baby: thus, while Hassan seems to concede, when he agrees to allow Brabantio to 'oversee the management of all Tarik's properties remaining here in Venice after [we] have safely departed with the child' (99), Hassan reveals at the play's end that he has already sold Othello's properties and pocketed the proceeds, thereby ensuring the child's inheritance.

While the play thus ends on an optimistic note, what is perhaps *Fortunes*' most powerful response to *Othello* is contained in less hopeful lines, which were delivered by the townspeople in the Abibigromma production – lines that did not find their way into the printed text, but nevertheless seem to underpin the revision. Specifically, an Abibigromma script in the archive shows that, as the production opens, the townspeople, who are divided into three groups, cannot seem to agree on how to proceed.[46] Group A announces that 'We are here to present a play', Group B immediately questions the need to 'perform a sequel to *Othello*', Group C declares that 'Four hundred years ago we were condemned to wear Othello's mask', and eventually the groups find themselves in full disagreement:

GROUP B   I will not wear Othello's mask.
GROUP C   You have no choice. When they look at you, they see Othello's mask.
GROUP B   I do not deserve to wear Othello's mask.
GROUP C   You may not wish to claim Othello's legacy, but Othello's legacy claims you.
GROUP A   None of us deserve to wear Othello's mask.[47]

Through this scene of disharmony – which offers something like what playwright Djanet Sears, in another context, terms 'a choir of African voices, chanting a multiplicity of African experiences'[48] – the play suggests that, for people of African descent,

---

[46] Barbara Molette and Carlton Molette, '*Fortunes of the Moor*, July 13, 1997', MP Box 21, Folder 9.
[47] Molette and Molette, '*Fortunes of the Moor*, July 13, 1997', p. 2.
[48] Djanet Sears, 'Notes of a colored girl: 32 short reasons why I write for the theatre', in *Harlem Duet* (Toronto, 1997), p. 12.

the Shakespearian legacy may be an unwanted – and, indeed, impossible – one. As the Prologue ends, the townspeople at last speak in unison, but all that they agree on is the immense scale of what they face: 'We are swallowed in the ocean of Othello's legacy.'[49] Rather than solving the Shakespeare problem, in other words, the play instead speaks to a sense of engulfment, as though *Othello* were a force like the vast waves that, thanks to climate change, have been sweeping away entire West African communities.[50] Acknowledging the harm that Shakespeare's tragedy continues to do, *Fortunes* nevertheless proceeds, redressing that injury with its Afrocentric and potentially curative re-telling.

WELCOMING

The revised version of *Fortunes* opens with the townspeople and the Griot/Hassan figure repeating the Ghanaian word 'Akwaaba', which, as the townspeople explain, means 'you are welcome' (1). This greeting seems particularly apt in light of the fact that *Fortunes* has been appreciatively received by many theatre artists of African descent. The play's first staged reading occurred in March 1995 at the Frank Silvera Writers' Workshop (FSWW), an acclaimed Harlem-based organization founded in 1973 by playwright/director Garland Lee Thompson, Sr, and actor Morgan Freeman to support Black playwrights. The FSWW presented a second reading of *Fortunes* in August 1995 at yet another celebrated venue: the National Black Theatre festival, which was established by Larry Leon Hamlin in 1989 and brought thousands to North Carolina for a week-long gathering of Black and diasporic theatre, film and television artists. *Fortunes* returned to New York in November and December 1995, where FSWW sponsored an Equity Showcase production directed by Charles E. Wise, which won the Audelco Writers'/Directors' Award, an honour often referred to as the Black theatre community's Tony Awards. In 1996, Von H. Washington, Sr, a veteran of the Black Arts movement, directed a production at Western Michigan University Theatre, and in 1997, the playwrights collaborated on a workshop production directed by Allie Woods, Jr, at Connecticut Repertory Theatre, the professional theatre associated with the University of Connecticut, Storrs, where Carlton Molette was then teaching drama and African American studies.

In 1997, the revised *Fortunes* directed by Carlton Molette premiered with Abibigromma at both the University of Ghana in Legon and the National Theatre in Accra, and then was chosen to represent Ghana at the third Pan-African Theatre Festival in Cape Coast. In 1998, Anthony Hill, a scholar of African American theatre, directed *Fortunes* at the Ohio State University, and Elmo Terry-Morgan presented a staged reading at Rites and Reason Theatre, a Black theatre organization housed at Brown University. In 1999, Runako Jahi directed *Fortunes* at the eta Creative Arts Foundation, a Chicago institution focused on African American aesthetics. In 2001, the Africana Studies Department at Agnes Scott College in Decatur, Georgia, gave *Fortunes* a staged reading; Nefertiti Burton directed the play at the University of Louisville under the auspices of one of the oldest African American theatre programmes in a predominantly white institution; and Harvey Johnson directed the play at Pittsburgh's Kuntu Repertory, which had been founded to support the Africana Studies Department at the University of Pittsburgh. In 2002, *Fortunes* was given a staged reading at Morgan State University, the largest of Maryland's HBCUs. This represented the last performance before the 2016 Emory reading, which was put on in collaboration with the late Pellom McDaniels III, curator of the African American Collections of the University's Rare Book Library.

Significantly, in staging *Fortunes*, virtually all these productions found ways to reimagine *Othello* from Black perspectives. Thus, not only was *Fortunes* performed at theatres founded by

---

[49] Molette and Molette, *'Fortunes'*, p. 2B, MP Box 21, Folder 9.
[50] Matteo Fagotto, 'West Africa is being swallowed by the sea', *Foreign Policy*, 21 October 2016: foreignpolicy.com/2016/10/21/west-africa-is-being-swallowed-by-the-sea-climate-change-ghana-benin.

people of colour for BIPOC audiences, it was performed as part of Black History month celebrations and in connection with exhibitions of Black theatre. Its staging was preceded by the singing of James Weldon Johnson's 'Lift Every Voice and Sing'. And it was also followed by professional development activities for teachers, talkbacks for audiences, and classroom discussions that invited students to reflect on how *Fortunes* engaged *Othello*. Repeatedly, audiences were urged to look at Shakespeare with new eyes – as, for example, when the late scholar of African American literature Ruthe T. Sheffey assigned her Morgan State students the creative exercise of 'Suggest[ing] in one sentence the plot for another play that rewrites a Shakespearean play from an Afrocentric viewpoint.'[51]

Why has *Fortunes* been warmly embraced by Black theatre artists and scholars while remaining excluded from the canon of Shakespeare appropriations? To answer that question, we might turn again to the archive – specifically the Molettes' folder of rejections from predominantly white theatre companies to whom they offered to send the manuscript, none of which mentions race in their reply. Consider, for example, the polite note from the artistic associate of a leading off-Broadway theatre that reads like a riddle: 'No, Thank you. Interesting, but we only do translations & adaptations of classics, rather than new plays based on classic themes.'[52] In making sense of this rejection, we might be tempted to conclude that the decision had to do with the fact that *Fortunes* aligns more with appropriation than with adaptation, for, as Julie Sanders has suggested, adaptation 'signals a relationship with an informing source text or original' while appropriation 'frequently affects a more decisive journey away from the informing source into a wholly new cultural product and domain'.[53] But recourse to that distinction does not in fact explain this particular rejection, for the theatre in fact staged several appropriations by non-Black playwrights, including in 1992–3 the *Othello*-inspired work of Ann-Marie MacDonald, *Goodnight Desdemona (Good Morning Juliet)*, a feminist comedy with no interest in race.[54]

Rather than parse the decisions of individual theatres to pass over *Fortunes*, it is perhaps more productive to contemplate the reception of *Fortunes* by returning again to its origins – specifically, to the fact that the Molettes were first inspired to write the play in the mid-1970s when they encountered debates about transracial adoption in the United States.[55] As legal scholar Twila Perry has observed, this controversy, which followed a statement by the National Association of Black Social Workers in 1972 that only Black families should be permitted to adopt Black children, pitted 'liberal colorblind individualism' against 'color and community consciousness'.[56] Building on Perry's analysis, Ruth-Arlene W. Howe showed that, while the public sphere framed this debate in terms of a standoff between the welcome offered by white parents and the hostility represented by Black separatism, in fact the debate was 'about establishing a new right or entitlement for certain white adults who wish to become parents by any means they select', rather than about meeting the needs of Black children.[57] To meet the needs of Black children, Howe maintained, systemic change in adoption policies was required; equally

---

[51] Dr Ruthe T. Sheffey, 'Discussion questions on *Fortunes of the Moor*', MP Box 20, Folder 10.
[52] L. Champagne, Artistic Associate, Classic Stage Company (CSC), undated postcard, MP Box 20, Folder 8.
[53] Julie Sanders, *Adaptation and Appropriation* (London and New York, 2006), p. 26.
[54] Other such appropriations in the CSC repertory in the mid-1990s include Phyllis Nagy's feminist rewriting of *The Scarlet Letter*, staged in 1994–5, and Susan Yankowitz's *Phaedra in Delirium*, an updating of the Greek myth, staged in 1997–8.
[55] Molette and Molette, 'Overcoming double consciousness', p. 104.
[56] Twila L. Perry, 'The transracial adoption controversy: an analysis of discourse and subordination', *New York University Review of Law and Social Change* 21 (1993–4), 33–108. 'The National Association of Black Social Workers position statement on trans-racial adoptions', dated September 1972, is available at cdn.ymaws.com/www.nabsw.org/resource/collection/E1582D77-E4CD-4104-996A-D42D08F9CA7D/NABSW_Trans-Racial_Adoption_1972_Position_(b).pdf.
[57] Ruth-Arlene W. Howe, 'Redefining the transracial adoption controversy', *Duke Journal of Gender Law & Policy* (1995), 131–64; p. 138.

important, she argued, was a widespread recognition that to overlook race in adoption placements would be to pose a danger to young Black lives. Rather than unilaterally oppose transracial adoption, however, she implored white prospective parents to become racially competent and recognize that Black children need to live in close community with others of African descent who can help them to thrive within a racist society.

In returning to the transracial adoption debate, *Fortunes* clearly associates the family of Tarik/Othello with colour and community consciousness, and associates Brabantio not only with the language of individual rights – 'My birthright entitles me to raise this child and control Othello's fortunes as his own' (38) – but also, counterintuitively, with 'color-blindness', for he contends that his wealth and status can overpower Venetian racism and the racial 'defect' he associates with the child (96). In other words, the play insists that an individualist, rights-based ideology is wholly congruent with anti-Blackness, putting the child – like his father – gravely at risk in Venice. In line with this, the play emphasizes that the matter of 'belonging to' is inextricably bound up with larger racialized structures of inequity: indeed, the play intimates parallels between the Venetian trade in enslaved Africans and the fact that, today, children of colour are far more likely than white children both to face violence and to be turned into commodities in an adoption 'market'. Clearly, these issues are fraught and audiences may resist the play's nuanced engagement with them – as, for example, a Chicago reviewer did when she ignored *Fortunes*' focus on the nurturing strength of Black community, instead projecting onto the play a much simpler message of her own: 'the play's moral conviction [is] that children with any African blood should be raised by black families'.[58] But *Fortunes*, as I have been arguing, offers not a separatist agenda but, rather, a paean to kinship and community. Indeed, it offers a love ethic not unlike that of the epistolary memoirs of James Baldwin, Ta-Nehesi Coates and Imani Perry, for it is addressed to those who love Black children even while fearing for their future in a world that does not always recognize their humanity.[59]

My larger point in turning to *Fortunes*' intervention in the transracial adoption debate is to emphasize that Brabantio's sense of a birthright that entitles him to control Othello's fortunes may speak to how white supremacy operates in Shakespearian scholarship and theatre. As such, the play might move us to a fundamental questioning of how race might matter to the staging and reception of *Othello* and its appropriations, going forward. What would it mean for a predominantly white Shakespeare industry to give up its right to *Othello*? What would it mean for white scholars to give up that racial entitlement and begin to centre dramas by Black theatre artists who, like Carlton and Barbara Molette, have engaged with *Othello* and created Othello's kin: from C. Bernard Jackson's *Iago* to Djanet Sears's *Harlem Duet* to Toni Morrison's *Desdemona* to Keith Anthony Cobb's *American Moor*? When will the field of Shakespeare studies properly acknowledge and welcome Black artists who have turned to *Othello*, recognizing that, as Kim Hall has written, 'Black love of Shakespeare is a site of profound struggle and *Othello* its most vexed object'?[60] Regrettably, only a small percentage of predominantly white Shakespearian theatre companies have responded to the coalition of BIPOC theatre workers who, in their 2020 document 'We see you, White American theatre', called out racist practices in their industry.[61] But now, more than ever, Shakespeare's future and fortunes depend on enacting transformative change precisely, as the Molettes have shown, by welcoming Othello's kin.

---

[58] Carol Burbank, '*Fortunes of the Moor*', *Chicago Reader*, 28 January 1999: chicagoreader.com/arts-culture/fortunes-of-the-moor.

[59] James Baldwin, *The Fire Next Time* (New York, 1963); Ta-Nehesi Coates, *Between the World and Me* (New York, 2015); and Imani Perry, *Breathe: A Letter to My Sons* (Boston, MA, 2019).

[60] Kim F. Hall, 'Introduction' to Keith Hamilton Cobb, *American Moor* (London, 2020), n.p.

[61] For the demands, see 'Our demands' at www.weseeyouwat.com/demands; for respondents' pledges, see the 'WSYWAT accountability report', 11 February 2021, available at issuu.com/wsywat/docs/wsywat_accountability_report_website.

'MORE FAIR THAN BLACK': OTHELLOS ON BRITISH RADIO

ANDREA SMITH

In 1933, as the BBC prepared to air its latest radio production of *Othello*, the critic and playwright Herbert Farjeon wrote an article for the *Radio Times* headlined: 'Othello was a black man.' In it, he states that, 'in most present-day stage versions of the play, this all-important point is blunted. The broadcast version will enable us, if not to see, at least to imagine Othello the colour Shakespeare first painted him.'[1] However, for almost another seven decades, imagining was all that audiences *could* do, as a succession of white actors continued to play the role. Examining the part of Othello as played on BBC radio charts the changing attitudes as to who could, and should, play him. This article will look at some of the key productions over the BBC's 100-year history, reaction to them, and the changing attitudes to a character referred to in the text as 'more fair than black' (*Othello*, 1.3.290).

Almost from the very beginning of the BBC's history, Shakespeare's works were an integral part of its output. Within three months, scenes from Shakespeare were being broadcast: within six, the first full-length play, *Twelfth Night*, aired in London.[2] At this point, the BBC was operating as a series of individual stations based in cities around the UK: within a year of *Twelfth Night*'s broadcast, at least thirty other productions of Shakespeare's plays had aired, from Aberdeen to Cardiff. On the 360th anniversary of Shakespeare's birth, the Birmingham station produced the first BBC *Othello*.[3] The eponymous hero was played by William Macready, grandson of the great Shakespearian actor of the same name.[4] Although not as famous as his ancestor, he was highly regarded, with a publication in the following year stating that he and his wife Edna Godfrey Turner had a 'Shakespearean repertoire of over 300 scenes, which are given without the aid of the book', adding that 'they have indeed made broadcast drama the triumph it is'.[5] The casting of a star actor in the role of Othello on radio was to set a pattern for decades to come.

It was eight years before *Othello* was performed again on the BBC. When it did return in 1932, Othello was played by Henry Ainley, an actor described as 'a prominent theatrical celebrity'.[6] The producer, Val Gielgud, later wrote: 'I think it is fair to claim that during the early thirties the prestige of broadcast plays and playing rose by leaps and bounds. Henry Ainley played "Othello" to my brother John's "Iago".'[7] Peggy Ashcroft was also in the production as Desdemona. Val Gielgud was delighted to have secured Ainley: 'I was

---

[1] Herbert Farjeon, 'Othello was a black man', *Radio Times*, 6 October 1933, p. 9.
[2] John Drakakis, 'Introduction', in *British Radio Drama*, ed. John Drakakis (Cambridge, 1981), pp.1–36; pp. 2–3.
[3] 'Shakespeare birthday performance of "Othello"', *Radio Times*, 18 April 1924, p. 140.
[4] 'Birmingham dramatic programmes', *Gloucester Citizen*, 25 April 1924, p. 5.
[5] 'Broadcasting and drama', *The Wireless Constructor*, April 1925, pp. 508–10; p. 510.
[6] Brian McFarlane, *The Encyclopedia of British Film* (London, 2003), p. 9.
[7] Val Gielgud, *Years of the Locust* (London, 1947), p. 92.

particularly proud to find myself working with an idol of my boyhood, the acknowledged possessor of the most beautiful voice in the English Theatre of the time.'[8] However, the great theatre actor was not a natural on radio, mistakenly attempting to project his voice to the thousands of listeners. His performance left an indelible impression on Val Gielgud: 'the importance of reasonable proximity to the microphone was so lost upon Henry Ainley that it was necessary to station a couple of Effects boys, one at each elbow, to lead him back into position whenever he moved to address an imaginary auditorium'.[9]

Ainley returned to the part seven years later, although, as this was at the beginning of World War II, the BBC was restricting drama productions to half an hour, to ensure there was enough air-time for other information and entertainment.[10] Ainley had remained a big star, with the *Radio Times* writing that attracting him to the part was 'a remarkable achievement for wartime broadcasting'.[11] His vocal quality was also the great selling point. A review of the play in the *Manchester Guardian* stated that 'Mr Ainley gives the feeling which is not the case with most actors that it would be perfectly satisfactory to hear him alone simply reciting passages from the play.'[12] Grace Wyndham Goldie in *The Listener* commented that 'in Mr Ainley's splendid voice, even when it rages, [there is] a mellow richness which speaks an inner satisfaction and which continually denies the dark violence of Othello's impulse to destroy'.[13]

Despite the wartime upheaval, an audio extract from the production has survived: the first recording in the BBC archives of a radio performance of *Othello*.[14] The opening section is missing, with the audio beginning at Othello's line 'It is the cause' (*Othello*, 5.2.1). Ainley's delivery is melodramatic and declamatory, with much vibrato in his voice. It is also easy to picture the scene described by Gielgud that had occurred seven years earlier. Although Ainley is not overmodulated, which must be a tribute to the sound engineers, he is louder than any other actor in the production.[15] It has the feel of a stage performance, and perhaps one that even in 1939 might have seemed rather old-fashioned. His delivery of 'O, O, O!' (5.2.205) is like a musical chromatic scale from high to low, three times in a row, each time covering almost an octave.[16] The *Manchester Guardian* reviewer wrote of Ainley's voice that it had 'an extraordinary range of tone and is one of the most musical they [the audience] are ever likely to hear'.[17] Even three decades later, Ainley's performance was still remembered for his distinctive delivery:

If you listen to an example of that old-style musical rendering of Shakespeare – to a recording in 1939 of Henry Ainley as Othello, for example – there is a splendid light and shade, and you can hear how the metre and rhythm relate. But the words are dragged up and down the scale. It is too poetic by half: your senses are not so much seduced as raped, and you realise that no one ever spoke or felt like that in his life.[18]

G. Wilson Knight wrote in 1930 about 'The *Othello* music', but was commenting on the poetry in the play, which 'holds a rich music all its own'.[19] Ainley takes the idea of music to a different level, turning some lines almost into opera.

Ainley's performance may also have affected other members of the cast, in particular Martita Hunt, who

---

[8] Val Gielgud, *Years in a Mirror* (London, 1965), p. 53.
[9] Val Gielgud, *British Radio Drama 1922–1956* (London, 1957) p. 123.
[10] Gielgud, *British Radio Drama 1922–1956*, p. 97.
[11] 'Both sides of the microphone – great names', *Radio Times*, 17 November 1939, p. 5.
[12] 'Review of broadcasting: Mr Henry Ainley as Othello – a scrapbook revival', *Manchester Guardian*, 6 December 1939, p. 8.
[13] Grace Wyndham Goldie, 'Critic on the hearth – Broadcast Drama: Here's Great Acting', *The Listener*, 7 December 1939, p. 1141.
[14] *Othello* (extract: act 5, scene 2), a.k.a. 'Put out the light', 2 December 1939 (unpublished, BBC Sound Archive).
[15] Overmodulation is the distortion that occurs when a sound source is too loud for the receiving microphone.
[16] *Othello* (extract), 1939, 0:12:52.
[17] 'Review of broadcasting: Mr Henry Ainley as Othello', *Manchester Guardian*, 6 December 1939.
[18] Noel Annan, 'How should Shakespeare be spoken?', *The Listener*, 5 October 1972, p. 435.
[19] G. Wilson Knight, *The Wheel of Fire* (London, 2001), p. 110.

played Emilia. Hunt was an actor described as 'playing all kinds of commanding roles (if they weren't commanding when she got them, they certainly were when she'd done with them)'.[20] But in this production, Hunt's performance veers away from commanding to simply melodramatic. She virtually screams at Othello 'thou art a devil' (*Othello*, 5.2.142) and spits out 'ignorant as *dirt*' (*Othello*, 5.2.171, emphasis mine).[21] She shouts 'odious, *damnèd* lie' (*Othello*, 5.2.187, emphasis mine) with vitriol, and her speech beginning 'Villainy, villainy, villainy!' (*Othello*, 5.2.197) borders on the hysterical.[22] However, despite the melodrama of the production, the moments of violence are almost hidden from the audience. Desdemona's death is completely silent.[23] Neither Ainley nor Hermione Hannen, who played his wife, make any noise, and there are no sound effects or music to give any indication that he has smothered her. When Hunt's Emilia is stabbed, she makes only a strange, quiet wail-cum-whimper.[24] And even Ainley makes no noise when Othello stabs himself. The reason for this is unclear, although it might have been because of concerns about taste and decency, particularly at a time when people were dying in conflict. Whatever the decision behind this, it is something that would change greatly in later productions.

Ainley was not the only actor to perform the role of Othello on BBC radio during the 1930s. Another star of the stage also took on the part. In 1933, Godfrey Tearle was described by the *Radio Times* as 'one of the few modern actors with the physique and presence for Othello, a part that requires qualities not very popular on the stage today'.[25] This was a slightly strange description of an actor who was about to appear in a radio production, particularly as this was to be his first appearance on radio, although he had performed the role on stage as far back as 1921.[26] Just as Farjeon had previewed the play by extolling its suitability for radio, so a reviewer from *The Times* also found radio 'preserved' the 'merits' of the play, despite being 'spoken by disembodied voices'.[27] The unnamed critic added that, even if it had been 'less well suited for wireless', they would have welcomed it anyway, 'for the opportunity it gave listeners to hear Mr Godfrey Tearle play the Moor'.[28] They praised Tearle's voice for being 'rich and resonant and without a touch of bombast', although they admitted that he 'remained high above the plane of pure realism'.[29] Meanwhile, weekly publication *The Era* described the production as an 'enormous radio success', while the *Hull Daily Mail* told readers of 'Godfrey Tearle's superb acting'.[30] Unfortunately, no audio of this production exists in the BBC archives, or of Tearle's second performance as Othello for BBC radio fifteen years later.

In 1948, Tearle was appearing in *Othello* at the Stratford Memorial Theatre. At the end of the season, an abridged version of the play was broadcast in the Midlands region.[31] This had been pre-recorded, still something of a novelty at this time, and was aired 'at the same moment' that the final stage performance was taking place.[32] Roderick Mann reported that it was 'timed to end as the curtain falls at Stratford. Listeners will then be taken over to the stage to hear a description of the scenes and speeches by leading members of the company.'[33] This must have been a technically tricky feat, especially for a regional station, but unfortunately there are no reviews to indicate

---

[20] McFarlane, *The Encyclopedia of British Film*, p. 327.
[21] *Othello* (extract), 1939, 0:09:25, 0:11:00.
[22] *Othello* (extract), 1939, 0:11:54, 0:12:22.
[23] *Othello* (extract), 1939, 0:05:40.
[24] *Othello* (extract), 1939, 0:15:15.
[25] 'Gifted idol', *Radio Times*, 29 September 1933, p. 734.
[26] 'Mr Godfrey Tearle in "Othello"', *Manchester Guardian*, 21 September 1933, p. 10; '"Othello"', *Observer*, 24 April 1921, p. 11.
[27] 'Broadcast drama, Mr Godfrey Tearle as Othello', *The Times*, 9 October 1933, p. 12.
[28] 'Broadcast drama', *The Times*.
[29] 'Broadcast drama', *The Times*.
[30] 'Radio drama advances', *The Era*, 11 October 1933, p. 3; '"Julius Caesar", short excerpts by famous Shakespearean actors', *Hull Daily Mail*, 27 October 1933, p. 16.
[31] 'Farewell tributes to Sir Barry', *Coventry Evening Telegraph*, 1 November 1948, p. 3.
[32] Roderick Mann, 'Dinner party under water', *Birmingham Gazette*, 29 October 1948, p. 2.
[33] Mann, 'Dinner party under water'.

how it was received. However, the theatre production was covered widely and this gives an indication of the performance Tearle is likely to have given on air, and it seems probable that it would have resonated with Ainley's. Local newspaper, the *Coventry Evening Telegraph*, reported that 'Godfrey Tearle agrees with Shaw that "Othello" is "pure melodrama"', adding that his performance was 'distinguished by dignity of poise, richness of voice and grandeur of expression'.[34] And Tearle's vocal tone, like Ainley's, is frequently referred to in reviews. *The Times* wrote: 'A noble presence and a rich, resonant voice are Mr Tearle's natural gifts ... the great speeches that a Salvini would hurl out as though they were one with the music of the spheres; Mr Tearle tunes down his vocal magnificence to draw from them quieter harmonies which lie closer to dramatic meaning.'[35] And the *Manchester Guardian* highlighted 'that providential instrument his voice, schooled and perfected by years of experience and tradition'.[36] Even in his obituary five years later, the way Tearle sounded in this production was commented on: 'he reminded a generation of playgoers who had forgotten how majestic and sonorous the verse could be without ever becoming artificial'.[37] In these early radio productions, voice and verse were considered the most important thing, rather than effective use of the medium or good storytelling. Othello had to sound beautiful, rather than reflect a particular character or ethnicity – a tendency that continued for some time.

Radio producers repeatedly raided the theatre for their Othellos. In 1949, Jack Hawkins, who would later go on to become a major British film star, took on the part. He had played Othello on stage two years earlier. If the reviews of that production are any indication as to how he might have played it on radio, he was quite unlike his predecessors. *The Stage* reported that 'people who have become accustomed by some recent performances to thunderings in the major key may regard this as a too subdued rendering. But Mr Hawkins uncommonly touches the emotions.'[38] *The Tatler* was more forthright, complaining it 'stops short of what is required':[39] 'It stops short of the poetry ... Without the music Othello's passion appears to be constantly held in check, no matter how well an actor may suit the action to the word, and without the full swell of passion a spectacle which should thrill the nerves and shake the heart inevitably loses its force.'[40] Although clearly not what critics had expected on stage, this lower-key style would have suited radio much better. However, the BBC quickly reverted to big performances and big voices.

In the Queen's coronation year, 1953, Valentine Dyall was radio's next Othello. He was already well known to audiences for telling 'spine-tingling, sinister-voiced stories' as the Man in Black.[41] The point was not lost on Emery Pearce in the *Daily Herald*, who told readers 'creepiness apart, he is a fine actor, and it is a quaint coincidence that the Man in Black will tonight start as the black Moor, Othello'.[42] A review of the production stated: 'The full majesty and power of "Othello" could hardly be expected to come over through sound alone. The marvel is that so much of it made an impact.... Valentine Dyall had nobility of voice as Othello, with range enough for both rage and pathos.'[43] Again, no audio exists of this production. And, three years later, there was another broadcast, this time starring the American actor Alfred Drake. The *Radio Times* pointed out that, 'although this will be his first major tragic role on radio', he had more than two decades' experience on stage

---

[34] 'Godfrey Tearle's Othello crowns Stratford season', *Coventry Evening Telegraph*, 31 July 1948, p. 2.
[35] 'Stratford Festival "Othello"', *The Times*, 2 August 1948, p. 6.
[36] '"Othello" at Stratford', *Manchester Guardian*, 2 August 1948, p. 3.
[37] 'Obituary: Sir Godfrey Tearle', *Manchester Guardian*, 10 June 1953, p. 4.
[38] 'London theatres: The Picadilly', *The Stage*, 3 April 1947, p. 7.
[39] Anthony Cookman, 'At the theatre', *The Tatler*, 16 April 1947, pp. 68–9; p. 68.
[40] Cookman, 'At the theatre'.
[41] Emery Pearce, 'Margaret has warned Frankie ... ', *Daily Herald*, 30 November 1953, p. 6.
[42] Pearce, 'Margaret has warned Frankie ... '.
[43] 'On the air: "Othello"', *The Stage*, 3 December 1953, p. 10.

playing characters including 'Petruchio, Antony and Malvolio'.[44] A review of the production described 'the bravura effect of the playing of Alfred Drake'.[45] In all these cases, from Macready through to Drake, the BBC seemed to be casting for vocal majesty, rather than radio acting technique, with the possible exception of Hawkins. And at no point does there seem to have been any consideration about the ethnicity of the character or whether it was appropriate for a white actor to play him.

By the 1970s, it was still unlikely an audience would see a Black actor playing Othello on stage. Paul Robeson had taken the part at the RSC in 1959.[46] But blacking-up remained the norm. In 1972, perhaps the most prestigious BBC radio production of the play – certainly the most repeated and listened to – was broadcast. And there was never a thought to cast a Black actor. Producer John Tydeman said the colour of the actor playing the part 'doesn't come into it. It's no problem on radio. Othello's not actually black, he's a Moor, an Arab type, a gypsy. The thing is that he's different. It's not about blackness or white.'[47] And so he cast Paul Scofield in the part, someone he considered the best actor to do Shakespeare on radio 'because of the remarkableness of his voice'.[48] Scofield had appeared in Tearle's Stratford production in 1948 as Roderigo, and even then had made an impression with at least one reviewer: 'I am not sure that Antony Quayle's bluff Iago is altogether a success; I found myself wondering whether Paul Scofield would not have made a better and more truly distinguished job of the part.'[49] However, he had never played the title role. Ahead of the broadcast, he told Robert Ottaway:

I have undertaken Othello now because I feel I am ready to do it justice. It is a question of one's maturity and experience. I was 39 when I first played Lear, who is an old man. The power the part needs can only be attained by a younger man. But Othello benefits from being played by an actor of the correct age.... the radio production has the entire text. I do feel that any problem presented by Shakespeare should be tackled, not shirked.[50]

Like Tydeman, Scofield was not thinking about the character's background and colour, but about experience. His claim to be the 'correct age' is also debatable: while there are references in the text to Othello being older than Desdemona, Scofield was 50 at the time of this recording. Later radio, and stage, Othellos were generally much younger.

Tydeman was delighted with his 'magnificent cast', which included Nicol Williamson as Iago.[51] But once they were assembled, he had a problem: 'When we had the read-through, I thought "Oh, god". They sounded very alike [Scofield and Williamson]. Same timbre. Paul said "I can drop my voice and Moor it up a bit."'[52] Listening to the opening scene of the play between Iago and Roderigo, it would be easy to mistake Williamson's voice for Scofield's. When Scofield appears, his accent is inconsistent. Often it is difficult to be sure where Othello is supposed to be from. At other times, the accent seems to be white South African, a sort of Afrikaans voice, such as when he delivers 'I ran it through even from my boyish days' (*Othello*, 1.3.131).[53] He also delivers his lines in quite a sing-song fashion, for example when he says 'Most potent, grave, and reverend signors' (*Othello*, 1.3.76).[54] In this

---

[44] 'Othello in sound', *Radio Times*, 24 February 1956, p. 1.
[45] Maxwell Sweeney, 'Radio review', *Irish Independent*, 3 March 1956, p. 11.
[46] 'RSC performances: Othello', Shakespeare Birthplace Trust: https://collections.shakespeare.org.uk/search/rsc-performances/oth195904/search/play_title:Othello/page/1/view_as/grid.
[47] John Tydeman, private phone conversation, 18 February 2020.
[48] Tydeman, phone conversation.
[49] '"Othello" at Stratford', *Manchester Guardian*, 2 August 1948, p. 3.
[50] Paul Scofield quoted in Robert Ottaway, '"I have undertaken Othello now because I feel I am ready to do it justice"', *Radio Times*, 9 November 1972, p. 3.
[51] Tydeman, phone conversation.
[52] Tydeman, phone conversation.
[53] *Othello*, BBC Radio 3, 12 November 1972: https://learningonscreen.ac.uk/ondemand/index.php/prog/RT3A618D?bcast=119210276, 0:20:22.
[54] *Othello*, 1972, 0:17:35.

speech, his voice covers an octave and a half and fluctuates greatly. In many ways, his delivery is not unlike that of the only earlier recording to exist, that of Ainley, in its musical style, although Ainley does not affect an accent. However, Scofield's delivery of Othello's 'O, O, O!' (*Othello* 5.2.205) is different.[55] The first two are delivered relatively quietly, with a suggestion of puzzlement, while the third takes inspiration from Emilia's line in the text, 'lay thee down and roar' (5.2.205), starting quietly but developing into a near-scream.

Reviewers had slightly mixed feelings about the production. Gillian Reynolds wrote that it 'measures the heartbeats of the play most exactly and to stunning effect'.[56] Yet David Wade, writing about Scofield's later *The Tempest*, remembered that: 'There has always been something as it were impromptu, chancy about Mr Scofield's Shakespearean performances on radio: in his Othello, even his Macbeth, there was a faint throw-away quality to the speaking as if he had read the lines for the first time and were wondering what they might mean – curious yet in both cases effective.'[57] However, the BBC had no concerns. Most productions get one repeat, some get two. This had three, with the last being in 1988, almost sixteen years after its initial airing. It was also one of the first four plays the BBC released on audio cassette.[58] The next production was not until the new millennium and the producer of that, Jeremy Mortimer, says Tydeman's tenure as head of radio drama until 1994 may have been a factor, adding that 'it was quite hard to come up with another idea for an *Othello*'.[59] There were also commercial considerations: 'BBC Enterprises, which became BBC Worldwide, kept on reissuing those cassettes or CDs and it was so irritating because just when you thought somebody might have forgotten them, they got reissued, and that was, kind of, "you can't do another one because they're selling these ones".'[60] And while 1988 may seem late for the BBC to continue to repeat a production where Othello was played by a white actor, it was only five years after the BBC Television Shakespeare production of the play, which featured Anthony Hopkins in the role, although Hopkins's casting was not without controversy. Peter Plouviez, the general secretary of actors' union Equity, wrote to the *Independent* in 1990 describing what he understood to have happened:

> The BBC had said that it was obliged to cast a black actor, for without one it could not sell the programme to America. The BBC went on to say that in its view there were no black actors in Britain capable of playing the part.... Despite the fact that, only days before, the BBC had been maintaining that the part could only be played by a black actor, it then cast Anthony Hopkins.[61]

It seems likely that radio producers and executives may also have believed there were few suitable actors in the 1980s and 1990s, as Mortimer says that, even when he came to cast his production, 'there was a feeling that the field of possible Othellos was not huge'.[62] However, in 2001, BBC radio finally did broadcast a production of the play with a Black actor in the title role.

Ray Fearon was no stranger to *Othello*: he had played the role for the RSC in 1999. Robert Gore-Langton reported that this had been 'the third time he'd played the part, first at drama school and then at the Liverpool Everyman at 24'.[63] Fearon's experience with the role was part of the appeal for Mortimer: 'I cast him really because he'd done it at the RSC and I knew that he really knew the text.'[64] But Fearon was not the immediate choice. Mortimer says that there were 'only half a dozen people who could possibly be considered' and that he auditioned actors for the part.[65] And it was not

---

[55] *Othello*, 1972, 2:48:30.
[56] Gillian Reynolds, 'The sound of silence', *The Guardian*, 11 November 1972, p. 10.
[57] David Wade, 'Aural experiences', *The Times*, 30 March 1974, p. 10.
[58] James Green, 'Taping up nicely', *The Stage*, 22 September 1988, p. 18.
[59] Jeremy Mortimer, private Zoom conversation, 7 April 2021.
[60] Mortimer, private conversation.
[61] Peter Plouviez, 'Letter: casting Othello', *Independent*, 3 August 1990, p. 16.
[62] Mortimer, private conversation.
[63] Robert Gore-Langton, 'Black: could Olivier play Othello today?', *The Times T2*, 9 February 2004, pp. 16–17; p.16.
[64] Mortimer, private conversation.
[65] Mortimer, private conversation.

a foregone conclusion that on this occasion Othello would be played by a Black actor. Mortimer says he 'went through a kind of period of really doubting whether Othello was a Black African or whether he was, as it were, Moorish, and whether, actually, he was from the near east'.[66] However, he says he was happy with his eventual choice.

Fearon's stage performance had not been greeted with great enthusiasm. Michael Billington in the *Guardian* gave the production three stars, adding that 'although Fearon is a perfectly capable Othello, he lacks seniority and weight'.[67] *The Times* did not award a rating, although the reviewer described Fearon as 'youthful', adding that 'he compensates for his lack of weight and authority with an unusually touching performance'.[68] Michael Coveney in the *Daily Mail* gave it just two stars.[69] But he also pointed out that Scofield, who was being honoured with a 'luncheon' in Stratford during the week the show opened, 'was a mediocre Othello, so there is no particular shame attached to Ray Fearon, a well-spoken 31-year-old, failing to scale the heights'.[70] Coveney's preference in an Othello was for 'a much more baritonal, awe-inspiring vocal rush. And we haven't had all that, frankly, since Laurence Olivier's blacked-up musical savage more than 30 years ago.'[71] However, not everyone agreed. Five years later, Gore-Langton wrote: 'It's not as though the 20th-century history of white actors in the role has been one long parade of delirious hits.... The whole romantic English tradition of blacked-up, barnstorming Othellos – from Edmund Kean to Donald Sinden – finally died with Michael Gambon in Scarborough in 1990.'[72] In comparing Fearon and Scofield, Coveney could not have known he was writing about two actors who would play consecutive Othellos for BBC radio, although the radio audience was reminded of Fearon's predecessor by the *Radio Times* ahead of the broadcast. Peter Barnard wrote that this would be 'the first production of *Othello* to be staged for Radio 3 since Paul Scofield memorably played the role in 1972'.[73] It seems expectations for Fearon were not high.

Playing Othello had been a personal issue for Fearon. He told Gore-Langton: 'At drama school I wrote a thesis on integrated casting at the National, RSC and the Royal Court ... Nobody black had played a title role in Shakespeare at any one of those places. This was in 1991! I loved Shakespeare and I said to myself, these people have got to let me have a go at these parts.'[74] It seems particularly fitting, then, that he was the first Black actor to play the role on BBC radio.[75] Reviews of Fearon's stage performance repeatedly reference his youth, and age was a factor in Mortimer's casting decision. Like Scofield, he believed in casting someone of the 'right age', but for Mortimer this was not an actor in their fifties. He says: 'I had this question in my mind about Othello's age and I sort of wanted a young Othello but he shouldn't sound young. [I wanted him] to have the right authority.'[76]

The casting of Othello was not the only thing that Mortimer did differently. Barnard points out that he 'set the play in the mid-20th century, Othello plays jazz records to Desdemona and news of the destruction of the Turkish fleet is broadcast on Radio Cyprus'.[77] Barnard also describes the production as 'likely to be controversial among traditionalists'.[78] Radio critics did not

---

[66] Mortimer, private conversation.
[67] Michael Billington, 'Military classic', *The Guardian*, 22 April 1999, p. 18.
[68] 'Curtain call – Othello', *The Times – Metro Supplement*, 8–14 May 1999, p. 37.
[69] Michael Coveney, 'Bad guys finish first', *Daily Mail*, 23 April 1999, p. 49.
[70] Coveney, 'Bad guys finish first'.
[71] Coveney, 'Bad guys finish first'.
[72] Gore-Langton, 'Black: could Olivier play Othello today?', p. 16.
[73] Peter Barnard, 'Othello', *Radio Times*, 27 September 2001, p. 140.
[74] Gore-Langton, 'Black: could Olivier play Othello today?', pp. 16–17.
[75] There had been two black television Othellos: the RSC production with Willard White was shown in 1990, and Colin McFarlane voiced Othello for the *Animated Tales* in 1994.
[76] Mortimer, private conversation.
[77] Barnard, 'Othello'.
[78] Barnard, 'Othello'.

review the broadcast, but, four years later, Andrew Dickson singled it out as one of his recommended audio productions of the play:

Ray Fearon provided one of the most memorable of recent Othellos at the RSC. On tape he is less vocally resonant than some ... but nevertheless manages to deliver an interpretation of the role which is both intelligent and terrifyingly sad ... Fearon's hero is young and virile, but comes to pieces with almost startling ease: listening to the bleached-out monotone of his voice in the latter stages of the play you sense that his revenge will be terrible and unstoppable – that of a man who has confronted his devils and will not return.[79]

Fearon's Othello is calm and controlled. There is no attempt at vocal gymnastics or musical delivery. Instead, Fearon is clear and allows the text to speak for itself without exaggeration. His delivery of 'Most potent, grave, and reverend signors' is controlled.[80] He presents a man who is a quietly successful commander, with no need to overstate his power. He maintains this when Iago first introduces the idea of jealousy. Rather than being dismissive of Iago, he is confident in himself and his marriage (*Othello*, 3.3.181).[81] However, by the time Iago leaves him, his tone has changed; there is now an edge to Fearon's voice and, when Desdemona enters, there is a hint of irritation subtle enough for the audience to pick up on, but for his wife plausibly to be unaware (*Othello* 3.3.292–3).[82] Even when he is about to kill her, he remains reasonably calm: he sounds genuine while delivering 'makes me call what I intend to do / A murder, which I thought a sacrifice' (*Othello*, 5.2.69–70).[83] In the moment before he carries out the killing, he does sound angry and shouts a little. Afterwards, he whispers 'My wife, my wife!', (*Othello*, 3.3.106) in a delivery surprisingly close to that of Henry Ainley.[84] But, where Ainley's voice then escalates with anger as he reaches 'I have no wife', Fearon remains quiet and is near to tears. Fearon was not only the first Black actor to play Othello on BBC radio, but also the first to give a truly audio-based performance, using the intimacy of the medium to the advantage of the character.

In an interview at the time of the RSC production, Fearon told Nicci Gerrard: 'Othello says, "I am black." You can't get round that. He's black in a world of white people, insecure, other, paranoid. Only his blackness makes sense of the play.'[85] Just like Farjeon nearly seventy years earlier, Fearon was very aware of the references to colour in *Othello*. And the following two BBC radio productions also cast Black Othellos, importing both from the theatre. In 2008, Chiwetel Ejiofor, who had put 'himself into the front rank of modern Othellos' at the Donmar Warehouse, played the part for BBC Radio 3.[86] Michael Billington's review of the theatre performance highlighted that 'what Ejiofor gives us, unfashionably, is Othello's word-music. In his talk of "the spirit-stirring drum, th' ear-piercing fife" he relishes the Moor's self-conscious rhetoric.'[87] And two years later, Lenny Henry, in his first Shakespearian role, performed it on BBC Radio 4. In both cases, the casts were imported wholesale from their respective theatres. Michael Grandage had directed the Donmar production and, according to the *Radio Times*, was 'a huge fan of radio drama'.[88] So, when he was approached, he happily agreed to the transfer. BBC producers tweaked the script to make sure that the production would not 'flounder' when it moved from 'stage to studio'.[89] The magazine's radio editor, Jane Anderson, concluded that

---

[79] Andrew Dickson, *The Rough Guide to Shakespeare* (London, 2005), p. 271.
[80] *Othello*, BBC Radio 3, 30 September 2001: https://learningonscreen.ac.uk/ondemand/index.php/prog/00148EA5?bcast=411815, 0:18:20.
[81] *Othello*, 2001, 1:23:52.
[82] *Othello*, 2001, 1:30:38.
[83] *Othello*, 2001, 2:43:39.
[84] *Othello*, 2001, 2:45:59; *Othello* (extract), 1939, 0:06:53.
[85] Ray Fearon quoted in Nicci Gerrard, 'Shakespeare and love', *Observer*, 25 April 1999, p. 34.
[86] Michael Billington, 'Othello – Donmar Warehouse, London', *The Guardian*, 5 December 2007: www.theguardian.com/stage/2007/dec/05/theatre.shakespeare.
[87] Billington, 'Othello – Donmar Warehouse, London'.
[88] Jane Anderson, 'Does Shakespeare ever work on the radio?', *Radio Times*, 1 May 2008, p. 118.
[89] Anderson, 'Does Shakespeare ever work on the radio?'.

those involved 'should feel immensely proud of this drama. It is produced, acted and directed both wisely and well.'[90] And Stephanie Billen in the *Observer* described the play as 'probably the most powerful production on radio this week'.[91]

Lenny Henry had come to *Othello* via a radio documentary. Director Barrie Rutter later told the *Independent*: 'At the end of a two-hour session directing Lenny Henry doing Othello's last speech for his BBC Radio 4 programme *Lenny and Will*, he asked me if he'd passed the audition.'[92] Henry was not being entirely serious, but the experience got the pair thinking, and Henry went on to play Othello for Rutter's company, Northern Broadsides. Henry won the *London Evening Standard* theatre award for best newcomer for his performance, as well as general acclaim, with theatre reviewer Lynne Walker writing that 'his voice carries and, while his timing is sometimes still a little shaky, his verse-speaking can sing'.[93] Rutter also thought Henry had 'a marvellous resonant voice' for the part.[94] Having originated through a radio programme, it was only natural that the production should find its way back onto the medium. Celine Bijleveld in the *Guardian* suggested the radio production was 'your chance to find out why' the stage version had been so successful. She added: 'For those unsure about Henry in the role, listening to him (as opposed to watching him) does allow you to put some distance between the Shakespearian character and his previous comic incarnations.'[95] Both Ejiofor and Henry were praised for their vocal delivery, and reviewers seemed to have forgotten that only a decade earlier it had been unusual for a Black actor to play the role on a major UK stage, let alone on the radio. It was now assumed that Othello could only be played by someone of African or Caribbean heritage. However, on radio at least, the next decade would see this change.

In 2020, Emma Harding's production of *Othello* finally decided to examine the idea that Mortimer had been considering twenty years previously, and academics had posited even earlier: that Othello might not be Black at all.[96] Harding picked an actor of Arab heritage, Khalid Abdalla, to play Othello: the first time this had happened on the BBC. This is also a rare occurrence in the theatre: none of the UK's major Shakespeare companies (RSC, Shakespeare's Globe or National Theatre) have yet chosen to cast in this way. The idea that the word 'Moor' could refer to an Arab was articulated immediately before the broadcast in a short introduction from Birmingham City University's Islam Issa: 'A Moor could have been any person with darker skin or who wasn't Christian, but it was a religiously loaded often derogatory term that usually referred to Mahometans.'[97] Issa goes on to suggest that Othello 'converted to Christianity' and 'adopts a militantly Christian tone to overcompensate for his otherness'.[98] Othello's possible Islamic background is suggested in this production during the drinking scene in act 2, scene 3. Lucy Popescu describes it as 'reminiscent of raucous male bonding down the pub; one knows it will end in trouble'.[99] Instead of the two songs sung

---

[90] Anderson, 'Does Shakespeare ever work on the radio?'.
[91] Stephanie Billen, 'Radio choice: Drama on 3, Othello', *Observer TV and Radio*, 4 May 2008, p. 5.
[92] Barrie Rutter, 'The day I cast Lenny as Othello', *Independent Extra*, 8 September 2009, p. 14.
[93] Lynne Walker, 'Henry shines as a stand-up tragedian with star quality', *Independent*, 19 February 2009, p. 20.
[94] Rutter, 'The day I cast Lenny as Othello'.
[95] Celine Bijleveld, *The Guardian*, 5 March 2010: https://advance.lexis.com/api/permalink/c126308a-91f1-430e-befd-6470ac7643a3/?context=1519360&federationidp=VJX3C459626.
[96] See Ferial J. Ghazoul, 'The Arabization of Othello', *Comparative Literature* 50 (1998), 1–31; p. 1; Walter Cohen, 'Othello [introduction]', in *The Norton Shakespeare*, 3rd ed., ed. Stephen Greenblatt, Walter Cohen, Suzanne Gossett, Jean E. Howard, Katharine Eisaman Maus and Gordon McMullan (London, 2016), pp. 2073–9; p. 2073.
[97] Islam Issa, 'Introduction' to *Othello*, BBC Radio 3, 19 April 2020: https://learningonscreen.ac.uk/ondemand/index.php/prog/15E01903?bcast=131740325.
[98] Issa, 'Introduction'.
[99] Lucy Popescu, 'Radio: bold Bard without stage distraction', *Camden New Journal*, 16 April 2020: http://camdennewjournal.com/article/radio-bold-bard-without-stage-distraction.

by Iago in Shakespeare's text, a single, modern song, sung by a rowdy group of men is inserted:

> (singing to the tune of 'My Old Man's a Dustman')
> Ali Khan's a Muslim
> He wears a Muslim's cap
> His father wears a burka *(singing continues, indistinct)*[100]

Reviewer Maryam Philpott states that 'Harding was keen to explore how the play's concept of "otherness" ... links to what may once have been a Muslim faith.'[101] By inserting this scene, Harding suggests that, not just Iago, but the majority of Othello's soldiers have no real respect for him, increasing the 'otherness' already present in the text, as well as situating it in a 21st-century world many people will recognise.

Harding also cuts most of the references to Othello's colour. 'Black' – or variants of it – appears eleven times in Shakespeare's text, but Harding cuts it to only four. Among those that are removed are the Duke's suggestion that Othello is 'far more fair than black', and Othello's assertions 'Haply for I am black' and 'As Dian's visage, is now begrimed and black / As mine own face', as well as 'sooty bosom' (*Othello*, 1.3.290, 3.3.267, 3.3.392–3, 1.2.71). In Harding's production, it might be suggested she is substituting Islam for 'Blackness', something particularly pertinent in a radio production where the colour of Othello's skin cannot be seen. Writing in 2016, Ayanna Thompson suggests that 'recently, black actors have expressed a belief that Othello is not actually about race'.[102] Harding's reinterpretation of the text along lines of religion rather than race would seem to fit with 21st-century ideas of reframing the play in other ways.

Harding also changes the ethnicity of Desdemona. Shakespeare's text repeatedly refers to the character as 'fair' and, notoriously, as a 'white ewe' being tupped by a 'black ram' (*Othello*, 1.1.88–9).[103] By casting Cassie Layton, a woman of colour, in the part of a character almost always played by a pale-skinned, blonde actor on stage, Harding is reversing decades of casting in this play: instead of a white man playing a Black character, a woman of colour is playing a white character. However, as Layton is not a star-name actor, unless the audience had seen her previous stage or screen work, it is unlikely that they would have been aware of this fact. Just as reviewers had commented about Lenny Henry that not being able to see him meant listeners were less likely to expect him to break into his comic persona, so radio can enable an actor of any heritage to play a part without their appearance being a significant factor in their casting, although, until the mid-1990s, little use has been made of this opportunity.

Harding's textual changes and direction of her actors also affect character. Desdemona's murder is particularly brutal. Lasting almost a full minute without words, there are sounds of her struggling, choking, gasping and slapping Othello.[104] Harding says that she 'wanted the murder to feel completely devastating' and 'hear the full horror' of what was happening to Desdemona.[105] She says that, to do this, she had 'one of the most upsetting studios' she had ever experienced:[106]

> We had Khalid and Cassie on the floor with pillows. I discussed how we were going to do it with the actors and they wanted to do it, kind of, for real. We practised a way of doing it so that it wasn't really going to hurt her, he wasn't pressing very hard, and we recorded the sound through the pillow of that happening.[107]

After Desdemona's death, Harding chooses not to have her revive, removing her final lines. The character no longer takes responsibility for her own death nor absolves Othello (Emilia: 'O, who hath done this deed?' Desdemona: 'Nobody,

---

[100] *Othello*, 2020, 0:37:59.
[101] Maryam Philpott, 'Othello – Drama on 3', *Cultural Capital*, 27 April 2020: https://maryamphilpottblog.wordpress.com/tag/khalid-abdalla.
[102] Ayanna Thompson, 'Introduction', in William Shakespeare, *Othello*, rev. ed., ed. E. A. J. Honigmann (London, 2016), pp. 1–116; p. 90.
[103] For references to Desdemona being 'fair', see *Othello*, 1.1.124, 1.2.67, 1.3.125.
[104] *Othello*, 2020, 1:47:37.
[105] Emma Harding, private Zoom conversation, 27 May 2021.
[106] Harding, private conversation.
[107] Harding, private conversation.

I myself' (*Othello*, 5.2.132–3)). Othello's line: 'For nought I did in hate, but all in honour' (*Othello*, 5.2.301) is also cut. In doing so, Harding ensures that Othello has no excuse for what he has done and, alongside the brutality of the killing, presents a much less sympathetic character than is usually heard on radio or seen on stage.

The presentation of the character of Othello on BBC radio over the last 100 years charts the changing attitudes both on air and beyond to the portrayal of Shakespeare's Moor of Venice. For most of the twentieth century, the only actors deemed fit to play him were white: race was not considered important, despite early twentieth-century critics and academics arguing that Othello was definitely Black.[108] It would be easy to suggest that radio facilitated the perpetuation of white actors playing the role as it is not a visual medium: Farjeon suggests that the 'difficulty' of Othello's colour 'does not arise in broadcasting'.[109] But there is nothing to suggest that producers gave the issue any thought at all. Their preference was for established, mature leading actors from the theatre, and as these were almost always white, it is no surprise that radio's Othellos were too.

Radio seems to have been particularly keen on actors with a sonorous or musical vocal quality. Producer Felix Felton points out that, on radio, actors cannot fall back on the tricks of the theatre – make-up, costume and gesture – putting more emphasis on voice.[110] However, he also acknowledges that acting for radio is not playing to 'a massed audience stretching back into the recesses of a vast auditorium, but to millions of individual listeners, each so close that he could touch them'.[111] As such, it requires a subtler acting style for a convincing performance. This fact seems to have been missed by many of his colleagues, who repeatedly chose actors who appeared to be broadcasting to the back row of the stalls. As such, they may have delivered the verse beautifully, but did not engage listeners in the characters.

It was not until the new millennium that attitudes as to who could play Othello and how they should play him began to change, with the casting of BBC radio's first Black actor in the role. And while Fearon, Ejiofor and Henry were not stalwarts of the Shakespearian theatre, all three had played the role on stage prior to their radio appearances, suggesting producers remained unwilling to take risks with actors unfamiliar with the part. It is only with Abdalla that casting has reached beyond those who have already been successful on stage as Othello, or who even have a back catalogue of Shakespearian lead roles, to establish their credibility.[112] Of the eleven actors to play Othello on BBC radio, seven were white; historically he has been played by men 'more fair than black'. However, the prevailing desire for old, white men with musical voices seems to have finally been eradicated – at least for the part of Othello. So far, no actor of colour has played an English king, or almost any other leading male Shakespearian role, on radio.[113] So there is still some way to go before radio fully embraces the opportunities of diverse casting.

---

[108] See A. C. Bradley, *Shakespearean Tragedy: Lectures on Hamlet, Othello, King Lear, Macbeth* (London, 1904; repr. 1950), p. 198; Harley Granville-Barker, *Prefaces to Shakespeare*, vol. 2 (Princeton, 1947; repr. 1978), pp. 148–9.
[109] Farjeon, 'Othello was a black man.'
[110] Felix Felton, *The Radio Play: Its Techniques and Possibilities* (London, 1949), p. 129.
[111] Felton, *The Radio Play*, p. 12.
[112] Although Abdalla had performed in *The Duchess of Malfi* and *Tamburlaine the Great* on stage, Othello was his first Shakespearian role.
[113] David Harewood is perhaps the only exception, having played Antony in the 2002 production of *Antony and Cleopatra*.

'THIS FAIR PAPER': *OTHELLO* AND THE ARTISTS' BOOK

AGNIESZKA ŻUKOWSKA

Love's Labour's Lost contains a delightfully absurd vision of human obtuseness, which is rendered in some strikingly visceral terms: the character of Dull is here described as the one who 'hath never fed of the dainties that are bred in a book. / He hath not eat paper, as it were, he hath not drunk ink. His intellect is not replenished' (4.2.24–6). For all its exaggerated humour, Shakespeare's playful definition of the ignorance of books of wisdom draws attention to the inherent physicality of the reading act, which is usually overshadowed by the mental experience it offers. A type of book that does justice to both modes of reading is the artists' book, a cross-generic form which appeals not only to the mind of its viewers-turned-readers but also to their senses, necessitating the recognition of its own materiality. Its concern with the book as a thing, also as an art object, makes the artists' book a perfect vehicle for a creative response to Shakespeare's *Othello*, a play built up around one of his most memorable props, the strawberry-spotted handkerchief, and featuring a troupe of increasingly objectified characters. As book artists enter into a creative dialogue with the Shakespearian text, they arrive at a variety of forms, ranging from the abstract to the figurative, or, to move from the province of the image to that of the word, the wordless to the verbose. What they all have in common, though, is that they position themselves against the established conventions and standards in book production, while at the same time reaching for a text with a particularly rich publication history.

THE (UN)BOOKISH: KATE CRONIN'S *A JEALOUSY SO STRONG, THAT JUDGEMENT CANNOT CURE*

Its plain cardboard slipcase stamped with Iago's words, 'a jealously so strong / That judgement cannot cure' (*Othello*, 2.1.300–1), the British artist and illustrator Kate Cronin's artists' book immediately announces itself as addressing the key theme of Shakespeare's tragedy of passion. In one of his villainous soliloquies, though, Iago confesses that the jealousy that he means to excite in Othello is supposed to be 'unbookish' (4.1.100), referencing here the general's lack of knowledge of the books of love, or even his ignorance of the Elizabethan psychology of love.[1] When set in this context, Cronin's choice of medium might seem rather puzzling. However, it is not coincidental. According to the letter and word artist Ward Tietz:

artists' books start from a position of either viewing or reading and must move toward, or gesture toward, an opposing reconciling position. Artists' books, then, achieve their final coherence in this space between viewing and reading, in an imagined space where pictorial representation fills in the representation of the text through metaphor, through synecdoche, through the representation of whole by part. We will find, interestingly, that pictures frequently disrupt a text and break its coherence, but also ultimately repair it.[2]

---

[1] See Lily B. Campbell, *Shakespeare's Tragic Heroes: Slaves of Passion* (London, 1961), p. 169.
[2] Ward Tietz, 'Artists' books: between viewing and reading', *The Journal of Artists' Books* 21 (2007), 17–26; p. 26.

'THIS FAIR PAPER': *OTHELLO* AND THE ARTISTS' BOOK

3 Kate Cronin, *A Jealousy So Strong, That Judgement Cannot Cure*. Image courtesy of the artist.

As they defy the audience's expectations, forcing them to oscillate between the positions of readers and viewers, artists' books are, by definition, 'unbookish'.

Cronin's visual rendering of the theme of jealousy is also 'unbookish' in the most obvious sense of being wordless. With the removal of the slipcase emerges a set of unbound sheets of paper, each folded in half, reminiscent more of notes or letters than of a codex-shaped book as we know it today. When unfolded, the book's pages reveal a network of crisscrossing black lines, which are initially sparse – the first page contains only a single black spot – but grow more intricate with each consecutive page (Figure 3). When confronted with the text of Shakespeare's play, the increasingly more complex webbing will quickly become associated with Iago's 'little … web', which the manipulative arch-villain uses to 'ensnare as great a fly as Cassio' (2.2.71–2). Upon being incorporated into the artists' book, the black webbing has its materiality highlighted by structural measures: it is not limited to two-dimensional screen-printed representation, as some of it is actually handsewn. Cronin's book thus references one of the crucial elements of the imagery of Shakespeare's *Othello* and an important cultural phenomenon in its own right – namely, the art of needlework and, by extension, embroidery.

In a striking combination of railing and praise, the enraged Othello describes Desdemona as one 'delicate with her needle, an admirable musician', also admitting that 'she will sing the savageness out of a bear – of so high and plenteous wit and invention' (4.1.183–6). The arts of singing and embroidery, here conflated, seem to be very different: singing is vocalized, short-lasting and processual, while embroidery is wordless but renders tangible effects in the form of the textile. However, both are potentially ornamental and inherently narrative; in historical terms, they are also part of the educational experience of early modern women of a higher social standing.[3] Writing of other

---

[3] Heather Wolfe, 'Letter writing and paper connoisseurship in elite households in early modern England', in *Working with Paper: Gendered Practices in the History of Knowledge*, ed. Carla Bittel, Elaine Leong and Christine von Oertzen (Pittsburgh, 2019), p. 22.

traditionally feminine skills, the book artist and cultural theorist Johanna Drucker enumerates 'the fields of calligraphy, binding, writing, painting and printing', of which she further notices that they 'are in many ways connected to the traditionally sanctioned women's pursuits of keeping diaries, sewing, fancy needlework, elaborate decorative tasks, and the careful preservation of memory'.[4] For all its emphasis on the domestic and the private, which are traditionally thought to be the province of women, Shakespeare's *Othello* subverts the conventional associations of sewing with the female sex, as the play's web of lies is spun by the male character of Iago. In one of his trademark soliloquies, the villain reveals to the reader that his plan is to 'out of [Desdemona's] own goodness make the net / That shall enmesh them all' (2.3.352–3). The figure of Desdemona, by contrast – for all her accomplishment, virtue and heroic integrity – does not spin the thread of her own fate; she rests instead under the double dramatic control of the real playwright Shakespeare and the fictional playwright-like figure of Iago. The latter is also suggested to be the author of the webbing in the artists' book, which is indicated by the fact that his lines are used in the place of the writer's or artist's name and title on the slipcase.

Desdemona's lack of agency is indicative of her general objectification, which is also reflected by the play's imagery. It is a scholarly commonplace that there exists a peculiar affinity between the heroine and the world of objects, especially the strawberry-spotted handkerchief, which finds its prolongation in the wedding sheets Desdemona wants to be shrouded in. She is also likened to a book: in one of his most memorable feats of jealousy, Othello exclaims: 'Was this fair paper, this most goodly book, / Made to write "whore" upon?' (4.2.73–4). Shakespeare's verbal accomplishment here results in the impression that, to quote Dympna Callaghan, Desdemona herself 'becomes an object – a sheet – where she is literally positioned as a text'.[5] A powerful literary image as it is, though, the association of Desdemona's flesh with the pages of a book is nothing more than a metaphor when used in the dramatic text. Kate Cronin's work, by contrast, makes it possible to move beyond the constraints of literary signification and give actual substance to Shakespeare's literary portrayal of a fictional character, which is also what happens during a theatrical staging. What emerges in the course of the artistic process is a Desdemona-as-book-object, an uncannily tangible concretization of the early modern idea of the lover as a book.[6]

The sensory reading of Cronin's work is much aided by the fact that reference to human corporeality rests at the very core of the medium of the artists' book. As noted by Gary Frost, the bodily experience of artists' books is distinguished by the:

haptic concern ... follow[ing] from the peculiar essence of the book as hand held art. Books are only read at arms' length and are notoriously intractable in gallery display. This is a legacy of writing as a picture of speech and its early use as a handheld prompt.... The whole environment of this experience is tactile, manipulative, confined, tricky and surprising.... This primary corporeal nature, both as an analogy to human anatomy and as a hand-held object, provides a primary descriptor of the physical book.[7]

Viewed in this context, the material make-up of Cronin's book becomes meaningful: the dark lines soiling its white sheets can be seen as a pendant to Othello's painful realization that his 'name, that was as fresh / As Dian's visage, is now begrimed and black / As [his] own face' (3.3.391–3). Using the webbing as a visual sign of the ongoing process of

---

[4] Johanna Drucker, 'Intimate authority: women, books, and the public–private paradox', in *The Book as Art: Artists' Books from the National Museum of Women in the Arts*, ed. Krystyna Wasserman (New York, 2007), p. 14.

[5] Dympna Callaghan, 'Looking well to linens: women and cultural production in *Othello* and Shakespeare's England', in *Marxist Shakespeares*, ed. Jean E. Howard and Scott Cutler Shershow (London, 2001), p. 72.

[6] For a discussion of the lover as a book motif in Shakespeare, see Eric Jager, *The Book of the Heart* (Chicago, 2000), pp. 147–8.

[7] Gary Frost, 'Reading by hand: the haptic evaluation of artists' books', *The Bonefolder: An E-Journal for the Bookbinder and Book Artist* 2 (2005), 3–6; p. 3.

moral degeneration – or, rather, of Othello's erroneous conviction about his wife's supposed infidelity – the artist thus gives material substance to what is, in Peter Erickson's terms, 'implied images of black ink on white paper' and an indispensable element of the play's depiction of the 'white–black racial dynamic'.[8]

Analysing Shakespeare's treatment of his central prop, Callaghan draws attention to the 'culturally proximate nature of the textual and the textile' in the early modern period, noticing that the handkerchief in *Othello* 'serves as a visual text which is treated like a printed book ... repeatedly described with the scribal term "copy"'.[9] A comparably dualist impression is created by the black webbing in the artists' book. Although it exists solely in a single copy, Cronin's work follows the structural principle of replication. The actual thread its pages are sewn through with finds its visual equivalent, or 'copy', in the screen-printed lines marring the white paper of Desdemona-as-book-object. The artist's choice and handling of the materials can also be seen as recalling, albeit in a somewhat perverse manner, one of the early modern practices involved in the sealing of letters. As observed by Heather Wolfe, some of the more elaborate royal and aristocratic correspondence, especially of a more private nature, was bound with silk floss, which was 'either wrapped around the fore edge of the folded packet multiple times and sealed in place on both sides of the packet or woven through a hole or holes in the packet, if extra security was desired'.[10] Wolfe also makes note of the importance of colour symbolism in silk-flossing: pink floss was thus a sign of fidelity, while black floss had mortuary connotations as it was used by senders in mourning.[11] The folded pages of Cronin's book are also pierced and tied with black thread, which is suggestive of the repeated violation and the eventual death of Desdemona at the hands of her own husband. In fact, in the original play, there is also a certain affinity suggested between Desdemona and the letter: of the four kisses that Othello bestows in the tragedy, three are meant for his wife (including the parting kiss conferred upon her corpse) and one is directed at a letter, referred to as 'the instrument of ... pleasures' (4.1.216).

A general property of artists' books, many of which draw on the book arts and on the art of sculpture, and hence often approximate art objects, is that they provoke what Gary Frost terms 'haptic conflict': they are 'quick to open [their] covers, but reluctant to open [their] contents'.[12] The overall tactile experience offered by Cronin's book is quite in line with the above definition. Its pages are left unbound; however, every consecutive sheet is harder to open because of the increasingly tighter sewing. A fitting answer to Shakespeare's poetics of confinement in *Othello*, Cronin's work defies the reader's general expectations as to the basic form of the book as we know it today – a codex whose pages are turned by a reader taking no account of their colour or texture and usually totally oblivious to the very act of turning them. By physically resisting its readers, Cronin's book sends a clear signal that it needs them to activate their senses, including the sense of touch, in order to explore its inextricable merger of form and content.

At this point, it is interesting to note that the motif of the net or web was a standard element of the early modern emblematic representations of the sense of touch. Associable with the tale of the weaver Arachne, whose pride over the tapestry depicting the gods' amorous exploits brought about her tragic end, the spiderweb motif also served as a warning against the dangers of sensual pleasures, a visual reminder of 'the snare in which the unwary love may be trapped'.[13] Apart from its admonitory appeal, the spiderweb was also thought to possess certain cognitive properties: as noted by Jennifer Rae McDermott, it stood for 'both

---

[8] Peter Erickson, 'Images of white identity in *Othello*', in *Othello: New Critical Essays*, ed. Philip C. Kolin (London, 2002), p. 141.
[9] Callaghan, 'Looking', p. 72. See also Catherine Bates, 'Weaving and writing in *Othello*', *Shakespeare Survey 46* (Cambridge, 1993), 51–60.
[10] Wolfe, 'Letter writing', p. 22.
[11] Wolfe, 'Letter writing', p. 23.
[12] Frost, 'Reading by hand', p. 4.
[13] Sharon Assaf, 'The ambivalence of the sense of touch in early modern prints', *Renaissance and Reformation* 29 (2005), 75–98; p. 89.

touching and knowing because its outward-reaching tactile filaments allow the perceiver to gather "intelligence"', an association stemming from 'a long philosophical tradition that likened the fibrous skin to a net and further used that simile to explain "intellectual apprehension"'.[14] Its folded pages containing several webbings, Cronin's book also stimulates cognitive experience: it hints at the existence of some secret one is expected to unfold. Note, in passing, that in Shakespeare's *Othello* the verb 'to unfold' is used only with reference to the characters of Iago – who 'knows more, much more, than he unfolds' (3.3.248) – and Desdemona – who asks the Duke of Venice to 'lend [his] prosperous ear' to her 'unfolding' (1.3.245). Its material make-up meant to trigger the viewer's mental activity, Cronin's work turns out to be remarkably consistent with Monica Carroll and Adam Dickerson's general view of artists' books as '*spaces, structures* or *loci* for inviting or encouraging certain kinds of epistemic activities in a reader'.[15]

In Shakespeare's play, the ultimate unfolding, or revelation, of Desdemona's goodness and Iago's vice comes at the price of cutting threads of multiple lives, a metaphor which is actually used with reference to Brabanzio, whose 'old thread' was 'shor[n] ... in twain' by grief (5.2.212–13). A tangible reflection of the denouement of Shakespeare's play is to be found on the final page of the artists' book, where the black webbing is cut open (Figure 4). The artist's gesture echoes here the symbolic splitting apart of the colours black and white in the tragedy: as noted by Peter Erickson, at the conclusion of the play 'Desdemona's "fair paper" is preserved as an unmarred field of pure whiteness – "Yet I'll not shed her blood / Nor scar that whiter skin of hers than snow" (5.2.3–4) – while Othello's blackness is sealed off in the image of "a malignant and a turbaned Turk" whose elimination is acted out in his suicide.'[16]

THE (IN)HUMAN: BORBONESA'S *OTHELLO: A BESTIARY*

Another work which enters into creative dialogue with Shakespeare's play, while at the same time demonstrating a strong awareness of the medium of the artists' book, is *Othello: A Bestiary – With Floral Additions*, a collaborative project by art collective Borbonesa, co-authored by Matt Fleming, Lee Shearman and Ian Whitmore, with hand-cut paper illustrations by Whitmore (2011). While Cronin focuses on two of *Othello*'s powerful images – the web and the book – through Whitmore's illustrations, Borbonesa's concertina distils from the Shakespearian text a much larger body of literary allusion – its references to animals – and renders them as screen-printed silhouettes and body fragments, originally hand-cut from black paper (Figure 5). The first page of the book proper,[17] for instance, bearing the image of a donkey head, refers to Iago's verbal manipulation of Roderigo: 'Many a duteous and knee-crooking knave / That, doting on his own obsequious bondage, / Wears out his time much like his master's ass' (1.1.45–7). Among the representations to follow are, for instance, on the next two pages: the flies Brabanzio is to be 'plagu[ed] with' (1.1.71) upon hearing the news of his daughter's elopement; the heads of the 'old black ram' and the 'white ewe' (1.1.88–9) of Iago's obscenely reductive picture of sexual intercourse; and the three horses of his nightmarish vision of Brabanzio's family tree: 'you'll have your daughter covered with a Barbary horse, you'll have your nephews neigh to you, you'll have coursers for cousins and jennets for germans' (1.1.113–15). The book's black-and-white inside also incorporates floral designs, referencing some of the plants mentioned in the Shakespearian text, including, for instance, the mandragora and the poppy, which, after his mistreatment by Iago, will not 'medicine [Othello] to

---

[14] Jennifer Rae McDermott, '"There's magic in the web of it": skin, mind, and webs of touch in *Othello*', in *Embodied Cognition and Shakespeare's Theatre: The Early Modern Body-Mind*, ed. Laurie Johnson, John Sutton and Evelyn Tribble (New York, 2014), p. 157.

[15] Monica Carroll and Adam Dickerson, 'The knowing of artists' books', *The Journal of Artists' Books* 43 (2018), 10–13; p. 13.

[16] Erickson, 'Images', p. 141.

[17] The concertina also includes a five-page foreword by the artist and printer Anna Fewster.

'THIS FAIR PAPER': *OTHELLO* AND THE ARTISTS' BOOK

4 Kate Cronin, *A Jealousy So Strong, That Judgement Cannot Cure*. Image courtesy of the artist.

5 Borbonesa, *Othello: A Bestiary – With Floral Additions*, I.3. Image courtesy of the artists; photo by Lee Shearman.

that sweet sleep / Which [he] owedst yesterday' (3.3.336–7); the willow of Desdemona's and Emilia's sorrowful songs; and, naturally, the ill-omened strawberries.

The natural detail, summary yet realistic, is also complemented with two types of nonfigurative elements – screen-printed irregular shapes, coloured back, and a number of specks of red – whose presence adds another layer of meaning to the entire work. As specified on the verso of the front cover, the irregular shapes, which are based on offcuts left over from the making of the animal figures, are meant to represent the references to monsters or unspecified creatures in the Shakespearian original. The red dots are supposed to stand for Shakespeare's allusions to the devil, which can in fact be seen as a departure from the tragedy, which conflates devilishness with blackness rather than redness: in many of its scenes, to quote from Doris Adler's study of the rhetoric of black in the play, 'the *black* of race and the *black* of devil are combined'.[18] A speck of red is thus placed, for instance, by the heads of the ram and the ewe of the second page of the book proper, where it corresponds to Iago's warning that the "devil will make a grandsire of [Brabanzio]' (1.1.91). Both types of nonfigurative material accompany the three horses visualizing the contamination of Brabanzio's bloodline by the inter-racial union of Desdemona and Othello. Suspended over the equine figures is a single speck of red, corresponding to one of Iago's taunts directed at Desdemona's father: "swounds, sir, you are one of those that will not serve God if the devil bid you' (1.1.110–11). At the bottom of the page, in turn, figures an organic-looking yet essentially nonrepresentational offcut, which, when confronted with the Shakespearian text, turns out to address Iago's famously phantasmagorical vision of a lovemaking couple as 'the beast with two backs' (1.1.118–19). Other examples soon follow.

Its pages teeming with animal forms, the concertina not only draws on the Shakespearian tragedy but also addresses a larger body of texts, associable with the classically rooted tradition of bestiaries. Compendia of all creatures, bestiaries were especially popular in the Middle Ages, but they continued to be read well into the early modern period, the most famous English examples being Edward Topsell's *The History of Four-Footed Beasts* (1607) and *History of Serpents* (1608). Whether handwritten or printed, bestiaries are notable for a certain type of structural regularity: the beings described can thus be grouped into various categories or simply follow the alphabetical order, and individual descriptive entries are usually accompanied by illustrations. In their *Othello*-based bestiary, the Borbonesa artists disrupt this balance by removing the text, save for the title and a short quotation from the play at the back of the cover wrapper. Also the treatment of individual designs, as well as their arrangement on the consecutive pages of the concertina, is much freer than the rigid ordering of animal entries in a standard bestiary or, for that matter, the ordering of material within any kind of a regular printed book. A certain degree of artistic licence is visible, for instance, in the overall design for the animal representations, which are rendered in varying scales and come both as entire silhouettes and heads, as well as other bodily fragments. The animal representations also partially disregard the book's page divisions, some of the tails or feathers projecting out to the next page.

Leafing through a book, one expects to find a certain form of ocular regularity, with black lines of print neatly inscribed into the white rectangle of the page. This is clearly not the case with the *Othello*-based concertina, which is notable not only for its compositional irregularities but also for the unusual prominence of the empty spaces between its figurative detail, sometimes amounting to entire blank pages (Figure 6). However, the inclusion of act and scene references to Shakespeare's text clearly indicates that Borbonesa aim at achieving some form of coherence: their intention, in fact, is to reflect the pattern of delivery of animal metaphors in the successive scenes of the play, or, to be more precise, in its Penguin

---

[18] Doris Adler, 'The rhetoric of *black* and *white* in *Othello*', *Shakespeare Quarterly* 25 (1974), 248–57; p. 251.

'THIS FAIR PAPER': *OTHELLO* AND THE ARTISTS' BOOK

6 Borbonesa, *Othello: A Bestiary – With Floral Additions*, III.4–IV.1. Image courtesy of the artists; photo by Lee Shearman.

edition by Kenneth Muir (1968). Seen from this perspective, the puzzling gaps in the overall composition of the bestiary acquire structural meaning: an entire page of the concertina or its large portion is left empty when no animal reference is to be found in a corresponding scene or its fragment in *Othello*. Thus, for instance, the first three pages of the book proper, boasting several animal designs, are succeeded by as many as four blank pages, which are a visible response to the lack of animal imagery in the Shakespearian source text.

The semiotization of empty space in Borbonesa's bestiary corresponds to the general tendency in the book arts to acknowledge what Nola Farman calls 'negative space', which includes 'the supporting material, the props, the space between the lines of text', and – which is particularly pertinent to the discussion of *Othello* – 'reverses light and dark'.[19] As observed by Farman, owing to their recognition and appreciation of all of the components of the page, including its negative spaces, artists' books depart rather far from the Western pictorial tradition, in which 'the background is the negative part of the field or picture plane. The main subject is the positive. It is the focal point; it is considered to be exceptional; it is consecrated.'[20] It is also interesting to note that even the positive element in the concertina – i.e., the animal silhouettes and plant detail – has a negative aspect to it, having been modelled on elements made using the paper-cutting technique. Paper-cutting involves subtraction, and not addition, of the material used: as part of the process, paper is removed – as opposed to, for instance, the art of painting, which depends for its effect on the application of the often multiple layers of paint onto the canvas.

The decorative impulse at its very core, paper-cutting is sometimes viewed as a sister art to embroidery, the latter being an important point of reference for the imagery devised for Shakespeare's *Othello*. Note, in passing, that paper-cutting also happens to

---

[19] Nola Farman, 'The artists' book and negative space', *International Journal of the Book* 3 (2005/6), 1–3; pp. 1–2.
[20] Farman, 'The artists' book', p. 2.

have some bookish connotations. In early modern Europe, paper- or parchment-cutting was sometimes used for the purposes of book decoration: one of the most famous examples here is Marie de' Medici's prayerbook, now in the collection of The Walters Art Museum, Baltimore, whose margins are decorated with hauntingly beautiful lace-like cutouts. Vivid and organic, the animal figures produced by Whitmore are stylistically closer, though, to Chinese animalistic paper cuts, while also bearing some resemblance to stencil graffiti – an art form which can provide spectacular aesthetic effects but can also be of a potentially disruptive character. The latter is a particularly fitting association for a work which breaks so many conventions of regular book design, to a spectacular aesthetic effect.

In his study of the relationship between word and image in the artists' book, Martin Sundberg observes that this hybrid art object 'consist[s] of an inextricable weave of the three main parts: the book as material object and structure, the book as sequence, and the book as page. Material, sequence and page constitute three parts that are inseparable and that together become meaningful – as book.'[21] However, as also noted by the theorist, there is a certain paradox involved in this seemingly neat definition, because the three parts can rarely be appreciated simultaneously by the viewer. Accordingly, the artists' book is also characterized by a 'double-sided effect of simultaneously stabilising and destabilising the structure'.[22] The same complexity is a property of Borbonesa's visual response to the poetics of animality in Shakespeare's play. It would appear that the concertina fulfils all the criteria for the artists' book as a 'weave'. When spread, it is not an entirely flat strip of paper; its gentle folds and tilted pages give it an almost sculptural look, which is further accentuated by the play of light and shadow on its surface and is likely to draw the viewer's attention to the concertina's materiality. The other element of Sundberg's book-as-a weave theory, the sequence, is reflected in the elongated shape of the entire bestiary, which is horizontally oriented and invites left-to-right reading. Finally, the format of the concertina does not hamper the reception of the 'book as page': page divisions are visibly highlighted by means of the vertical folds across its single sheet. This having been said, it is impossible for the viewer to appreciate all these qualities at a time; the experience of looking at a book of fifty-four pages is by necessity kaleidoscopic, which means that the viewer is constantly made to shift between different receptive modes.

The reception of Borbonesa's Shakespeare-inspired bestiary is further enriched when one considers the relationship that evolves between its inside and outside. The book's cover is stamped with a single red strawberry, which is pictured against a green background reverberating the tragedy's key theme of jealousy. Emerging at the removal of the book's black-and-white decorative cover wrapper, this design is a clear reference to Desdemona's strawberry-spotted handkerchief. In fact, as it reappears inside the concertina, the colour red is more immediately associable with the strawberry motif from the wrap-around than with Shakespeare's demonic allusions, which it was originally meant to represent. With its strawberry-like specks of red, the entire concertina thus invites analogies with the play's central prop, the embroidered love token – after all, Borbonesa's book is a single folded sheet, echoing the play's textile symbolism. It is interesting to note, in passing, that, while in his play Shakespeare makes a number of references to red-coloured motifs, including strawberries, blood or hellish fires serving to illustrate the characters' emotional turmoil, the words 'red', 'scarlet' or 'crimson' are conspicuously absent from the dramatic text.

As the Borbonesa artists expand the chromatic vocabulary of the Shakespearian original to include the actual colour red, they also question the established conventions of book design: in its most basic form, a printed page should be black and white. Distorting the relationships between print and paper, word and image, readership and viewership,

---

[21] Martin Sundberg, 'The collapse of the word–image dichotomy: towards an iconic approach to graphic novels and artists' books', *Konsthistorisk tidskrift / Journal of Art History* 86 (2017), 31–44; p. 33.
[22] Sundberg, 'The collapse', p. 34.

the concertina has an air of ambiguity about it, which is another reason why it can be seen as a material replacement for the fictional Shakespearian handkerchief. When it comes to the latter, it is also possessed of an ambiguous nature, which is visible on many levels. For instance, while most readers and theatre makers imagine it to be white, Ian Smith famously observes that it is actually black, 'a fitting, virtually self-explanatory symbol of the play's central but controversial interracial marriage'.[23] A further level of complexity is added by the somewhat uncanny symbolism behind the strawberry motif. While it is associable with innocence – being an indispensable detail of, for instance, the depictions of the *hortus conclusus* – the fruit can also stand for treachery and deceit, because of the possible presence of a serpent underneath its innocent-looking leaves.[24] Finally, being an object that Desdemona talks to and kisses, the strawberry-spotted textile is not only a love token but also a replacement for the absent Othello, which makes it assume the status of the mediator between the worlds of people and objects. A similar mediatory function is performed by the concertina, or, for that matter, a large body of artists' books, which invite readerly engagement and interaction on many levels.

THE (UN)SPOKEN: EMILY MARTIN'S *DESDEMONA, IN HER OWN WORDS*

Emily Martin's unbound book *Desdemona, In Her Own Words* gives much prominence to the verbal element of Shakespeare's tragedy, which is incorporated into the work, albeit in a changed form. As part of her project, the Iowa-based artist extracted the lines spoken by Desdemona from the Shakespearian source text and used them to script a completely new play. The lines composed were then incorporated into a series of prints, an artists' book, and a stop-motion animation involving hinged puppets. This is how Martin recounts the initial stage of her creative process on the colophon sheet:

I isolated Desdemona's lines and made a set of individual word magnets so I could arrange and rearrange her words to see what else she might say. While I cannot make Desdemona say some of the things I wished she would, she speaks for herself here, not as anyone's pawn. And I found that in the time I have spent with Desdemona's words I developed a greater appreciation for the language of the play. The result is this very short play consisting of a prelude, five acts and a coda.[25]

Martin's play inscribed into the pages of the artists' book is distinguished by a rigid regularity of structure, which gives it an incantational, almost litany-like appeal. Apart from the Prelude, which contains a statement of Desdemona's newly vocalized independence and can be read as an assertion of the heroine's humanity ('I am not some token to be moved between men with motives of their own'), the rewritten text is made up solely of questions addressed to the remaining characters of Shakespeare's play:

Act I: 'When did your heart lose faith so your ears hear but guilt and your eyes see me not'
Act II: 'Where is this beguiling monster that he never speaks slander to my face'
Act III: 'Why did no one speak on my behalf before all was lost to violence'
Act IV: 'Who is this miserable man that he taints my truth and makes such fatal sorrow'
Act V: 'What wretched husband believes false speech and feels just in killing his loyal wife'

There is a structural symmetry behind the arrangement of these lines: the play proper starts and ends with a question addressed to Othello (Acts I and V), while the central query, directed at Emilia, Cassio and Brabanzio (Act III), is flanked by two questions posed to Iago (Acts II and IV). The entire sequence is closed off by a Coda, consisting of two rhetorical questions: 'How can love die this easily was it ever even truly love.'

Martin's decision to present Desdemona's reconstructed lines in the artists' book, a form

---

[23] Ian Smith, 'Othello's black handkerchief', *Shakespeare Quarterly* 64 (2013), 1–25; p. 24.
[24] On the snake and strawberries emblem, see, for instance, Frances N. Teague, *Shakespeare's Speaking Properties* (London, 1991), p. 26.
[25] Emily Martin, *Desdemona, In Her Own Words* (Iowa City, 2014), colophon.

with a vigorous interest in all matters related to materiality, makes it possible to highlight the new play's syntactic and structural regularities using visual measures. Each of the sections scripted by the artist is thus contained within a separate folder, its cover bearing the number of the act (or a reference to the Prelude or Coda) and – in all but one folder – a single word heralding its content. The two elements listed on the outside of each folder are always separated with a colon, as in 'Act I: When'. The only departure from this pattern is the Prelude, whose cover is inscribed with two words, 'I am', instead of one. This is a telling discrepancy: the first printed words of the play proper make one think not only of Desdemona's mistreatment and silencing in the Shakespearian original, but also of the general status of the fictional figure in the dramatic text. Still, from a structural viewpoint, this minor irregularity does not destroy the book's overall impression of coherence, which is further accentuated by the visual parallels between the individual folders. Each of the principal parts of Martin's work comprises a letterpress-printed picture of Desdemona.

Shown in profile, which is in itself a confrontational pose, Shakespeare's heroine is pictured gesticulating violently, her lips parted as if she were screaming (Figure 7). For all the emotional impact of such gestures, their repertoire is rather limited: Desdemona is shown either crossing her arms or raising them against the sky. Resulting from technical limitations – in the letterpress printing process, the artist used wire to delineate the shape of Desdemona's body – the linear silhouette of the female figure has an almost archaic quality about itself. In fact, she bears some resemblance to the figure of the mourner, not unlike ones from the *prothesis* scenes on ancient Greek ceramics, pictured in the traditional gesture of lamentation – with arms raised above the head. A somewhat different source of inspiration is here cited by the artist: in the early stages of the project, Martin also made a hinged puppet of Desdemona, reminiscent of Indonesian shadow puppets, *wayang kulit*;[26] more puppets of this kind can be seen in the stop-motion animation.

One of the striking properties of shadow theatre, apart from its overall aestheticization, is that the characters' emotions and passions are primarily expressed by means of gesture. In the artists' book, Desdemona's passionate reactions are also demonstrated using fairly conventionalized gestures, which is illustrative of a larger tension between organizational rigour and freedom of expression that makes itself felt in Martin's work. A peculiar kind of tension is thus visible in the overall structure of the piece, whose central sections purport to follow the five-act pattern delineated by Shakespeare but, in fact, can also be rearranged at will with no change to the meaning of the entire play. According to the artist, while the principal elements of her work are so ordered as to 'denote [their] place in this new play', the overall structure of the unbound book 'of individual pages ... allow[s] each of Desdemona's statements to be seen as stand-alone declarations'.[27]

Martin's book is so designed as to accord a considerable degree of autonomy to its readers, who are not only invited to co-create the text by rearranging its parts but also encouraged to compose it anew. This is made possible by a set of word magnets corresponding to all of the words spoken by Desdemona in Shakespeare's play, which can be attached to the inner sides of the clamshell box, lined with sheet metal and covered in paper, containing the entire unbound book (Figure 8). If Martin's book were limited to its letterpress-printed inside, the resultant impression could easily be that the authorial plan to liberate Desdemona from the constraints of the dramatic text has proved a failure. The heroine's words would only be used as building blocks of a new text, once again encapsulated in print. Passed from the hands of one author to another, the figure of Desdemona would still seem strikingly passive, which is exactly what the artist wanted to avoid. However, the inclusion of the magnets in the book

---

[26] Genevieve Trainor, 'Desdemona redux: Emily Martin explores animation at CSPS', *Little Village: Iowa City, Cedar Rapids News, Culture & Events*: https://littlevillagemag.com/desdemona-redux-emily-martin-explores-animation-at-csps.

[27] Emily Martin, 'Desdemona in her own words', 2015 MCBA Prize Entries: https://mcbaprize.org/martin.

'THIS FAIR PAPER': *OTHELLO* AND THE ARTISTS' BOOK

Why did no one speak on my behalf before all was lost to violence

7 Emily Martin, *Desdemona, In Her Own Words*, act 3: Why. Image courtesy of the artist.

is a clear signal that Martin's printed play is just one of the many verbal combinations possible, which gives the entire work an air of potentiality. There is also a close affinity to be noticed between the reader and the fictional figure of Desdemona, as they are both empowered by the artist. This is made possible by the emancipation of the printed word, as if in answer to the early modern conviction about the corporeal nature of the verbal, which was thought to have material dimensions.[28]

***

Inherently predisposed to give tangible substance to literary allusion, yet also capable of addressing a wide range of extra-literary, often

---

[28] See Gina Bloom, *Voice in Motion: Staging Gender, Shaping Sound in Early Modern England* (Philadelphia, 2007), p. 2, and Judith H. Anderson, *Words that Matter: Linguistic Perception in Renaissance English* (Stanford, 1996), p. 19.

AGNIESZKA ŻUKOWSKA

8 Emily Martin, *Desdemona, In Her Own Words*, detail of the word magnets. Image courtesy of the artist.

self-referential issues, the artists' book can thus be seen as a fully fledged conversation partner for the dramatic text. When in the artist's hands, 'this fair paper, this most goodly book' does not necessarily have to be 'writ[ten] ... upon' or covered with lines of print to generate meaning. Addressing Shakespeare's *Othello*, the three contemporary books discussed turn out to be strongly receptive to its overlapping textual and textile imagery, its poetics of animality, and its concern with the silencing of women. Sharing the play's interest in artifice and objectification, they seamlessly enter into creative dialogue across the media and the ages.

OTHELLO: A DIALOGUE WITH THE BUILT ENVIRONMENT

YIK LING YONG

In her *Shakespeare After All*, Marjorie Garber reminds us of the 'geographical shift ... from a civilized place to a wild one, from a locale of order and law to a place of passion and confusion' that *Othello* presented.[1] In view of the role architecture plays in constructing the sense of place and locale, this article further sorts out how specific architectural components of the built environment enrich the play's representation of reason and passion, and values and rights. In this interdisciplinary, architecturally centred enquiry, I examine the way these components help to shape themes, focusing on imagery of built forms as a visual counterpart to the play's verbal narrative. I argue that there is an architectural 'narrative' alongside verbal narrative in the play, and these narratives complement one another in the phasal portrayal of Othello's tragedy. Examining the representation of forms and functions of architectural creations, I focus on the set of generated spatial meanings, demonstrating that strong architectural impressions as well as the interplay between built forms and narrative are pertinent to the delivery of the play's key themes and idea, helping to build up a purposeful, intricate system of ethical reasoning and assertions. Assigning the built environment a prominent role and value for reading and understanding, I hope to offer a refreshingly revisionist, architectural perspective on the set of challenges that Othello faces in the institutional system within which he functions.

The role of the built environment as among the investigative methods for cultural geography and material culture to explore actions in Shakespearian plays and other early modern dramas has been usefully explained by Julie Sanders and Catherine Richardson.[2] However, although domestic space and items have been discussed for specific scenes of Shakespeare's plays, for *Othello* there is a lack of focused examination on how architectural creation as a concept defines, generates and represents its complex ethical atmosphere. Henri Lefebvre has written that created space is a 'social product' with meanings embedded in metaphors, social reference or cultural association.[3] In view of the process and characteristics of spatial production that generate 'complex symbolisms' for human interactions, it would be worthwhile to examine portrayed physical spaces more closely, placing our understanding of invoked built forms in the context of societal, institutional influences for the play's underlying considerations.[4]

The place name 'Venice' in the formal title *Othello, the Moor of Venice* is a potent symbol in the light of the play's political-economic and morality discourse. Sean Benson emphasizes its exotic,

---

[1] Marjorie Garber, *Shakespeare After All* (New York, 2005), p. 589.
[2] See Julie Sanders, *The Cultural Geography of Early Modern Drama, 1620–1650* (Cambridge, 2011), and Catherine Richardson, *Domestic Life and Domestic Tragedy in Early Modern England* (Manchester, 2006).
[3] Henri Lefebvre, *The Production of Space*, trans. Donald Nicholson-Smith (Oxford, 1991), p. 26.
[4] Lefebvre, *Production of Space*, p. 33.

'locative' value, suggesting that, as a geographical referent, it indicates 'royal status – until one considers that "Moor" is an indicator of ethnicity rather than aristocracy'.[5] The 'added recognition' of the place name, to use Benson's words, alerts us geographically to a 'foreign and exotic' environment foregrounding Othello's ascendancy, which is problematic – how he could hold significant authority but still be distrusted?[6] In the play's early scenes, endemic inequality in terms of existing systemic privilege is spatialized through the means of an intricate environmental system. Beginning its actions on a street in Venice, geographical implications are first emphasized through the mention of – and tension set up by – the contrast of the city with Florence: 'But he ... a Florentine' (*Othello*, 1.1.12–19). Here, our attention is drawn to the two places, due to Iago's emotive, emphatic 'but'. He feels hard done by at having been passed over for promotion in Venice even though he is a local of the place. Alleging that city has a biased administrative system, he claims that, owing to its senators' foiled 'personal suit to make me his lieutenant' (1.1.9), instead of him, another person has been promoted. Native emotion, coming through via the juxtaposition of Venice and Florence, connects his discontent with the perceived administrative system currently in place, introducing what special privilege might bring in the context of a city perceived to be run by a system of fair government. Setting one metropolitan city (Venice) against another (Florence) creates the impression of fair competition among peers, infusing a vision that enables social mobility. However, the unfortunate fact is that, instead of him, who is a native Venetian, another metropolitan – Cassio, a Florentine, an outsider – has been cherry-picked. Everything being equal, one tends to sympathize with Iago.

What follows claimed injustice is the threat to upend the institution. Alluding to the urbanism of Venice, built forms have been exploited to depict actions: 'Proclaim him in the streets; incense her kinsmen, / And, though he in a fertile climate dwell, / Plague him with flies' (1.1.69–71), says Iago, threatening to carry out a major public protest against the system. Through this, the streets of Venice have been invested with the power to 'proclaim' (1.1.69) rumours, 'incense' (1.1.69) the public, and 'plague' (1.1.71) the reputation of the powers that be in order that suffered inequality can be heard. At the heart of this strong protest is experienced urban space in Venice. Sophia Psarra has usefully spoken of the urban fabric that inspired the '*Myth of Venice*', which is 'a collection of beliefs and official histories that described Venice as the most serene Republic'.[7] Essentially, Venice's extensive network of connected streets incorporated, as a visual fulcrum, the long and wide Piazza San Marco, which was the central administrative centre. The Piazza had been carefully designed such that its featured long and wide street had a tapering shape generating an illusion of perspective for pedestrians. It was, moreover, flanked by the large and ceremonious Duke's Palace, which held the Great Council, the Basilica, and the loggia façade of the Procurators of San Marco. Visually, reinforced by the Piazza's long tapering shape, the area's overall perspectival quality, as Psarra suggests, 'unifies' public space, making them 'synchronically accessible to the eye'.[8] Because of this spatial quality, San Marco is said to have been '[c]onfigured to accommodate performances and processions', being 'the heart of ceremonious occasions, from processions to festivals ... expressing the ritual structure of society and the social order of justice'.[9]

It is possible to imagine the above architectural backdrop as a background image for the play-scene. First, there is the political imagery that

---

[5] Sean Benson, *Shakespeare, 'Othello', and Domestic Tragedy* (London, 2011), p. 94.
[6] Benson, *Domestic Tragedy*, p. 94.
[7] Sophia Psarra, 'The role of spatial networks in the historic urban landscape: learning from Venice in the fifteenth and sixteenth centuries', *The Historic Environment: Policy and Practice* (2018), 249–73; p. 255.
[8] Psarra, 'Role', p. 256.
[9] For Venice's urban network see Psarra, 'Role'. Venice's urban space was constituted of an extensive, pedestrian system and squares known as 'campi'. The Duke's Palace (Palazzo Ducale), its administrative centre, represented the highest authority.

links to houses of rulers. Iago's description, 'he in a fertile climate dwell' (1.1.70), alludes to the comfortable, eminent house of 'Signor Brabanzio' (1.1.78), calling to mind actual senators in the Great Council. The imagery helps to contextualize Iago's claim of unfair practice in the political map of Venice, represented at three levels of government: the 'duke' in 'council' (1.2.94) stands for monarchical elements; the senators, the aristocracy; and the council, the democracy. One feature of such a system is that senators can be approached freely by the plebeian any time – enacted in act 1, scene 1 when Brabanzio is being roused at night at his house (1.1.74–80) by Iago and Roderigo. The image of two plebeians' effrontery to 'yell' (1.1.75) under his window paints a vivid picture of Venice running a democracy that is rather efficient, showing a regime that not only is untyrannical, but instead promotes freedom. Through urban fabric and built forms identified with San Marco – the historical and architecturally prominent Duke's Palace, its great council chamber, streets and squares – the setting helps to define actions in the scene as a civic concept. Due to the historical usage and political reputation attached to the built forms, some very particular ideas about the symbolism of Venice as a place and entity become audible. It is supposed to be what Felix Gilbert terms as 'the city of liberty', a city that aroused the admiration of foreign countries for its reputed 'justice, power, wealth and splendour'.[10]

In the way that social practice of space has been exploited to build up jarring personal experience, the created dual image of Venice – democracy as well as inequality – casts a long shadow over Venetian lives. Iago claims that Brabanzio has 'a voice potential / As double as the Duke's' (1.2.13–14): the senator has two votes in the council in the person of one, suggesting political arbitrariness that militates against a fair system. Iago's threatened stump oratory takes advantage of Venice's unique open space to portend troubling destabilization. His specific action verbs – 'proclaim' (1.1.69) Brabanzio, and 'incense' (1.1.69) his kinsmen – shape the perception of city space. The relationship between streets and actions, and between streets and the Duke's residence (Great Chamber) / senator's residence calling forth stirring public protests, recalls and requires the spatial logic of specific urban form – the tapering street that gives perspective focus on the speaker. Placing standing orators' threatening gestures and facial expressions in crosshair sights, the generated spatial imagery that is simultaneously metaphorical and literal calls up contemporary built forms, which in turn gives meaning to actions, and the intertwining relationship has a particular visual resonance. Instead of foreign dignitaries coming through Venice, attracted in awe of its political system as well as its unique streets, we can now imagine angry crowds thronging them to hear dissidents' fiery speech and to rebel.

Yet invoked street imagery also sets Iago up as a low-ranking naval soldier, as against those in power. He is seen moving about, nursing a grievance about 'Preferment [that] goes by letter and affection, / And not by old gradation' (1.1.35–6). Such a visual impression situates him in the struggles of working-class plebeians, presenting his 'downward mobility', to use Benson's words.[11] As Benson has argued, in contemporary practice it was difficult to move from a 'nonaristocratic status to ascend the military hierarchy'.[12] This is the situation for Iago. The street, seen as what Karen Malone describes as a 'contested domain of cities', the 'terrain of social encounters and political protest', is a fitting form that symbolizes his tenuous climbing of the greasy pole to 'get his place' (1.3.385).[13] Iago's social status, his quandary and his opportunity are interlinked with the physical environment which he occupies – the naval institution that is expected to put a premium on merit, rather than personal background, allowing for social mobility.

---

[10] Felix Gilbert, 'The Venetian Constitution in Florentine political thought', in *Florentine Studies: Politics and Society in Renaissance Florence*, ed. Nicolai Rubinstein (London, 1968), pp. 463–500; p. 466.
[11] Benson, *Domestic Tragedy*, p. 101.
[12] Benson, *Domestic Tragedy*, p. 101.
[13] Karen Malone, 'Street life: youth, culture and competing uses of public space', *Environment and Urbanization* 14 (2002), 157–268; p. 157.

Investing the scene with event spatiality, the architectural imagery is a natural, logical communicative strategy in the context of physical data for a 'spatial turn' for exploring social mobility.

There is also discourse on building typology in connection with users, and it is difficult to miss the point about social status that is in step with corresponding built forms. Roderigo, a member of the gentry, hints that he owns a landed house when he says, 'I'll sell all my land' (1.3.374). Here, the indication of wealth and status helps to shape the imagination that he has a gentleman's house, or a residence of the elite, which in turn suggests Iago's desirous nature. In trying to make Roderigo squander away his wealth, Iago's success in coercing him to part finally with his estate turns him into a homeless aristocrat. His move to dispossess Roderigo perhaps underlines his own passion for an elite house and the value attached to it. Lena Orlin writes that, during Elizabethan times, such passion has its roots in the 'trickling-down of aspiration' of the common people as they encountered the architectural achievements perceived in the Great Rebuilding.[14] Since Roderigo's dispossession is contrived by Iago – the innocent gentleman sells his estate simply for the latter's vague promise of Desdemona's love – his coerced dispossessed situation perhaps points to Iago's own disgruntled stripped condition. Iago only has a 'lodging' (1.3.372), which, as Emma Smith has suggested, is an 'implicit contradistinction to the word "house" associated with Brabanzio', due to its connoted temporariness.[15] In light of Iago's own stripped opportunity, Roderigo's forced dispossession by him points to a way of compensating for hurt feelings, suggesting Iago's artificiality. It seems, then, that he is not sincere about the espoused true and fair rule of competition that he claims he has fallen foul of. The imagery that he has previously pictured for us – the democratic system – is thus only smoke and mirrors intended to conceal his intention of getting 'evened with' (2.1.298) Othello.

In presenting the physical living environment, the play works with four distinct built forms – streets, houses, coastal structure and a castle. As a physical domain, for Brabanzio's residence, architectural space is developed after the building has been identified and its atmosphere brought up, giving a sense that it has been 'worked' to communicate meaning. After his comfortable, eminent house that Iago's 'fertile climate dwell' (1.1.70) builds up, Roderigo plays upon the perceptual difference between two environments' spatiality – noisy streets and a quite large house – plotting out spatial distance, evoking the insulation of the senator from ongoing injustice, a theme that is extended and developed through a retelling of architectural spaces. 'Here is her father's house' (1.1.74), uttered by Roderigo, informs us that the residence is by the street. Below this structure, Iago and Roderigo need to 'call aloud' (1.1.74), in 'timorous accent and dire yell' (1.1.75), in order to rouse Brabanzio. We can derive a series of spatial images from created spatial dynamics. First, physical space cuts Brabanzio off from the outside atmosphere, suggesting a peaceful home that is remote from street disturbances, bringing to light a senatorship that is tone-death to injustice on the ground. Power and prestige conferred to Brabanzio may first be perceived through allusion to held public office and physical location. He has 'place' (1.1.105) and 'power' (1.1.105), which can 'make this bitter' (1.1.106) to Iago and Roderigo, his influence being physically portrayed by his position *at a window above* (s.d. 1.1.80), where he speaks dismissively, staring down upon the two who are below. Architectural cachet comes to the fore when he compares his Venetian home to a farmhouse: 'This is Venice. / My house is not a grange' (1.1.107–8). Setting 'house' against 'grange', the typological analogy suggests preoccupation with eminence and security: he is affronted by the mere thought of living in a farmhouse, rather than a secured mansion which is not likely be 'rob[bed]' (1.1.107). Yet 'grange' may also indicate his owned invaluable goods, which may point

---

[14] Lena Cowen Orlin, *Locating Privacy in Tudor London* (Oxford, 2008), p. 4.
[15] Emma Smith, *Othello* (Horndon, 2005), p. 59.

to his daughter, Desdemona. Emma Whipday emphasizes the architectural undertone that may be associated with the daughter, suggesting that 'grange', as a storehouse or repository for grain, also connotes 'goods', and by this Brabanzio is 'registering the reading of grange as a secure storehouse from which goods can only be accessed by the owner of those goods: his house is "no grange" because it has already "yield[ed] everything" – as has, he is soon to fear, his daughter'.[16]

Historically, country houses had gatehouses for porters, as distinct from the farmhouses which were ungated.[17] Several related architectural themes recur, speaking to security and control, emphasizing Brabanzio's seat. One area is estate control and the consequence of its breach. When Brabanzio is roused, he initially feels sure of his safety despite the intrusion, certain about the estate's order and 'reason' (1.1.82). 'What is the reason of this terrible summons?' (1.1.82) asks the senator with magisterial aplomb when Iago yells, 'Thieves, thieves!' (1.1.81). Iago's provocative question about his house's security lapse, 'Are your doors locked?' (1.1.85), is discarded by Brabanzio's self-assured demands, instead of alarm. His responses, 'Why, wherefore ask you this' (1.1.85) and 'What have you lost your wits' (1.1.92), strike a note of built-in confidence, even though the consequence is serious: Iago tells him he has been robbed, and his daughter raped by 'an old black ram' (1.1.88). Even so, 'Upon malicious bravery dost thou come / To start my quiet' (1.1.101–2) – his reply at this stage implies that he is more concerned about the serenity of his estate, the emblematic guarded residence giving him order and judicial calmness.

When Brabanzio appears at the *'window'* (s.d. 1.1.80), the architectural feature frames up his current location, registering a charged moment in our mind. The spatial logic of placing him at this feature draws our attention to its function and materiality. The external walls of medieval and Renaissance houses were made of strong masonry. Their windows, by contrast, were often of decorated glass that is much more breakable. Being at the boundary of buildings, they also form a transitional space between outside and inside. In introducing the theme of hostile intrusion, windows suggest the point of failure, and thus vulnerability and danger. Whipday draws a metaphorical link between the window's transitional space and the 'threshold' space for the scene, suggesting that 'by presenting the father rather than the daughter in a liminal position at the threshold of the home, Shakespeare recasts the elopement from the point of view of the abandoned father'.[18] Drawing from the nature and use of this built form for *Merchant of Venice* and *Much Ado about Nothing*, Whipday further identifies the form's repeated pattern in constructing danger associated with elopement. In 'Clamber not you up to the casements then / Nor thrust your head into the public street' (2.5.31–2) in *Merchant*, the father refers to the dangerous potential that comes with Jessica's planned elopement; in 'What man was he talked with you yesternight / Out of your window betwixt twelve and one? / Now if you are a maid, answer to this' (4.1.84–6) in *Much Ado*, Claudio similarly hints at the danger of the loss of reputation if Hero's chastity is violated. In these examples, window space acts as a visual representation of a father figure's vulnerability, a feeling which, according to Whipday, may be felt when 'a young man attempts to penetrate the house of the senex in order to woo the ... daughter'.[19] For her, the feature, due to its associated transitional sense of space, signifies that the 'boundaries of his [Brabanzio's] home have become permeable'.[20]

After the safe and quiet atmosphere that architectural references ironically establish, allusions to Desdemona's room further reveal the kind of domestic living that may be expected in such a facility. '[S]he

---

[16] Emma Whipday, *Shakespeare's Domestic Tragedies* (Cambridge, 2019), p. 122.
[17] The country house, according to architectural historians, is the residence 'of the ruling class', a house type typically arranged in a U shape layout having building blocks around a courtyard. See Mark Girouard, *Life in the English Country House: A Social and Architectural History* (New Haven, 1994), p. 2.
[18] Whipday, *Domestic Tragedies*, p. 125.
[19] Whipday, *Domestic Tragedies*, p. 122.
[20] Whipday, *Domestic Tragedies*, p. 125.

be in her chamber' (1.1.140), uttered by Roderigo, indicating that she possesses a room of her own, creates spatial dynamics whose meanings are provocatively paradoxical. First, as Orlin has suggested, individual bedrooms are considered 'specialized' and can 'construct personalities'.[21] 'Particularized room uses are the grounds from which discussions of early modern privacy generally proceed', says Orlin.[22] As a specialized room, 'chamber' introduces independence and privacy to characters. Desdemona's accorded bedroom of her own impresses on us that she may carry out private activities in solitude, suggesting her independence. Yet the private space also aims at commenting upon her enjoyed freedom or lack of it by placing her private moments in the crosshairs of Brabanzio. Examining the social practice of space in the early modern elite house, Orlin helpfully writes for us that the owners of elite houses typically adopted shared occupancy as a sleeping arrangement, for the sake of companionship or for personal security.[23] 'Shared occupancy was the norm even for gentry; the navigator Sir Martin Frobisher, for example, spoke of the bedroom occupied by his wife's daughter, waiting women, and chambermaids', writes Orlin. Bedrooms' highly 'specialized' nature allows owners to switch 'identities and functions as required, to suit family exigencies and life passages' such as for 'mutual surveillance'.[24] The way in which Desdemona's bedroom is infused with the mood of surveillance – by 'watch' (1.1.125) and 'guard' (1.1.126) – creates an atmosphere of observation for the room. Because she is expected to be found there whenever called for, the evoked, specific kind of sleeping arrangement for her seems to be a spatial means of exerting patriarchal control over her freedom by erecting a physical boundary and a system of surveillance around her. Yet it also has interesting resonances with Orlin's concept of 'the site of illicit liaison' due to the need for surveillance.[25] It is reminiscent of an early modern secret 'liaison' room, as actions are being organized around it as the focus of attention, characters using it as a tool to turn on Desdemona's elopement.

And yet actions around the bedroom also give voice to the futility of surveillance, presenting the powerlessness of a powerful father in the face of the inevitable 'com[ing] of my despisèd time' (1.1.163). It stings Brabanzio to the quick when he is informed that Desdemona cannot be found in her room: 'If she be in her chamber or your house, / Let loose on me the justice of the state / For thus deluding you' (1.1.140–2). Startling Brabanzio into a frenzied search for Desdemona, Iago's provocation sets two architectural concepts – space-owning, and its social practice – directly on a collision course, creating a great tension. Her chamber might suggest an observation chamber, yet it is also an exclusive room in which its owner may decide creatively the way she wants to use the room. The latter impression – that she is now the master of her own place and 'At this odd-even and dull watch o' th' night, / Transported ... / To the gross clasps of a lascivious Moor' (1.1.125–8) – cuts to the heart of Brabanzio, who instantly exclaims 'Give me a taper, call up all my people. / This accident ... / Belief of it oppresses me already' (1.143–5). Recall that Brabanzio is still certain of the house's security when the housebreaking is announced to him and we get the sense that, despite such confidence, he is less sure about his power over Desdemona. Actions surrounding room ownership, developing the conflict between her independent spirit and her father's controlling inclination, thus reveal a strong underlying desire and anxiousness. If his daughter has eloped, the consequence is horrible for him not least because, according to Roderigo's insinuation, his daughter, a 'white ewe' (1.1.89) will be with a 'black ram' (1.1.88), signifying a disaster of lineage for Brabanzio, dramatized in his emotional 'O treason of the blood' (1.1.171). As such, he is no longer able to contemplate a domestic presence with any degree of equanimity. Smith reminds us that

---

[21] Orlin, *Locating Privacy*, p. 146.
[22] Orlin, *Locating Privacy*, p. 96.
[23] Orlin, *Locating Privacy*, p. 172.
[24] Orlin, *Locating Privacy*, p. 172.
[25] Orlin, *Locating Privacy*, p. 172.

'domestic tragedies usually dramatize female transgression that splits apart the household'.[26] 'As women took control of the household ... the idea of the home as man's dominion, securely within the compass of patriarchal power, was under increasing threat', says Smith.[27] In the scene's generated quality of space, the duality of architectural impression enables this kind of heightened emotion. Smith fruitfully connects the loss of patriarchal control to the idea of a hollow house. For her, with the escape of the daughter, 'the view of the patriarch that the house is a place of security under masculine control has been shattered, revealed as a hollow complacency', and the 'irrevocable separation of the female from the domestic' has taken place.[28] By this, it may be argued that the house is 'empty'; Desdemona's bedroom, helping to frame the discussion about Brabanzio's surveillance and defiance, conveys the threat that he feels about future generations, lineage and purity.

The image of the house's interior also helps to initiate the shattering of the household for the play. When we next see Brabanzio's frightened scramble for lights, an energized, radiant house in dark night bursts onto the scene. Called forth by imagery of illumination, the edifice is highly symbolic, acting as a kind of rung tocsin for actions, readied for the purpose of 'apprehend[ing]' (1.1.179) Desdemona and Othello. Portrayed moving light sources and gathering servants allow us to explore the house's basic arrangement. Brabanzio's 'call up all my people' (1.1.143), implying the presence of rule and order, first suggests a rather large house population. The emphasis on illuminants – 'tinder' (1.1.142), 'taper' (1.1.143) – and the repeated calls for more lights – 'Light, I say, light!' (1.1.146) – indicate the need to traverse through dark corridors and halls. When the household gathers, Brabanzio and his servants, who are '*below*' (s.d. 1.1.161), evoke a large, open area on ground level. A staged event needs a particular kind of space, and we may infer that the action happens in the courtyard, especially since the servants are holding strong lights – '*torches*' (s.d. 1.1.161) – rather than candles, for brighter ambience. Significantly, the action to capture Desdemona and Othello involves calling at 'every house' (1.1.182). A powerful dual architectural imagery – power house versus 'every house' – has thus been set up. The gathering of personnel in the courtyard recalls the event of mustering troops preparing to march out to put down a rebellion, symbolizing that the chaos that is about to descend is not only at Brabanzio's house but on existing order, presaging actions that threaten the wider social contract.

Architectural potency afforded to individual characters also happens in regard to Othello's straddled background. Benson suggests that, as a general, Othello 'seems to outsize' the use of nonaristocratic protagonists in 'domestic tragedies', yet he is always 'on the fringe of respectability' because of his birth, and thus his claim to social standing is 'problematic'.[29] What architectural forms are exploited to explore his problematic background in comparison to the Venetian householders? Interestingly, when Othello first appears, he is said to be 'unhoused' (1.2.26), his place of residence being the 'tented field' (1.3.85), an unpropertied situation which is rich with metaphorical implications. His 'free' (1.2.26) unhoused condition, which is linked to the 'seas' worth' (1.2.28), besides adding the point that he exists in military and seafaring exploits, gives voice to how identities and interests are variously expressed from the distinct perceptions of different characters. For Othello himself, moving military quartering that is 'free' represents vastness and bounty that he experiences as the romantic extent of his feeling for Desdemona. Associating the extent of his love with the boundless sea and then contrasting it with 'circumscription and confine' (1.2.27), he brings out infinity and freedom, which he says is the 'worth' (1.2.28) of his love.

As a mobile housing form, 'tented field' (1.3.85) is a forum for discussing his preferred style of living, which is non-aristocratic. Smith emphasizes its

---

[26] Smith, *Othello*, p. 51. [27] Smith, *Othello*, p. 51.
[28] Smith, *Othello*, p. 55.
[29] Benson, *Domestic Tragedy*, p. 105.

architectural subtext, fruitfully linking Othello's disdain for comforts to the distinction between the architecture of the war council and the 'tented field'. The 'temporary military encampments are implicitly contrasted with the stones and mortar of the Venetian war council.... this soldier disdains the comforts of home: he is used to making "the flinty and steel couch of war / My thrice-driven bed of down" (1.3.229–30)', writes Smith.[30] In the scene, Othello goes on to say that he prefers hardness to the hollow, soft materials: 'I do agnize / A natural and prompt alacrity / I find in hardness' (1.3.230–2). Flint and steel are hard stone and metal, respectively, evoking the hardship of war. By contrast, 'bed of down' is light, the feather composition meaning there is space within it. It is therefore a hollow, soft and warm fabric, a material which is central to the construction of elite households and identity. The comparison of materials recalls and expands the theme of the hollow house previously identified. Initially, the hollow house acquires its meaning from the departure of the daughter. Here, arguably, the hollowness of the feather bed takes on the additional sense of worth, or its lack, as Othello only derives life's value from solid, hard materials.

It comes across as ironic, given Othello's expressed anti-aristocratic stance, that his thought of the accommodation for Desdemona during his stay in Cyprus to fight the Turks stresses 'Due reference of place and exhibition' and 'such accommodation ... / As levels with her breeding' (1.3.236–8). Emphasizing 'exhibition' and 'breed', thus invoking elite living, he may be seen as backpedalling on his earlier rejection of living in comfort. The Duke suggests that Desdemona return to 'her father's' (1.3.239) house, but this is rejected by Brabanzio. The rejection perhaps also suggests that Desdemona has passed the point of 'reintegration into Brabantio's household', to borrow Orlin's suggestion, which states that, by rejecting, the father 'jumps to restore the integrity of his house'.[31] Indeed, as Smith pertinently puts it, the rejection suggests a 'reversibility of the step' since 'the domestic is ... lost forever to Desdemona, as she has chosen to leave her father's protection'.[32]

For Brabanzio, on the other hand, it is the imminent loss of his daughter that concerns him. Alluding to the shore's specific physical defensive texture and materiality, he likens his grief to storm water that 'engluts and swallows' when coastal floodgates are opened, imagining that 'my particular grief / Is of so flood-gate and o'erbearing nature / That it engluts and swallows other sorrows' (1.3.55–7). The architectural imagery provides us with a palpable coastal geography of Venice, although it involves only a set of metaphorical built forms that map emotions to mechanical functions. The city, constituted of lagoons, relied historically on canal navigation for trade, and floodgates were vertical seawalls built to prevent flooding, being strategically emplaced massive concrete structures, turning beaches into protected shorelines.[33] The image of floodgates, which pictures raised barriers in violent weather proleptically suggests destruction. The imagined 'stol'n' (1.3.60) daughter will be like storm water that 'engluts and swallows' (1.3.57) everything above it, devastating love and family.

Portrayed coastal architecture further links Venice intricately with Cyprus. In act 2, scene 1, when Cassio refers to Cyprus's high vertical seawalls, hoping Jove will 'bless this bay with [Othello]'s tall ship' (2.1.80), imagery pertaining to deep-sea harbours physically establishes Venice as a shipping entrepôt that has ventured into Cyprus. The harbour also points to Venice's military ambition, through Cyprus's fortified image as an island fortress. We are informed of this architectural form through the local governor, Montano: 'A fuller blast ne'er shook our battlements' (2.1.6),

---

[30] Smith, *Othello*, p. 58.
[31] Lena Cowen Orlin, 'Desdemona's disposition', in *Shakespearean Tragedy and Gender*, ed. Shirley Nelson Garner and Madelon Sprengnether (Bloomington and Indianapolis, 1996), pp. 171–92; p. 176.
[32] Smith, *Othello*, p. 57.
[33] For details on the historical development of the floodgates in Venice, see Oscar Ravera, 'The Lagoon of Venice: the result of both natural factors and human influence', *Journal of Limnology* 59 (2000), 19–30.

which directly protect a 'castle' (2.1.202). Following the portrayal of Venice in its street-lined form earlier, this new scene sets up a strong opposition between two physical fabrics: street-lined city (Venice) versus storm fortress (Cyprus). Visually, the 'blast' (2.1.6) of the wave poignantly reminds us of the 'flood-gate' (1.3.56). With the perceived ferocity of the wave now hitting the fortress of Cyprus, we are invited to imagine whether the Venetian floodgates, which are now being transposed to Cyprus, will break apart when the pressure of the island tide becomes a force that is too great.

Ernst Honigmann argues that act 1's distinctive and lengthy introduction of characters is 'detachable' from the rest of the play.[34] The new architectural form that is introduced, the high fortress, which produces a 'screen refresh' for the play, shifts our attention from act 1 to Othello's new encounter in the new scene. That the fortress is built on a high point is inferable from Montano's line, 'What from the cape can you discern at sea?' (2.1.1).[35] New forms introduce new themes, which begin with celebrated love registered through an open space in the harbour. The sense and need of space in the beginning of this act, accompanied by and emphasized through atmosphere and mood, suggest an assembling space of celebrated arrivals before welcoming crowds. The atmosphere of a cheering crowd infuses the scene when a gentleman says, 'The town is empty. On the brow o'th' sea / Stand ranks of people and they cry "A sail!"' (2.1.54–5). An eager mood is injected when a third gentleman says, 'every minute is expectancy' (2.1.42). These lines strongly suggest that the scene is the arrival space or deck in the harbour. Onto this deck, Desdemona makes her first step, signalling her much-anticipated arrival, expressed verbally in 'O behold, / The riches of the ship come on shore' (2.1.83–4).

Othello's arrival, also long-awaited – which is after Desdemona, and moreover is celebrated by the sounding of a trumpet – reemphasizes the strong sense of purpose in the scene's depiction of individual arrivals. Since the two arrive separately, each arrival drawing an eager response from the crowd, the sense of place helps to shape the individuality and greatness of the two characters. Showing the couple's embrace and loving exchange in full view of the implied deck, space helps to communicate the apex of love. Othello's 'O, my fair warrior!' (2.2.183) upon arrival recalls Desdemona's admiration of his 'valiant parts' (1.3.253) that her 'soul and fortune consecrate' (1.3.154). Both are 'warriors' in the other's mind. Love and harmony, the injected mood and atmosphere of space seem to impart, are very much in both their minds. At the scene's emotional heart is, therefore, the arrival space, which is powerful in presenting personal feelings intertwined with publicly displayed emotions, importantly forming part of the impression of the couple's love in the play.

From the arrival space, Othello's invitation, 'Come, let us to the castle' (2.1.202), brings us into his new residence, a castle that ironically recalls the aristocratic house that he earlier said he disdained. But, while still waiting for Othello's arrival, Iago first forges an interior image of its architecture, striking up an engaging and certainly humorous conversation about 'housewifery' (2.1.115) with Emilia, his wife, and Desdemona:

> You are pictures out of door,
> Bells in your parlours; wildcats in your kitchens,
> Saints in your injuries; devils being offended,
> Players in your housewifery, and hussies in your beds.
> (2.1.112–15)

Clustering around the above imagery is elite architecture. The castle interior features the long gallery, a room for entertaining and displaying collections of family portraits. The parlour is also a dedicated space for leisure. Even so, for Iago, a commoner, these rooms seem to be a privilege afforded not only to Desdemona but also to him: the metaphor is directed at Emilia, his wife. In this

---

[34] William Shakespeare, *Othello*, ed. E. A. J. Honigmann (London, 1997), p. 62.

[35] Cliffside castles commanded excellent views of the distant sea. A castle protruding from a cliff, especially, was an effective deterrent due to the increased difficulty of access. See T. E. McNeill, *Castles* (London, 2006), p. 103.

way, he projects ownership and privilege on to himself even though he remains only an ensign. Since he does not seem to be working on improving his competency to a more commensurate level, it strikes us that his previous claim of unfair treatment has been undermined. Unfair competition, the cornerstone of his accusation that Cassio had been unduly privileged, has been laid bare, transforming what appears to be a potentially justifiable anger to malignity. Benson notes he has many reasons for his duplicity, including 'class envy', whether in terms of stripped position or of others' felt innate superiority over him, displayed during various casual conversations – such as when Cassio says, 'the lieutenant is to be saved before the [ancient]' (2.3.91–2), in relation to faith, as Benson has pointed out.[36] The conjured rooms, then, accompanied by allegations that 'the lusty' Othello 'hath leapt into my seat' (2.1.295), and that his competitor, Cassio, might also have slept with his wife ('For I fear Cassio with my nightcap, too', 2.1.306), register a displaced architectural ideal, suggesting that he is contemplating a revenge – one that centres upon sexual deceit in the castle.

And yet the imagery also comes over as an outline of a feminine ideal, an ideal whose controvertibility perhaps adds to his desire to harm. Iago's conjured architectural interior may be seen as the woman's body in total control of itself, and, with that, her sexuality. She is free to go out of its 'doors' (2.1.112) into the gallery, becoming a displayed 'picture' (2.1.112), pleasant to be looked at. But once she is in the 'parlours' (2.1.113) or 'kitchens' (2.1.113), she is capable of becoming a spit-fire or 'wildcat' (2.1.112), loud and fiery. Yet she can choose to laze around, or be active in bed. Read in the context of suggested adultery, Othello's castle now appears to be a large bawdy house or fleshpot. Within, Iago, by envisioning women's actions that he feels will happen 'for surety' (1.3.382), appears to be pre-experiencing the imagined knavery, and that, in turn, impresses on us that he has been seized by the experience, disclosing to us the direction of his scheme, the 'wife for wife' (2.1.298) revenge that is the mainspring of his plot.

From the couple's arrival, to the fortress, and then to the emerging accusatory motifs that metaphorical interior establishes, we are thus oriented linearly to the path of Iago's persecuting method. In act 2, scene 2, architectural allusions portray space in the kitchen via an announced celebratory feast for the couple's new arrival and marriage: 'All offices are open, and there is full liberty of feasting from this present hour of five till the bell have told eleven' (2.2.8–10), declares Othello. The castle is initially redolent of claustrophobia created by its tall blank concrete blocks, called forth at first by Brabanzio's reference to 'the fortitude of the place' (1.3.221), and afterward retold through the locals' 'shook our battlements' (2.1.6) and repeated 'citadel' (2.1.97, 210). Yet the portrayed kitchen undoes the unfavourable impression by its entertaining 'offices' (2.2.8). The reversal, which is through a welcoming mood, offers new opportunity for actions and thoughts. The great kitchen evokes the practice of hospitality, presenting multifunctional space for communal eating, drinking, entertainment for visiting attendants.[37] The scene shows that Othello lays great store on hospitality. Whether guests are from Cyprus or Venice, he is open and generous to them, an act that reveals he is making the effort to establish himself in Cyprus through the ritual of hospitality. Through this move, his new residence is situated in a bi-physical domain that displays exerted zonal control. The established custom of Venice decides the forms and ritual of domestic rule in Cyprus, announcing the coming measures taken by him as he grapples with new situations.

After the short kitchen scene, actions move to the castle's base-court, its spatiality having been shaped by the practice and discipline of estate management. In act 2, scene 3, references to guarding and its space appear eleven times; 'guard' (2.3.1, 209) appears twice, 'platform' (2.3.112) once, and 'watch' (for example, 2.3.12) seven times – the

---

[36] Benson, *Domestic Tragedies*, p. 100.
[37] See McNeill, *Castles*, p. 54, for illustrations of the offices that enable the communal activities.

paucity of other named space helping to focus the presence of the place. The atmosphere of guardedness affords an organized appearance and formal impression, imparting that a certain standard of estate ruling is to be maintained, and that Othello is one who adheres to rules and order. In this space, Othello warns Cassio 'Not to outsport discretion' (2.3.3) when inspecting the 'guard' (2.3.1). His command to his attendants enacts estate governance involving the division of labour that forms part of the hierarchy for castles' efficient management. Othello's command, 'Look you to the guard' (2.3.1), alludes to the constable's task of inspecting the estate and the duty of standing guards. Cassio's reply, 'Iago's hath direction what to do' (2.3.4), on the other hand, implies the latter has been assigned other designated duties, such as patrolling or supervising. It is this kind of impression – formality, decorum and discipline – that he inspires for the estate, striking an attitude that signals he will not let passion disrupt 'serious and great business' (1.3.267).

Ironically, the hint of anomie in 'Not to outsport discretion' (2.3.3) is one upon which Iago's 'wife for wife' (2.1.298) vindication is predicated. It is the habitual breach of duty that becomes a mark for the baiting of knavery under Cassio's 'watch' (2.3.12) and 'guard' (2.3.1). In the way that the base-court is set up for this action, the space dramatizes social practice, which is the 'custom of entertainment' (2.3.32) by the 'flock of drunkards' from the kitchen (2.3.55) who form the base-court population. Depicted architectural space therefore reflects upon a social unit that is specific, an entity which Othello regretfully calls 'wild' (2.3.207) – one in which 'private and domestic quarrel' happens 'In night, and on the court and guard of safety' (2.3.208–9).

As a space, the zonal quality that the base-court gives is distinct from that of the bedroom. In the middle of the commotion involving Cassio injuring Montano (machinated by Iago) in this space, arousing first Othello, and then Desdemona, movements between two zones give a number of effects. First, that the couple should come out from the bedroom each by themselves builds up and re-emphasizes movement between two domains, creating the sense of inner/outer spatial relationship. When the inner zone is adverted to, a sense of withdrawal is produced. Coming out of the bedroom, Desdemona asks, 'What's the matter … ?' (2.3.245), and Othello answers, 'All's well now, sweeting. / Come away to bed' (2.3.246–7). For some reason, he tries to draw Desdemona apart from the external zone. The zonal space acquires a certain poignancy that may be linked to a purposive act of concealing. Thus, in addition to – and because of – the sense of movement between them, the two zones stand out, the cause of disturbance having been emphasized. And since the object of the concealment is Cassio, the 'night-brawler' (2.3.189), tension generated by the two zones feeds into the feeling that he is going to be the central figure of the coming conflict. His behaviour, especially, will become a focus for creating the conditions under which Iago can execute his announced revenge.

And if we see the base-court as a place-image for the very kind of behaviour its space implies, then the words and actions of Iago further brand it as diabolical. After the short scene in act 3, scene 2 informing us that Othello will go out to inspect Cyprus's fortifications, so he is not present when Cassio asks Desdemona to intercede in his punishment for the brawl, the scene segues smoothly into continuing actions. In act 3, scene 3, due to the large number of terms associated with hell, space acquires a sinister air, being shaped as a breeding ground for evil, insinuating intention. The scene deals with Othello's increasing vigilance triggered by Iago's pretended exclamation, 'Ha! I like not that' (3.3.33), when they observe Cassio leaving Desdemona 'guilty-like' (3.3.38). It suggests covertly that Othello guards against something, leading him to decline three times Desdemona's request to consider reinstating Cassio. Othello's vigilance is first accompanied by hell imagery: 'Perdition catch my soul … Chaos is come again' (3.3.91–3). This then leads to an existential 'World', mentioned four times in the scene (for example, 3.3.335), which has been emphatically tied with Iago's insinuating thoughts. Initially,

Iago's 'thought' (3.3.111) about Cassio's 'honest[y]' (3.3.105) appears for Othello as 'some monster . . . / Too hideous to be shown' (3.3.111). However, echoed by Iago's 'beware . . . It is the green-eyed monster', it plays up Othello's 'jealousy' (3.3.169–70). Thence, Iago's insinuation slowly takes hold of Othello. 'Monstrous world' (3.3.382) breeds his thought of descending from 'Perdition' (3.3.91) into 'Death and damnation' (3.3.401), finally exclaiming, 'O, monstrous, monstrous!' (3.3.431) as he stares down the barrel of the eventuality of hinted betrayal, his insecurity having been impregnated by Iago's stoking insinuation.

Yet this 'world' develops into a 'dungeon' (3.3.275) and, later, a 'hollow hell' (3.3.451), as Othello wrestles with 'monstrous' existence. After Desdemona and Cassio leave the scene, so only Iago is with him in the 'world', physical space calls to mind that of an echo chamber. Such a reality has been suggested when Iago says 'thou echo'st' me' (3.3.110). He has pretended to ask Othello whether Cassio knew beforehand of the latter's love for Desdemona:

IAGO   Did Michael Cassio, when you wooed my lady,
       Know of your love?
OTHELLO   He did, from first to last. Why dost thou ask?
IAGO   But for a satisfaction of my thought,
       No further harm.
OTHELLO   Why of thy thought, Iago?
IAGO   I did not think he had been acquainted with her.
OTHELLO   O, yes, and went between us very oft.
IAGO   Indeed?
OTHELLO   Indeed? Ay, indeed. Discern'st thou aught in that?
       Is he not honest?
IAGO   Honest, my lord?
OTHELLO   Honest! Ay, honest.
IAGO   My lord, for aught I know.
OTHELLO   What dost thou think?
IAGO   Think, my lord?
OTHELLO   'Think, my lord?' By heaven, thou echo'st me.

(3.3.96–110)

The invoked echo chamber is at the centre of this play not least because it happens halfway through it, but also because it is at the heart of its thematic development. It has been explored that Othello's emerging vigilance is a result of Iago's insinuation. Yet here the image presents vividly the moment of Othello's realization of its resonance: 'By heaven, thou echo'st me' (3.3.110). His thought about Desdemona is shared with Iago's mind. The realization has a significant impact on the play's development since, for the first time, Othello is explicit about her betrayal, saying that she is 'gone' (3.3.271) soon after Iago leaves the scene. The image sharpens the effect of successful insinuation. Iago has raised Othello's suspicions of Desdemona's fidelity, the echo chamber helping to reverberate the former's suggestion through the latter's mind.

And yet the echo chamber later combines with the 'dungeon' (3.3.275) to form a 'hollow hell' (3.3.451), from which arises 'black vengeance' (3.3.451), and in which Othello surrenders to 'tyrannous hate' (3.3.453). The fact that Othello first experiences an echo chamber as Iago's insinuation, then descends into a dungeon before finally emerging into a cell not only defines moments of Othello's uncertainty, but also helps to develop it into something more concrete. 'Hollow cell' signifies a cell with high bare concrete walls.[38] It appears after Iago further insinuates into Othello's mind a far more lurid eroticized picture involving a fabricated dream concerning Desdemona in which Cassio dreams up 'lay[ing] his legs o'er my thigh' (3.3.428), drawing his belief that 'this denoted a foregone conclusion' (3.3.433). A hollow cell symbolizes the complete loss of hope. 'Hollow' cell conjures up reverberative soundwaves bouncing off bare surfaces, relaying the effect of the insinuated dream imagery on Othello's mind, dramatized in his exclamation, 'monstrous, monstrous' (3.3.431). It is perhaps revealing that the occurrence of the 'dungeon' is sandwiched between that of the echo chamber and the cell. As a spatial means to explore Othello's progressive state of mind, it is fruitful to distinguish the architecture of a 'dungeon' (3.3.275) and a cell. A hollow cell calls

---

[38] Kenneth Muir (Harmondsworth, 1968) adopted 'hollow cell' instead of 'hollow hell' in his edition.

up total destruction, a dystopic existence devoid of life and interactions except hearing one's own voice. By contrast, 'dungeon' denotes a moist basement chamber having 'vapour' (3.3.275), supporting underground life, the 'toad' (3.3.274). Initially, Othello would rather be locked away in the dark, dank dungeon than be cheated by Desdemona: he would rather 'live upon the vapour of the dungeon / Than keep a corner in the thing I love' (2.3.275–6). Importantly for him, there remain hopes for Desdemona's loyalty at this stage (before the dream), hopes that project onto 'life' in the dungeon: there is still life since there is as yet no 'ocular proof' (3.3.365) that can establish Desdemona's betrayal. Representing his thought with the dungeon is also a rather fitting project because of its racial subtext: a deep underground space that is dark may hint at the hidden anxiety about skin colour. He first floats the idea that it is because he is 'black' that he has 'not those soft parts of conversation / That chamberers have' (3.3.267–70). Perhaps the underlying anxiety is the disadvantage that he is 'black' (3.3.267). The first time that he mentions his racial disadvantage, the depth and darkness of the dungeon has a particular significance that signals to us how far Iago's temptation has come over him at this stage.

Yet racial discrimination is only a flitting thought since Othello refutes it right afterwards, saying 'yet that's not much' (3.3.270). The dungeon's supporting system helps to convey that at this stage race does not dominate his thought. He does not quite think of himself in self-abhorrent terms, soon saying, perhaps self-vindicatingly, that he is a 'great' (3.3.277) man, arguing that "tis the plague of great ones' (3.3.277). This again begs the question: why, inside a dungeon, does he still profess the optimism of feeling 'great' (3.3.277)? As has been discussed, although the space of a dungeon is oppressive, it provides living conditions in which one can still 'live upon vapour' (3.3.275). 'Dungeon' for him is not as hostile as a 'hollow' cell, and from this we can infer that his feeling of ethnic discrimination does not take hold.

Whereas architectural imagery hitherto serves either to contextualize events or as a visual counterpart to characters' states of mind, in the scene involving the discussed dream that leads to Othello's initial suspicion, architectural creation is exploited primarily to enact realism. Othello's need for 'ocular proof' (3.3.365) of Desdemona's insinuated infidelity requires Iago to fabricate truth. However, to let Othello see Desdemona and Cassio in bed together is 'a tedious difficulty' (3.3.402). Since Iago cannot create an affair whose validity he cannot establish, he can only lead Othello to discover the authenticity of presented events, expressed in his 'door of truth' (3.3.422). For this, Iago creates realistic social circumstances to help secure Othello's 'living reason' to suspect (3.3.44). The dream's aim, which is for Othello to think up a shared bed wherein lie Desdemona and Cassio, successfully constructs plausible experience, enacting the practice of living communally as it works with space and events to enhance reality, giving authentication to Othello's imagination.

But although the realistic, provocative vision plays up Othello's suspicion, Iago knows that Othello has not crossed the psychological threshold of believing the 'truth', and therefore he continues to pile up more evidence to weigh down on Othello. In act 3, scene 4, words suggesting 'lodging' are dense, appearing multiple times in its first eleven lines, launching characters into an imaginative search for a handkerchief's travelled path:

DESDEMONA Do you know, sirrah, where Lieutenant Cassio lies?
CLOWN I dare not say he lies anywhere.
DESDEMONA Why, man?
CLOWN He's a soldier, and for one to say a soldier lies, 'tis stabbing.
DESDEMONA Go to. Where lodges he?
CLOWN To tell you where he lodges, is to tell you where I lie.
DESDEMONA Can anything be made of this?
CLOWN I know not where he lodges ...

(3.4.1–11)

The dense locative references to track down Cassio's lodging, and thus Desdemona's lost handkerchief, sets up the adverted temporary housing form as an architectural symbol. Desdemona's dropped handkerchief, which Othello gave her as a nuptial token, is believed to be in Cassio's house; it has been picked up by Emilia, who then gave it to Cassio. Othello has asked for it, and Desdemona cannot produce it. A marriage handkerchief is, according to John Hodgson, 'an emblem of her reputation'; if it is to be found in Cassio's lodging, it is a sign that it has been 'stained' by him (5.1.37).[39] Thus, when Desdemona next asks, 'Where should I lose that handkerchief?' (3.4.23), tension set up by her question has a particular resonance: the expectation that the handkerchief is at Cassio's lodging and the implication that she has been 'stained'. Marriage tokens need to stay where they belong and be displayed when asked, so 'To lose't it give't away were such perdition ... ' (3.4.67). Smith notes that the temporariness of the housing form has been linked to the repeated punning on 'lies' and 'lodges', connoting 'deceit ... sexuality and penetration'.[40] Indeed, at Bianca's residence, her interrogative 'O Cassio, whence came this?' (3.4.177) when bid to copy its design for him, feeds into sexual tension. Exchanges, made up of Cassio's question, 'What make you from home? ... I was coming to your house' (3.4.166–8), and Bianca's 'And I was going to your lodging' (3.4.169), suggest an intimate relationship between the two persons. And with Cassio's subsequent response, 'I know not neither. I found it in my chamber' (3.4.185), we discover assignations at Bianca's and Cassio's lodging through the mutual visitations. And since their exchange concentrates on Desdemona's handkerchief, references to their lodging have the effect of associating the handkerchief, and therefore Desdemona, with rendezvous and debauchery. The sense of tempo – first one, and then the other – of the handkerchief entering and leaving separate residences in this way builds up into the actions an aura of betrayal and deceit.

In the way that sexually connotative architectural typology recurs as a symbol, the pattern of its recurrence parallels purposeful echoing discussed earlier. Keenly aware of the agonizing impact of the loss of the handkerchief on Othello, Iago forthwith plays up Othello's anxiety. '[B]eing hers, / She may ... bestow't on any man' (4.1.12–13), says Iago of the handkerchief, pretending to trivialize the situation. But it only hardens Othello's misunderstanding. 'By heaven ... O, it comes o'er my memory / As doth a raven o'er the infectious house' (4.1.19–21), exclaims Othello. What comes through for him is reflective of Iago's earlier suggested bawdy house. The castle has now become an 'infected house' (4.1.21), casting our mind back to Iago's conjured fleshpot in act 2, scene 1. Smith emphasizes the sexual undertone of the invoked built forms, suggesting that 'it is the closed door of the bedroom behind which Othello imagines the most monstrous of events', fruitfully connecting Othello's subsequent experience of epilepsy to Freud's notion of 'the uncanny' that relates to familiar previous frightening events, creating the blurring of imagination and reality that induces Othello's epileptic fits.[41]

Iago seizes the opportunity provided by the breakdown to execute his next plan, whose constructed architectural space further denigrates Othello's image – at least visually. During Othello's trance, Iago stages a dumb show in which occurs a manipulated conversation between Cassio and Bianca. In this show, Othello can see but cannot hear Cassio's jokes about Bianca's sexual advances, and thus misinterprets them as about Desdemona. Othello also needs to stoop low to hide when observing them. The setting has the air of a space before the castle. We may imagine a place in front of a castle where Cassio could naturally happen upon Othello's epilepsy, during which Iago instructs Cassio to return after Othello recovers. It is also a place where Bianca would appear naturally with Desdemona's handkerchief, berating Cassio for giving her a handkerchief that is another woman's love token. It is possible to imagine this space as the series of external

---

[39] John Hodgson, 'Desdemona's handkerchief as an emblem of her reputation', *Texas Studies in Literature and Language* 19 (1977), 313–22.
[40] Smith, *Othello*, p. 59. [41] Smith, *Othello*, p. 60.

protruding walls or buttresses at the front walls of castles, due to spatial dynamics. These structures step up from the bottom to the top of the walls, being widest at their base, forming recesses which may offer hiding places. When Othello withdraws into this space to watch Cassio, the created image paints a comic, unnatural posture, demeaning his status as a respected governor. As he 'confine[s]' (4.1.74) and 'encave[s]' (4.1.80) himself behind these recesses, restrictive space contrasts markedly with the castle's open courtyard where he used to issue peremptory commands authoritatively. Now, instead of confronting his opponent openly, he descends into voyeurism and stealth, his strained posture discrediting him by representing, visually, mental degradation that undermines his governorship. It raises serious doubt about his ability to rule by posing the question of just how judicious he may be. Iago's comments on his behaviour, 'his unbookish jealousy must conster / Poor Cassio's smiles ... in the wrong' (4.1.100–2), speak to his incompetent performance, his inability to see through deception and to look beyond his own jealousy, condensed in the physically constrained space in which he finds himself.

In light of watching and misunderstanding Desdemona from Othello's strained position, architectural space may further shed some light on the conception of Desdemona's murder. Smith writes that, 'after talking about catching the pair *in flagrante*, Iago pushes Othello's mind towards the door of their adulterous chamber'.[42] The discourse about the chamber, its doors and their components is instrumental in the construction of Othello's path to Desdemona's destruction. In the scene, Othello first swears 'I will chop her into messes' (4.1.195), then changes tack to poisoning her (4.1.199), but finally sees Iago's 'justice' (4.1.204) of 'strangl[ing] her in her bed' (4.1.203), which has been 'contaminated' (4.1.203). This reveals the physical reasoning of his planned murder: Desdemona 'plucked him [Cassio] to my chamber' (4.1.138), so in the chamber she will die. In act 4, scene 2, accusing Emilia of being Desdemona's 'bawd' (4.2.21) or pimp, his mind turns to the fastening contraption of the chamber's door –

lock and key. Smith argues that, when Othello says 'a subtle whore, / A closet lock and key of villainous secrets' (4.2.22–3) and then dismisses her, saying 'Leave procreants alone and shut the door' (4.2.30), the imagery associates 'illicit sex' with 'terrible fertility', as he imagines adulterous 'procreants' behind closed doors.[43] Here, perhaps, the shut room also indicates his conclusive belief in Desdemona's guilt, closing the door on the evidence of her innocence just as a prison warden firmly locks away confirmed criminals.

And since there is a contestation between the bedroom and other unspecified spaces for Desdemona's killing, the significance of this space comes to the fore. Shortly after Othello has smothered Desdemona on her bed, Emilia calls from outside the room and Othello replies:

> I had forgot thee. – O, come in, Emilia. –
> Soft, by and by. Let me the curtains draw.
> *He closes the bed-curtains*
> Where art thou?
>
> (5.2.112–14)

The above image showing Othello drawing the bed-curtains hastily to conceal Desdemona from Emilia's view heightens the tension of the murder. Presenting Desdemona's dying moments, two distinct spaces stand out – the dying Desdemona within, and Emilia's imminent discovery without. Desdemona seems to die twice – first when Othello strangles her before he closes the curtain, and the other time when Emilia '*opens the bed-curtains*' (s.d. 5.2.129). When Emilia finally sees her, the former exclaims:

> EMILIA   O, who hath done this deed?
> DESDEMONA   Nobody, I myself. Farewell
>   Commend me to my kind lord ...
>
> (5.2.132–134)

When she faces the curtains, her line of sight, which is towards their fabric, projects onto us. If bed hangings of the Elizabethan times could be a visual reference, what we see on the textile

---

[42] Smith, *Othello*, p. 60. [43] Smith, *Othello*, p. 61.

hanging is a wall of silk featuring rich embroidered illustrations of nature. These woven fabrics' materiality, as well as the warmth infused by embroidered patterns, reflects a domestic environment and virtues. Because the curtains surround Desdemona on all four sides, they suffuse her in an atmosphere of these virtues. Orlin argues that such hangings conjure up 'the woman disappeared into her work', which is a 'badge of virtue'.[44] The curtains in the scene therefore have the effect of making her orchestrated death even more tragic. She is, in fact, kind to a fault. Having been wronged, yet at her moment of death, she lies for Othello, looking kindly upon him. When we encounter the play's final imagery, 'Look on the tragic loading of this bed. / This is thy work' (5.2.373–4), it is clear that the intended imagery is arranged for us to see and to reflect on the killing of a woman who is a 'perfect chrysolite' (5.2.152).

Projected fabric materiality also builds up melodramatic realism. Smith notes that 'Othello is preoccupied that Emilia will enter the room and "speak" – the word occurs three times in a dozen lines. His line "Soft, by and by. Let me the curtains draw" (5.2.113) combines an injunction to silence – "soft" – with an attempt to reseal and close off the bed curtains.'[45] Indeed, Othello says 'soft' while touching the side of the curtains, the moment drawing our attention to the point at which the skin touches the soft fabric. The scene acts out vividly the moment of Othello's attempt to get her to listen in the very moment of witnessed crime. It is as if he is trying to touch Emilia's 'soft spot', so as to win her over – she whose shriek, 'foul murder's done' (5.2.115), conveys shock at the deed which she needs to 'report' (5.2.137). Towards the end of the play, aware of the magnitude of the deed after Emilia reveals the truth to him, a crippling emotional moment grips him: 'Blow me about in winds, roast me in sulphur, / Wash me in steep-down gulfs of liquid fire' (5.2.286–7). Yet, due to space, we feel that his lamentation goes beyond guilt as he signals that he will go to her bed. 'Do you go back dismayed? 'Tis a lost fear ... where should Othello go?' (5.2.276–8), he asks, bringing our sight back to the bed as he '*touches*' (s.d. 5.2.282) her body. It is as though he is trying to redeem himself by painting a passionately devoted vision, making accommodation to his loss before stabbing himself, hoping to be seen as one who 'loved not wisely but too well' (5.2.353), and to be remembered as one who has bent over backward to do the necessary when preyed upon. In this way, the spiritual implications of his actions are bound up with the scene's plotted occupied spaces, materiality and generated spatial dynamics, giving them particular significance and presence.

In *Othello*, it is therefore possible to discover two forms of narratives – verbal and architectural – that are mutually complementary, the one depicting echoes and insinuations, the other context and actions, the intertwining imagery enabling a deepened discourse through which the wider implications of actions may be explored. I focus on the built environment as a perspective from which to examine specific themes of passions and emotional and spatial experience that permeate the narratives, engaging in an imaginary architectural reconstruction, fruitfully suggesting the way in which the reasoning and behaviour of Othello have been tied to conflicting values and interests. To understand more fully how they are delivered effectively, this article presents architecturally centred reading as a tool and a way of seeing how pertinent questions are framed in intertwining forms of narratives, offering a new lens to broaden and focus the scope for reading.

---

[44] Lena Cowen Orlin, 'Three ways to be invisible in the Renaissance: sex, reputation, and stitchery', in *Renaissance Culture and the Everyday*, ed. Patricia Fumerton and Simon Hunt (Philadelphia, 1998), pp. 183–203; pp. 185–6.
[45] Smith, *Othello*, p. 69.

'[A] MAID CALLED BARBARY': *OTHELLO*, MOORISH MAIDSERVANTS AND THE BLACK PRESENCE IN EARLY MODERN ENGLAND

IMAN SHEEHA

Scholarly discussions of race in *Othello* have almost exclusively focused on the eponymous character.[1] Often forgotten is another Moorish character the play evokes, even if she does not make an appearance on the stage: Barbary, the maidservant Desdemona remembers in the Folio version and with whose tragic story she identifies to process her own experience of rejection and grief.[2] Barbary is an example of

---

[1] For a survey of the criticism, see *Othello*, ed. Michael Neill (Oxford, 2006), pp. 113–30. In using the category 'race', I agree with critics who see it as applicable to the early modern period. See Peter Erickson, 'Invisibility speaks: servants and portraits in early modern visual culture', *Journal for Early Modern Cultural Studies* 9 (2009), 23–61; p. 26; 'Representations of Blacks and Blackness in the Renaissance', *Criticism* 35 (1993), 499–527; 'The moment of race in Renaissance studies', *Shakespeare Studies* 26 (1998), 27–36; 'The representation of race in Renaissance art', *The Upstart Crow* 18 (1998), 2–9; '"God for Harry, England and Saint George": British national identity and the emergence of white self-fashioning', in *Early Modern Visual Culture*, ed. Peter Erickson and Clark Hulse (Philadelphia, 2000), pp. 315–45; p. 315. For studies that trace the development of race consciousness in the period, see Kim F. Hall, *Things of Darkness: Economies of Race and Gender in Early Modern England* (Ithaca, NY, 1995); Dympna Callaghan, 'Othello was a white man', in *Shakespeare without Women: Representing Gender and Race on the Renaissance Stage* (London, 2000), pp. 75–96; George M. Fredrickson, *The Black Image in the White Mind* (Middletown, CT, 1987). For a survey of the scholarly literature on race in *Othello*, see Imtiaz Habib, '*Othello*: the state of the art', in *Othello: A Critical Reader*, ed. Robert C. Evans (London, 2015), pp. 84–7. For early modern perceptions of Africans, see *Othello*, ed. Neill, p. 123; Alden T. Vaughan and Virginia Mason Vaughan, 'Before Othello: Elizabethan representations of sub-Saharan Africans', *The William and Mary Quarterly* 54 (1997), 19–44. On the slipperiness of the term 'Moor' in this period, see Jack D'Amico, *The Moor in English Renaissance Drama* (Tampa, 1991); Virginia Mason Vaughan, *Performing Blackness on English Stages, 1500–1800* (Cambridge, 2005), p. 25; Emily C. Bartels, 'Imperialist beginnings: Richard Hakluyt and the construction of Africa', *Criticism* 34 (1992), 517–38; p. 523; Michael Neill, '"Mulattos", "Blacks", and "Indian Moors": Othello and early modern constructions of human difference', *Shakespeare Quarterly* 49 (1998), 361–74; pp. 364–5.

[2] Ambereen Dadabhoy writes that 'Othello is the only figure who represents non-European identity' in the play. See 'Two faced: the problem of Othello's visage', in *Othello: The State of Play*, ed. Lena Cowen Orlin (London, 2014), pp. 121–47; p. 123. There has been some discussion of the absent Black woman, the female counterpart of Othello. See Celia R. Daileader, *Racism, Misogyny, and the 'Othello' Myth: Interracial Couples from Shakespeare to Spike Lee* (Cambridge, 2005), p. 13; Kim F. Hall, 'Reading what isn't there: "Black" studies in early modern England', *Studies in Early Modern Philosophy* 3 (1993), 23–33. In a rare discussion of Barbary, Salkeld suggests that she may not have been entirely fictional, referencing the prosecution of Barbary Moore, alias Browne, on 10 February 1598/9 for fornication (Imtiaz Habib and Duncan Salkeld, 'The Resonables of Boroughside, Southwark: an Elizabethan black family near the Rose Theatre', *Shakespeare* 11 (2015), 135–56; p. 148). Barbary was famously given a voice in Toni Morrison's reimagining of the play, *Desdemona* (London, 2012). While the critical consensus seems to be that 'Barbary' is simply an alternative to 'Barbara', I agree with Michael Neill's 2006 edition – that 'we should think of Barbary as a black maid', p. 357, n. 24.

those women about whom Kim F. Hall wondered: why, '[w]hile feminists are increasingly uncovering the voices and presence of white Englishwomen', do 'women of color ... [even though] clearly a presence in ... sixteenth- and seventeenth-century England, ... remain "invisible women" existing at the margins of English culture and current critical practice[?]'.[3] Barbary's near absence from the critical response to the play is paralleled by the excision of her story in the early decades of the twentieth century when act 4, scene 3 was routinely cut from performances.[4] This article seeks to fill this gap by arguing that Barbary, a figure with no counterpart in Shakespeare's principal source, Giraldi Cinthio's *Hecatommithi* (1565), is crucial to the play's engagement with race and gender. Through Barbary, *Othello* challenges stereotyped racist and sexist representations of Moorish female servants on the early modern stage, often characterized by contempt for their alleged lustfulness, treachery, and unfaithfulness to (often) white mistresses.[5] *Othello*'s depiction of Barbary also subverts contemporary visual and theatrical portrayals of Moorish maidservants that reduce them to figures of Otherness whose Black skin serves as a racial background against which the whiteness of their mistresses' skin – and so those mistresses' privilege, status and virtue – shine.[6] By contrast, Desdemona and Barbary find a bond that transcends both the racial and status divides, a depiction that acts as a counterbalance to offset the racism of the characters who pass comment on Othello himself.

Barbary, furthermore, in both her African origins, suggested by her name, and her position as a domestic servant, speaks to the experiences of many members of the early modern audience – not least, Black female servants among them.[7] Scholars researching the Black presence in early modern England are increasingly alerting us to the importance of taking Black people into account when writing about early modern theatre.[8] It is time to revise statements such as 'Recipients of the negative image [of Africans] were mixed in gender as well as socio-economic class', to include 'race' as well.[9] Attending to the *potential* Black

---

[3] Cited in Betty S. Travitsky and Adele F. Seeff, *Attending to Women in Early Modern England* (Newark, 1994), p. 284.

[4] Colleen Ruth Rosenfeld, 'Shakespeare's nobody', in *Othello: The State of Play*, ed. Orlin, pp. 257–79; p. 258.

[5] For associations between Blackness and lustfulness, see Karen Newman, '"And wash the Ethiop white": femininity and the monstrous in *Othello*', in *Critical Essays on Shakespeare's Othello*, ed. Anthony Barthelemy (New York, 1994); Ania Loomba, *Shakespeare, Race, and Colonialism* (New York, 2002).

[6] Vaughan traces the way in which blackened skin operated in medieval and early modern culture as a signifier of otherness (Vaughan, *Performing Blackness*, p. 3). While not considering the tradition I am exploring here, Carol Chillington Rutter draws attention to the way in which twentieth-century performances of *Antony and Cleopatra* cast an often white-washed Cleopatra against Black Charmian and Iris, a practice that I see as carrying this tradition over into modern performance. See Carol Chillington Rutter, *Shakespeare in Performance: Antony and Cleopatra* (Manchester, 2020), p. 17.

[7] Barbary, or Mauretania, the region in North Africa, was associated with Arab-Berber people (Nabil Matar, *Britain and Barbary, 1589–1689* (Gainesville, 2005), pp. 3, 5). For the interest in Barbary in this period, see Emily Bartels, *Speaking of the Moor: From Alcazar to Othello* (Philadelphia, 2008), pp. 21–44. For Black servants, see Peter Fryer, *Staying Power: The History of Black People in Britain* (London, 2018), chs. 1 and 2. Vaughan has highlighted a shift in stage representations of Black people in the late seventeenth century, motivated, she argues, by personal experience of Black people (Vaughan, *Performing Blackness*, p. 167).

[8] Matthew Steggle, 'Othello, the Moor of London: Shakespeare's Black Britons', in *Othello: A Critical Reader*, ed. Evans, pp. 103–24. Miranda Kaufmann has identified over 360 African individuals living across Britain between 1500 and 1640. See Miranda Kaufmann, 'Africans in Britain: 1500–1640' (D.Phil. thesis, Oxford University, 2011). Imtiaz Habib earlier listed 362 records of Black people between 1500 and 1640 in *Shakespeare and Race: Postcolonial Praxis in the Early Modern Period* (Lanham, 1999). My article is not the first to attempt to read the play in light of the experiences of Black people in early modern England. Habib, for example, contextualized it within the experiences of Black military men. See Imtiaz Habib, 'Othello, Sir Peter Negro, and the Blacks of early modern England: colonial inscription and postcolonial excavation', *Lit: Literature Interpretation Theory* 9 (1998), 15–30. My interest, unlike Habib's, lies in the Black people who led more ordinary lives and to whom Barbary would have been of particular interest.

[9] Vaughan and Vaughan, 'Before Othello', p. 43. See Lois Potter, '"All's one": Cinthio, *Othello*, and *A Yorkshire Tragedy*', in *Othello: The State of Play*, ed. Orlin, pp. 46–62; p. 60.

presence in the early modern playhouse complicates such statements – made within the context of an analysis of *Othello* – as: 'Dramatists manipulated the ... spectacle [of Blackness] to evoke a range of responses, including ethnocentric contempt and ambivalent curiosity or revulsion.'[10] Identification, sympathy and recognition, it seems, cannot be imagined as potential responses to the 'spectacle' of Blackness on the early modern stage. The implicit assumption here, as Matthew Steggle points out, is that this was 'a play produced by an all-white theatre for an all-white audience'.[11] This assumption erases the experiences of playgoers who were not white, a segment of the early modern audience that is not entirely impossible to imagine. A Black family, the Resonables, lived between 1579 and 1592 in Boroughside, Southwark, and St. Olave, Tooley Street, which lay on the south bank of the Thames, a precinct immediately adjacent to Southwark with its rich theatrical connections, including Phillip Henslowe's Rose playhouse which opened in 1587 and Shakespeare's own residence nearby. The Resonables shared a neighbourhood with twenty-six actors of the Rose and, later, the Globe. Previously, they had lived in St Bride's parish in Farringdon Ward Without, which boasted two theatres, the Bel Savage Inn on the parish's north side and the first Blackfriars theatre to its south.[12] It is not entirely inconceivable that a member of this family might have enjoyed the nearby theatres. *Othello*, and particularly its representation of Barbary, would have spoken differently to such an audience member, with his or her personal experience of being a Black person in early modern England, from how it did to their white counterparts. Barbary's African roots trope her as an Other who, thus, speaks to fellow Black playgoers. However, she is also troped as familiar. As a serving maid, Barbary taps into the experiences of many audience members who were employed as domestic servants and who, like her, experienced the common ordeal of seduction and rejection. By evoking her as experiencing a dilemma only too familiar to white female servants, the play undermines contemporary constructions of race as an indelible marker of Otherness and challenges perceptions of Moors as 'exotic Others', 'associate[d] [with] barbarian culture, physical monstrosity, moral shortcomings, and, in some instances, divine wrath', against whom the self (English, White, Christian, Protestant) is defined by way of contrast.[13] Instead, Barbary is offered as a figure with whom the self is encouraged to identify and with whose experience of rejection, grief and tragic death it

---

[10] Vaughan and Vaughan, 'Before Othello', p. 29. See also Jean E. Howard, 'An English lass amid the Moors: gender, race, sexuality, and national identity in Heywood's *The Fair Maid of the West*', in *Women, 'Race', and Writing in the Early Modern Period*, ed. Margo Hendricks and Patricia Parker (London, 1994), pp. 101–17. A notable exception is Matthew Steggle who argues that Black people 'might, in theory at least, have been present at an early performance of [*Othello*]' (Steggle, 'Othello, the Moor of London', p. 104).

[11] Steggle, 'Othello: the Moor of London', pp. 105–6. Steggle does not consider Barbary. Interestingly, while the myth of an all-male early modern professional theatre has been exploded, the notion of its being an all-white institution persists. For women's contribution to the early modern professional playhouse, see Natasha Korda, *Labors Lost: Women's Work and the Early Modern English Stage* (Philadelphia, 2011).

[12] Habib and Salkeld, 'The Resonables of Boroughside, Southwark', pp. 135, 139, 138.

[13] Richard Helgerson calls this 'nation formation'. See Richard Helgerson, *Forms of Nationhood: The Elizabethan Writing of England* (Chicago, 1994); Vaughan and Vaughan, 'Before Othello', pp. 19, 29. See also Howard, 'An English lass amid the Moors', p. 102. Vaughan writes that 'the "black-faced devils" of the homiletic tradition had become amalgamated with the figure of the black Moor of Africa in a conventional symbol of the qualities – barbarism, ignorance, impudence, and falsehood – in opposition to white Englishness and true religion' (Vaughan, *Performing Blackness*, p. 71). Critics have long recognized the way the play challenges contemporary stereotypes about Moors. See, for example, G. K. Hunter, 'Elizabethans and foreigners', *Shakespeare Survey 17* (Cambridge, 1964), 37–52; p. 51); Martin Orkin, 'Othello and the "plain face" of racism', *Shakespeare Quarterly* 38 (1987), 166–88; Lynn Enterline, 'Eloquent barbarians: Othello and the critical potential of passionate character', in *Othello: The State of Play*, ed. Orlin, pp. 149–76; p. 152; Dadabhoy, 'Two faced', p. 140. The way Barbary, too, contests dramatic and pictorial traditions of representing Black women, however, has not been recognized.

could sympathize, as proven by Desdemona, who models this response for the audience.[14]

Using archival sources, the pioneering and groundbreaking work of Imtiaz Habib has demonstrated that Black people were 'a pervasive, repetitive, and accelerating presence in Elizabethan London'.[15] 'Black Tudors' – Africans in Tudor England – as later scholars building on Habib's work have shown, 'were not only present, but played an active part in some of the best-known stories of the age.'[16] Scholars cite such relatively well-known Africans as John Blanke, the trumpeter depicted in the Westminster Tournament Roll of 1511; Jacques Francis, one of the salvage operators employed to recover the ordinance from the wreck of the *Mary Rose* in 1546; Thomasen, a Black maid in Elizabeth I's court (1574–7); and the Moroccan ambassador to Elizabeth I, Abd el-Ouahed ben Messaoud ben Mohammed Anoun, often credited with being Shakespeare's inspiration for Othello.[17] Research, however, is increasingly revealing that the Black presence in the period was not restricted to those few who made it to such prestigious positions.[18] As Miranda Kaufmann shows, '[t]he Africans found at court and in noble and gentry households were, in fact, a tiny minority. We have more evidence of Africans living in merchant households.'[19] African men and women who led more ordinary lives, as Peter Fryer and Imtiaz Habib have also shown, were a common sight in early modern England.[20] Far from being merely 'human menageries' – in G. K. Hunter's memorable phrase – status markers and decorative objects in the houses of the high and mighty, as early research suggested, Africans often performed functional roles as porters, gardeners, musicians, cooks or laundresses.[21] Examples include Edward Swarthye, alias Nigro, who worked as a porter in the 1590s at Whitecross Manor in Lydney, Gloucestershire; Grace Robinson, a blackamoor, who worked as a laundress for the Lady Anne Clifford between 1613 and 1624; and 'John Morockoe, a blackamoor' employed by the third Earl of Dorset, in his kitchen and scullery at Knole in the 1620s. Africans were also employed as domestic servants, carrying out duties comparable to those performed by their white counterparts. Among their ranks were Suzanna Peiris, 'a blackamoore servant to John Despinois, a hatbandmaker' who was buried at St Botolph Aldgate in 1593; Symon Valencia, 'a black moore', who was recorded as being 'servant to Stephen Drifyeld a nedellmaker' at his burial in the same year; Augustina Patra, a Black maidservant, who, interestingly, belonged to the household of the daughter of Henry Carey, patron of Shakespeare's theatre company between 1594 and 1596; and, interesting for my purposes, 'Barbaree', servant to a Master Smith, who was buried in St Peter, Paul's Wharf, in 1623.[22] Recent research has also uncovered the case of a 12-year-old 'Polonia

---

[14] Critics have observed the way Desdemona models excessive emotional investment for the audience when she falls in love with the hero Othello portrays in his life story. See Laurie Maguire, 'Othello, theatre boundaries, and audience cognition', in *Othello: The State of Play*, ed. Orlin, pp. 17–43.

[15] Imtiaz Habib, *Black Lives in the English Archives, 1500–1677: Imprints of the Invisible* (Aldershot, 2008), p. 116.

[16] Miranda Kaufmann, *Black Tudors: The Untold Story* (London, 2017), p. 262. Scholars often cite Elizabeth I's decrees in 1596 and 1601 expelling Black people from England as evidence of their increased numbers in the period. See, for example, Habib, *Black Lives*, p. 112. Kaufmann has recently argued that Elizabeth's government never intended to expel the Black population. See 'Caspar van Senden, Sir Thomas Sherley and the "Blackamoor Project"', *Historical Research* 81 (2008), 366–71.

[17] E. A. J. Honigmann, 'Introduction' to *Othello*, Arden Third Series (London, 1997), pp. 1–112; pp. 2–4, 14–17; Habib, *Black Lives*, p. 2.

[18] For Africans in English and Scottish courts between 1500 and 1640, see Kaufmann, 'Africans in Britain', in *Black Tudors*, p. 160.

[19] Kaufmann, 'Africans in Britain', p. 160.

[20] Fryer, *Staying Power*, p. 8.

[21] G. K. Hunter, 'Othello and colour prejudice', *Proceedings of the British Academy* 53 (1967), 139–63; p. 145. See also Paul Griffiths, *Lost Londons: Change, Crime, and Control in the Capital City, 1550–1660* (Cambridge, 2008), p. 74; Kaufmann, 'Africans in Britain', pp. 162–3. For Black servants as decorative objects, see Habib, *Black Lives*, p. 68.

[22] Kaufmann, 'Africans in Britain', pp. 176–80; Steggle, 'Othello: the Moor of London', pp. 117, 121; Habib and Salkeld, 'The Resonables of Boroughside, Southwark', p. 150; Habib, *Black Lives*, p. 3.

blackmor maid', whose mistress consulted Simon Forman about her maid's illness on 5 May 1597. Forman concluded that the girl was suffering from 'Moch pane syd[e] stom[ach]' and was 'Lyk to vomit' and had, like *Othello*'s Barbary, a 'fa[i]nt harte, full of melancoly & cold humors mixed with collor [i.e. choler]'.[23] Some Black people pursued trades such as needle-making or silk-weaving, and even lived on their own as independent single men and women.[24] Examples include Lambert Waterson, a Moroccan trader who lived in London and was described in 1568 as 'denizen, barbaryen, tenaunte of Gabriell Levesy, grocer'; Resonable Blackman, mentioned above, an independent craftsman; and the various African women explored by Kaufmann who seem to have been prosperous enough to possess property to leave in their wills to family and friends.[25]

The Africans in whom I am interested are those who, like Barbary, were employed in domestic service and who, like many servants in this period, might have frequented the playhouse and seen the original production of *Othello* at the Globe.[26] Attending to this demographic of early modern society and entertaining the *possibility* that Africans might have formed part of the early modern playgoing population allows us to approach the question of the original reception of the play from a fresh perspective and opens up the play to new questions. '[O]ur new understanding of the historical context', as Kaufmann writes, commenting on our increased awareness of the Black presence in the period, 'may affect not only our discussions of the language of early modern plays, but also our understanding of their performance, and audience.'[27] If we at least accept the possibility that an African maidservant could have attended the original production of *Othello*, fresh questions about the play and its reception emerge. What would the tragic story of an abandoned African maidservant mean to an African maidservant in the audience? How does attention to this other African character complicate our understanding of *Othello*'s portrayal of race? How does the fact that Barbary's story is only accessible to the audience through the fond memory of her white mistress engage with contemporary dramatic and pictorial conventions for representing relationships between white mistresses and Moorish maidservants? In a society where 60 per cent of the population aged 15 to 24 was employed in domestic service, how does the figure of a Black domestic servant signify?[28] These are the questions that concern me in this article.

In act 4, scene 3 of the Folio version, known as the 'willow scene' in reference to Barbary's song, Shakespeare both borrows from and subverts conventions of representing mistresses and maidservants in domestic spaces. While the relationship between Desdemona and Emilia in this scene conforms to dramatic convention, it is by introducing Barbary that Shakespeare challenges it. Early modern drama offers many examples of this convention at work. The elements constituting them are often the same: the mistress is often younger, less experienced, bashful, and thus scandalized by her maidservant's more worldly and sexually uninhibited worldview. The two women are usually depicted sharing a private conversation that takes place while they engage in some domestic activity and occupy settings that, in Eamon Grennan's words,

---

[23] Cited in Gustav Ungerer, 'The presence of Africans in Elizabethan England and the performance of *Titus Andronicus* at Burley-on-the-Hill, 1595/96', *Medieval & Renaissance Drama in England* 21 (2008), 19–55; p. 24.

[24] Kaufmann, 'Africans in Britain', p. 201.

[25] Kaufmann, 'Africans in Britain', pp. 209–12; Habib and Salkeld, 'The Resonables of Boroughside, Southwark', p. 136.

[26] For servants as playgoers, see Andrew Gurr, *Playgoing in Shakespeare's London*, 3rd ed. (Cambridge, 1987), pp. 57, 66, 77, 79, 233, 238, 250, 272; Bernard Capp, 'Playgoers, players and cross-dressing in early modern London: The Bridewell evidence', *The Seventeenth Century* 18 (2003), 159–71.

[27] Miranda Kaufmann, '"Making the beast with two backs" – interracial relationships in early modern England', *Literature Compass* 12 (2015), 22–37; p. 32.

[28] Ann Kussmaul, *Servants in Husbandry in Early Modern England* (Oxford, 1981), p. 3; Peter Laslett, *The World We Have Lost: Further Explored* (London, 2001), pp. 13–16; Alan Bray, *Homosexuality in Renaissance England* (New York, 1995), pp. 45, 51.

function as 'protected enclosure[s] where the women may, for a few minutes free of a world that puts checks upon their voices, speak (or sing) their minds and hearts'.[29] In *Much Ado about Nothing*, for example, Hero, preparing for her upcoming (fateful) wedding, engages in a private conversation with her maidservant, Margaret, in which, rightly as it turns out, she voices her apprehensions about the impending wedding night: 'God give me joy to wear it', she sighs, indicating the wedding gown, 'for my heart is exceeding heavy' (3.4.23–4). The maidservant responds with the sexually explicit remark, "Twill be heavier soon by the weight of a man', a statement that enrages and embarrasses the bashful mistress who scolds: 'Fie upon thee, art not ashamed?' (3.4.25–6). The exchange is specifically designed and placed to stress Hero's chastity (crucially important as she will shortly be accused by her fiancé of infidelity), and Margaret's sexual laxity (a useful trait as Don John will soon realize for his plot to slander Hero) and perhaps, given her inferior status, greater freedom to pursue romantic and/or sexual adventures.[30] This pattern of pitting a chaste mistress against a sexually uninhibited serving woman is repeated in John Ford's *'Tis Pity She's a Whore* (1630s). The serving woman here is specifically described as being older than her mistress, in a move that registers contemporary anxieties about older, experienced women corrupting younger maidens.[31] Annabella's 'old' guardian, suggestively named 'Putana' ('whore'), encourages her mistress to embark on an incestuous relationship.[32] She dismisses her mistress's hesitation with the remark: 'fear nothing, sweetheart, what though he be your brother? Your brother's a man I hope, and I say still, if a young wench feel the fit upon her, let her take anybody, father or brother, all is one' (2.1.46–9). Putana's uninhibited nature has already been on display in 1.2 when, observing her mistress's suitors, she warns Annabella against marrying a soldier on the grounds that his sexual performance will not be adequate: 'I do not like him, and be for nothing but for being a soldier: one amongst twenty of your skirmishing captains but have some privy maim or other that mars their standing upright' (1.2.79–82). Though she gives the opposite advice, Zanthia in John Fletcher, Philip Massinger and Nathan Field's *The Knight of Malta* (1616–19) is true to type as she approves her mistress's choice to marry a soldier, because, she says, he will be 'a perpetuall guard upon her honour', a service that she will want to 'reward' with 'her own Exchequer / Which he finds ever open'.[33] Checked by her scandalized mistress ('Be more modest', 'Thou talkst of nothing'), Zanthia retorts, 'Why, we may speak of that we are glad to taste of', adding: 'Of nothing Madam? You have found it something' – 'nothing' and 'something' clearly sexually suggestive (3.2.54–7). Virginia Mason Vaughan's comment on John Marston's *Sophonisba* (1604–6)

---

[29] Eamon Grennan, 'The women's voices in *Othello*: speech, song, silence', *Shakespeare Quarterly* 38 (1987), 275–92; p. 282. As has been amply discussed in the literature, this scene differs between the texts of the First Quarto (1622) and of the First Folio (1623). See Scott McMillin, 'The mystery of the early *Othello* texts', in *Othello: New Critical Essays*, ed. Philip C. Kolin (New York, 2002), pp. 401–24; E. A. J. Honigmann, *The Texts of Othello and Shakespearian Revision* (London, 1996), pp. 10–12, 39–40; *Othello*, ed. Neill, pp. 405–33; Scott McMillin, ed., *The First Quarto of Othello* (Cambridge, 2001); Denise A. Walen, 'Unpinning Desdemona', *Shakespeare Quarterly* 58 (2007), 487–508; p. 489.

[30] I am grateful to this journal's reader for suggesting this reading to me.

[31] For this trope, see the gossips pamphlets by Samuel Rowlands, such as *Tis Merry when Gossips Meet* (London, 1602) and *A Crew of Kind Gossips All Met to be Merry Complayning of their Husbands* (London, 1613).

[32] Putana is described as 'old' in 4.3.175, 226, 231; 5.6.124. All quotations are from Derek Roper's edition, *'Tis Pity She's a Whore* (London, 1975); subsequent references in parentheses. For 'Putana' meaning 'whore', see John Florio, *Queen Anna's New World of Words or Dictionarie of the Italian and English tongues* (London, 1611), sig. Mm2v.

[33] John Fletcher, Philip Massinger and Nathan Field, *The Knight of Malta*, 3.2.46, 52–5. All quotations are from the edition by George Walton Williams in *The Dramatic Works in The Beaumont and Fletcher Canon*, vol. 8 (Cambridge, 1992); subsequent references in parentheses.

applies here: the serving woman's 'frank sexuality is crucial in the construction of [her mistress] as the chaste heroine'.[34]

The convention became so familiar that some dramatists counted on their audience recognizing its elements, only to deliver a twist. Thomas Middleton's *The Changeling* (1622), for example, offers the familiar formula: Beatrice-Joanna and her waiting woman, Diaphanta, occupy the private space of a closet in act 4, scene 1. The twist is that the mistress is not the conventional chaste maiden, but one who has lost her virginity and is casting about for a virgin to replace her in the marital bed on her wedding night. Middleton introduces another twist: the maidservant, unlike her analogues, is a virgin, a fact that qualifies her for the position of her mistress's replacement.[35] Despite these twists, the play preserves the tradition of representing maidservants as lustful, a choice that sits rather awkwardly with the fact of Diaphanta's virginity. Finding her mistress in Alsemero's closet and learning that she 'c[a]me hither ... / To look my lord', Diaphanta reveals her lustfulness by stating in an aside: 'Would I had such a cause to look him, too!' (4.1.56–8). It is not surprising, then, that Diaphanta offers herself as the proxy virgin that Beatrice-Joanna seeks – 'Madam, what say you to me, and stray no further? / I've a good mind, in troth, to earn your money' (4.1.76, 93–4) – eagerly anticipating the wedding night, as her reading her mistress's remark regarding the weighty 'business' on which they are about to embark in a sexual sense shows: 'I shall carry't well, because I love the burden' (4.1.124–5). Similarly, in John Webster's *The White Devil* (1612), Vittoria is far from being the mistress of the tradition whose virtue shines against her waiting woman's lustfulness. She is the 'white' version of her waiting woman, Zanche, who serves as an embodiment of the stereotype of the promiscuous serving woman, lusting after two men, Flamineo and the Duke of Florence, disguised as a Moor, and sharing with the latter a highly suggestive dream in which he 'lay down by [her]'.[36]

In the willow scene, Shakespeare offers a version of this pattern. Desdemona, a chaste woman bewildered by her husband's outbursts of rage, shares a private conversation with her waiting woman, Emilia, in the intimate space of the bedchamber, while the latter performs domestic tasks, undressing her mistress, fetching sheets and laying them on the bed (4.3.20–1). Carol Chillington Rutter has read this scene against contemporary discourses on 'gossips' – female friends – inserting it within a tradition of representations of such friendships that encapsulates Chaucer's Wife of Bath, Titania's Indian votress, and the witches in *Macbeth*. Rutter argues that 'these gossips inhabit bodies that constantly exceed the texts they occupy in scenes that celebrate dangerous female intimacy and alliance even as, by suggesting insubordination, they demystify male authority'.[37] I also wish to draw attention to the way the encounter between Desdemona and Emilia in this scene conforms to the pattern I am tracing here. Much as in the scenes discussed above, Desdemona's scandalized enquiry as to whether 'there be women do abuse their husbands / In such gross kind?' is answered by the more experienced and worldly Emilia in the positive: 'There be some such, no question' (5.1.60–1). Emilia adds that she herself is willing to 'do such a deed' (62), dismissing her mistress's shocked disbelief ('In truth, I think thou wouldst not') with the emphatic: 'In truth, I think I should' (69–70).[38]

---

[34] Vaughan, *Performing Blackness*, p. 87.
[35] Thomas Middleton, *The Changeling*, ed. Douglas Bruster, in *Thomas Middleton: The Collected Works*, ed. Gary Taylor and John Lavagnino (Oxford, 2007), 4.1.95–121; subsequent references in parentheses.
[36] John Webster, *The White Devil*, ed. John Russell Brown (London, 1960), 5.3.231; subsequent references in parentheses.
[37] Carol Chillington Rutter, *Enter the Body: Women and Representation on Shakespeare's Stage* (London and New York, 2001), p. 158.
[38] It is perhaps this tradition that stands behind some editors' decision to reassign Desdemona's line 'This Lodovico is a proper man' (4.3.34) to Emilia. Honigmann, following M. R. Ridley, explains his decision in these terms: 'For Desdemona to praise Lodovico at this point seems out of character' (*Othello*, ed. Honigmann, p. 291, nn. 34–5); Ridley had earlier mused: 'One is tempted to wonder whether there has been a misattribution of speeches, so that

Desdemona's innocence and readiness to forgive her husband's cruelty ('my love doth so approve him, / That even his stubbornness, his checks, his frowns – / ... have grace and favour in them' (4.3.18–20)) are counterbalanced by Emilia who recognizes her society's double standards for what they are (83–102).

At the heart of this scene, as with its analogues, lies a misogynistic tendency to pit women against each other. All three mistress–maidservant relationships examined above suggest the fragility of female bonds, especially when forged across status lines, and feature some form of betrayal. Margaret, intentionally or not, ends up being party to a plot that discredits her mistress (4.1). Diaphanta, in her eagerness to enjoy the wedding night with her mistress's husband, stays in his bedchamber beyond the set time previously agreed on with her mistress ('About midnight you must not fail to steal forth gently, / That I may use thy place' (4.1.126–7)) and thus sends her mistress into a panic that only subsides when Beatrice-Joanna allows her servant-lover to set Diaphanta's chamber on fire and thus force her exit from the marital chamber, eventually killing her (5.1). Similarly, Webster's Zanche offers to betray her mistress to the disguised Moor in a bid to win his love, promising to 'rob Vittoria' and so 'In coin and jewels ... make good unto [Francisco's] use / An hundred thousand crowns' (5.3.252, 257–9). She, furthermore, betrays her mistress by 'reveal[ing] a secret' that seals Vittoria's fate (5.3.243). Emilia, too, despite her fierce loyalty in the final scene, contributes to her mistress's demise. The handkerchief she hands over to Iago in act 3, scene 3 is arguably the only piece of 'evidence' that Othello will ever accrue. Desdemona, too, withdraws from the temporary bond she shared with Emilia when discussing women's lot in a patriarchal society, recoiling, as Emilia exits, from their encounter, and seeking divine assistance so as 'Not to pick bad from bad, but by bad mend' (5.1.104). 'Emilia's "gossip"', as Rutter observes about Trevor Nunn's 1989 *Othello*, 'was [thus] discredited as "bad"', and when Emilia (Zoe Wanamaker) 'exited, she and Desdemona [Imogen Stubbs] were as far apart as ever'.[39] Against this context, both external and internal to the play, the movement in the willow scene towards Barbary gains special importance.

While the differences between the Folio and Quarto versions of this scene have long been observed, the way the longer Folio version allows an important comparison with the scenes discussed above, and works to challenge contemporary perceptions and representations of relationships between mistresses and serving women, has not been remarked upon.[40] Absent from the Quarto, Desdemona's relationship with Barbary in the Folio stands in stark contrast to the trope of pitting mistress against maidservant. Facing rejection and experiencing grief over lost love, Desdemona turns to a memory of this maidservant to process her own feelings, remembering a song that 'expressed her fortune' (5.1.28). Instead of being contrasted with Barbary in terms of her chastity, and thus superior virtue, Desdemona is depicted as identifying with this woman, sharing with her – in Grennan's memorable phrase – a 'sisterhood of grief', and forming with her – to borrow Niamh J. O'Leary's phrase – 'a virtual female community'.[41] Rendered,

---

this line as well as the next should be Emilia's' (*Othello*, ed. M. R. Ridley (London, 1965), p. 166, n. 35).

[39] Rutter, *Enter the Body*, p. 173.

[40] Critics have noticed the thematic differences between the two versions, remarking on the way in which the Folio presents Desdemona and Emilia as complex characters and depicts Emilia as an insightful woman (Walen, 'Unpinning Desdemona', p. 487); Carol Chillington Rutter, 'Unpinning Desdemona (again) or "Who would be toll'd with wenches in a shew?"', *Shakespeare Bulletin* 28 (2010), 111–32. E. A. J. Honigmann has long wondered whether the song was cut because the boy actor who played Desdemona left the company or lost his singing voice at this point (Honigmann, *Texts of Othello*, pp. 10–12, 39–40).

[41] Grennan, 'The women's voices in Othello', p. 279. Niamh J. O'Leary distinguishes between 'actual' and 'virtual' female communities, referring to women 'com[ing] together and self-identify[ing] as like-minded group members' and as 'imagined or virtual, often invoked by a single woman in a moment of need', respectively. O'Leary does not consider the way her useful categories apply to Othello's women. See Niamh J. O'Leary, 'Virtual and actual female alliance in The Maid's Tragedy and The Tamer Tamed', in *The Politics of Female Alliance in Early Modern England*, ed. Christina Luckyj

through her 'unpinning', in Rutter's words, 'smaller', 'vulnerable', 'perhaps sacrificial', experiencing excessive grief and anticipating (?) her imminent death ('If I do die before thee', she instructs Emilia, 'prithee shroud me / In one of these same sheets' (5.1.23–4)), Desdemona is reminded of another woman whose rejection-induced grief proved fatal.[42] 'My mother had a maid called Barbary, / She was in love, and he she loved proved mad, / And did forsake her', she says, introducing Barbary, illuminating their shared experience of suffering that resulted from a lover's rejection (5.1.25–7). Her designation of Barbary's lover as 'mad' links the two women as it directly echoes Iago's anticipation earlier in the same act that her own lover, Othello, 'shall go mad' when he mistakenly takes Cassio's smiles when Bianca is mentioned as triggered by a memory of Desdemona (4.1.99). More strikingly, Desdemona *embodies* this absent woman on stage, stepping for a minute into her body, substituting her voice for the absent maid's, performing her bodily gestures and restaging the scene of female grief and abandonment that she had presumably witnessed as a child: 'I have much to do / But to go hang my head all at one side / And sing it, like poor Barbary' (5.1.30–2). She embodies the 'poor soul [Barbary/ the song speaker] [who] sat sighing by a sycamore tree', 'Her hand on her bosom, her head on her knee' (5.1.38, 40). Desdemona thus identifies with the serving woman in a way that inverts the power dynamics between mistresses and maidservants in the scenes discussed above, insisting instead on the commonality of their experiences. In those scenes, mistresses often put the transgressive maidservants in their place, thus reasserting their power and superiority: Desdemona's own dismissal of Emilia at the end of this scene with her 'Good night, good night' (5.1.103), simultaneously putting an end to the dangerous conversation and reasserting her control over access to her person and claims on her time and space, is a case in point. But Desdemona's treatment of Barbary as an example to be followed and a source of instruction to be heeded also subverts contemporary theorization on the mistress–servant relationship. In early modern household manuals, mistresses operate as models for their servants, their conduct being an example to be followed. This was exactly why preachers often expressed a concern that a wife who failed in her duty to obey her husband also served as a negative model for her servants. William Gouge, to cite one example, thundered that a wife's disobedience had disastrous consequences for all bonds of duty within the household: disobedient wives 'thwart Gods ordinance, peruert the order of nature, deface the image of Christ, ouerthrow the ground of all dutie, hinder the good of the family'.[43]

In his depiction of Desdemona's relationship with Barbary, Shakespeare not only subverts the power dynamics that theoretically structured mistress–servant relationships. He also, as critics have noted, changes the genders in his probable source of the song, where the singer is gendered male and the false lover, female. By making this change, he stresses the topic of women's mistreatment by men and highlights the shared experience of female grief and 'sympathy' that, in Carol Thomas Neely's words, 'stretches from Emilia and Desdemona to include Barbary and the protagonist of the song – all victims of male perfidy'.[44] In pairing Desdemona and Barbary, then, Shakespeare subverts the pattern of pitting mistress against maidservant and prepares the way for Emilia's identification with her mistress later on, and her willingness to die defending her. Just as Desdemona physically reproduces Barbary's bodily gestures while she remembers her song, Emilia replays Desdemona's final moments, singing 'Willow' as she dies (5.2.255) and 'evoking', as Grennan observes, 'Desdemona, Barbary, and the infinite line of women undone by love and men'.[45] Desdemona's identification with Barbary gains

---

and Niamh O'Leary (Lincoln and London, 2017), pp. 68–85; p. 68.
[42] Rutter, 'Unpinning Desdemona', p. 117.
[43] William Gouge, *Of domesticall duties* (London, 1622), p. 287.
[44] Rosenfeld discusses the original version in 'Shakespeare's nobody', p. 266; Carol Thomas Neely, *Broken Nuptials in Shakespeare's Plays* (New Haven, 1985), p. 123.
[45] Grennan, 'The women's voices in *Othello*', p. 291.

further importance when we consider the way it challenges another early modern convention: dramatic and pictorial representations of white mistresses and their African maidservants.

In contemporary visual culture, representations of maidservants and mistresses often had racialized dimensions.[46] As Peter Erickson writes, in early modern visual culture, 'black and white are relational'.[47] Portraits of white patrons featuring a Black servant or attendant, as Erickson points out elsewhere, depict 'the servant appeal[ing] to us to see him or her as a person, a potential subject. As a clearly identified social subordinate and implied racial inferior, [however,] the servant is typecast in the role of object ... appurtenance, status symbol, exotic touch.'[48] This became an established visual convention dubbed by Erickson: 'the motif of the black servant'.[49] The Black attendant in these portraits often 'operates as a literal extension and physical appendage of the white subject'.[50] Kim F. Hall, following Michelle Cliff, describes this strategy as a process of 'objectification' whereby 'people are dehumanized, made ghostlike, given the status of Other'.[51] In contemporary paintings, white mistresses are pitted against African maidservants, the positioning of the latter designed to emphasize the whiteness of the mistress's skin and so her privilege, power and superiority. She is, in Habib's words, 'the white woman's negative index'.[52] Nor was this strategy a novelty in this period. An English proverb that could be traced back to the early fifteenth century decides that 'Black best sets forth white.'[53] Peter Paul Rubens's *Venus Before the Mirror* (1616), based on Titian's *Venus with a Mirror*, is a case in point. Venus's white body, which dominates the painting and thus pushes the Black servant to the margin, is a stark contrast to her attendant's, a Black figure that Rubens added to the original version.[54] 'Her presence', as Erickson observes, 'sets up a black–white juxtaposition.'[55] The Black attendant's gaze 'makes us focus our attention on Venus's face', thus rendering the servant literally marginal and visibly subordinate.[56] Rubens's *Diana and Callisto* (1637–8) repeats this motif, as Diana and her Black female servant form a similar pair contrasted by skin colour as well as posture: Diana's, authoritative; the servant's, submissive. The Black woman's inferior status is indicated by the cap which contains her hair, in contrast to the other women in the painting whose hair runs free, and her servile role is captured in her diligent protection of her mistress against the menacing dog lurking in the margin. The same technique can be seen in Titian's *Diana and Actaeon* (1556–9) where Diana's white body is contrasted by the Blackness of that of her female servant. Both women are depicted in a similar position to stress the Black/white binary that frames their portrayal. This is a process that Erickson calls 'white self-fashioning', and Vaughan describes as 'contribut[ing] to the construction of a normative English female "fairness"' that 'coded her as an object of desire'.[57] This pictorial strategy works simultaneously to emphasize the mistress's whiteness and the Black servant's racial difference, and, by extension (by implication?), her inferiority. These images, while not necessarily accessible to all members of the early modern audience, are, nonetheless, suggestive and helpful in understanding cultural tropes at work in artistic representations of white mistresses and African maidservants.

---

[46] Peter Erickson alerts us to the time lag involved in representations of Black figures in British art when compared to Continental art. See Erickson, 'Representations of Blacks', p. 516.
[47] Erickson, 'Representations of Blacks', pp. 521, 505.
[48] Erickson, 'Representations of race in Renaissance art', pp. 4–5; Erickson, 'Invisibility speaks', p. 24. See also Kim F. Hall, 'Object into object? Some thoughts on the presence of Black women in early modern culture', in *Early Modern Visual Culture*, ed. Erickson and Hulse, pp. 346–79; p. 348.
[49] Erickson, '"God for Harry"', p. 324.
[50] Erickson, 'Invisibility Speaks', p. 34.
[51] Hall, 'Object into object?', p. 346.
[52] Imtiaz Habib, '"Hel's perfect character"; or the Blackamoor maid in early modern English drama: the postcolonial cultural history of a dramatic type', *Lit: Literature Interpretation Theory* 11 (2000), 277–304; p. 284.
[53] Quoted in Vaughan, *Performing Blackness*, p. 6.
[54] Erickson, 'Representations of Blacks', p. 510.
[55] Erickson, 'Representations of Blacks', p. 510.
[56] Quoted in Hall, 'Object into object?', p. 355.
[57] Erickson, 'Representations of race in Renaissance art', p. 322; Vaughan, *Performing Blackness*, pp. 59, 65.

The theatre too participated in this tradition, offering a parallel to the pictorial pattern explored above.[58] 'In the theatrical realm', Alden T. Vaughan and Virginia Mason Vaughan observe, 'Africans seem initially to have been introduced for their visual power. They were literally spectacular, ... [and] audiences could instantly see the difference between the black character's real or contrived skin color and the other actors' lighter hue.'[59] Habib has argued that the treatment of the Moorish woman on the early modern stage is different from that of her male counterpart, identifying her as a 'dramatic type', a figure who is 'demoniz-[ed]', whose sexuality is 'bestially coded', and whose 'only cultural visibility ... is in her brutalized dramatic reproduction as the treacherous and lascivious blackamoor maid'.[60] Early modern drama often maps the binary of chastity/lustfulness onto the categories of white and Black embodied by mistresses and maidservants, respectively.[61] The '[female] Moor', as Vaughan observes about *Sophonisba*, 'deflects anxieties about female desire onto herself, accentuating her mistress's white virtue'.[62] Shakespeare has already employed this binary in *The Merchant of Venice*, in which Jessica's chastity, ensured through her surrendering her virginity only within the confines of marriage, is contrasted with the Moorish maidservant seduced, made pregnant and then abandoned by Gobbo (3.5.1759–64).[63] As Vaughan writes: 'The black servant [whom Gobbo impregnates] epitomizes English concerns about amalgamation and opens a space for Jessica, the Jew's daughter, to slip inside the Christian polity.'[64] Such a pair also appears in Webster's *The White Devil*, where Zanche, a Moorish maidservant, is identified by her dark skin, in stark contrast to her mistress's whiteness. Where Vittoria is 'fair' (1.2.6, 37; 2.2.50; 4.2.10), and her 'cheek' is 'red and white' (3.2.52), Zanche is described as a 'devil' (customarily imagined as Black) (5.1.89, 156), a 'foul nest' (5.1.232), and condemned as 'infernal' (5.3.216). *The Knight of Malta* offers another such pair where Zanthia, a treacherous Moorish maidservant, is specifically depicted as the polar opposite to her mistress's whiteness and chastity, traits that in the world of the play go hand in hand. Oriana is chaste. Her 'faire hands', in the words of one character, reflect her chastity: 'As white as this I see your Innocence, / As spotlesse, and as pure' (2.5.68–70). By contrast, the lustful Zanthia offers herself to her lover, Mountferrat, and is puzzled by his rejection: 'Am I not here / As lovely in my blacke to entertaine thee, / As high, and full of heat, to meet thy pleasures?' (2.3.11–3). Her lustfulness is, thus, inevitably (resultantly?) linked with her Blackness. Zanthia's Blackness is at the centre of her characterization, and she is referred to by different characters as a 'black cloud', a 'black swan', a 'black pudding', and 'my little labour in vain', the latter a reference to the common early modern proverbial expression: 'it is impossible to wash an Ethiop (or blackamoor) white' (1.1.164, 190; 1.2.61–2).[65] She is consistently described as a 'devil' and 'hels perfect character' (2.3.18; 4.1.65, 82).[66] By contrast, Oriana, her mistress, is

---

[58] Erickson, 'Invisibility speaks', p. 33.
[59] Vaughan and Vaughan, 'Before Othello', p. 29. Vaughan, *Performing Blackness*, ch. 2, surveys Black characters on the early modern stage. Matar, *Britain and Barbary, 1589–1689*, ch. 1, argues for a shift in the dramatic representation of Moors over this period, from dangerous figures into dull natives or noble savages (p. 10).
[60] Habib, '"Hel's perfect character"', p. 280.
[61] For the association between Blackness and lustfulness, see Vaughan, *Performing Blackness*, pp. 43–50; Hall, *Things of Darkness*, p. 97.
[62] Vaughan, *Performing Blackness*, p. 87. Similarly, Lynda E. Boose has argued that the 'depiction [of the lascivious Black servant] literalizes the patriarchal fear of the darkness of female sexuality'. See Lynda E. Boose, '"The begetting of a lawful race": racial discourse in early modern England and the unrepresentable Black woman', in *Women, 'Race', and Writing in the Early Modern Period*, ed. Margo Hendricks and Patricia Parker (London and New York, 1994), pp. 35–54; p. 47.
[63] Some critics have suggested that 'more than reason' is a reference to the family of Resonable Blackman, mentioned above. See Habib and Salkeld, 'The Resonables of Boroughside, Southwark'.
[64] Vaughan, *Performing Blackness*, p. 76.
[65] Morris Palmer Tilley, ed., *A Dictionary of the Proverbs in England in the Sixteenth and Seventeenth Centuries* (Ann Arbor, 1950), E186, p. 190.
[66] Vaughan, *Performing Blackness*, p. 19.

described in terms of her whiteness: her hands are 'faire', she is a 'faire Jewell' and her very name and soul are described as being 'white' (4.2.174; 2.5.118). The contrast in skin colour between mistress and maidservant is shown to be an index of their characters: just as Oriana's 'faire hands' represent her chastity, Zanthia's Blackness is seen as an externalization of her character, her 'black shape' presaging her 'blacker actions' (4.1.63). In fact, Black and white operate independently in the play, acquiring negative and positive attributes, respectively. Thus 'destruction' is 'black' while 'vertue' is 'white' (2.5.117, 180). It is a commonplace of the scholarly literature that 'black' and 'white' operate in a similar way in the rhetoric of the racially motivated characters in *Othello*. Thus, Desdemona's purity is manifested in 'that whiter skin of hers than snow / And smooth as monumental alabaster' (5.2.4–5), in contrast to Othello who is an 'old black ram', 'the blacker devil' who has a 'sooty bosom' and 'thick-lips', and Desdemona's 'filthy bargain' (1.1.88; 5.2.140; 1.3.71; 1.1.66; 5.2.164).

Desdemona's identification with 'poor' Barbary subverts this pattern of pitting white against Black, since, apart from the ethnic origins suggested by her name and her adoption of the Willow Song, already associated with Dido, an African queen, Barbary's skin colour is not discussed at all, whether on its own terms or in relation to Desdemona's whiteness.[67] It also subverts the tradition of pitting white mistress against Moorish serving woman, insisting, instead, on the two women's shared experience of abandonment and grief. *Othello* constructs a community of women betrayed in love and united by solidarity and empathy, undermining the tradition that depicts racial difference as a barrier to identification between mistress and maidservant or, indeed, as an index of social and moral inferiority. Desdemona's empathetic response to Barbary models this reaction to the audience who are thus encouraged to adopt a similar attitude to her plight, and it is to the audience that the final section of this article turns.

Stories of audiences' excessive emotional investment and identification form an important part of *Othello*'s reception history, more so than for any other Shakespearian play.[68] One such example appears in Samuel Pepys's diary, where he describes seeing *The Moor of Venice* at the Cockpit Theatre on 11 October 1660. Pepys's attention is caught by the emotional response that a 'very pretty lady' displays: she 'call[s] out' in distress 'to see Desdemona smothered'.[69] Perhaps the most extreme example appears in Stendhal's report of an 1822 performance in Baltimore, when an American soldier shot at the actor playing Othello.[70] Such documented responses seem to have often revolved around the central couple: audiences pity the innocent Desdemona or, swayed by racism, are angered when they witness a Black man murdering a white woman. In this final section, I want to suggest that, through the inclusion of Barbary, the play encourages another avenue for audience identification. Barbary, simultaneously exotic and familiar, speaks to the experiences of domestic servants in early modern England – often victims of sexual abuse and abandonment – at the same time that she makes visible the experiences of *Black* servants, whose plight in service might have been made even more acute by their status as Other.

The identity of Barbary's lover remains anonymous, and there is no indication in the snippets of information that Desdemona remembers about the maidservant as to whether the man who seduced and abandoned her was a fellow servant or household master. Her tragic story, however, resonates with many similar stories experienced by servants in this period, who were abandoned by their lovers and often left to face destitution, and worse. 'The most common profile of a bastard-bearer', as David Cressy explains, 'was

---

[67] Patricia Parker, 'Fantasies of "race" and "gender": Africa, Othello and bringing to light', in *Women, 'Race', and Writing*, ed. Hendricks and Parker, pp. 84–100; p. 97.
[68] Maguire, '*Othello*, theatre boundaries, and audience cognition', p. 27. See also Edward Pechter, *Othello and Interpretive Traditions* (Iowa City, 1999), ch. 1.
[69] Gamini Salgado, *Eyewitnesses of Shakespeare: First Hand Accounts of Performances, 1590–1890* (London, 1975), p. 49.
[70] Cited in *Othello: The State of Play*, ed. Orlin, p. 1.

a single woman in her twenties, employed away from home as a domestic maid or servant in husbandry, who succumbed to the pressures or promises of her master or fellow servants.'[71] The sexual abuse of maidservants by their masters was a sad reality for many in this period.[72] Keith Wrightson has estimated that some 14–23 per cent of women who had illegitimate children in seventeenth-century Essex or Lancashire named their master as the father.[73] This abuse was enabled by the nature of the maidservant's tasks (making and warming beds, for example), by the architectural realities of the early modern house (no corridors, rooms opened into each other, servants not allowed to lock the rooms in which they slept), the vulnerable position of servants, and the absence of privacy (in short supply even to employers).[74] Since servants formed a sizeable portion of the early modern playgoing population, it would not be surprising if servants watching the original performance identified with Barbary and, like Desdemona, empathized with her suffering and pitied her tragic death. Such identification pushes her racial difference to the background and renders it a less important aspect of her character than her status as a servant with a recognizable plight and a familiar story, often told by the kitchen fire or even experienced first-hand. Through Barbary, then, *Othello* challenges early modern prevalent notions of race as a marker of Otherness and irreconcilable difference. Barbary's race is less relevant to at least some members of the audience than is her vulnerable position in service and experience of rejection and betrayal.

While Barbary's story could thus have spoken to a large portion of its early modern audience employed in service, it is possible that it also spoke even more directly to a smaller demographic: Black female domestic servants. The experience of the Black female servant who was seduced and abandoned was, as Kaufmann has shown, 'common'. She cites the case of 'Marey a negroe' who, in March 1606, informed the Bridewell Court that 'one John Edwards ... had the use of her body twice & she is with child by him'. Mary, Kaufmann adds, 'was just one of 30 African women known to have borne illegitimate children in England between 1578 and 1640'.[75] Habib, commenting on this same population, speculates that these women were sexually abused by their masters.[76] If Black female servants, as I am speculating here, found the playhouse as enticing as their white fellows did, then it is not completely inconceivable that the original performance of *Othello* might have been experienced by African servants. Such audience members would have responded to Barbary's tragic history in a more personal way. They would have seen a story similar to ones they experienced or knew about: a story that involved living as a Black person in a white society, seduction and abandonment. They would also have observed a refreshing departure from the theatrical tradition that involved characters who looked like themselves. This is because, in its sympathetic treatment of the plight of a Moorish maidservant, *Othello* validates the experiences of Black servants and refuses to participate in the mockery of these experiences that is usual in contemporary dramatic representations.[77] We need only think

---

[71] David Cressy, *Birth, Marriage, and Death: Ritual, Religion, and the Life-Cycle in Tudor and Stuart England* (Oxford, 1999), p. 74.

[72] See Tim Meldrum, 'London domestic servants from depositional evidence, 1660–1750: servant–employer sexuality in the patriarchal household', in *Chronicling Poverty*, ed. Tim Hitchcock, Peter King and Pamela Sharpe (London, 1997), pp. 47–69; Laura Gowing, 'The haunting of Susan Lay: servants and mistresses in seventeenth-century England', *Gender and History* 14 (2002), 183–201; Joaneath Spicer, ed., *Revealing the African Presence in Renaissance Europe* (Baltimore, 2012), p. 26.

[73] Keith Wrightson, 'The nadir of English illegitimacy in the seventeenth century', in *Bastardy and Comparative History*, ed. Peter Laslett, K. Oosterveen and R. Smith (Cambridge, 1980), p. 187. See also Bernard Capp, *When Gossips Meet: Women, Family, and Neighbourhood in Early Modern England* (Oxford, 2003), pp. 144–9.

[74] Laura Gowing, *Common Bodies: Women, Touch and Power in Seventeenth-Century England* (New Haven and London, 2003), p. 60; Amanda Flather, 'Gender, space, and place', *Home Cultures* 8 (2011), 171–88; p. 181.

[75] Kaufmann, '"Making the beast with two backs"', pp. 27–8.

[76] Habib, *Black Lives*, p. 200.

[77] For a survey of the representations of Black figures in the drama and in the contemporary travel literature, see Vaughan and Vaughan, 'Before Othello'.

of *The Merchant of Venice* for an example where the 'negro' impregnated by Gobbo is evoked and dismissed in the same breath. Her plight of seduction and resultant pregnancy (a situation that is likely to earn her a whipping and land her in Bridewell) is treated as a joke by the clown, Gobbo, and potentially by the play since, as some critics have suggested, she might have been solely introduced for the sake of the pun on Moor/more.[78] The joke here, as Habib and Salkeld write, is 'at her expense', for '[Will] Kemp's [the actor playing Gobbo] lines slander the woman as "less than honest" and cheap while exculpating him: "if she be less than an honest woman, she is indeed more than I took her for" (3.5.37–8)'.[79] Carolyn Prager has suggested that this conversation evokes '[a]nti-African sentiment in the last decade of the sixteenth century' and 'alludes to … English hostility to London's growing number of blacks'.[80] Nor is she the only example of such treatment in the drama. In *Sophonisba*, Zanthia faces a similar fate as she is sentenced to die by the man who had bribed her earlier to betray her mistress. Unsurprisingly, having completed her task, Zanthia is dismissed in terms that equate her with refuse, with the 'dung, excrement, or compost' used to fertilize the soil: 'When Plants must flourish', Syphax informs her, 'their manure must rot.'[81] The metaphor, of course, literalizes the common association between female servants and the lower body. Those Black female servants' plights are dismissed as unworthy of sympathy or, indeed, stage time. Their stories are soon forgotten as they are dropped from the plots without comment.

Against this context, then, *Othello*'s treatment of Barbary's story must have stood out for a Black female servant playgoer as an instance of a respectful, empathetic and serious engagement with the experience of someone like herself. Seen from the perspective of this particular playgoer, *Othello*'s representation of race is far more nuanced and complicated than a focus on Othello alone would allow. Critics are still debating whether the play is 'racist' or 'anti-racist' ('I think this play is racist, and I think it is not', writes Vaughan), basing their views on its depiction of Othello. Including Barbary in this discussion and contemplating the potential Black presence in the early modern playhouse significantly changes the terms of this debate.[82] Whereas Othello's association with Barbary (the geographical region) evokes, at least in Iago's rhetoric, the 'barbarian' (1.3.354), setting him apart from 'civilized' Venice, Barbary's African roots do not mark her as inferior or hinder her white mistress's sympathy and identification. Unlike Othello, a man in a position of power, a 'wheeling stranger / Of here and everywhere' and thus far removed from the experiences of the majority of the play's original audience (1.1.138–9), Barbary, as a maidservant, occupies a more relatable position. The grounds on which a white playgoer identified with Barbary might have been different from those of a Black playgoer, but, through encouraging audience identification with her, the play challenges constructions of Africans as beings utterly different from the self. No analysis of *Othello*'s representation of race is complete without taking Barbary into account.

---

[78] William Shakespeare, *The Merchant of Venice*, ed. John Russell Brown (London, 1955), p. 99.

[79] Habib and Salkeld, 'The Resonables of Boroughside, Southwark', p. 154.

[80] Carolyn Prager, 'The Negro allusion in *The Merchant of Venice*', *American Notes and Queries* (1976), 50–2; p. 50.

[81] John Marston, *The Wonder of Women or the Tragedy of Sophonisba*, ed. William Kemp (New York and London, 1979), 4.1.89. Cf. *OED Online*, 'manure, n.', sense 1a.

[82] Virginia Mason Vaughan, *Othello: A Contextual History* (Cambridge, 1994), p. 69.

'THE MOOR'S ABUSED BY SOME MOST VILLAINOUS KNAVE, SOME BASE NOTORIOUS KNAVE, SOME SCURVY FELLOW': LEGAL SPACES, RACIAL TRAUMA AND SHAKESPEARE'S *THE TRAGEDY OF OTHELLO, THE MOOR OF VENICE*

LISA M. BARKSDALE-SHAW

In the early morning hours on 12 October 2019, an African American man, who later identified himself as James Smith, was woken by his niece and nephew who informed him that the front door to a neighbour's home was ajar. Out of concern, he contacted the non-emergency line for the Fort Worth police in the hopes that officers might conduct a 'wellness check'.[1] Mr Smith told the non-emergency operator that not only was the front door ajar, but also lights were visible and two vehicles, which he described as sedans, were in the driveway.[2] An officer who was dispatched to the location immediately pulled his weapon when arriving on the scene, as he approached the house. He saw the lights on inside the house. Unbeknown to the occupant of 1203 East Allen Avenue, Atatiana Jefferson, who was playing the *Call of Duty* video game with her 8-year-old nephew, her family would change irreversibly that night.[3] They both heard 'someone prowling in the bushes' of the backyard, where they had the door open to catch the night-time breeze. While her nephew wanted to look out the window to see whence the sound came, Atatiana Jefferson, a 28-year-old pre-med biology graduate from Xavier University, refused to let him do so and went herself to check on the source of this disruption to their evening. She was not unfamiliar with the neighbourhood, as she had recently moved into her mother's home to care for her. Her mother, who was hospitalized because of complications related to her congestive heart failure, was not in the house – it was just Atatiana Jefferson and her nephew; his mother was also hospitalized, recovering from recent heart surgery. So she went to investigate the disturbance. Without identifying himself as a police officer, Aaron Dean demanded: 'Put your hands up. Show me your hands.'[4] Then, according to the body-camera video, a 'split-second' later, he shot through the screen window – killing Atatiana Jefferson. This shooting would become

---

[1] Stephanie Hegerty and Atatiana Jefferson, 'Why I will no longer call the police', *BBC News*, 16 June 2020.
[2] WFAA, 'SOUND: the non-emergency phone call about Atatiana Jefferson before she was killed in her own home', YouTube, 13 October 2019. WFAA Channel 8 is an ABC affiliate.
[3] Jamie Stengle, 'Who was Atatiana Jefferson? The woman killed in her home by a Texas cop was devoted to her family, relatives say', *Chicago Tribune*, 15 October 2019.
[4] Hayley Miller, 'Atatiana Jefferson's 8-year-old nephew witnessed her killing, lawyer says', *Huffington Post Black Voices*, 14 October 2019.

the seventh officer-involved shooting between June and October 2019 for the city of Fort Worth, Texas. Officer Dean, 34 years old, joined the city's police force in 2018 – he resigned before FWPD officials fired him. Later, a weapon was discovered beside Atatiana Jefferson's bloodied body; apparently, she had grabbed a handgun before walking to the window to look in the backyard. Merely one month after her death, her father, Marquis Jefferson, having no previous health issues, died – succumbing to a heart attack.[5] Two months later, her mother, Yolanda Carr, who no longer had the care that her daughter provided, would die in the same house where her daughter met a violent end.[6] Late in the night, Atatiana Jefferson's older sister, Amber Carr, the mother of her two nephews, cries herself to sleep, comforted by her son, the 8-year-old who witnessed the end of his beloved aunt's life. He consoles his mother, wraps his arms around her, and encourages her to breathe.

Each family member suffers from some heart sickness. While this 8-year-old boy attempts to console his mother, who ministers aid to his trauma after he witnessed the violent end to his aunt's life, and the loss of the matriarch and the patriarch of these families? Who heals his psychic wounds? What happens when such mental injuries are unresolved and carried over into manhood? What does a wellness check look like for a person from the African diaspora? What does it mean to have others outside of this community who have care or concern for people of African descent? Historically, within the community, the treatment of the trauma has been almost non-existent.[7] The commodification of African bodies has meant that, as property, they possess no feelings, no emotions, no wounds, nor heartbreak. The confrontation with legal institutions and/or their agents, as evidenced above, make the trauma worse. We will keep those questions in mind as we consider the young boy, Othello, who appears in Venice as a man in Shakespeare's seventeenth-century drama.

This article submits that the socio-psychological and the clinical psychiatric effects of racial trauma on Moors not only emerge on the early modern stage, but also manifest themselves in both legal and cultural consequences for the Moor, and reap identifiable behaviours characterized by the larger society.[8] By focusing on the psychological perspective, I investigate how racial injury affects the perception of the Blackamoor as the stereotypically aggressive and cruelly violent warrior, as framed in legal spaces.[9] While racial trauma has been acknowledged, this narrative has not been read with the Moor, as a military figure across several dramas and playwrights.[10] Specifically, I argue that the space where Othello shares his traumatic narrative is complicated and unsafe. Second, Iago functions as a tool to safeguard ideas of supremacy by racially traumatizing Othello within a conspiratorial framework. Finally, I submit that Othello's suicide and Desdemona's murder serve to represent violent self-hatred and betrayal that stem from the preceding trauma the audience witnesses in the play. I consider the impetuous murder of Desdemona by 'the

---

[5] Bob D'Angelo, 'Atatiana Jefferson shooting: victim's father dies of heart attack, family says', *The Atlanta-Journal Constitution*, 10 November 2019.
[6] Erica Pettway, 'Mother dies months after her daughter, Atatiana Jefferson, killed in house by Fort Worth officer', *CBS42.com*, 9 January 2020.
[7] Alex Pieterse, 'Perceived racism and mental health among Black American adults', *Journal of Counseling Psychology* 59 (2012), 1–9.
[8] I presented an earlier version of this article before medical professionals as an Erikson Scholar at the Austen Riggs Center at Stockbridge, Massachusetts, on 26 September 2016.
[9] Naomi Inoue, 'Evaluation of a treatment outcome', *Rorschachiana* 30 (2009), 180–218.
[10] Some scholars have discussed racial trauma in different contexts, including African literature, by Zoe Norridge, *Perceiving Pain in African Literature* (London, 2013), p. 87, and psychology, by Christopher Lane, 'The psychoanalysis of race: an introduction', *Discourse* 19 (Winter 1997), 3–20; p. 7.

warlike Moor' Othello (2.1.27). Even amidst written proofs of Roderigo and Iago's conspiracy, by the play's denouement Othello alone bears the weight of the prosecution. Examining these spaces through multidisciplinary lenses offers an opportunity to represent the past by unpacking the past and the present using literature, medicine and law. 'To say that "what is known" must include the present will seem self-evident, but it may be less obvious that historical authenticity resides not in the fidelity to an alleged past but in an honesty vis-à-vis the present as it re-presents that past.'[11] Ultimately, I am developing a theory of racialized trauma that evolves among these warriors as they navigate within these early modern dramas, and that yields a method for this society to read and receive this warring Moor.

As I consider legal institutions, I must also embrace how medicine measures trauma.[12] Racial trauma – a persistent consequence of historical trauma – and its effects emerge as devastating across the African diaspora.[13] In effect, this trauma inflicts 'real and perceived danger, threats', bystander harm, or events both shameful and humiliating to similar members of the global majority, which include circumstances that are sudden, uncontrollable and 'emotionally overwhelming'.[14] Racial trauma may present itself in response to racism, including but not limited to discrimination and microaggressions that provoke stress and trauma reactions – and may be recurring, systemic and intergenerational. The effects of racial trauma may devastate one's wellbeing and physical health, and lead to psychological distress, and a psychosocial impact (i.e., poor self-image and self-hatred), and erosion of familial and communal relationships.[15]

This evolution in the field of psychology yields a framework for discussing William Shakespeare's play *Othello*, and the critical scholarship offers different interventions for examining the play's psychological dynamics. Traditionally, and for varied reasons, students, scholars and actors across the

[11] Michel-Roph Trouillot, *Silencing the Past: Power and the Production of History* (Boston, MA, 1995).

[12] For discussion on measuring trauma, see R. Mollica, L. MacDonald, M. Massagli and D. Silove, 'Measuring trauma – measuring torture: healing the wounds of mass violence: Harvard Trauma Checklist revised (Cambodian version)', Harvard Program in Refugee Trauma, 1998.

[13] Compare Post-Traumatic Stress Syndrome: post-traumatic stress disorder, as defined by the American Psychiatric Association's *Diagnostic and Statistical Manual of Mental Disorders*, involves events that are 'generally outside the range of usual human experience, such as rape, military combat, bombing, torture, kidnapping, incarceration as a prisoner of war or in a death camp, and accidents or natural catastrophes involving serious and widespread physical injury'. Such events, or 'stressors' regularly produce a variety of related symptoms, among them 'recurrent painful, intrusive recollections of the event' and dreams or nightmares during which the event is re-experienced; psychic numbing; sleep disorders; hyperalertness; irritability, anxiety, and depression. DSM-IV foregrounds the intrusive recollections and their disruptiveness and expands on the term 'disassociativelike states'. Recurrent, intrusive recollections, commonly termed flashbacks, can take varying forms, but in general they tend to be powerfully visual, even photographic': American Psychiatric Association, *Diagnostic and Statistical Manual of Mental Disorders DSM-IV* (Washington, DC, 1994), p. 26. See also Cathy Caruth, *Unclaimed Experience: Trauma, Narrative, and History* (Baltimore, 1996).

[14] In 1970, Joseph L. White, considered by many as the 'godfather' of the field of Black psychology, published his article 'Toward a Black psychology', in which he argued the need to develop a theory of Black psychology that would not have the pitfall that white psychology seems to utilize to analyse the African diaspora (*Ebony* (1970), 5). See also Reginald Jones, *Black Psychology* (New York, 1998). During the late twentieth century, several figures contributed to advancing this field with their work: Frances Cress Welsing's book *The Isis Papers: The Keys to the Colors* (London, 1991) confronts the truth about the sociopolitical creation of race categories; and Linda James Myers's book *Understanding an Afrocentric Worldview: An Introduction to an Optimal Psychology* (Washington, DC, 1996) advances the conversation around Africana-centred psychology. See also 'The Cress Theory of color-confrontation', *The Black Scholar* 5 (1974), 32–40 by Frances Cress Welsing.

[15] Nkechinyelum A. Chionesо, Carla D. Hunter, Robyn L. Gobin, Shardé McNeil Smith, Ruby Mendenhall and Helen A. Neville, 'Community healing and resistance through storytelling: a framework to address racial trauma in Africana communities', *Journal of Black Psychology* 46 (2020), 95–121.

diaspora find the play difficult to receive.[16] Ostensibly, we can hearken back to the concern with the mythology that saturates the oppression of the African diaspora.[17] My article endeavours to dispel these myths, which have been globalized to support racist notions to advance a capitalist agenda. The hijacking of the 'idea of Africa', which emerges as the title of V. Y. Mudimbe's book, speaks to the myth-making phenomenon by actors outside of the diaspora in terms of the continent.[18] We find these notions occur in Shakespeare's *Othello*, and perhaps earlier in Giraldi Cinthio's *Hecatommithi* as well.[19] I think we should start from the place where Ben Okri, in his book *A Way of Being Free*, suggests that *Othello* must be viewed as 'the white man's myth of the black man'.[20] Kim Hall addresses the manipulation of the conceptions of Blackness in the introduction to her edition of *Othello: Texts and Contexts* (p. 3). In her play *Desdemona*, Toni Morrison extends this mythology as she explains the illogical manner in which Desdemona creates a fantastical narrative about Othello, and delivers an intergenerational exploration of racial trauma. Likewise, Keith Anthony Cobb re-narrates the play in his text *American Moor*, in whose Introduction Kim Hall says: 'With effort, we can undo and redo the Shakespeare scripts, the scripts about Shakespeare that we have inherited, and the scripts of Anglo-American life.' Exploring the trauma and the myth-making, Morrison and Cobb take up the cause with this play.[21]

In this article, I examine legal spaces, racial trauma and how we evaluate those circumstances as they evolve from one moment to the next in Shakespeare's *Othello*. Simply put, I ask: 'How does Othello defend himself against propaganda, conspiracy, and the weight of evidence amidst these psychic injuries?'

DEVELOPING OTHELLO'S THEORY OF DEFENCE

'For an abuser of the world, a practiser / Of arts inhibited and out of warrant.' (Brabantio, 1.2.78–9)

Upon the entrance of Brabantio and Othello to the Senate in act 1, scene 3, the Duke of Venice asks: 'What's the matter?' (1.3.59)[22] In essence, the

---

[16] See Imtiaz Habib, 'Racial impersonation on the Elizabethan stage: the case of Shakespeare playing Aaron', *Old Dominion University Commons* (2007), 32. See also Keith Hamilton Cobb's *American Moor* (London and New York, 2020); and Ayanna Thompson's 'Introduction' to William Shakespeare, *Othello*, rev. ed., ed. E. A. J. Honigmann (London, 2016), p. 90, where she discusses Adrian Lester's approach to playing the title role.

[17] See also Hugh Butts, who opens discussion on racial trauma in the twenty-first century in his article entitled 'The Black mask of humanity: racial/ethnic discrimination and post-traumatic stress disorder', *Journal of the American Academy of Psychiatry and the Law* 30 (2002), 336–9, in which he emphasizes the problematic tendency of European Americans to cleave to myths and stereotypes about people from the African diaspora (p. 336).

[18] V. Y. Mudimbe, *The Idea of Africa* (Bloomington and Indianapolis, 1994).

[19] See Kim Hall's 'Introduction' to Kim F. Hall, ed., *Othello, the Moor of Venice: Texts and Contexts* (Boston, MA, 2007), where she discusses 'Stories of race and place' (pp. 2–10).

[20] Ben Okri, *A Way of Being Free* (London, 2015), p. 63. See Thompson's discussion of Okri in her 'Introduction' to *Othello*, ed. Honigmann (pp. 63–4). Please note that, hereafter, when discussing the *Othello* Arden edition with Thompson's 'Introduction', I will refer to it as *Othello Arden Revised*.

[21] Edward Pechter's 2004 edition (New York and London) discourses upon the problematic discussions of Othello's Blackness, particularly in its performance history, by scholars on both sides of the pond (p. 173). In his 2006 Oxford edition of Shakespeare's play, Michael Neill discusses the vexed and contradictory audience responses to Blackness or 'colour' in the early modern performances (p. 2). Leah Marcus observes the danger of Othello's Blackness and its proximity to others in her book *How Shakespeare Became Colonial: Editorial Traditions and the British Empire* (London, 2017), pp. 19, 43. While Katharine Eisaman Maus examines some issues of psychology, she emphasizes the legal aspects of proof and consequences in her book *Inwardness and the Theater in the English Renaissance* (Chicago and London, 1995). Virginia Mason Vaughan's *Othello* yields rigorous discussion on the concept of the early modern cultural understanding of 'Moor' (Vaughan, *Performing Blackness on English Stages, 1500–1800* (Cambridge, 2005) p. 5), while Ian Smith's discussion, in his article 'We are Othello: speaking of race in early modern studies' (*Shakespeare Quarterly* 67 (2016), 104–24), engages in this notion that investigates the critical and cultural conversations around this tragic figure.

[22] This question possesses not only legal echoes, but historical ones. See *The Destruction of Black Civilization: Great Issues of a Race from 4500 B.C. to 2000 A.D.* (Chicago, 1987) by

entire scene unfolds like a courtroom where the court disposes of multiple matters. Before the entrance of Othello and Brabantio, the Senate deals with the matter of the Ottomans, Cyprus and the imminent attack which poses a threat to Venice. At the temporary close of this issue, this body turns its attention to the matter of *Senator Brabantio of Venice versus General Othello the Moor*. Here, Shakespeare offers the audience a scene that we do not receive in Giraldi Cinthio's source novella, *Hecatommithi* (1565). Briefly, Cinthio mentions the reluctance of Desdemona's family regarding the marriage between her and the Moor, writing: 'Although the Lady's relatives did all they could to make her take another husband, they were united in marriage' (p. 376). Instead, Shakespeare presents what in 21st-century nomenclature would be considered a high-profile political case that appears to read as a domestic civil case. Amidst the political and domestic dynamics, Othello must develop a legal theory of defence to address Brabantio's accusations.[23] The accused has two options for his defence: (1) deny those facts (or one of them) as explained by the plaintiff, here Brabantio; or (2) admit those facts and demonstrate that the plaintiff is not entitled to succeed.[24]

In response to the Duke's inquiry, Brabantio explains to the court how Othello the Moor with some mysterious dark arts, 'by spells and medicines bought of mountebanks' (1.3.62), has pilfered his honourable and cherished daughter Desdemona from the safety of his protection and household. In this scene, Brabantio, like Iago throughout this drama, plays upon the stereotypes about Africanness. Several scholars proffer explanations to illuminate these stereotypes. 'The African figure', Mudimbe writes, 'was an empirical fact, yet by definition it was perceived, experienced, and promoted as the sign of the absolute otherness' (p. 38). 'Racial otherness allows white man to lump all 'others' (male and female) into another, less valued, group' (Hall 182). This concept of otherness rests upon the institutional foundation of colonialism or colonization, which derives from the Latin meaning, 'to cultivate' or 'to design' (Mudimbe 1). This design or cultivation of Africa prefaces 'depopulation' using violence and genocide by the colonizers.[25] In *Racecraft: The Soul of Inequality in America*, Karen E. Fields and Barbara J. Fields explain:[26]

A colonial rule does not just want the natives to bow down and render obeisance to their new sovereign. The natives must also grow food, pay taxes, go to work in mines and on estates, provide conscripts for the army and help to hold the line against rival powers. In effect, the colonizers and natives negotiate a 'social terrain', which maps the boundaries of the relationship and if the terrain changes, so must their activities and the map.

In early modern Italy, most representations of Africans depicted them as either enslaved or formerly enslaved.[27] Perhaps, to understand these dynamics and their history, we should ask – as previous legal scholars such as Derrick Bell have – 'How does the human spirit accommodate itself to desolation? How did they? What tools of the spirit were in their hands with which to cut a path through the wilderness of their despair?'[28] Do the answers provide the secrets to survival of racial

---

Chancellor Williams, where he asks: 'what had happened? How was this highly advanced Black Civilization so completely destroyed that its people for our times and for some centuries past have found themselves not only behind the other peoples of the world, but as well, the color of their skin a sign of inferiority, bad luck, and the badge of the slave whether bond or free?' (p. 18). See also Trouillot, *Silencing the Past*. Trouillot applies the interrogatory – 'what happened' – to how we perceive the concept of 'history' (p. 2).

[23] See also Mitchell N. Berman, 'Justification and excuse, law and morality', *Duke Law Journal* 5 (2003), 1–77. This article addresses some of the legal theories of defence, which not only are used during a trial, but may also be used by courts for instructing juries.

[24] J. H. Baker, *An Introduction to English Legal History*, 3rd ed. (London and Boston, MA, 2004), p. 91.

[25] Sven Lindqvist examines the nineteenth century in his book *Exterminate All the Brutes*, trans. Joan Tate (London, 1997), pp. 122–3. See also Raoul Peck's HBO documentary *Exterminate All the Brutes* (2021).

[26] Karen E. Fields and Barbara J. Fields, *Racecraft: The Soul of Inequality in America* (London, 2012), pp. 139–40.

[27] See T. F. Earle and K. J. P. Lowe, *Black Africans in Renaissance Europe* (Cambridge, 2005), p. 282.

[28] Derrick Bell discusses how to decolonize the mind, and Dr Howard Thurman's questions, in his book *And We Are*

oppression passed from the humanity of African ancestors (p. 217)?

These multiple lenses – legal, medical and racial – provide additional ways of reading this scene before the Senate in this matter of *Brabantio* versus *Othello*. For example, let us not forget how Brabantio threatens Othello with 'peril' (1.2.81) and 'prison' (1.2.85) at 1.2 before arriving at the Senate. After having been exposed to dangerous and deadly stressors, 'what are the impacts of generations of slavery and oppression on a - people?'[29] First, what are the effects of slavery and oppression for Othello? Whether Othello with his words seems undaunted by the threat made before witnesses – particularly, one of his men, Iago – is not definitive. Second, the very important fact here is that Brabantio has threatened the life of Othello and seeks the law to help him to carry out his threat. In essence, he seeks to weaponize the law for his personal benefit. In answering these questions, an examination of the speech that Othello makes before the Venetian Senate, which I address later, is quite instructive.

Even more compelling is the *effect* of the text on Othello – the commentary that Keith Anthony Cobb presents in his play *American Moor* complements the analysis of the words from the perspective of an actor grounded within the African diaspora and playing this pivotal role. Cobb's play presents the audience at least two opposing mentalities – confidence, and crippling fear and foreboding – which Othello embodies: 'Othello enters that scene like I just entered this dingy-ass, empty, cold motherfucking' room, under scrutiny, his boyhood dreams now unrealizable, those of adulthood clearly in jeopardy, and immediately aware that who he *is* is not the *he* either sought or seen by those he stands before' (p. 37). With both fear and fearlessness, Othello, according to Cobb, confronts Brabantio and the Senate. Faced with Brabantio's vengeful outrage, General Othello enters the Venetian Senate and is presented with a quandary: does he share his intimate thoughts with these stately men? Othello the Moor is always cognizant of his minoritized position, yet he must place, even temporarily, his consternation aside and unpack the depth of his humanity with this political body:

In his heart, he is an invincible, indestructible powerhouse of a boy, with a deep, boyish desire to please, to be praised, to make people proud of him ... he shouts from the shore from the bottom of his voice to the top of his mighty lungs so as they hear him back across the Strait of Gibraltar, in Morocco, Mauritania and back through the ages of his people's glorious past, 'Have I not done well? Am I not wonderful just as you?' (p. 37)

Within this space, past and present oscillate for Othello.[30] He calls on his ancestors, and seeks their approval and their strength. With this ancestral power accompanying Othello, will these senators and the Duke see the wonder of Othello the Moor, or his many accomplishments? '*This* is what stands before that senate, his human being seeping out of every pore. And I suspect that among them they would say, because I have heard them say it of me, with words and without, "Where does he get his balls so big to act like *everything* that he is?"' (p. 37).

I think Cobb's question is answered by the ancestral power, which exudes from Othello the Moor – this general presents himself as the epitome of leadership, honour, fidelity and strength. At the same time, we find the problematic word 'resilience' seems relevant, but ever more powerful is an unabating and immovable hope planted by his African ancestors. At the same time, he also describes another feeling – less confident and grandiose: 'in all those other once so impregnable places not quite head and not quite heart of a body begun

---

Not Saved: The Elusive Quest for Racial Justice (New York, 1989), pp. 215–31.

[29] Dr Joy DeGruy, in her book *Post-Traumatic Slave Syndrome: America's Legacy of Enduring Injury and Healing* (Milwaukie, OR, 2005), asks this question. Using the *Diagnostic and Statistical Manual of Mental Disorders V*, she describes the criterion A stressor for PTSD, stating 'the person was exposed to: death, threatened death, actual or threatened serious injury, or actual threatened sexual violence either directly, as a witness, indirectly, or repeated or extreme indirect exposure to aversive details of the event(s)' (pp. 101–2).

[30] See also Toni Morrison's *Desdemona*, lyrics by Rokia Traoré, Oberon Modern Plays (London, 2012).

to betray him, he knows he is old ... He knows he is epileptic ... He knows by now that no one is going to erect a statute on the Rialto to the memory of the great General Othello, the Moor' (p. 37). The actor, Keith Anthony Cobb, describes a level of introspection and transparency to reveal this character, Othello, that shifts focus from physical to medical impediments. Even further, this description uncovers, through a series of rhetorical questions, Othello's vulnerable mental faculties:

What did you call his situation, 'dire'? He smiles, compensating for despair that you have no clue, nor the first genuine concern what is, in fact, dire about his situation. His smile is like an involuntary spasm on the edge of insanity. How does one maintain one's sanity when so much of what one is has forever been held in such strict and unnecessary abeyance by others' fears and the rules that one never agreed to? You want mental fragility, all the tiny little cracks in Othello's armor that might make him finally snap completely and kill someone, even if that someone were the solitary love of his life?

(pp. 37–8)

In this moment amidst all these complicated emotions of fear, fragility and violence, Othello presents his theory of defence to Brabantio's allegations that refutes his father-in-law's slanderous remarks before the Senate. He embraces, assents to and raises the stakes of the judicial body's judgment. Yet, problematically, this space does not embody a place for truth and justice, but one where – in order to defeat this threat to his life, liberty and humanity – Othello must re-enact his life-long history of trauma. He understands that the only way the Senate will displace the evil depiction that Brabantio's allegations have created is for him to perform, re-enact, the painful trauma that has heretofore hastened his arrival in Venice. Before General Othello enters this space, he realizes his worth to the Senate as a warrior to defeat the Turks and save Venice, for he knows his 'services ... shall out-tongue [Brabantio's] complaints' (1.2.17–18). Nevertheless, this factor does not mean he does not experience the fallout from revisiting the trauma, 'on the edge of sanity' (p. 38), which he must enact again and again to justify his presence, liberty and purpose.

Within this Venetian court, Othello embarks upon what Cathy Caruth calls 'an unconscious historical testimony', creating a site for historical memory and offering 'notions of what it means to remember'.[31] Yet I submit that, especially for this Venetian court, Othello's testimony is quite conscious. Michel-Roph Trouillot suggests that 'the past is constantly evoked as the starting point of an ongoing trauma and as a necessary explanation to current inequalities suffered by blacks'.[32] The moment demonstrates this 'ongoing trauma' when Othello begins with a backstory in the monologue that he presents to the assembly to explain and defend his secret marriage to the Venetian Senator Brabantio's daughter, Desdemona, and rebutt arguments of a mystical seduction:

OTHELLO Her father loved me, oft invited me,
Still questioned me the story of my life
From year to year – the battles, sieges, fortunes
That I have passed.
I ran it through, even from my boyish days
To th' very moment that he bade me tell it,
Wherein I spake of most disastrous chances,
Of moving accidents by flood and field,
Of hair-breadth scapes i'th' imminent deadly breach

(1.3.129–38)

The performance of this narrative reads with multiple layers of complications. As outlined above, while Othello shares his love story, most conspicuously he reveals that Senator Brabantio invited him as a guest into his home. Othello is not, as Brabantio depicts, a thief or an interloper. The general's narrative tells how the hospitality moves from his being a dinner guest to being a trusted friend, and, eventually and predictably, to a noble suitor. At the same time, this stately locale creates

---

[31] See Cathy Caruth, *Listening to Trauma: Conversations with Leaders in the Theory and Treatment of Catastrophic Experience* (Baltimore, 2014), p. xiii.
[32] See Trouillot's discussion in *Silencing the Past*, p. 17, which also extends to the African diaspora.

what resembles a legal trial after his interrogation by Brabantio from the earlier scene. Desdemona's father, Brabantio, invites Othello to share 'the story of [his] life / From year to year' (1.3.130–1). Othello the Moor begins this narrative from his 'boyish days' (1.3.133) until the present day. This character hearkens back to his stage predecessor, Aaron the Moor, a 'combat survivor and prisoner of war and victim of slavery' in *Titus Andronicus*,[33] and simultaneously speaks to a 21st-century child soldier, Agu, navigating violence in a war-torn, fictional West African country in Uzodinma Iweala's novel *Beasts of No Nation*.[34]

In a hostile setting, Othello shares the tales of his victories, particularly those 'battles, sieges, fortunes', through 'epithets of war' (1.1.13), 'the trade of war' (1.2.1) and shifts from the 'most disastrous chances / Of moving accidents by flood and field' (1.3.135–6) with natural catastrophes to the most deadly ones. These embattled phrases evoke for me the figure of the playwright Terence who is depicted in an image, entitled, 'Terence exchanging his comedies for freedom'.[35] Using his own tragic memories, Othello also exchanges an autobiography filled with the 'flinty steel couch of war' (1.3.230) not only for the entertainment of Brabantio and the audience, but for his liberty as well. Othello tells:

> Of being taken by the insolent foe
> And sold to slavery; of my redemption thence
> And portance in my travailous history;
> Wherein of antres vast and deserts idle,
> Rough quarries, rocks and hills whose heads
>   touch heaven
>
> (1.3.139–43)

He presents the audience two tales – one elicits the 'romance' of war, and the other lays bare its soul-crushing trauma. Within this journey, we learn from Othello that he was not always the leader of men on the battlefield, nor on the seas, but he was taken captive by the enemy 'and sold to slavery' (1.3.139). Again, we can connect his autobiography/testimony to those shared about Terence, by way of Suetonius – emphasizing the rise from slavery to affluence – and Petrarch – distinguishing himself from Terence the senator.[36] Othello describes an epoch that is difficult – emotionally and geographically, which evokes Raoul Peck's visually stunning portrayal of the geography of genocide, the suffering in slavery, and the tumult of trauma in his 2021 HBO four-part documentary *Exterminate All the Brutes*.[37] The story explains a global and historical phenomenon, including the little boy from Haiti who determined to narrate this story. Instead of Peck's 'Everyman' who stands in place of the white colonizer, here, we have, in Shakespeare, Othello the Moor, who stands in place of the indigenous colonized. While he does not share the specific circumstances of his own slavery, nor the details of his redemption, Othello refers to this chapter in his narrative as his 'travailous history' (1.3.140). From vast caves and deserts, he navigates rough terrains filled with quarries, rocks and hills of tremendous heights whose peaks 'touch heaven' (1.3.142). Othello faces the demands found from man as well: 'It was my hint to speak – such was my process' (1.3.143). In his travels, he discovers vast representations of culture, behaviour and violence – which also brings us into remembrance of Shakespeare's Caliban and his relentless servitude in *The Tempest*.[38] Peck's documentary and Shakespeare's drama through Caliban examine the nature of oppression and supremacy and how it is perceived by the indigenous populations and colonizers, and essentially exposes the

---

[33] Deborah Willis, 'Gnawing vulture, revenge, trauma theory, and Titus', *Shakespeare Quarterly* 53 (Spring 2002), 21–52; p. 25.
[34] Uzodinma Iweala, *Beasts of No Nation* (New York, 2005). See also Morrison's reference to Othello as a child soldier in her re-imagining of Shakespeare's play, *Desdemona* (p. 36).
[35] Misha Teramura, 'Black comedy: Shakespeare, Terence, and Titus Andronicus', *ELH* 85 (Winter 2018), 877–908; p. 887.
[36] Teramura, 'Black comedy', p. 881.
[37] See Lindqvist, *Exterminate All the Brutes*.
[38] See also Hortense Spillers's reference to Caliban as he echoes in the works of Césaire's *Discourse on Colonialism*, Fanon's *Black Skin, White Masks* and Mannoni's *Psychology of Colonialism* (*Black, White, and in Color: Essays on American Literature and Culture* (Chicago and London, 2003), p. 577, n. 10).

binaries of slavery and capitalism which exist within this society of exploration, and which Shakespeare portrays through his plays, such as *Othello*. Peck 'describes a different representation of the indigenous figure'. In her review, Jo Livingstone observed: 'In it, [Peck] lays out the history of race-based violence as defined by postcolonial scholars of history, such as Gayatri Chakravorty Spivak and Frantz Fanon, who have worked to dismantle the myths (the white man's burden, manifest destiny, Aryanism, et al) that disguise whiteness as "natural" or a default state of being.'[39] In the same way that Raoul Peck presents those binaries in his documentary, we see them evoked not only in the legal dynamics before the Venetian Senate and the Duke, but over the course of the play as well.

Within this drama, Shakespeare provides us with this kind of figure in Othello, who teeters on the edges of this popular imagery across five acts. As the chronicle of his life continues, Othello yields a testimony that seeks to persuade the Venetian court in a way that contravenes social history: 'They do not tell us just what such a study would look like, and why centuries of testimony by people of color regarding their experiences, including individuals like Frederick Douglass, W.E.B. DuBois, Charles Wright and Toni Morrison, are not measure enough.'[40] The effect of testimony can unfold as creating a historical narrative, empathy, or trauma pornography. In contravention to lived experience, here in this play, Othello weaves a tale that not only persuaded Desdemona but attempts to convince the state's highest officials:

> This to hear
> Would Desdemona seriously incline,
> But still the house affairs would draw her thence,
> Which ever as she could with haste dispatch
> She'd come again, and with a greedy ear
> Devour up my discourse; which I, observing,
> Took once a pliant hour and found good means
> To draw from her a prayer of earnest heart
> That I would all my pilgrimage dilate,
> Whereof by parcels she had something heard
> But not intentively. I did consent,
> And often did beguile her of her tears
> When I did speak of some distressful stroke
> That my youth suffered.
>
> (1.3.143–56)

Does his story echo the more recent songs of 'ongoing trauma' from figures such as Lucy Terry Prince, whose story is detailed by Nafissa Thompson-Spires in *Four Hundred Souls*[41] or even the traumatic lyrics crafted by Rokia Traoré in Morrison's *Desdemona*? For General Othello the Moor, the anecdotes from his life took a turn when his audience changed from Brabantio to his daughter, Desdemona. He was moved by her desire to hear his story and often would expand this discourse on his 'pilgrimage' (1.3.154). Seducing tears from Desdemona, Othello could not ignore the emotional impact of his words for 'some distressful stroke / That my youth suffered' (1.3.155–6). By presenting impending war as a backdrop in the play, Othello's war trauma appears accessible, but 'slavery yielded stressors that were both disturbing and traumatic, exacting a wound upon the African American psyche that continues to fester'.[42] Yet most of the African diaspora experienced these psychic wounds, including Othello. Even in this 21st-century moment, we have 'ocular proof' (3.3.363) of slavery, in the case of Libya, and tepid global responses to that tangible evidence.[43] This proof is 'the strongest kind of evidence in both English and Continental courts'.[44] How does the audience beyond the Venetian assembly respond to Othello's wounds?

---

[39] Jo Livingstone, 'Raoul Peck's *Exterminate All the Brutes* insists on telling what really happened', *The New Republic*, 16 April 2021.

[40] Bell, *And We Are Not Saved*, p. 81.

[41] Nafissa Thompson-Spires, 'Lucy Terry Prince, 1744–1749', in *Four Hundred Souls*, ed. Ibram X. Kendi and Keisha N. Blain (New York, 2021), p. 117.

[42] De Gruy, *Post-Traumatic Slave Syndrome*, p. 101.

[43] Patrick Wintour, 'Fake news: Libya seizes on Trump tweet to discredit CNN slavery report', *The Guardian*, 28 November 2017.

[44] Maus, *Inwardness and the Theater*, p. 118.

Arguably, the playwright, the patient or the speaker wants the audience's, the doctor's and the listener's empathy. Some studies of trauma refer to 'empathy' as 'an undeniable miracle', along with 'love', in response to experienced trauma.[45] Even Desdemona could not quell the empathetic effect of Othello's annals upon her:

> My story being done
> She gave me for my pains a world of sighs,
> She swore in faith 'twas strange, 'twas passing strange,
> 'Twas pitiful, 'twas wondrous pitiful;
> She wished she had not heard it, yet she wished
> That heaven had made her such a man. She thanked me
> And bade me, if I had a friend that loved her,
> I should but teach him how to tell my story
> And that would woo her.
>
> (1.3.159–67)

In the sharing of his own journey to Venice, Othello found that Desdemona's response was not merely 'passing strange' and 'wondrous pitiful', but she was open to being wooed by this Moor – she knew him and loved every detail of his life. She does not surrender mere empathy, but something perhaps more significant – that is, humanity. The fight against Brabantio's unadulterated rage, supremacy and oppression relies upon humanity. In this trial or hearing, does Othello's recitation of his life history and his history with Desdemona recover the humanity that earlier scenes with Brabantio, Iago and Roderigo attempt to destroy?[46]

Clearly, this shift in Othello's story from the autobiographical slave narrative to a Venetian romance should not be overlooked. It is the slave narrative that consumes Brabantio. It is the slave narrative that captures the imagination of the attendees in the audience. It is the slave narrative that finances the global voyages to begin the racial capitalism that builds nations. The shift to the romantic disturbs Brabantio. The shift to the romantic disturbs some attendees, based on their 'hostile' reception to Ira Aldridge's performance of Othello.[47] The distaste for the shift to the romantic serves as the basis for anti-miscegenation laws not only in the United States but across the African diaspora.[48] Othello's response was swift and life-altering:

> Upon this hint I spake:
> She loved me for the dangers I had passed,
> And I loved her that she did pity them.
> This only is the witchcraft I have used
>
> (1.3.165–8)

Here, we have a report on his childhood, a history of battle, and his courtship of Desdemona. In a seemingly therapeutic and socially engaging way, Othello retells the traumas of war, violence, capture and enslavement. Does Othello share this story in a safe space, amongst confidants, allies and loved ones? Will we see that, after the telling of his story, he has won the day with this audience that possesses ulterior motives? Notably, Othello possesses a very special skill set that is needed to maintain the safety of the Venetians – is he only truly imperilled after he is no longer needed to secure the state's physical and economic safety? What is the cumulative effect of dismissing, ignoring or refusing to engage substantively with the story of Othello? Yet this drama does not limit the engagement with this narrative through Iago's soliloquies, but also stages the re-enactment of battle with the 'clink and fall of swords' (2.3.230) in the fight scenes between Othello's lieutenant, Cassio, and the former governor of Cyprus, Montano, in this 'town of war' (2.3.209) at 2.3. In the following section, we will examine how Iago's soliloquies and monologues instigate Othello's continued trauma, through what might be called Othello's

---

[45] For discussion on why more than empathy is needed, see Françoise Davoine and Jean-Max Gaudillière, *History beyond Trauma* (New York, 2004), p. 59.
[46] See Christina Sharpe, *In the Wake: On Blackness and Being* (Durham and London, 2016), p. 55.
[47] See Ayanna Thompson's Introduction to *Othello Arden Revised*, p. 1.
[48] See discussion of miscegenation in Leah S. Marcus, 'The two texts of "Othello" and early modern constructions of race', in *Textual Performances: The Modern Reproduction of Shakespeare's Drama*, ed. Lukas Erne and Margaret Jane Kidnie (Cambridge, 2004), pp. 24–5.

own post-traumatic distress disorder, to demonstrate how white supremacy requires consistent instigation of racial trauma.[49]

It is this constant demand to justify himself that brings to mind a statement by Toni Morrison:

The function, the very serious function of racism is distraction. It keeps you from doing your work. It keeps you explaining, over and over again, your reason for being. Somebody says you have no language, and you spend twenty years proving that you do. Somebody says your head isn't shaped properly so you have scientists working on the fact that it is. Somebody says you have no art, so you dredge that up. Somebody says you have no kingdoms, so you dredge that up. None of this is necessary. There will always be one more thing.[50]

In spite of its effect on the community of the African diaspora, what occurs within social structure, or publicly, is distraction, trauma and an attempt to redirect one's energy. For example, here, instead of preparing for the upcoming battle against the Turks, Othello is justifying how he was successfully able to court Desdemona when others, including Roderigo, failed. It has long been recognized as a devastatingly harmful pattern. It is harmful to the African diaspora, and it is harmful to the larger community, for, by demanding participation in the pointless justification of one's existence, success, station and presence in white spaces, everyone participates in a futile process that does not address the larger problem of the uncomfortability with blackness in any space.

Othello's presentation of his lifelong trauma wrapped in a love story serves to fight injustice and move the Senate to sympathy against the rash and defamatory statements levelled at him by Brabantio, his wife's father. His narrative dispels the gaps, the inconsistencies and the unsubstantiated story that Brabantio creates to fell Othello. At the end of the arguments, Brabantio's case evolves as outlandish in its execution and racist at its foundation. While I will address Iago's motivations later, I examine not only Othello's motives here, but, more importantly, Brabantio's motives within this scene.

Eventually, the Duke and the Senate are persuaded by the account of Othello and its responsiveness to Brabantio's allegations. What is the verdict that the Senate should reach after hearing both Brabantio's and Othello's accounts of this matter? The Senate has every reason to move against Brabantio, who did not bother to come to the Senate about the matter of the Turks, and to favour Othello who would help to see them resolve this military matter. In addition, General Othello is reputed as not only a capable warrior, but an honourable one. The Duke refers to the general as 'Valiant Othello' (1.3.49), but Senator 1 even more conspicuously calls him the 'valiant Moor' (1.3.48). This assembly has no reason to doubt the word of Othello – and they may have, based on previous interaction with Brabantio, reason to doubt his word. Here, Brabantio's allegations appear grounded not only in false claims of witchcraft and potions, but – more subtly – race and economics. To Brabantio's arguments, the Duke replies: 'To vouch this is no proof' (1.3.107). Is it possible that the issue becomes one of integrity, where Othello possesses a great measure and Brabantio's measure has been placed in question, particularly based on his performance before the Senate?

In sum, Othello's legal defence here emerges as successful against Brabantio's half-baked concoctions based in fiction, falsehoods and propaganda. At the end of this scene, rather than a celebratory tone after Othello wins the day, there is a sense of foreboding–foreshadowing. His father-in-law not only has placed (verbally) poison into his ear regarding Desdemona, but has in essence disowned her because she has confirmed Othello's story before the Senate. Brabantio's position is disturbingly disappointing and more complicated than it would appear:

---

[49] Della Mosley, Candice N. Hargons, Carolyn Meiller et al., 'Critical consciousness of anti-Black racism', *Journal of Counseling Psychology* (2021), 1–16.

[50] Toni Morrison, 'A humanist view', Oregon's Public Speakers Collection, Black Studies Center Public Dialogue, Part 2, 30 May 1975, Portland State University Library, Portland, Oregon. Keynote Speech.

> Look to her, Moor, if thou hast eyes to see:
> She has deceived her father, and may thee.
> (1.3.293–4)

He is not just a father who has had 'property', in terms of his daughter, taken without his permission, but a man who has determined for less honourable reasons to disown his daughter and his new son-in-law because of the latter's blackness. Ironically, Desdemona and Othello both know what it is to be propertied – based on gender and race.[51]

EXAMINING IAGO'S CONSPIRACY

> As I confess it is my nature's plague / To spy into abuses, and oft my jealousy / Shapes faults that are not.
> (*Iago*, 3.3.149–51)

In this examination of legal spaces, 1.1 presents a setting outside that of the courtroom hearing. Seemingly more truthful than a soliloquy, the following monologue exposes the oppressive machinations that occur away from public spaces.[52] With almost every sense, we, the audience, see, hear and feel Iago's animus that surpasses petty jealousy. In essence, the conversation, which we encounter between Iago and Roderigo at the outset of the play, presents two co-conspirators who determine to destroy Othello the Moor by any means necessary. For the purpose of this discussion, I define the concept of conspiracy as an 'agreement between two parties, who develop a partnership to commit some illegal act, and that has divided families, friends, and countrymen and women, as history and literature have proven'.[53]

While the nature of the underlying crime varies, the crime of conspiracy, its elements, its case law and its statutory prohibitions continue to evolve from its early fourteenth-century origins.[54] For example, Iago suggests an alternate scheme to Roderigo where Iago 'trimmed in forms and visages of duty', by 'keep[ing] yet their hearts attending on themselves', increases his economic and sociopolitical circumstances by 'throwing but shows of service on their lords' (1.1.49–51).

Although there exists an irrationality to the social construction of race if separated from its agenda of racial capitalism, by considering both racism and capitalism together, we provide a more effective institutional analysis of supremacy and oppression and how they manifest – for example, in unlawful behaviour.[55]

While some might argue that Cassius manoeuvred within a similar ethos when he served Julius Caesar, for Cassius the motive was power – Iago's motives emerge as more complex and sinister. Nevertheless, the final part of this speech delivers the violent rhetoric that defines Iago's commitment to his notions of supremacy: his 'nature's plague' and his 'jealousy'. Iago divulges two key facts in this portion of the speech: (1) 'In following [the Moor] I follow but myself'; and (2) 'I am not what I am' (1.1.57, 64). Iago articulates an intentional plan to wage a multi-tiered warfare against an unsuspecting Othello. This speech embodies the angry white male syndrome to supplant and

---

[51] See also Lisa M. Barksdale-Shaw, '"Did not great Julius bleed for justice' sake?"': examining a theory of social justice through will-making in Shakespeare's *Julius Caesar*', *Shakespeare in Southern Africa* 33 (2020), pp. 74–87 (n. 25).

[52] Recall the 2009 Matthew Shepard and James Byrd, Jr. Hate Crimes Prevention Act, which was signed into law by President Barack Obama on 28 October 2009. See also Tariro Mzezewa, 'Regardless of the verdict, Arbury murder suspects still face federal hate-crime charges', *New York Times*, 23 November 2021.

[53] See Lisa Barksdale-Shaw, '"That you are both decipher'd": revealing espionage and staging written evidence in early modern England', in *A Material History of Medieval and Early Modern Ciphers: Cryptography and the History of Literacy*, ed. Katherine Ellison and Susan Kim (New York and London, 2018), pp. 118–36.

[54] See also Baker's discussion on intimidation and conspiracy (*An Introduction to English Legal History*, pp. 523–9).

[55] Cedric J. Robinson, *Cedric J. Robinson: On Racial Capitalism, Black Internationalism, and Cultures of Resistance*, ed. H. L. T. Quan (London, 2019). He writes 'Only the clever manipulation of the threat of black dominance has kept the underprivileged white masses and the privileged upper classes of the South from coming to a parting of the political ways' (p. 177). See his discussion of studying racism and capitalism together (p. 77).

destroy his target.[56] Here, the target is Othello, his superior – not a head of state, as in *Julius Caesar*. It begs the questions: 'Why is the white man so angry? Why is he being so careless about the impact of his anger? Why doesn't he notice the effect this outburst is having on the few people of color in the room?'[57] Is the issue for Iago truly hatred? Nevertheless, Iago's actions serve as proxy for treason against Venice, which hired General Othello to safeguard its nation state.[58] Iago seeks to topple Othello, not merely for the purse that Roderigo supplies, but for his own dissatisfaction and reasons that bear no proof in the action on the stage. Not unlike the Duke of Venice's protestations for proof of Brabantio's allegations about Othello's witchcraft: 'Without more certain and more overt test / Than these thin habits and poor likelihoods / Of modern seeming do prefer against him' (1.1.108–10). In the same way, Iago has no rational bases upon which to ground his hatred, his enmity, his detestation, his ill will and malevolence.

Typically, the motives of this conspiracy are not jealousy, but something much more insidious. Iago evolves as the vehicle whereby racial oppression, antagonism and decimation run throughout the drama. By colonizing the political against those who are marginalized by race, he wages a war against Othello, which results in a devastating attack at the very core of his person – his personal life and his career.[59] We should not overlook, underestimate or dismiss the use of white supremacy – to do so would encourage reading this scene and the entire play without the extremely nuanced gradations that Shakespeare provides, intentionally or not, in this complicated play centring General Othello the Moor of Venice. From Samuel Coleridge to Kyle Grady, an examination of Iago's motives entails a long history in literary scholarship.[60] Yet, in this analysis, we examine motivation through legal, psychological and racial lenses that reveal more than poetic licence: sinister and malevolent implications, which possess real-life consequences.[61]

Within this play, Iago introduces an ideological framework that exists during this early modern moment. Race and racecraft emerge as a global project of colonialism, imperialism and capitalism, which essentially devastates every continent.[62] The need for African bodies to serve capitalist projects on a global scale becomes prescient and sufficient to alienate and dehumanize. With the Spanish Inquisition and the discovery doctrine, this ideology spreads in methods from every institution – religious, social, financial and political.[63]

The mythology of the superiority of whiteness remains foundational as the antithesis to recognizing

---

[56] See Carol Anderson, *White Rage: The Unspoken Truth of Our Racial Divide* (New York and London, 2017). She observes that 'Republican South Carolina senator Lindsey Graham, taking stock of the nearly inevitable apocalypse, put it best: "We're not generating enough angry white guys to stay in business for the long term"' (p. 139).

[57] Robin DiAngelo, *White Fragility: Why It's So Hard for White People to Talk about Racism* (Boston, MA, 2018), p. 1.

[58] See Rebecca Lemon, *Treason by Words: Literature, Law, and Rebellion in Shakespeare's England* (Ithaca and London, 2006). Consider her discussion of the 1534 Treason Act (p. 8).

[59] For discussion of decolonizing the political, see Mahmood Mamdani, *Neither Settler nor Native: The Making and Unmaking of Permanent Minorities* (Cambridge, MA, and London, 2020), p. 23.

[60] See Elinor S. Shaffer, 'Iago's malignity motivated: Coleridge's unpublished "Opus Magnum"', *Shakespeare Quarterly* 19 (1968), 196; Kyle Grady, 'Othello, Colin Powell, and post-racial anachronism', *Shakespeare Quarterly* 67 (2016), 68–83; p. 68; Harold Bloom, *Iago* (New York, 1992), p. 3; Matt Carter, 'Othello's white sword: stage properties, race, and performance', *Shakespeare Bulletin* 38 (2020), 245.

[61] See Karen Attiah, 'Opinion: George Floyd has become the Emmett Till of this moment', *The Washington Post*, 6 June 2020.

[62] Peter Fitzpatrick, 'Racism and the innocence of law', *Journal of Law and Society* 14 (Spring 1987).

[63] See Chouki El Hamel, *Black Morocco: A History of Slavery, Race, and Islam* (Cambridge, 2013), pp. 12, 55, 78, 99. See also Peter Fitzpatrick, 'Document of discovery', in *A Companion to Racial and Ethnic Studies* (Oxford, 2001). For a discussion of different conditions of genocide, see Raoul Peck's 'Exterminate All the Brutes', where he includes contempt for aliens, fanaticism, exploitation, slavery, and conquest.

a collective humanity.[64] While the presentation of Othello's story – including his history, his romance with Desdemona, and his status as a general – would appear to yield a powerful way to centre the protagonist of this tragedy, what unfolds becomes the reification of a dominant narrative that is crafted from the outset of the play until the five acts reach their conclusion. In the two passages that I discuss below, the dominant narrative of superiority offers stunning models for dismantling Othello's psyche and marginalize him before his men and the Venetian society. Specifically, Iago, Othello's ensign, embarks upon a character assassination unequalled in all the fields of battle, to belie Othello's reputed valiant reputation. Through racial epithets, racialized metaphors and hatred, 'good Iago' (2.1.97) manages, for several purses from Desdemona's rejected suitor Roderigo, to create a breach between Desdemona and Othello and mount an assault against the 'wronged Othello' (3.3.470) that sends him on an emotional, legal and political descent from which he will not recover. Iago not only weaponizes the tools of this descent, but emerges as Othello's 'false friend'.

As an unabashed proclamation, Iago simply states: 'I am not what I am' (1.1.64). He explains his plan to Roderigo. This plan involves him offering a perception of himself that is false. Iago is the dangerous figure in the play, but through propaganda, psychological warfare and slander, he marshals a diabolical assault on Othello that destroys him. We witness an intergenerational transmission of racial trauma from this tale, and those of classical playwright Terence, to the narratives of twentieth-century writers James Baldwin and Ralph Ellison. At every turn, the psyche of the man from the African diaspora endures the attacks from the turmoils of slavery to those of Jim Crow. As he explains to Roderigo, Iago has no idea what ills or misdeeds Othello may have committed, but he declares emphatically and repeatedly: 'I hate the Moor' (1.3.366–7, 385). While Roderigo is aware of the plans against Othello, he does not realize that he will finance this great project to his own economic ruin. I recall a former American president, Lyndon B. Johnson, who said: 'If you can convince the lowest white man he's better than the best colored man, he won't notice you're picking his pocket. Hell, give him somebody to look down on, and he'll empty his pockets for you.'[65] Iago intimately understands this premise.

Within the criminal project, this conspiracy to fell Othello contains several schemes. Initially, we are introduced to the conspiracy between Iago and Roderigo. In five acts, we watch Iago use several unwitting actors to advance this conspiracy. First, we have the moment in 2.3 where Iago convinces Cassio to talk to Desdemona to assist him in getting Othello to retract the demotion and return his position as Othello's lieutenant.[66] He ultimately wants Cassio to have access to Desdemona, so she seems guilty of having made Othello a cuckold. Second, in 3.3, Iago convinces his wife Emilia to steal the handkerchief, so he might prove Desdemona's infidelity.[67] Third, in 1.1, Iago uses Brabantio to level accusations against Othello to taint his reputation, motives and leadership, and demonstrate that he poses a threat not only to Brabantio's family at the local level, but also to the nation state of Venice.

Rather conspicuously, the attack on Cassio mirrors the concerted attacks on Othello, but these moments are quite distinct – like Desdemona, Cassio serves as a pawn to dismantle Othello. For instance, the attack on Cassio is merely to remove the lieutenant from his position, for it is Iago's belief – or so he says – that the Florentine 'arithemetician' and 'bookish theoric' (1.1.18, 22) Cassio possesses neither the experience nor the character that leadership demands. Some may suggest that Iago was right, as Cassio indulged in the alcohol-induced revelry with the other men despite his own self-knowledge that he was susceptible to

---

[64] Laura Quiros, Rani Varghese and Todd Vanidestine, 'Disrupting the single story: challenging the dominant trauma narratives through a critical race lens', *Traumatology* 26 (2020), 160–8.
[65] Bill Moyers, 'What a real president was like', *Washington Post*, 13 November 1968.
[66] See the discussion that begins at line 310.
[67] See the discussion that begins at line 217.

overdrinking. However, Iago does not rest at Cassio's alcohol-fuelled binge, but uses the state of intoxication as a moment for Roderigo to launch a physical attack against Cassio to incense Othello against his lieutenant. Yet the attack against Cassio extends further, for, after the lieutenant's demotion, Iago encourages him to seek restoration of his position through Othello's wife instead of seeking out Othello directly. This pursuit of Desdemona for his cause makes Cassio look even more egregiously guilty in Othello's eyes and has the added benefit of making Desdemona look unfaithful as well.

With relentless fervour, Iago also recruits his wife Emilia to implicate Desdemona further by having Emilia pilfer a cherished handkerchief given to Desdemona by Othello. Of all the pawns that Iago chooses in these multiple schemes, Emilia is the one who expresses the greatest distrust of or doubt about his attentions. Or perhaps she is the most sceptical about the sincerity of his intentions? She is never heard referring to her husband as 'honest Iago', as Othello does (1.3.295).[68] Actually, her husband impugns her honesty as well. Early in this scene, Iago suggests that Othello has even made him a cuckold with his wife Emilia – sexual jealousy is not separated from race. Iago's motives appear to return to the propaganda associated with supremacy. Nevertheless, throughout the play, Othello refers to him as 'honest Iago', but in the opening scene Iago explains his ideals of supremacy by reinforcing well-crafted narratives of hierarchy, capitalism and confidence tricks:[69]

> I follow him to serve my turn upon him.
> We cannot all be masters, nor all masters
> Cannot be truly followed. You shall mark
> Many a duteous and knee-crooking knave
> That, doting on his own obsequious bondage,
> Wears out his time much like his master's ass
> For naught but provender, and when he's old, cashiered.
> Whip me such honest knaves!
>
> (1.1.41–8)

In these lines, Iago provides a persuasive diatribe to Roderigo in an attempt to dispel the notion that duty is rewarded. In fact, he argues that blindly following one's prescribed duties results in ruin. Maybe the character Bosola from John Webster's *The Duchess of Malfi* might agree after serving two years in the 'galleys' (1.1.34) because he followed the bidding of his masters. In Shakespeare's *Julius Caesar*, Cassius delivers a similar speech at 1.2 to convince Brutus to join the conspiracy against Caesar. Apparently, Emilia knows something about her husband that the rest of the characters do not. Nevertheless, she gives the handkerchief to him despite her concerns. Is Iago so convincing and intimidating, or is she merely the obedient wife? Ultimately, Iago's placement of Desdemona's handkerchief in Cassio's rooms solidifies the ultimate assassination attempt against Cassio – authorized by Othello, planned by Iago, and executed by Roderigo.

In act 1, Brabantio's role in this conspiratorial scheme sets off these multitudinous plots against Othello. While Brabantio appears the most vested in the cause against Othello, his arguments also advance more than a fatherly protective stance on behalf of his daughter, Desdemona. It inculcates his notions of supremacy. Even at the end of his case, he advises Othello not to trust his daughter because she has betrayed him.

Finally, Othello becomes the last unwitting partner in his own demise. Several moments unfold – for instance, Iago directs him: 'Do it not with poison, strangle her in her bed – / even the bed she hath contaminated' (4.1.204–5). The most devastating part of this conspiracy to destroy Othello the Moor is for Iago to make himself seem the friend, the counsellor and the advisor to Othello. Instead of helping him, Iago's every utterance advances his plot against Othello. Even when Iago witnesses the trance that Othello slips into at 4.1, he is unfazed by it as he responds: 'Work on, / My medicine, work!' (4.1.44–5). He has no sympathy. His sociopathy does not allow him to extend

---

[68] Othello makes this reference in acts 1, 2 and 5.
[69] Steven Roberts and Michael Rizzo, 'The psychology of American racism', *American Psychologist* (2021), 475.

any sense of concern for Othello's mental or physical state when he witnesses this traumatic episode.[70]

Overall, these multiple conspiracies become significant because they are not crafted merely to destroy Othello, demote Cassio, defame Desdemona and discombobulate Brabantio. Most importantly, they are constructed to make Othello become what Iago thinks of him as: unworthy, alien and a monster. 'Monstrous intimacies', whether defined as 'strange', 'violent' or even 'interracial' coupling, encompass the 'original trauma' and 'subsequent repetitions post-slavery'.[71] Iago has proven that he will use any excuse to explain his hatred of Othello the Moor.

CREATING A COURT RECORD OF IAGO'S AND RODERIGO'S CRIMES

I swear 'tis better to be much abused / Than but to know't a little.

(*Othello* 3.3.338–9)

Where the 1.3 court scene evolves as Iago's attempt not only to assassinate Othello's character, but also perhaps to instigate an even more deadly result, this final scene of the play accomplishes that goal. Even further, we see what may be read as the prosecution of Othello. In a brief summary, 5.2 opens with Othello approaching his marital bed to murder his wife Desdemona for her alleged unfaithfulness. By line 123, Desdemona expires after Othello strangles her. What proceeds involves an exchange between Emilia and Othello where she defends Desdemona's faithfulness and Othello insists upon his wife's unfaithfulness. Emilia remains steadfast until, eventually, she is violently stabbed by her husband before witnesses at line 231, after a failed attempt by Othello to save her. Immediately, Iago is removed and escorted off stage, and we are left with Othello and a dying Emilia who finally expires at line 249.

Echoing the Duke in 1.2, Gratiano asks the same question: 'What is the matter?' (5.2.257). More importantly, 'what is their crime? And what is to be their punishment?'.[72] Here again, the scene opens like a courtroom scene where Venetian nobles, Gratiano and Lodovico, Desdemona's kin, pass judgment. Absent are the Duke of Venice and Brabantio. Nevertheless, we have other Venetian nobles to enforce the law, to return order and to assess this macabre tragedy that has unfolded. In brief, Othello confesses all, including the attempted murder of Cassio and the murder of Desdemona. Iago chooses to stand mute. Othello commits suicide.

When comparing the hearing in act 1 with this hearing in act 5, we have conspicuously different types of proofs. 'The law of proof required the (professional) judge of facts to decide on the basis of an objectively fixed quantum of proof – two concurring independent witnesses of good character, or an equivalent combination of proofs.'[73] Whereas, in act 1, Brabantio levels accusations – more accurately, defamation – here, in this final scene, written evidence appears, which reads as relevant, reliable and persuasive. In act 1, the Iago–Roderigo conspiracy was in its infancy, but by act 5, the conspiracy has blossomed into the full manifestation of its goals – to fell Othello. These written, evidentiary proofs in act 5 may be considered in terms of their reliability, credibility and objectivity.[74] In effect, these two hearings illustrate the evolution of the trial process, with the court relying on more substantive evidence.[75] Iago's conspiracy does not reveal jealousy, but an animus

---

[70] For discussion of Iago's sociopathy, see Burton Raffel's 'Introduction' to *Othello, The Annotated Shakespeare* (Connecticut, 2005), p. xxxii.
[71] Sharpe, *In the Wake*, pp. 25, 65, 190.
[72] For further discussions of these questions that circulate around the procession of subjugated African bodies, see Saidiya V. Hartman, *Scenes of Subjection: Terror, Slavery, and Self-Making in Nineteenth-Century America* (Oxford, 1997); quotation from p. 32.
[73] Michael R. T. Macnair, *The Law of Proof in Early Modern Equity* (Berlin, 1999), p. 15.
[74] For a discussion of competence of witnesses and admissibility of documents, see Macnair, *The Law of Proof*, p. 21.
[75] See Baker's discussion of proof, trial by ordeal and the evolution of the trial process: *An Introduction to English Legal History*, p. 85.

grounded in an oppression revealed by a healthy, written record. The crimes of Roderigo and Iago, and eventually Othello, do not become substantiated until the letters are discovered. Across the scenes in the five acts of the play, this scene becomes the one that offers substantive evidentiary proofs – letters – to confirm all that has been confessed by Othello, attested to and witnessed by Cassio and Emilia, and suppressed by Iago.

Roderigo's First and Second Letters

Shakespeare 'papers' the final moments of the play with letters. Even Othello's words return in phantasmagoric fashion to haunt the proceedings: 'Was this fair paper, this most goodly book / Made to write "whore" upon?' (4.2.72–73).[76] These letters reveal the extent of the conspiracy between Roderigo and Iago.[77] At 5.2.306, Lodovico shares two of Roderigo's letters just after Iago chooses silence:

> Here is a letter
> Found in the pocket of the slain Roderigo,
> And here another: the one of them imports
> The death of Cassio, to be undertook
> By Roderigo.
>
> (5.2.306–9)

To his co-conspirator's downfall, Roderigo makes a written record of the conspiracy – not only are these records discovered, but displayed and read to the entire assembly at the end of the scene. This court-like scene offers two written exhibits from Iago's co-conspirator. Now, it does not matter that Iago chooses to stand silent, as Roderigo admits in great detail each conspiracy, beyond the confessions offered by Othello and Emilia. These legal exhibits – and stage props – give the audience a narrative around the production and the presentation of written evidence. These two letters not only confirm Emilia's testimony, but also implicate Othello in his attempt to murder Cassio by the hand of the contract killer Roderigo.[78]

Roderigo's Third Letter

With Roderigo slain by Iago, he cannot testify in this final scene of the play. The letters appear to serve effectively against Iago, perhaps better than Roderigo would – for at every turn in this drama, the rejected swain-turned-killer followed Iago's cue. Where Emilia's testimony served as a surrogate for Desdemona, here Roderigo's final letter supplants the words that either he or Iago could speak. Notably, at line 311, Lodovico explains:

> Now here's another discontented paper
> Found in his pocket too, and this, it seems,
> Roderigo meant t'have sent to this damned villain
> But that, belike, Iago in the nick
> Came in, and satisfied him
>
> (5.2.311–15)

The pockets of Roderigo unravel this disturbing narrative in a way that leaves almost no unanswered questions, save one: why would Roderigo memorialize these unlawful schemes in several letters? Only the final letter, apparently, was meant for the bloodthirsty Iago's eyes. Even further, at line 322, Cassio adds to Lodovico's explanation of Roderigo's letter. For Cassio, the letter emerges as the proof needed to understand the devices behind his own conspicuously rapid, yet inexplicable, downfall:

> There is besides in Roderigo's letter
> How he upbraids Iago, that he made him
> Brave me upon the watch, whereon it came
> That I was cast; and even but now he spake,
> After long seeming dead, Iago hurt him,
> Iago set him on.
>
> (5.2.322–7)

Cassio not only learns of the contract for his death, but that his demotion was also a part of the conspiratorial plot between Iago and Roderigo. While some scholars expressed consternation by Shakespeare's use of these letters as a mere 'conceit' at the end of the scene, they serve a powerfully persuasive presentation of the facts – as the audience knows them, but the

---

[76] See Alan Stewart, *Shakespeare's Letters* (Oxford and New York, 2008), p. 48.
[77] See Stephen Alford, *The Watchers: A Secret History of the Reign of Elizabeth I* (New York and London, 2012).
[78] See also Stewart, *Shakespeare's Letters*, p. 292. He mentions all three letters from Roderigo.

characters on the stage do not.[79] They invoke the legal shift from witness testimony to written proofs. Here Othello also wants letters to help to remedy this sad end by testifying to his character. Unlike Iago's earlier admission in act 1, 'I am not what I am', Othello asks here in act 5:

> I pray you, in your letters,
> When you shall these unlucky deeds relate,
> Speak of me as I am.
>
> (5.2.338–40)

Yet, the final 100 lines of the play do not sufficiently recover the character of Othello after the audience has watched him kill his innocent wife. Not only does the audience experience this visibly wrongful death in front of them, not off stage as in the Greek tradition, but Othello must rest with the revelations that Roderigo's words, a written admission, evoke.

After the reading of Roderigo's letters, Lodovico passes judgment upon Iago, determining to torture him, but delays a sentence against Othello in order to weigh his culpability based on what they now know from the testimony of the witnesses – and, most importantly, the letters of Roderigo, Iago's co-conspirator. Shakespeare – using Othello, of course – removes the need to make the determination against Othello where he punishes himself with suicide.[80] At first glance, this act tries to return some measure of honour to this fallen general. Yet this act presents as insufficient after the audience witnesses his trauma by Iago's machinations across five acts of this drama.

In these 360 lines of the play's final scene, we are not sufficiently recovered – neither is Othello, for he determines to take his own life as a result of Roderigo's admissions. While we have watched the stealth targeting of Othello by Iago for the entire play, and Othello succumbing to these underhanded acts, we are not fully satisfied with the result – where the scene should prosecute Iago, instead we have the prosecution of Othello. Why does the scene read like the culpability ultimately rests upon Othello? For example, there exists an underlying sense that he should have detected the malevolent machinations of Iago supported by the incompetent Roderigo.[81]

Nevertheless, I find this reading most problematic. We have witnessed Iago unravel the life of Othello at every turn – yet, at the end of the conspiracy, in its successful conclusion, we still place most of the blame upon Othello, not Iago. I make this declaration because the scene presents as if we are reading not the unfolding of Iago's conspiracies, but the prosecution of Othello as a fallout or consequence of Iago's conspiracy. Iago is silent. Iago silences his detractors, including his wife, Emilia. We do not get the live testimony of Roderigo or the complete testimony of Emilia – Othello remains the solitary, culpable figure on the stage after the bodies of Emilia and Desdemona have fallen. The women are not safe. The state is not safe. The play gives us an answer in which the once noble general kills himself. With Cassio's character restored, Othello must confront his attempts to kill his two closest champions.

CONCLUSION

I am abused.

(Othello 3.3.271)

How do we protect the little boy within the African diaspora from weaponized trauma? In 1944, a state court in South Carolina held a multiple murder trial for the killings of two little girls, the alleged perpetrator being George Stinney, Jr, 14 years old.[82] The trial lasted 3 hours. The jury returned a guilty verdict in 10 minutes.[83] Little or no defence was provided to counter the narratives filled with accusations, a rush to judgment, and the execution of the youngest person in the state. In 2014, this verdict was finally overturned. How do

---

[79] For the discussion of Ann Pasternak Slater and Thomas Rymer's response to the presentation of these letters, see Stewart, *Shakespeare's Letters*, pp. 292–3.
[80] For discussion of honour suicide, see Davoine and Gaudillière, *History beyond Trauma*, p. 17.
[81] Shaffer, 'Iago's malignity motivated', p. 196.
[82] Karen McVeigh, 'George Stinney was executed at 14. Can his family now clear his name?' *Guardian*, 22 March 2014.
[83] Linsey Bever, 'It took 10 minutes to convict 14-year-old George Stinney, Jr. It took 70 years after his execution to exonerate him', *Washington Post*, 18 December 2014.

we respond to the trauma filling 'the lines of Shakespeare's 17th-century play, the 21st-century story of Atatiana Jefferson's 8-year-old nephew, or even the 20th-century tragedy of 14-year-old George Stinney, Jr, where, after almost 70 years, someone spoke for him. Here, allies refused to be complicit. Protests and legal strategies were mobilized to address what Michelle Alexander called 'structural harm traceable to our racial history'.[84] The trauma was abated – for a moment. In these seamless examples – fictional and factual – from Shakespeare's *Othello* to Ms Jefferson's 8-year-old nephew, we possess evidence of repeated trauma to African bodies: boys, men, girls and women.[85] When does trauma cease?[86] Almost as if in answer to my question, in the final pages of *Black Skin, White Masks*, Frantz Fanon wrote: 'I, the man of color, want only this: That the tool never possess the man. That the enslavement of man by man cease forever. That is, one by another. That it be possible for me to discover and love man, wherever he may be.'[87] From *Titus Andronicus* and *Othello* to *The Tempest*, we continue to prosecute African bodies – they remain the site of violence. We find no justification in the nuances of these different characters – whether written during the Tudor or the Stuart era. We are left with Othello's statement: 'I am abused.' Where are the allies who fight relentlessly for life, liberty and humanity – *before* the abuse? Ultimately, we must find a way to protect those little boys and girls who become men and women.

---

[84] Michelle Alexander, *The New Jim Crow: Mass Incarceration in the Age of Colorblindness* (2012), p. xxx.

[85] Isabel Soto, 'I knew that Spain once belonged to the Moors: Langston Hughes, Race and the Spanish Civil War', *Research in African Literatures* 45 (2014), 130–46.

[86] Cynthia Young, 'Black ops: Black masculinity and the War on Terror', *American Quarterly* 66 (March 2014): 35–67.

[87] Frantz Fanon, *Black Skin, White Masks* (New York, 1952), pp. 205–6. See also Spillers, *Black, White, and in Color*, p. 387.

BEN JONSON'S *SEJANUS* AND SHAKESPEARE'S *OTHELLO*: TWO PLAYS PERFORMED BY THE KING'S MEN IN 1603

JOHN-MARK PHILO[1]

In 1603, Shakespeare was booed off the stage. He was performing alongside Richard Burbage in one of the period's most notorious flops: Ben Jonson's *Sejanus*. No fewer than four contemporary witnesses, including Jonson himself, attest to the heckles, jeers and hisses with which the play was greeted by its first audience at the Globe, who apparently had little patience for Jonson's meticulous reconstruction of imperial Rome.[2] By contrast, Shakespeare's *Othello*, written in the same period and performed by the same company, gained immediate and lasting popularity, and, as Samuel Pepys attests, was one of the first plays to be performed when the theatres reopened in 1660.[3] So, too, the plays appear to be at odds in their choice of and approach to source material. From direct quotations from little-known Greek tragedies to extensive translation of Roman historiography, *Sejanus* is self-consciously erudite.[4] For the main plot, Jonson followed Tacitus' account of Tiberius' influential favourite, Sejanus, and his fall from the emperor's grace, as recounted in Books III to VI of the *Annales*. The lost sections of Book V he supplemented with material from Cassius Dio and Suetonius. In addition to these, Jonson turned to Juvenal, Martial, Pliny, Seneca, Persius and Lucan to flesh out his reimagining of Tiberian Rome.[5] Shakespeare, on the other hand, took as the foundation for *Othello* a novella included by Giraldi Cinthio in his *Hecatommithi* (1565), a collection of romantic vignettes and short stories which also provided him with a plot for *Measure for Measure*.[6] *Othello* wears its classical learning lightly. Iago's apposite appeal to Janus, the two-faced Roman god – one of only two such instances across Shakespeare's work – is made in passing, and when Shakespeare draws on

---

[1] I would like to express my thanks to the readers for their invaluable feedback and to the copy-editors for the care with which they prepared this piece for publication. I owe a debt of gratitude to Dr Thomas Roebuck for inviting me to deliver a lecture on *Sejanus*, from which this research ultimately emerges.

[2] As Everard Buckworth recalls in the commendatory verse prefacing the Quarto and Folio editions of the play, when he attended a performance 'in the Globes faire Ring', he witnessed 'the Peoples beastly rage, / Bent to confound thy grave, and learned toile'. Almost half a century later, Francis Osborne (1593–1659) would recall how he 'amongst others hissed *Sejanus* off the stage': Everard Buckworth, 'To the most understanding poet', in Ben Jonson, *Seianus His Fall* (London, 1605), sig. A3v; Francis Osborne, *The True Tragicomedy Formerly Acted at Court: A Play by Francis Osborne*, ed. Lois Potter (New York and London, 1983), p. 4.

[3] Samuel Pepys, *The Diary of Samuel Pepys*, vol. 1: *1660*, ed. Robert Latham and William Matthews (October 1660), p. 264, via Oxford Scholarly Editions Online, DOI: 10.1093/actrade/9780004990217.book.1.

[4] Tiberius quotes a fragment from a lost tragedy in the second act: Εμου θανοντος γαια μιχθητω πυρι ('Once I have died, let the world be consumed by fire') (Jonson, *Sejanus*, 2.330). All quotations from the text of the play are taken from the edition prepared by Tom Cain for *The Cambridge Edition of the Works of Ben Jonson Online*, ed. David Bevington, Martin Butler and Ian Donaldson (Cambridge, 2012): https://universitypublishingonline.org/cambridge/benjonson/k/works/sejanus/facing/#. Further references to this edition appear in parentheses.

[5] For a discussion of Jonson's sources, see Ben Jonson, *Sejanus His Fall*, ed. Philip J. Ayres (Manchester, 1990), pp. 10–16.

[6] Geoffrey Bullough, *Narrative and Dramatic Sources of Shakespeare*, vol. 7 (London, 1973), p. 194; Kenneth Muir, *The Sources of Shakespeare's Plays* (London, 2005), p. 183.

Pliny for Othello's description of the Pontic Sea, he does so quietly.[7]

At first glance, then, there is little that connects Jonson's *Sejanus* and Shakespeare's *Othello*. This article argues, however, that there are indeed close points of contact between the two plays, not least of all their shared cast. Though often referred to simply as 'Shakespeare's Company', between 1598 and 1611 the Lord Chamberlain's / King's Men were responsible for staging no fewer than six of Jonson's works, including *Every Man in His Humour*, *Every Man out of His Humour*, *Sejanus*, *Volpone*, *The Alchemist* and *Catiline*.[8] As explored below, the company appears to have performed productions of Jonson and Shakespeare back-to-back when touring, encouraging at least some audience members to think of their plays as the work of the company as a whole, as opposed to that of a specific playwright. There are also some compelling thematic parallels between *Sejanus* and *Othello*. In both cases, a manipulative servant provides the main driving force for their respective plots, and the action performed on stage is prompted by the interventions of Sejanus/Iago. In both plays, the most important plot device is the beguiling of a social superior – that is, of Othello and Tiberius. The plays share the same emphasis on exploiting the fears of the victim, and of cultivating a sustained sense of alarm or anxiety. Both Iago and Sejanus take a keen interest in the emotional impulses and motivations of those around them. While Iago is able to lecture Roderigo in detail on 'the blood and baseness of our natures' (1.3.318),[9] Sejanus is described as 'well-read / In man and his large nature' (3.694–5). Following an exchange with Tiberius in the second act, Sejanus predicts a trajectory for his victim which we might readily apply to Othello: 'His fear will make him cruel; and once entered, / He doth not easily learn to stop, or spare / Where he may doubt' (2.388–90). Indeed, the fear which Iago inspires in Othello similarly works to 'make him cruel'. It is only in the final moments of the play that Othello comes to be associated with the word, when he weeps 'cruel tears' (5.2.21), and is, in his own description, 'cruel ... yet merciful' (5.2.89), and, in Emilia's, 'cruel Moor' (5.2.246). Beyond a common modus operandi, Iago and Sejanus share a way of speaking of, and to, their intended victims, and, as is explored below, they both appeal to what is a strikingly similar lexicon of manipulation. Sejanus and Iago ultimately derive from the tradition of the stage Machiavel, the skillful deceiver who is able to exploit those around him to serve his own turn, as employed by Marlowe in the *Jew of Malta* and the *Massacre at Paris*, by Shakespeare in *Titus Andronicus*, *Richard III* and *Hamlet*, and by Jonson in *Volpone* (and perhaps also in Jonson's own version of 'Richard crockback').[10] But, even allowing for a shared tradition, there are compelling and specific parallels in the depiction of manipulation in *Othello* and *Sejanus* which warrant further study. This shared idiom and shared company raise some intriguing questions about the relationship between the two plays, as well as possible avenues of influence between Jonson and Shakespeare. There is more in common, this article suggests, between Shakespeare's tragic romance and Jonson's imperial Rome than first meets the eye.

The parallels between the dramatic works of Jonson and Shakespeare have received detailed critical attention.[11] In his lecture series on the two

---

[7] 'By Janus, I think so' (Jonson, *Sejanus*, 1.2.32). Cf. *The Merchant of Venice*, 1.1.53. For Shakespeare's use of Pliny in *Othello*, see Muir, *Sources*, pp. 188–90.

[8] See, for example, Andrew Gurr, *The Shakespeare Company, 1594–1642* (Cambridge, 2004); Steven Urkowitz, 'Did Shakespeare's Company cut long plays down to two hours playing time?' *Shakespeare Bulletin* 30 (2012), 239–62.

[9] All quotations from *Othello* are taken from *The New Oxford Shakespeare*, ed. Gary Taylor, John Jowett, Terri Bourus and Gabriel Egan (Oxford, 2016).

[10] Philip Henslowe, 'Life records 26: Dulwich College Archive – Philip Henslowe's diary', fol. 106v: https://universitypublishingonline.org/cambridge/benjonson/k/life/26_L1602_10_Dulwich.

[11] See, for example, the essays gathered by Ian Donaldson in *Jonson and Shakespeare* (London, 1983), and those edited by James Loxley and Fionnuala O'Neill Tonning for their special issue of *Shakespeare* 12 (2016). For individual studies, see Nancy S. Leonard, 'Shakespeare and Jonson again: the comic forms', *Renaissance Drama* 10 (1979), 45–69; Russ McDonald, *Shakespeare & Jonson, Jonson & Shakespeare* (Lincoln, NE, 1988); Mark Robson, 'Jonson and Shakespeare', in *Ben Jonson in Context*, ed. Julie Sanders

playwrights, Sidney Musgrove identified allusions to *Henry V*, *The Tempest* and *Hamlet* across Jonson's plays.[12] Brian Tyson has highlighted some persuasive parallels between *Othello* and Jonson's *Volpone* (1606), citing verbal echoes, overlapping themes and Jonson's burlesque treatment of the handkerchief.[13] More recently, Ian Donaldson has compared representations of jealousy by the two playwrights, observing that 'Jonson's irrationally jealous husband, Thorello, in *Every Man in His Humour*, is intriguingly refashioned in Shakespeare's Othello, whose very name is a near anagram of his.'[14] For Tom Cain, the importance of *Sejanus* to Shakespeare was the fact that it offered 'a new way of treating the contemporary as well as the historical political scene', reflecting that 'without *Sejanus* it is difficult to see Shakespeare's later Roman plays, or *Measure for Measure*, *King Lear*, and *Macbeth*, treating the uses and abuses of power as they did'.[15] So, too, the points of contact between *Sejanus* and *Julius Caesar* have been explored in some considerable detail.[16] It is rare, however, that *Othello* and *Sejanus* are mentioned in the same breath, still less compared to one another.

For R. A. Foakes, *Othello* 'stands in contrast to *Sejanus*', and, to date, David Farley-Hills has undertaken the closest comparison of *Othello* and *Sejanus*, suggesting that the latter 'was certainly an influence on *Othello* and has to be taken into account in understanding the dramatic climate in which *Othello* was conceived and executed'.[17] The relationship between the emperor and his most intimate advisor, 'where Sejanus constantly attempts to weave textures of deception around his master, must have provided more than a few clues in developing the relationship of Iago and Othello'.[18] For Farley-Hills, however, the similarities between the two plays stop short of verbal resonance: 'Jonson's lines must certainly have been running in Shakespeare's head at the time, but in spite of this it is remarkable that we can detect little verbal influence of *Sejanus* on *Othello*.'[19] This article argues that there is, in fact, enough verbal overlap between *Othello* and *Sejanus* to warrant a detailed comparison of the two plays. Such a comparison will help to nuance our understanding of how these two playwrights, and indeed the Lord Chamberlain's / King's Men, were operating in the final years of Elizabeth's reign, and at the beginning of James's. By considering the original staging of these two plays by the King's Men and by examining the idiom of manipulation employed by Iago and Sejanus, this article explores how dramatic material and stage practice could be repurposed in what are ostensibly very different contexts.

Sejanus was first published in quarto in 1605, and was subsequently included in the Folio *Workes* of 1616. According to the title page in the folio version, the play was first performed by the King's Men in 1603 – that is, at some point between 25 March 1603 and 24 March 1604, according to the old calendar.[20] E. K. Chambers suggests that, given 'the theatres were probably closed from Elizabeth's death to March 1604, the production may have been at Court in the autumn or winter of 1603'.[21] Tom

---

(Cambridge, 2010), pp. 57–64; Warren Chernaik, 'The dyer's hand: Shakespeare and Jonson', in *The Cambridge Companion to Shakespeare and Contemporary Dramatists*, ed. Tom Hoenselaars (Cambridge, 2012), pp. 54–69; Richard Dutton, 'Jonson and Shakespeare: Oedipal revenge', *Ben Jonson Journal* 23 (2016), 24–51.

[12] Sidney Musgrove, *Shakespeare and Jonson* (Auckland, 1970), pp. 12–20.
[13] Brian F. Tyson, 'Ben Jonson's black comedy: a connection between Othello and Volpone', *Shakespeare Quarterly* 29 (1978), 60–6.
[14] Ian Donaldson, 'Looking sideways: Jonson, Shakespeare, and the myths of envy', *Ben Jonson Journal* 8 (2001), 1–22; p. 12.
[15] Tom Cain, 'Introduction', in Jonson, *Sejanus*, ed. Cain.
[16] Edward Pechter, 'Julius Caesar and Sejanus: Roman politics, inner selves, and the powers of the theatre', in *Shakespeare and his Contemporaries: Essays in Comparison*, ed. E. A. J. Honigmann (Manchester, 1986), pp. 60–78; Ian Donaldson, '"Misconstruing everything": Julius Caesar and Sejanus', in *Shakespeare Performed: Essays in Honour of R. A. Foakes*, ed. Grace Ioppolo (Newark, 2000), pp. 88–107.
[17] R. A. Foakes, 'The descent of Iago: satire, Ben Jonson, and Shakespeare's Othello', in *Shakespeare and his Contemporaries*, ed. Honigmann, pp. 16–30; p. 24; David Farley-Hills, *Shakespeare and the Rival Playwrights, 1600–1606* (London and New York, 1990), pp. 127–8.
[18] Farley-Hills, *Rival Playwrights*, p. 130.
[19] Farley-Hills, *Rival Playwrights*, p. 128.
[20] *The Workes of Benjamin Jonson* (London, 1616), p. 355.
[21] E. K. Chambers, *The Elizabethan Stage*, 4 vols. (Oxford, 1923), vol. 3, p. 367.

Cain has recently cast doubt on a court debut of *Sejanus*, citing a lack of evidence for such a performance as well as the Master of Revels's preference for plays which had already been tried and tested on the public stage. Cain suggests persuasively a narrow window in the first half of 1603, namely 9–16 May, during which the play's earliest attested audience members – Everard Buckworth, William Fennor and Esmé Stuart – could all reasonably have attended its first performance at the Globe.[22]

The dating of *Othello* proves more challenging still. The play appears in the Stationers' Register in an entry for 6 October 1621 as 'The Tragedie of Othello, the moore of Venice'.[23] A quarto edition appeared in 1622, and in the following year it was included in the First Folio. The earliest reference to a performance of the play is preserved in the Revels Accounts for 1604–5, where an entry for 1 November 1604 records the performance of 'A play in the Banketinge: house att whitehall Called The Moor of Venis'.[24] There is no critical consensus, however, as to the precise date of its composition. E. A. J. Honigmann in the third Arden edition of *Othello* posits a date 'at some point in the period from mid-1601 to mid-1602', while Norman Sanders, editing the play for the New Cambridge Shakespeare Series, suggested that it 'was probably written *circa* 1602–4'.[25] More recently, the editors of *The Oxford Shakespeare* have highlighted Shakespeare's use of Richard Knolles's *History of the Turks* as a source for *Othello*, which was 'published no earlier than 30 September 1603, so Shakespeare probably completed his play some time between that date and the summer of 1604'.[26] Matters are complicated, however, by an allusion to *Othello* identified by Brandon Centerwall in the prefatory verse included in a work entitled *Saint Marie Magdalens Conversion*, dating to January 1603.[27] Here, among what appear to be allusions to Shakespeare's *Lucrece*, *Troilus and Cressida* and *Richard III*, the author includes: 'the rage, / Wherwith that passion is possest withall, / When ielousie with loue doth share apart'.[28] With the evidence as it stands, however, it may not be possible to settle on a definitive date for *Othello*, or indeed for *Sejanus*. If we assume that *Othello* predates *Sejanus*, we might imagine that Jonson was inspired by Shakespeare's staging of the manipulator–manipulated relationship in his dramatic adaptation of Tacitus. If, on the other hand, *Sejanus* predates *Othello*, one might reasonably suggest that Shakespeare, while he himself was performing in Jonson's play, was taken by the dramatically satisfying prospect of a servant who deceives his master, and by an idiom of manipulation which draws on the figurative use of opiates, poisons, charms, work and practice. The aim of this article, however, is not to demonstrate definitively a flow of influence in one direction or the other. Instead, it seeks to identify and embrace the various ways in which the two tragedies are interconnected, drawing attention to the porous nature of plays which were developed in the same social and professional contexts. The comparison of the two tragedies and the environments from which they emerged will thus provide a better understanding not only of the interests and practice of the playwrights at the turn of the century, but of the company as a whole.

---

[22] Cain, 'Introduction', in Jonson, *Sejanus*, ed. Cain.

[23] *A Transcript of the Registers of the Company of the Stationers of London: 1554–1640*, vol. 4, ed. Edward Arber (London, 1877), p. 21.

[24] The National Archives, 'Accounts etc. Parts 13 to 33', AO 3/908/13, doi.org/10.37078/385. For a history of the debate concerning the authenticity of the Revels's Accounts, see Edmund K. Chambers, *William Shakespeare: A Study of Facts and Problems*, vol. 2 (Oxford, 1930), pp. 331–2.

[25] William Shakespeare, *Othello*, ed. E. A. J. Honigmann (Walton-on-Thames, 1977), p. 345; Shakespeare, *Othello*, ed. Norman Sanders (Cambridge, 1984), p. 1.

[26] William Shakespeare, *The Oxford Shakespeare: The Complete Works*, 2nd ed., ed. John Jowett, William Montgomery, Gary Taylor and Stanley Wells (Oxford, 2005), p. 873. For a discussion of Shakespeare's use of Knolles's *History*, see Bullough, *Narrative and Dramatic Sources*, pp. 212–13.

[27] Brandon S. Centerwall, 'An allusion to Othello, 31 January 1603', *Notes and Queries* 62 (2015), 113–16.

[28] I. C., *Saint Marie Magdalens Conversion* ([England]: 1603), sig. A3r. It is possible, however, that the last four lines of the first stanza are in fact referring to one and the same play concerning 'louers giddy fancies'. This is certainly how 'and' functions in the stanza that follows.

'FALL'N INTO THE FINEST COMPANY':[29] BEN JONSON AND THE LORD CHAMBERLAIN'S / KING'S MEN

Sejanus is one of the few plays in which Shakespeare himself is known to have performed. According to the cast list preserved in Jonson's *Workes* (1616), when the tragedy 'was first acted, in the yeere 1603 By the Kings Maiesties Servants', the 'principall Tragœdians' included first and foremost 'Ric. Burbadge' and 'Will. Shake-speare'.[30] Given their prominence in the list of players, Burbage most probably took the part of Sejanus, and Shakespeare the part of Tiberius, or vice versa. Burbage himself offers another link between the two plays, performing in *Othello* as 'the greued Moore'.[31] As indicated by the cast lists included in the Folio edition of Jonson's *Workes*, Burbage in fact acted in no fewer than five of Jonson's plays, each of which was staged by the Lord Chamberlain's / King's Men:

(1) *Every Man in His Humour*, first performed in 1598 at the Curtain Theatre in Shoreditch, in which Burbage was acting opposite Shakespeare[32]
(2) *Every Man out of His Humour*, first performed in the winter of 1599 at the newly founded Globe Theatre, Bankside
(3) *Sejanus*, performed at the Globe in 1603, in which Burbage again took a leading role opposite Shakespeare
(4) *Volpone*, performed at the Globe in spring 1606, in which he most probably took the title role (he is listed first among 'the Principall Comœdians')
(5) *The Alchemist*, first performed in 1610, perhaps staged, as Lucy Munro suggests, at the company's newly acquired playhouse at Blackfriars, with a production in Oxford in the same year[33]

These playwrights and actors were then messily interconnected: Shakespeare, performing in *In His Humour*, was acting at the same theatre, The Curtain, where Jonson had first tried his hand at writing and performing, albeit with little success.[34] Though we are now wont to refer to 'Shakespeare's Globe', Jonson's *Every Man out* was in fact one of the first plays to be acted at the new theatre in the winter of 1599, which had opened its doors only a few months before.[35] Jonson would return to the Globe with *Sejanus* and *Volpone*, in which Burbage also took leading roles. If Burbage was important to realizing the plays of Shakespeare, he was no less important for those of Jonson, for whom the name 'Burbage' became synonymous with 'best actor'.[36] As noted above, the first recorded performance of *Othello* is from a court context, but it is not unreasonable to assume that it debuted, as with *Sejanus*, at the Globe, where it would be staged again in 1610.[37]

Another potential bridge between *Othello* and *Sejanus* is Alexander Cooke, a company shareholder in the King's Men who took female roles in his early days as a boy actor.[38] As David Kathman has persuasively argued, Cooke can be identified as the 'Saunder' mentioned in the handwritten cast

---

[29] Ben Jonson, *Bartholomew Fair*, ed. John Creaser, in *The Cambridge Edition of the Works of Ben Jonson*, 4.3.91.
[30] Jonson, *Workes*, p. 438.
[31] Quoted by Gabriel Egan in *The Oxford Companion to Shakespeare*, ed. Michael Dobson and Stanley Wells (Oxford, 2001), p. 58.
[32] David Bevington, '*Every Man in His Humour*: stage history': https://universitypublishingonline.org/cambridge/benjonson/k/essays/stage_history_EMI. Cf. National Archives, 'Accounts etc. Parts 13 to 33'.
[33] Lucy Munro, '*The Alchemist*: stage history': https://universitypublishingonline.org/cambridge/benjonson/k/essays/stage_history_Alchemist/1.
[34] According to John Aubrey's 'Brief life', having completed military service in the Netherlands, Jonson 'came over into England, and acted and wrote at The Green Curtaine, but both ill': John Aubrey, 'LR95d (early lives) – Aubrey's Life of Jonson', ed. Kate Bennett, p. 1: https://universitypublishingonline.org/cambridge/benjonson/k/life/95d_Aubrey.
[35] Randall Martin, '*Every Man out of His Humour*: stage history': https://universitypublishingonline.org/cambridge/benjonson/k/essays/stage_history_EMO/1.
[36] *Bartholomew Fair*, 5.3.64–7.
[37] For Hans Jacob Wurmsser von Vendenheym's note on the 1610 performance of *Othello*, see British Library MS Add. 20001, fol. 9v: https://shakespearedocumented.folger.edu/resource/document/german-prince-sees-othello-globe-1610.
[38] For the evidence for Cooke as shareholder, see 'Will of Alexander Cooke', The National Archives, PROB 11/123/410, in which he leaves to his unborn child 'Fiftie poundes alsoe which is in the hands of my fellowes as my share of the stocke': fol. 385r.

list for *The Seven Deadly Sins*, where he was playing the Queen opposite Burbage's King.[39] He seems to have played opposite Burbage once again in *Sejanus*, where he appears at the end of the cast list, suggesting that he played a female role, either Agrippina or Livia, alongside Burbage's Sejanus/Augustus.[40] If we accept that they were acting opposite one another in *Deadly Sins* and, later, in *Sejanus*, it does not seem unreasonable to suggest that the company reprised their coupling for *Othello*, with Cooke taking the role of Desdemona alongside Burbage's Othello. As actors in the Lord Chamberlain's / King's Men, Shakespeare and Burbage – and perhaps also Cooke – thus appeared as leading roles in *Sejanus* and *Othello* alike.

At the turn of the century, the King's Men were associated with the plays of both Jonson and Shakespeare. In the last of the Parnassus Plays, performed between 1598 and 1602 by the students of St John's College, Cambridge, two actors from the King's Men, Richard Burbage and Will Kemp, appear as characters. They are holding auditions for the sometime students, Philomusus and Studioso, who, having failed to secure work following graduation, turn to 'the basest trade'.[41] Burbage is quietly optimistic. Even if the dramatic technique of these student actors requires some correction, 'a little teaching will mend these faults, and it may bee besides they will be able to pen a part'.[42] Of note here is how quickly Burbage slips from acting to playwrighting: clearly it seemed reasonable that an aspiring actor might also assist in developing new works for the company, as was the case with Shakespeare. Kemp, however, remains unconvinced:

Few of the university pen plaies well, they smell too much of that writer *Ouid*, and that writer *Metamorphosis*, and talke too much of *Prosperpina* & *Iuppiter*. Why heres our fellow *Shakespeare* puts them all downe, I and *Ben Ionson* too. O that *Ben Ionson* is a pestilent fellow, he brought up *Horace* giving the Poets a pill, but our fellow *Shakespeare* hath given him a purge that made him beray his credit.[43]

For the author of the Parnassus Plays at least, Shakespeare and Jonson were connected by competition, and there is a curious chiasmus here as Kemp slips from Shakespeare to Jonson, and from Jonson to Shakespeare. With the image of '*Horace* giving the Poets a pill', he nods to the climax of *Poetaster*, which sees the Roman poet Horace administer a purgative to the would-be poet Crispinus to help him to vomit up his 'terrible windy words'.[44] The allusion asks the audience to think of Jonson and Shakespeare as sharing a similarly agonistic relationship, with Shakespeare implicitly re-cast as the true poet, Horace, and Jonson as Crispinus. If, as Dan Blank argues, the university audience could reasonably be expected to recognize Kemp and Burbage as having starred in the plays of Shakespeare, then so too this same audience may also have recognized them from the plays of Jonson, who is, after all, cited here in the same breath.[45] As detailed above, Burbage performed in no fewer than six of Jonson's plays, including *Sejanus*, while Kemp is recorded in the cast list for *Every Man in His Humour* alongside Shakespeare and Burbage.[46]

---

[39] David Kathman, 'Reconsidering *The Seven Deadly Sins*', *Early Theatre* 7 (2004), 13-44; pp. 34–5.
[40] Jonson, *Workes*, p. 438.
[41] Anonymous, *The Returne from Pernassus* (London, 1606), sig. G4r.
[42] Anonymous, *Returne from Pernassus*, sig. G3r.
[43] Anonymous, *Returne from Pernassus*, sig. G3r.
[44] Ben Jonson, *Poetaster*, ed. Gabriele Bernhard Jackson, in *The Cambridge Edition of the Works of Ben Jonson*, 5.3.441.
[45] Dan Blank, '"Our fellow Shakespeare": a contemporary classic in the early modern university', *Review of English Studies* 71 (2020), 652–69; pp. 661–5.
[46] Jonson, *Workes*, p. 72. Jonson enjoyed a closer relationship to the universities than Shakespeare. According to Thomas Fuller's *Worthies of England* (1662), Jonson had matriculated at St John's College, Cambridge, 'where he continued but few weeks for want of further maintenance'. In 1607, Jonson dedicated *Volpone*, with Burbage most probably starring in the titular role, to 'The Two Famous Vniversities', drawing special attention to 'Their Love and Acceptance Shew'n to his Poeme in the Presentation'. In the dedicatory epistle addressed to the Universities of Oxford and Cambridge, Jonson again nods to previous performances of the play in the two towns, referring to *Volpone* as 'my latest WORKE: (which you, most learned Arbitresses, have seene, iudg'd, & to my crowne, approu'd . . .)': Thomas Fuller, *The Histories of*

The King's Men were also staging consecutive performances of plays by Jonson and Shakespeare. In a letter of September 1610, the scholar Henry Jackson (1586–1662) attended a series of plays at Oxford performed by the company: 'The King's actors have been here for the last few days. They performed to much applause and a full theatre. But to pious and learned men they seemed, with good reason, to be impious, because, not content with belittling the Alchemists, they most obscenely violated holy scripture.'[47] Today, the importance of Jackson's letter lies in its eye-witness testimony of Shakespeare's *Othello*: he goes on to mention the 'tragedies which they elegantly and fitly performed', including a drama featuring 'that lady Desdemona, killed before us by her husband'.[48] Of interest to the discussion here, however, is the fact that Jackson makes no mention of either playwright: from Jackson's perspective, he went to see a handful of plays by the King's Men, and he consistently speaks of the company as a whole rather than the work of a specific playwright: 'they were here ... they performed ... they seemed ... they violated' ('adfuerunt ... egerunt ... visi sunt ... violarint [etc.]'). Intriguingly, in the case of *The Alchemist*, Jackson associates the moral responsibility for the play's content not with its author, but rather with the players themselves. It is the actors who have smeared alchemists and scripture alike and whom he subsequently accuses of 'depravity' ('improbitas'). Jackson's identification of these plays by their content, by their actors, and by their characters, but not their authors, has intriguing implications for how early modern audiences may have identified parallels across different plays, especially when such plays were being performed in succession.

The King's Men also juxtaposed the plays of Jonson and Shakespeare for their audience at court. According to the accounts for 1604–5 prepared by Edmund Tylney, Master of Revels, 'on the 7 of January was played the play of Henry the fift', followed the next day by 'A play Cauled Euery on out of his umor'.[49] Intriguingly, these plays are identified not by their authors, but rather their company, performed, as Tylney notes, 'by his Ma*jes*ties plaiers'.[50] These plays were followed on 2 February by another production by the King's Men: 'On Candelmas night A playe Euery one In his Umor'. Once again, the play is not identified as Jonson's, but rather recorded by Tylney as 'By his Ma*jes*ties plaiers'.[51]

Between 1598 and 1605, Shakespeare and Jonson inhabited the same intellectual, creative and social space. Examining the relationship between *Othello* and *Every Man in*, Donaldson remarks: 'if Jonson could learn from Shakespeare, Shakespeare could also learn from Jonson. One thinks of the two men working and talking together, watching and pondering each other's inventions, observing and retaining certain phrases, ideas, names, turns of plot'.[52] This image of a shared creative milieu is supported by the documentary evidence. The anonymous 'Notes for my Perambulation in and round the Citye of London', preserved at Edinburgh University Library and identified by Martha Carlin in 2014, place Jonson, Shakespeare, Burbage and 'ye rest of their roystering associates' at the Tabard Inn, Southwark.[53] This was the same inn from which Chaucer's pilgrims began their journey in the *Canterbury Tales*, and it is not difficult to imagine its appeal for Jonson and his peers. The literary and creative opportunities afforded by such an environment are suggested by 'Master Francis Beaumont's Letter to Ben Jonson', dated to the summer of

---

the *Worthies of England* (London, 1662), p. 243; Ben Jonson, *Volpone Or The Foxe* (London, 1607), sigs. ¶r and ¶3v.

[47] 'Postremis his diebus adfuerunt Regis Actores Scenici. Egerunt cum applausu maximo, pleno theatro. Sed viris piis et doctis impii merito visi sunt, quod non contenti Alcumistas perstringere, ipsas sanctas Scripturas foedissime violarint' – 'Henry Jackson to D.G.P.', Corpus Christi MS 304, fol. 83v: https://shakespearedocumented.folger.edu/file/ms-304-folio-83-verso-and-84-recto.

[48] 'Tragoedias, quas decoré, et apté agebant ... Desdemona illa apud nos a marito occisa': 'Henry Jackson to D.G.P.', fol. 83v.

[49] The National Archives, 'Accounts etc. Parts 13 to 33'.
[50] The National Archives, 'Accounts etc. Parts 13 to 33'.
[51] The National Archives, 'Accounts etc. Parts 13 to 33'.
[52] Donaldson, 'Looking sideways', p. 12.
[53] Edinburgh University Library MS La. II 422/211, fol. 8r.

1605, in which Beaumont writes to Jonson from the countryside, where, he explains: 'I lye, and dreame of your full Mermaide wine.'[54] The Mermaid Tavern, located to the east of St Paul's, was, according to Beaumont, a nourishing environment for the literary minded:

> What things haue we seene?
> Done at the Mermaide? heard wordes that haue beene
> So nimble, and so full of subtle flame,
> As if that euery man from whom they came
> Had meant to put his whole wit in one ieast[55]

While Shakespeare was not known to have socialized with Jonson and Beaumont at the Mermaid, it is not unreasonable to imagine a similar atmosphere enjoyed by the two playwrights and their 'roystering associates' at the Tabard Inn, Southwark. Beyond their shared social and professional spaces, we might add that by 1601, a selection of Jonson's and Shakespeare's poems had been printed alongside one another as an appendix to Robert Chester's *Loves Martyr* (1601), though whether these appeared with the consent of either dramatist is uncertain.[56]

The ways in which actors might contribute to the development of a given play within such a milieu are suggested by Aubrey's account of Jonson's exchanges with John Lacy (c.1615–81), the actor, dramatist and choreographer whose earliest known role was Ananias in *The Alchemist*. Aubrey records that Jonson 'tooke a Catalogue from Mr Lacy (the Player) of the Yorkshire Dialect – 'twas his Hint for Clownery, to his Comœdy called, The Tale of a Tub. This I had from Mr Lacy.'[57] Whether this was exceptional or representative of wider conversations between actors and playwrights, it is, without Lacy's comment, difficult to say. It does reinforce, however, the impression of a collaborative and consultative environment in which these plays were written, in which conversations between actors and dramatists (who were, as in Shakespeare's case, at times one and the same) were understood to contribute to the content of the plays themselves. In this vein, it is worth noting that Shakespeare himself has been posited, not unreasonably, as the 'second pen' to which Jonson refers in the address 'To the Readers' prefacing the quarto edition of *Sejanus*:

> Lastly I would informe you, that this Booke, in all numbers, is not the same with that which was acted on the publike Stage, wherein a second Pen had good share: in place of which I have rather chosen, to put weaker (and no doubt lesse pleasing) of mine own, then to defraud so happy a *Genius* of his right, by my lothed usurpation.[58]

For Anne Barton, the most obvious candidate was the resident playwright for the company that would be staging the play: 'Shakespeare, who in any case was going to act in *Sejanus*, would seem a logical choice as someone who could alter the text, with Jonson's cooperation, for performance.'[59] This explanation certainly chimes with the picture painted by the documentary evidence of a shared and collaborative milieu. As Gary Taylor and Rory Loughnane observe in their discussion of Shakespeare's possible contribution to *Sejanus*, 'He and Jonson were the most successful playwrights writing for the Chamberlain's Men between 1598 and 1603, and collaboration between them would have seemed to make obvious sense to a company trying to impress a new royal family.'[60] Given his proximity to the play in production and his importance as a writer for the

---

[54] Francis Beaumont, 'Beaumont's first letter – 1605: literary record 15, line 6': https://universitypublishingonline.org/cambridge/benjonson/k/litrecord/litrecord_beau_001.

[55] 'Beaumont's first letter', lines 47–51.

[56] Robert Chester, *Loves Martyr, or Rosalins Complaint* (London, 1601), pp. 172–83.

[57] 'Aubrey's Life of Jonson', fol. 54r / p. 4.

[58] Jonson, *Sejanus* (1605), sig. ¶2v.

[59] Anne Barton, *Ben Jonson, Dramatist* (Cambridge, 1984), p. 94. For the suggestion that this 'second pen' was George Chapman, see Fredrick Gard Fleay, *A Biographical Chronicle of the English Drama 1559–1642*, 2 vols. (London and Edinburgh, 1891), vol. 1, p. 372; R. P. Corballis, 'The "second Pen" in the stage version of "Sejanus"', *Modern Philology* 76 (1979), pp. 273–7.

[60] Gary Taylor and Rory Loughnane, 'The canon and chronology of Shakespeare's works', in *The New Oxford Shakespeare: Authorship Companion*, ed. Gary Taylor and Gabriel Egan (Oxford, 2017), pp. 417–602; p. 541.

company more generally, Shakespeare does indeed appear to be 'the most plausible candidate'.[61] In the above, Jonson insists that he has removed these additions, yet it remains a tantalizing possibility that the verbal echoes across these plays, as explored below, may in fact represent the traces of this 'second Pen'.

For at least one early audience member, there was something directly comparable about *Sejanus* and *Othello*. In the verse which prefaces the 1640 edition of Shakespeare's *Poems*, Leonard Digges (1588–1635) compared Jonson's *Catiline* unfavourably with Shakespeare's *Julius Caesar*, and *Sejanus* with *Othello*:

> So have I seene, when Cesar would appeare,
> And on the Stage at halfe-sword parley were
> *Brutus* and *Cassius*: oh how the Audience,
> Were ravish'd, with what wonder they went thence,
> When some new day they would not brooke a line,
> Of tedious (though well laboured) *Catilines*;
> *Sejanus* too was irksome, they priz'de more
> Honest *Iago*, or the jealous Moore[62]

Digges has grouped together four plays which deal with persuasion and betrayal at both a personal and public level. With the comparison of *Julius Caesar* and *Catiline*, Digges harnesses two plays exploring a similar subject matter – that is, political intrigue and conspiracy at Rome – and comments on the success with which each playwright has executed the staging of this material. The contemporary audience was apparently 'ravish'd' by Shakespeare's treatment of the 'halfe-sword parley' of the conspirators in *Julius Caesar*, while 'tedious' and 'well laboured' *Catiline* left something to be desired. It is not unreasonable to assume that Digges wished to make a similar comment with his contrast of *Sejanus* and *Othello* – namely, that both playwrights had employed comparable subject matter, but had executed them with differing degrees of success. It is worth noting in this regard how readily Digges slips from 'irksome' Sejanus to 'Honest Iago', the two 'vipers' of their respective dramas (the term is used by both Shakespeare and Jonson: *Othello*, 5.2.281; *Sejanus*, 5.660). Once again, it is useful to think in terms of overlapping casts: each of the plays mentioned by Digges was performed by the Lord Chamberlain's / King's Men. The fact that the same actors were performing across these plays may well have reinforced the comparison for Digges, laying yet further emphasis on the respective success and failure of the two plays.

Before examining some of the verbal parallels linking the two tragedies, it is worth underlining that *Othello* certainly left an impact on Jonson, as is suggested by his nod to the tragedy in the *Discoveries* (1641). Here he glances back to Iago's assessment of Othello's credulity, applying the same wording to Shakespeare in a passage which, though it speaks fondly of the playwright, takes him to task for some infelicities of phrasing in *Julius Caesar*.

> The Moor is of a free and open nature
> That thinks men honest that but seem to be so
> (*Othello* 1.3.370–1)

He was, indeed, honest and of an open and free nature.[63]

In his critique of Shakespeare's style, Jonson thus remembered one of Shakespeare's most celebrated plays, which had, even in its immediate reception, dwarfed Jonson's own tragedy of the same year. The section that follows considers the verbal and thematic overlap between the two tragedies, and how these parallels might have been underlined for an early modern audience by the theatrical practice of the company as a whole, as well as the physical presence of the same actors on the stage.

---

[61] Taylor and Loughnane, 'Canon and chronology', p. 541.
[62] William Shakespeare, *Poems* (London, 1640), sig. *3v. For a discussion of Digges and the commendatory verse which prefaces the *Poems* and First Folio, see John Freehafer, 'Leonard Digges, Ben Jonson, and the beginning of Shakespeare idolatry', *Shakespeare Quarterly* 21 (1970), 63–70.
[63] Ben Jonson, *Discoveries (printed 1641)*, ed. Lorna Hutson, in *The Cambridge Edition of the Works of Ben Jonson*, lines 474–5: https://universitypublishingonline.org/cambridge/benjonson/k/works/discoveries/facing/#.

BEN JONSON'S *SEJANUS* AND SHAKESPEARE'S *OTHELLO*

IDIOMS OF MANIPULATION: MEDICINE, POISON AND PRACTICE

The same 'cunning, and fine words' (1.506) which pervade *Sejanus* are also to be found in *Othello*, where Iago displays a manipulative dexterity comparable to his Roman counterpart. In both plays, 'medicine', 'charms', 'poison', 'work' and 'practice' are invoked in a figurative sense of persuasion or coercion, and the language of manipulation forms another key layer of contact between the two plays. These verbal parallels may well have been reinforced, this section argues, by the physical presence of the same actors across both performances, as well as a shared theatrical practice developed by the King's Men and put to work in both *Sejanus* and *Othello* alike.

Iago and Sejanus are acutely aware of the persuasive force of insinuation, and speak of their actions in very similar terms. Iago's aside in the third act, in which he meditates on his plans for the handkerchief, serves as a useful illustration of how these shared idioms converge in *Othello*:

> I will in Cassio's lodging lose this napkin,
> And let him find it. Trifles light as air
> Are to the jealous confirmations strong
> As proofs of holy writ. This may do something.
> The Moor already changes with my poison.
> Dangerous conceits are in their natures poisons,
> Which at the first are scarce found to distaste,
> But, with a little act upon the blood,
> Burn like the mines of sulphur.
> *[Enter Othello]*
> I did say so:
> Look where he comes. Not poppy nor mandragora
> Nor all the drowsy syrups of the world
> Shall ever medicine thee to that sweet sleep
> Which thou owned'st yesterday.
> (*Othello*, 3.3.315–27)

This is, in fact, the only appearance of 'poppy' across Shakespeare's works. It is also used, however, in a strikingly similar context in *Sejanus*:

> Well, read my charms,
> And may they lay that hold upon thy senses
> As thou hadst snuffed up hemlock, or ta'en down
> The juice of poppy and of mandrakes. Sleep,
> Voluptuous Caesar, and security
> Seize on thy stupid powers, and leave them dead
> To public cares.
> (*Sejanus*, 3.595–601)

Although it is difficult to establish with certainty whether *Sejanus* predates *Othello*, the fact that Shakespeare's only appeal to 'poppy' was deployed in the same context and in the same sense by a similar character is certainly suggestive. We might note also that these speeches occur in roughly the midway point in both plays, and feature similar action on stage: in both instances, the speech offers the villain an opportunity to interact one-on-one with the audience, and both speeches reach a climax with the re-entry of their victim on stage. These opiates are used to a subtly different end in *Othello*, however. Whereas, in *Sejanus*, they are invoked to dull Tiberius' senses – 'Sleep, Voluptuous Caesar' – in *Othello*, they are invoked in a promise to rob Othello of 'his peace and quiet' (2.1.284).

Iago's reflection in the above that 'Trifles light as air / Are to the jealous confirmations strong / As proofs of holy writ' (3.3.316–18) echoes Sejanus' remark in the second act that: 'whisp'ring fame / Knowledge and proof doth to the jealous give' (2.195–6). Both men thus share a keen understanding of how best to exploit 'imputation, and strong circumstances' (*Othello*, 3.3.400), namely by planting and fostering jealousy in their respective victims. So, too, Iago's suggestion that 'Dangerous conceits ... with a little act upon the blood, / Burn like the mines of sulphur' (3.3.320–3) has its equivalent in Jonson's tragedy, where Sejanus explains: 'The way to put / A prince in blood is to present the shapes / Of dangers greater than they are' (2.383–5). In both cases, the method 'to put a prince in blood' (or in Iago's case, a general) is to play upon imagined fears (Iago's 'dangerous conceits' echo Sejanus' 'shapes of dangers'), as presented by this pair of 'subtle whisperers' (*Sejanus*, 3.15).

Iago's figurative appeal to 'my poison' is found elsewhere in *Othello*. In the opening scene, Iago bids Roderigo 'poison his delight' (1.1.66), and, in the following act, he describes how his suspicion that Othello has made a cuckold of him 'Doth, like a poisonous mineral, gnaw my inwards' (2.1.271). In the final moments of the play, Lodovico describes the product of Iago's machinations as a kind of poison in itself: 'The object poisons sight' (5.2.363). As mentioned above, at the climax of their respective dramas, both Iago and Sejanus are referred to as 'viper' (*Othello*, 5.2.281; *Sejanus*, 5.660). In addition to its figurative use, poison has an altogether more literal application in *Sejanus*. In the second act, Sejanus devises with Livia and her physician to administer a 'potion' (2.9) to Drusus, one which will give the appearance of a natural death: 'so prepare the poison / As you may lay the subtle operation / Upon some natural disease of his' (2.108–10). So too it is with the threat of poison that Sejanus persuades Agrippina to mistrust Tiberius: '[he] put those doubts in her; sent her oft word, / Under the show of friendship, to beware / Of Caesar, for he laid to poison her' (4.187–9). Even in this example, however, the literal sense of poison is enmeshed with the figurative, tied to Sejanus' 'la[ying] doubts' in Agrippina. In both plays, then, poison is invoked in a figurative sense with regard to deception.

Sejanus' 'charms', which he refers to as tools of persuasion ('Well, read my charms . . . ') are also to be found in Shakespeare's tragedy. Here, however, it is Othello who is first accused of harnessing 'foul charms', 'drugs' and 'minerals', when Brabantio dubs him 'a practiser / Of arts inhibited and out of warrant' (1.2.77–8). A little later, he will describe his daughter to the Duke as 'corrupted / By spells and medicines' (1.3.60–1). Othello takes the literal sense of these charges of 'drugs [and] charms' and reworks them as a metaphor for their courtship: 'She loved me for the dangers I had passed, / And I loved her that she did pity them. / This only is the witchcraft I have used' (1.3.166–8). In both plays then, drugs, medicine and charms are employed, much like poison, in relation to deception and persuasion.

Sejanus and Iago also share a manner of speaking to, and of, their victims. Sejanus's blunt exhortation to Tiberius – 'be not secure' (2.206) – is treated more subtly in the hands of Iago: 'Wear your eyes thus: not jealous, nor secure' (3.3.194). While Sejanus' victim 'permits himself / Be carried like a pitcher, by the ears' (1.416–17), Othello 'will as tenderly be led by th'nose / As asses are' (1.3.372–3). In both cases, a servant pays lip-service to the duty he owes his superior, while consistently keeping an eye to his own advantage. Iago counts himself among those:

Who, trimmed in forms and visages of duty,
Keep yet their hearts attending on themselves,
And, throwing but shows of service on their lords,
Do well thrive by them, and when they have lined their coats,
Do themselves homage.

(*Othello*, 1.1.48–52)

Sejanus similarly performs 'shows of service' in the pursuit of his own ambition, and Tiberius describes his servant in precisely these terms in the final act: 'under a pretext of service to us he doth but remove his own lets' (*Sejanus*, 5.580–1). Both Iago and Sejanus profess their 'service' to their masters in equally effusive terms. Sejanus declares to Tiberius that 'Myself / Have no ambition farther than to end / My days in service of so dear a master' (3.527–9). At what is the same midway point in *Othello*, Iago kneels before his general: 'Witness that here Iago doth give up / The execution of his wit, hands, heart / To wronged Othello's service' (3.3.457–9). The performance of service thus serves as another verbal, and visual, link between the two plays.

Both tragedies appeal to the sense of 'work' and 'practice', as both noun and verb, in the sense of exerting influence over or beguiling another.[64] There is, for instance, a persuasive resonance between Iago's 'work on; my medicine works' (4.1.41) and Sejanus' 'Work then my art on Caesar's fears' (2.399). In an early speech, Iago remarks that 'He holds me well: / The better shall my purpose work on him' (1.3.361–2), while the 'Argument' prefacing *Sejanus* describes how he 'worketh with all his engine to remove Tiberius

---

[64] See *OED Online*, 'work, v.', senses VI.38a–b, 39a.

from the knowledge of public business' ('Argument', lines 18–19). Referring to Lygdus, the eunuch who will administer poison to Drusus, Sejanus promises Livia and her physician 'I'll work him' (2.24), while in the final scene of *Othello*, Lodovico states bluntly to Iago: 'This is thy work' (5.2.363). In both plays, woven work is also associated with entrapment. As Arruntius remarks of Sejanus and his flatterers, 'now they work; / Their faces run like shuttles; they are weaving / Some curious cobweb to catch flies' (3.22–4). In *Othello*, the handkerchief becomes a symbol and visual reminder of Iago's 'work' as it travels from Desdemona to Emilia, and from Iago to Cassio, and finally to Bianca. The embroidery of the handkerchief is first referred to as 'work' in the third act, when Emilia stumbles upon it (3.3.290–1). Cassio refers to its 'work' twice in the next scene (3.4.169; 178), while Bianca refers insistently to its 'work' four times in succession in act 4 (4.1.141–5). The handkerchief's 'work' is at once a pattern of embroidery and also Iago's 'work' as described by Lodovico in the final moments of the play, as cited above. This woven work is also remembered in the 'net' which Iago promises to make of Desdemona's virtue: 'So will I ... out of her own goodness make the net / That shall enmesh them all' (2.3.322–4), which itself suggests something of Arruntius's 'cobweb to catch flies'.

'Practice' has a similar function in both plays. The 'Argument' prefacing the printed versions of *Sejanus* records how 'Sejanus practiseth with' Livia ('Argument', lines 8–9), while, at the end of the first act, Sejanus declares that 'What was my practice late I'll now pursue / As my fell justice' (1.580–1). In the second act, Sejanus describes his duty as 'to sound, t'explore, / To watch, oppose, plot, practise, or prevent' (2.365–6), which will be echoed in Tiberius' exhortation to Macro to 'Explore, plot, practise' (3.704). In *Othello*, Iago similarly describes himself as 'practising upon his peace and quiet / Even to madness' (2.1.284–5), while Lodovico will lament in the final scene: 'O thou Othello, that was once so good, / Fall'n in the practice of a cursèd slave' (5.2.287–8). There is some dramatic irony in Desdemona's observing of Othello that 'some unhatched practice ... Hath puddled his clear spirit' (3.4.131–3), which chimes with Silius' suspicions in *Sejanus* over 'some subtle practice' (2.472). The charges which Brabantio makes against Othello bring together the idioms of medicine, charms and practice: 'Thou hast practised on her with foul charms, / Abused her delicate youth with drugs or minerals / That weakens motion' (1.2.72–4). Much like 'work', 'practice' thus forms another key part of the lexis of manipulation and persuasion shared by *Othello* and *Sejanus*.

But the two plays most probably shared more than a merely verbal overlap of 'work' and 'practice'. Beyond the audience's visual recognition of the actors themselves, it is not unreasonable to imagine that the shared practice and stage work of the company as a whole may have reinforced these verbal parallels. Might the staging of the interactions between Sejanus and Augustus, for instance, have provided a visual cue linking to those between Iago and Othello? In the last of the Parnassus Plays, as cited above, Kemp draws an implicit contrast between the stilted delivery employed by student actors and that of their professional counterparts, as represented on stage by Burbage and Kemp: 'it is a good sport in a part to see them neuer speake in their walke, but at the end of the stage, iust as though in walking with a fellow we should neuer speake but at a stile, a gate, or a ditch, when a man can go no further'.[65] According to Kemp, the university actor has to reach his mark before he feels comfortable delivering his lines, posing awkwardly 'at the end of the stage'. There is an implicit suggestion here that Kemp and Burbage, as professional urban actors, are capable of delivering their lines in a more natural manner, 'speak[ing] in their walke'. This emphasis on physicality as a means of differentiating between different types of actor opens up an intriguing possibility – namely, that the stage practice of a given company may have been distinctive and recognizable to the contemporary audience. The practice-based learning from which these

---

[65] Anonymous, *Returne from Pernassus*, sig. G3r.

actors, including Shakespeare, presumably benefitted as members of the King's Men offers another level of connection between the two plays.

Iago and Sejanus both speak of their designs in terms of birth. Iago resolves himself to his purpose: 'I have't. It is ingendered. Hell and night / Must bring this monstrous birth to the world's light' (1.3.374–5). Iago had already appealed to a figurative parturition in his remark to Roderigo that 'There are many events in the womb of time, which will be delivered' (1.3.348–9). Sejanus employs a similar idiom when he promises to father 'a race of wicked acts' (2.151). In terms of a more general overlap in the vocabularies of deception and villainy, we might also compare Jonson's 'plant our engines' (3.491) with Shakespeare's 'devise engines' (4.2.207), and Iago's appeal to 'Hell and night' to Lepidus' appeal to the same: 'hell and lasting night' (5.837).

More broadly, both plays are keenly interested in the gap between what Iago refers to as 'outward action' and 'the native act and figure of my heart' (1.1.59–60); or, as Arruntius exclaims, 'the space, the space / Between the breast and lips' (3.96–7). In the first act, Iago explains: 'Though I do hate him as I do hell pains – / Yet for necessity of present life / I must show out a flag and sign of love, / Which is indeed but sign' (1.1.150–3). Here 'sign' carries the sense of a military banner, while 'show out' is used in the specialist sense of displaying or unfurling a flag as a symbol of one's allegiance, the martial imagery picking up Iago's reference to 'the Cyprus wars' several lines above (1.1.146).[66] This image has a special significance for Iago, who is referred to repeatedly as Othello's 'ensign' – that is, Othello's standard-bearer (1.2.48; 1.3.121; 1.3.278; 2.1.67; 2.1.96; 5.1.50). The signs and flags of love, as used of an outward show or pretence, also appear in Jonson, where Arruntius remarks of Laco as he rushes to pay homage to Sejanus: 'Ay, go, make haste ... With the pale troubled ensigns of great friendship / Stamp'd i'your face!' (5.431–6). Iago's emphasis in the above on the 'necessity' of silence chimes closely with Sejanus' reflection that 'Revenge is lost, if I profess my hate' (1.579). Iago returns to the contrast of outward performance and hidden intent when, having urged Cassio to entreat Desdemona, he remarks: 'When devils will the blackest sins put on, / They do suggest at first with heavenly shows, / As I do now' (2.3.313–15).

In *Sejanus*, Jonson presents a city in which feigning and manipulation have become formalized in the operation of state business, and the intrigues of the imperial palace have seeped into the law courts. Thus, Arruntius remarks of Afer in the second act:

> Ay, there's the man, Afer the orator!
> One that hath phrases, figures, and fine flowers
> To strew his rhetoric with, and doth make haste
> To get him note, or name, and any offer
> Where blood or gain be objects; steeps his words,
> When he would kill, in artificial tears –
> The crocodile of Tiber!
> (2.418–24)

Deceit and the cultivation of fear function in *Sejanus* as tools of the law courts and of the state more generally, where 'subtle practice' (2.472) is part and parcel of Roman political life and orators deploy a 'mercenary tongue and art' (3.177). It is not only the 'corrupted ministers o' the state' who deal in obfuscation and double-speak, but even the emperor himself (3.236). While the orators of *Sejanus* use these skills to entrap political opponents – as Arruntius puts it, 'they are weaving / Some curious cobweb to catch flies' (3.23–4) – Iago harnesses them to settle private vendettas: 'With as little a web as this will I ensnare as great a fly as Cassio' (2.1.163–4). And, while Afer in the above uses 'artificial tears' to condemn innocent men in the public courts as 'the crocodile of Tiber', it is behind closed doors that Othello brings the same charge against womankind: 'If that the earth could teem with woman's tears, / Each drop she falls would prove a crocodile' (4.1.227–8).

Once again, however, there is less distance between the two plays than first it seems. Much like Iago, Sejanus also aims to settle a private vendetta. While Iago suspects that he has been

---

[66] See *OED Online*, 'sign, n.', senses 3a–3b; 'show, v.', sense II.3f.

cuckolded by Othello ("twixt my sheets / He has done my office', 1.3.358–9), Sejanus pursues his 'vengeance' against Drusus for a personal slight – namely, that 'the prince struck him publicly on the face' ('Argument', lines 31, 6). The impetus behind the action on stage has as much to do with the personal and the private as it does with Sejanus' ambitions for public life. As with Sejanus, Iago's manipulation of those around him has tangible, albeit indirect, consequences for the public sphere, from the interruption of a counsel of war to the driving of Venice's greatest general to distraction.[67]

It is worth noting that the lexicon of manipulation and deception which can be heard across *Othello* and *Sejanus* does not feature in Cinthio's *Hecatommithi*, Shakespeare's primary source for *Othello*. Although Cinthio at one moment refers to the ensign's 'orditi inganni' (literally 'woven tricks' or 'hatched schemes'), there is no suggestion of the figurative use of medicine, poison, opiates, practice and work shared by *Othello* and *Sejanus*.[68] This shared idiom of manipulation suggests then that Shakespeare had an eye to Jonson's Roman tragedy when he was reworking Cinthio's tale for the stage. Nor is the loathing which Iago and Sejanus reveal for their superior expressed by the villain of Cinthio's novella. Here, the ensign's hatred is directed exclusively towards Disdemona, with whom 'he fell most passionately in love'.[69] Disdemona, faithful to her husband, scorns the soldier's advances, and thus 'the love that he bore for this woman changed into bitterest hate'.[70] The dramatically satisfying plot device of a servant who secretly despises his superior was not to be found in Cinthio but, rather, in Jonson, suggesting another link between *Othello* and *Sejanus*.

One possibility worth entertaining is that *Sejanus* does indeed predate *Othello*, and that Shakespeare, when he came to write *Othello*, was echoing expressions and turns of phrase which he himself had delivered and heard being delivered (and, indeed, had perhaps helped to develop as 'second Pen') when he was acting opposite Burbage in *Sejanus*. If, as Farley-Hills suggests, '*Sejanus* is a kind of purist's "answer" to *Julius Caesar* in exhibiting a treatment of Roman history that gives greater priority to both historical accuracy and statement', in this light we might similarly view *Othello* as the liberal adapter's reply to *Sejanus*, in which Shakespeare demonstrated successfully the dramatic appeal of a play devoted to the machinations of a devious servant and a duped master.[71] The fact that Shakespeare's only use of 'poppy' occurs in a strikingly similar context to where it appears in Jonson gently suggests the possibility that the composition of *Sejanus* might predate that of *Othello*, or perhaps even that the same actor-writer was responsible for its appearance in two strikingly similar moments across two different plays. Whether Shakespeare originally had a hand in developing parts of the play, or whether his involvement was limited to starring alongside Burbage, it is clear that these plays share meaningful points of contact in their casting and staging, but also in the idiom with which they treat persuasion and manipulation, appealing to a familiar lexis of poison, medicine, work and practice.

CONCLUSION

As the examples explored here suggest, *Othello* and *Sejanus* are messily interconnected. *Sejanus* was, after all, a play in which Shakespeare himself performed, probably in the role of Tiberius opposite Burbage's Sejanus. This was not Shakespeare's first role in a play by Jonson: in 1598, he had performed in *Every Man in His Humour*, also acting alongside Burbage. Shakespeare may even have contributed to an early version of *Sejanus* as the 'second Pen',

---

[67] 'Public sphere' in the sense developed by Jürgen Habermas in *The Structural Transformation of the Public Sphere*, trans. Thomas Berger and Friedrich Lawrence (Cambridge, 1989), pp. 3–5.
[68] Giraldi Cinthio, *De Gli Hecatommithi di M. Giovanbattista Gyraldi Cinthio* (Mandovì, 1565), p. 575.
[69] 's'innamorò ... ardentißimamente': Cinthio, *Hecatommithi*, p. 574.
[70] 'Mà mutò l'amore, ch'egli portaua alla Donna, in acerbißimo odio': Cinthio, *Hecatommithi*, p. 575.
[71] Farley-Hills, *Rival Playwrights*, p. 129.

offering his services not merely as a lead actor, but also in the development of the script. Staged by the same company in the same year, the two tragedies also share compelling parallels in theme, imagery and phrasing. Iago and Sejanus employ a similar way of speaking of and to their intended victim, drawing on a figurative use of charms, opiates, poison, work and practice. The physical presence of the same actors on the stage, as well as the shared theatrical practice of the company as a whole, may well have underlined these internal similarities for the early modern audience. Certainly, for Leonard Digges, there was something comparable about *Othello* and *Sejanus*, not least of all their respective success and failure with the public. There are then rich extra- and intratextual links between the two plays, which speak of the wider social and professional contexts shared by these two playwrights at the turn of the century.

This article will, it is hoped, prompt further discussion of how Shakespeare's experience as an actor in Jonson's plays may have inflected the composition and production of his own. So, too, there remains more to be explored in terms of a practice-based learning within early modern theatre companies, and the creative opportunities this might have afforded to playwright-cum-actors as they slipped between performance and composition. In a similar vein, the correspondence of Henry Jackson raises some intriguing questions vis-à-vis the relationship between company, playwright and audience. To what extent did early modern spectators feel they were viewing a performance by a particular company, as opposed to a particular playwright? Might the name of the company have carried at times a similar weight to – or perhaps an even greater one than – that of the author? And what role did the audience play in the production and layering of meaning as they recognized a given actor and his technique across, for example, *Sejanus* and *Othello*? By examining these two plays in relation not merely to their authors, but to the company that first staged them, this article has underlined some new points of contact between Shakespeare and Jonson, as well as the importance of recognizing the King's Men as a company entwined with both playwrights at the turn of the seventeenth century.

IAGO AND THE CLOWN: DISASSEMBLING THE VICE IN *OTHELLO*

NICOLE SHERIKO

THE MOST FORGETTABLE CHARACTER IN SHAKESPEARE

Few characters have been more maligned than the Clown in Shakespeare's *Othello* – that is, when anyone remembers he exists.[1] He has been labelled the 'most forgettable character of his class in Shakespeare', and a tonally confusing theatrical requirement rightly cut from most performances.[2] Even critical work that champions minor clown characters justifies his removal, calling him 'a distraction from the audience's experience of the play itself'.[3] Because the criticism has nothing nice to say about the Clown, it often says nothing at all. Cutting this clown is part of a larger trend in removing clown characters; over 150 years of *King Lear* productions without the Fool is perhaps the starkest example. But this critical and directorial approach to *Othello*'s Clown flies in the face of everything we know about early modern clown actors. As recent actor-centred criticism has shown, such men were leading solo and company performers with celebrity that made them as important as well-known straight actors – if not more so.[4] How, then, can *Othello*'s Clown be so poorly regarded, even when scholarship has long celebrated other clown characters?

First, scholarly emphasis on clown actors as either comic doubles of the main action or singular solo performers adjacent to the theatrical fiction define clown roles as easily removable stock characters.[5] A minor clown who seems both alien

---

[1] In this article, I use the capitalized 'Clown' to refer to the specific character in *Othello* by that name, as distinct from 'clown' as a general dramatic term.

[2] Richard Levin, 'Shakespearean defects and Shakespeareans' defenses', in *'Bad' Shakespeare: Revaluations of the Shakespeare Canon*, ed. Maurice Charney (Rutherford, NJ, 1988), pp. 23–36; p. 25. See also Peter Holland, 'The resources of characterization in Othello', *Shakespeare Survey* 41 (Cambridge, 1989), 119–32; p. 126. On clown as requirement or failed comic relief, see Bente A. Videbaek, *The Stage Clown in Shakespeare's Theatre* (Westport, CT, 1996), p. 17; Levin, 'Defects', p. 31; and Thomas Marc Parrott, *Shakespearean Comedy* (New York, 1949), pp. 290–1. On cuts, see Arthur Colby Sprague, *Shakespeare and the Actors: The Stage Business in his Plays (1660–1905)* (Cambridge, MA, 1945), p. 202.

[3] Videbaek, *Stage Clown*, p. 7 and p. 17.

[4] Alexandra Halasz, '"So beloved that men use his picture for their signs": Richard Tarlton and the uses of sixteenth-century celebrity', *Shakespeare Studies* 23 (1995), 19–38; and Andrew Gurr, *The Shakespearean Stage, 1574–1642*, 3rd ed. (Cambridge, 1992), p. 86. Recent actor-focused criticism on clowning is exemplified by Nora Johnson, *The Actor as Playwright in Early Modern Drama* (Cambridge, 2003), pp. 16–53; and Richard Preiss, *Clowning and Authorship in Early Modern Theatre* (Cambridge, 2014). See also Robert Weimann, *Shakespeare and the Popular Tradition in the Theater: Studies in the Social Dimension of the Dramatic Form and Function* (Baltimore, 1978), pp. 151–60.

[5] The earlier thematic readings of clown characters as foils were advanced by, e.g., C. L. Barber, *Shakespeare's Festive Comedy: A Study of Dramatic Form and Its Relation to Social Custom* (Princeton, 1959), pp. 12–14; and François Laroque, *Shakespeare's Festive World: Elizabethan Seasonal Entertainment and the Professional Stage*, trans. Janet Lloyd (Cambridge, 1993), p. 42. For more recent metatheatrical criticism, see previous note.

and alienable is particularly at risk for neglect when his textual part seems too small to explain itself. Second, *Othello* does not reject all clownishness alongside the Clown. The Clown's absence typically results in exaggerating the clownishness of Iago, isolating the play's clownish energies instead of maintaining those energies' early modern dispersal across the play. Exploiting villainy's comic potential can prove challenging for audiences, however, as one typically puzzled reviewer writes of Iago's portrayal in a 2019 Stratford Festival production: 'Instead of a multifaceted performance, however, [Gordon S.] Miller delivers one that seems at war with itself. He is a naturally funny actor, but seems to be restraining himself – not always with success – from a comic delivery of lines. When he leans too hard into villainous, however, a cartoonish quality seeps in.'[6] Iago acting alone as a clownish character changes the play's balance of comedy and villainy. In addition, audience confusion or too easy complicity in his evil suggests the Clown offers something Iago cannot fully absorb into his own character.[7] Audiences and reviewers use comedy and villainy as essential reference points for describing performance, suggesting that Iago and the Clown exist as vital counterpoints in the play. Objectors to *Othello*'s Clown seem to think he can be excerpted from the play, but redistribution of the comic element he should supply suggests the essential and mobile qualities of clowning.

This mobile clownishness is made possible by the development of dramatic character across early theatre history, through processes of assembling and disassembling different theatrical modes in ways that embed early modern clowns in a larger network of character types. What exactly constitutes a dramatic character is in flux over that history as the changing scale of playing companies produced characters ranging from collectives (like Mankind) to ideas (like Envy) to people (like Hamlet), and some characters were built out of other characters (like the Vice). Both the Clown and Iago descend from the Vice character of morality drama, the forerunner of great stage villains and clowns as virtuoso roles for the playing company's best players. While critics have studied the Vice as ancestor to both villains and clowns, none has yet considered how dividing the Vice's theatrical labour among characters works in conjunction.[8] In other words, how do villains and clowns channel the same Vice figure to different ends within the same play, and how does this sharing shape dramaturgy? As the Stratford review makes clear, the audience needs no awareness of Vice conventions to be subject to their effects, so a re-examination of the Vice offers critical and performance insight into a particularly potent dramatic force. *Othello* provides a useful case study of these dynamics because it distributes Vice performance qualities across different character types. Together, *Othello*'s leading roles demonstrate the

---

[6] J. Kelly Nestruck, 'Stratford Festival 2019: an Othello with no heroes, or set, to lean on', *The Globe and Mail*, 28 May 2019: www.theglobeandmail.com/arts/theatre-and-performance/reviews/article-stratford-festival-2019-an-othello-with-no-heroes-or-set-to-lean-on.

[7] On Iago's clownish audience appeal, another review comments, 'But it's Miller who anchors the production. His Iago is not the wiry, scary, silent type, but a flip and glib menace, who appears to be ragging Othello for pure sport.... a great performance as a happy-go-lucky shit disturber, more sly than vicious, who should by no means be underestimated. He's almost likeable – and that's a real feat': Susan G. Cole, 'Stratford Festival review: modern take on Othello deepens Shakespeares [sic] tragedy', *Now Toronto*, 4 June 2019: https://nowtoronto.com/culture/theatre/stratford-festival-review-2019-othello-2.

[8] On the connection between Vices, clowning and fooling, see Enid Welsford's pioneering study of clowning, *The Fool: His Social and Literary History* (London, 1935; repr. 1961), pp. 285-8, as well as Olive Busby, *Studies in the Development of the Fool in Elizabethan Drama* (Oxford, 1923), pp. 12–14, 26–30 and 48–52; Sandra Billington, *A Social History of the Fool* (Brighton, 1984), pp. 25–7; David Wiles, *Shakespeare's Clown: Actor and Text in the Elizabethan Playhouse* (Cambridge, 1987), pp. 1–10; David N. DeVries, 'The Vice figure in Middle English morality plays', in *Fools and Jesters in Literature, Art, and History: A Bio-Bibliographical Sourcebook*, ed. Vicki Janik (Westport, CT, 1998), pp. 471–84; and Preiss, *Authorship*, pp. 65–7. On Vice and villainy, see L. W. Cushman's pioneering study *The Devil and the Vice in the English Dramatic Literature before Shakespeare* (Halle, 1900), and Bernard Spivack, *Shakespeare and the Allegory of Evil* (New York, 1958).

IAGO AND THE CLOWN: DISASSEMBLING THE VICE IN *OTHELLO*

Vice's importance as an assemblage of performance traditions that casts a long shadow over early modern character and dramatic structure.

This article argues for the centrality of clowning to dramatic character by reconstructing the intertheatricality of character produced by the Vice's development across early theatre history. Intertheatricality itself posits that the play is not the dominant unit of theatrical meaning, identifying instead smaller units – actors' parts, tropes, stage images and more – recurring across plays to give drama shape.[9] I take a similar approach to character, influenced by recent intertheatrical criticism like repertory studies, which help us to see character as another networked element of drama constructed in part beyond any one play.[10] As an aggregated character, the Vice's consolidation means that inheriting a piece of the Vice means inheriting the residue of its other pieces. Rather than seeing Iago and the Clown as fully discrete people, we instead see character emerge as a relation of shared theatrical tools wielded for different ends. Vice influence manifests these and other characters as assemblages of performance modes that occur in different combinations across early theatre history. More narrowly, I argue that what critics isolate as clownishness is an older theatricality more widely dispersed across diverse kinds of characters and, as a result, scholarship on clowning has wider applicability than it has seen. Recent critical interest in clowns has complicated their roots, techniques and actorly contributions, but this work has not yet been brought to bear on other kinds of characters or longstanding narratives about the development of character. If we treat clowns more like other major characters played by leading actors, we should also see those characters as more clown-like, recognizing that shared actorly inheritance manifests across the play in ways not fully documented by the text. The dynamics of a few Vice descendants in one play thus model how dramatic character developed in the broader context of theatre history, and invite us to reconsider how company practice shaped the intercharacter dynamics of early modern drama.

I begin with a brief history of the Vice's late medieval and early modern development as it aggregates and disaggregates different theatrical modes. Then I turn to *Othello* as a case study for the Vice's early modern dispersal. First, the interplay of Iago's and the Clown's scenes illustrates a few shared performance modes that descend from the Vice and thus exceed narrow categorization as clowning. Lingering on one such mode – the typically clownish knack for audience engagement – demonstrates the restructuring of Vice modes as essential to the play's plot and effect on the audience. Finally, I look beyond clown and villain to expand the Vice's family tree in the play, turning to Othello's blackness and Roderigo's foolishness. Rethinking the intersections of these four characters reveals the Vice as a vital network of theatrical energies shaping early modern drama.

THE VICE AND THEATRE HISTORY

The history of the Vice is one of consolidation and dispersal. David Bevington argues that the 'early "Vice" derives his bag of tricks from the several divisions and subdivisions of sin in medieval allegorical drama, all compressed into a single generic or root evil', and Peter Happé's checklist of Vice characters charts this arc.[11] Bevington links the

---

[9] William N. West, 'Intertheatricality', in *Early Modern Theatricality*, ed. Henry S. Turner (Oxford, 2013), pp. 151–72; p. 155. See also, for example, Simon Palfrey and Tiffany Stern, *Shakespeare in Parts* (Oxford, 2007).

[10] For an introduction to repertory studies, see Lucy Munro, 'Early modern drama and the repertory approach', *Research Opportunities in Renaissance Drama* 42 (2003), 1–33. For model studies, see Scott McMillin and Sally-Beth MacLean, *The Queen's Men and Their Plays* (Cambridge, 1998); Roslyn Knutson, *The Repertory of Shakespeare's Company* (Fayetteville, AR, 1991), and *Playing Companies and Commerce in Shakespeare's Time* (Cambridge, 2001); and Munro, *Children of the Queen's Revels: A Jacobean Repertory Approach* (Cambridge, 2005).

[11] David Bevington, *From 'Mankind' to Marlowe: Growth of Structure in the Popular Drama in Tudor England* (Cambridge, MA, 1962), p. 122; Peter Happé, 'The Vice: a checklist and annotated bibliography', *Research Opportunities in Renaissance Drama* 22 (1979), 17–35; pp. 17 and 19–23.

Vice's consolidation to changing structural features of drama: 'the need to fit a previously expansive representation of vice into the limited capabilities of a small troupe, and the emergence of a leading player whose acting talents suited the engrossing tactics of the Vice manipulator'.[12] The Vice is thus a rich figure because it consolidates the theatrical techniques of multiple players in one lead actor, who can exploit different 'tricks' strategically as the play unfolds. This leading actor, then, stage-manages a suite of disparate performers in one character and adds to it his own conventional function as stage manager of the play. Though critics typically locate the Vice as a medieval or Tudor phenomenon, John D. Cox traces its existence up through the beginning of permanent commercial theatres, and Peter Holland sees Vice characters lingering into seventeenth-century provincial drama.[13] Patterns of Vice inheritance thus underscore how characters were shaped by an ongoing negotiation with older, but still contemporary, morality play models in this transitional period of theatre history. Because Vice characters manifest the continuity between medieval and early modern drama, audiences of a play like *Othello* (*c.*1603–1604) would have easily recognized the Vice in this consolidated form as a stage figure.

Even as the Vice proper lingered, however, the playing conditions that produced it changed and redistributed its theatrical energies. As playing companies grew in the late 1560s and 1570s, they expanded beyond more than one leading player, who Bevington sees shift from the Vice to the increasingly important human hero role, sometimes taking a bit of the Vice with him.[14] Having shifted the leading actor elements to the protagonist, the Vice retains much of his villainy and comedy, which ultimately descend into other characters – often villains and clowns. Lest we fall into too strict an evolutionary taxonomy, however, we should remember that the Vice assembled his bag of tricks from a range of performers, so it makes sense that a similarly wide range emerged from that theatrical repository. Such a range is clear in the mix of characters critics describe as Vice descendants: villains such as Marlowe's Barabas and Ithamore, or Shakespeare's Richard III, Aaron, Don John, Antonio (*Tempest*) and Iago, and comic characters such as Falstaff and the company of Hal, or Doctor Faustus's servant Wagner and the clown.[15] Bernard Spivack's influential study of evil names Iago as the most significant, though that may be because he combines the most recognizable Vice traits.[16] Others describe characters like Richard III and Iago as clown-like rather than as Vices, seeing borrowed performance modes rather than their shared origins.[17] This slippage occurs because, though villains and clowns are both recognized as Vice relations, the people most frequently connected to the Vice are celebrity clown actors. One contemporary laments, 'Now *Tarleton's* dead the Consort lackes a vice', and Nashe's *An Almond for a Parrat* calls Will Kemp 'Jest monger and vice-gerent generall to the Ghost of Dick Tarlton', seeing the Vice tradition pass down from one famous clown to another.[18] Privileging the clown in accounts of the Vice is typical, but limiting. Attributing all but the most obviously evil Vice qualities to the clown distorts the picture of how the Vice as a theatrical form is redistributed more widely across an early modern play.

The Vice itself is readily recognized by early modern audiences and critics alike, but its many names and modes make it difficult to pin down

---

[12] Bevington, '*Mankind*', p. 122.
[13] John D. Cox, *The Devil and the Sacred in English Drama, 1350–1642* (Cambridge, 2000), p. 8. Peter Holland, 'Theatre without drama: reading REED', in *From Script to Stage in Early Modern England*, ed. Peter Holland and Stephen Orgel (Houndmills, 2004), pp. 43–67; pp. 54–5.
[14] Bevington, '*Mankind*', pp. 82–3.
[15] For lists of Vices, see Leah Scragg, 'Iago – Vice or Devil?' *Shakespeare Survey 22* (Cambridge, 1969), 53-66; p. 53; Happé, 'Checklist', pp. 21–3.
[16] Spivack, *Allegory*.
[17] For example, Videbaek, *Stage Clown*, p. 4. Cf. W. H. Auden, 'The Joker in the pack', in *The Dyer's Hand and Other Essays* (New York, 1962), pp. 246–72.
[18] Anon., *A Whip for an Ape: Or Martin displaied* (London, 1589), sig. A2v; Thomas Nashe, *An Almond for a Parrat* (1590). Citing these, Margreta de Grazia describes Tarlton's 'dual role as Clown and Vice' surviving through Kemp, in *Hamlet without Hamlet* (Cambridge, 2007), p. 180.

IAGO AND THE CLOWN: DISASSEMBLING THE VICE IN *OTHELLO*

exactly what the Vice is or does.[19] The Vice is less a discrete theatrical entity than a conceptually useful and historically delimited consolidation; as Happé puts it, 'the role was really a convention depending for its success upon immediate recognition on the stage, visually and theatrically, and not upon the naming only'.[20] The Vice character is defined as a function rather than a person, and clowns work similarly – less as a fixed type than as a storehouse of theatrical modes from which individual clown characters draw a subset. This mutability applies more widely to other character types, such as villains and human heroes, which form in relation to the Vice's evolution. Some clownish modes come from clown actors' status as leading actors (like the Vice) so we might usefully understand such modes as a function of actorly importance, rather than part of an idealized clownishness. Holland calls for a theory of character that recognizes the distinctiveness of leading players' performance modes, and one could borrow from clowning scholarship to think about the characterological effects of celebrity.[21] Critics have seen most easily in clowns a quality vital in the Vice and across early modern plays: character and actor intertwine. The wide distribution of Vice theatricality further suggests that changing actor dynamics affects intercharacter dynamics, especially among leading roles in a play. In this way, the strategies of modern repertory studies refine Bevington's older account of playing company dynamics by focusing more narrowly on the interactions of one group of characters and actors, rather than defining the Vice by aggregating an already aggregated character across a large sweep of theatre history. In this case, the distributed qualities of Vice performance that I will track in *Othello* offer theories of character and histories of playing company evolution as both shape the play's theatricality and its effect on audiences.

CLOWNS AND VILLAINS AS THEATRICAL SIBLINGS

So what was in the Vice's bag of tricks? What theatrical functions or performance styles did he encompass? Let us turn to *Othello* as a play that distributes a range of Vice tricks across seemingly disparate characters. In this play, the Clown and Iago have a strong family resemblance. The Clown appears twice to perform hijinks that echo and interpret Iago's own, both times showcasing their shared Vice traits. The most noted examples are in the thematic overlaps of their wordplay.[22] The Clown's appearances flank *Othello*'s pivotal scene, where Iago first conditions Othello as a suspicious reader (3.3), to tackle its issues in a comic vein. He first appears in 3.1 when Cassio brings musicians to win back Othello's favour after drunkenly misbehaving. The Clown interrupts to speak a series of sexual innuendos at the group's expense:

CLOWN   Why, masters, ha' your instruments been in Naples, that they speak i'th' nose thus?
MUSICIAN   How, sir, how?
CLOWN   Are these, I pray you, wind instruments?
MUSICIAN   Ay, marry are they, sir.
CLOWN   O, thereby hangs a tail.
MUSICIAN   Whereby hangs a tale, sir?
CLOWN   Marry, sir, by many a wind instrument that I know.

(3.1.3–11)

This is almost a stock sketch – it resembles a scene performed by Peter, the domestic servant clown in *Romeo and Juliet* – but here plays to an audience about to learn hyper-vigilance for sexual potential from Iago in the next scene. Despite the musicians clinging to the literal sense of their musical instruments, the Clown insistently renders the objects bawdy, a kind of wordplay critics see as typical of Vices and clowns. Upon hearing the nasal sound of the music, the Clown suggests they have come from a hotbed of venereal disease. When the

---

[19] On slippage in whom we consider a Vice character, see Scragg, 'Iago', p. 61.
[20] Happé, 'Checklist', p. 17.
[21] Holland, 'Characterization', p. 121.
[22] See, for example, Leonard Prager, 'The Clown in *Othello*', *Shakespeare Quarterly* 11 (1960), 94–6, and Robert A. Watts, 'The comic scenes in *Othello*', *Shakespeare Quarterly* 19 (1968), 349–54. For a critique of this approach, see Levin, 'Defects', pp. 27–8.

baffled musicians cannot respond, he links their 'wind instruments' to flatulence and the anus via a tail/tale pun and then sends the musicians away.[23] The Clown dissolves the ordered musicians into unruly bodies, turns their musical instruments into sexual ones, and uses those tactics to undercut Cassio's project to please Othello. Despite Cassio's intentions, the Clown sexualizes Cassio's medium for appeal, much like how, despite Desdemona's intentions, Iago and later Othello sexualize her language of appeal for Cassio. Iago and the Clown share innuendo as a typical Vice tactic, though for different reasons. Iago's use of innuendo thus borrows an element of Vice performance associated with the Clown, so the Clown's conventional bawdy jokes are implicated directly in Iago's plot. After all, innuendo is not thematic set dressing but plot action that sets the tragedy into motion. Iago and the Clown's mutual borrowing is at the core of *Othello*'s dramatic structure.

When the Clown reappears in 3.4, he echoes Iago's sinister invocation of sexuality from the intervening scene, linking bawdy jokes to death in a series of puns on 'lie'. Though this too can feel like a stock sketch – it uses 'one of the tritest of Elizabethan puns' – here again it responds to the play's immediate concerns and links the play's comedy and villainy:[24]

DESDEMONA   Do you know, sirrah, where Lieutenant Cassio lies?
CLOWN   I dare not say he lies anywhere.
DESDEMONA   Why, man?
CLOWN   He's a soldier, and for me to say a soldier lies, 'tis stabbing.
DESDEMONA   Go to. Where lodges he?
CLOWN   To tell you where he lodges is to tell you where I lie.
DESDEMONA   Can anything be made of this?
CLOWN   I know not where he lodges, and for me to devise a lodging and say he lies here, or he lies there, were to lie in mine own throat.

(3.4.1–13)

Desdemona asks where Cassio 'lies' – where he lives – but the Clown 'dare[s] not say he lies anywhere' because 'for [him] to say a soldier lies, 'tis stabbing'. The Clown turns Desdemona's question into two possibilities: (1) that soldiers lie down in death from stabbings; or (2), the Clown questioning a soldier's truthfulness will be punished by stabbing. The first offers a threatening vision of Cassio's future, and the second links unclear speech to death, describing how the first vision will be fulfilled. Moving from broader innuendo humour to a nimble wordplay exchange also common in clowning, the Clown reinforces the patterns of misinterpretation produced by Iago's attention to innuendo. In the similarity between the Clown's and Iago's wordplay, comic and tragic misunderstanding are two sides of the same coin.

When Desdemona clarifies her question, the Clown continues his multiplication of 'lie' to emphasize truth-telling further. As he explains, he would have to lie to answer her question because he does not know the answer. But as he has already primed us to see in earlier pun games, the Clown also links this deception to sexual possibility where the Clown and Cassio 'lie' together at the same lodging ('where he lodges … is where I lie'). The Clown's response raises uncertainty, core to the play, of the relationships between people and knowledge, something Iago himself highlights when he says 'I lay with Cassio lately' to claim he knows of sexual intimacy between Cassio and Desdemona (3.3.418). This ongoing deconstruction of Desdemona's query about Cassio thus creates a series of thematic puns that link threats of death, sex and truth-telling – threats intertwined in the previous scene with Iago and Othello and in Iago's ongoing plot.[25] These themes extend the Clown's earlier pun on 'honest':

---

[23] 'Tail' here suggests both male and female genitalia as well as buttocks. *OED* 'tail, n.', senses 1, 5c and 5a. On musical instrument jokes, see R. King, '"Then murder's out of tune": the music and structure of Othello', *Shakespeare Survey 39* (Cambridge, 1987), 149–58; and L. J. Ross, 'Shakespeare's "dull clown" and symbolic music', *Shakespeare Quarterly* 17 (1968), 107–28.

[24] Prager, 'Clown', p. 95.

[25] On this Clown as thematic interpreter here, see also Prager, 'Clown', p. 96.

IAGO AND THE CLOWN: DISASSEMBLING THE VICE IN *OTHELLO*

CASSIO   Dost thou hear, my honest friend?
CLOWN   No, I hear not your honest friend, I hear you.

(3.1.21–2)

'Honest' is the epithet most associated with Iago in the play, as William Empson elaborates in his influential 1951 essay.[26] As the audience knows, however, Iago's double-dealing renders this 'honest' epithet ironic because in Iago's hands the question of everyone's honesty – linking truthfulness and chastity – becomes suspect. As the Clown jests here, 'honest' as a label becomes easily detached from its proper subjects, a reflection on the epithet as well as the Clown's ongoing wordplay.

Critics noting these thematic resonances have often explained them away as part of a structure wherein the clownish scenes comically echo the main plot (as a 'b plot' or 'comic underplot') but I resist the persistent secondary status such readings attribute to clowns.[27] In the thematically linked wordplay, it is more useful to see the same trick – a purposeful misinterpretation – used for different ends, by Iago for deception that raises the stakes of the Clown's jesting, and by the Clown for an entertaining didacticism that helps to illuminate Iago's evil. Thus, the play embeds the Clown not as a thematic duplicate of Iago, but as a figure with similar theatrical practices who acts as an agent of demystification for the audience. Collapsing the play's clownishness wholly into Iago distorts the tragedy in part because he cannot contain the conflicting ends of their shared techniques: entertaining and undermining, teaching and deceiving, mystifying and demystifying.

VICE DESCENDANTS AND THE AUDIENCE

The functional overlap between the Clown and Iago extends beyond the stage in the ways they engage the audience, a mainstay of Vice performance that feeds directly back into the goals of the play.[28] Both the Clown and Iago deploy teaching, singing and laughter to draw the audience into the play. The clown-as-teacher model is a familiar one. Numerous scenes in Shakespeare involve teacher characters who are clowns (e.g., *Love's Labour's Lost*'s Holofernes) or comic education scenes (e.g., the English language lesson in *Henry V*). As Happé puts it, the Vice is a 'didactic showman', and we see this in the Clown's wordplay with Desdemona, where he walks her step by step through an explanation of his 'lie' puns.[29] The implicit teaching that the Clown had performed with Cassio by modelling linguistic ambiguity becomes an explicit form of teaching here. To underscore this didacticism, the Clown ends by invoking a catechism ('I will catechize the world for him; that is, make questions, and by them answer' (*Othello*, 3.4.16–17)). As Hornback explains in his discussion of 'parroting', Vice-like teaching can happen through a repetition of lines or words back and forth, as we see in the Clown's catechism.[30] An alternative to the catechism model of question-and-answer dialogues appears when Iago uses clownish 'theames'. As a kind of entr'acte entertainment passing the time before Othello arrives in Cyprus, Desdemona asks Iago questions about how to praise different kinds of women and Iago answers wittily (2.1.120–67). In doing so, Iago plays a post-performance game we know clown actors played with audiences, in which they improvised witty responses to questions or 'theames' shouted by the onlookers.[31] An editor calling this

---

[26] William Empson, 'Honest in Othello', in *The Structure of Complex Words* (London, 1951), pp. 218–49.
[27] For a summary of this critical approach, see Richard Levin, 'Elizabethan Clown Subplots', *Essays in Criticism*, 16 (1966), 84–91 and Weimann, *Popular*, pp. 237–46.
[28] On the Vice's audience engagement, see Robert C. Jones, 'Dangerous sport: the audience's engagement with Vice in the moral interludes', *Renaissance Drama* 6 (1973), 45–64; R. C. Johnson, 'Audience involvement in the Tudor interlude', *Theatre Notebook* 24 (1970), 101–11; pp. 107–11; and Weimann, *Popular*, p. 157.
[29] Peter Happé, 'A guide to criticism of medieval English theatre', in *The Cambridge Companion to Medieval English Theatre*, ed. Richard Beadle (Cambridge, 1994), pp. 312–43; p. 335.
[30] Robert Hornback, *Racism and Early Blackface Comic Traditions: From the Old World to the New* (New York, 2018), pp. 156–8.
[31] William Dodd likens this scene to such exchanges collected by Armin in his *Quips upon Questions*: William Dodd, 'Character as dynamic identity from fictional interaction script to performance', in *Shakespeare and Character: Theory, History, Performance,*

scene 'One of the most unsatisfactory passages in Shakespeare' echoes judgements of the Clown, but this scene also invokes a clownish didacticism by offering misogynist lessons on female behaviour, the kind of socially conservative moral work done through the Vice in morality drama.[32] Both scenes with Desdemona may also be sites of actorly teaching. Iago and the Clown both sing, and Catherine Henze posits that boy actor singers (like the boy acting Desdemona) were likely rehearsed by the adult male singers (clowns, in her analysis) who shared scenes with them.[33] In each of these cases, teaching blends on- and off-stage audiences, either by directing attention at both simultaneously (the Clown's language learning) or by using a strategy for engaging one in the other, as when offstage 'theames' become onstage action, or onstage action enables offstage vocal training. As on- and off-stage intertwine, we also see playing company practice shaping dramatic character dynamics.

Mixing on- and off-stage audiences plays a key role in the Vice's transformation of audience engagement to audience complicity in service of a play's plot. Engaging the audience is a well-recognized feature of clowns, whose metatheatrically interpretive stance and personal celebrity easily reached beyond the play world. This feature is often described as an outward-facing extratheatrical element distinct from plot-moving activity, but, in a Vice context, morality plays stage the abstract, universalized human struggle of the audience, so addressing audience members means addressing the subject of the play. Specifically, producing complicity is a conventional feature of the Vice, a technique we see deployed when Titivillus in *Mankind* (1465) demands money from the audience to enter, or when he says he will go invisible to other characters, testing audience complicity via suspension of disbelief. Even more than teaching, singing by the Clown and Iago demonstrates this Vice inheritance. First, singing itself engages the audience by operating in a presentational mode that blurs the line between play and playhouse worlds; and, second, its participatory nature draws audiences in. A song for the Clown is not scripted but, as David Wiles points out, the Clown likely performs with the musicians in his scene with Cassio because entr'acte musical performance was a common clown contribution to the performance event.[34] Though we do not know the exact nature of the Clown's song, Robert A. Watts links it to Iago's earlier drinking song to suggest that 'the Clown *is* Iago in that both the Clown and Iago share means, but not ends. What the clown does for the sake of comedy, Iago does for tragedy', a dynamic we already saw in their wordplay.[35] While the Clown's song may be merely annoying or entertaining, Iago's drinking song has a more sinister tragic purpose, enticing Cassio into drinking enough to cause trouble. Especially since Iago's song is based on a popular tune, the audience likely sings along and thus becomes part of the song's efficacy on stage. As Iago uses the song to pull Cassio into harm, he echoes a moment in *Mankind*, when the Vice's company draws the audience into singing a scurrilous song. Singing clowns are more common than singing villains in Shakespeare, but Iago demonstrates how adopting this often comic element of the Vice can be part of tempting characters and audiences alike.

Iago's success in coercing audience complicity is clear from audience responses to the play across theatre history. Ayanna Thompson's revised introduction to the Arden 3 *Othello* valuably collects many revealing responses.[36] In them, we see audience discomfort: a soldier in 1822 shooting at the actor playing Othello to prevent the murder, and a young girl in 1943 whispering 'Oh God, don't let

---

and *Theatrical Persons*, ed. Paul Yachnin and Jessica Slights (Houndmills, 2009), pp. 62–79. Giorgio Melchiori likens this to the exchange between a court lady and her jester or fool, and sees a similar pattern in Desdemona's bedroom conversation with Emilia: Giorgio Melchiori, 'The rhetoric of character construction in Othello', *Shakespeare Survey 34* (Cambridge, 1982), 61–72; p. 67. On 'theames', see *Tarlton's Jests* (London, 1613), sigs. B2r–v, and Preiss, *Authorship*, pp. 88–98.

[32] William Shakespeare, *Othello*, ed. M. R. Ridley (London, 1958), 2.1.117–64n.

[33] Catherine A. Henze, *Robert Armin and Shakespeare's Performed Songs* (New York, 2017), pp. 114–54.

[34] Wiles, *Clown*, p. 162. [35] Watts, 'Comic', p. 352.

[36] Ayanna Thompson, 'Introduction', in *Othello*, ed. E. A. J. Honigmann, revised ed. (London, 2016), pp. 1–116; pp. 41–3.

him kill her', do not want to be complicit in Desdemona's death.[37] We also see actor discomfort: Antony Sher playing Iago in 2004 is uneasy that audiences often remain silent observers and wishes someone would step in.[38] Audiences that witness without speaking up are by far more common, but even they are often coerced into audibly supporting Iago's evil when they laugh at his violent or offensive humour. Audiences often rely on elements like verbal emphasis, pitch, cadence, gesture and facial expression to follow the action when dialogue is difficult to hear or understand, and thus laugh at things that look or sound like humour. Iagos use this to their advantage, encouraging the audience to treat Iago as a clown, even when he is leaning into the villainy of the Vice. The entanglement of clown and villain manifests repeatedly in their shared techniques and shapes engagement with the play as audience responses become a vital part of the environment it creates.

GROWING THE VICE FAMILY TREE

The dispersal of Vice traits occurs across a wider range of characters than just a clown/villain dyad and affects further structural features of early modern drama. In morality plays, the conventional dynamics of complicity and investment in leading actors pull the audience towards the Vice just as the Mankind figure is tempted likewise. The threat of Mankind succumbing to the Vice is even more complicated in *Othello* because the play's Mankind figure also inherits Vice qualities. This brings me to a kind of Vice figure least recognized in the scholarship – leading clown characters and hyperbolic villains are the most discussed descendants of the Vice, but not the only ones. Iago and the Clown inherit overlapping Vice qualities but neither inherits the Vice's conventional blackness, which passes to another leading actor role: Othello. The Vice's blackness is itself an amalgamation of symbolic religious, moral and racial qualities that can be dispersed across plays in performance, offering a complex microcosm of the Vice's more broadly mutable appearance and attributes. The Vice participates in a long iconographic tradition of representing attributes such as Christian allegorized evil through complexion. As critical race scholars have elaborated at length, the blackface paint that visually marked Vice and devil figures drew on associations of sin with blackness and purity with whiteness that often mapped on to race.[39] Such paint was also used to indicate the Vice's influence over Mankind, as in Francis Merbury's Tudor interlude *The Marriage Between Wit and Wisdom* when a Vice figure paints Wit's face black to indicate his folly, but this typically indicates a temporary state (Wit later wipes it off when he regains his senses).[40] In *Othello*, the transfer of this key Vice attribute is much more complete, and thus reconfigures the relationship of Vice with race in ways that could subvert audience expectation. For instance, other characters retain the connection between blackness and villainy – Shakespeare's Aaron, Marlowe's Ithamore – but *Othello* works differently by decoupling multiple types of blackness from Vice, casting Othello as the Mankind figure to Iago's villainous tempter.[41] As a result, this particular redistribution of the Vice changes the dynamics of audience identification that had relied on Mankind's unmarked whiteness in all its manifold meanings. It also changes the

---

[37] Stendhal, *Racine and Shakespeare* [1823], trans. Guy Daniels (New York, 1962), p. 22; and Margaret Webster, *Don't Put Your Daughter on the Stage* (New York, 1972), pp. 114–15, quoted in Thompson, 'Introduction', p. 43.

[38] Antony Sher, 'Iago', in *Performing Shakespeare's Tragedies Today: The Actor's Perspective*, ed. Michael Dobson (Cambridge, 2006), pp. 57–69, 64 and 69, quoted in Thompson, 'Introduction', p. 43.

[39] See, for example, Sujata Iyengar, *Shades of Difference: Mythologies of Skin Color in Early Modern England* (Philadelphia, 2005); Farah Karim-Cooper, *Cosmetics in Shakespearean and Renaissance Drama* (Edinburgh, 2006); and Robert Hornback, 'Folly as proto-racism: blackface and the "natural" fool tradition', in *The English Clown Tradition from the Middle Ages to Shakespeare* (Woodbridge, Suffolk, 2009), pp. 24–62, and 'Emblems of folly in the first *Othello*: Renaissance blackface, Moor's coat, and "Muckender"', *Comparative Drama* 35 (2001), 69–99.

[40] Francis Merbury, *The Marriage Between Wit and Wisdom* [1966], ed. Trevor N. S. Lennam (repr. Oxford, 1971), 9.41.

[41] On the play's psychomachia, see Hornback, *Racism*, p. 188.

relationship of race to moral evil, making the play's greatest threat a conspicuous whiteness, a dynamic that many critical race scholars and Black actors alike have identified.[42] The consequences of this Vice distribution of different kinds of blackness alone extend far beyond the scope of this article, and in doing so demonstrate the significance of choices about how to divide the Vice's many theatrical duties to the play's effects and audience dynamics.

As Othello demonstrates further nuance in the play's use of the Vice, we should note that he inherits more than forms of blackness and is thus entangled with other unexpected intercharacter dynamics. In part through its relation to the Vice, blackness is also linked to the comic traditions that descend through the Vice to the early modern clown. Othello inherits bits of clownishness – though stripped of their humour – in his status as a gull. 'O gull' (5.2.159), Emilia calls him at the end of the play, the same scene where Othello looks for devil's hooves on Iago, each character pinning the others to stock theatrical types. The Mankind figure of morality drama is often a gull, conventionally duped by the Vice, so Othello's own duping follows that model and sometimes elicits the audience's unsettling laughter at Othello's expense. In addition to channelling Mankind as gull, though, Othello bears a strong resemblance to another gull who is not a universalized Mankind figure but a foolish man occupying one of the clown's traditional places in early modern drama: Roderigo. Critics across the centuries have praised what they identify as the 'intensity' of *Othello* as a play with no b-plot, but Roderigo's plot serves that conventional function. The main plot involves Iago duping Othello by persuading him that Desdemona really loves somebody other than she claims and urging him to murder; the b-plot involves Iago duping Roderigo in the same way. In this similarity, Roderigo also valuably demonstrates the decoupling of Vice clownishness from humour. In echoing Othello's plot, Roderigo takes the interpretive position of the clown vis-à-vis the main plot (as the Clown does vis-à-vis Iago) and suggests such an interpretive function need not be comic. In this context, *Othello* demonstrates how the proximity of Vice and Mankind threatened in the morality structure can be fulfilled as tragic structure with the Vice redistributed. If we compare Othello and Roderigo as we did Iago and the Clown, we see again similarities that separate theatrical mode from character type. In stressing the amalgamated nature of Vice descendants like these, I argue for networks of character wherein social status or personal relationship (who characters are) is necessarily shaped by theatricality (how they operate in the drama).

As Othello overlaps with Roderigo, we see another cross-current in the network of character attributes the Vice bequeaths to the play, and yet another way of imagining the Vice's inheritors. We are expanding the Vice family tree. As Iago and Othello show us that Vice inheritance touches more than just clowns, Roderigo reminds us that there is more than one way to play a clown character. The richness and porousness of clowning is made visible by the mobility of Vice elements and attention to the company dynamics that shape character. Though criticism has tended to focus on the singularity of a few celebrity clown performers – Tarlton, Kemp, Armin – and their characters as a singular type, we should remember that most early modern plays have multiple clown characters played by the multiple clown actors each company contained.[43] *Othello* includes the named Clown performer as well as Roderigo. More obvious examples appear in Shakespeare's *Much Ado about Nothing*, where Kemp's Dogberry is part of a comic duo with Verges, or in plays with clown troupes such as *Love's Labour's Lost* (Holofernes, Don Armado, Costard) and *Twelfth Night* (Armin's Feste, Sir Toby Belch, Sir Andrew Aguecheek). This last – Sir Andrew – resembles

---

[42] The Stratford Festival's programme and reviews, for example, explicitly point to societal racism as the play's chief concern.

[43] See, for example, Andrew Gurr, 'Appendix 1: the players', in *The Shakespeare Company, 1594–1642* (Cambridge, 2004), pp. 217–46, and 'Appendix 2: the players', in *Shakespeare's Opposites: The Admiral's Company 1594–1625* (Cambridge, 2009), pp. 274–88.

IAGO AND THE CLOWN: DISASSEMBLING THE VICE IN *OTHELLO*

Roderigo as another character being fleeced by other clowns and not in himself particularly funny (perhaps even a bit tragic). These comic troupes are both assemblages of the Vice's many component parts, and replicas of the way Vice characters themselves often work with an entourage of devils. While one of these characters was often played by one of the better-studied clowns such as Kemp or Armin, their partners were played by clown actors celebrated in their own moment though not well remembered in ours. More work remains to be done on lesser-known clown performers and their playing styles, which borrow differently from older Vice performance traditions. Such work is part of studying how the Vice disperses a range of essential theatrical functions across plays in ways less clear-cut than critics have assumed, creating affinities between seemingly opposite characters as moral and theatrical agents. Whether for clown, villain or even hero, tracing the wider range of theatrical modes that a core dramatic figure like the Vice can encompass prompts a rethinking of intercharacter dynamics among seemingly distinct characters, and a more expansive view of roles often seen as discrete stock types.

The Vice reminds us that intertheatricality was vital to early modern drama's effects but can be difficult for modern critics and audiences to access to the same extent. Criticism in repertory studies like the intertheatrical work on clowning emphasizes how much dramatic material and meaning is transferred outside of textuality and in the lightly documented relationships between performances. For this reason, scant textual record does not justify cutting but rather invites exploration in performance, and thus modern performance offers a useful counterpoint to critical work on Vice inheritance. Consider, for instance, the evocative illustrations of clownish dispersal in the universal whiteface clown make-up used in Emma Rice's 2017 *Romeo and Juliet* and by Brazilian theatre troupe Clowns de Shakespeare in other plays. Borrowing old and creating new theatricalities of Vice inheritance embraces the value of minor characters to major plays. Such theatricalities are a nod not just to the theatre historians in the audience, but also to the general audience member responsive to the effects of performance regardless of those effects' origins. Recapturing the cross-pollination of characters descended from the Vice can help to recreate the complex patterns of identification and complicity that are so crucial to a play's effects. Re-embedding the Vice's family tree for modern audiences can thus both excavate the past and reanimate an important part of how early modern plays leverage their audiences in performance.

PITYING DESDEMONA IN FOLIO *OTHELLO*: RACE, GENDER AND THE WILLOW SONG

JOSHUA R. HELD[1]

Pity is a major emotion in Shakespearian tragedy, but its relation to critical race studies and gender studies has been comparatively under-examined.[2] Pity fundamentally depends on an exchange of sympathy between the pitying, often in a position of advantage or at least of security, and the pitied, typically in a position of disadvantage. In Shakespeare's era, and in many before and since, differences in race and gender have entailed certain advantages and disadvantages: in his England, white male figures (at least those of a certain class) typically possessed more legal advantages than female figures or persons of other races.[3] Attentive to difference regarding both race and gender, *Othello* draws pity from audiences through its portrayals of these intertwined concerns, brought together pointedly through the marriage of Othello and Desdemona.[4]

In 1610, Henry Jackson commented on a production of *Othello* in Oxford: 'although she [Desdemona] pleaded her cause superbly throughout, nevertheless she moved [us] more after she had been murdered, when, lying upon her bed, her face itself implored pity [*misericordiam*] from the onlookers'.[5] Building on a history of especially sympathetic response to Desdemona, which I revisit in the conclusion, I argue that Desdemona is especially pitiable in the Folio version of the play because of several related elements that are uniquely available (or further highlighted) in that text: her defence of her own

---

[1] I wish to thank Emma Smith and the anonymous readers at *Shakespeare Survey* for their immense help with this article, especially for the encouragement to think more about race in *Othello*. I am also indebted to participants in a 2021 Shakespeare Association of America seminar for comments on an earlier version of this argument.

[2] For an overview of pity and emotion in Shakespeare, see David Hillman, 'The pity of it: Shakespearean tragedy and affect', in *The Oxford Handbook of Shakespearean Tragedy*, ed. Michael Neill and David Schalkwyk (Oxford, 2016), pp. 135–50. See also Bridget Escolme, *Emotional Excess on the Shakespearean Stage: Passion's Slaves* (London, 2015); Allison P. Hobgood, *Passionate Playgoing in Early Modern England* (Cambridge, 2014); and Gail Kern Paster, *Humoring the Body: Emotions and the Shakespearean Stage* (Chicago, 2004).

[3] On race and gender, see Ania Loomba, *Gender, Race, Renaissance Drama* (Manchester, 1989); Margo Hendricks and Patricia Parker, eds., *Women, 'Race', and Writing in the Early Modern Period* (New York, 1994), especially the essay by Loomba, 'The color of patriarchy: critical difference, cultural difference, and Renaissance drama', pp. 17–34; Kim F. Hall, *Things of Darkness: Economies of Race and Gender in Early Modern England* (Ithaca, NY, 1995); Dympna Callaghan, *Shakespeare Without Women: Representing Gender and Race on the Renaissance Stage* (New York, 1999); Joyce Green MacDonald, *Women and Race in Early Modern Texts* (Cambridge, 2002); and various essays in *The Oxford Handbook of Shakespeare and Embodiment: Gender, Sexuality, and Race*, ed. Valerie Traub (Oxford, 2016).

[4] On the juncture of race and gender in the play, see Karen Newman, '"And wash the Ethiop white": femininity and the monstrous in *Othello*', in *Shakespeare Reproduced: The Text in History and Ideology*, ed. Jean Howard and Marion F. O'Connor (New York, 1987), pp. 143–62; and Heinz Antor, 'Constructing alterity: race, gender, and the body in Shakespeare's *Othello*', in *Performing the Renaissance Body: Essays on Drama, Law, and Representation*, ed. Sidia Fiorato and John Drakakis (Boston, MA, 2016), pp. 73–106.

[5] Jackson's letter was first printed in Geoffrey Tillotson, '*Othello* and *The Alchemist* at Oxford in 1610', *Times Literary Supplement*, 20 July 1933, p. 494; cited with translation from 'Documents', in *The Norton Shakespeare*, ed. Stephen Greenblatt, Walter Cohen, Jean E. Howard, Katharine Eisaman Maus, Gordon McMullan and Suzanne Gossett (New York, 1997), pp. 3321–63; p. 3336. The brackets around 'us' are editorial.

feminine perspective, her identification with the Black maid Barbary, and her performance of the Willow Song. The Folio underscores these features of Desdemona especially in act 4 – the part of a Shakespearian play that Kenneth Burke calls the 'pity' act – in anticipation of the climactic outpouring of pity, and terror, at her death, and the death of Othello.[6]

Many argue that Othello gains great respect – and pity, adds Dennis Austin Britton – in part because of his ability to act heroically while enduring the race prejudice directed at him, especially by Iago.[7] Likewise, criticism of the late twentieth and early twenty-first centuries emphasizes Desdemona's strong feminine will and robust self-confidence, all while retaining great pity for her.[8] I am emphasizing that Desdemona, to the degree that she welcomes a Black identity not just by marrying Othello but also, in a Folio-only portion, by following the model of her mother's maid Barbary, obtains a double portion of pity – as a Black woman.[9]

By underscoring Desdemona's shared Black identity with Othello, I am diverging from a strand of scholarship of the mid twentieth century and after that, having established the presence and influence of Black Africans in Shakespeare's England, nevertheless generally emphasizes Othello's difference from other characters in the play.[10] This difference,

---

[6] Kenneth Burke, 'Othello: an essay to illustrate a method', The Hudson Review 4 (1951), 165–203; p. 174. See also Edward Pechter, 'The "pity" act', in Othello and Interpretive Traditions (Iowa City, 1999), pp. 113–40. On pity in the play more broadly, see Shawn Smith, 'Love, pity, and deception in Othello', Papers on Language and Literature 44 (2008), 3–51.

[7] Dennis Austin Britton, 'Contaminatio, race, and pity in Othello', in Rethinking Shakespeare Source Study: Audiences, Authors, and Digital Technologies, ed. Dennis Austin Britton and Melissa Walter (New York, 2018), pp. 46–64. Respect for Othello develops relatively early in studies of race in the play: see G. K. Hunter, 'Othello and color prejudice', Proceedings of the British Academy 53 (1967), 139–63; Ruth Cowhig, 'Blacks in English Renaissance drama and the role of Shakespeare's Othello', in The Black Presence in English Literature, ed. David Dabydeen (Manchester, 1985), pp. 1–25; and Emily C. Bartels, 'Making more of the Moor: Aaron, Othello, and Renaissance refashionings of race', Shakespeare Quarterly 41 (1990), 433–54. On Iago, see Janet Adelman, 'Iago's alter ego: race as projection in Othello', Shakespeare Quarterly 48 (1997), 125–44.

[8] A foundational argument for Desdemona's strong character is Carol Thomas Neely, 'Women and men in Othello: "what should such a fool / Do with so good a woman?"' Shakespeare Studies 10 (1977), 133–58. Such a view formed into something of a critical consensus by the 1980s: see W. D. Adamson, 'Unpinned or undone: Desdemona's critics and the problem of sexual innocence', Shakespeare Studies 13 (1980), 169–86; Jane Adamson, 'Othello' as Tragedy: Some Problems of Judgment and Feeling (Cambridge, 1980), pp. 214–63; Ann Jennalie Cook, 'The design of Desdemona: doubt raised and resolved', Shakespeare Studies 13 (1980), 187–96; Eamon Grennan, 'The women's voices in Othello: speech, song, silence', Shakespeare Quarterly 38 (1987), 275–92; and Lena Cowen Orlin, 'Desdemona's disposition', in Shakespearean Tragedy and Gender, ed. Shirley Nelson Garner and Madelon Sprengnether (Bloomington, 1996), pp. 171–92. For a relatively extensive literature review of (and response to) scholarship on this topic, see Will Stockton, 'Chasing chastity: the case of Desdemona', in Rethinking Feminism in Early Modern Studies: Gender, Race, and Sexuality, ed. Ania Loomba and Melissa E. Sanchez (New York, 2016), pp. 195–211. For an earlier view that emphasizes Desdemona's weaknesses, see Margaret Loftus Ranald, 'The indiscretions of Desdemona', Shakespeare Quarterly 14 (1963), 127–39.

[9] For a study of 'Desdemona's Blackness', see Lara Bovilsky, Barbarous Play: Race on the English Renaissance Stage (Minneapolis, 2008), pp. 37–66. I emphasize the effect of this in the Willow Song, which is not central to Bovilsky.

[10] For foundational modern studies of Othello amid broader considerations of racial difference, see Eldred Jones, Othello's Countrymen: The African in English Renaissance Drama (Oxford, 1965), esp. pp. 86–109 on Othello; Jones, The Elizabethan Image of Africa (Charlottesville, 1971); Anthony Gerard Barthelemy, Black Face, Maligned Race: The Representation of Blacks in English Drama from Shakespeare to Southerne (Baton Rouge, 1987); and Jack D'Amico, The Moor in English Renaissance Drama (Tampa, 1991). The recent scholarship on race in Othello is vast, as my notes will suggest, and can be polemically engaged. See, for example, Ian Smith, 'We are Othello: speaking of race in Early Modern Studies', Shakespeare Quarterly 67 (2016), 104–24. For a defence of race as a pertinent concept in Shakespeare's England, see Ayanna Thompson, 'Did the concept of race exist for Shakespeare and his contemporaries? An introduction', in The Cambridge Companion to Shakespeare and Race, ed. Ayanna Thompson (Cambridge, 2021), pp. 1–16. More recently, some scholars are showing the still earlier histories of race and its influences: see Geraldine Heng, The Invention of Race in the European Middle Ages (Cambridge, 2018), and Hannah Barker, That Most Precious Merchandise: The Mediterranean Trade in Black Sea Slaves, 1260–1500 (Philadelphia, 2019).

many stress, is especially visible through his Blackness, a colour that – at least one critic has contended – he shares with the fateful handkerchief.[11] Yet the emphasis on Othello's uniqueness threatens to occlude his established position in the Venetian state, and to wall him off from the other characters, including Desdemona. Whereas many scholars have shown Othello's belonging within the religious and social structures of Venice, I emphasize his more intimate connection with his wife.[12] This article argues that Desdemona, by performing lyrics that she learns from – and identifies with – a Black woman, elides some of the difference between her and Othello, and shares with him the pity that develops principally for her in the Folio's Willow Song.

PITY IN THE FOLIO

The Folio (F: 1623) version of *Othello* differs significantly from the Quarto (Q: 1622), containing not just upward of 1,000 variants, but also 160 new lines. This article reveals that several of these variants cohere to elicit greater pity for Desdemona, especially in the longest F-only passage, the Willow Song (see Table 1 below). The focus on this portion helps bring into perspective several other F-only passages that also affect an interpretation of Desdemona, the husband who accuses and ultimately kills her, and the villain who deceives him.

Scholars generally believe that Shakespeare may have revised *Othello*, whether by excising portions from a longer version (ultimately printed as F) to form a shorter, performance-oriented text (ultimately as Q), or by expanding Q. Those who argue for expansion do so with the rationale that Shakespeare would hardly have cut certain portions so dramatically effective as the Willow Song, much less without also expunging all the references to it.[13] Yet several others favour cuts, reasoning that it would have been unfeasible to add substantial portions to an already long text.[14] Richard Dutton proposes that Shakespeare composed lengthy plays such as *Othello* for performance

---

[11] On Blackness, see, inter alia, Kim F. Hall, '*Othello* and the problem of Blackness', in *A Companion to Shakespeare's Works*, vol. 1: *The Tragedies*, ed. Richard Dutton and Jean E. Howard (Malden, MA, 2003), pp. 357–74; and Ian Smith, 'Seeing Blackness: reading race in Othello', in *The Oxford Handbook of Shakespearean Tragedy*, ed. Neill and Schalkwyk, pp. 405–20. See also Ian Smith, 'Othello's black handkerchief', *Shakespeare Quarterly* 64 (2013), 1–25. An abridged version of this argument appears in Lena Cowen Orlin, ed., '*Othello*': *The State of Play* (London, 2014), pp. 95–120. Smith is arguing against a view such as that of Lynda E. Boose, 'Othello's handkerchief: "the recognizance and pledge of love"', *English Literary Renaissance* 5 (1975), 360–74.

[12] On Othello's fit in Venice, see Dennis Austin Britton, 'Re-"turning" *Othello*: transformative and restorative romance', *ELH* 78 (2011), 27–50; and Britton, *Becoming Christian: Race, Reformation, and Early Modern English Romance* (New York, 2014), pp. 112–41. Also on his religion, see Julia Reinhard Lupton, 'Othello circumcised: Shakespeare and the Pauline discourse of nations', *Representations* 57 (1997), 73–89; and Daniel J. Vitkus, 'Turning Turk in *Othello*: the conversion and damnation of the Moor', *Shakespeare Quarterly* 48 (1997), 145–76. On the possibility that Othello is not the only character in the play from Africa, see Jane Donawerth, 'Bianca: the other African in *Othello*', in *Roman Literature, Gender and Reception: Domina Illustris*, ed. Donald Lateiner, Barbara K. Gold and Judith Perkins (New York, 2013), pp. 232–50.

[13] See Nevill Coghill, *Shakespeare's Professional Skills* (Cambridge, 1964), pp. 164–202; Balz Engler, 'How Shakespeare revised *Othello*', *English Studies* 57 (1976), 515–21; and John Jones, *Shakespeare at Work* (Oxford, 1995), pp. 239–54.

[14] See W. W. Greg, *The Shakespeare First Folio: Its Bibliographical and Textual History* (Oxford, 1955), pp. 357–74; Scott McMillin, 'The *Othello* Quarto and the "foul-paper" hypothesis', *Shakespeare Quarterly* 51 (2000), 67–85; Scott McMillin, 'The mystery of the early *Othello* texts', in '*Othello*': *New Critical Essays*, ed. Philip C. Kolin (New York, 2002), pp. 401–24; and Scott McMillin, 'Introduction', in *The First Quarto of Othello*, ed. Scott McMillin (Cambridge, 2001), pp. 1–47, esp. pp. 8–15. Edward Pechter, 'Crisis in editing?' *Shakespeare Survey* 59 (Cambridge, 2006), 20–38, finds difficulties in both Greg and McMillin (pp. 21–8). Yet others also support this position: Pervez Rizvi, 'Evidence of revision in *Othello*', *Notes and Queries* 45 (1998), 338–43; and David Lake and Brian Vickers, 'Scribal copy for Q1 of *Othello*: a reconsideration', *Notes and Queries* 48 (2001), 284–7. For an early iteration of this position, see E. K. Chambers, *William Shakespeare: A Study of Facts and Problems*, vol. 1 (Oxford, 1930), pp. 457–63. E. A. J. Honigmann initially favoured

PITYING DESDEMONA IN FOLIO *OTHELLO*

Table 1 F-only passages of three lines or more

	TLN	Arden 3	#	Speaker / Topic
1	134–50	1.1.119–35	17	Roderigo defames Othello
2	290–5	1.2.72–7	6	Brabantio accuses Othello
3	2029–36	3.3.386–93	8	Othello requests proof
4	2103–10	3.3.456–63	8	Othello vows before Iago
5	2415–20	4.1.38–43	6	Othello falls in a trance
6	2769–72	4.2.74–7	4	Othello accuses Desdemona
7	2865–78	4.2.153–66	14	Desdemona claims innocence
8	3001–22 3024–6 3030–5	4.3.29–52 4.3.54–6 4.3.59–62	31	Desdemona: Willow Song
9	3059–76	4.3.85–102	18	Emilia critiques men
10	3425–30	5.2.147–50	6	Emilia defends Desdemona
11	3468–78	5.2.181–90	10	Emilia cries villainy
12	3545–7	5.2.244–6	3	Emilia: willow reprise
13	3566–72	5.2.264–70	7	Othello explains

Note: Line number totals (#) are from F.

at court, where long performances were welcome, and where Othello was performed in 1604.[15] Yet Dutton takes no sides regarding the priority of F or Q *Othello*, finding even the slightly shorter Q quite long enough for court performances.[16]

I, likewise, do not occupy a definite position regarding the chronology of the texts, focusing instead on the features of the Folio that highlight its different set of values from the Quarto. Many editors prefer F since it contains the fuller text, while others contend that both versions are theatrically viable.[17] In either case, F presents a significantly different text in some important points of the play, and many of its changes were used in the next quarto printing (Q2: 1630) and became accepted in almost all subsequent texts.[18] It is tempting to speculate further regarding the origins of the F additions. Yet Emma Smith illustrates the usefulness of 'reorient[ing] the discussion' of F changes 'away from causes, to think instead about effects'.[19] This article does just that, particularly regarding the conjoined issues of pity, gender and race.

Before proceeding to my argument, however, I want to clarify my relationship to two important textual studies of race and gender in the play. Leah Marcus contends that the Folio presents a decidedly more racist version of the play than does the Quarto.[20] She asserts, 'Most of the key

---

addition but later accepted the possibility of cuts: 'Shakespeare's revised plays: *King Lear* and *Othello*', *The Library*, 6th ser., 4 (1982), 142–73; E. A. J. Honigmann, *The Texts of 'Othello' and Shakespearean Revision* (New York, 1996); and E. A. J. Honigmann, 'The textual problem', in *Othello*, Arden Third Series, ed. E. A. J. Honigmann (London, 1997), pp. 351–67.

[15] Richard Dutton, *Shakespeare, Court Dramatist* (Oxford, 2016). On the 1604 court performance of *Othello*, see Jason Lawrence, 'Jacobean royal premieres? *Othello* and *Measure for Measure* at Whitehall in 1604', in *Performances at Court in the Age of Shakespeare*, ed. Sophie Chiari and John Mucciolo (Cambridge, 2019), pp. 92–106.

[16] See, for example, Dutton, *Shakespeare, Court Dramatist*, p. 266.

[17] In favour of F, see Alice Walker, 'The 1622 Quarto and the First Folio texts of Othello', *Shakespeare Survey 5* (Cambridge, 1952), 16–24; Alice Walker, *Textual Problems of the First Folio: 'Richard III', 'King Lear', 'Troilus and Cressida', '2 Henry IV', 'Hamlet', 'Othello'* (Cambridge, 1953), pp. 138–61; *Othello*, ed. Alice Walker and John Dover Wilson (Cambridge, 1957); and Stanley Wells and Gary Taylor, *William Shakespeare: A Textual Companion* (Oxford, 1987), pp. 476–8 (Wells edited *Othello*). McMillin (see note 14) approves of both Q and F.

[18] On the importance of Q2, see Thomas L. Berger, 'The Second Quarto of *Othello* and the question of textual authority', in *'Othello': New Perspectives*, ed. Virginia Mason Vaughan and Kent Cartwright (Rutherford, NJ, 1991), pp. 26–47, *contra* Charlton Hinman, 'The "copy" for the Second Quarto of *Othello* (1630)', in *Joseph Quincy Adams Memorial Studies*, ed. James G. McManaway, Giles E. Dawson and Edwin Eliott Willoughby (Washington, DC, 1948), pp. 373–89.

[19] Emma Smith, 'Reading the First Folio', in *The Cambridge Companion to Shakespeare's First Folio*, ed. Emma Smith (Cambridge, 2016), pp. 155–69; p. 157. On this point, see also Ed Pechter, 'Against attribution', *Shakespeare Quarterly* 69 (2018), 228–55.

[20] 'To imagine "gentle Shakespeare" as a reviser who began with a text resembling Q, then amplified and refocused it into a text resembling F, is to imagine a Shakespeare who

passages critics have repeatedly cited to define the play's attitude towards blackness, miscegenation, and sexual pollution, derive from the First Folio version of the play, and do not exist in the quarto.'[21] This statement is simply inaccurate, and misrepresents Marcus's own evidence, which rests largely on the Folio's first long addition, Roderigo's defamation of Othello. This passage, she claims, provides 'the lines that critics most often rely on to establish Othello's (stereotypical) Moorish lust and his marginality to Venetian culture even at the beginning of the play'.[22] These lines, indeed, contain a depiction of Brabantio's 'faire Daughter' in 'the grosse claspes of a lasciuious Moore' (TLN 135, 139; 1.1.120, 124), and some critics cite them for the purpose that Marcus observes.[23] Yet both Quarto and Folio contain, still earlier in the play, several other pertinent lines, such as Iago's warning that 'Euen now, very now, an old blacke Ram / Is tupping your white Ewe' (B2 v 4–5; 1.1.87–8; cf. TLN 96–7), in which the 'tupping' / topping pun emblematizes the vivid conjunction of putative sexual, racial and bestial defilement.[24] Just lines later, Iago develops the juncture of race and animal imagery: 'youle haue your daughter couered with a Barbary horse; youle haue your Nephewes ney to you; youle haue Coursers for Cousens, and Iennits for Iermans' (B2 v 29–31; 1.1.109–12; cf. TLN 123–6). Iago then brings these smears to a climax in the lurid prediction that Brabantio's 'daughter, and the Moore, are now making the Beast with two backs' (B2 v 35–6; 1.1.114–15; cf. TLN 128–9). These lines offer still more frequent, potent illustrations of racism (and some are more frequently cited by critics) than the F-only lines that Marcus highlights, in which Roderigo merely recycles the racial slanders he has seen modelled by Iago.[25]

Since Marcus believes that the Folio exacerbates the problem of racism, its additional identification of Desdemona with Blackness holds, for her, negative potential: 'Through the differences between Q and F Desdemona is not only blackened, she is also rendered alien from her previous self.'[26] I agree that Desdemona is 'blackened', and perhaps even to some degree 'rendered alien' in certain portions unique to F, but I emphasize that, in the F-only Willow Song, Desdemona herself confirms – and extends – the 'blacken[ing]' that

---

deliberately intensified what look from our modern perspective like racist elements of the play': Leah S. Marcus, 'The two texts of *Othello* and early modern constructions of race', in *Textual Performances: The Modern Reproduction of Shakespeare's Drama*, ed. Lukas Erne and Margaret Jane Kidnie (Cambridge, 2004), pp. 21–36; pp. 22–3; and Leah S. Marcus, 'Constructions of race and gender in the two texts of Othello', in *Rethinking Feminism*, ed. Loomba and Sanchez pp. 113–32; p. 116. While appreciating Marcus's fresh attention to gender (as well as race) in the later essay, I consider the two essays together, since she calls the earlier an 'abridged' version of the later ('Constructions', p. 118, n. 14), and since they share many of the same evidences and claims (such as that above).

[21] Marcus, 'Constructions', p. 116. This claim repeats one from 'Two texts', p. 22, except that it emends 'towards' to 'toward', adds 'First' before 'Folio', and inserts a comma after 'pollution'.

[22] Marcus, 'Constructions', p. 117; 'Two texts', p. 24.

[23] See, for example, Newman, '"And wash the Ethiop white"', p. 151; Martin Orkin, 'Othello and the "plain face" of racism', *Shakespeare Quarterly* 38 (1987), 166–88; p. 168; Michael Neill, 'Unproper beds: race, adultery, and the hideous in *Othello*', *Shakespeare Quarterly* 40 (1989), 383–412; p. 396; and Hall, '*Othello* and the problem of Blackness', p. 368. F is cited throughout by through line number (TLN) from *The Norton Facsimile: The First Folio of Shakespeare*, ed. Charlton Hinman (New York, 1968). I cross-reference TLNs from F (and citations from Q) with citations by act, scene, and line number from Honigmann's Arden Third Series edition of *Othello*.

[24] Citations from Q1 are by signature and line number from Shakespeare, *The Tragoedy of Othello, The Moore of Venice* (London, 1622), as printed in *Shakespeare's Plays in Quarto*, ed. Michael J. B. Allen and Kenneth Muir (Berkeley, 1981). On 'tupping', see Jeffrey Masten, 'Glossing and t*pping: editing sexuality, race, and gender in Othello', in *The Oxford Handbook of Shakespeare and Embodiment*, ed. Traub, pp. 567–85.

[25] At least some of these lines common to Q and F are cited to illustrate a racist perspective in the play by all the critics listed in note 23, as well as by some who do not cite the F-only lines: e.g., Bartels, 'Making more of the Moor', p. 448; Adelman, 'Iago's alter ego', p. 125; and Britton, 'Re-"turning" Othello', p. 33. The only aforementioned passage cited by all these is common to F and Q: 'an old blacke Ram / Is tupping your white Ewe'.

[26] Marcus, 'Constructions', p. 128.

Marcus portrays (through the passive voice) as something forced on her. Desdemona's deliberate self-blackening through the Willow Song renders her at once more powerful in choosing her own fate and more pitiable in enduring its consequences, quite unlike the character that Marcus sees in the Folio, and more striking than in an interpretation by Lois Potter in the second textual study of importance to my argument.[27] Potter maintains that 'someone – probably the author, but possibly not only him – was uncertain about how to achieve a balance between Desdemona's sexuality and her innocence'.[28] I argue, however, that, regarding the pity an audience feels for Desdemona, any reviser(s) quite certainly were not striving for 'balance': F presents a decidedly more pitiable female lead.

KNEELING: DESDEMONA'S SELF-DEFENCE IN 4.2

Several F-only portions in the first two scenes of act 4 contribute to a unique understanding of Desdemona, even before the F-only Willow Song: Othello's F-extended mad trance (4.1), his F-extended accusation of Desdemona (4.2) and Desdemona's kneeling defence of her innocence to Iago and Emilia (4.2). This last speech occurs in a crucial moment in act 4, just after the play's first intimate conference between her and Othello, who verbally abuses her. To show how the F-only lines shift the direction of the scene, this section starts with the two other F additions named above before focusing on Desdemona's long added defence in F. The section ultimately shows that this speech prepares for the still more piteous F-only Willow Song in the following scene (4.3).

In act 4, scene 1, Othello reaches the onstage zenith of his madness more visibly in F through additional repetitions that function in sequence with those in his imminent interview with Desdemona, and that suggest serial revision for this effect. Iago impugns Desdemona by reporting to Othello a putative conversation he had with Cassio. He feeds Othello just one word, 'Lye', and Othello springs: 'With her?' (TLN 2409–10; 4.1.33). Iago again responds with consummate ambiguity, 'With her? On her: what you will' (TLN 2411; 4.1.34), detonating Othello's reaction, extensive even in Q: 'Lie with her, lie on her? We say lie on her, when they bely her; lye with her, Zouns, that's fulsome, handkerchers, Confession, handkerchers' (I3 v 18–20; 4.1.35–7). F as usual omits the oath ('Zouns'), apparently in deference to the 1606 Act of Abuses, but it adds several lines that repeat the already confused language of 'Confession' and 'handkerchers', illustrating what one critic calls Othello's 'dismemberment of syntax'.[29] F thus reveals Othello's greater departure from what G. Wilson Knight characterizes as his 'magnificent rhetoric', and highlights instead his obsessive rage:[30] 'To confesse, and be hang'd for his labour. First, to be hang'd, and then to confesse: I tremble at it. Nature would not inuest her selfe in such shadowing passion, without some Iustruction [sic]. It is not words that shakes me thus, (pish) Noses, Eares, and Lippes: is't possible. Confesse? Handkerchiefe? O diuell' (TLN 2415–20; 4.1.38–43). In Q, Othello reveals a paranoia about the 'handkerchers' that F extends in the rant on this 'Handkerchiefe'. Yet F also extends the preoccupation to the process of confession itself, beginning the additional segment 'To confesse' and including another 'to confesse' and 'Confesse?' before the final 'Handkerchiefe'. And between these repeated single words that illustrate an unhealthy focus on minutia, Othello also reimagines the physical organs

---

[27] The phrase 'self-blackening' riffs on Stephen Greenblatt, *Renaissance Self-Fashioning: More to Shakespeare* (Chicago, 1980).

[28] Lois Potter, 'Editing Desdemona', in *In Arden: Editing Shakespeare, Essays in Honour of Richard Proudfoot*, ed. Gordon McMullan and Ann Thompson (London, 2003), pp. 81–94; p. 92.

[29] See Kenneth Gross, 'Slander and skepticism in *Othello*', *ELH* 56 (1989), 819–52; p. 829.

[30] G. Wilson Knight, *The Wheel of Fire: Interpretation of Shakespeare's Tragedies* (1930; repr. Cleveland, 1964), p. 103. For a more recent appraisal of Othello as the 'grandest high-style speaker in Shakespeare', see Richard Strier, 'The 2019 William B. Hunter Lecture of the SCRC: paleness versus eloquence – the ideologies of style in the English Renaissance', *Explorations in Renaissance Culture* 45 (2019), 91–120; p. 112.

by which Desdemona putatively proved unfaithful: 'Noses, Eares, and Lippes'.

Othello's more intense madness in act 4, scene 1, aligns with extra accusatory rhetoric in some F-only lines of scene 2, which ultimately show Othello more crazed, less open to Desdemona's attempts to persuade him of her virtue. During the heated interview between husband and wife at the centre of the scene, Othello in Q accuses her:

> Was this faire paper, this most goodly booke,
> Made to write whore on? – What, committed?
> Heauen stops the nose at it, and the Moone winkes,
> The bawdy wind, that kisses all it meetes,
> Is husht within the hallow mine of earth,
> And will not hear't: – what committed, – impudent strumpet.
>
> (K4 r 14–19; 4.2.73–82)

The dashes in Q perhaps suggest additional gestures to accompany Othello's fury, which ends in a Q-only barb: 'impudent strumpet'.[31] F, however, inserts four extra lines that begin after the first 'What commited' (Q: 'What, committed?') and expatiate on that keyword of adultery from the Ten Commandments ('Thou shalt not commit adultery', Exodus 20.14), and included in the English church canons of 1604.[32] The F-only lines show Othello fixating on Desdemona's presumed fault in a way that Q does not:

> Committed? Oh, thou publicke Commoner,
> I should make very Forges of my cheekes,
> That would to Cynders burne vp Modestie,
> Did I but speake thy deedes. What committed?
>
> (TLN 2769–72; 4.2.74–7)

In Q, Othello speaks the question 'What, committed?' twice at a line end, bracketing the extended imagery of natural phenomena – 'Heauen', 'the Moone', 'The bawdy wind', 'earth' – that are astonished at Desdemona's licence. In F, he speaks the phrase four times, the two additional instances framing the imagery of the 'Forges of [Othello's] cheekes', which previews the imagery of the natural 'wind' in the lines shared with Q. Especially in the first F-only repetition, the word 'Committed' clangs across the line with the other hard gutturals in the derogatory epithet 'publicke Commoner'. Although Q suggests Othello's excessive rage in the closely repeated 'committed', F intensifies this effect, highlighting the madness that Othello had demonstrated most starkly in the previous scene.

As a result of Othello's conversations with Iago early in act 4 (and in act 3), which feed his growing obsession with his wife's chastity, he explodes at her in a private interview in the middle of act 4, scene 2, repeatedly calling her a 'Whore' (TLN 2768, 2783, 2788; 4.2.73, 88, 91). It is this recurrent charge of 'whore', Lisa Jardine observes, that particularly abets the continued downward spiral of the plot, since Desdemona, accused persistently of effectual adultery, does not sufficiently combat these slanders, especially not in Q.[33] Desdemona responds in some fragmented assertions of her innocence, while Othello grows still more enraged and leaves soon after the re-entry of Emilia, who was to guard the door against any intrusion. Then, after Iago enters, Desdemona in both F and Q turns to Othello's confidant with a desperate plea:

> Alas *Iago*,
> What shall I do to win my Lord againe?
> Good Friend, go to him: for by this light of Heauen,
> I know not how I lost him.
>
> (TLN 2862–5; 4.2.150–3)

---

[31] On the potentially rich performative cues in the dashes of early modern dramatic texts, see Claire M. L. Bourne, *Typographies of Performance in Early Modern England* (Oxford, 2020), pp. 77–136.

[32] *The English Church Canons of 1604, with Historical Introduction*, ed. C. H. Davis (London, 1869), pp. 97–8, section 109: 'Notorious Crimes and Scandals to be certified into Ecclesiastical Courts by Presentment'.

[33] Lisa Jardine, '"Why should he call her whore?" Defamation and Desdemona's case', in *Reading Shakespeare Historically* (London, 1996), pp. 19–34. Dympna Callaghan observes that 'whore' is 'probably the worst name you can call a woman in Shakespeare's England': 'Introduction', in *A Feminist Companion to Shakespeare*, ed. Dympna Callaghan (Malden, MA, 2000), pp. xi–xxiv; p. xiii. See also Kay Stanton, '"Made to write 'whore' upon?" Male and female use of the word "Whore" in Shakespeare's canon', in *A Feminist Companion to Shakespeare*, pp. 80–102.

Desdemona implies that she wishes Iago to find 'how [she] lost' Othello and report back to her so she can 'win [her] Lord againe': the desired action is clear, as is the appeal to a putative 'Good Friend'. This is the end of her speech in Q, but in F she adds an extensive repudiation of the 'whore' slurs:

> Heere I kneele:
> If ere my will did trespasse 'gainst his Loue,
> Either in discourse of thought, or actuall deed,
> Or that mine Eyes, mine Eares, or any Sence
> Delighted them: or any other Forme,
> Or that I do not yet, and euer did,
> And euer will, (though he do shake me off
> To beggerly diuorcement) Loue him deerely,
> Comfort forsweare me. Vnkindnesse may do much,
> And his vnkindnesse may defeat my life,
> But neuer taynt my Loue. I cannot say Whore,
> It do's abhorre me now I speake the word,
> To do the Act, that might the addition earne,
> Not the worlds Masse of vanitie could make me.
>
> (TLN 2865–78; 4.2.153–66)

This added speech divides into two rhetorically powerful segments: in the first, Desdemona vows the constancy of her 'Loue' (TLN 2866–73; 4.2.154–61) and reasons that she is impermeable to Othello's 'vnkindnesse' (TLN 2873–5; 4.2.161–3); in the last portion she recoils at the hideous epithet ('Whore') Othello has hurled at her (TLN 2875–8; 4.2.163–6). Throughout the speech, she kneels, an utterly poignant gesture to which I will return.

Desdemona begins her self-defence with a complex vow that extends across eight lines, the conditional 'If ere' leading to a prodigious list of faculties and features that attest to her faithfulness. She first calls her 'will' to account and then her 'Eyes', 'Eares, or any Sence', concluding with her 'Loue', which itself answers to her earlier mention of the 'Loue' of 'his' that she asserts she did not 'trespasse 'gainst'. Likewise, she asserts her constant 'Loue' across all time – present, past and future: 'I do ..., and euer did, / And euer will'. Desdemona furthermore emphasizes the intensity of her 'Loue' by encompassing not only 'actuall deed' but also 'discourse of thought', attempting to make visible her inner intentions.[34] Desdemona concludes this elaborate formal vow with a stirring consequence should she lie about her complete and persisting 'Loue' for Othello: 'Comfort forsweare me'. Although the 'Comfort' of a peaceful life with her spouse may seem already strained, Desdemona makes her truthfulness guarantor of all the rest of her 'Comfort', including apparently her eternal salvation, as she had earlier ventured: 'No, as I am a Christian' (TLN 2779; 4.2.84). In such comprehensive vows, Desdemona stakes her life on her honesty. From this vow, she draws some implications that also affect her very existence: whereas she cannot guarantee what 'may' happen to her 'life', she controls her 'Loue', and determines 'neuer' to 'taynt' it – the 'neuer' reworking the iterations of 'euer' in the previous lines. For her, love is better than life.

In the final segment of the speech, the possibility of 'taynt' raises the spectre of the foul term that haunted the early portion of the scene: 'Whore'. Desdemona says it only to deny it, à la *occultatio* ('I cannot say Whore') and then, apparently ruing its appearance, attempts to mask the unwanted syllable within a pun: 'It do's abhorre me now I speake the word'. Yet the 'Whore'/'abhorre' pun is so raw that it only attracts more attention to the very word that Desdemona would bury. Still warily backing away from the explosive term, Desdemona reasons from the lesser to the greater that if she 'abhorre[d]' even the word, then 'To do the Act, that might the addition earne, / Not the worlds Masse of vanitie could make' her (TLN 2877–8; 4.2.165–6). Although the last few lines of Desdemona's speech seem to trip over themselves, they reveal a rhetorically sophisticated attempt to convey sincerity, which in this play especially is much more difficult than slick deceptions. She speaks in assertions that occasionally overlap, quite unlike the loosely inferential logic of Iago, who acts on what he only

---

[34] On the problem of discerning intention in the play, see Katharine Eisaman Maus, *Inwardness and Theater in the English Renaissance* (Chicago, 1995), pp. 104–27. On the relation between love and self-control in the play, see James Kuzner, *Shakespeare as a Way of Life: Skeptical Practice and the Politics of Weakness* (New York, 2016), pp. 49–79.

'suspect[s]' 'as if for Surety' (TLN 1078, 736; 2.1.293, 1.3.389).[35] And yet, ironically, Iago is the one Desdemona is calling on to present her case.

Julian C. Rice accuses Desdemona of unwarranted self-confidence in this speech: 'Her reference to her "discourse of thought" and to her "senses" as having been perfectly pure is another example of pride, since the mind and the senses were notoriously fickle from the Skeptical and Calvinistic points of view.'[36] But, arguably, Desdemona does not emphasize that she is 'perfectly pure' so much as that she has steadfast 'Loue' – nor, if she did, would her audience necessarily hold her to the standards of the 'Skeptical and Calvinistic points of view'. In a more positive assessment of the speech, Eamon Grennan proposes that '[w]hen Othello is not present to stifle her speech, Desdemona remains capable of utterance that constitutes a potent assertion of her freedom to love and to express that love'.[37] Yet even if Desdemona's speech were somehow to win Iago, and even if she favourably impresses her indirect audience (God, in her vow), any success only highlights the fact that the one she most needs to persuade is absent. For this reason, Desdemona can win pity from an audience while also not necessarily detracting from the pity that extends to Othello, who is not privy to the same careful defence.

During this additional speech in F, Desdemona 'kneele[s]' before Iago, presenting an eminently pitiable posture, especially so since Iago has no intention of helping her.[38] For an audience, and for Desdemona herself, such kneeling may very well recall that same action earlier in the scene, as soon as Emilia had left to give private conference between Othello and Desdemona, when she had knelt before him to aver her ignorance of any accusations: 'Vpon my knee, what doth your speech import? / I vnderstand a Fury in your words' (TLN 2723–4; 4.2.31–2). It is at this very moment in the scene that Desdemona's speech could have had its most powerful effect, applying all her persuasive powers to convince her husband – rather than her foe – of her faithfulness. Yet she delivers it only later to Iago who has no intention of conveying to Othello any of this elegantly crafted speech, and so Desdemona's appeal gets her nowhere with the character she most needs to impress.

The additional prominence of Desdemona's kneeling in F's version of the scene also retroactively highlights – and draws connections to – Othello's own kneeling before Iago three scenes earlier, in a passage also much expanded in F. Near the end of act 3, scene 3, Iago continues to gull Othello, calling him disingenuously to 'Patience' towards Desdemona: 'your minde may change' (TLN 2102; 3.3.455). Othello rejects the proposal in a brusque speech in Q: 'Neuer: / In the due reuerence of a sacred vow, / I here ingage my words' (H3 v 28–30; 3.3.456, 464–5). Othello either kneels at this 'vow', or perhaps earlier (as the Q stage direction may indicate), continuing the posture through the 'vow'. In F, Othello combines kneeling with a much longer, more impassioned speech:

> Neuer Iago. Like to the Ponticke Sea,
> Whose Icie Current, and compulsiue course,
> Neu'r keepes retyring ebbe, but keepes due on
> To the Proponticke, and the Hellespont:
> Euen so my bloody thoughts, with violent pace
> Shall neu'r looke backe, neu'r ebbe to humble Loue,
> Till that a capeable, and wide Reuenge
> Swallow them vp. Now by yond Marble Heauen,
> In the due reuerence of a Sacred vow,
> I heere engage my words.
>   (TLN 2103–12; 3.3.456–65)

The longer speech either prepares the kneeling at the 'vow' more elaborately (if the kneeling occurs at the vow itself) or sustains the kneeling for longer (if the kneeling occurs earlier in the speech). Yet, however long Othello has been kneeling, Iago calls

---

[35] On the importance of inference and presumption in the play (especially its rhetoric), see Joel B. Altman, *The Improbability of 'Othello': Rhetorical Anthropology and Shakespearean Selfhood* (Chicago, 2010).
[36] Julian C. Rice, 'Desdemona unpinned: universal guilt in *Othello*', *Shakespeare Studies* 7 (1974), 209–26; p. 218.
[37] Grennan, 'The women's voices in *Othello*', p. 288.
[38] On the gesture of kneeling and the act of supplication in the Renaissance, see Leah Whittington, *Renaissance Suppliants: Poetry, Antiquity, Reconciliation* (Oxford, 2016).

him to remain thus still longer as he joins in the vow, showing his solidarity with Othello at once in their common posture and their shared verse line:

> Do not rise yet:
> Witnesse you euer-burning Lights aboue,
> You Elements, that clip vs round about,
> Witnesse that heere *Iago* doth giue vp
> The execution of his wit, hands, heart,
> To wrong'd *Othello*'s Seruice. Let him command,
> And to obey shall be in me remorse,
> What bloody businesse euer.
>
> (TLN 2113–20; 3.3.465–72)

Iago here clinches his vow with the echo of 'bloody' (TLN 2120) from Othello's speech in F (TLN 2107), where shared diction and the more nearly equal speech lengths suggest the fuller partnership of the two plotters. Insofar as Desdemona's posture of kneeling revisits these earlier moments of kneeling in the play, both of herself to Othello and of Othello to Iago, it only highlights the ineffectiveness of her plea to the common antagonist Iago. The F-only portions in the first two scenes of act 4 therefore highlight the difficulties Othello undergoes in his struggle to think clearly, and spotlight Desdemona's still more extensive, failed attempts to gain pity from him. In all these textual changes, F presents a more pitiable Desdemona, a character with more ability – but less opportunity – to clear her name.

SINGING: THE WILLOW SONG IN 4.3

Against the backdrop of the earlier F-only portions in act 4 (and act 3), the more famous F-only Willow Song takes on additional significance, especially for an interpretation of Desdemona. Immediately after her first sustained private dialogue with Othello in 4.2, audiences see her longest stretch of private dialogue with Emilia in 4.3, turning the focus to a special female intimacy, unique in the play.[39] Besides the song itself, F contains several other unique segments, and the scene is the most radically reshaped in the play, growing from 61 lines in Q (L2 r 27 – L3 r 14) to 112 lines in F (TLN 2968–3079). These additions reveal Desdemona's greater recognition of her danger and yet her unflinching commitment to her previous course of action, which entails continued trust in Othello. Many scholars have examined the Willow Song and its pertinence to an interpretation of Desdemona, several of them considering the differences between Q and F, especially regarding the staging of Desdemona's undressing.[40] I emphasize the pity that F adds, and insist that it be read in connection with other material unique to F that primes the pity pump.

The simple fact that Desdemona sings the song is highly significant. In both F and Q, she observes that her mother's maid Barbary 'dy'd singing it' (TLN 3000; 4.3.28); then in Q she does not sing the song, while in F she sings it. Coghill favours F here because he reasons that if Shakespeare had not included the song itself, he 'would successfully have ousted *all* reference to' it.[41] But, rather than evidence a sloppy cut (or a tempting nub for an addition), both Q and F convey significant implications in an informal syllogism. Based on the parallel between Barbary and Desdemona herself, if she sings the song, she will die; if she does not, she will not die. In F but not Q, Desdemona sings the song and thus fulfils the minor premise that suggests her fatal conclusion.

Furthermore, when Desdemona sings the song, she performatively embodies an affiliation with Blackness that reorients some of the other (potentially adverse) associations with Blackness that Lara

---

[39] See Evelyn Gajowski, 'The female perspective in Othello', in *'Othello': New Perspectives*, ed. Vaughan and Cartwright, pp. 97–114; p. 107: 'When we enter the willow song scene, we enter a world of women from which men are excluded.'

[40] For the argument that the song was cut (to form the text of Q) when the play was done indoors at Blackfriars, see Denise A. Walen, 'Unpinning Desdemona', *Shakespeare Quarterly* 58 (2007), 487–508. Carol Chillington Rutter, 'Unpinning Desdemona (again) or "Who would be toll'd with Wenches in a shew?"' *Shakespeare Bulletin* 28 (2010), 111–32, disputes this. See also Clare McManus, '"Sing it like poor Barbary": *Othello* and early modern women's performance', *Shakespeare Bulletin* 33 (2015), 99–120.

[41] Coghill, *Shakespeare's Professional Skills*, p. 192.

Bovilsky has noted.[42] In one such instance, where Othello in F fitfully deems Desdemona a 'weed' (TLN 2762), he in Q condemns her as a 'blacke weede' (K4 r 10; 4.2.68), which one editor calls 'a striking touch'.[43] In the central scene of Q's act 4, Desdemona is associated with a negative valence of Blackness by her own Black husband. In F, however, and in the very next scene, she performs the Blackness that forecasts her continuing identification with him, and that – in the lyrics – reveals her abiding commitment to love him at any price, including her reputation, and by inference her life.

Several other aspects of the scene in F also affect the pity an audience may feel for Desdemona, including the fragmentary delivery of the song, and the melancholy conversation that precedes it.[44] In both Q and F, Desdemona explains its ominous import:

> My mother had a Maid call'd *Barbarie*,
> She was in loue: and he she lou'd prou'd mad,
> And did forsake her. She had a Song of Willough,
> An old thing 'twas: but it express'd her Fortune,
> And she dy'd singing it. That Song to night,
> Will not go from my mind …
> (TLN 2996–3001; 4.3.24–9)

Given the precedents in Shakespeare's England, the name '*Barbarie*' quite surely designates the maid's origin from the Barbary coast, a Moorish region of Africa the play had already connected to Othello and his Blackness through Iago's pejorative description of the Moor as a 'Barbary horse' (TLN 124; 1.1.110).[45] It is probable that the maid Barbary served as an early entrée for Desdemona into an interest in her own husband, himself apparently from this region or near it. After naming the maid, Desdemona opens up an allegorical vista that extends right into her song, for all that she says of Barbary applies as well to herself: 'She was in loue: and he she lou'd prou'd mad, / And did forsake her'.[46] Desdemona does not state or even suggest that the maid's lover killed her; yet she telescopes the maid's failed love affair with a song of death, which 'express'd her Fortune'. Desdemona states that the maid 'dy'd singing it', perhaps in rueful memory of her 'mad' lover, and confesses that 'That Song to night, / Will not go from my mind'. Desdemona not only explores the persona of an intimately remembered Black woman, but also begins to align her fate with this persona.

After Desdemona explains the history and symbolic importance of the Willow Song, F diverges markedly from Q, ultimately creating more space for Desdemona's self-reflection, centred on the song. F orients the scene around the melancholy refrain of 'Willough', mitigating her agitation at Othello's imminent return, which governs the mood more fully in Q. Accordingly in Q, Desdemona more promptly follows Othello's instructions, 'Get you to bed on th'instant, I will be return'd forthwith: dismisse your Attendant there: look't be done' (TLN 2975–7; 4.3.5–7). In both texts, she punctually conveys these instructions to Emilia: 'He saies he will returne incontinent, / And hath commanded me to go to bed, / And bid me to dismisse you' (TLN 2980–2; 4.3.10–12). Despite Emilia's fussy response, 'Dismisse me?' (TLN 2983; 4.3.12), Desdemona presses: 'It was his bidding: therefore good *Aemilia*, / Giue me my nightly wearing, and adieu. / We must not now displease him' (TLN 2984–6; 4.3.13–15; cf. Q L2 v 5–7). But in Q, Desdemona maintains more constant pressure on Emilia to leave, prodding her seventeen lines later, 'Now get thee gone, good night' (L2 v 24; 4.3.57; cf. TLN 3027), which

---

[42] See Bovilsky, *Barbarous Play*, pp. 37–66.

[43] McMillin, ed., *The First Quarto of Othello*, p. 126.n.

[44] For an emphasis on the song's being 'broken off', see Rosalind King, '"Then murder's out of tune": the music and structure of *Othello*', *Shakespeare Survey 39* (Cambridge, 1987), pp. 149–58; p. 157.

[45] For records of Black people named Barbary in England, see Imtiaz Habib, *Black Lives in the English Archives, 1500–1677: Imprints of the Invisible* (Burlington, VT, 2008) – e.g., pp. 107–8. On the name 'Barbary', see also Peter Erickson, 'Race words in *Othello*', in *Shakespeare and Immigration*, ed. Ruben Espinosa and David Ruiter (Burlington, VT, 2014), pp. 159–76.

[46] On the allegorical dimension of the song, see Martha Ronk, 'Desdemona's self-presentation', *English Literary Renaissance* 35 (2005), 52–72; pp. 61–7.

comes more than forty lines later in F. Desdemona in F punctuates the song by two additional reminders – 'prythee dispatch' and '(Prythee high thee: he'le come anon)' (TLN 3003, 3019; 4.3.31, 49) – and yet Emilia's final exit ('Good night good night'; L3 r 13; 4.3.103; cf. TLN 3077) comes fifty lines after the last reminder to do so in F, rather than only twenty-six lines later in Q. Although Desdemona seems committed to complying with Othello's wishes in either text, in Q this commitment is interrupted merely by Emilia's garrulousness, while in F the longest delay is Desdemona's extensive Willow Song, which creates a pause that Emilia exploits further in her own reflections at the end of the scene (especially in F).

Desdemona earns considerable pity through the complex weave of song with spoken dialogue that reveals her preoccupation with its portents. After she explains the import of the song, which 'Will not go from [her] mind', she in Q immediately calls out, 'harke, who's that knocks?' (L2 v 22), and Emilia calms her, 'It is the wind' (L2 v 23). In Q, this exchange short-circuits any impulse Desdemona might have to sing the song, and she next – despite reminding Emilia to 'get thee gone' (L2 v 24; 4.3.57) – calls her back with a query, 'Mine eyes doe itch, does that bode weeping?' (L2 v 25; 4.3.57–8). Perhaps the 'itch[ing]' eyes result from the attempt to suppress the song that in F flows in several stanzas, though not before some additional conversation unique to F:

DESDEMONA   I haue much to do,
    But to go hang my head all at one side
    And sing it like poore *Brabarie* [sic]: prythee dispatch.
EMILIA   Shall I go fetch your Night-gowne?
DESD.   No, vn-pin me here,
   This *Lodouico* is a proper man.
EMILIA   A very handsome man.
DESD.   He speakes well.
      (TLN 3001–8; 4.3.29–36)

Desdemona specifies her efforts to suppress emotion ('much to do'), avoiding the extreme posture of the maid who sang the song with her 'head all at one side'.[47] Perhaps further to distract herself from the memory of the song that haunts her, despite efforts to dismiss it, Desdemona abruptly asserts of her kinsman, '*Lodouico* is a proper man.' Some scholars see her considering Lodovico as a potential suitor, though any such consideration seems short-circuited in her subsequent conversation.[48] When Emilia attempts to develop the topic in a titillating direction ('A very handsome man'), Desdemona attenuates 'handsome' to refer to 'speak[ing] well'. Temporarily stymied, Emilia tells her own quixotic story to match Desdemona's of Barbary: 'I know a Lady in Venice would haue walk'd barefoot to Palestine for a touch of his nether lip' (TLN 3009–10; 4.3.37–8). The proposition of 'walk[ing] barefoot to Palestine' suggests pilgrimage, and it is tempting also to see this Folio portion faintly preparing the F-variant 'Iudean' (TLN 3658; 5.2.345) in Othello's final speech, implicating Desdemona twice over in a misbegotten deal brokered in the Holy Land.

Although Desdemona attempts various stratagems to distract herself from the Willow Song, probably squelching tears in Q and in F, and raising a new topic, she does not ultimately evade it in the Folio. When Emilia presents Lodovico as a love interest, Desdemona turns to the song, embarking on what one critic has called the 'fullest expression of her chaste and mature sexuality':[49]

---

[47] *Contra* S. N. Garner, 'Shakespeare's Desdemona', *Shakespeare Studies* 9 (1976), 233–52; p. 248: 'She [Desdemona] not only foreshadows her death but also expresses an unconscious desire for it.... That the song will not go from her mind and that she has "much to do" to keep from hanging her head and singing it suggest the insistence of a death wish.' Such a view undercuts Desdemona's continuing vitality in this scene and certainly in the last.

[48] Ruth Vanita, '"Proper" men and "fallen" women: the unprotectedness of wives in *Othello*', *Studies in English Literature, 1500–1900* 34 (1994), 341–56; p. 347, overviews a range of interpretations including some more salacious options, ultimately presenting Desdemona's comment as deliberately 'ironical', undercutting Lodovico. Samuel Johnson (*The Plays of William Shakespeare*, ed. Johnson, vol. 10 (London, 1765), p. 446), thinks that Desdemona simply 'endeavours to change her train of thoughts'.

[49] Rochelle Smith, 'Admirable musicians: women's songs in *Othello* and *The Maid's Tragedy*', *Comparative Drama* 28 (1994), 311–23; p. 320.

The poore Soule sat singing, by a Sicamour tree.
  Sing all a greene Willough:
Her hand on her bosome her head on her knee,
  Sing Willough, Willough, Willough.
The fresh Streames ran by her, and murmur'd her moanes
  Sing Willough, &c.
Her salt teares fell from her, and softned the stones,
  Sing Willough, &c.
                                    (TLN 3011–18; 4.3.39–46)

The images in the song project sorrow onto the natural landscape, the '*Streames*' that '*murmur'd her moanes*' and the '*teares*' that '*softned the stones*' confirming the reflexive posture of '*Her hand on her bosome her head on her knee*', which mimic the drooping willow itself. These images and the plaintive refrain develop a poignant mood for Desdemona. As she sings the song, she mimetically becomes its subject, the '*poore Soule*' who '*sat singing*', while the '*moan[ing]*' and '*teares*' correspond to, or metaphorically stand for, her own.

In the next stanzas, Desdemona attempts to continue her singing while also conversing with Emilia, and so loses her place in the song. F marks her snatches of conversation with parentheses:

(Lay by these)
Willough, Willough. (Prythee high thee: he'le come anon)
Sing all a greene Willough must be my Garland.
Let nobody blame him, his scorne I approue.
(Nay that's not next. Harke, who is't that knocks?)
                                    (TLN 3018–22; 4.3.47–52)

That the refrain '*Willough, Willough*' directly follows an earlier iteration of it ('*Sing Willough, &c.*'; TLN 3018; 4.3.46) suggests that Desdemona may merely hum the tune during the strophe while she comments '*Lay by these*', resuming the refrain, which she interrupts again with a still longer comment to Emilia: '*Prythee high thee: he'le come anon*'. After another iteration of the refrain, Desdemona adds a new tag from the original song ('*must be my Garland*') and then begins a new verse that apparently goes awry: '*Nay that's not next*.' Desdemona's precise slip is hard to discern, since her lyrics after the first couplet differ significantly from the original Tudor set.[50] But whatever lyrics Desdemona thinks should come 'next', the ones she sings – '*Let nobody blame him, his scorne I approue*' – not only suggest her immediate anxiety at not being prepared when Othello returns, but also adumbrate the larger uncertainties about what he will do, given his manic accusations of her infidelity.

After interrupting herself, Desdemona is disturbed by the impression that someone 'knocks', which answers her anxiety revisited just three lines earlier that 'he'le come anon'. The knock comes in a line shared with Q, though in that text it obviates the song while in F it arrests the wandering tune and so gives Desdemona a chance to continue afresh. This mangled set of strophes, broken by interjected conversation, mistaken lyrics and imagined disruptions, allows great flexibility in performance to extend the potentially long process of undressing Desdemona, perhaps even by interpolating extra verses not printed in F.[51] Although Desdemona maintains remarkable self-control throughout the play, these broken lines and her visible agitation amid them convey the confusion she experiences, baring her soul even as the 'vn-pin[ning]' exposes her body for her night with Othello.

Even after multiple interruptions, Desdemona regains her composure to finish the song. She concludes with a most revelatory couplet, unprecedented in the Tudor lyrics:

I call'd my Loue false Loue: but what said he then?
  Sing Willough, &c.
If I court mo women, you'le couch with mo men.
                                    (TLN 3024–6; 4.3.54–6)

In departing from the available lyrics, or anything like them, Desdemona more overtly than before reveals herself as the subject of the lyrics. By ending with a couplet that highlights '*Loue*', Desdemona

---

[50] For the Tudor lyrics (in two alternative versions) that inform F's, see Ross W. Duffin, *Shakespeare's Songbook* (New York, 2004), pp. 467–70. On some differences between F's song and the original lyrics, see Ernest Brennecke, '"Nay, that's not next!": the significance of Desdemona's "Willow Song"', *Shakespeare Quarterly* 4 (1953), 35–8.

[51] See Walen, 'Unpinning Desdemona', p. 495.

returns to a chief concern of her long F-only speech in the previous scene, where she not only asserts that she does 'Loue him [Othello] deerely', but also that no 'vnkindnesse' of his could 'taynt [her] Loue' (TLN 2872, 2874–5; 4.2.160, 162–3). The first half of the couplet asks for a response from the '*false Loue*', and so the second half comes from the persona of that man, returning to the orientation of the original lyrics, which are sung by a man who mourns his unfaithful beloved. By placing the final line in the mouth of the male lover, Desdemona not only suits those original lyrics but also recalls the cynical attitude Othello had demonstrated in the previous scene, and foreshadows his coming putative justice. Indeed, the last phrase, '*you'le couch with mo men*', prefigures some crucial (imagined) evidence for Othello in his soliloquy as he weighs the option of killing Desdemona asleep on their bed: 'Yet she must dye, else shee'l betray more men' (TLN 3245; 5.2.6). This unique segment in F thus strengthens the supposed logic, and real pathos, of much else in the play.

Having finished the song, Desdemona embarks on a lengthy conversation with Emilia that reflects the concerns of that song, and of her imminent conversation with Othello. Despite Desdemona's obvious anxiety, Emilia proves by turn cold, unhelpful and ominously ironic, perhaps directing further pity towards the increasingly desolate Desdemona. Desdemona's bidding to Emilia, 'So get thee gone, good night', may suggest that they have finished her preparation for Othello's return, at which point Emilia was (per Othello's instructions) to leave. Yet, as in Q, Desdemona calls her back with a question: 'mine eyes do itch: / Doth that boade weeping?' (TLN 3027–8; 4.3.57–8). Whereas in Q (as seen above) the 'itch[ing]' eyes obviate the song, in F they indicate Desdemona's attempt to quell the emotions it has conjured in her, and prompt her to continue conversation with Emilia, who responds evasively, ''Tis neyther heere, nor there' (TLN 3029; 4.3.58). In F (only), Desdemona responds to her own question ('I haue heard it said so') and then presents a new query that aligns the song lyrics with her own mistreatment in the previous scene:

> O these Men, these men!
> Do'st thou in conscience thinke (tell me *AEmilia*)
> That there be women do abuse their husbands
> In such grosse kinde?
>
> (TLN 3030–3; 4.3.59–62)

Desdemona's pointed interjection, '(tell me *AEmilia*)', reveals her increasing efforts to elicit a definite response from Emilia, who nevertheless returns an equally vague answer: 'There be some such, no question' (TLN 3034; 4.3.62). Although Desdemona thought she could count on Emilia for definite support of her newly (and temporarily) questioning approach to 'husbands', and by implication Othello, Emilia turns reticent.

Apparently not content with Emilia's answers, Desdemona reformulates the previous question and puts it to Emilia directly: 'Would'st thou do such a deed for all the world?' (TLN 3034; 4.3.63). In this line and the following ones, F and Q coincide again, though they reflect quite differently on the relationship of the two speakers. In F, Desdemona appears exasperated with Emilia's taciturnity; in Q, her abrupt question – without the context of the previous four lines – relies on Emilia to understand the more covert reference to adultery ('such a deed'). That she does so validates Desdemona's confidence in her, and highlights their camaraderie. In the succeeding lines, common to F and Q, Emilia puns at Desdemona's expense, inverting Desdemona's oath 'by this Heauenly light' (TLN 3037; 4.3.64) into a context of trickery: she would rather cuckold her husband 'i'th'darke' (TLN 3039; 4.3.66). In Q, which has just highlighted Desdemona's and Emilia's solidarity, this witticism proves more jovial than in F, where it feels more strident, even cross. The increasing dissonance between Emilia and Desdemona here and elsewhere in the second half of the scene, particularly in F, intensifies the vulnerability of the latter, and the sympathy an audience may grant her.

In the ensuing dialogue of nearly twenty lines (TLN 3040–58; Q L2 v 32 – L3 r 12; 4.3.67–84), common to both F and Q, Emilia finally engages Desdemona more fully, though she is anything but encouraging to Desdemona's faithfulness. Emilia ultimately proposes that any woman who would prepare for her future ('store the world', TLN 3058; 4.3.84) would venture hoodwinking her husband. Then, in F, Emilia continues her rejoinder in an additional eighteen lines that disclose a more bitter approach to marriage than any of her previous responses. This long, added portion reveals more in F not just of Emilia but also of Desdemona, who, though impatient to have Emilia leave, listens to the protracted lecture. Emilia shifts from answering Desdemona's persistent questions to taking a position more fully her own:

> But I do thinke it is their Husbands faults
> If Wiues do fall: (Say, that they slacke their duties,
> And powre our Treasures into forraigne laps;
> Or else breake out in peeuish Iealousies,
> Throwing restraint vpon vs: Or say they strike vs,
> Or scant our former hauing in despight)
> Why we haue galles: and though we haue some Grace,
> Yet haue we some Reuenge. Let Husbands know,
> Their wiues haue sense like them: They see, and smell,
> And haue their Palats both for sweet, and sowre,
> As Husbands haue. What is it that they do,
> When they change vs for others? Is it Sport?
> I thinke it is: and doth Affection breed it?
> I thinke it doth. Is't Frailty that thus erres?
> It is so too. And haue not we Affections?
> Desires for Sport? and Frailty, as men haue?
> Then let them vse vs well: else let them know,
> The illes we do, their illes instruct vs so.
>   (TLN 3059–76; 4.3.79–104)

Emilia's thesis – 'it is their Husbands faults / If Wiues do fall' – at once transmutes Desdemona's sympathies towards her husband and returns to her own forceful imagery from act 3, scene 4. There she imagines husbands as 'all but Stomackes, and we all but Food, / They eate vs hungerly, and when they are full / They belch vs' (TLN 2256–8; 3.4.105–7). Since Emilia has just witnessed Othello's insulting of the innocent Desdemona in the previous scene, her bitterness towards men in the present scene is especially understandable. Yet her hostility seems gratuitous, hardly calculated to persuade Desdemona – instead, apparently attempting only to justify herself, and to vent her festering acrimony. That Desdemona endures the rant without interrupting it – even when she could take just occasion at one of its many rhetorical questions – illustrates her willingness to humour a friend, and perhaps once more to consider the possibility of rejecting Othello.

Emilia supports her feminist manifesto first by presenting some simulations of various ways that husbands might offend their wives. The off-hand manner of Emilia's evidence ('Say') belies the stiff accusations against those who 'slacke their duties, / And powre our Treasures into forraigne laps', licentious activities that seem relatively distant from both Iago and Othello. Emilia seems to target Othello more fully in the next salvo, against those who 'breake out in peeuish Iealousies', or who 'strike' their wives, as Othello had done to Desdemona in act 4, scene 1. Whereas, in the opening lines of F's addition, Emilia attends at least partially to Desdemona's struggle with Othello, her first-person plural pronoun (us, our) that previously seemed to concern primarily her and Desdemona opens to encompass all women in a thrice-repeated 'we': 'Why we haue galles: and though we haue some Grace, / Yet haue we some Reuenge' (TLN 3065–6; 4.3.91–2). In the emphasis on revenge and on the appeal to shared human 'sense' – 'They see, and smell, / And haue their Palats both for sweet, and sowre, / As Husbands haue' (TLN 3067–9; 4.3.93–5) – Emilia resonates with the spite of another slighted Venetian, Shylock, who asks, 'Hath not a Iew eyes? hath not a Iew hands, organs, dementions, sences, affections, passions … ?' (TLN 1270–2; 3.1.53–5). After the initial accusations and then the rationale for revenge, Emilia raises a series of rhetorical questions to critique male offences regarding 'Sport', 'Affection' and 'Frailty' (TLN 3070–2; 4.3.96–8). Emilia pinpoints three specific categories that contribute to the confusions of romantic relationships and that, she asserts, belong equally to husband and wife. Her long speech against men highlights Desdemona's own patience.

Emilia concludes with a couplet proverb that distils an action from her previous harangue: 'Then let them vse vs well: else let them know, / The illes we do, their illes instruct vs so' (TLN 3075–6; 4.3.101–2). Despite this resounding conclusion, and despite the exceeding depravity of Iago, Emilia does not seem to have planned anything devious against him, her own specimen of a husband; if precedent holds, she might instead find some trifle to favour him with, since she at least very recently considered herself 'nothing, but to please his Fantasie' (TLN 1934; 3.3.303). Perhaps it is because Desdemona senses this mismatch between design and action that she lets Emilia carry this speech to such lengths. Or perhaps it is because Desdemona finds the logic compelling, however little she ultimately acts on it. In any case, since Desdemona stands by quietly while Emilia denounces men, the play presents the possibility of a woman's defection from her husband for several possible reasons, made more persuasive by their arrangement together in one long speech, at the very point that Desdemona must face the crux of her fate with Othello. An audience of F may well wonder, however fleetingly, during Emilia's speech: will Desdemona accept this view and desert Othello, perpetuating the tale of a forsaken African, like Barbary?

F, like Q, concludes the scene with a brief send-off from Desdemona, though this functions quite differently in the two texts. Having just endured a twenty-line excoriation of men in F, Desdemona gathers her wits for a curt dismissal:

> Good night, good night:
> Heauen me such vses send,
> Not to picke bad, from bad; but by bad, mend.
> (TLN 3077–9; 4.3.103–4; cf. Q L3 r 13–14)

In F, Desdemona's lack of a response to Emilia's long speech is itself significant, the valediction 'Good night, good night' repeated perhaps to confirm that no further discussion is welcome, and a pithy couplet tacked on to gloss as salutary what Emilia had put so deleteriously. In Q, Desdemona's valediction ends the conversation much earlier, after just the first two lines of Emilia's speech, sending her out with good wishes and a proverb that attempts to make some sense of their briefer disagreement. In either text, Desdemona seems to imply that she determines not to imbibe Emilia's deceptive logic ('Not to picke bad, from bad') but perhaps, instead, to use their discourse as a general encouragement ('by bad, mend'). Alternatively, or additionally, this proverb might gloss the whole preceding scene, which itself reflects on the nightmarish scene before it: Desdemona proceeds into the play's final scene with a sustained geniality that not even the mournful Willow Song or captious critiques from her friend Emilia can dislodge. But the fact remains that, in F, Desdemona has just experienced a much longer attack explicitly directed towards men and implicitly aimed at her own acceptance of her husband. In F, although Desdemona asks the initial questions and prods Emilia to answer them, Emilia ultimately seizes the right to ask the questions and then – knowing that Desdemona will give responses just as dissenting as those she received – answers her own questions, folding them into a sustained diatribe. Accordingly in F, her conciliatory final response to Emilia carries more rhetorical weight, warding off future conflict rather than (in Q) simply ending a back-and-forth question-and-answer in which Desdemona asked all the questions and Emilia gave increasingly desultory answers. Thus, in the close of this scene, and in several additions in act 4 of F, Desdemona reveals her rhetorical aptitude and yet intensifies her embrace of a destiny marked out more by her affiliation with her husband than by her own abilities.

The most famed portion of act 4, scene 3, the Willow Song, recurs in the final scene in a passage again unique to F, at once reinforcing the power of this song across the play and freshly emphasizing pity for Desdemona, and for Emilia, who sings it after her mistress's death and in premonition of her own. In both F and Q, Emilia asks, 'oh lay me by my Mistris side' (TLN 3534; 5.2.235; cf. M4 v 9). When she next speaks, in F she recalls Desdemona's song: 'What did thy Song boad Lady? / Hearke, canst thou heare me? I will play the Swan, / And dye in Musicke: *Willough,*

Willough, Willough' (TLN 3545–7; 5.2.244–6). The music, already accurately foretelling Desdemona's death, now haunts other characters and the whole stage, 'twisting in and out', Erin Minear observes, 'of the minds of characters and audience'.[52] Emilia, presumably lying near the dead Desdemona, thus overtly calls attention once more to Desdemona's own 'boad[ing]' lyrics. In Q, without the 'Willow' reprise, Emilia's next statement – 'Moore, she was chaste' (TLN 3548; 5.2.245; cf. M4 v 20) – rings more loudly as an accusation against Othello; in F, with its previous focus on Desdemona, Emilia's claim feels more rueful, tempering her critique of the 'cruell Moore' (TLN 3548; 5.2.245; cf. M4 v 20).

I have argued that, whereas F presents a more pitiful conclusion for Desdemona, and Emilia, it also sharpens the sting of Othello's death. In F, at a famed crux, Othello speaks of himself in his last speech as 'one, whose hand / (Like the base Iudean) threw a Pearle away / Richer then all his Tribe' (TLN 3657–9; 5.2.344–6). In Q, he portrays himself as the 'base *Indian*' (N2 r 8), also exotic but creating mercantile rather than religious overtones. Each reading has its defenders, and influences; the most significant impact of F is the arguably increased pity for Othello, who depicts himself most guiltily as 'the' Judean, Judas, who accepted a 'base' bribe to deliver Christ – the 'Pearle' who is 'Richer then all his Tribe' – into the hands of executioners.[53] In terms of Othello's analogy, Desdemona is the Christ 'Pearle', and Othello the one whose 'hand' not only destroyed the innocent but also commits suicide, as did Judas in remorse (Matt. 27.5). Othello's heavy self-condemnation may help to allay the guilt an audience attributes to him; whereas Judas is understood to be thoroughly evil, inspired by Satan (John 13.2), Othello's transgression, as he believes, was the fault of one who 'lou'd not wisely, but too well' (TLN 3655; 5.2.342).

CONCLUSION

At the end of *Othello*, pity is powerful, cutting as deep as the sword that the titular protagonist thrusts into his own entrails. This article has examined several F-only segments of the preceding act to argue that these serial shifts reveal a unique, coherent version of Desdemona and, ultimately, of the plot that culminates in her death and the death of her husband. Near the end of act 4 in F, but not in Q, Desdemona sings the melancholy Willow Song that deepens at once her premonition of her death and her commitment to face it. Earlier in the act, F uniquely includes her longest defence of her chastity – delivered, ironically, to the villain Iago. Whereas in Q Desdemona may seem unable adequately to defend herself, especially in her brief counter-charges to Othello in act 4, scene 2, F reveals that she can do so to even her most cunning enemy. The Willow Song in F thus capitalizes on other F-only portions that generate respect and pity for Desdemona, further implicating her as a cause of pitying emotions an audience experiences in the final deaths.

Starting with Henry Jackson in 1610, audiences through the centuries have registered – in sometimes quite different ways – the play's emotional force.[54] Samuel Pepys reported of an early Restoration performance on 11 October 1660 that 'a very pretty lady that sot by me cried to see Desdimona [*sic*] smothered'.[55] In the next century, Samuel Johnson commented of the same incident: 'I am glad that I have ended my revisal of this dreadful scene. It is not to be endured.'[56] And in the century after that, William Hazlitt remarked more broadly that the play 'excites our sympathy in

---

[52] Erin Minear, 'Music and the crisis of meaning in *Othello*', *Studies in English Literature, 1500–1900* 49 (2009), 355–70; p. 366.

[53] In favour of Q here, see Richard Levin, 'The Indian/Iudean crux in *Othello*', *Shakespeare Quarterly* 33 (1982), 60–7. In favour of F, see Joan Ozark Holmer, 'Othello's Threnos: Arabian trees and "Indian" versus "Judean"', *Shakespeare Studies* 13 (1980), 145–67.

[54] On historically conditioned differences in audience reaction to Desdemona, starting with Jackson, see Paul Yachnin, *Stage-Wrights: Shakespeare, Jonson, Middleton, and the Making of Theatrical Value* (Philadelphia, 1997), pp. 26–35.

[55] Samuel Pepys, *The Shorter Pepys*, ed. Robert Latham (Berkeley, 1985), p. 86.

[56] *The Plays of William Shakespeare*, ed. Johnson, vol. 10, p. 458.

an extraordinary degree'.[57] By the mid twentieth century, so universally acknowledged was sympathetic power for Desdemona that W. H. Auden admitted, 'Everybody must pity Desdemona', even while he himself begrudged this: 'but I cannot bring myself to like her'.[58] In more recent decades, several female playwrights have written dramatic extensions of Desdemona's character, from Ann-Marie MacDonald's *Goodnight Desdemona (Good Morning Juliet)* (1988) to Paula Vogel's *Desdemona: A Play about a Handkerchief* (1993), and especially Toni Morrison's *Desdemona* (2011), which – among other things – imagines Desdemona's learning the Willow Song from Barbary, performed in the premier by a singer-songwriter from Mali, Rokia Traoré.[59] Morrison, to get inside Desdemona's perspective, draws on a connection to a Black woman and her song, which the Folio first provides, and which becomes central to the long history of pity for Desdemona.

---

[57] William Hazlitt, *Characters of Shakespear's Plays*, 2nd ed. (London, 1818), p. 43.

[58] W. H. Auden, 'The Joker in the pack', in *The Dyer's Hand and Other Essays* (1962; repr. New York, 1968), pp. 246–72; p. 268.

[59] See Ann-Marie MacDonald, *Goodnight Desdemona (Good Morning Juliet)* (Toronto, 1990) – the play premiered in 1988 in Toronto; Paula Vogel, *Desdemona: A Play about a Handkerchief* (New York, 1994) – the play premiered in 1993 in Sag Harbor, NY; Toni Morrison, *Desdemona* (London, 2012) – the play premiered in 2011 in Vienna. See also Ayanna Thompson, '*Desdemona*: Toni Morrison's response to *Othello*', in *A Feminist Companion to Shakespeare*, 2nd ed., ed. Dympna Callaghan (Malden, MA, 2016), pp. 494–506.

DESDEMONA'S HONEST FRIEND

JEREMY LOPEZ[1]

Emilia is a cipher. Shakespeare repeatedly asks us to scrutinize her reticence: at the quayside; after she gives Iago the handkerchief; when she does not tell Desdemona where the handkerchief has gone; as she prepares Desdemona for bed. At the same time, Emilia is candid. Shakespeare repeatedly asks us to marvel at her outspokenness: after Othello interrogates Desdemona about the handkerchief; at the end of the 'Willow' scene; in the face of Iago's threats after the truth of the handkerchief plot has been revealed. On the whole, critics have synthesized the competing demands of Emilia's character into a sympathetic interpretation: if she errs in giving the handkerchief to Iago and concealing its whereabouts, she does so without malice (possibly under compulsion) and more than redeems herself when, in the final scene, she speaks out for the honesty of Desdemona and against the villainy of the men who have destroyed her. Often, Emilia's relationship to Desdemona is characterized as one defined by loyalty, devotion, friendship and even love.[2] Often, as well, her actions and speech are represented as circumscribed or overdetermined by the dramatic or social roles – lower-class foil to Desdemona, leery wife of a vicious husband, clear-eyed 'shrew' in a misogynist world – to

---

[1] I am grateful to Ted Leinwand, Paul Menzer, Ed Pechter, Chris Warley and the members of the Harvard Shakespeare Seminar for extensive commentary on earlier versions of this article. Katherine Chu, Nate Crocker and Claire Ellis at the University of Toronto provided invaluable research assistance at various points throughout a long process of writing and rewriting.

[2] Even Thomas Rymer, perhaps thinking more of Cinthio than Shakespeare, refers to Emilia as Desdemona's 'friend and confident', in *A Short View of Tragedy* (London, 1693), p. 127. For a diverse array of sympathetic descriptions of Emilia, especially in her relation to Desdemona, see: A. C. Bradley, *Shakespearean Tragedy*, 2nd ed. (London, 1922), pp. 240–2; Thomas D. Bowman, 'In defense of Emilia', *The Shakespeare Association Bulletin* 22 (1947), 99–104; Marvin Rosenberg, *The Masks of Othello* (Berkeley, 1961), p. 29; M. R. Ridley's introduction to the Arden Second Series edition (London, 1964), p. lxvii; Norman O. Sanders's introduction to the New Cambridge edition (Cambridge, 1984), pp. 36–7; E. A. J. Honigmann's introduction to the Arden Third Series edition (London, 1997), pp. 54–5; Carol Thomas Neely, 'Women and men in *Othello*: "what should such a fool / do with so good a woman?"' in *The Woman's Part: Feminist Criticism of Shakespeare*, ed. Carolyn Lenz and Carol Thomas Neely (Urbana, 1980), pp. 211–39; Edward Pechter, *Othello and Interpretive Traditions* (Iowa City, 1999), pp. 116–20; James Schiffer, '*Othello* among the Sonnets', in *Othello: New Critical Essays*, ed. Philip C. Kolin (New York, 2002), pp. 325–45, esp. pp. 327–8 and 334; Marguérite Corporaal, '"Moor, she was chaste. She loved thee, cruel Moor": *Othello* as a starting point for alternative dramatic representations of the female voice', *Comitatus* 33 (2002), 99–111, esp. pp. 102–3; Michael Neill, *Servile Ministers: Othello, King Lear, and the Sacralization of Service* (Vancouver, 2004), esp. pp. 25–7; Linda Anderson, *A Place in the Story: Servants and Service in Shakespeare's Plays* (Newark, DE, 2005), pp. 125, 183, 238, and 240; Harold Bloom's essay at the end of the *Yale Annotated Othello* (New Haven, CT, 2005), pp. 219–20; David Schalkwyk, *Shakespeare, Love and Service* (Cambridge, 2008), pp. 245–61; and Anna Kamaralli, *Shakespeare and the Shrew: Performing the Defiant Female Voice* (London, 2012), pp. 143–52.

which she is readily consigned.[3] In this article, I offer a somewhat less sympathetic view of Emilia, though it is also one in which she has a bit more to do – she is, at any rate, perfectly capable of doing Desdemona harm without being coerced by, or trying to please, her husband. The Emilia that emerges from my reading is not mutually exclusive of the Emilias that other critics have created, and will probably both broaden and be broadened by those interpretations that find the character more constrained, fearful, affectionate or heroic than I do.[4] My reading particularly emphasizes her role as Desdemona's servant and, in so doing, it rejects the possibility – pervasively endorsed in the critical literature and in the theatre – that the two women share, or come to share, an affective bond that constitutes a form of resistance to the homosocial (and, indeed, the *social*) tensions that drive this violent tragedy so explicitly concerned with the 'curse of service'.[5] It is just possible that Emilia seeks – either out of admiration from the outset, or out of regret after Desdemona begins to suffer – to transcend the class relation that separates her from her mistress, but, if she does, as I shall argue, Desdemona resists her at every turn. Our final image of Emilia – fearless, free-speaking, loyal to the death – is an image that she constructs as carefully as the one her husband constructs for Othello. Perhaps this has generally been hard to see because it would be too painful to admit that Emilia and Desdemona not only do not, but do not want to, speak the same language, and that even the moments of Desdemona's most abject suffering are not free of class-inflected resentment and affectation.[6]

*

---

[3] Bradley's view that Emilia's silence on the handkerchief demonstrates a 'stupidity' that is in keeping with her 'coarseness of nature' (Bradley, *Shakespearean Tragedy*, p. 240) has largely been transmuted into an argument that she is afraid of her husband (see Hongimann's Arden introduction, p. 46, for a typical instance); when she speaks out in the final scene, it is in part because she sees that there is nothing left to fear. Lynda Boose sees Emilia's actions as part of a 'strongly gendered pattern that this play goes to considerable lengths to construct. For despite Emilia's clear dislike of her husband and resentment at his contempt, she nonetheless strives to win his approval by stealing the handkerchief' (Lynda Boose, '"Let it be hid": the pornographic aesthetic of Shakespeare's *Othello*', in *Othello: Contemporary Critical Essays*, ed. Lena Cowen Orlin (Basingstoke, 2004), pp. 22–48; p. 41). Evelyn Gajowski makes a similar argument to Boose: see Evelyn Gajowski, '*Othello*: female subjectivity and the Ovidian discursive tradition' in *The Art of Loving: Female Subjectivity and Male Discursive Traditions in Shakespeare's Tragedies* (Newark, DE, 1992), pp. 51–85. Joel Altman finds that Emilia is virtually hypnotized by Iago's injunction that she '[b]e not acknown' on the handkerchief: it causes her 'to lose ... her link to the handkerchief as she renders it up in service to him' (Joel Altman, *The Improbability of Othello: Rhetorical Anthropology and Shakespearean Selfhood* (Chicago, 2010), p. 241). Another view of Emilia is that she is, at first, merely an instrument of the dramatic design. Pechter, *Othello and Interpretive Traditions*, p. 116, suggests that Emilia, before she picks up the handkerchief, merely 'fills a place in the plot ... the play doesn't encourage any deeper interest on our part'. In a similar vein, Harry Berger, Jr, has argued that her character follows 'two different trajectories ... In the first, she is a faithful attendant, in the second a closemouthed watcher' (Harry Berger, Jr, 'Impertinent trifling: Desdemona's handkerchief', *Shakespeare Quarterly* 47 (1996), 235–50; p. 246).

[4] Emilias most similar to the one I offer in this article can be found in Berger, 'Impertinent trifling'; Carol Chillington Rutter's chapter on Trevor Nunn's 1989 RSC production (with Zoe Wanamaker as Emilia and Imogen Stubbs as Desdemona) in her *Enter the Body: Women and Representation on Shakespeare's Stage* (London, 2001), pp. 141–77; and in Aveek Sen, 'What Emilia knew: Shakespeare reads James', in *Blind Spots of Knowledge in Shakespeare and His World: A Conversation*, ed. Subha Mukherji (Berlin, 2019), pp. 100–12. The Emilia I postulate perhaps knows more of what she does (and is less directly influenced by her husband) than that of Berger or Sen; and she and Desdemona do not arrive at the sense of solidarity (fleeting and grim though it is) that Rutter found in the relationship as represented by Wanamaker and Stubbs.

[5] Othello, ed. Russ McDonald in The Complete Pelican Shakespeare, ed. A. R. Braunmuller and Stephen Orgel (London, 2002), 1.1.34. Unless otherwise noted, all citations of the play, hereafter given parenthetically, will be taken from this edition.

[6] In 'The Jacobean Shakespeare: some observations on the constructions of the tragedies', Maynard Mack briefly makes a point that is related to my argument here and that is taken up in various ways by Berger, Rutter, Altman, Sen and others: 'The alabaster innocence of Desdemona's world shines out beside the crumpled bedsitters of Emilia's ... but the two languages never, essentially, commune – and, for this reason, the dialogue they hold can never be finally adjudicated.' In *Jacobean Theatre*, ed. John Russell Brown and Bernard Harris (New York, 1960), pp. 22–3. See also Collen Rosenfeld, 'Shakespeare's nobody', in *Othello: The State of Play*, ed. Lena Cowen Orlin (London, 2014), pp. 257–79.

For Desdemona, Emilia is a new servant. Othello appoints her to the position when his wife decides to accompany him to Cyprus.

> Honest Iago,
> My Desdemona must I leave to thee.
> I prithee let thy wife attend on her
> And bring them after in the best advantage.
>
> (1.3.294–7)

Since Brabantio does not know who Iago is (1.1.113), and since even Iago seems to have been kept in the dark about Othello's marriage (1.1.4–6) and was not party to their wooing (3.3.93–100), we can assume that neither he nor Emilia has had any contact with Desdemona before they take her aboard the Cyprus-bound ship. In bringing Emilia into the play to 'attend on' Desdemona, Shakespeare has demoted the ensign's wife from what she is in Cinthio: a 'beautiful and virtuous young woman' who comes to Cyprus 'because she was Italian [and] she was dearly loved by the Moor's wife and spent the greater part of the day with her'.[7] The gesture is subtle, but it provides essential context for the first time we see Emilia, 2.1, a scene in which she is both marginal and central.[8]

At the quayside in Cyprus, Emilia is caught first between Cassio and Iago, next between Iago and Desdemona, in arguments about, and competing idioms of, breeding. ''Tis my breeding', Cassio insists as he kisses Iago's wife, 'That gives me this bold show of courtesy' (2.1.98–9). In the refined habits of a Florentine arithmetician, a kiss is just a kiss. Iago will have none of it:

> Sir, would she give you so much of her lips
> As of her tongue she oft bestows on me,
> You would have enough.
>
> (100–2)

Hinting that his wife's verbal incontinence is of a piece with her sexual voraciousness (he gets more of her tongue than he can stand), Iago establishes a satirical, corporeal idiom that will silence Cassio for sixty lines. Although the only thing that we know about Emilia at this point – that her husband thinks she's a scold – might lead us to expect that she will spar with Iago, she is reticent, and notably so: 'Alas, she has no speech!' Desdemona remarks (102), and proceeds herself to speak the part that Iago had marked out for his wife. As she encourages Iago in his alehouse paradoxes, Desdemona attempts to leave behind the 'breeding' that Othello was so solicitous to accommodate in the middle of the previous scene (1.3.239); she is ready to embrace the flinty and steel couch of war, and in mixed company to give as good as she gets. I think that we are supposed to admire Desdemona's behaviour here – it is further confirmation that she is independent, free-speaking and open to experience – but also to notice how much she overshadows Emilia, who speaks only three half-lines in the entire scene: 'You have little cause to say so' (2.1.108, refusing to take Iago's bait); 'You shall not write my praise' (116, a tentative gesture, warned away by Iago's 'No, let me not'); and 'How if fair and foolish?' (135, perhaps a surgical strike in Iago and Desdemona's game, aimed at Desdemona herself). It is hard to know what Emilia thinks in this scene, but easy to speculate: she is irritated that her husband is flirting with Desdemona; she is embarrassed that Iago is speaking insinuatingly about their marriage in front of the general's wife; she is bored with a routine that she has heard before; she herself is silently flirting with Cassio. The reticence that enables this speculation, that puts her inscrutable subjectivity at the centre of the scene, is framed in class terms from the moment her mistress notes it. 'Marry, *before your ladyship*,' Iago explains to Desdemona, 'She puts her tongue a little in her

---

[7] Cinthio is quoted from the translation at Internet Shakespeare Editions: https://internetshakespeare.uvic.ca/doc/Cinthio_M/index.html.

[8] For a related discussion of Shakespeare's Emilia as opposed to Cinthio's (which arrives at somewhat different conclusions from my argument), see Timothy Burns, 'One that loved not wisely but too well: devotional love and politics in *Othello*,' in *The Soul of Statesmanship: Shakespeare on Nature, Virtue, and Political Wisdom*, ed. Khalil M. Habib and L. Joseph Hebert, Jr (Lanham, MD, 2018), pp. 3–22.

heart / And chides with thinking' (105–7, emphasis mine). It is a question of breeding. The relation between mistress and servant enfolds the relation between husband and wife.

The next time we see Emilia, in 3.1, she is different. With Cassio, and without Desdemona, Emilia is comfortable. I think that Shakespeare imagines the three, Iago, Emilia and Cassio, to have known each other for some time, which is why Iago thinks he can 'set [Emilia] on' to 'move for Cassio to her mistress' (2.3.370–1). Whether or not she has acted on Iago's urging (we never actually see her speak on Cassio's behalf to Desdemona) – whether or not she is really in a position to 'move' her mistress or merely to provide access to her – Emilia is full of information in 3.1:

> Good morrow, good lieutenant. I am sorry
> For your displeasure, but all will sure be well.
> The general and his wife are talking of it,
> And she speaks for you stoutly. The Moor replies
> That he you hurt is of great fame in Cyprus
> ...
>   but he protests he loves you,
> And needs no other suitor but his likings
> To bring you in again.
> ...
>   Pray you come in.
> I will bestow you where you shall have time
> To speak your bosom freely.
>
>   (3.1.41–54)

She is sufficiently trusted by Desdemona to be present for arguments between the mistress and her husband (we will soon see this first-hand), but not so discreet that she will not share what she has learned to the advantage of her own husband or, as she thinks, his friend. To say that, as a faithful attendant, Emilia somewhat resembles Iago here, following her mistress in order to serve her own turn, is not necessarily to impute malice to her motives. It is, however, to emphasize that the service relation between Desdemona and Emilia determines what happens between Cassio and Iago, and Desdemona and Cassio.

Does Desdemona expect Emilia to bring Cassio to speak to her? It is hard to tell at the beginning of 3.3, where we are party only to their meeting's end. What is clear in this scene is that Desdemona has no intention of crediting the servants for any reconciliation between Cassio and her husband. Again, it is a question of breeding. Here, as throughout the play, Desdemona speaks with authority, takes for granted the utility of her subordinates, and evinces a careful concern that everything occupy its rightful place. 'Be thou assured, good Cassio,' she says, using the familiar second-person pronoun, 'I will do / All my abilities in thy behalf' (3.3.1–2). Ever so slightly jarringly, it is Emilia, not Cassio, who replies, shifting the emphasis of the putative negotiation towards herself and her husband: 'Good madam, do. I warrant it grieves my husband / As if the cause were his' (3–4). Desdemona's reply, 'O, that's an honest fellow' (5), is perfunctory, possibly dismissive, and she turns immediately back to Cassio, now using the formal *you*, as though to remind herself and Emilia that this is a discussion of business rather than a conversation between friends.

> Do not doubt, Cassio,
> But I will have my lord and you again
> As friendly as you were.
>
>   (5–7)

Miserable Cassio, always verging on hyperbole, insists for two short speeches upon his own servitude – to Desdemona (9) and to Othello (18) – and this seems to draw Desdemona back to the familiar *thee* and *thou* (20–8), going so far as to enlist Emilia as a witness to both her sway with her husband and her solidarity with Cassio:

> Before Emilia here
> I give thee warrant of thy place. Assure thee,
> If I do vow friendship, I'll perform it
> To the last article.
>
>   (19–22)

Even if Emilia were planning to respond with enthusiasm, all she has time for is a very deferent 'Madam, here comes my lord' (29) as the general and Iago enter.

In this scene, as in 2.1, Shakespeare's touch is very light: the social dynamics that structure Desdemona's attempt to establish herself as mistress, Emilia's attempt to establish herself as faithful attendant, and Cassio, Emilia and Iago's attempt to accommodate the presence of Desdemona in their circle are subtle and ritualized.[9] We do not need to imagine – and there is little in the play's critical or theatrical history to suggest that anyone has imagined – that Emilia bridles, inwardly or visibly, at being treated merely as an accessory to Desdemona's mistress-ship, nor that Desdemona explicitly or implicitly puts her in her place. The place that each occupies dramatically and socially, indeed the service-relation itself, feels natural and conventional. But, in *Othello* as in most early modern drama, the fidelity of servants cannot be taken for granted and the service-relation is often highly fraught. Iago is the most obvious example in this play, though perhaps not the best one to adduce here, since, for all his talk of the curse of service, he generally seems to occupy a position of mastery, leading Othello tenderly by the nose (1.3.393). A more apposite example is provided by the somewhat mysterious Clown, whose insouciant reply to Cassio in 3.1 might give us a hint at how Desdemona's 'O that's an honest fellow' sounds in Emilia's ears:

CASSIO   Dost thou hear, my honest friend?
CLOWN   No, I hear not your honest friend, I hear you.
(3.1.21–2)

The Clown knows what William Empson observed about the word 'honest' in *Othello* and throughout Shakespeare's work: that it is never used between equals, and that it always carries a feeling of condescension or contempt.[10] He bridles because he understands that his presumed honesty is a projection of his interlocutor's social superiority. The Clown's first appearance immediately precedes the moment where Emilia offers to make herself useful to Cassio. His second appearance, in 3.4, immediately precedes Emilia's lie about the handkerchief: perhaps not coincidentally, Desdemona first asks the Clown (whom she addresses as 'sirrah', 3.4.1, the unique instance of the word in the play) if he knows where Cassio is, and then asks Emilia if she knows where the handkerchief is. The reply is the same in each case: 'I know not' (3.4.11, 24). In both of his scenes, it is unclear whether the Clown actually performs the errand with which he is tasked (Emilia arrives by herself in 3.1, and Cassio arrives with Iago in 3.4) and it is very clear that he has no interest in doing it. Deferent only as far as he need be, resentful but apparently impotent, subordinate but obviously independent, and radiating the sense that he knows more than he says, the Clown is an epitome of the figure of the servant in *Othello* and can help us, perhaps, explain Emilia's strange behaviour in the matter of the handkerchief.

Taking up Desdemona's dropped handkerchief, Emilia perceives a divided duty. 'I am glad I have found this napkin', she begins (3.3.290), and perhaps we might expect her shortly to pursue her just-departed mistress to return it to her. 'This was her first remembrance from the Moor' (291) – all the more reason to perform the obvious service. Still, she delays, considering: 'My wayward husband hath a hundred times / Wooed me to steal it' (292–3). The implications of 'glad' from the first line start to pull in another direction – 'I am glad to have the opportunity to do the thing my husband has been after me to do' – though 'wayward' and

---

[9] Sen, 'What Emilia knew', pp. 105–7, provides a fine reading of the social dynamics of the quayside scene. See also Ralph Berry, *Shakespeare and Social Class* (Atlantic Highlands, NJ, 1988), pp. 95–121, for a discussion of 'the relations between military rank and social class' (p. 112) in the play.

[10] See William Empson, *The Structure of Complex Words* (Cambridge, MA, 1989), pp. 218–49. 'Four columns of *honest* in the Shakespeare Concordance', Empson writes, 'show that he never once allows the word a simple hearty use between equals.' The 'nearest case' of a use between equals is in the exchange between Desdemona and Emilia at the beginning of 3.3, but 'Emilia is butting into the talk with Cassio, and Desdemona, in this careless reply to silence her, has a feeling that Iago though reliable and faithful is her social inferior' (pp. 218–19). See also Iago's 'Whip me such honest knaves' (1.1.48), where 'honest knaves' describes the kind of faithful servants who allow their masters to take advantage of them.

'steal' suggest that, in this regard, as in regard to his loose talk about their marriage, Emilia is more resistant to than complicit with her husband.[11] Her resistance is confirmed by the adversative beginning of her next clause: 'but she so loves the token / (For he conjured her she should ever keep it) / That she reserves it evermore about her / To kiss and talk to' (293–6). In the very act of revealing the important history of the object we are seeing for the first time, Emilia sends a strong signal – probably not deliberately, in her capacity as a fictional person, but formally, as a part of the play's epitasis – that she is not going to return the handkerchief.[12] But the nature of her intervention into the mechanics of the plot remains ambiguous: 'I'll have the work ta'en out / And give't Iago' (296–7). Presumably she would give her mistress the original (Desdemona, so fond of the object, would probably recognize a substitute), though the pronoun in 'give't' leaves the question open. In either case, Emilia seems to be angling for a dual reward – attempting to play the part of both faithful attendant and indulgent wife ('I nothing but to please his fantasy', 299). The possibility that the play will henceforth contain two handkerchiefs suggests that Emilia is undertaking a piece of servant's wit, and one whose consequences will depend upon dilatory time.

But Emilia is not given the time she needs to do whatever it is she imagines she will do with the handkerchief. Iago's unexpected arrival causes her to play her double game more rapidly, and for different stakes. In most modern editions, including the one I have used for this article, Emilia and Iago's lewd, flirtatious negotiation over the handkerchief (301–15) ends with an editorial stage direction indicating that Iago '*Snatches*' it from Emilia – where the verb efficiently suggests both theft and sexual violence, conflating Iago's coercion of his own wife with his crime against Othello's. It might be more interesting, however, if – as is suggested in the notes of the earlier Arden editions – Emilia simply gives the handkerchief to her husband.[13] If Emilia seeks, at first, to be rewarded for both faithful attendance and wifely obedience, she focuses, once Iago arrives, more singly on the latter: a bird in the hand. 'I have a thing for you', she announces immediately upon his arrival, and then, a few lines later, she asks: 'What will you give me now / For that same handkerchief?' (301, 305–6). Clearly, she expects something in return, even if, perhaps, it is only knowledge of Iago's purpose: 'What will you do with't . . . ?' (314); 'If't be not for some purpose of import, / Give't me again' (316–17). Nonsuited,

---

[11] Berger paraphrases this part of the speech as 'my husband is a little weird ("wayward") and is probably up to some mischief, but it's none of my business' ('Impertinent trifling', p. 245).

[12] For the handkerchief as a 'snowballing signifier', see Karen Newman, *Fashioning Femininity and English Renaissance Drama* (Chicago, 1991), p. 91. See also Berger, 'Impertinent trifling', pp. 243–4, for a discussion of the handkerchief's entrance into the action and a response to Newman; and Altman, *Improbability*, pp. 239–41.

[13] Nicholas Rowe (1709, p. 1604) inserted the stage direction '[*Snatching it*]' at Iago's line 'Why, what's that to you?' (3.3.315 in the Pelican edition). The Furness Variorum notes that Edwin Booth incorporated this direction into the business of his production: 'BOOTH: Pause mysteriously, "Why—," as if about to give her some wonderful reason. Then snatch it, with "What's that to you?"' (*A New Variorum Edition of Shakespeare*, 2nd ed., ed. Horace Howard Furness, vol. 6 (Philadelphia, 1886), n. to 3.3.368). Honigmann's 1997 Arden edition reproduces Rowe's stage direction and indicates that 'Some Iagos snatch the handkerchief, others get it by coaxing.' The only modern editions I could find that do not direct Iago to snatch the handkerchief are those of Alvin Kernan (Penguin, 1986), Stanley Wells (Oxford, 1986), Nick de Somoygi (Nick Hern, 2002), and Edward Pechter (Norton, 2016), all of which direct him, in some form, to '[*Take*]' it. Both of the earlier Arden editions (H. C. Hart, 1903, and M. R. Ridley, 1958) reproduce Rowe's direction but express dissatisfaction with it. 'Emilia's immediate purpose is to give it', says Hart, 'and she seems to me to do so, when she says "here it is" in the previous line but one. Though effective on the stage, it seems an excrescence in the study. Moreover, Iago is too calmly subtle to be betrayed into impolitic impetuosity' (Hart, ed. *Othello*, n. to 3.3.316). Ridley says that the stage direction 'is now so traditional a piece of stage business that I have let it stand; but it is needless, since Emilia's "What will you do with it?" is natural enough even if she *gives* the handkerchief to Iago (which is her expressed intention). She is still, as yet, too much under his thumb to dare make an answer to her question a condition of surrendering it' (Ridley, ed. *Othello*, n. to 3.3.320).

deprived of the possibility of reaping any reward without bringing punishment on herself, Emilia falls back upon a rhetoric, that of the loyal and sympathetic servant ('Poor lady, she'll run mad / When she shall lack it', 317–18), that is guaranteed not to impress Iago: 'Be not acknown on't', he tells her (319), and sends her away. The possibility of defining Emilia's relation to Desdemona by means of some positive action disappears into Iago's mysterious motivations.

In giving her the theatrical task of disclosing the handkerchief's importance, and then making her responsible (whether or not under duress) for its movement in the plot, Shakespeare pins Emilia to her identity as servant. He then proceeds, much as Othello does with Desdemona once he suspects her with Cassio, relentlessly to test her fidelity. Emilia fails every test, and does so in a way similar to how Desdemona fails – that is, she retires into a class-specific idiom that obfuscates rather than illuminates her will. The first instance in this parallel development is Emilia's slightly mysterious and never-realized plan to duplicate the handkerchief, which comes towards the end of the scene in which – in front of Emilia – Desdemona has overwhelmed her laconic, surly husband by speaking up for Cassio with a frothy, ironic verbosity that can only confirm Othello's suspicion of a conspiracy: 'Why then tomorrow night, or Tuesday morn, / On Tuesday noon or night; on Wednesday morn' (3.3.60–1); 'What? Michael Cassio, / That came a-wooing with you, and so many a time, / When I have spoke of you dispraisingly, / Hath ta'en your part' (70–3); 'Why this is not a boon! ... Nay, when I have a suit / Wherein I mean to touch your love indeed, / It shall be full of poise and difficult weight' (77–82). Berger has argued – correctly, I think – that Desdemona 'grasps the meaning of Othello's little disquisition on her hot hand' with not 'a jot less clarity than the editors who gloss his adjectives', and that she 'acts in a manner calculated to evoke from him the signs of thinking that denote the passion she won't acknowledge'.[14] His ensuing analysis of the argument is primarily interested in describing the psychosexual dynamics between husband and wife, but it describes social dynamics as well: the well-bred Venetian newlywed cannot even acknowledge that her actions on behalf of a well-bred gentleman friend could be a cause for jealousy. Like Emilia, Desdemona seems to have difficulty *not* expressing a divided loyalty, and the reason for this seems to lie in her social position.

Later, in 3.4, again under the watchful eye of Emilia, it is Othello who is verbose and Desdemona who is laconic, repulsed rather than enchanted by her husband's exotic stories of origin, wilfully ignoring the obvious meaning of his words as she attempts to shift the ground of their quarrel back to matters of professional courtesy: 'This is a trick to put me from my suit. / Pray you, let Cassio be received again' (3.4.87–8). This argument is framed within an argument Desdemona has with Emilia about whether Othello is jealous. Just slightly worried about the handkerchief, Desdemona reassures herself that her husband is 'made of no such baseness / As jealous creatures are', to which Emilia replies 'Is he not jealous?' (3.4.27–9). If Emilia's tone in this question is meant (as I suspect it is) to be careful and neutral, skirting Desdemona's careless intimation that jealousy disappears with social elevation, the incredulity that she suppresses erupts to the surface when, after Othello storms out, she does not inform her mistress, sheepishly, apologetically, even worriedly that she might have some idea of the handkerchief's whereabouts. Rather, she reiterates her question with new force: 'Is not this man jealous?' (98). What follows seems to me a moment of clear aggression on Emilia's part as, emboldened by her mistress's discomfiture, she articulates a truth that she would have transcend the symbolism of any trifling token between lovers.

> 'Tis not a year or two shows us a man.
> They are all but stomachs, and we all but food;
> They eat us hungerly, and when they are full
> They belch us.
>
> (102–5)

---

[14] Berger, 'Impertinent trifling', p. 238.

DESDEMONA'S HONEST FRIEND

Much like Iago when he talks to Roderigo, or when he talks to Desdemona in 2.1, Emilia adopts an idiom that both insists upon and pretends to breach the social barrier between herself and her mistress. With or without a magical handkerchief, Desdemona can expect nothing more than to be chewed up and spat out; this is the way for masters and mistresses as it is for their servants; as in the 'lame and impotent conclusion' of Iago's riddling (2.1.161), where elegant ladies who don't use sex to their advantage are no better than barmaids, gender and sexual appetite seem to enfold and occlude class difference. 'Us', Emilia says; 'we'; 'us' again. It is a statement of solidarity that seems meant to bring Desdemona down to her level – and in any case to the level of base appetite (the wine they all drink is made of grapes). Emilia speaks with the experience of a disappointed wife and the freedom of a perspicacious servant. She expresses a common identity with Desdemona based on gender while implicitly rebuking her for her delicately cultivated illusions. Informed by an experience of servitude that Desdemona has not been able to imagine for herself, Emilia speaks with authority, and the advice she gives is probal to thinking. She speaks as Desdemona's honest friend.

*

Emilia is the focal point of the middle part of 2.1, although she tries to remain invisible. Minding her place, she stands by almost silently as her husband parades his aggressive wit before her new mistress, but in her silence she is watchful. Here, as in 3.3 where Othello has a headache, and as in 3.4 where Othello demands the handkerchief and tells a story of its provenance, we are meant to watch Emilia as she watches, and to wonder what she is thinking. If she does not seem obviously jealous in 2.1; if she does not seem obviously opportunistic when, in 3.1, she promises Cassio access to Desdemona; and if she does not seem resentful when, in 3.3, Desdemona freezes her out of the conversation with Cassio – she might begin to seem all of these things when, later in 3.3, caught between anger and curiosity about her husband's interest in her mistress's linen, she seizes the handkerchief and passes it along to Iago. She may, in that scene, be sufficiently uncertain of her own designs, or sufficiently at the mercy of her husband's seductive, coercive manner, that she can plausibly disown knowledge of the handkerchief's destructive potential; and she may, at the beginning of 3.4, be sufficiently fearful of Desdemona's anger, and still hopeful of learning Iago's purpose, that she buys herself additional time by directly disowning knowledge of its whereabouts. But Shakespeare takes away all of Emilia's excuses after he makes her witness to the confrontation between Othello and Desdemona. At the same time, he gives Desdemona lines that, if we hear them with Emilia's ears, might readily explain the surprising tack the servant takes. 'Believe me,' Desdemona says after asking where the handkerchief might be, 'I had rather have lost my purse / Full of crusadoes' (3.4.25–6). A purse filled with money! Iago's own crassness haunts the casual analogy that Desdemona makes with her love token, perhaps only confirming Emilia's estimation of its triviality, her intuition that the young, rich Venetian girl is in over her head. The next part of Desdemona's speech is even worse.

> And but my noble Moor
> Is true of mind, and made of no such baseness
> As jealous creatures are, it were enough
> To put him to ill thinking.
>
> (26–9)

It is not just the absurdity of her ruling out the possibility of jealousy entirely, but the obviously classed terms with which she does it – contrasting her 'noble' Moor to those 'base' creatures susceptible to jealousy (we know Iago to be a jealous husband) – that might cause these lines to rankle. As Cassio seems to have done with Iago, Desdemona obliviously and with the best will in the world flaunts the daily beauty in her life that makes Emilia ugly. In her decision to disown knowledge of the handkerchief, Emilia might be animated by the same malicious, envious spirit that animates her husband, but she also might be merely interested: she wants to see what it will take to widen the horizon of her mistress's experience beyond what Desdemona is able to conceive.

In act 4, the difference between Emilia's and Desdemona's knowledge – about both the ways of men in general and the mechanics of the plot in particular – becomes increasingly stark, as does the destructive potential of that difference. At the beginning of 4.2, Othello quizzes Emilia on Desdemona's interactions with Cassio. He invests in his wife's servant something like the same confidence he invests in his own – Shakespeare insists on this by making the beginnings of 4.1 and 4.2 closely parallel – but he treats her much more definitely like a servant. Desdemona, he asks, never sent 'you out o' th' way?' – not 'To fetch her fan, her gloves, her mask, nothing?' (4.2.7–9). When Emilia goes in to fetch Desdemona, Othello refers to her as a 'simple bawd' (20), and once Desdemona has arrived he dispatches Emilia with rough condescension.

> Some of your function, mistress.
> Leave procreants alone and shut the door.
> Cough or cry hem if anybody come.
> Your mystery, your mystery! Nay, dispatch!
> (27–30)

His language is even uglier after his terrible interview with Desdemona:

> You, mistress,
> That have the office opposite to Saint Peter
> And keep the gates of hell! ... You, you, ay, you!
> We have done our course; there's money for your pains:
> I pray you turn the key, and keep our counsel.
> (90–4)

He assumes (correctly, as it turns out) that Emilia has been listening at the keyhole and gives her a tip to buy her silence, ironically figuring his violent encounter with his wife as an illicit sexual encounter ('We have done our course') facilitated by a bawdy 'mistress'. This is the first time in the play that Othello has had any direct interaction with Emilia, and throughout he imputes to her the secret knowledge to which he imagines serving-women must be privy. Emilia disavows this knowledge (in rather exaggerated terms, it seems to me) because she understands its implications – 'I durst, my lord, to wager she is honest'; and 'if she be not honest, chaste, and true / There's no man happy' (12, 17–18) – and because she begins to understand the point of the game she has helped Iago to play: 'If any wretch hath put this [i.e. Desdemona's dishonesty] in your head, / Let heaven requite it with the serpent's curse' (15–16). Surprised at how far and how quickly things have progressed, angry with her husband, leery of blame, Emilia must be reeling as Othello exits. But, perhaps quietly putting in her purse the money he has just given her, she recovers quickly, and, with remarkable cruelty, resumes her performance of ignorance. 'How do you, madam? How do you, my good lady?' she asks the stunned Desdemona (96) – questions that would seem less performative if they were not preceded by another, utterly disingenuous: 'Alas, what does this gentleman conceive?' (95).

Emilia knows what Othello conceives. He told her at the beginning of the scene: Othello suspects Desdemona with Cassio. However a reader or actor might interpret it, Emilia's silence on this point arises from and illuminates a fraught class relation.[15] Perhaps she is ashamed, and fearful of punishment, because she can no longer deny her complicity in Othello's suspicion and Desdemona's distress: abusing the privileges of her subordinate position, she has not only worked to give Cassio access to Desdemona but also helped to misplace the love token that enables Othello's jealousy. Perhaps, resentful of Desdemona's wealth and beauty, impatient with her naivety, Emilia enjoys her mistress's discomfiture and, to herself, actively

---

[15] Berger, 'Impertinent trifling', p. 246, discusses this scene: 'This is the second time she fails to report something she has seen or heard, though here, as before, she is well positioned to know that her failure can increase Desdemona's jeopardy along with Othello's jealousy.' Although he finds these 'lapses' to be 'deeply problematic', Berger 'hasten[s] to add that none of this should be construed as reflecting adversely on Emilia's loyalty and devotion to Desdemona' – construing the ambiguity as a formal problem arising from the tension between her 'well-stenciled and recognizable position' as the servant who abets her mistress in a love affair and her much less readily legible relationship with Iago.

disavows her own complicity: the handkerchief is a mere trifle, a convenient excuse for the Moor's predictable, inevitable violence. Perhaps, alternatively, Emilia is torn between anxiety about telling Desdemona what she knows (because to do so would be to implicate herself) and fear of her own seething, suspicious husband, who seems to prize the handkerchief almost as much as Othello; the potential parallel between servant and mistress as victims of domestic violence gives the lie to Desdemona's fatuous opposition between the 'noble' and the 'base' in matters of jealousy. If any one of these possibilities, or any combination of them, might plausibly admit, as well, a feeling of solidarity between the women that transcends social position, Emilia seems to sacrifice that feeling for the malicious pleasures of surreptitious hostility when her husband arrives on the scene.

We do not have to believe that Iago and Emilia are happily married, or even that they are co-conspirators, to see that they speak the same language.[16] This is clear for the first time in 3.4, and it becomes even more obvious when the pair enter together midway through 4.2. Listen with Desdemona's ears as Emilia, drawn out by Iago's unobtrusive queries and gentle promptings, hammers on the epithet she heard (while listening at the keyhole) Othello use for his wife: 'my lord hath so bewhored her' (115); 'He called her whore' (120); 'Hath she forsook so many noble matches ... To be called whore?' (125–7); 'Why should he call her whore?' (137).[17] As in 3.4, Emilia implicitly reproaches Desdemona for her lack of experience, summoning forth a range of unsavoury types to characterize and explain Othello's behaviour – 'A beggar in his drink / Could not have laid such terms upon his callet' (120–1); 'I will be hanged if ... Some cogging, cozening slave, to get some office, / Have not devised this slander' (130–3); 'The Moor's abused by some most villainous knave, / Some base notorious knave, some scurvy fellow' (139–40) – and identifying herself with the all-seeing eye of heaven that 'such companions [ought to] unfold' (141). With her references to the 'cozening slave' and the 'villainous knave', Emilia quite possibly (as at 15–16) betrays an awareness of her own husband's machinations – though if she does, she keeps it veiled beneath satirical generalizations. At line 145, however, Iago suddenly, explicitly becomes the target of Emilia's anger:

> Some such squire he was
> That turned your wit the seamy side without
> And made you suspect me with the Moor.
> (145–7)

It is a moment of astonishing cruelty: the servant figures herself as an object, however notional, of her mistress's husband's desire at the same moment that she searches, with relentless candour, for a reason the mistress has fallen out of favour with her husband. Although Desdemona never speaks directly to Emilia in this scene, and barely acknowledges anything she says, the servant's words effect a discomfiture and a physical lowering – Desdemona kneels (151) to affirm her love and fidelity – that is as surprising and pathetic as when Othello, in 4.1, falls into a fit as he is tormented by Iago.

Not only does Desdemona not speak directly to Emilia in 4.2, she seems actively to exclude her from her conversation and confidence. To Emilia's concerned queries just after Othello exits, Desdemona replies 'Do not talk to me, Emilia' (102) – understandable enough, perhaps, given her distracted state ('I cannot weep, nor answers have I none / But what should go by water', 120–1), but, after instructing Emilia to put the wedding sheets on her bed, she tells her to 'call thy husband hither' (106). Then, at the end of their conversation, just before she kneels in her vow of

---

[16] Tom McAlindon makes a similar point: see Tom McAlindon, 'Othello, the Moor of Venice' in *Iago: Major Literary Figures*, ed. Harold Bloom (New York, 1992), pp. 59–63, esp. pp. 59–60.

[17] Discussing this scene, Bradley glances in the direction of the kind of aggression I am imputing to Emilia: 'If one were capable of laughing or even of smiling when this point in the play is reached, the difference between Desdemona's anguish at the loss of Othello's love, and Emilia's recollection of the noble matches she might have secured, would be irresistibly ludicrous' (Bradley, *Shakespearean Tragedy*, p. 241).

fidelity, Desdemona says hopelessly: 'Alas, Iago, / What shall I do to win my lord again? / Good friend, go to him' (148–50). Good friend! How startling these words must be to Emilia – how much they must confirm her sense of her mistress's naivety and of the social disruption caused by Desdemona's advent in Othello's inner circle. Desdemona, I think, intends to startle Emilia with these words, because she has noted the aggression in Emilia's insinuations about Othello's desire for her – just as she has noted and been disturbed (perhaps especially in retrospect, after hearing Emilia's insinuations) by his coarse, familiar language with Emilia when he called her into and sent her out of the room. Like the conversation at the quayside in 2.1, this scene dramatizes shifting, competing intimacies – real, imagined, projected – just barely visible at the edges of a palpable silence between mistress and servant. Emilia, of course, has the last laugh. With friends like Iago, Desdemona hardly needs the enemy she has made of her own servant.

Perhaps 'enemy' is an exaggeration, but I do not think it is much of one. Shakespeare gives Emilia not one but two opportunities to tell Desdemona what she learns, at the beginning of 4.2, about Othello's suspicions about Cassio. And if, in the first instance, her silence might be justified by Desdemona's discomfiture and then Iago's presence, in the second she has Desdemona all to herself and, briefly and tentatively, Desdemona seems to invite her into her confidence. The third scene of act 4 contains a number of mysteries: why does Desdemona abruptly refer to Lodovico as a 'proper man' (4.3.35)? What is the sound that interrupts her song (52)? What does the song of willow portend – does Desdemona foresee her own death (see 24–5, 30–1) or does she merely fear that he she loves is 'mad' and will soon 'forsake' her (27–8)? The cryptic quality of the scene creates a new tone in the interaction between mistress and servant. They seem to share some unspoken understanding; Emilia is gentle and matronly ('Come, come, you talk!' 25); Desdemona's many commands – 'Give me my nightly wearing' (16), 'Prithee, unpin me' (21), 'unpin me here' (34) –

'Prithee, hie thee' (48), 'get thee gone' (57) – are not peremptory but, in the light of Othello's ominous commands, seem to implore Emilia for her presence. It is this scene more than any other that has created the impression that the key element of Emilia and Desdemona's relationship is their gendered likeness rather than their classed difference. But, for an Emilia who is responsible, and conscious of her responsibility, for the missing love token; who has perhaps more than an inkling of how her husband has deployed that token as a disruptive force in her mistress's marriage; who withholds information about Othello's suspicions that would enlighten and benefit Desdemona; and who has since their first scene together been quietly antagonizing her mistress with the barbed quillets of open-eyed, resentful servitude – for this Emilia, the impression of female solidarity, an impression that she might at this point in the action find comforting or even exonerating, must be fleeting indeed.

It does not even last the entire scene. From the beginning, Emilia is alert for opportunities to force Desdemona to speak at her level. 'I would you had never seen him', she says boldly at line 18, but Desdemona does not take the bait. To Desdemona's 'That Lodovico is a proper man' (35) – which might simply be a way of expressing relief that the self-composed emissary from Venice still treats her husband with professional respect (1–2) – Emilia replies with sexual insinuations, but Desdemona changes the subject. Perhaps the willow song gives Emilia the opportunity to reflect with regret upon the desperate pass to which she has helped bring her mistress – but if she does, she keeps it to herself; any sense of camaraderie between the women depends upon Emilia's continuing to hoard her secret knowledge. And when Desdemona offers her own reflections on the willow song – 'Dost thou in conscience think ... / That there be women do abuse their husbands / In such gross kind' (60–2) – the voice of the honest servant bursts forth once more. Like Iago with Othello (or Roderigo), Emilia in lines 68–103 compulsively satirizes Desdemona's idealistic morality and gradually shifts the focus to her own transactional view of the world, daring her interlocutor to disagree. How are we to imagine Desdemona understands Emilia's harsh candour? Merely as the taunt, the reprimand for her mistress's naivety, that it is clearly meant to be? As a confirmatory glimpse into the promiscuous lives of base, jealous people? As (more sinisterly now) another allusion to the lusts of Othello to which Iago and Emilia have been privy; an attempt to draw out an admission of Desdemona's own secret desires; an invitation, in her insistent use of the first-person plural (84–103), to female confession, conspiracy and revenge? Whatever Desdemona hears, or thinks she hears, and whatever she thinks about what Emilia says, remains a mystery: the oblique couplet with which she ends the scene once again puts her servant by and reaffirms the yawning gulf between them. They have no shared experience, or none that they can speak of. The next time they are in the same room together, in the play's final scene, Emilia reveals all the knowledge that she could not or would not in 4.3, but now it is over Desdemona's dead body.

In 5.2, Emilia speaks in a new way. Shakespeare keeps a tight rein on the character for the first half of the play and gradually slackens his grip. By the time the final scene arrives, Emilia – character as well as actor – is dying to speak. It is no wonder, as Lois Potter has noted, that there was some question among actresses and audiences in the nineteenth century whether Emilia or Desdemona was the starring female role.[18] One feature of Emilia's new language in 5.2 is that she openly expresses affection for Desdemona, whom she repeatedly refers to as 'my mistress' (5.2.168, 186, 238). 'Sweet Desdemona, O sweet mistress, speak!' she cries when she learns that Desdemona is dead (122). Othello calls his wife a 'liar gone to burning hell'; Emilia retorts that Desdemona, in her martyrdom, is an 'angel' (130–2) and that she was 'heavenly true' (136). As Othello gradually reveals that Iago's insinuations made him suspect Desdemona with Cassio, Emilia apostrophizes her dead mistress: 'O mistress, villainy hath made mocks with love' (152). When Iago's villainy is exposed, Emilia tells Othello that he has killed 'the sweetest innocent / That e'er did lift up eye' (200–1). It is possible that Shakespeare wanted, with this new Emilia-language – so insistent in its representation of a close mistress–servant relation, so uncharacteristically naive in its conception of wifely virtue – to show Emilia suddenly realizing, and trying to make amends for, her complicity in Desdemona's destruction. It is also possible, and I think more likely, that he wanted to show Emilia acting. The giveaway, to my ear, is in the other new feature of Emilia's language: the explicit, brutal, racist contempt she expresses for Othello. With her mistress dead and Othello hemmed in by his own crime and, shortly thereafter, the Venetian authorities, Emilia can indeed speak 'as liberal as the north' (221). Othello is 'the blacker devil' for killing his wife (132), a 'gull', a 'dolt', and 'ignorant as dirt' for being deceived by Iago (164–5): a 'dull Moor' (226) and the object of Desdemona's 'filthy bargain' (158). With Othello, Emilia plays the part of the servant who saw clearly, and loved her mistress, as the master could not. With Iago (who knows better) and everyone else (who does not), she plays the part of the servant who is loyal to the death and beyond. Her death speech – in which she announces that she will 'play the swan', co-opts Desdemona's willow song, admonishes Othello for being blind to his wife's chastity, commends her own soul to heaven, and insists once more on her candour and honesty (247–52) – is remarkably, almost comically grandiloquent.[19] Regretful, remorseful, angry at both Iago and

---

[18] See Chapter 2 ('Desdemona's play') of Lois Potter, *Shakespeare in Performance: Othello* (New York, 2002), esp. pp. 50–2. Of particular note is the story of Clara Morris who, as Emilia, received top billing alongside Salvini in two of his American productions in 1883. Morris seems to have 'made the most of every opportunity to control the situation'. Her Emilia 'intended to steal the handkerchief from the outset and even showed some anxiety in case Desdemona should notice that she dropped it' (p. 52). In the final scene, she stole the show.

[19] Sen, 'What Emilia knew', finds there to be 'something excessive', perhaps even 'slightly comic', about Emilia's dying moments, which speak 'of a torment different from that of being married to an evil man' (p. 112).

Othello, surprised at the catastrophic turn of events: all of these things Emilia may be in 5.2, but she is also fully taking advantage of her moment centre stage. Like Othello in his own death speech, Emilia takes advantage of this central position to shape our memory of her around the service she has faithfully performed.

Emilia's climactic moment in 5.2 offers another parallel with Othello: this is her story of the movements and the meaning of the handkerchief, the long-delayed revelation of the truth that leads more or less directly to her death.

EMILIA: O thou dull Moor, that handkerchief thou speak'st of
I found by fortune, and did give my husband;
For often, with a solemn arnestness –
More than indeed belonged to such a trifle –
He begged of me to steal 't.
IAGO: Villainous whore!
EMILIA: She give it Cassio? No, alas, I found it,
And I did give 't my husband.
IAGO: Filth, thou liest!
EMILIA: By heaven, I do not, I do not, gentlemen.
O murd'rous coxcomb! what should such a fool
Do with so good a wife?
(226–35)

Othello's first 'recognizance and pledge of love', the 'antique token' given by his father to his mother (217–18), becomes in Emilia's retelling a mere 'trifle'. The word (which echoes Iago's own, spoken just after Emilia has delivered him the handkerchief and left the stage, 3.3.322) is aggressively pitched at Othello, whose history of the token Emilia heard, together with Desdemona, in 3.4. Whatever magical properties the 'dull Moor' might attribute to the handkerchief, Emilia knows where it has actually been and demonstrates – in a remarkably mischievous bit of scene-stealing – that its real significance is for the bond between herself and her husband. *She* gave it to *him*, because he *begged* her to, with *solemn earnestness*. Editors sometimes insert a stage direction '[*To Othello*]' before Emilia's last two lines, but these might just as appropriately be addressed to Iago – or Iago might plausibly hear a reference to himself as his wife lambastes Othello. Emilia may not be innocent, but she is as good a wife as Desdemona. Performing her fidelity to Desdemona, Emilia also demonstrates her fidelity to Iago, much as Othello, in his death speech, implies his fidelity to Desdemona by performing his fidelity to the Venetian state. If Emilia's candour is courageous, it is also self-aggrandizing. And if Desdemona – who must play out the rest of the scene silently, trapped on a bed between two professed lovers who did so much to ensure her destruction – could speak, she might ask the question that underlies her horrified reaction, in 3.4, to Othello's story about the handkerchief: why didn't you tell me this before?

*

Early modern actors and audiences probably would have been more alert than modern ones to the fact that everything Emilia says or does not say is framed by the service relation – by the order from Othello in 1.3, which precedes her appearance in the play, that she 'attend on' Desdemona. But Shakespeare is characteristically perverse in his representation of the women's relationship: he dramatizes it largely from Emilia's point of view, always suggesting that it might be, or become, more socially equal. It is Desdemona herself who resists any movement towards equality, even of a merely rhetorical kind, and this resistance is an integral part of her tragedy. Desdemona will not speak to Emilia on equal terms; Emilia, aware that the situation cannot be otherwise, acts according to the demands of the moment – now deferent, now crafty; now plain-speaking, now guarded; now self-seeking, now loyal – and keeps her options open. Whether or not she would help her mistress, she must almost inevitably reveal any secret knowledge belatedly. An analogous situation, though framed by quite different social restrictions, happens with Desdemona and Roderigo, whose function in the play is partly to remind us of Desdemona's class (in another kind of play, she would be Olivia to his Andrew Aguecheek, with Iago as Toby Belch), and who belatedly speaks the truth of Iago's guilt (5.2.362–74, 383–7). Desdemona, then, remains completely aloof from those who hold information that might save her, and is most at ease – speaks on equal terms – with those who (wittingly or not) draw her to destruction: Iago and Cassio. The tragic significance of these ironies, the fact that Desdemona is to some extent the victim of her own social position – the senator's daughter who manages the 'house affairs' (1.3.147), puts by the suits of the 'wealthy curlèd darlings' of Venice (1.2.68) and pursues her heart's desire with an utterly clear sense of where her 'duty' lies (1.3.181) – is easier to see if you can see that Emilia exploits that social position as she chafes against her own.

If we cannot see these things, as critical and theatrical history suggests for the most part we cannot, it is perhaps because Shakespeare, in this bleak and subtle variation on city comedy, dramatizes an attitude towards social position that persists into our own historical moment: half ashamed, half brutally realistic, unwilling to admit that it tells the whole story yet hard pressed to deny its power when we are forcefully made aware of our own. Consider, by way of conclusion, the terrible moment of Desdemona's murder:

OTHELLO: I saw the handkerchief.
DESDEMONA: He found it then.
I never gave it him. Send for him hither.
Let him confess a truth.
OTHELLO: He hath confessed.
DESDEMONA: What, my lord?
OTHELLO: That he hath used thee.
DESDEMONA: How? Unlawfully?
OTHELLO: Ay.
DESDEMONA: He will not say so.
OTHELLO: No, his mouth is stopped.
Honest Iago hath ta'en order for't.
DESDEMONA: O, my fear interprets. What, is he dead?
OTHELLO: Had all his hairs been lives, my great revenge
Had stomach for them all.
DESDEMONA: Alas, he is betrayed, and I undone!

(5.2.66–76)

With the benefit of dramatic irony, a reader or spectator can perceive in this exchange Desdemona's flat denial ('I never gave it him'); her confidence in her innocence ('Send for him hither'); her incredulity ('How, unlawfully?'); her dawning awareness of events beyond her control ('my fear interprets'); and, finally, her realization that she and her husband's loyal lieutenant have been caught in a trap ('he is betrayed, and I undone'). But listen to the passage with Othello's ears, and it sounds rather different: his wife is initially evasive ('He found it then'), and possibly brazen ('Let him confess a truth'); she is then alarmed when Othello calls her bluff ('What, my lord?'), surprised that Cassio would be indiscreet ('He will not say so'), concerned for her lover ('What, is he dead?'), and finally distraught that her secret has been discovered ('he is betrayed, and I undone'). Like Desdemona and Emilia, Othello and Desdemona do not speak the same language; they both know it, and they know that Desdemona's language is superior. Othello hardly dares speak plainly and, Iago-like, hangs out baits for Desdemona – 'He hath confessed', 'he hath used thee' – hoping that she will either acknowledge or destroy the monster in his thought. As in the scene where Othello diagnoses her moist palm, Desdemona knows what Othello wants her to say and, more importantly, the clarity with which he wants her to say it, but she refuses to give him what he wants. To do so would be to acknowledge – and, she might think, to hurt her husband by acknowledging – the difference in their social position: even at the point of death, she will not be reduced to giving voice to the possibility that her relationship with Cassio is anything more or less than what befits their breeding, nor will she admit that her husband has always already been so reduced. So, speaking as she thinks, she dies.

SUFFERING ECSTASY: *OTHELLO* AND THE DRAMA OF DISPLACEMENT

JENNIFER J. EDWARDS[1]

'When we lose certain people, or when we are dispossessed from a place, or a community,' writes Judith Butler in *Precarious Life*, 'we may simply feel that we are undergoing something temporary, that mourning will be over and some restoration of prior order will be achieved.'[2] But it is in this process of loss, she proposes, that 'something about who we are is revealed, something that delineates the ties we have to others'; we find that we are 'attached to others, at risk of losing those attachments, exposed to others, at risk of violence by virtue of that exposure', and that we are thus 'not only constituted by our relations but also dispossessed by them'.[3] The dangerous potentialities Butler describes ring through *Othello*, where social vulnerability is rife and fears of loss and dispossession run high. Read one way, this is a tragedy about being or feeling like an outsider, whether a racial other in Venetian high society like Othello, or a social outsider like Iago, whose very name, as Marianne Novy notes, 'suggests he is an outsider to Venice'.[4] Read another way, it is a drama of displacement, in which the anxiety of losing one's place is a central concern; 'I am worth no worse a place', Iago laments as he reveals how Othello turned down his 'personal suit' to be made lieutenant, promoting another outsider, 'one Michael Cassio, a Florentine' (1.1.11, 9, 19) to the post instead. In the play's opening scenes, Iago announces not only that Othello has denied him the place of the placeholder (*lieu*: place; *tenant*: holding), but that he suspects he has also replaced him in his marital bed: 'it is thought abroad that 'twixt my sheets / He has done my office', Iago claims; 'I do suspect the lusty Moor / Hath leapt into my seat' (1.3.379–80, 2.1.294–5). Iago is put out in every sense, and he seeks to ensure that others are similarly displaced.

If we find in a characteristically enigmatic claim such as 'were I the Moor I would not be Iago' (1.1.57) an instance of what Greenblatt terms 'hypothetical self-cancellation', then what we observe in Iago's subsequent line, 'I am not what I am' (1.1.65), is a subject who has not only endured self-cancellation, but been constituted by it.[5] It is this sense of self-displacement, of willed self-fracture, that interests me in what follows. For what Iago exhibits is a reflexive model of selfhood which establishes itself by negating the ipseic fixity that the claim 'I am' designates; this is a subject who resists subjective stability and singularity, for whom dispossession of place becomes constitution of self. Describing the death of his friend Étienne de la Boétie, Montaigne explains how his grief entails the irrecoverable loss of a second self; such a relationship enables a man to 'double himself', and to become so 'glued together' with one's second self that being 'sundred' from it is

---

[1] For their support and advice on this work in various forms, I would like to thank Eric Langley, Deana Rankin, Harry Newman, Farah Karim-Cooper and Kiernan Ryan. Research for this publication was supported by the Huntington Library.
[2] Judith Butler, *Precarious Life: The Powers of Mourning and Violence* (London, 2006), pp. 22, 24.
[3] Butler, *Precarious Life*, pp. 20, 24, 23.
[4] Marianne Novy, *Shakespeare and Outsiders* (London, 2013), p. 88.
[5] Stephen Greenblatt, *Renaissance Self-Fashioning: From More to Shakespeare* (Chicago, 1980), p. 235.

an intensely painful experience which 'pull[s] away some piece of our owne'. Montaigne's response to this traumatic bereavement – 'I was so accustomed to be ever two, and so enured to be never single, that me thinks I am but halfe my selfe' – is to fashion a second self in the *Essayes*, and Iago's reaction to the sundering of his dual identity is much the same.[6] Believing that Othello 'Hath leapt into [his] seat' and dispossessed him of Emilia, his loving *alter idem* – 'the thought whereof / Doth, like a poisonous mineral, gnaw my inwards' (2.1.295–6) – Iago responds by replacing his lost second self with a perverse other.

Acknowledging himself to be thrown out of and beside himself, Iago becomes a model of divided, diffuse identity, capable of projection and introspection in a way that would later become the hallmark of modern, cynically inflected subjectivity – 'I think therefore I am' – and that was already being forged in Montaigne's *Essayes*: 'Every man looks before him selfe, I looke within my selfe; I have no businesse but with my selfe ... I roule me into my selfe.'[7] If, in declaring 'I am not what I am', Iago 'provides a succinct description of tragic subjectivity',[8] he also provides a succinct description of the proto-modern, ecstatic subject: knowingly beside himself and enjoying his coalesced detachment. In these circumstances, the enigmatic claim 'I am not what I am' is a declaration not only of duplicity, of being two-faced, but of being inherently duplicate, dislocated from self.

In stating 'I am not what I am', then, Iago presents himself as a subject who has mastered the art of constituting himself through displacement, and he will spend the play encouraging others into his rhetorical structure. This experience of radical displacement, of fractured selfhood, is best understood by enlisting a term whose etymology captures the essence of what it involves: ecstasy, from the Greek ἐκ (out of, away from, beyond) and στάναι (to stand, to place). In early modern thought, this experience was considered a state of divine or erotic union, in which the subject is temporarily thrown beside itself as the soul or mind wanders free from the body. In Saint Teresa's words, it is 'an extasy, by which the soul seemeth to goe out of her self with a servour of spirit, to be transformed into her beloved'.[9] In *Othello*, a play which gradually undermines any faith in loving interlocutors, this capacity of the subject to fracture and lose itself, to be displaced and transformed, is tragically exploited, as characters are induced into ecstasies with profound physiological and pathological consequences. Taking my cue from critics such as Michael Neill, who suggests that Othello suffers 'a violent induction into this new discourse of interiority', and Janet Adelman, who has observed the 'extent to which [Iago] works to replicate his own self-division in Othello',[10] I argue in what follows that the ecstasies suffered by the play's central subjects – from Cassio's drunkenness to Othello's trance – exemplify the tragedy's dramatization of this radical fragmentation of the self.

UNDER THE INFLUENCE: CASSIO'S 'UNHAPPY BRAINS'

> Some wine, ho!
> (*Sings*) And let me the cannikin clink, clink,
> And let me the cannikin clink
> A soldier's a man,
> O, man's life's but a span,
> Why then, let a soldier drink.
> Some wine, boys!
> (*Othello*, 2.3.63–8)

---

[6] Michel de Montaigne, *Essayes*, trans. John Florio (London, 1613), I.27.94, I.38.121.
[7] Montaigne, *Essayes*, II.17.371.
[8] Garrett A. Sullivan, Jr, 'Tragic subjectivities', in *The Cambridge Companion to English Renaissance Tragedy*, ed. Emma Smith and Garret A. Sullivan (Cambridge, 2010), pp. 73–85; p. 73.
[9] Saint Teresa of Avila, *The Third Part of the Soule's Delight*, trans. R. F. Paul (Antwerp, 1654), p. 105.
[10] Michael Neill, *Issues of Death: Mortality and Identity in English Renaissance Tragedy* (Oxford, 1997), p. 159; Janet Adelman, 'Iago's alter ego: race as projection in *Othello*', *Shakespeare Quarterly* 48 (1997), 125–44; p. 128.

If the mind is to attain the heights of contemplation, writes Montaigne in his essay 'Of drunkenness', it 'must quit it[self] and raise hir selfe a loft, and taking the bridle in hir teeth, carrie and transport hir man so farre, that afterward hee wonder at himselfe, and rest amazed at his actions'.[11] Here, Montaigne reflects on alcohol's ability to facilitate the act of self-departure, on the way wine enables the subject to take an intoxicated step beyond itself. But, intrigued though he is by the parallels between drunken excess and spiritual ecstasy, Montaigne is no advocate of inebriation: 'drunkennesse ... appeareth to mee a grose and brutish vice'.

Other vices but alter and distract the understanding, whereas this utterly subverteth the same, and astonieth the body.... The worst estate of man, is where he looseth the knowledge and governemen[t] of himselfe. And amongst other things, it is said, that as must wine boyling and working in a vessell, workes and sends upward what ever it containeth in the bottome, so doth wine cause those that drinke excessively of it, [to] worke up, and breake out their most concealed secrets.[12]

Drinking, in these terms, causes us to lose knowledge and control of ourselves. 'Beware of drink', warns the divine Samuel Speed, because 'where Drunkenness reigns, Reason is an exile'.[13]

As early modern accounts of ancient Bacchic revelry repeatedly stress, alcohol could provide an opportunity for ecstatic unity – with the 'grapegod Bacchus', as Ovid's Pythagoras calls him – but could also occasion a violent loss of self.[14] '[T]he Bacchinalls', writes Thomas Heywood, 'were women that were usually drunke in the celebrations of the feasts of *Bacchus* ... extasied in their devine furor'.[15] *Antony and Cleopatra*'s 'Egyptian bacchanals' (2.7.100) demonstrate how this kind of intoxicated ecstasy could cut either way:

> Come, thou monarch of the vine,
> Plumpy Bacchus, with pink eyne!
> In thy vats our cares be drowned,
> With thy grapes our hairs be crowned!
> Cup us till the world go round,
> Cup us till the world go round!
> (2.7.110–15)

Temporarily setting their grievances to one side, this intoxicated travesty of a sacred rite brings Rome and Egypt together in a fleeting state of harmonious concord: 'all take hands', says Antony, 'Till that the conquering wine hath steeped our sense / In soft and delicate Lethe' (103–5). Yet to drink and dance to such excess can also result in a loss of self-control; 'strong Enobarb / Is weaker than the wine', complains Caesar, 'and mine own tongue / Splits what it speaks' (119–21). 'This wild disguise', he declares, 'hath almost / Anticked us all' (121–2); like Hamlet's 'antic disposition' (*Hamlet*, 1.5.173), alcohol threatens to dispossess the Romans of themselves. In *Antony and Cleopatra*, where the stoic confines of the Roman individual are always at risk of erosion under the liquid influence of Egyptian epicureanism, the literal fumes of wine are metaphorically felt in moments where 'surfeits' and 'lascivious wassails' (1.4.27, 56) gradually dissolve the defined structures of the 'firm Roman' (1.5.43), and melt the 'man of steel' (4.4.33). Put simply, alcohol is a catalyst for the ecstatic experience, for better and for worse. As Maria warns Sir Toby in *Twelfth Night*, 'that quaffing and drinking will undo you' (1.3.13). We recognize, therefore, the potential for 'distempering draughts' (*Othello*, 1.1.100) to 'undo' and 'distemper' the consumer.

The fine line between ecstatic communion and ecstatic self-abjection, between an experience that is blissfully social and one that is painfully alienating, is central to the presentation of drinking in act 2 of *Othello*. Taking his cue from the Herald's entreaty – 'It is Othello's pleasure ... that ... every man put himself into triumph' in celebration of both the 'perdition of the Turkish fleet' and

---

[11] Montaigne, *Essayes*, II.2.192.
[12] Montaigne, *Essayes*, II.2.187–8.
[13] Samuel Speed, *Prison-pietie, Or, Meditations Divine and Moral* (London, 1677), sig. B6v.
[14] Ovid, *Shakespeare's Ovid: Being Arthur Golding's Translation of the Metamorphoses*, ed. W. H. D. Rouse (London, 1961), XV.455.
[15] Thomas Heywood, *Gynaikeion: Or, Nine Bookes of Various History* (London, 1624), pp. 148–9.

Othello's 'nuptial[s]' – Iago cajoles Cassio into raising a glass and joining the 'night of revels' enjoyed by their comrades: 'happiness to their sheets ... to the health of black Othello' (2.2.1–7, 2.3.39, 26–9). As Rebecca Lemon observes, 'this custom of health drinking ... was a prevalent one, associated with male communities bound in political–military unity'.[16] At the outset of the scene, drinking is presented as a means of achieving social unity and celebrating. But when Cassio reveals the adverse effects that alcohol has on him – 'I have very poor and unhappy brains for drinking' (30–1) – Iago's insistence on his drinking with their friends is no longer motivated by a desire to achieve social harmony, but by an attempt to capitalize on the violent ecstasy that drinking can produce. Like the philosopher and Protestant divine William Ames, Iago is well aware that 'drunkennesse doe consist in the losse of the use of reason by Drinking':[17]

> If I can fasten but one cup upon him,
> With that which he hath drunk tonight already,
> He'll be as full of quarrel and offence ...
> Now 'mongst this flock of drunkards
> Am I to put our Cassio in some action
> That may offend the isle.
>
> (44–57)

Seeking to manipulate Cassio's 'infirmity' for his own nefarious ends, Iago proceeds to 'fluster' Cassio 'with flowing cups' and cause him to lose himself ''mongst [a] flock of drunkards' (37, 54, 55).

Cassio has 'unhappy brains for drinking' (31), not simply because he is 'unfortunate in the infirmity' (37), but because drinking makes his brain unhappy. As a number of early modern writers are at pains to point out, 'excessive drinking of wyne' can 'troble & distemper the brain & judgement of the drinker', for wine 'blow[s]' and 'spoiles the braine'.[18] In his *Methode of Phisicke*, Philip Barrough goes so far as to draw parallels between drinking and conditions such as apoplexy:

The Apoplexie is caused of a flegmaticke humour, that is cold, grosse and tough, which doth at one time aboundantly fill the principal ventricles of the braine, which humour ouermuch crudities, and chiefly dronkennes doth engender. Also it is caused by a fall or a blow which shaketh & bruiseth the braine, and causeth humours to flowe thither.[19]

Drinking violently disturbs and distempers the brain. Observing how 'the vapour of wine mount[ed] up into the brain', Tomaso Garzoni discusses in a chapter 'Of Drunken Fooles' how wine could 'overwhelm' the subject, 'tak[ing] from a man sight, knowledge, and judgement ... in an instant'.[20] For Pierre de la Primaudaye, the stakes of insobriety are even higher:

[W]ine is hurtfull for the braine, for the marrow of the back bone, and the sinewes that grow out of it. Whereby it falleth out, that this principall part beeing hurt, there succeede in time, great and dangerous maladies thereupon, to wit, the apoplexie, the falling evill, the palsie, shakings, numbnes of members, convulsions, giddines of the head, shrinking of ioints, the incubus, the catalepsia, lethargie, frensie, rheumes, deafenes, blindenes, and shrinking of mouth and lips.[21]

Perhaps influenced by Galen's conclusion that 'by drunkennesse commeth astonishment of the brayne, the Falling sicknesse, or some mayme either to Sense or Motion', these writers underscore the extent to which drinking can damage the subject.[22] Diagnosing the effects of wine as the symptoms of a 'dangerous maladie', they bring into focus how the experience of being drunkenly beside oneself was perceived in medical terms. Acknowledging the tendency of the 'distempering

---

[16] Rebecca Lemon, *Addiction and Devotion in Early Modern England* (Philadelphia, 2018), p. 118.
[17] William Ames, *Conscience with the Power and Cases Thereof Divided into V Bookes* (Leydon and London, 1639), p. 80.
[18] Antonio de Guevara, *The Dial of Princes*, trans. T. North (London, 1568), p. 127; John Hoskins, *Sermons Preached at Pauls Crosse and Else-where* (London, 1615), p. 31; Richard Young, *The Drunkard's Character* (London, 1638), p. 235.
[19] Philip Barrough, *The Methode of Phisicke* (London, 1583), p. 25.
[20] Tomaso Garzoni, *The Hospital of Incurable Fooles* (London, 1600), p. 27.
[21] Pierre de la Primaudaye, *The Third Volume of the French Academie* (London, 1601), p. 363.
[22] Stephen Bradwell, *A Watch-Man for the Pest* (London, 1625), p. 31.

draught' to alter his temper, because he has 'unhappy brains for drinking' a fluid that was itself understood to make the brain unhappy, Cassio perceives the ecstasy of intoxication not as a joyous state of social unity, but as an intensely disruptive physical experience of estrangement.

Drinking, then, makes Cassio unhappy, and it is in this unhappiness that he loses himself. The word 'hap' and its variants, as well as denoting moments of chance and fortune (as in 'happenstance', or 'haply') are also used in relation to contact and proximity: 'haptic' involves touch (from the Greek *haptikos*: to come in contact with) and, for early moderns, to 'hap' could mean 'to take' or 'seize' something (*OED*, *v.*, sense 3, now obsolete). 'Happiness', as Sara Ahmed writes, 'puts us into intimate contact with things.'[23] In this sense, ecstasy is an experience that drives the subject towards such 'hap-py' moments: a union with the divine or the beloved, or a moment when subjects feel more 'in touch' with the world around them. For Cassio, however, the ecstasy of intoxication does not bring him intimate contact or happy union, but instead catalyses self-dissolution and unhappy conflict:

MONTANO: What's the matter, lieutenant?
CASSIO: A knave teach me my duty? – I'll beat the knave into a twiggen bottle.
RODERIGO: Beat me?
CASSIO: Dost thou prate, rogue?
MONTANO: Nay, good lieutenant, I pray, sir, hold your hand.
CASSIO: Let me go, sir, or I'll knock you o'er the mazard.
MONTANO: Come, come, you're drunk.
CASSIO: Drunk?
They Fight
(140–9)

Where Viola is 'happy' at the end of *Twelfth Night* because 'place, time, fortune, do cohere and jump' (5.1.247, 250), Cassio's unhappiness renders him 'drunk', 'speak[ing] parrot' (*Othello*, 2.3.273), and lacking coherence. 'Unhappy brains' lead to un-hap-py actions that will in turn only intensify his feelings of unhappiness.

As Cassio attempts to assert his authority over Iago – reminding him that 'The lieutenant is to be saved before the ensign' – while also trying to maintain control of himself – 'I am not drunk now ... You must not think then that I am drunk' – Iago exploits his 'unhappy' disposition (102–3, 107–8, 110–11). Craving his lieutenancy, Iago seeks to displace Cassio in order to take the place that he considers to be rightfully his. Cassio's claims not to be drunk are therefore countered by Iago's assuring Montano that the lieutenant's intoxication is 'evermore his prologue to his sleep' (121), a lie that seeks to sever Cassio from his 'reputation' and cause it to be 'lost without deserving' (261, 263–4). Exploiting the fact that Cassio is 'unfortunate in the infirmity', Iago inducts Cassio into his model of self-fracture by eroding 'the immortal part of [him]self', employing the 'invisible spirit of wine' to 'steal[s] away [his] brains' (257, 275, 284–5). Cassio laments 'that men should put an enemy in their mouths' and thus 'transform [them]selves into beasts' (284–5, 286). Richard Young – anatomizing the problem of drunkards and the evils of drink in his jeremiad *The Drunkard's Character* (1638) – argues that 'drunkards are *worse* then beasts, in that beasts remaine the same they were created; whereas Drunkards ... suffer themselves to be transformed by drinke into swine'.[24] 'I have lost the immortal part of myself, and what remains is bestial' (257–8): pouring drink down Cassio's throat, Iago inflicts his own unhappiness on this 'unfortunate' subject, and demonstrates how easily his own experience of self-fracture can be artificially inflicted on others.

'I am not drunk now. I can stand well enough' (107–8): '[s]wagger[ing]' (274) in his drunken state, Cassio is unable to balance 'I' and 'I', signifiers that lack stability because their dizzy referent cannot stand still. In this way, the 'voluble' (2.1.238), changeable subject is transformed from 'a sensible man, by and by' into 'a fool, and presently a beast! O, strange!' (2.3.298–300). The

---

[23] Sara Ahmed, 'Happy objects', in *The Promise of Happiness* (Durham, NC, 2010), p. 23.
[24] Young, *Drunkard's Character*, p. 14 (emphasis mine).

'sinne which cracks mens credits' is felt particularly strongly by Cassio, as cracks start to show in the foundations of his identity; as Young would put it, 'hee *looseth* his *credit* and *good name, for drunkennes defames* a man, and takes away his reputation'.[25] As Cassio laments: 'Reputation, reputation, reputation – O, I ha' lost my reputation' (256–7). By a drink that 'dislikes' him, Cassio is estranged from himself – 'how comes it, Michael, you are thus forgot?' (181) – to the point where he is no longer like himself, and no longer likes himself: 'one unperfectness shows me another to make me frankly despise myself' (290–1). Having successfully displaced Cassio – 'never more be officer of mine' (242), commands Othello, having been woken by the drunken revelry – Iago strives to make that place his own: 'Now art thou my lieutenant' (3.3.481), Othello will subsequently assure him. Alcohol has exiled Cassio from himself and he mourns the loss, desperately trying to recover himself: 'I will ask him [Othello] for my place again' (3.1.296). It was loss of place that brought about Iago's self-division, and it is apt, an unhappy coincidence, that Cassio's self-shattering now causes him to lose his.

Like wine, Iago is a transformative substance, having 'at [his] disposal apparently plastic powers' that can drive the play's subjects into ecstatic fracture, 'invisibly inducing physic discord', as Eric Langley puts it.[26] While Iago might be able to sustain a protean model of ecstatic plurality ('*I* am not what *I* am'), Cassio's unhappy self-estrangement forces him into a violent state of self-loss. Unlike Iago, who is paradoxically able to maintain a sense of self through the experience of self-division, Cassio's ego is brittle. He might not know the subjective flux that drunkenness facilitates, but Iago does: 'good wine is a good familiar creature, if it be well used' (302–3). Under the influence of both alcohol and Iago, Cassio's sense of self is shattered. Iago demonstrates how easily the dynamics of ecstasy can be thrown into discord, how easily self-knowledge can be corrupted, and how easily the subject can be distempered.

Having considered how Cassio's 'unhappy brains' make him vulnerable to a negative, pathological ecstasis, an experience of self-loss rather than self-location, let me turn now to consider the fragmentation that Iago inflicts upon Othello in similar pathological terms. If, as Robert Ritchie Simpson suggests, 'th[e] use of a medical situation to enhance ... dramatic effect is an absorbing theme, worth more detailed study',[27] then what follows examines Othello's 'ecstasy' (4.1.78) alongside medical treatises of epilepsy in order to suggest the extent to which Shakespeare's conflation of these states reflects the play's larger concerns about subjectivity and integrity.

'*FALLS IN A TRAUNCE*': OTHELLO'S EPILEPTIC ECSTASY

Earthquakes and falling sickness have the same causes. Falling sickness is not a disease coming from nature in its regular course, or from ill health in the organism of destruction of the humors, but solely from the same causes as earthquakes, for the motion of the earth is also the motion of man and is experienced by all which grows on the earth.... if the living spirit boils due to faults in its properties, it produces vapors which make the whole body tremble.[28]

CASSIUS: And when the fit was on him, I did mark
How he did shake ...

(*Caesar*, 1.2.122–3)

Lost in a corporeal storm, as Paracelsus has it, the epileptic subject is shaken by internal eruptions; they tremble, lose control and, as described above, suffer internal fragmentation as the storm rages. Behind this metaphor lies the notion that the

---

[25] Young, *Drunkard's Character*, pp. 27, 66.
[26] Roland Barthes, *Mythologies*, trans. Annette Lavers (London, 2000), p. 58; Eric Langley, *Narcissism and Suicide in Shakespeare and his Contemporaries* (Oxford, 2009), p. 266.
[27] Robert Ritchie Simpson, *Shakespeare and Medicine* (Edinburgh, 1959), p. 160.
[28] Paracelsus, *Four Treatises of Theophrastus Von Hohenheim Called Paracelsus*, trans. C. Lillian Temkin, George Rosen, Gregory Zilboorg and Henry E. Sigerist (Baltimore, 1996), pp. 144–5.

body operates as a microcosm of the world – 'earthquakes and falling sickness have the same causes' for, as John Donne has it, 'every Man is a little world'.[29] Understood in these terms, storm and body are seen to operate in similar ways; both exist in a state of flux, at the mercy of external influence: 'For a while the body of a thunderstorm is surrounded by a shell or skin, and as long as the body remains whole, the effect of mercury, sulphur and salt remains enclosed in it. But when the time comes, thunder disrupts its shell and breaks forth.'[30] The subject must therefore remain hermetically sealed off if the storm is to be constrained. For while sulphur lies dormant in the body, it may be ignited by an outside force and produce vapours which, 'communicated to the brain', stupefy the senses and throw the subject into 'Epilepsie, and trembling'.[31]

Only a handful of seizures or fits are depicted on the early modern stage. In Ben Jonson's *Volpone* (1606) and *The Devil is an Ass* (first performed 1616), feigned seizures are used to comic effect. In *Volpone*, Voltore feigns being possessed by a demonic parasite, and in act 5, scene 7, the eponymous protagonist in disguise orchestrates the simulated fit before an audience:

VOLPONE: They said, you were possessed; fall down, and seem so: I'll help to make it good.
[*Voltore falls.*]
[*Aloud to the court*] God bless the man!
[*Aside to Voltore*] Stop your wind hard, and swell. [*Aloud*] See, see, see, see!
He vomits crooked pins! His eyes are set Like a dead hare's hung in a poulter's shop! His mouth's running away! Do you see, Signor?
Now 'tis in his belly.[32]

Voltore falls when he is told, comes to when he is told – 'Look! He comes t'himself!' (33) – and adopts the rhetoric of a tranced subject who has suffered a temporary absence from the body: 'Where am I?' (34). Here, as Alan C. Dessen has considered, Volpone highlights various symptoms and other characters 'reinforce the effect', treating the audience 'to one of the funniest scenes in the play'.[33] In *The Devil Is An Ass*, by contrast, Fitzdottrel is the author of his own feigned seizure:

[*Fitzdottrel*] *begins his fit.*
FITZDOTTRELL: Gi'me some garlic, garlic, garlic, garlic!
MERECROFT: Hark the poor gentlemen, how he is tormented!
FITZDOTTRELL: My wife is a whore, I'll kiss her no more; and why?
Mayst not thou be a cuckold, as well as I?
Ha, ha, ha, ha, ha, ha, ha, ha, etc.
. . .
SIR POL: That is the devil that speaks and laughs in him.[34]

In this lengthy 'fit', his observers (many of whom are in on the trick) note 'how he changes' (32), 'how he foams!' and 'swells!' (33–4), and '[g]ive him more soap to foam with' (68). Since the Middle Ages, soap had been a useful tool in imitating epileptic attacks; as Ambrose Paré describes, explaining how beggars were wont to simulate epilepsy to earn alms: 'by putting sope into their mouths, they foam at the mouth like those that have the falling sickness'.[35] Using '[a] little castle-soap' (5.3.3) – a hard, Spanish soap made with soda and olive oil, here 'rub[bed]' on the 'lips' (4) – Fitzdottrel mimics the physical

---

[29] John Donne, *The First Sermon Preached to King Charles* (London, 1625), p. 29.
[30] Owsei Temkin, *The Falling Sickness: A History of Epilepsy from the Greeks to the Beginnings of Modern Neurology* (Baltimore, 1945), pp. 173–4.
[31] Ambrose Paré, *The Works of That Famous Chirurgion Ambrose Parey*, trans. Thomas Johnson (London, 1634), p. 1169.
[32] All quotations from the text of the play are taken from the edition prepared by Richard Dutton for *The Cambridge Edition of the Works of Ben Jonson Online*, ed. David Bevington, Martin Butler and Ian Donaldson (Cambridge, 2012), 5.7.21–8. Further references to this edition appear in parentheses.
[33] Alan C. Dessen, 'On stage allegory and its legacy: *The Three Ladies of London*', in *Locating the Queen's Men, 1583–1603: Material Practices and Conditions of Playing*, ed. Helen Ostovich, Holger Schott Syme and Andrew Griffin (London, 2009), pp. 147–58; p. 157.
[34] All quotations from the text of the play are taken from the edition prepared by Anthony Parr for *The Cambridge Edition of the Works of Ben Jonson Online*, ed. David Bevington, Martin Butler and Ian Donaldson (Cambridge, 2012), 5.8.24–9.
[35] Paré, *Workes*, p. 995.

effects of seizure, as well as other commonplace traits such as inarticulate stammers – 'Buzz, buzz, buzz, buzz'; 'Oh, oh'; 'Hum!'; 'Yellow, yellow, yellow, yellow, etc.' (4, 48, 72, 74) – and speaking in foreign tongues (a feature of some prophetic trances known as *glossalalia*). Both plays employ commonplace markers of these fits, feigning demonic possession for comic effect.

Othello's genuine seizure, by contrast, intensifies the tragedy, marking a moment of unbearable anguish and shattered subjectivity as he succumbs to Iago's insinuation that Desdemona has cuckolded him with Cassio. For early moderns, the subject who trembled in epilepsy tested the limits of medical understanding; this was an experience which blurred the boundaries between natural and supernatural, divine and demonic, with discussions about the causes and cures of epilepsy repeatedly resisting stable definition. Indeed, the play's interest and investment in this altered state and the desire to diagnose it are evidenced by the significant alterations to this speech between its appearance in the 1622 Quarto (Q1) and its reproduction in the First Folio (F1) the following year:

Q1: Lie with her, lie on her? We say lie on her, when they bely her; lye with her, Zouns, that's fulsome, handkerchers, Confession, hankerchers.
He fals downe.[36]

F1: Lye with her? lye on her? We say lye on her, when they be-lye-her. Lye with her: that's fullsome: Handkerchiefe: Confessions: Handkerchiefe. To confesse, and be hang'd for his labour. First, to be hang'd, and then to confesse: I tremble at it. Nature would not invest her selfe in such shadowing passion, without some Instruction. It is not words that shakes me thus, (pish) Noses, Eares, and Lippes: is't possible. Confesse? Handkerchiefe? O divell.
Falls in a Traunce.

(4.1, TLN 2412–20)

In F1, the speech is expanded to include references to Othello's physical state, to trembling, shaking and the additional specification that when '*He fals downe*' (Q1), it is '*in a Traunce*' (F1). It is almost as though Ralph Crane, the scribe who is generally assumed to have prepared *Othello* for publication in the Folio, felt compelled to diagnose Othello's fall, rescripting and clarifying it as a tranced experience of altered consciousness.

The critical compulsion to diagnose this condition is shared by the text itself, presenting a moment that straddles the medical and the non-medical. For Othello's epileptic body, as Iago diagnoses it, is also curiously ecstatic in both Q1 and F1: 'I ... laid good 'scuse upon your ecstasy' (4.1.77–8), Iago tells Othello when he returns to himself. In *Julius Caesar*, epilepsy is used as a metaphor for political weakness, as Cassius reports Caesar to have suffered a fit in Spain and recalls how 'I did mark / How he did shake. 'Tis true, this god did shake / ... As a sick girl' (1.2.122–30). In these circumstances, using epilepsy as a ''scuse' for ecstasy has the deliberate effect of undermining Othello's strength, as both a man and a military leader. What interests me here, however, is the unexplored affinity between these two states – epilepsy and ecstasy – and how these altered states of consciousness intersect with issues of subjectivity, emotion, race and affect. Elsewhere in early modern culture, we find ecstasy most often associated with experiences of religious rapture, frenzied madness and erotic bliss, in which the soul would temporarily leave the body; here it figures in the convulsive tremors of pathological seizure. Whereas diagnostic readings of the play have focused on and taken issue with Iago's claim that 'my lord is fall'n into an epilepsy' (4.1.48), the following examines this claim alongside Iago's subsequent statement that this was simply a cover, an excuse laid upon Othello's ecstasy. To view these states in tandem, I argue, highlights the place of ecstasy within an increasingly medicalized lexicon of conscious experience, and provides a lens through which to understand the significance

---

[36] William Shakespeare, *Othello*, Q1 (London, 1622), sig. I3v, ll. 18–20.

of Othello's violent physical seizure and the destabilized sense of self.

The fact that Iago describes Othello's 'trance' as both 'epilepsy' and 'ecstasy' has received little critical attention. This has mostly been due to the lack of evidence for the former diagnosis, unless, as Sujata Iyengar notes, 'we take [Othello's] headache as a migrainous aura preceding the attack' rather than a symbolic expression of his supposed cuckoldom.[37] Furthermore, she writes, 'Iago appears to be bolstering outdated associations among epilepsy, madness, and hysteria, confirmed by his anticipation of Othello's "savage madness" if disturbed before the fit outlives its course.'[38] In his recent study of fainting, Giulio J. Pertile reflects this diagnostic uncertainty when he writes that 'whether or not it is medically accurate, Iago's description of what befalls Othello as "an epilepsy" is uncannily appropriate': one that early moderns would have recognized as hallmarks of 'the falling sickness'.[39] David Hoeniger, however, discredits views of the episode as an epileptic one; he contends that 'Othello's fit is merely a short-lived trance caused by his overwrought emotional state', that 'Shakespeare knew the symptoms of epilepsy, and that they do not suddenly appear because a man is overcome with passion'.[40] And yet, by also calling Othello's seizure an 'ecstasy', Iago seems to suggest otherwise: 'Whilst you were here, o'erwhelmed with your grief ... Cassio came hither. I shifted him away, / And laid good 'scuse on your ecstasy' (4.1.75–8). Here, Shakespeare does indeed present a kind of ecstatic epilepsy that results from overwhelming emotion, and furthermore reflects a range of contemporary theories concerning these altered states.

For Stephanie Moss, Othello's epilepsy represents 'the pinnacle of [Iago's] manipulations', a state that marks Othello's shift 'from a subject to an object, from an assimilated black man to an outsider'.[41] Understood in these terms, Othello's epilepsy figures as an experience of radical alienation and expulsion, not only from the self, but also from society; what it shares with ecstasy is a sense of abjection, of being thrown beyond subjective and social borders. This ecstatic epilepsy compounds Othello's 'otherness'. As Justin Shaw observes, with Othello's seizure the racialized terms used earlier in the play to describe Othello as a 'wheeling stranger' and 'erring Barbarian' become medicalized, as 'wheeling' and 'erring' take on an additional sense of mental distraction.[42] Othello's trance marks him as an outsider: it is an experience of literal and mental ecstasy that both disables and racializes him. Whether or not this is an isolated incident or an ongoing condition, disability, race, gender and emotion intersect here and invert the play's martial power relations, as a Black general suffers a 'passion most unsuiting such a man' (4.1.76), falls down and suffers convulsions as his healthy white ensign is positioned above him.

Discussing Othello's anxieties about narration and self-presentation in the play's closing stages, Ian Smith argues that 'Othello understands that, given the play's imperial geopolitics, the members of his immediate audience will revert to seeing in his blackness the enemy "Turk" within.'[43] In this tranced state, such anxieties are likewise at stake, as narrative agency is lost to verbal incoherence and physical convulsions that highlight the tension between Othello's split identities as Christian and

---

[37] Sujata Iyengar, *Shakespeare's Medical Language: A Dictionary* (London, 2014), p. 121.
[38] Iyengar, *Shakespeare's Medical Language*, p. 121.
[39] Giulio J. Pertile, *Feeling Faint: Affect and Consciousness in the Renaissance* (Evanston, IL, 2019), p. 96.
[40] David Hoeniger, *Medicine and Shakespeare in the English Renaissance* (London, 1992), p. 204.
[41] Stephanie Moss, 'Transformation and degeneration: the Paracelsan/Galenic body in *Othello*', in *Disease, Diagnosis and Cure on the Early Modern Stage: Literary and Scientific Cultures of Early Modernity*, ed. Stephanie Moss and Kaara L. Peterson (Aldershot, 2004), pp. 151–70; p. 153. See also Sid Ray, 'Staging epilepsy in *Othello*', in *Stage Matters: Props, Bodies, and Space in Shakespearean Performance*, ed. Annalisa Castaldo and Rhonda Knight (Madison, 2018), pp. 56–71.
[42] Justin Shaw, '"Rub him about the temples": *Othello*, disability, and the failures of care', *Early Theatre* 22 (2019), 171–84; p. 173.
[43] Ian Smith, 'We are Othello: speaking of race in Early Modern Studies', *Shakespeare Quarterly* 67 (2016), 104–24; p. 111.

Muslim, Venetian and Turk, European and Moor. For, in labelling his trance an 'epilepsy' (whether or not we agree that such a diagnosis is accurate), Iago marks Othello as racially other to both the immediate onlooker (Cassio) and the early modern audience in the theatre, connecting him with Islam and the epilepsy of the Prophet Mohammed:

Nowe *Mahumet* beinge taughte al kinde of vngraciousnes of his detestable Maister, throughe intemperant liuinge and continuall drunkennes, fell at the length into the fallinge sicknes, the whiche his wife could not wel suffer for the often coming therof. Wherfore the olde dissemblinge knaue to deliuer himselfe from that infamie, doth hide and cloke his disease: sayeinge it to be the meruailous brightnes of *Gabriell* the aungel & messenger of God, of whom he being put in that traunce did receiue and learne most secret & straunge things, and that hee was not able to abyde the presence of him: with a manifest lye he affirmed it.[44]

Anti-Islamic writers of Christian texts repeatedly presented Mohammed as a false prophet who claimed divine inspiration in order to explain or 'cloke' his seizures: a 'marvellous brightness' to cover 'intemperant living and continual drunkenness'. Curiously, however, the opposite happens when Iago publicly labels Othello's trance as 'epilepsy' in order to ''scuse ... ecstasy'. If Othello's seizure echoes that of the 'Ur-Moor', Mohammed, then it also inverts it, as Iago presents himself falsely to Othello as an angelic informer from whom he will 'learn most secret and strange things'.[45] But the ensign is no 'messenger of God'. 'When devils will the blackest sins put on, / They do suggest at first with heavenly shows, / As I do now' (2.3.342–4) – this is, indeed, the divinity of hell. This is ecstasy re-scripted: not a religious experience, nor the 'plague of an high-hand' or marker of 'a very sinful soule', as Edward Kellet argues of epilepsy, but rather a pathological condition – a violent reminder that, as Butler puts it, 'we are constituted by our relations but also dispossessed by them as well'.[46] As ecstasy has been overlooked in diagnostic approaches to Othello's seizure, I want to conclude by considering ecstasy's place within an increasingly medicalized lexicon of disorientation.

In one of the few studies of the affinity between ecstasy and epilepsy, Jesús López-Peláez Casellas touches on the ecstatic nature of Othello's epilepsy, but does so more as a means of rejecting the medical diagnosis than developing it; 'Othello experiences an uncontrollable sexual arousal', he writes, that 'leads not necessarily to an epileptic fit ... but to an episode that resembles an orgasm'.[47] The term 'ecstasy' here is sexually rather than medically charged. But, as the physician Helkiah Crooke suggests, an epileptic fit and an orgasm need not be treated as distinct categories. In fact, it is the ecstasy of 'natural pleasure in generation' that binds them together: 'For were it not that the God of Nature hath placed heerein so incredible a sting or rage of pleasure, as whereby wee are transported for a time as it were out of our selves ... and wee overtaken with an extasie, which *Hippocrates* calleth a little *Epilepsie* or falling sicknesse.'[48] Ecstasy and epilepsy are here presented as connected states, and Crooke is not alone in his identification of the similarity between the two. For they were considered to be not only similarly difficult to classify, but also similar in their very nature: both 'import a distraction of the senses, a violent alienation of the mind'; both throw the subject beside itself.[49] It is difficult, it would seem, to distinguish between

---

[44] Sebastian Münster, *Cosmographia*, trans. Richard Eden (London, 1572), fol. 63.

[45] Daniel Vitkus, 'Turning Turk in Othello: the conversion and damnation of the Moor', *Shakespeare Quarterly* 48 (1997), 145–76; p. 155. See also Matthew Dimmock, *Mythologies of the Prophet Muhammad in Early Modern English Culture* (Cambridge, 2013).

[46] Edward Kellet, *A Retvrne from Argier. A Sermon Preached at Minhead in the County of Somerset the 16. of March, 1627* (London, 1628), p. 23.

[47] Jesús López-Peláez Casellas, 'Shakespeare's *Othello* and Freud's *Degradation in Erotic Life*', in *Into Another's Skin: Selected Essays in Honour of Maria Luisa Dañobeitia*, ed. Mauricio D. Aguilera Linde, Maria Jose de la Torre Moreno and Laura Torres Zúñiga (Granada, 2012), pp. 35–46; p. 42.

[48] Helkiah Crooke, *Mikrokosmographia: A Description of the Body of Man* (London, 1615), p. 200.

[49] Meric Casaubon, *A Treatise Concerning Enthusiasme* (London, 1655), p. 62.

someone 'falling into Trances and *Ecstasies*' and those who 'lye in Trances like men having the falling sickness': between those who in 'wild extasies' endure the 'swelling of their bodies and foaming at the mouth' and 'they that are in a swoune [and] foaming under a Epilepsie'.[50] Indeed, as Thomas Newton writes in 1570, translating Augustine Curio's discussion of Mohammed's epilepsy, 'he often fell grouelong on the ground, foming and froathing at the mouth (for he had the fallyng sicknes) and laye in a horrible extasie or distraction of minde'.[51] To suffer epilepsy could be to lie in horrible ecstasy.

It is not surprising, therefore, that these tranced states were, for a number of early modern writers, inextricably linked and often prone to conflation: 'I pray what is the difference between a *Trance*, and a *fainting* or *swooning*', asks the scholar and divine Meric Casaubon (1599–1671), explaining that 'there is so much affinity, that the words may probably be confounded sometimes'.[52] For Casaubon, as for a number of members of both medical and theological disciplines, this was precisely the problem. As Allison P. Hobgood notes in her consideration of Julius Caesar's 'falling sickness', 'with increased conversion of the populace to Christianity, epilepsy's connections to divine prophecy ... and ecstatic possession became more pronounced', with medieval Christianity 'recasting ... epileptic fits as divine ecstasy'.[53] In much the same way, with increased medical interest in the cause and nature of epilepsy, ecstasy began to take on a medical identity, and would later earn its place under an index of 'distempers of the brain', in a chapter on 'Inward Diseases, and Distempers of the Body' in Alderman Randle Holme's encyclopaedic work *The Academy of Armory*.[54] In short, the lines between natural and numinous ecstasy became blurred: lines which Casaubon – who held 'every true, natural, and perfect ecstasie, to be a degree or *species* of epilepsie' – would seek to clarify by resituating conceptions of the ecstatic experience in discussions of disease.[55] In these circumstances, the textual changes to *Othello* outlined above reflect a broader compulsion to diagnose these altered states: states which simultaneously captured and evaded the early modern medical imagination.

Subscribing to a more naturalistic understanding of ecstasy, Casaubon wonders whether it might function like any other disease:

I will not make question of it ... but I desire only to propose it, that learned Naturalists and Physicians may (if they please) consider it; Whether it be probable or possible, that naturall Ecstasies and Enthusiasms ... should be contagious: though not contagious in the same manner as the Plague, or the Pox is; yet contagious in their kind.[56]

Ecstasy, he suggests, could beget ecstasy. This is a theory that would come to occupy the next generation of critics of enthusiasm, a state of divine inspiration which was understood as what Daniel Lindmark terms 'the preaching disease' in his discussion of contagious ecstasy in eighteenth-century Sweden.[57] Here he quotes Olof Celsius, president of the Stockholm Consistory, writing of what was by 1776 not merely a theory, but an established diagnosis: 'The consequences of this enthusiasm may be less dangerous as long as the infection is restricted to certain individuals. But since it has really proved to be contagious, just like certain diseases, it is believed that entire crowds of people may be easily infected in the meanwhile, damaging

---

[50] Bureau d'adresse et de rencontre, *Another Collection of Philosophical Conferences of the French Virtuosi*, trans. G. Havers and J. Davies (London, 1665), p. 385; Ephraim Pagitt, *Heresiography* (London, 1645), p. 33; Henry More, *An Explanation of the Grand Mystery of Godliness* (London, 1660), p. 111; Thomas Adams, *A Commentary, Or, Exposition upon the Divine Second Epistle* (London, 1633), p. 712.

[51] Augustine Curio, *The Notable Histories of the Saracens*, trans. Thomas Newton (London, 1575), III.4.

[52] Casaubon, *Treatise*, p. 64.

[53] Allison Hobgood, 'Early modern ideologies of ability', in *Beholding Disability on the Renaissance Stage* (Michigan, 2021), pp. 20–48; p. 35.

[54] Randle Holme, *The Academy of Armory* (Chester, 1688), p. 432.

[55] Casaubon, *Treatise*, p. 95. [56] Casaubon, *Treatise*, p. 100.

[57] Daniel Lindmark, 'The preaching disease: contagious ecstasy in eighteenth-century Sweden', in *Imagining Contagion in Early Modern Europe*, ed. Claire L. Carlin (Basingstoke, 2005), pp. 139–53.

the country and agitating the congregation.'[58] A century later, then, studies of ecstatic phenomena continued to situate themselves between medical and theological thought. Here we find answers to Casaubon's question as to whether ecstasy might be in some sense contagious, most notably in works such as the French physician Philippe Hecquet's pamphlet on those suffering *les maladies de l'epidémie convulsionnaire* (1733). Hecquet regards convulsions not as brought about by divine or demonic intervention, but rather as psychological phenomena born of an agitated imagination: 'an actual soul fever', to borrow a phrase from the German philosopher Christoph Martin Wieland.[59] What was merely a passing thought for Casaubon would be explored in depth a century later as debates about the ecstatic condition continued.

These debates had already preoccupied a number of early modern writers for some time. Wieland's sense of epilepsy as 'soul fever', for example, had been explored by the French theologian Pierre Charron, who described the falling sickness as something that 'ariseth from the force of imagination, which enforcing and bending it self with too deep an attention about a thing, carrieth away the whole strength and power of the *Soule*'.[60] Read this way, it is Othello's enforced attention that drives him to distraction. Similarly, the idea that ecstasies could be 'contagious in their kind' would have been by no means alien to an early modern audience. Informed by Longinus's theories about the sublime impact of words upon the body, a number of early modern writers considered the potential for one state of ecstasy to beget another. In his treatise on poetry, for instance, Henry Dethick (1547/8–c.1613) celebrates poets who could experience 'a burning ardor of mind, as if in a kind of violent impulse', and could bring about a similar experience for their listeners.[61] In *An Apology for Poetry*, Philip Sidney likewise observes the 'heart-ravishing' potential of poetry which could 'strike, pierce' and 'possesse' the soul.[62] The ecstasy of a poet could bring about ecstasies in his audience; as the French poet and priest Pontus de Tyard remarks, following the Neoplatonist Marsilio Ficino, 'the divine furor not only makes a good poet, but also drenches with its liquor … those who listen to these verses'.[63] Elsewhere, in *Hamlet* – a play that repeatedly identifies the ear as a location of danger, as a vulnerable point of entry into the body and the mind – Ophelia's 'speech' is reported as having the potential to 'move / The hearers to collection' (4.5.8–9). Subject and soul could all too easily be moved, for better or for worse, by words that entered the ear.

We might, therefore, set Casaubon's suggestion alongside the early modern medical discussions in which epilepsy was understood as emanating from harmful vapours. This is precisely what underpins Casca's fears that the cause of Caesar's fit might also pose a threat to him:

CASCA: And still as he [Caesar] refused [the crown], the rabblement hooted, and clapped their chapped hands, and threw up their sweaty nightcaps, and uttered such a deal of stinking breath because Caesar refused the crown that it had almost choked Caesar; for he swooned and fell down at it. And for mine own part, I durst not laugh, for fear of opening my lips and receiving bad air.
CASSIUS: But soft, I pray you. What, did Caesar swoon?
CASCA: He fell down in the market-place, and foamed at mouth, and was speechless.
BRUTUS: 'Tis very like: he hath the falling sickness.
(*Caesar*, 1.2.243–54)

Here epilepsy is emphasized as a pathological rather than divine state: as a transmissible medical condition. In his belief that the 'infection of air' is capable of creating 'most contagious diseases, as the falling sicknesse', Casca reflects an early modern

---

[58] Lindmark, 'Preaching disease', p. 139.
[59] Quoted in Lindmark, 'Preaching disease', p. 142.
[60] Pierre Charron, *Of Wisdome*, trans. Samson Lennard (London, 1608), I.33.
[61] Henry Dethick, *Oratio in Lauden Poësoes* [1575], trans. J. W. Binns in *Latin Treatises on Poetry from the Renaissance* (Fairmount, 1999), pp. 32–3.
[62] Philip Sidney, *An Apologie for Poetrie* (London, 1595), sigs. B4r, D3r.
[63] Pontus de Tyard, *Solitaire Premier* (Paris, 1575), p. 23.

anxiety about the contagious nature of epilepsy.[64] Assuming 'stinking breath' to be the cause of Caesar's falling sickness, he insists upon the geohumoral quality of this altered state, aligning it with infectious utterances, foul air. What early modern medical treatises termed 'noxious vapours' are here called 'bad air', which is capable of having the same violent effect on the body.[65]

Shakespeare dramatizes the full potential of these fears when he comes to write *Othello*, where the bad air that circulates is equally dangerous. As Londoners faced repeated outbreaks of plague (especially the major outbreak in 1603 from which it was still recovering), contagious breath was, of course, less a metaphor and more a threatening reality for the playgoer; 'what will not kill a man, if a *vapor* will?' asks Donne, voicing a common anxiety about man's vulnerability to his environment.[66] As Longaville puts it in *Love's Labour's Lost*, 'Vows are but breath, and breath a vapour is' (4.3.65), which adumbrates the dangers of the 'vapour-vow' (67) sworn by Othello and Iago:

OTHELLO: Now, by yon marble heaven,
In the due reverence of a sacred vow
I here engage my words.
IAGO: Do not rise yet.
         Iago kneels
Witness you ever-burning lights above,
You elements that clip us round about,
Witness that here Iago doth give up
The execution of his wit, hands, heart
To wronged Othello's service. Let him command,
And to obey shall be in me remorse,
What bloody business ever.

(3.3.63–72)

In a play that makes the power of words all too clear – where 'hearts are piercèd through the ear' (1.3.218) and the art of telling stories is deemed no less powerful than witchcraft (1.3.127–69) – danger lurks in these exchanges. For the act of hearing, as Crooke explains, involves a violent invasion, whereby 'sound sealeth or stampeth in the ayre the species or forme of the sound, and ... driueth it on vnto the instrument of hearing which ... receiue[s]

those species, and must like-wise be mooued'.[67] 'My Lord,' says Iago, feigning concern, 'I see you're moved' (3.3.229): given the early modern anatomist's conception of the mouth and the ear as connected in a 'circulatory system, through which the "inward air" of the ear is constantly refreshed and replaced', Iago's interruptions throughout act 3, scene 3 can be understood as preventing Othello from expelling the poisoned air which, 'implanted in the instrument of hearing', is trapped inside his body.[68] A common feature of early modern plague literature, the process of purgation is delayed by the ensign's astute interjections in *Othello*:

IAGO: I know not that, but such a handkerchief –
I am sure it was your wife's – did I today
See Cassio wipe his beard with.
OTHELLO: If it be that –
IAGO: If it be that, or any that was hers,
It speaks against her with the other proofs.

(3.3.442–46)

If 'it is by stopping the mouth of this dazzling storyteller and, at the same time, stuffing his ears with poison that Iago works upon him', as Allison Deutermann contends, then Othello's trance signals the moment when Iago's pestilent words take full effect.[69] As Thomas Blount explains in his *Glossographia*: '*Epilepsie (epilepsia)* the Fallingsickness ... is caused by some humor or vapour; suddenly stopping the passage of spirits in the brain, which the brain striving to expel, causeth the

---

[64] Simeon Partlicius, *A New Method of Physick: Or, A Short View of Paracelsus and Galen's Practice*, trans. Nicholas Culpeper (London, 1654), p. 503; Joseph du Chesne, *A Breefe Aunswere of Iosephus Quercetanus Armeniacus, Doctor of Phisick, to the Exposition of Iacobus Aubertus Vindonis* (London, 1591), p. 64.
[65] Henry More, *Enthusiasmus Triumphatus* (London, 1656), p. 26.
[66] John Donne, *Devotions vpon Emergent Occasions* (London, 1624), pp. 284–5.
[67] Crooke, *Mikrokosmographia*, p. 611.
[68] Allison K. Deutermann, 'Hearing Iago's withheld confession', in *Shakespearean Sensations: Experiencing Literature in Early Modern England*, ed. Tanya Pollard and Katharine Craik (London, 2013), pp. 47–63; p. 54; Crooke, *Mikrokosmographia*, sig. Ddd6r.
[69] Deutermann, 'Hearing Iago's withheld confession', p. 54.

patient to fall down and commonly foam at the mouth.'[70] Iago's poisonous words confuse and destabilize Othello, forcing his speech to collapse into incoherent prose before his body collapses in a trance. 'I tremble at it' (4.1.38): his body vibrating in an uncontrollable convulsion, Othello is no longer 'the noble Moor ... Whom passion could not shake' (266–8). For, as Iago's 'medicine' takes effect (43), a 'bloody passion' begins to 'shake ... [Othello's] very frame' (5.2.47) under the external pressure of the words Iago crams into his ears and the internal pressure of 'the lethargy [which] must have his quiet course' (4.1.51). 'If not', asserts Iago, adopting the discourse of diagnosis, 'he foams at mouth' (52). Understood in these terms, Othello's ecstatic epilepsy could be seen as caused by the '*Grossenesse* of [Iago's] *Vapours*, which rise and enter [through the ear and] into the *Cells* of [his] *Braine*'.[71] It could also be seen as a dramatic forerunner of Casaubon's belief that ecstasy, like enthusiasm and epilepsy, might be transmissible: a displacement of the self that could be inflicted on others.

Shakespeare employs this enigmatic trance state in *Othello* to enhance his dramatization of the violent fracturing of the self, the radical displacement of identity, suffered by the play's tragic protagonist. Following Janet Adelman, who argues that Iago 'transfer[s] his own sense of hidden contamination' to others, and Eric Langley, who reads Iago as a figure 'whose psychopathology spreads pathologically, who spreads his influence like a plague',[72] I have suggested that the play's representation of ecstatic experience contributes to the play's depiction of contagiously ruptured subjectivity. Whereas Iago inhabits an ecstatically reflexive form of being – 'I am not what I am' – Othello's ecstasy enacts a violent shattering of the self from which he never recovers: 'That's he that was Othello. Here I am' (5.2.290). As Kiernan Ryan notes, 'the entire tragedy is contained in the gulf that divides those two pronouns'.[73] By the play's conclusion, Othello is tragically dislocated, driven outside himself, only able to restore a simulacrum of a unified self through a suicidal gesture:

OTHELLO: Set you down this;
And say besides that in Aleppo once,
Where a malignant and a turbaned Turk
Beat a Venetian and traduced the state,
I took by th' throat the circumcisèd dog
And smote him thus.

He stabs himself

(5.2.360–5)

With that 'thus' Othello brings his fractured selves into violent contact in a gesture that fuses not only language and action, but also self and self. Drawn into Iago's world of plural, diffuse identity, Othello acknowledges his divided identity as both Turk and Venetian and strives to reunite his disparate selves. 'Speak of me as I am. Nothing extenuate' (351): what Othello seeks in his last moments is coherence – words that are accurate, selves that cohere.

What 'ecstasy' offers us is a term whose etymology captures perfectly the sense of fractured, displaced selfhood *Othello* dramatizes so powerfully. It provides a way of thinking afresh about the construction and destruction of identity and selfhood – about what Butler calls 'this disposition of ourselves outside ourselves [that] seems to follow from bodily life, from its vulnerability and its exposure'.[74] Here, in a play where subjects variously exhibit the self-shattering potential of 'precarious life', Shakespeare offers dangerous exemplars of what it means to live interpersonally, to be taken outside and beyond oneself, to suffer ecstasy.

---

[70] Thomas Blount, *Glossographia* (London, 1656), sig. P3r.
[71] Francis Bacon, *Sylva Sylvarum* (London, 1627), p. 259.
[72] Adelman, 'Iago's alter ego', p. 131; Eric Langley, *Shakespeare's Contagious Sympathies: Ill Communications* (Oxford, 2018), p. 121.
[73] Kiernan Ryan, *Shakespeare* (Basingstoke, 2002), p. 89.
[74] Butler, *Precarious Life*, p. 25.

OTHELLO'S SYMPATHIES: EMOTION, AGENCY AND IDENTIFICATION

RICHARD MEEK[1]

In *The New Found Worlde, or Antarctike*, which was translated into English in 1568, André Thevet describes the people of France Antarctique, a French colony in Brazil:

> As touching their maners even so as is the temperatnesse of the ayre according to the diversitie of places, also the people themselves doe cause varietie of temperance, and by folowing of maners for the *Simpathie* that the soule hath with the body, as *Galian* sheweth in the booke that he hath write. Likewise we see in *Europia*, in divers Kingdomes, the varietie of maners and customes, the *Africans* in general are crafty, as the *Syrines* covetous, the *Sicilians* willy, and the *Asians* voluptuous.[2]

Citing Galen as an authority, the text offers an environmental and physiological explanation for the 'varietie of maners and customes' of different peoples. The word '*Simpathie*' – which in its earliest usages referred to affinity and correspondence – is used to describe the relationship between the soul and the body, and between a person's 'temperance' and the 'temperatnesse of the ayre'.[3] According to Early English Books Online (EEBO), this is the first appearance of *sympathy* in an English printed text; and, as with other early examples, the term is capitalized and italicized to emphasize its status as an innovative loanword, borrowed from the French.[4] Thevet uses the word to suggest the ways in which an individual's habitual behaviour and conduct are shaped by their physical environment. People from particular places have a distinct nature or character, which is determined by the physical conditions of that place rather than the individuals themselves – although

Thevet does concede that there are exceptions to his list of categorizations by adding the qualifying phrase 'in general'.[5]

Such essentializing tendencies are also evident in chapter 16, which describes the people of Ethiopia, and explains that the heat of the air 'draweth out the natural heat of the heart, and other interior parts, & therfore they remain colde within ... and onely burned outwarde'. This 'inward coldnesse' leads to a lack of 'hardinesse and manhoode', which is explained in meteorological and humoral terms, and is in direct contrast to the English, whose

---

[1] An earlier version of this article was delivered at the autumn meeting of the Deutsche Shakespeare-Gesellschaft in Bochum in November 2018. Thanks to Andreas Höfele, Claudia Olk, Felix Sprang and Roland Weidle for their hospitality and feedback. I am also grateful to Katharine A. Craik, Brett Greatley-Hirsch, Jane Rickard and the anonymous reader at *Shakespeare Survey* for commenting on earlier drafts.

[2] André Thevet, *The New Found Worlde, or Antarctike*, trans. Thomas Hacket (London, 1568), fols. 4–5. Further references appear in parentheses.

[3] See the *OED*'s primary definition of *sympathy*: 'A (real or supposed) affinity between certain things, by virtue of which they are similarly or correspondingly affected by the same influence ... (esp. in some occult way), or attract or tend towards each other' (*OED Online*, sense 1a; first cited usage 1586).

[4] The word '*Simpathie*' is a slight Anglicization of the original French *sympathie*, which appears in Thevet's original text: 'pour la sympathie qu'il y a de l'ame avec le corps' (André Thevet, *Les singularitez de la France Antarctique* (Antwerp, 1558), sig. B5v).

[5] As Thevet puts it, 'En general, lon trouve les Africains cauteleux ... ' (sig. B5v).

mediocre climate causes them to be 'cold without, but marvelous hot within, to be hardy, couragious, & ful of great boldnesse' (fol. 25). Thevet goes on to make an additional point about Ethiopians that is especially germane to the theme of the present article: 'These *Ethiopians & Indians* use Magike bicause they have many herbes & other things proper for that exercise. And it is certaine & true, that there is a certain *Sympathia* in things, and hid *Antipathia*, the which cannot be known but by long experience' (fol. 25). Here, Thevet refers to the hidden system of sympathies and antipathies – described by classical writers and early modern philosophers – thought to exist in nature.[6] Ethiopians and Indians can use magic to access this mysterious system through their use of herbs and other natural substances; in other words, these races have a certain (and potentially advantageous) knowledge of and power over the natural world that is alien to most Europeans.

Thevet's invocation of these two forms of sympathy – between the soul and the body, and between things in the natural world – speaks to my own interest in the representation of sympathy in *Othello*. While not a direct source of Shakespeare's play, *The New Found Worlde* was nevertheless part of a set of texts that formed Elizabethan and Jacobean views of Africa and the New World.[7] The idea that individuals have a particular 'nature' that dictates their emotions and behaviour is a central concern of *Othello*; the play also invokes the idea of sympathetic magic, most explicitly in Brabantio's worries about Othello's courtship of Desdemona. But *Othello* does not endorse either of these ideas, and interrogates the belief that a person's nature is shaped by their physical environment or humoral physiology. It is true that the play's characters sometimes evoke humoral theory as a way of explaining each other's behaviours, including references to choler, spleen and gall.[8] However, it seems to me that these descriptions of the bodily aspects of emotion are treated sceptically, or even ironically, in the play. Indeed, *Othello*'s presentation of Galenic discourse is part of its radical scepticism regarding stereotypes of various kinds: racial, gender and humoral.

The present article considers the representation of sympathy and identification within the play – not merely as a contagious or magical phenomenon, but as a form of intersubjectivity. In so doing, it seeks to complicate two critical commonplaces about *Othello*: first, that its portrayal of interpersonal relations is predominantly bleak or pessimistic. This viewpoint was powerfully articulated by Stephen Greenblatt in *Renaissance Self-Fashioning* (1980), which focuses not on sympathy but on its later counterpart empathy, describing its representation in the play as a 'ruthless displacement and absorption of the other'. Greenblatt continues: 'in *Othello*, where all relations are embedded in power and sexuality, there is no realm where subject and object can merge in the dramatic accord affirmed by the theorists of empathy'.[9] For Greenblatt, then, there is no possibility of empathy or human agency, which have disappeared into the power structures that the play depicts.[10] Similarly, Mary Floyd-Wilson has written that the closest Iago gets to 'affective communion is his manipulation and perversion of other people's passions'.[11] Yet, as we

---

[6] Hacket uses the earlier Latin terms *sympathia* and *antipathia* as equivalents for Thevet's *sympathie* and *antipathie*: 'Et est certain qu'il y à quelque sympathie es choses & antipathie occulte, qui ne se peut cognoistre que par longue experience' (Thevet, *Les singularitez de la France Antarctique*, sig. E5v). On sympathetic magic, see Ann E. Moyer, 'Sympathy in the Renaissance', in *Sympathy: A History*, ed. Erik Schliesser (Oxford, 2015), pp. 70–101.

[7] See Alden T. Vaughan and Virginia Mason Vaughan, 'Before *Othello*: Elizabethan representations of sub-Saharan Africans', *The William and Mary Quarterly* 54 (1997), 19–44; p. 23.

[8] For two influential readings of the play's humoralism, see Mary Floyd-Wilson, *English Ethnicity and Race in Early Modern Drama* (Cambridge, 2003), pp. 132–60, and Gail Kern Paster, *Humoring the Body: Emotions and the Shakespearean Stage* (Chicago and London, 2004), pp. 60–76. See also Eric Langley, *Shakespeare's Contagious Sympathies: Ill Communications* (Oxford, 2018), pp. 152–88, and Emily Weissbourd, '"Search this ulcer soundly": sex as contagion in *The Changeling* and *Othello*', in *Contagion and the Shakespearean Stage*, ed. Darryl Chalk and Mary Floyd-Wilson (London, 2019), pp. 105–25.

[9] Stephen Greenblatt, *Renaissance Self-Fashioning: From More to Shakespeare* (Chicago and London, 1980), p. 236.

[10] See John Lee, 'Agency and choice', in *A Handbook of English Renaissance Literary Studies*, ed. John Lee (Hoboken, NJ, 2017), pp. 56–69, p. 62.

[11] Floyd-Wilson, *English Ethnicity and Race*, p. 144.

shall see, Shakespeare also presents us with a more optimistic model of sympathy, in which the self is able to partake in and imagine the emotions of the other. And, second, while some critics have argued that *Othello* points to 'the pneumatic character of premodern life and the humoral subject', the play itself problematizes both sympathetic magic and Galenic humoralism as ways of understanding human behaviour and emotions.[12] However, if sympathy is more flexible and agential than these concepts might suggest, then individuals can choose not to be sympathetic, or be persuaded to harden their hearts against others.

The article begins by considering the appearance of the term 'sympathy' in the play, which is used in the context of Desdemona and Othello's union. This moment implicitly reflects upon the question of emotional agency, and thus taps into the wider interpretive and ethical problems that the play explores. It goes on to examine *Othello*'s most significant references to humoral theory and bodily sympathy, and argues that these statements – many of which are spoken by Iago – are often revealed to be mendacious or mistaken within the world of the play. The final section considers several moments that describe a sympathy between people and the natural world, and proposes that these should not be seen as literal descriptions of natural or environmental sympathy but rather as metaphorical ways for the play's characters to articulate and conceptualize human feelings and relationships. Early modern sympathy emerges as a complex frame for thinking about how people relate to one another and understand themselves.

I

By the time Shakespeare wrote *Othello* in the early seventeenth century, the concept of sympathy as affinity or correspondence had appeared in various natural philosophical texts and translations of classical works. For example, Philemon Holland's translation of Pliny's encyclopaedic *Natural History* (1601), which appears to have been a significant influence upon *Othello*, describes how 'in everie coast and corner of the world there may be observed both sympathies and antipathies (I meane those naturall combinations and contrarieties in those her creatures)'.[13] This phenomenon explains why certain pairings of wild trees – such as the oak and the olive tree, or the colewart and the vine – do not thrive if grown together:

Thus you see what enmity & discord there is in some things. Contrariwise, we may observe in others, how wonderfully they accord and agree together: for pitch will dissolve, spread, and be drawne out with oile, being both as they are of a fatty nature; oile alone will incorporat and mingle well with lime; & they hate water, the one as well as the other.[14]

Such naturally occurring sympathies and antipathies explain why certain things are attracted to or repelled from each other. At the same time, however, other texts from this period used the term 'sympathy' in a more affective sense to describe human emotions and relationships. Holland's 1603 translation of Plutarch's *Morals* suggests that emotional affinity is part of the union of matrimony, and describes how a wife 'ought to have a fellow-feeling (by way of sympathie and compassion) of her husbands calamities, and the husband of his wives, much more'.[15] Similarly,

---

[12] Paster, *Humoring the Body*, p. 66. The present article thus aligns itself with recent work that has argued for a more active and pluralistic conception of early modern emotions. See, for example, Brian Cummings and Freya Sierhuis, eds., *Passions and Subjectivity in Early Modern Culture* (Farnham, 2013); Richard Meek and Erin Sullivan, eds., *The Renaissance of Emotion: Understanding Affect in Shakespeare and His Contemporaries* (Manchester, 2015); R. S. White, Mark Houlahan and Katrina O'Loughlin, eds., *Shakespeare and Emotions: Inheritances, Enactments, Legacies* (Houndmills, 2015); and Cora Fox, Bradley J. Irish and Cassie Miura, eds., *Positive Emotions in Early Modern Literature and Culture* (Manchester, 2021).

[13] Pliny, *The Historie of the World. Commonly Called, The Naturall Historie of C. Plinius Secundus*, trans. Philemon Holland (London, 1601), Second Tome, p. 175. On the influence of Pliny on the play, see, for example, William Shakespeare, *Othello*, ed. Michael Neill (Oxford, 2006), pp. 19–20.

[14] Pliny, *The Historie of the World*, p. 176.

[15] Plutarch, *The Philosophie, Commonlie Called, The Morals*, trans. Philemon Holland (London, 1603), p. 318.

OTHELLO'S SYMPATHIES: EMOTION, AGENCY & IDENTIFICATION

Thomas Dekker's *The Bachelers Banquet* (1604) describes what happens 'when a Young man ... meetes with a Wife of like yeeres, fresh, lustie, Faire, kinde, and gracious'. He writes that 'Nature hath framed such Simpathy betweene them, that if the one bee ill at ease or discontented, the other is so likewiss.'[16]

Such concepts of sympathy – both the natural philosophical and the interpersonal – were clearly an important influence upon *Othello*, which sometimes uses the former model as a way of describing the latter. There is one intriguing moment, as we shall see below, when Desdemona invokes the concept of physiological sympathy in her description of Othello's troubled emotions. But we might begin by exploring the appearance of the term 'sympathy' itself within the play. It is used by Iago in 2.1 in one of his descriptions of the relationship between Othello and Desdemona. However, as we might expect from Iago, this is not the loving fellowship and communion described by Plutarch or Dekker:

> When the blood is made dull with the act of sport, there should be again to inflame it, and to give satiety a fresh appetite, loveliness in favour, sympathy in years, manners, and beauties, all which the Moor is defective in. Now, for want of these required conveniences, her delicate tenderness will find itself abused, begin to heave the gorge, disrelish and abhor the Moor. Very nature will instruct her in it and compel her to some second choice.   (*Othello*, 2.1.227–35)

Here Iago uses 'sympathy' in its earlier sense of agreement and affinity to suggest that the Moor and Desdemona are ill matched. He states that there should be a sympathy in 'years, manners, and beauties' but this is absent. Iago implies that the union of Othello and Desdemona is a temporary one, and that she will soon find her husband distasteful. As Iago describes it, Desdemona's antipathy towards Othello will result in a physical sickness ('heave the gorge') and she will come to 'disrelish' him. What is especially striking in this passage is Iago's suggestion that Desdemona's choice is not entirely her own; rather, she will be 'instruct[ed]' and 'compell[ed]' by '[v]ery nature' to select someone else. This is one of several statements in the play in which a character is said to be bound by the rules of nature, or to have acted against their nature. But, of course, we have to treat Iago's statement sceptically because it is part of his rhetorical strategy to persuade Roderigo that Cassio is next in line in Desdemona's affections. In other words, Iago's argument that human beings are driven by their bodies – and the natural rules of sympathy and antipathy – should not necessarily be regarded as a reliable indicator of his own or early modern beliefs on the subject.

Iago's comments about Desdemona's nature recall Brabantio's anxieties about his daughter, expressed in act 1. But while Iago suggests that Desdemona's nature will compel her to reject Othello in favour of Cassio, Brabantio points to her attraction to Othello as evidence that her nature has been corrupted. He characterizes Desdemona's elopement as a 'treason of the blood' (1.1.171), suggesting both a betrayal of her family and a triumph of passion over reason.[17] Brabantio's explanation for her behaviour is shaped by accounts of magical spells that he has read: 'Is there not charms / By which the property of youth and maidhood / May be abused? Have you not read, Roderigo, / Of some such thing?' (1.1.173–6). Brabantio goes on to claim that Othello has enchanted Desdemona and bound her in 'chains of magic' (1.2.66), which recalls the mysterious system of sympathies and antipathies mentioned by Thevet. He suggests that her 'delicate youth' has been abused 'with drugs or minerals / That weakens motion' (1.2.75–6). In other words, her 'motion' – her desires and emotions, including the natural antipathy that she should feel towards Othello – has been altered by medical or supernatural means. Brabantio refers to Desdemona's 'motion' once again in 1.3:

---

[16] Thomas Dekker, *The Bachelers Banquet: or A Banquet for Bachelers* (London, 1604), sig. I3v.

[17] See William Shakespeare, *Othello*, ed. E. A. J. Honigmann (Walton-on-Thames, 1997), 1.1.168n.

> A maiden never bold,
> Of spirit so still and quiet, that her motion
> Blushed at herself – and she in spite of nature,
> Of years, of country, credit, everything,
> To fall in love with what she feared to look on!
> (1.3.94–8)

Brabantio characterizes his daughter as a maiden with a still and quiet 'spirit' – perhaps referring literally to the liquid spirits within her body.[18] Even her own impulses or desires ('her motion') would cause Desdemona to blush. Yet she has been made to fall in love with another 'in spite of nature' – which again may suggest her own nature or the rules of the material world.[19] Like Iago, Brabantio emphasizes the incompatibility of the pair, and states that Othello must have used 'witchcraft' (64) and 'mixtures powerful o'er the blood' (104) to enflame Desdemona's feelings. In this lurid vision of Othello's courtship of Desdemona, Brabantio's obsession with his daughter's blood and spirits leaves little room for agency or choice. It might be going too far to suggest that he resembles a 'new humoralist' critic of the play, but certainly Brabantio is presented as being overly keen to find a materialist explanation for Desdemona's actions, desires and emotions.[20] For him, sympathy is a dangerous power that draws individuals together without their consent, and has the capacity to assimilate the self into the other.

However, Brabantio's simplistic and involuntary model of sympathetic attraction does not describe accurately the more active forms of intersubjectivity that the play depicts. When Othello is finally given the chance to explain himself, it turns out that he used no witchcraft at all – or at least no literal witchcraft or potions. He describes how he won Desdemona through storytelling, in an extended piece of narrative that recalls Aeneas' account of the Trojan war that wins the affections of Queen Dido.[21] In Othello's description of their courtship, which is essentially a story about the affective power of narrative, he recounts how Desdemona wept for the tragic tales of his youth: 'My story being done, / She gave me for my pains a world of kisses [sighs Q]' (1.3.157–8). Othello's account of Desdemona's response includes a fascinating representation of an imagined other:

> She thankèd me,
> And bade me, if I had a friend that loved her,
> I should but teach him how to tell my story,
> And that would woo her. Upon this hint I spake.
> She loved me for the dangers I had passed
> And I loved her that she did pity them.
> This only is the witchcraft I have used.
> (1.3.162–8)

This curious substitution of selves enables Othello to imagine himself in the place of the imaginary friend described by Desdemona, which prompts him to woo her. In this way, their love has its origins in a complex combination of rhetoric, storytelling and role-playing, and chimes with Nancy Selleck's description of Renaissance speakers and writers who 'share a tendency to locate selfhood beyond subjective experience, in the experience of an *other*'.[22] This is very much an interpersonal rather than humoral model of selfhood: Desdemona's love for Othello is based on her imaginative and affective response to his narrative, while he in turn loves her because of this piteous response. Sympathy is thus figured as a form of imaginative and empathetic reciprocity, rather than as a natural or magical process.

---

[18] See *Othello*, ed. Neill, 1.3.96n.
[19] The former sense is suggested by the *OED*'s fifth definition of *nature*: 'The inherent dominating power or impulse in a person by which character or action is determined, directed, or controlled' (sense 5a). It is suggested that this sense is 'Sometimes referred to as if having an independent existence or character', which would fit with Brabantio's understanding of his daughter's nature.
[20] See Richard Strier's characterization of 'the new humoralists' in *The Unrepentant Renaissance: From Petrarch to Shakespeare to Milton* (Chicago and London, 2011), pp. 16–23.
[21] See Lynn Enterline, 'Eloquent barbarians: *Othello* and the critical potential of passionate character', in *Othello: The State of Play*, ed. Lena Cowen Orlin (London, 2014), pp. 149–76; pp. 158–62; and Colin Burrow, *Shakespeare and Classical Antiquity* (Oxford, 2013), pp. 56–7.
[22] See Nancy Selleck, *The Interpersonal Idiom in Shakespeare, Donne, and Early Modern Culture* (Basingstoke, 2008), pp. 1–2.

At this point in the play, then, Shakespeare would appear to be questioning the idea that human beings are at the mercy of mysterious forces beyond their control, both those that come from outside and those within the self. This sceptical view is articulated later in the same scene by Iago, who offers some further reflections on human nature and the question of emotional agency. Iago is once again addressing Roderigo, who says that he is ashamed to be so foolish in his passion for Desdemona, but protests that it is not in his 'virtue' (meaning his power or moral strength) to amend it. Iago disagrees:

> Virtue! A fig! 'Tis in ourselves that we are thus or thus. Our bodies are our gardens, to the which our wills are gardeners; so that if we will plant nettles or sow lettuce, set hyssop and weed up thyme, supply it with one gender of herbs or distract it with many, either to have it sterile with idleness or manure with industry, why, the power and corrigible authority of this lies in our wills.
>
> (1.3.319–26)

This is clearly a very different view of human nature from the one that Iago articulates in his comments in 2.1 about Othello and Desdemona. Here, Iago uses the natural world as a metaphor for the self – although this is nature presented as a garden, ripe for human cultivation. It is, as Charlotte Scott has written, a celebration of 'subjective determination above a preconditioned body'.[23] The image of the self-as-garden often appeared in Christian writings and sermons, usually to suggest that only the righteous person profits from his or her cultivation.[24] However, in Iago's mock-sermon there is no Christian morality or sense of collective endeavour, but simply an emphasis upon individual will. Yet his insistence that people are entirely self-determining is complicated by his own metaphor, which suggests that they must work with naturally occurring plants or herbs – or, by extension, the natural workings of their own bodies. The plants that Iago mentions were regarded as complementary opposites – either dry or wet – and thus thought to aid each other's growth.[25] Recalling Pliny's description of sympathetic and antipathetic plants, Iago's elaborate metaphorical scheme implies that managing the self is akin to balancing the natural qualities of flowers and herbs.

Iago goes on to make some provocative comments about human emotions: 'If the beam of our lives had not one scale of reason to poise another of sensuality, the blood and baseness of our natures would conduct us to most preposterous conclusions. But we have reason to cool our raging motions, our carnal stings, our unbitted lusts' (1.3.329–31). As Iago has it, reason should be able to triumph over the passions, which are described here as 'raging motions'. We have already seen that Brabantio uses 'motion' in connection with Desdemona's bodily nature, which may point to the kinetic aspects of this earlier term for emotions.[26] Certainly, there are several sixteenth- and seventeenth-century usages of *motions* that describe violent or disorderly forces within the body, such as Levinus Lemnius's *The Touchstone of Complexions* (1576): 'reason is not able easily to subdue the lewd affections, and unbrydled motions, that grow by immoderate gurmandyze, surphet, and dronkennesse'.[27] Similarly, a passage in Plutarch's *Morals* – which Iago's comments closely resemble – describes 'the minde of a temperate person' and 'the marvellous tranquillitie … when reason had once extinguished the excessive, furious, and raging motions of the lusts and desires'.[28] But while such examples

---

[23] Charlotte Scott, *Shakespeare's Nature: From Cultivation to Culture* (Oxford, 2014), p. 3.
[24] See Scott, *Shakespeare's Nature*, p. 3, and *Othello*, ed. Honigmann, 1.3.321n.
[25] See William Shakespeare, *Othello*, updated ed., ed. Norman Sanders (Cambridge, 2003), 1.3.315–16n., and Vivian Thomas and Nicki Faircloth, *Shakespeare's Plants and Gardens: A Dictionary* (London, 2014), under 'hyssop'.
[26] Paster suggests that Iago's usage of the term 'primarily refers to movements and changes in state such as putrefaction or vivification' (Paster, *Humoring the Body*, p. 31).
[27] Levinus Lemnius, *The Touchstone of Complexions*, trans. Thomas Newton (London, 1576), sig. B2v.
[28] Plutarch, *The Morals*, trans. Holland, p. 71. On Shakespeare's knowledge of the *Morals*, see Burrow, *Shakespeare and Classical Antiquity*, p. 211.

associate 'motions' with base and bodily impulses, in other contexts the word could refer to what Katharine Craik has called 'integral features of the self or spirit'.[29] In *Henry VIII*, for example, Buckingham specifically distinguishes his 'motions' from humoral anger as he describes his assessment of Cardinal Wolsey to Norfolk: 'this top-proud fellow – / Whom from the flow of gall I name not, but / From sincere motions' (1.1.151–3). While the term 'motions' looks back to the earlier conception of the passions as a movement within the body, then, it also points forward to the later word 'emotions', which implies an outward movement from the individual. The shift from *motions* to *emotions* in the seventeenth century is part of a wider cultural shift, whereby the passions are increasingly seen as things that emerge from the self rather than forces that act upon it.[30]

In this way, the first act of *Othello* opens up some complex questions regarding the source and nature of human feelings. Do passions come from within the self or from outside? Are they beyond our control or can they be cultivated? Iago asserts that our raging motions can be controlled or allowed via 'a permission of the will' (1.3.334–5). However, as several critics have noted, Iago himself seems to be unable to put his theories of emotion into practice. He admits in 2.1 that his jealousy of Othello cannot be regulated and affects his body 'like a poisonous mineral' (2.1.296), which complicates his own and the play's position on this matter.[31] These questions regarding emotional agency are thus tied to the larger interpretive and ethical dilemmas that *Othello* poses, including the source and nature of Iago's hatred and Othello's jealousy. Iago tells Roderigo that 'These Moors are changeable in their wills' (1.3.346), suggesting, in a somewhat paradoxical claim, that it is in the nature of all Moors to be changeable. Yet this racial stereotype – reminiscent of Thevet's essentialism – is another piece of rhetorical misdirection, inasmuch as it is designed to change the will of Roderigo, who is, if anything, far more fickle and open to persuasion than Othello. Indeed, as we shall see in the next section, Iago exploits others' belief in the idea of a fixed human nature, together with their belief in humoral theory, as one of his key rhetorical and persuasive strategies.

II

In 2.1, Iago notes the sweet harmony between Othello and Desdemona: 'O, you are well tuned now, / But I'll set down the pegs that make this music, / As honest as I am' (2.1.200–2). Here Iago alludes to the idea of musical sympathy, in which the strings of an instrument were observed to vibrate in sympathetic harmony with each other. Juan Luis Vives describes this phenomenon in his treatise on the passions, *De Anima et Vita*: 'The feeling of sympathy is like the plucking of a faculty to which similar faculties are attuned, as they say about the strings of two different lyres, that, when the same note is played on them, seem to blend and respond to each other.'[32] Like Vives, Iago applies this phenomenon to human sympathies – yet he resolves to disturb this sympathy by 'set[ting] down the pegs' – that is, loosening the strings – of this metaphorical instrument. Iago plans to do this by disrupting Othello's ability to temper his raging motions: he will 'put the Moor / At least

---

[29] Katharine A. Craik, 'Introduction' to *Shakespeare and Emotion*, ed. Craik (Cambridge, 2020), pp. 1–16; p. 3.

[30] Christopher Tilmouth writes that 'the Renaissance conceptualizing of affectivity ... encompassed a struggle to develop precisely this active notion of affection, an innovation that, from the seventeenth through to the eighteenth century, gradually transformed *passions* into *emotions* and *sentiments*' (Christopher Tilmouth, 'Passion and intersubjectivity in early modern literature', in *Passions and Subjectivity*, ed. Cummings and Sierhuis, pp. 13–32; p. 29). See also Susan James, *Passion and Action: The Emotions in Seventeenth-Century Philosophy* (Oxford, 1997), and Thomas Dixon, *From Passions to Emotions: The Creation of a Secular Psychological Category* (Cambridge, 2003).

[31] See Timothy M. Harrison, who suggests that – unlike some early modern theorists of the passions – Shakespeare refuses to compartmentalize passions and rationality: 'In *Othello* ... reason brings passion into being and intensifies its effects' (Timothy M. Harrison, 'Confusion', in *Shakespeare and Emotion*, ed. Craik, pp. 330–43; p. 333).

[32] Juan Luis Vives, *The Passions of the Soul: The Third Book of 'De Anima et Vita'*, trans. Carlos G. Noreña (Lampeter, 1990), p. 46.

into a jealousy so strong / That judgement cannot cure' (2.1.299–31). Othello himself acknowledges that there are times when his emotions threaten to overtake his judgement, for example in his comments following Cassio's drunken fight with Roderigo and Montano:

> Now, by heaven,
> My blood begins my safer guides to rule,
> And passion, having my best judgement collied,
> Essays to lead the way.
>
> (2.3.197–200)

Othello states that his judgement has been placed under pressure because of the unruliness of his soldiers: it has been 'collied' – that is, 'begrimed; blackened; darkened, murky' (*OED*) – by his passion. While some critics have emphasized the racial connotations of this term, others have read it as a pun on 'choler', one of the four humours of the body, which was thought to produce irritability or irascibility.[33] We might suggest, however, that the central conceit in this passage is martial rather than racial or humoral, and that Othello uses the metaphor of a military expedition in which his blood threatens to overrule his 'safer guides' and tries to assume command. Othello thus implies that the soldiers' insubordination is replicated within him – but this choice of metaphor makes it difficult to locate the source of his passions, and whether they derive from an internal or external conflict. Either way, this passage demonstrates the challenges of reading emotions in *Othello*, and reminds us that the language of blood and humours can be hard to disentangle from other metaphorical frameworks.

When we turn to the more explicit references to humoral theory in the play, we find that they raise further questions about emotional agency, racial identity and stereotypes. In some cases, we find characters putting too much faith in Galenic terms and concepts, while in others the use of those concepts is shown to be misleading or even deceptive. In 3.4, for example, Desdemona expresses the view articulated by Thevet and other early modern writers that being exposed to the sun in southern climes made the body cool and dry:

EMILIA: Is he not jealous?
DESDEMONA:
Who, he? I think the sun where he was born
Drew all such humours from him.

(3.4.29–31)

According to this humoral model, Othello's native constitution and physiology mean that he cannot be jealous.[34] Such views were contradicted by Leo Africanus, whose *Geographical Historie of Africa*, translated into English by John Pory in 1600, asserts that 'No nation in the world is so subject unto jealousie; for they will rather leese their lives, then put up any disgrace in the behalfe of their women.'[35] The play thus reflects two competing stereotypes about people from Africa: one drawing upon humoral theory and physiology, and one supposedly based on observation of social practices, both bound up with emergent ideas about race. As Floyd-Wilson has suggested, 'the play sustains a conflict between an emerging racial stereotype of African sexuality and an older geohumoral discourse'. It seems to me, however, that both of these forms of essentialism are being interrogated in *Othello*. In her geohumoral reading, Floyd-Wilson asserts that Othello is '[h]umorally cold and arid' and that he 'possesses a fixed and undivided nature'.[36] But the fact that Othello

---

[33] Paster compares this passage to the gloomy verbal portrait of Pyrrhus in *Hamlet*, writing that, 'as we have seen with Pyrrhus roasted black as his purpose, choler "blackened" the consciousness of anyone caught in its grip' (Paster, *Humoring the Body*, p. 67).

[34] See Neill's long note to 3.4.28–9 (*Othello*, ed. Neill, p. 466).

[35] Leo Africanus, *A Geographical Historie of Africa*, trans. John Pory (London, 1600), p. 40. On the relationship between Africanus's *Historie* and *Othello*, see Emily C. Bartels, *Speaking of the Moor: From Alcazar to Othello* (Philadelphia, 2008), pp. 138–54.

[36] Floyd-Wilson, *English Ethnicity and Race*, pp. 147, 150. For further discussion of racial stereotypes and essentialism in the play, see, for example, Ania Loomba, *Shakespeare, Race, and Colonialism* (Oxford, 2002), pp. 91–111; Stephen Cohen, 'I am what I am not: identifying with the other in *Othello*', *Shakespeare Survey 64* (Cambridge, 2011), pp. 163–79; Ayanna Thompson, *Passing Strange: Shakespeare, Race, and Contemporary America* (Oxford, 2011); and Carol Mejia LaPerle, 'Race in Shakespeare's tragedies', in *The Cambridge Companion to Shakespeare and Race*, ed. Ayanna Thompson (Cambridge, 2021), pp. 77–92.

changes in the course of the play suggests that Shakespeare is questioning the very idea of a fixed and undivided nature. As Iago suggests in an offhand comment to Roderigo, 'base men being in love have then a nobility in their natures more than is native to them' (2.1.216–18). Here Iago implies that Roderigo can change his lowly status through being in a particular emotional state, but his comments can also be applied to his attempts to debase and deceive Othello by altering the nature that is supposedly 'native' to him.

In this way, Desdemona is arguably blinded by a racial and geohumoral stereotype, even if it appears to be a positive one, and fails to acknowledge that Othello's identity is more malleable and changeable than her materialist reading suggests. When Othello appears in the same scene and takes Desdemona's hand, he notes that it is hot and moist. He already suspects Desdemona of infidelity at this point and interprets the qualities of her hand accordingly:

> This argues fruitfulness and liberal heart.
> Hot, hot and moist – this hand of yours requires
> A sequester from liberty; fasting, and prayer,
> Much castigation, exercise devout,
> For here's a young and sweating devil here
> That commonly rebels.
>
> (3.4.38–43)

Recalling his earlier speech to his troops, Othello figures excessive passion as a kind of rebellion, and states that Desdemona needs to be shut away from liberty and temptation. But his belief that a moist hand indicates lustiness, which was proverbial at the time, is presented as an interpretive error.[37] As Julie R. Solomon has suggested, Othello's 'belated humoral diagnosis' of Desdemona's behaviour implies that Shakespeare wanted his audiences 'to see beyond the frame of humoral materialism'.[38] Indeed, both Desdemona and Othello are guilty of misreading in this scene, or at least of putting too much faith in physiological interpretations of the other.

Later in 3.4, Desdemona says to Cassio that now is not a good time for her to appeal to Othello on his behalf: 'My advocation is not now in tune. / My lord is not my lord, nor should I know him / Were he in favour as in humour altered' (3.4.121–3). Echoing Iago's language in 2.1, and therefore implicitly reflecting his success in untuning the pair, Desdemona states that she does not recognize Othello in terms of his appearance or his 'humour'. Her explanation to Emilia is that an external cause – a matter of political or public affairs – has affected his inner self:

> Something sure of state,
> Either from Venice or some unhatched practice
> Made demonstrable here in Cyprus to him,
> Hath puddled his clear spirit; and in such cases
> Men's natures wrangle with inferior things,
> Though great ones are their object.
>
> (3.4.138–43)

Once again, one character seeks to explain another's behaviour by appealing to beliefs about human nature: it is the nature of men, Desdemona suggests, to 'wrangle with inferior things' when they are more concerned with greater matters. She states that something has 'puddled' Othello's 'clear spirit', which could potentially refer to the animal spirits, the source of all sensation and movement in the body, which have been fouled or muddied.[39] But we might also argue that Desdemona is using the term figuratively, recalling Othello's metaphorical use of 'collied', suggesting that something has corrupted Othello's usually clear understanding.[40]

---

[37] See Morris Palmer Tilley, ed., *A Dictionary of the Proverbs in England in the Sixteenth and Seventeenth Centuries* (Ann Arbor, 1950), H86: 'A moist hand argues an amorous nature (fruitfulness).'

[38] Julie R. Solomon, 'You've got to have soul: understanding the passions in early modern culture', in *Rhetoric and Medicine in Early Modern Europe*, ed. Stephen Pender and Nancy S. Struever (Farnham, 2012), pp. 195–228; p. 198.

[39] See Neill's note to 3.4.139. According to Paster, Desdemona is 'thinking here in material terms about how passions ... work within the body' (*Humoring the Body*, p. 62).

[40] The *OED* notes that 'puddled', in the sense of 'To pollute or contaminate (water)' (3a; first cited usage 1593), was chiefly used in figurative contexts. It also suggests that the word meant 'to muddle, confuse, or corrupt (a person or his or her outlook, imagination, understanding, etc.)' (3b, citing this passage).

Desdemona expands upon her account of Othello's mood by making an analogy with the natural affinities between different parts of the body:

> 'Tis even so;
> For let our finger ache and it indues
> Our other, healthful members even to that sense
> Of pain. Nay, we must think men are not gods,
> Nor of them look for such observancy
> As fits the bridal.
>
> (3.4.143–8)

Desdemona suggests that an ache in a small part of a person, such as a finger, can cause their whole person to be affected. This passage is not usually glossed or explained in editions of the play, but this is clearly Desdemona using the concept of physiological sympathy, which we find invoked by preachers and other writers in the period. For example, in a sermon preached at Paul's Cross on 9 November 1589, William James uses the term 'sympathie' to describe an emotional affinity between members of the church, as if they are part of the same body:

> as in the griefe of the bodie, the very heart sigheth, the eies shead teares, the head aketh, the stomacke refuseth foode, the whole bodie is made feeble, though it be but the griefe of a finger, or of a toe: so in the church there ought to be a sympathie, and fellowe feeling, to weepe with them that weepe, to rejoice with them that rejoice.[41]

Recalling Romans 12.15, James uses the idea of bodily sympathy as a way of binding together his listeners. Similarly, Gervase Babington writes that there is a 'simpathy and mutuall affecting of parts of the same body, though they be divers and much distant in place one from an other'.[42] It seems clear that Shakespeare was aware of such usages, and understood that the physiological conception of sympathy could be used as a metaphor for relationships between people. The irony, however, is that Desdemona is mistaken about the source of Othello's discontent, which is his lack of sympathy for and trust in Desdemona herself. Shakespeare thus demonstrates that the earlier idea of sympathy as automatic correspondence, while attractive to some of his characters, could be a limited and potentially misleading way of understanding others.

It is worth emphasizing in this context, then, that another character in *Othello* who frequently invokes humoral terms is Iago. Daniel Juan Gil has argued that Iago employs a 'cognitive theory of the emotions', as opposed to a humoral one, and that this is 'central to his project of exploding the geo-social coordinates that are conventionally carried by emotional experience'.[43] We might go further, however, and observe that there are several moments in the play when Iago specifically uses humoral terminology in order to persuade and beguile his interlocutors. The first occurs in 2.1 when Iago informs Roderigo that Cassio is especially prone to bouts of anger: 'Sir, he's rash and very sudden in choler, and haply may strike at you' (2.1.271–2). Yet Cassio's anger seems to be caused by intoxication rather than a humoral imbalance. It is true that Brabantio has alluded to the dangers of 'distempering drafts' (1.1.100), while Cassio himself laments alcohol's ability to transform his nature: 'To be now a sensible man, by and by a fool, and presently a beast! O, strange!' (2.3.298–300). But there is no suggestion in 2.3 that such temporary beastliness is the product of Cassio's supposedly choleric disposition; rather, it is the result of being provoked by Roderigo – a hostile interpersonal encounter engineered by Iago.[44] Second, shortly after Othello's fit in 4.1, Iago threatens to tell others that Othello is splenetic: 'Marry, patience, / Or I shall say you're all-in-all in spleen, / And nothing of a man' (4.1.86–8). The spleen was thought to be the seat of melancholy and sudden or

---

[41] William James, *A sermon preached at Paules Crosse the IX. of November, 1589* (London, 1590), sig. G4r.

[42] Gervase Babington, *Certaine plaine, briefe, and comfortable notes upon everie chapter of Genesis* (London, 1592), sig. R2v.

[43] Daniel Juan Gil, *Shakespeare's Anti-Politics: Sovereign Power and the Life of the Flesh* (Basingstoke, 2013), p. 93.

[44] For an alternative reading, which sees Cassio's drunkenness as akin to or a cause of humoral imbalance, see David Houston Wood, *Time, Narrative and Emotion in Early Modern England* (Farnham, 2009), pp. 88–9.

violent passion, but Iago is evoking this idea as a way of further confounding Othello and questioning his masculinity. In other words, it is presented here – and specifically by Iago himself – as a means of commanding Othello to rein in his grief and anger, rather than an accurate identification of their source.

My third example occurs when Iago is discussing Othello's frame of mind with Desdemona in 4.2: 'I pray you, be content. 'Tis but his humour. / The business of the state does him offence, / And he does chide with you' (4.2.169–71). This passage recalls Desdemona's own assessment of Othello's troubled emotions: Othello is perturbed by state business and as a result is unkind to Desdemona. Here, Iago explicitly suggests that this behaviour is due to Othello's 'humour' or temporary mood. However, the cause of Othello's jealous passion is neither the business of state nor his humoral body but rather Iago's ability to persuade and manipulate. In all three of these examples, then, Galenic medicine is treated in a sceptical or cynical way – certainly by Iago, and perhaps by the play as well. Other critics have rightly noted the inconsistency between Iago's stated belief in self-determination and his repeated playing on 'everyone else's apparently deterministic belief in stereotype and inevitability, both about women and Moors'.[45] We might add that humoral theory – which is based upon deterministic beliefs about human nature and passions – involves another set of stereotypes that Iago exploits to create plausible narratives about people and their natures. In this way, humoral theory should not be regarded as a reliable guide to the emotions of the play's characters, but rather as an increasingly outmoded belief system that is invoked by Iago as a way of manipulating the emotions of others.

III

We have already seen that *Othello* is interested in the relationship between the idea of natural sympathy and the human world, and that the former can be used as a way of describing the latter. One important example of this is Cassio's description of the storm at the start of act 2. We learn that, while the storm has destroyed the Turkish fleet, it is remarkably benign and sympathetic towards Iago's ship:

> He's had most favourable and happy speed.
> Tempests themselves, high seas, and howling winds,
> The guttered rocks and congregated sands,
> Traitors ensteeped to clog the guiltless keel,
> As having sense of beauty do omit
> Their mortal natures, letting go safely by
> The divine Desdemona.
>
> (2.1.68–74)

The storm, rocks and sand banks – so fatal to the Turkish fleet – have a sense of beauty, and refrain from indulging their deadly or 'mortal natures'. This is yet another example of something being made to swerve away from its particular nature because of an external force. But in this case it is a human being, Desdemona, who is on board Iago's ship and causes these elements of the natural world to change. In other words, this is not an individual being affected by the environment, but an individual changing the environment around them. Rather than being a literal description of ecological or environmental passions, however, this speech might be regarded as an example of Cassio's metaphorical exuberance. Indeed, shortly before the speech, he suggests that Desdemona is a maid who 'excels the quirks of blazoning pens' (2.1.64), suggesting that this description of natural sympathy is a self-consciously poetic way of describing Desdemona's effect upon the social world around her. But it also reminds us of Desdemona's own capacity for sympathy, which is often neglected by critics who focus on the relationship between Iago and Othello, and regard her primarily as an object of pity and compassion.

Perhaps the most important example of Desdemona's capacity for fellow-feeling is her relationship with Emilia. The sympathy between these two women is most apparent in 4.3, in which

---

[45] Emma Smith, *Othello* (Horndon, Devon, 2005), p. 82. See also Marianne Novy, *Shakespeare and Outsiders* (Oxford, 2013), pp. 116–17.

Desdemona recalls a 'song of willow' (4.3.26) that was sung by her mother's maid, Barbary – whose name evokes the Barbary coast and suggests that she may have been a Moor.[46] According to Desdemona, the song captured and expressed Barbary's emotions: 'An old thing 'twas, but it expressed her fortune, / And she died singing it' (4.3.28–9). The song, which only appears in the Folio text, serves a similar function for Desdemona herself, who finds that this old folk ballad also expresses her misfortune, as well as prefiguring her tragic demise. She resolves to 'hang [her] head all at one side' and 'sing it, like poor Barbary' (4.3.31–2); in other words, Desdemona will adopt the traditional pose of love melancholy as she replicates the performance of a tragic precursor. But what is particularly suggestive about the song itself is that it describes an affinity between the 'poor soul', who laments her lost love, and the surrounding environment:

'The poor soul sat sighing by a sycamore tree,
    Sing all a green willow.
Her hand on her bosom, her head on her knee,
    Sing willow, willow, willow.
The fresh streams ran by her and murmured her moans,
    Sing willow, willow, willow.
Her salt tears fell from her and softened the stones,
    Sing willow' –
                                                    (4.3.38–45)

The willow tree was a traditional emblem for the grief of unrequited love, while the sycamore was prized as a shade tree, providing the shadows sought by a melancholy individual.[47] But, as well as these cultural associations and emblematic images of grief and love melancholy, the streams that run by the poor soul are said to have 'murmured her moans'. In addition, the woman's tears soften the stones around her; stones were proverbially unsympathetic, but it was also said that stones and flint could be softened by water.[48] The song thus contains two suggestive images of natural sympathy, in which the surrounding environment is affected by the poor lady's grief.

However, rather than simply endorsing the concept of natural sympathy, the play presents it as part of an old song, recalled at a time of intense anguish, and as a way for Desdemona to establish sympathy between herself and Emilia, Barbary and the tragic figure depicted within the song. The scene represents, as Clare McManus has suggested, a 'homosocial vision of feminine intimacy', which allows Desdemona to ventriloquize and borrow the emotions of these various female personae.[49] The possibility that Barbary was a Moor adds a layer of cross-cultural sympathy to Desdemona's appropriation of the song. And indeed, in the play's final scene, Emilia dies after singing it ('I will play the swan, / And die in music' (5.2.254–5)), further elaborating the network of sympathy between the women. These images of natural sympathy are thus a way for Desdemona both to express her grief and to elicit sympathy from others – including audiences and readers of the scene. Desdemona's performance of the Willow Song prompts her and Emilia to discuss gender roles and the nature of infidelity. Emilia offers an eloquent plea for sympathy between husbands and wives based on their physical resemblance: 'Let husbands know / Their wives have sense like them. They see, and smell, / And have their palates both for sweet and sour, / As husbands have' (4.3.92–5). On the one hand, then, Emilia suggests that men and women are alike, in terms of their physiology and their 'affections' (99) – another early modern term for emotions. On the other hand, however, this recognition of a shared human nature serves to highlight the antipathy between them. If men and women are

---

[46] See Kim F. Hall, ed., *Othello, the Moor of Venice: Texts and Contexts* (Boston MA, 2007), p. 260. The word is also used in a very different context by Iago to describe Desdemona being 'covered with a Barbary horse' (1.1.113–14).

[47] See Martha Ronk, 'Desdemona's self-presentation', *English Literary Renaissance* 35 (2005), 52–72; esp. pp. 65–8. See also Thomas and Faircloth, *Shakespeare's Plants and Gardens*, under 'sycamore', and *Othello*, ed. Neill, 4.3.37n.

[48] For the proverbs 'A heart of (as hard as a) stone (flint, marble)' and 'Constant dropping will wear the stone', see R. W. Dent, *Shakespeare's Proverbial Language: An Index* (Berkeley, 1981), H311 and D618.

[49] Clare McManus, '"Sing it like poor Barbary": *Othello* and early modern women's performance', *Shakespeare Bulletin* 33 (2015), 99–120; p. 107.

indeed alike, Emilia suggests, then women should emulate men in their infidelity: 'Then let them use us well, else let them know / The ills we do, their ills instruct us so' (101–2). Shakespeare implies that these supposedly innate differences between men and women – whereby women are frail and men are allowed to act upon their passions – are the result of culture and prejudice rather than nature or physiology.

The affective sympathies depicted in 4.3 contrast sharply with Othello's statements about his hard-heartedness. As Othello says to Iago as he contemplates murdering Desdemona, 'my heart is turned to stone; I strike it, and it hurts my hand' (4.1.178–9). Similarly, in the play's final scene, Othello suggests that Desdemona herself is the cause of his stony heart: 'O perjured women! Thou dost stone my heart' (5.2.68). In his last speech, however, Othello emphasizes his capacity for spontaneous weeping. He employs another natural-world image as he asks those present to write down his story in their letters, and to speak

> of one whose subdued eyes,
> Albeit unused to the melting mood,
> Drops tears as fast as the Arabian trees
> Their medicinable gum.
>
> (5.2.357–60)

Othello uses the idea of a naturally weeping tree as a way of describing his own emotions. Commentators have pointed out that this passage recalls Pliny's *Natural History*, in particular his account of the medicinal resins obtained by piercing certain Arabian trees; it thus prefigures Othello's imminent death by piercing or wounding.[50] According to Pliny, 'the Trees which beare the Myrrhe' are found 'in many quarters of Arabia', and 'sweat out of themselves a certain liquor called Stacte, which is very good Myrrh, and none better'. He goes on to describe the process of extracting gum by making an incision in the 'Baulme' or balsam: 'This feat being wrought, there issues out of the wound a juice or liquor, which they call Opobalsamum, of an excellent and surpassing sweet smell: but it comes forth by small drops: and as it thus weepes, the teares ought to be received in wooll.'[51] In this way, Othello's image is perhaps more ambiguous than he realizes, inasmuch as the trees he invokes are not necessarily fast-weeping and – certainly in the case of the balsam – require a skilful gardener to draw out their 'teares'. Pliny's metaphorical description also reminds us that apparently magical sympathies in nature often have a rational explanation and are the result of human intervention or imagination.

Thus, while Othello's image of weeping Arabian trees might seem to echo Desdemona's Willow Song, with its emphasis upon a sympathetic natural world that seems to feel human passions, it also recalls Iago's idea of the self-as-garden. It implies that sympathy is not simply spontaneous, but an art that needs to be cultivated – especially in one 'unused' to weeping like Othello. Moreover, rather than enabling sympathy for the other, Othello's simile seems to represent sympathy for the self. As with his earlier narrative regarding his courtship of Desdemona, he hopes that listeners will be moved by the emotional response described within the tale. In this case, however, it is his own tears he describes, rather than those of a figured audience. Othello does go on to place himself in the position of 'a malignant and a turbaned Turk' (5.2.362) he once killed. Yet imagining the other here results in Othello returning to and ultimately destroying himself. In other words, this form of sympathy results in Othello's suicide, rather than compassion for Desdemona or Emilia. The figurative language that connects the Willow Song and Othello's final speech invites us to compare these key moments, and to recognize that the play presents us with two contrasting representations of sympathetic engagement: one involving an outward movement from the self and a sharing of others' grief, and one involving a solipsistic – or even narcissistic – return to the self. This further

---

[50] See Joan Ozark Holmer, 'Othello's Threnos: "Arabian trees" and "Indian" versus "Judean"', *Shakespeare Studies* 13 (1980), 145–67.
[51] Pliny, *The Historie of the World*, pp. 368, 377.

suggests that the emotions of the play's characters are not produced by the natural forces of sympathy and antipathy, even if they are evoked metaphorically, but the result of their individuated responses to others.

Rather than simply subscribing to a humoral or physiological model of the passions, then, *Othello* implies that individuals have considerably more emotional agency than such concepts might suggest. And yet the fact that some of the play's characters believe in these earlier models of human nature leaves them particularly susceptible to manipulation. The play depicts a transitional world in which ideas of natural sympathy and the humours are starting to look arcane or redundant, but the more modern conception of a society formed of individual selves, bound together through imaginative sympathy, is an uncertain and unstable one. It is perhaps apt, therefore, that the single instance of the word 'sympathy' in the play is spoken by Iago, who uses it to describe and disrupt the harmony between Othello and Desdemona. But that harmony is also disrupted, ironically, by Desdemona's feelings of sympathy for another man. In 3.3, Desdemona pleads on behalf of Cassio, and attempts to move Othello to restore him to favour once again. She states that Cassio is 'so humbled / That he hath left part of his grief with me / To suffer with him' (3.3.53–5). This moving description of what we would now call sympathy – or even empathy – involves Desdemona taking part of Cassio's grief, which enables her to share in his suffering. Such moments remind us that sympathy in the play is neither absent nor impossible. But in the precarious world of *Othello*, where individuals do not possess a single or predetermined nature, and where their passions can be manipulated or misconstrued, sympathy in one pair of selves can lead to antipathy – and jealousy – in another.

WARNING THE STAGE: SHAKESPEARE'S MID-SCENE ENTRANCE CONVENTIONS

MARGARET JANE KIDNIE[1]

A stretch of dialogue in the last scene of *Hamlet* as printed in the second Quarto of 1604–5 (Q2) has long been considered something of a textual crux. In response to Hamlet's tale of rewriting the commission for his execution entrusted with Rosencrantz and Guildenstern, Horatio demands, 'Why what a King is this!' Hamlet then launches into an account, in both Q2 and F, of Claudius's offences. Figure 9 shows Hamlet's speech as printed in Q2.

Hamlet's speech as printed in F, by contrast, finds closure in a concluding part-line – 'is't not perfect conscience, / To quit him with this arme?' (F *Hamlet*, TLN 3571–2) – that makes explicit what is left unsaid in Q2. Philip Edwards comments that 'there is obviously something missing' from Q2, and G. R. Hibbard explains the difference between Q2 and F by arguing that this part-line was deliberately omitted by a Q2 compositor who found himself pressed for space due to faulty casting-off.[2] The Q2 passage looks odd to some editors because what it might 'stand' upon Hamlet now to do in 'perfect conscience' is left, as T. M. Parrott and Hardin Craig put it, 'hanging in the air'.[3]

The argument for textual corruption is difficult to make persuasively, however, because Hamlet's unspoken thought might seem to some readers a suggestive, even desirable, choice, or else Q2's punctuation immediately before Osric's entrance might be interpreted as interrupted speech. The pointing of a similar entrance earlier in Q2 (Figure 10) is illustrative. The King is manipulating Laertes in this scene to take revenge on Hamlet for Polonius's murder. His speech here closes with a full stop after 'imagine' that editors typically modernize to a dash, in order to clarify that the Messenger interrupts the King mid-sentence. To return to Osric's entrance, the courtier thus might intrude into the space provided by a pregnant pause and an implied intent, or one might suppose that he interrupts the Prince mid-sentence, just as the Messenger previously interrupted the King. (The structural correspondences between Osric's and the Messenger's entrances, I will argue, are significant, and I will draw further connections between them in the final section of this article.)

The longer version of Hamlet's exchange with Horatio as printed in F, in addition to extending Hamlet's speech to make explicit what is implicit in Q2, motivates the Prince's apology to Laertes before they fall to play in the tragedy's closing action. Figure 11 shows the passage leading up to

---

[1] I am immensely grateful to Sonia Massai, David McInnis and James Purkis, who read and provided helpful feedback on an early version of this article. The manuscript image reproduction was generously supported by the J. B. Smallman Research Fund at The University of Western Ontario.

[2] William Shakespeare, *Hamlet*, ed. Philip Edwards (Cambridge, 1985), p. 19; G. R. Hibbard, 'The chronology of the three substantive texts of Shakespeare's *Hamlet*', in *The Hamlet First Published (Q1, 1603): Origins, Forms, Intertextualities*, ed. Thomas Clayton (Newark, NJ, 1992), pp. 79–89, esp. pp. 85–6.

[3] *The Tragedy of 'Hamlet': A Critical Edition of the Second Quarto, 1604*, ed. T. M. Parrott and Hardin Craig (London, 1938), p. 229, quoted in Jesús Tronch-Pérez, *A Synoptic Hamlet* (Valencia, 2002), p. 379.

WARNING THE STAGE: MID-SCENE ENTRANCE CONVENTIONS

> *Hora.* Why what a King is this!
> *Ham.* Dooes it not thinke thee stand me now vppon?
> He that hath kild my King, and whor'd my mother,
> Pop't in betweene th'election and my hopes,
> Throwne out his Angle for my proper life,
> And with such cusnage, i'st not perfect conscience?
>   *Enter a Courtier.*
> *Cour.* Your Lordship is right welcome backe to Denmarke.

9 Detail from Q2 *Hamlet* (1604–5), sig. N2. STC 22276, Folger Shakespeare Library. Used by permission of the Folger Shakespeare Library under a Creative Commons Attribution – ShareAlike 4.0 International Licence.

> *King.* Breake not your sleepes for that, you must not thinke
> That we are made of stuffe so flat and dull,
> That we can let our beard be shooke with danger,
> And thinke it pastime, you shortly shall heare more,
> I loued your father, and we loue our selfe,
> And that I hope will teach you to imagine.
>
>   *Enter a Messenger with Letters.*
> *Messen.* These to your Maiestie, this to the Queenes;
> *King.* From *Hamlet*, who brought them?

10 Detail from Q2 *Hamlet* (1604–5), sig. L3 v. STC 22276, Folger Shakespeare Library. Used by permission of the Folger Shakespeare Library under a Creative Commons Attribution – ShareAlike 4.0 International Licence.

Osric's entrance as printed in F. Gary Taylor and Paul Werstine have independently suggested that Q2 and F craft distinctive portrayals of Hamlet's relationship with Laertes, and they argue, with different emphases, that variants between these texts in the final scene are evidence of an underlying process of textual revision.[4] This attention to character has perhaps overshadowed what is, from a practical script-writing point of view, yet another major variant between these passages as printed in the two versions. In F, Horatio sees Osric coming and warns his friend to silence; in Q2, Hamlet and Horatio only certainly notice Osric when he speaks to welcome Hamlet home to Denmark. This difference has implications for one's interpretation of Osric. According to Andrew Gurr and Mariko Ichikawa, Shakespeare allowed actors 'about four lines' to exit the stage from a position at the front (almost certainly where Hamlet and Horatio are engaged in dialogue), and they infer that this is likewise how long it would take an entering actor to trace the route in the other direction.[5] If Osric, in the version as printed in Q2, were to take up to four lines to approach the Prince, he would be on stage when Hamlet is justifying regicide.

---

[4] Gary Taylor, '*Hamlet*', in *William Shakespeare: A Textual Companion*, ed. Stanley Wells and Gary Taylor with John Jowett and William Montgomery (New York, 1997), pp. 396–420, esp. p. 400; Paul Werstine, 'The textual mystery of *Hamlet*', *Shakespeare Quarterly* 39 (1988), 1–26.

[5] Andrew Gurr and Mariko Ichikawa, *Staging in Shakespeare's Theatres* (Oxford, 2000), pp. 78–84, esp. p. 84. See also Mariko Ichikawa, *Shakespearean Entrances* (Houndmills, 2002), p. 44, and ch. 3.

> *Hor.* Why, what a King is this?
> *Ham.* Does it not, thinkft thee, ftand me now vpon
> He that hath kil'd my King, and whor'd my Mother,
> Popt in betweene th'election and my hopes,
> Throwne out his Angle for my proper life,
> And with fuch coozenage; is't not perfect confcience,
> To quit him with this arme? And is't not to be damn'd
> To let this Canker of our nature come
> In further euill.
> *Hor.* It muft be fhortly knowne to him from England
> What is the iffue of the bufineffe there.
> *Ham.* It will be fhort,
> The *interim's* mine, and a mans life's no more
> Then to fay one: but I am very forry good *Horatio*,
> That to *Laertes* I forgot my felfe;
> For by the image of my Caufe, I fee
> The Portraiture of his; Ile count his fauours:
> But fure the brauery of his griefe did put me
> Into a Towring paffion.
> *Hor.* Peace, who comes heere?
>   *Enter young Ofricke.*   (marke.
> *Ofr.* Your Lordfhip is right welcome back to Den-

11 Detail from F *Hamlet* (1623), sig. pp6 r, TLN 3566–87. STC 22273 F.1 no. 68, Folger Shakespeare Library. Used by permission of the Folger Shakespeare Library under a Creative Commons Attribution – ShareAlike 4.0 International Licence.

These variant stagings of the mid-scene entrance thus beg questions about the early modern performance conventions that guided both actors and the playwrights who wrote for them. What would one suppose an entering character would hear of the onstage dialogue? And how are actors alerted to an entrance that might well be staged behind (or above) them? Ichikawa has considered the first of these questions in a preliminary way. She speculates that 'When a character made an entrance or exit in an ordinary manner, despite the fact that he approached onstage characters or was still on stage, the audience was not invited to be concerned whether he heard them or not':

Presumably some convention operated on the Shakespearean stage concerning the relationship between onstage characters and entering or exiting characters. Shakespearean audiences knew that when a character turns his back and begins to move towards the tiring-house, the character is assumed to move out of earshot. On the other hand, since an entering character normally faced front-stage, the question may be more complicated.

It is my view that, unless the entering character makes a direct response to the onstage characters' dialogue, the Elizabethan audience would not have cared whether he hears them while he is walking towards the speaking characters.[6]

Ichikawa's conjectures about the audience's presumed indifference to what an entering character hears make sense in those many cases in which the introduction of a potentially listening character does not strain the logic of the scene. But in a tragedy dominated by various forms of spying and eavesdropping, would an Elizabethan audience really 'not have cared' whether Osric (over)hears Hamlet resolving to murder the King? It seems more likely, as Ichikawa suggests at the beginning of the passage quoted above, that 'some convention' guided mid-scene entrances, and so the semiotic logic of the stage.

---

[6] Ichikawa, *Shakespearean Entrances*, pp. 54–5.

WARNING THE STAGE: MID-SCENE ENTRANCE CONVENTIONS

The second question – how onstage actors were alerted to mid-scene entrances – has gone largely unexplored beyond Warren D. Smith's suggestion that the familiar 'How now' greeting prompts onstage actors to adjust their positioning in order to accommodate entering actors.[7] Discussion of mid-scene entrances has instead tended to consider from the perspective of the audience what Alan C. Dessen calls the 'interpretative potential' of early modern staging conventions, a focus that draws in consideration of actors' points of entry to the stage, and the number and arrangement of the tiring-house doors.[8] Peter Thomson, for example, comments that mid-scene entrances, positioned at the back of a deep stage, are 'almost always prepared for' by the dialogue in order to pull the spectator's gaze towards the doors.[9] The playwright's 'need to focus [audience] attention' on the entering actor(s) similarly explains, for Bernard Beckerman, the frequent coincidence of mid-scene entrances with summonses, music cues, processions and announcements of entries from the stage.[10] Beckerman takes special note of what he calls 'unprepared entrances' – Lear, for example, entering with the dead body of Cordelia – commenting that they 'are usually unannounced for dramatic purposes'.[11]

What would it mean, though, for a mid-scene entrance to be announced? No onstage character verbally anticipates Lear's approach, it's true, but he enters howling, riveting attention to himself. Onstage characters and (first-time) spectators, I would instead suggest, are 'unprepared' for what is an 'announced' entrance. The difference between this mid-scene entrance and Hamlet's entry to the King at prayer, for example, is instructive. In this latter example, the audience sees and hears Hamlet's entrance while the King remains oblivious throughout to the present threat to his safety: Hamlet's entrance is unprepared for, and, within the stage fiction, it also remains unannounced.[12] One presumes that tactics to redirect the audience's focus of attention during a performance existed in early modern English theatres as they do today, albeit differently resourced. But the pressing issue in this scene from *Hamlet* – as understood from the actor's, rather than the audience's, perspective – is surely not how the playwright guides the spectator's eye, but how he guides the *actor's* eye. How does the actor playing the King know not to look back (or over, or up) when Hamlet enters?

A sustained rehearsal process and access to a script of the play in its entirety provides modern actors with a contextual understanding of the scenes in which they perform. Early modern players, by contrast, were given only their individual part(s) to learn. Tiffany Stern argues that the bulk of an actor's rehearsal process in a part-based system was devoted to learning his lines and cues, leaving little time or incentive on the part of the actor to participate in ensemble rehearsals, which were, she suggests, infrequent.[13] In *Shakespeare in Parts*, Simon Palfrey and Stern suggest that ensemble rehearsals would have been turned over to 'particular *group* elements of the play' that could not be learned through solitary study, such as 'jigs, songs, dances, sword fights, perhaps crowd or climactic scenes'.[14] Dumb shows,

---

[7] Warren D. Smith, 'The Elizabethan stage and Shakespeare's entrance announcements', *Shakespeare Quarterly* 4 (1953), 405–10; pp. 408–9.

[8] Alan C. Dessen, 'Shakespeare and the theatrical conventions of his time', in *The Cambridge Companion to Shakespeare Studies*, ed. Stanley Wells (Cambridge, 1986), pp. 85–99, pp. 97; see also his *Elizabethan Stage Conventions and Modern Interpreters* (Cambridge, 1984). Leslie Thomson provides a considered account of the ongoing debate about two or three stage doors in *Discoveries on the Early Modern Stage: Contexts and Conventions* (Cambridge, 2018), pp. 213–41.

[9] Peter Thomson, *Shakespeare's Theatre*, 2nd ed. (London, 1992), p. 46.

[10] Bernard Beckerman, *Shakespeare at the Globe 1599–1609* (New York, 1962), pp. 180–1.

[11] Beckerman, *Shakespeare*, pp. 180–1.

[12] F *Hamlet*, TLN 2349–73; Q2 *Hamlet*, sigs. I1v–I2; Q1 *Hamlet* (1603), sigs. G1v–G2. Transcriptions from Shakespeare's Quartos are taken from *Shakespeare's Plays in Quarto: A Facsimile Edition of Copies Primarily from the Henry E. Huntington Library*, ed. Michael J. B. Allen and Kenneth Muir (Berkeley, 1981).

[13] Tiffany Stern, *Rehearsal from Shakespeare to Sheridan* (Oxford, 2000), see esp. ch. 3.

[14] Simon Palfrey and Tiffany Stern, *Shakespeare in Parts* (Oxford, 2007), p. 72 (emphasis original).

according to Leslie Thomson, may also have benefitted from rehearsal since they require 'more than each player's separate dialogue part' to ensure competent delivery.[15] It may have been the case, moreover, that some players practised together in small ad hoc groups. Scott McMillin has pointed to scenes involving novice actors, for example, suggesting that playwrights accommodated the rehearsal and training of boy actors by scripting scenes shared between a master and his apprentice(s).[16]

The scope and frequency of early modern rehearsal remains something of a question, mostly for lack of evidence. Depending on the scene and the actor, it seems not impossible that an actor's familiarity with the action might largely have amounted to a reading of the play by, or to, the company early in the preparation process, supplemented with possible access during performance to a backstage plot in which the general shape of sequential scenes was sketched.[17] No extant plot, however, indicates precisely where a mid-scene entrance falls.[18] If one assumes working conditions premised on limited and selective group rehearsal, then the challenge for players already onstage to know and remember other players' entrances into a scene – and, specifically, to know and remember how to interact with them – becomes acute. This difficulty would be compounded by an intensive repertory system that required actors 'to learn a new role every other week' while 'keep[ing] in mind thirty or forty others'.[19]

It seems inevitable that players who lacked a detailed knowledge of the scenes in which they appeared would at least sometimes have to rely on theatrical conventions to guide their response in performance to a mid-scene entrance. As Evelyn B. Tribble's work on distributed cognition indicates, such conventions would lower the load placed on actors (apprentices and adults alike), freeing up cognitive space for other demands on memory in a high-pressure theatrical environment.[20] It logically follows that *every* mid-scene entrance would have to conform to convention, or else represent an irregular entrance that would need special care and rehearsal. Such conventions, if they existed, would also presumably have guided playwrights, as well as the literary revisers and bookkeepers whose hands can be found in surviving playbooks. How would certain types of entrance shape in different ways what entering and onstage characters would notice and seem to hear? What *are* these entrance types?

In order to get some purchase on these questions, I compiled and analysed mid-scene entrances in twenty-six plays. Four of these texts are plays by Shakespeare written around the same time as *Hamlet* – *Henry V*, *Julius Caesar*, *As You Like It* and *Twelfth Night* – all of them as printed in the Folio. The fifth text, readied for performance in 1603 and so also contemporary with *Hamlet*, is the 1607 Quarto of Thomas Heywood's *A Woman Killed with Kindness*. I also included in this sample the surviving eighteen playhouse manuscripts, which range in date from about 1590 (*John a Kent*

---

[15] Leslie Thomson, 'Dumb shows in performance on the early modern stage', *Medieval and Renaissance Drama in England* 29 (2016), 17–45; esp. pp. 38, 34.

[16] Scott McMillin, 'The sharer and his boy: rehearsing Shakespeare's women', in *From Script to Stage in Early Modern England*, ed. Peter Holland and Stephen Orgel (Houndmills, 2004), pp. 231–45. Apprentice training is investigated further by Evelyn B. Tribble, *Cognition in the Globe: Attention and Memory in Shakespeare's Theatre* (New York, 2011), ch. 3, and John H. Astington, *Actors and Acting in Shakespeare's Time* (Cambridge, 2010), ch. 5.

[17] On 'Reading to the company', see Peter Holland in *Reading Plays: Interpretation and Reception*, ed. Hanna Scolnicov and Peter Holland (Cambridge, 1991), pp. 8–29.

[18] Tiffany Stern discusses the function of the backstage plot in *Documents of Performance in Early Modern England* (Cambridge, 2009), ch. 7, as does Paul Werstine in *Early Modern Playhouse Manuscripts and the Editing of Shakespeare* (Cambridge, 2013), pp. 108–13, and ch. 5. Transcripts of surviving plots can be found in David Bradley, *From Text to Performance in the Elizabethan Theatre: Preparing the Play for the Stage* (Cambridge, 1992), and digitizations of all of the plots except that for *The Battle of Alcazar* can be found in 'Plots and arguments', *The Lost Plays Database*: https://lostplays.folger.edu/Category:Plots_and_arguments.

[19] Beckerman, *Shakespeare*, p. 130. The 'rigorous' pace of early modern performance is detailed by Roslyn L. Knutson in 'The repertory', in *A New History of Early English Drama*, ed. John D. Cox and David Scott Kastan (New York, 1997), pp. 461–80, esp. p. 465.

[20] Tribble, *Cognition*.

WARNING THE STAGE: MID-SCENE ENTRANCE CONVENTIONS

and *John a Cumber*, transcribed and possibly also written by Anthony Munday) to about 1636 (*The Wasp*).[21] Unlike printed texts, whose provenance is clouded, these manuscripts indisputably show preparation by a bookkeeper for performance, and so offer especially good evidence of theatrical practices. The last three plays in the sample are the variant texts of *Hamlet*. This sample can be associated with seven or eight theatrical companies. *John of Bordeaux*, perhaps by Robert Greene, may have been performed by Lord Strange's and subsequently the Admiral's Men, Heywood's *Woman Killed* was written for Worcester's / Queen Anne's Men, and The Red Bull (Revels) Company owned *The Two Noble Ladies*. As many as four plays were in the repertory of Lady Elizabeth's Men (*The Honest Man's Fortune* by Nathan Field, John Fletcher and Philip Massinger, with Robert Daborne; Massinger's *Parliament of Love*; and perhaps Heywood's *Captives* and Thomas Dekker's *Welsh Ambassador*), with *Honest Man's Fortune* eventually migrating to the King's Men. The King's Revels Company played Henry Glapthorne's *Lady Mother* and the anonymous *Wasp*; Walter Mountfort's *Launching of the Mary* belonged either to the same company or else to Prince Charles's Men. Twelve of the playtexts in this sample are associated with the Chamberlain's / King's Men (all of Shakespeare's plays; perhaps the collaborative *Sir Thomas More*; *Second Maiden's / Lady's Tragedy*, attributed to Thomas Middleton; Fletcher and Massinger's *Sir John van Olden Barnavelt*; John Clavell's *Soddered Citizen*; Massinger's *Believe as You List*). The plays in this sample that cannot be associated with a particular company include *John a Kent*, *Edmund Ironside*, *Charlemagne* and *Thomas of Woodstock*.

While recognizing that any effort of categorization is inherently interpretive, this article identifies eight types of mid-scene entrance that emerge from study of every such entrance in the twenty-six plays in my sample. These eight types are divided into two broad categories that I term 'warned' (verbally announced in some manner to the actors on stage) and 'unwarned'; I work through each category in turn, returning thereafter to the specific instance of Osric's interruption of Hamlet in the final scene of Q2. All entrance types are compiled in tabular form in Table 2. My goal is to group together mid-scene entrances by certain clearly defined criteria in an effort to discern a potential stage logic that actors (and the playwrights who wrote for them) could have drawn on, either as a consciously learned skill or through immersion in their craft. Just as importantly for my purposes, I want to understand, if possible, how such conventions might *limit* dramatists' writing in specific ways. Conclusions about the conventions guiding mid-scene entrances are inevitably constrained by the size of my sample, and it seems not unlikely that investigation of more plays might reveal more subtleties of interpretation; given the huge number of plays that have not survived, this knowledge gap will always, to some extent, remain a factor to consider. There is evidence, even within this sample, that one theatrical company may have had distinctive practices compared to the others (discussed below), and conventions may have evolved over time. Despite these methodological qualifications, the consistency of patterning that emerges from this sample strongly implies that for the actor (as distinct from either the character or the spectator), *every* entrance is prepared for, even if – especially if – it is unannounced.

WARNED ENTRANCES

There are four types of warned entrance. The most commonplace entrance of all is one in which an onstage character verbally acknowledges another character's appearance or imminent appearance onstage. Orsino, for example, greets Valentine with 'How now what newes from her?' (*Twelfth Night*, TLN 28), and Henry V welcomes a fellow soldier the morning before Agincourt with 'Good morrow old Sir *Thomas Erpingham*' (*Henry V*, TLN 1858). The

---

[21] Details of authorship, dating and theatrical provenance follow Martin Wiggins, *British Drama, 1533–1642: A Catalogue*, 11 vols. (Oxford, 2012–), vols. 3–8.

Table 2 Types of mid-scene entrance (by percentage)

	Warned entrances				Unwarned entrances				
	HFS	HOE	SUM	PAM	SUS	SS	POS	WA	BOOS	AE
John a Kent (29) *†	48.3	13.8	17.2		17.2	3.4				
Bordeaux (29)	20.7	34.5	13.8	13.8	6.9	10.3				
Ironside (19)	31.6	26.3	21.1	10.5	5.3	5.3				
Henry V (38)	36.8	50.0	2.6		2.6	5.3		2.6		
Julius Caesar (40)	45.0	35.0	15.0		2.5			2.5		
As You Like It (30)	66.7	26.7	3.3		3.3					
Hamlet Q1 (41)	56.1	19.5		9.8	7.3			7.3		
Hamlet Q2 (53)	45.3	30.2	7.5	7.5	3.8			5.7		
Hamlet F (52)	51.9	21.2	5.8	7.7	5.8			1.9	5.8	
More (48)	52.1	25.0	4.2	10.4	4.2			4.2		
Twelfth Night (44)	47.7	31.8	9.1		2.3	2.3		2.3	4.5	
Woman Killed (36)	16.7	41.7	8.3		8.3	8.3	5.6	5.6	5.6	
Woodstock (44)	50.0	27.3	13.6	4.5	4.5					
SMT (39)	43.6	17.9	17.9		7.7	2.6	2.6		7.7	
HMF (32)	43.8	31.3			15.6			9.4		
Charlemagne (48)	58.3	29.2	2.1	2.1	4.2	2.1			2.1	
Barnavelt (47)	40.4	38.3	8.5		2.1	2.1	2.1	6.4		
Noble Ladies (26)	46.2	34.6	3.8	3.8	3.8	7.7				
Ambassador (43)‡	44.2	44.2	11.6							
Captives (36)	25.0	41.7	8.3	2.8	2.8	16.7			2.8	
Parliament (12)‡	66.7	8.3	16.7	8.3						
Soddered (37)	45.9	32.4	2.7		13.5			5.4		
Believe (32)‡	46.9	31.3	3.1		3.1	3.1		12.5		
Launching (28)	25.0	39.3	21.4		3.6	7.1			3.6	
Lady Mother (43)	34.9	41.9	7.0	4.7	7.0	2.3			2.3	
Wasp (36)	50.0	19.4	19.4		2.8	2.8			2.8	2.8

HFS: Hailed from stage
HOE: Hailing on entry
SUM: Summoned
PAM: Pre-arranged meeting
SUS: Sizing-up stage
SS: Simultaneous staging
POS: Pass over stage
WA: Wait attendance
BOOS: Blurred onstage/offstage space
AE: Anomalous entry

* Total number of mid-scene entrances given in brackets. Where an MS playbook provides revised and unrevised versions of the same scene, all mid-scene directions are compiled. Some MS playbooks are incomplete (missing pages).
† 2 damaged and unusable mid-scene entrances not listed.
‡ 1 damaged and unusable mid-scene entrance not listed.

stage is similarly warned if an onstage character, avoiding interaction with the newcomer, simply notes the entrance. Casca tells Brutus, 'Stand close a while, for heere comes one in haste' (*Julius Caesar*, TLN 574–5), while Anselmus notes to his best friend, Votarius, as his wife enters, 'yonder she comes'.[22]

Only slightly less common among warned entrances (even preferred in nearly a quarter of the sampled plays) are those entrances in which an entering character hails the stage. The Sheriff enters *Woman Killed* to arrest a distraught nobleman, for example, with the line, 'Sir *Charles*, I am made the vnwilling instrument / Of your attach and apprehension.'[23] Maria, by contrast, enters and gains the attention of late-night revellers in *Twelfth Night* by complaining, 'What a catterwalling doe you keepe heere?' (*Twelfth Night*, TLN 771).[24] Whether he hails or is hailed by the stage, an actor might potentially enter early in order to get into a central speaking position or to create an interpretively suggestive stage picture (or both).[25] If he were to enter early, however, as I will go on to explain in the context of unwarned entrances, he would be ignored – even if the other actor(s) happened to notice the entrance – until either he or one of those already onstage verbally warned of the entrance. (An actor left alone onstage with cued lines to deliver will undoubtedly anticipate an entrance, but that entrance, when it comes, is warned if the onstage character is to acknowledge it.)

The manuscript playbooks offer some evidence, moreover, that an audience might suppose that upon entry a character could, or at least might, hear any lines delivered during her approach. The importance of sustaining the perception that an intruding character does *not* happen to overhear sensitive stage dialogue is made especially clear in *The Honest Man's Fortune*. This playbook has been transcribed by the bookkeeper, Edward Knight, who presents his stage directions in a bold, oversized hand.[26] A scene towards the middle of the comedy cues an entrance in the left margin for two swaggerers, Laverdure and Lapoop. They enter to Dubois, who has promised to help them to kill his former master, Montagne. Unbeknown to the entering characters, however, Dubois only feigns hatred of Montagne in order to secure service, and the soliloquy on which they intrude unpacks his unswerving loyalty. Rather than gain space for a three-line entrance direction by positioning it slightly higher on his page, Knight begins it to the left of Dubois's closing line. He then clarifies its proper placement by connecting with lines the bottom of the entrance direction to the speech rule that marks the end of Dubois's speech. The entrance direction is badly cramped as a consequence, with its second and third lines over-running the column usually reserved for speech prefixes, so forcing a series of four speech prefixes towards, and in two cases into, the dialogue column (Figure 12).

Knight's layout of this entrance direction suggests that the bookkeeper-scribe is taking pains to make sure that Laverdure and Lapoop enter no earlier than the last line of Dubois's soliloquy, and possibly even not before the conclusion of that speech. The placement of the stage direction matters because the entering characters should not seem to overhear Dubois's praise of Montagne.[27]

---

[22] Thomas Middleton, *The Second Maiden's Tragedy*, ed. W. W. Greg (Oxford, 1964), line 335. Further references will be to *SMT*.

[23] Thomas Heywood, *A Woman Killed with Kindness* (London, 1607), sig. B4. Further references will be to *Woman Killed*.

[24] A unique example of this type found in *The Soddered Citizen* involves an entering character hailing the stage through ostentatious movement and gesture: Miniona '*comes w*th. *state*' towards Brainsick and his man, and she and her maid then '*salute*' them '*w*th. *seremony*', a compliment Fewtricks returns by addressing and kissing the maid (*The Soddered Citizen*, ed. J. H. P. Pafford (Oxford, 1936), lines 1606–11; further references will be to *Soddered*).

[25] On the potential interpretive effect of entrance directions that are printed somewhat in advance of the verbal warning to or from the stage, see Alan C. Dessen, *Recovering Shakespeare's Theatrical Vocabulary* (Cambridge, 1995), pp. 64–77.

[26] Nathan Field, John Fletcher and Philip Massinger, *The Honest Man's Fortune*, ed. Grace Ioppolo (Manchester, 2012), pp. x–xi, xiii. Further references will be to *HMF*.

[27] See also *SMT* (947) and *Charlemagne*, ed. J. H. Walter (Oxford, 1938), lines 1379–80 (further references will be to *Charlemagne*). These short directions show no special effort with regard to placement on the part of the scribe and author,

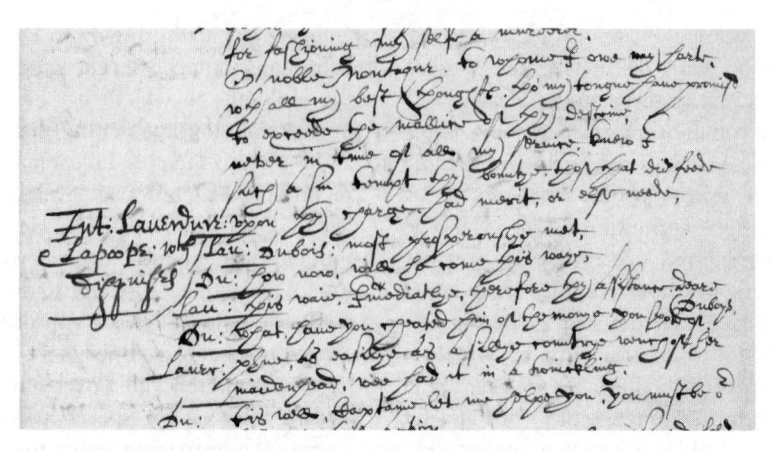

12 Detail from Nathan Field, John Fletcher and Philip Massinger, with Robert Daborne, *The Honest Man's Fortune* (8 February 1624), MS Dyce 25.F.9, fol. 14b, © Victoria and Albert Museum, London.

Implicit in Ichikawa's comment that the audience 'was not invited' to reflect on what an entering character hears is surely this occasional need for tact around the timing of an entrance – should spectators consider the question, they might well assume that an entering character could hear, or might hear, onstage dialogue. And indeed, as I will show below in the context of unwarned entrances, when it is essential that an entering character should hear what is said during their approach, bookkeepers again attend closely to the timing of the entrance, repositioning it, if necessary, somewhat earlier in the book.

A third type of warned entrance consists of those characters who enter in response to a call from the stage (not always the same character who was summoned to enter). Characters who have to be fetched by another character and characters who return after being sent on errand are not numbered among summoned entrances since onstage actors are unable to anticipate without additional warning the precise moment of that eventual entry. Warnings to the stage provided for the entrance of fetched and returning characters are sometimes oblique, however, leaning heavily on the contextual knowledge that a character has previously been sent on errand. In three instances, for example, servants announce their entrance through unscripted gesture, silently delivering the items for which they were sent on errand.[28] More typically, the prompt is verbal. In *The Book of Sir Thomas More*, the Sheriff's abrupt and unaddressed command – 'Bring them away to execution' – serves to warn a mid-scene entrance and guide the eye of the actor playing the Sheriff in a busy scene since he could only direct this instruction to the Officer returning, as the Sheriff supposes, with the prisoners from

---

respectively, but neither do they suggest that the entrance intrudes on the soliloquizing character. The scribe Ralph Crane's positioning of a five-line entrance direction for burghers and soldiers in *Sir John van Olden Barnavelt* might seem to imply this group enters while Leidenberch advises Barnavelt to 'stand a side' to avoid being seen (John Fletcher and Philip Massinger, *Sir John van Olden Barnavelt*, ed. T. H. Howard-Hill (Oxford, 1980), lines 601–5; further references will be to *Barnavelt*). The dialogue, however, makes clear that the entrance is yet to happen (Leidenberch specifies that he 'expect[s] them every mynutt') and so, in this particular instance, the last rather than first line of Crane's direction, aligned with Modesbargen's warning ('they are come'), might be supposed to signal the moment of entry.

[28] Philip Massinger, *Believe as You List*, ed. Charles J. Sisson (Oxford, 1928), lines 1112–19; Walter Mountfort, *The Launching of the Mary*, ed. J. H. Walter (Oxford, 1933), lines 1126–34; *John of Bordeaux*, ed. W. L. Renwick (Oxford, 1936), lines 466–71.

Newgate.[29] The onstage actor, whether or not he initially spots the entering actor, is thus guided through these various 'fetched' entrances.

The fourth and last type of warned entrance comprises pre-arranged meetings: onstage characters are alert to the meeting time and explicitly stand ready for the entrance. Prisoner transfers in *More* fall into this category, as does Friar John's entrance as though into D'Averne's home in *The Captives*, which is, he believes, preparatory to an assignation with Lady D'Averne but is actually a trap laid for him by the waiting D'Averne and his man.[30] Entrances made by actors performing in plays-within-plays (including spectacles summoned by magic) likewise fulfil pre-arranged meetings: within the inset play, an entrance might be the start of a new scene, but from the perspective of the onstage audience that entrance is anticipated by merit of the fact that they have gathered to watch a play.[31]

Entrances anticipated by offstage sounds are difficult to isolate as an independent category, in part because noises off only potentially warn of an entry. The '*Flourish, and Shout*' from the games are of concern to Brutus and Cassius, for example, but nobody enters to them until much later in the scene (*Julius Caesar*, TLN 174–9). Even a royal flourish does not certainly warn of an entrance.[32] And yet offstage sounds such as drums, flourishes, sennets, tuckets, loud music, bells, shouting, cries for help, and the not-infrequent cue for generalized 'noise' form an essential part of the crafting of some mid-scene entrances because they attract the attention of onstage characters to what is notionally happening just beyond the tiring-house walls. Should an entrance follow, characters are thus already alert to it without any need of further warning. The poise, for example, with which Henry V can enter to his men at Southampton – 'Now sits the winde faire, and we will aboord' – is shaped by the trumpets that herald his arrival (*Henry V*, TLN 641). A tucket likewise supports Mountjoy's entrance to the assembled English troops before the battle of Agincourt: 'Once more I come to know of thee King *Harry*, / If for thy Ransome thou wilt now compound' (*Henry V*, TLN 2325–6). Characters elsewhere comment on an offstage noise and then stand by to watch what might next unfold.[33] The stage is alerted to a potential entrance, however, even without explicit acknowledgement of the sound effect. John Ashburne, for example, makes no comment in *The Captives* on a 'tmult wth in and suddene noyse', but when two girls then enter in flight, asking each other where they might find safety, he intervenes to offer them his protection.[34] The noise cues the actor playing Ashburne to notice an entrance that he would otherwise ignore, so allowing his character to attend to the girls' dialogue as though they had hailed the stage upon entry.[35] Offstage noises thus occasionally stand in place of verbal warnings on the part of entering characters; more typically, however, they colour or enhance other types of warned entrance.

UNWARNED ENTRANCES

Not every entrance, however, is warned. When onstage actors are given no warning of an entrance, they ignore it either until they are hailed by the

---

[29] *The Book of Sir Thomas More*, ed. W. W. Greg (Oxford, 1911), line 594. Further references will be to *More*.
[30] *More*, 1603–40, 1861–73; Thomas Heywood, *The Captives*, ed. Arthur Brown (Oxford, 1953), lines 1747–74 (further references will be to *Captives*).
[31] Entrances in inset spoken plays are warned following the same patterns discerned in the framing text; on the staging complexities of dumb shows, see Thomson, 'Dumb shows'.
[32] *Charlemagne*, 73.
[33] *The Two Noble Ladies*, ed. Rebecca G. Rhoads (Oxford, 1930), lines 1146–9 (further references will be to *Two Noble Ladies*); *Captives*, 2032–6.
[34] *Captives*, 1496–1505.
[35] Even entrances that flow directly into onstage fighting are not necessarily verbally acknowledged by onstage actors if the entrances are anticipated by offstage noises; see *HMF*, 939–44 ('Clashing of weapons'), *Two Noble Ladies*, 2022–34 ('*Alarme*'), and *Edmond Ironside*, ed. Eleanore Boswell (Oxford, 1928), lines 1560–8 ('drum*m*s') and 1587–94 ('Alarum'). One suspects, however, that entrances with drawn swords might well have been at least minimally rehearsed.

entering character(s) or until an onstage character is cued to deliver a line that acknowledges the entrance. Onstage actors are thus under no pressure to keep one eye on the tiring-house doors; indeed, even if one of them should happen to catch sight of an unwarned entry, his character would remain ignorant of it until cued by the dialogue to attend to it. There are four types of unwarned entrance. The first of these might be described as characters 'sizing up the stage' upon entry. They enter, take stock of the onstage action and sometimes deliver lines, but do not demand the attention of the onstage characters. They then either exit unseen or else explicitly engage the onstage characters through direct address. Hamlet's consideration of the King at prayer on the way to his mother's closet, already discussed, is a familiar example of an unwarned, unacknowledged entrance. Henry V's intrusion on his troops immediately prior to his St Crispin's Day speech is another: Henry enters and listens unseen to Westmoreland mourn the absence on the field of 'But one ten thousand of those men in England, / That doe no worke to day' before announcing his presence with, 'What's he that wishes so?' (*Henry V*, TLN 2260–2). It is because onstage actors know to ignore unwarned entrances that a character – even a King – can catch their characters by surprise.

Trebonius's entrance immediately following the assassination of Caesar is the same type of unwarned entrance, played to very different effect. Cassius's query about Antony's whereabouts – not prompted specifically by sight of Trebonius, who enters without announcing himself – is addressed to the stage in general:

BRU. . . . let no man abide this deede,
   But we the Doers.
       Enter Trebonius.
CASSI. Where is *Antony*?
TREB. Fled to his House amaz'd:
       (*Julius Caesar*, TLN 1306–10)

This entrance brings nuance to a perception of Cassius's command of the stage traffic, perhaps suggesting on his part a moment of uncertainty or even alarm. From the perspective of the actor playing Trebonius, he simply enters, pays attention to the stage, and waits for his cue – he goes unnoticed (or at least unacknowledged) until he demands attention by providing the information Cassius seeks. From the perspective of the bookkeeper, however, this entrance brings risks with it: because the stage is given no warning of the entrance, the actor playing Cassius would have no reason to look for Trebonius prior to delivering his line (his cue is presumably part or all of Brutus's 'But we the Doers'). If the actor playing Trebonius should be late on his entrance, he would be in the position of replying to an unheard question. Evidence that dialogue that implicates a mid-scene entrance in this manner was indeed of concern to a bookkeeper is provided by an added marginal direction in the *John a Kent* playbook. A duped character concludes his uncertain explanation of how he became separated from his party with the claim that his information comes from a messenger sent by Cumber:

    That Griffin, Powesse and S^r. Gosselen denvyle,
    reskewed them from vs, how or when we knowe not,
Enter so sayd a deuill or boy sent to vs from Iohn a Cumber.

       Enter Iohn a Cumber pulling of his foole coat, lyke Kent still.
Cumber ffrom me young Lordes? alas you were deceiu'd,
    as you likewise, and all haue beene together.[36]

Cumber's entrance line contradicts Oswen's claim that the magician sent him a message by 'a deuill or boy'. As with the *Caesar* example, the timing of this entrance is an issue, and the bookkeeper, whose

---

[36] Anthony Munday, *John a Kent and John a Cumber*, ed. Muriel St Clare Byrne (Oxford, 1923), lines 1434–9. This entrance is discussed by William B. Long, who notes that 'Hand C-Bookkeeper 1 is quite precise with his lining' (William B. Long, '*John a Kent and John a Cumber*: an Elizabethan playbook and its implications', in *Shakespeare and Dramatic Tradition*, ed. W. R. Elton and William B. Long (Newark, 1989), pp. 125–43, esp. p. 135); my transcription reproduces for clarity the bookkeeper's marginal locating line as marked by Long.

hand is reproduced here in bold, takes care both to make the actor's entrance cue more visible by means of duplication and marginal lining, and to send him on stage, as William B. Long explains, 'moments before the [unannotated] text would have him there'.[37]

Characters who enter to size up the stage can be 'spotted' by the character(s) to whom they enter by means of the cuing system. In an early scene in *Honest Man's Fortune*, Montagne's creditors enter immediately after his lawyers tell him that his suit has failed and his fortunes are ruined. They eye Montagne but explicitly try *not* to attract attention in order to facilitate his arrest for debt – 'yf wee loose him now', one of them says, 'hees gone for ever'. One of them will therefore 'staye & dog him' while the other will 'go fetch the officers'. Part or all of this last phrase, however, is the cue line for Longavile, one of Montagne's loyal servants, who pulls his sword: 'dog you him bloodhounde, by this pointe / thou shalt more safelye dog an angrie lyon, / then attempt him'.[38] The actor playing Longavile would at first ignore the entrance (as would the other onstage actors), but his cue allows him to seem to spot the others, his character's extended riff on the creditor's metaphorical turn of phrase ('dog him') providing situational context for his noticing them.[39]

These 'sizing up the stage' entrances are distinguished from a second type of unwarned entrance by what the entering and onstage characters seem aware of in terms of the fictional action. Entering and onstage characters who are, or seem, oblivious to each other's presence generate an effect of simultaneous staging, each character (or group) sharing the stage space and often, but not necessarily, the same fictional location without knowledge of the other character (or group).[40] Their independent trains of dialogue are sustained until a cue crosses the groups, prompting a character to notice the bigger stage picture. A scene in *Woman Killed*, for example, features Sir Francis entering with Malby just as Sir Charles exits under arrest. Susan delivers a three-line complaint about the cruelty of her brother's creditor, and then Sir Francis, addressing his comments to Malby, triumphs in his enemy's misfortunes. Neither group shows any awareness of the other until Malby, prompted by his friend's determination to compound Sir Charles's troubles by ruining his sister, points to where Susan stands. Sir Francis looks to Susan and says 'a looke did flie / To strike my soule through with thy piercing eie', and Susan in turn, verbally recognizing her brother's enemy, runs away.[41]

Simultaneous staging in *Henry V* serves to shape the King's encounters with his men as he moves anonymously through the English camp the night before Agincourt. One of these meetings – Henry's extended exchange with Bates, Court and Williams – plays out much like the example from *Woman Killed* above: like Susan, Henry stands aloof, not acknowledging the soldiers' entrance, until Williams calls out 'Who goes there?' (*Henry V*, TLN 1941–2). The difference here between an onstage character 'not acknowledging' and 'genuinely not noticing' an entrance is a subtlety shaped by fictional context and audience reception; from a purely theatrical perspective, the actor simply ignores the entrance. This distinction between actor and character, or, to put it a different way, the distinction between what the actor hears and what an audience might suppose his character *seems* to hear, is brought even more sharply into focus in another example of this type in the same scene of *Henry V*. Here, Gower addresses Fluellen by name upon their entrance, his greeting prompting

---

[37] Long, 'Playbook', p. 135. [38] *HMF*, 371–6.
[39] This device of spotting a character who is sizing up the stage is relatively rare. The only comparable instances are found in *Soddered* (784–93, 2043–5) and Henry Glapthorne, *The Lady Mother*, ed. Arthur Brown (Oxford, 1959), lines 1088–93, 1148–54.
[40] The fleeing Edgar's entrance to Kent asleep in the stocks, which Dessen describes as a 'juxtaposition rich with potential meanings', is an example of simultaneous staging in which characters share stage space without, however, sharing a 'specific locale' (Dessen, 'Conventions', p. 97). Dessen develops his analysis of stage pictures that offer interpretively provocative juxtapositions in Dessen, *Recovering*, ch. 4. See also Tim Fitzpatrick's analysis of the 'split' stage in relation to stage doors in Tim Fitzpatrick, *Playwright, Space and Place in Early Modern Performance* (Farnham, 2011), pp. 128–34.
[41] *Woman Killed*, sigs. D2–D2v.

Fluellen to tell him to 'speake fewer' in case they are overheard by the enemy (*Henry V*, TLN 1913–14). Henry neither hails nor is hailed by the entering characters, and so Gower and Fluellen exit without ever knowing the King was there. As in the previous example, the actor playing Henry need behave no differently than he would if his character were entirely unaware of the other characters – he would ignore the entrance – and so what Henry seems to see and/or hear during the encounter remains entirely a matter of audience reception. That he *was* listening is confirmed only after the others exit, Henry's reflections on the encounter in effect writing over as eavesdropping the spectator's potential experience of simultaneous staging.

A third, somewhat rare type of unwarned mid-scene entrance comprises the highly stylized entrance of characters who 'pass over the stage'; presumably the entrance is ostentatiously presented to the character's sight, and so unmissable.[42] The fourth and final type is defined by characters who enter and wait attendance until they are summoned to speak. One of Lamyra's speeches in *Honest Man's Fortune* (a line and a half reply to Montagne) continues with '– from whence'. This cues a servant who entered two lines earlier to reply, 'from the lord of *Amience* madame'.[43] A similar effect is created by the staggered entrance given to the Ambassadors in the second scene of F *Hamlet*: they enter part-way through the King's opening speech and are ignored until the King turns to them and sends them on errand (F *Hamlet*, TLN 204–18).

As with other types of mid-scene entrance, onstage actors are not required to spot the arrival of a character who waits attendance since their characters' knowledge of the entrance is built into the dialogue. The implicit suggestion, however, is that these particular entering characters remain unacknowledged or 'invisible' because they lack status relative to the character who eventually calls on them (always to perform some service). These characters might be supposed therefore to overhear everything said onstage, but the audience is not invited (to draw on Ichikawa's phrasing) to dwell on the point. Williams's mid-scene entrance after Agincourt is another example of this type:

King. Good [God] keepe me so.
        Enter Williams.
Our Heralds go with him [Mountjoy],
Bring me iust notice of the numbers dead
On both our parts. Call yonder fellow hither.
Exe. Souldier, you must come to the King.
Kin. Souldier, why wear'st thou that Gloue in thy Cappe?

(*Henry V*, TLN 2645–52)

Williams is not 'waiting attendance', but he is clearly of inferior status. Henry is engaged with Fluellen and the French herald at the time of his entrance, and, like Claudius and Lamyra in my previous examples, his acknowledgement of Williams involves a sudden redirection of attention within one continuous speech. The actor playing Henry may well not have noticed, therefore, what is probably an inconspicuous entrance, but as he knows he will go on to ask about the glove, he knows whom to look for.

On the evidence of my sample, the circumstances in which an onstage character acknowledges an unwarned mid-scene entrance are thus few and heavily constrained. Characters who pass over the stage make themselves noticeable to those already onstage, while characters entering to wait attendance only become visible when their social superiors have occasion to notice them; stage group(s) who are conventionally oblivious to others' presence can be cued to notice each other. Consideration of these conventions explains why a theatrical reviser would bother to introduce a fairly bland bridging line to cover a passage that was cut from *Honest Man's Fortune*. Three would-be

---

[42] *Woman Killed*, sigs. C2v–C3 and F4; *SMT*, 928–30; and *Barnavelt*, 952–7. On this entrance type, see Ichikawa, *Shakespearean Entrances*, pp. 90–101, and Leslie Thomson, '"Pass over the stage" – again', in *Staging Shakespeare*, ed. Lena Cowen Orlin and Miranda Johnson-Haddad (Newark, 2007), pp. 23–44.
[43] *HMF*, 1416–18.

WARNING THE STAGE: MID-SCENE ENTRANCE CONVENTIONS

suitors to Lamyra enter seeking audience with the lady. In the unrevised version, Lamyra's servant, who enters with them, exits to announce them to his mistress, and while they wait, the suitors indulge in some coarse dialogue about how to get ahead in the world. One of them (Lapoop) cuts short their observations by interjecting 'the ladyes', a line that hails the entrance of Montagne '*bare*' (he now serves Lamyra), Lamyra, Lady Orleance, a maid named Charlotte, and Montagne's page, Viramour.[44] The next line, 'do ye smell nothing', is delivered by Montagne, and when Charlotte replies no, he claims 'the carrion of three knaves is verye strong in my nosthrill'.[45] This in turn is the suitor Laverdure's cue to praise Lamyra's beauty. When the whole of the suitors' comic dialogue is cut, including Lapoop's warning of the entrance from the stage, the theatrical reviser intervenes in the manuscript to interline an additional sentence at the end of the servant's arch refusal to take Malycorn's bribe of a 'tester' (a sixpence piece) prior to his exit (the added line is reproduced in italics):

yf you wolld haue too 3. pences for it sir,
to giue some of yor kindred as you ride, Ile see yf I can get em wee vse not (tho' servan*tes*) to take bribes. – *Exit.*
but I may spare my labour heeres my lady[46]

In both the revised and unrevised versions of this passage, there therefore exists a line delivered by an onstage actor warning the entrance of 'my lady' or 'the ladies', who are the object of Laverdure's next line. Without the bridging line, the ladies' entrance would remain conventionally unseen by the onstage characters since Montagne, a servant, does not demand the attention of the stage. The bookkeeper's intervention allows Laverdure to start his courtship of Lamyra through posture and gesture while waiting for his speaking cue, which eventually comes from Montagne, who slips in a snide insult, in effect as an aside.

Bookkeepers and theatrical revisers thus attended to the structure and timing of entrances. There is no surviving evidence, however, that their occasional repositioning of a mid-scene entrance had a textual life beyond the playbook: backstage plots, as already noted, do not precisely locate entrances within a scene, and neither does Orlando's part in Greene's *Orlando Furioso* (the only surviving professional actor's part from the period). The first two of three mid-scene entrances in Orlando's part are warned, Orlando either hailing or being hailed by the stage upon entry, and so, just possibly, the cue for speech might be understood also to cue the entrance. The third of his mid-scene entrances, however, which is unwarned (he sizes up the stage for four lines before he speaks), also lacks a cue to enter.[47] Noticing the challenge that an unscripted early entrance presents the actor who is working from the Orlando part, David Bradley supposes that actors would attend to the stage dialogue as it unfolds on the other side of the tiring-house wall and so intuit their moment of entry, a view shared by Stern.[48] The timing of an unwarned entrance, however, is difficult – perhaps even impossible – to determine without prior knowledge of the scene. One might posit that all such entrances were therefore rehearsed, but if actors were responsible for identifying their moment of entry, there would seem to be little motivation for bookkeepers to reposition entrances in the manuscripts. Werstine hypothesizes instead that the bookkeeper was responsible for 'tim[ing] the entrance in relation to the dialogue, as only he could do, for only he had a complete text of the play'.[49] In this latter scenario, the specific placement of an entrance only needed to reach – as a textual record – as far as the bookkeeper, who would cue actors to enter. Once on stage, actors' interactions with each other would be guided by theatrical convention.

---

[44] *HMF*, 1648–88. [45] *HMF*, 1689–91. [46] *HMF*, 1653–6.
[47] 'Appendix III: *Orlando Furioso*', in *Henslowe Papers, Being Documents Supplementary to Henslowe's Diary*, ed. W. W. Greg (London, 1907), pp. 155–71, line 104, 377, 422.
[48] Bradley, *From Text to Performance*, p. 25; Stern, *Documents*, p. 222.
[49] Werstine, *Playhouse Manuscripts*, p. 206.

ONSTAGE/OFFSTAGE SPACES

There are thus four types of warned entrance (characters hailed from the stage, characters hailing the stage, summoned entrances, and pre-arranged meetings) and four types of unwarned entrance (characters who enter to size up the stage unseen, entering and onstage characters who are oblivious to each other, and characters who pass over the stage or enter to wait in attendance). Blurred distinctions between onstage and offstage spaces, however, can disrupt assumptions about what counts as an entrance.[50] There are two 'arras' scenes in *Hamlet*, for example – Polonius and the King eavesdrop on Hamlet's interview with Ophelia, and Polonius eavesdrops on Hamlet's interview with his mother – but little consistency among the three texts about how to script this piece of stage business. In the first of these scenes, F includes both an exit and entrance direction for Polonius and the King, while Q1 and Q2 provide the cue for them to enter but no previous exit direction; in the closet scene, Q2 and F print neither exit nor entrance direction for Polonius, while Q1 cues an exit, but no entrance.[51] The physical staging of these two eavesdropping scenes in the earliest performances may well have been identical (character(s) step behind a wall hanging), but the textual notation varies both between texts and within each individual text.[52] *Second Maiden's Tragedy* presents a similar textual ambiguity. Anselmus has a direction to '*Exit*' into a closet in order to spy on his wife unseen, but there is no subsequent cue to bring him back on stage moments later to deliver an eight-line speech before he '*Locks him self in*'.[53] He is again unprovided of an entrance when his wife thereafter inadvertently stabs Votarius, even though he not only comments on his friend's death, but leaves his closet to kill the maid, Leonela.[54] The playbook is silent about the closet's location, but it was likely a space, perhaps behind a stage door, that for purposes of this scene was used as an extension of the onstage space. Mid-scene entrance directions are not 'missing' in this scene, nor is the exit direction necessarily wrong: the playbook finds a logic here in the context of a character who is positioned in a spot that might be considered both/either onstage and/or offstage. Anselmus's movements were seemingly as textually clear as they needed to be to guide performance since none of them is annotated by the bookkeeper.[55]

In cases such as these, a mid-scene exit and entrance, as distinct from a character shifting place within a possibly extended stage space, are a matter of textual representation.[56] Only once in my

---

[50] Ichikawa explains that 'marginal positions such as behind stage posts, near the stage doors, and even the space behind the *frons scenae* were sometimes treated as "onstage" and sometimes as "offstage"' (Ichikawa, *Shakespearean Entrances*, p. 132). In *The Shakespearean Stage Space*, she considers various ambiguously scripted stagings, concluding that the meaning of directions such as '*enter*', '*within*' and '*above*' sometimes requires 'taking into account the fictional locale or situation of the scene and the stage conditions in the playhouse where the version of the play was performed' (Mariko Ichikawa, *The Shakespearean Stage Space* (Cambridge, 2013), p. 154).

[51] F *Hamlet*, TLN 2383–405, 1708–1818; Q2 *Hamlet*, sigs. G2–G3v, I2; Q1 *Hamlet*, sigs. D4v–E2, G2.

[52] On the staging of arras scenes, see Gurr and Ichikawa, *Staging*, pp. 106–7, and Fitzpatrick, *Playwright*, pp. 124–7.

[53] *SMT*, 1998, 2023–30. [54] *SMT*, 2119–22.

[55] Anne Lancashire emends the playbook's exit as an error (5.1.12 s.d., 55–6) and adds without comment the direction '[*Coming from closet*]' (5.1.109) when Anselmus emerges from his hiding spot after Votarius's death (in Thomas Middleton, *The Second Maiden's Tragedy*, ed. Anne Lancashire (Manchester, 1978)). The logic of Anselmus's '*Exit*' is comparable to a cue in *Captives* for two young women to 'go in' to the back gate of the monastery to appeal in song for charity. How (or where) precisely they 'go in' is unclear, but when they are refused harbour, they fall out of view – at least as far as the playbook is concerned – for nearly forty lines, only to re-emerge from an apparently hidden 'onstage' position to rejoin the dialogue, like Anselmus, without a cue to enter (755–821).

[56] The flip side of onstage characters whose mid-scene movements are variably scripted are those characters who remain 'within', despite engaging in extended dialogue. In my sample, both Denis in *Captives* (2491–502) and Malvolio in *Twelfth Night* (TLN 2005) are cued to deliver substantial dialogue 'wth in/*within*'. On the staging of the dark house scene, see John H. Astington, 'Malvolio and the dark house', *Shakespeare Survey* 41 (Cambridge, 1988), 55–62; David Carnegie, '"*Maluolio within*": performance perspectives on the dark

sample does a blurred distinction between onstage and offstage spaces result in a mid-scene entrance that fails to conform, at least on the face of it, to the conventions of entry already outlined. When Sir Andrew seeks to evade the duel with Viola (in disguise as Cesario) by offering his horse in return for the youth's agreement to 'let the matter slip', Sir Toby replies:

> Ile make the motion: stand heere, make a good
> shew on't, this shall end without the perdition of soules,
> marry Ile ride your horse as well as I ride you.
>   *Enter Fabian and Viola.*
> I haue his horse to take vp the quarrell, I haue perswaded
> him the youths a diuell.
>   *Fa.* He is as horribly conceited of him: and pants, &
> lookes pale, as if a Beare were at his heeles.
>   (*Twelfth Night*, TLN 1805–12)

The entrance is unwarned, and yet Sir Toby registers the entering characters (the shift from 'your horse' to 'his horse' implicitly indicates that he is no longer speaking to himself). To put this a different way, if this Folio entrance plays out in performance from the perspective of the actor playing Sir Toby as an *actual* mid-scene entrance, then theatrical convention should guide him to ignore Fabian and Viola.

More likely, however, this is another example of a flexibly described offstage/onstage space. Editors since Capell have often omitted this entrance altogether, choosing also to cut the prior exit for Fabian and Viola when Sir Toby and Sir Andrew enter to the duel (*Twelfth Night*, TLN 1790). Elizabeth Donno retains these Folio directions but interprets the exit to mean that Fabian and Viola fall back to a position that might in other circumstances be considered offstage but here remains part of the extended playing space (she suggests they occupy the space behind an open stage door).[57] The cue that crosses from Sir Toby to Fabian thus marks an 'entrance' in the sense that it brings Fabian, and subsequently Viola, back into earshot of the others within the fictional action. The build-up to the duel, although challenging in terms of textually representing the shifting stage groupings that will suggest to an audience who hears what and when, would have been readily navigable in performance through verbal cues and theatrical convention so long as Fabian and Viola in their retired offstage/onstage position remain – like Polonius behind the arras, and Anselmus in the closet – continually present within the scene.

There is just one entrance in the whole of my sample that fails to conform to the conventions outlined above. In *The Wasp*, the Countess and Luce enter to Gilbert and his man, Howlett, who have been discussing Gilbert's son's dissipation. Immediately prior to their entrance, Gilbert instructs Howlett to 'go wet yor beak ithe butery y^{w}le sing the clerer'. The Countess then enters, asking Luce, 'w^t. thinkst thow of this country life my girle', going on to reflect on the pleasures of a retired life.[58] The women's entrance is especially abrupt – it is even more sudden in the revised version of this scene, which cuts the end of Gilbert's interview with Howlett, including the line of dialogue that guides Howlett to exit. The bookkeeper attended to this entrance, supplementing it in the margin with an exit direction for Howlett, but otherwise made no effort to adjust the warning structure. The precedent of the previous twenty-five texts – *Wasp* is the latest play in the sample, one of two surviving playbooks of the King's Revels Company – would indicate simultaneous staging: none of the actors has been prompted to take note of the other group. The oddity of this entrance becomes apparent when the Countess eventually asks after the whereabouts of the Wasp (Gilbert's disguised identity) and then spots him with the words 'here he comes himself' (he is wearing what he describes in soliloquy at the beginning of the scene as a 'fantastick / & ridiculous habit').[59] Where then does Gilbert come from? If he emerges from some notionally concealed onstage/offstage position, how does he

---

    house', *Shakespeare Quarterly* 52 (2001), 393–414; and Ichikawa, *Stage Space*, pp. 29–51.
[57] William Shakespeare, *Twelfth Night*, ed. Elizabeth Donno (Cambridge, 1985), 3.4.231 s.d.
[58] *The Wasp*, ed. J. W. Lever (Oxford, 1976), lines 1116–18. Further references will be to *Wasp*.
[59] *Wasp*, 1148–56; 1074–5.

know to retire himself at the moment of their entrance? By the time the cuing system allows him to notice their presence, the women have been on stage for eight lines. Perhaps they simply ignore him upon entry, but that possibility feels strained given his outlandish costume and sudden appearance to view.

I can only think that this mid-scene entrance was rehearsed or that the playwright and bookkeeper expected the actors to have a reliably good knowledge of this scene in advance of performance (just possibly, one might infer that some kind of instruction was written into Gilbert's part or other document sufficient to signal the kind of stage business that in other plays is conventionally handled through dialogue). While any early modern scene or part-scene might have been rehearsed, this example from *Wasp* stands out from other mid-scene entrances in this sample in that it seems to *require* rehearsal. Werstine has already pointed to certain features of the playbooks of the King's Revels that 'decisively separate' the work of this 1630s bookkeeper 'from earlier practice', and he notes that, despite the wide variety of annotation found in extant playbooks, 'it nevertheless seems possible to distinguish the King's Revels Company's way of conducting performances from those of other companies whose texts come down to us'.[60] This anomalous mid-scene entry supports that suggestion.

RASH INTRUDING FOOLS: OSRIC AND THE MESSENGER

Some inferences may be drawn from the preceding discussion. First, onstage actors are alerted to entering characters with whom they interact; if an entrance is not warned, onstage actors should assume their characters are not supposed to see the entrance until such time as they are addressed or the cuing system prompts them to take note of it. Second, characters who are called or fetched, who enter to wait attendance or to observe the stage unseen, or who hail the stage upon entry (even if they enter somewhat before their line) can hear – or, more precisely, might be thought to hear – dialogue spoken during their approach since they enter with the explicit purpose of engaging the stage action. These intuitive and flexible conventions of entry are able to support a wide variety of possible fictional situations, even deliberate 'misfires' that otherwise might seem to require some kind of group rehearsal. Jenkin in *Woman Killed*, for example, straightforwardly announces his entrance to his master, Wendoll, asking 'Did your worship cal?'[61] Under typical circumstances, a direct address would prompt the onstage character to notice the entrance. Wendoll, however, did not summon the entrance. So even though he is in the middle of what would otherwise be a soliloquy, in which he deliberates betraying his friend and patron, the actor playing Wendoll, supported by the knowledge that *he* eventually hails Jenkin from the stage, can accurately interpret the servant's line as a false demand for attention and ignore the entrance.[62]

If the theory is to hold that these conventions enabled a working method in which actors learning from parts were supported by minimal group rehearsal, then it would follow that a particular mid-scene entrance type could not be accommodated by the system. Specifically, playwrights would have to avoid scripting fictional situations in which entering characters are seen by onstage characters without first declaring themselves to, or being verbally acknowledged by, the stage. The problem with this type of entrance is that actors without a strong knowledge of a scene's fictional shape would be left with no means to distinguish those entrances their characters should see from

---

[60] Werstine, *Early Modern*, pp. 215–16.
[61] *Woman Killed*, sig. C3.
[62] David Wiles argues that Heywood wrote the part of Jenkin for Will Kemp. The comedy of the servant who comments on the stage soliloquy while waiting attendance is consistent with techniques of metatheatre and improvisation associated with Jenkin elsewhere in the tragedy (David Wiles, *Shakespeare's Clown: Actor and Text in the Elizabethan Playhouse* (Cambridge, 1987), pp. 82, 106–7).

those they should *not* see. This uncertainty would in turn disable playwrights' ability to shape layered stage pictures in which separate groups remain oblivious to each other, or in which characters enter to comment on action, unseen by the stage. And, indeed, it is precisely this entrance type that is absent from twenty-five of twenty-six of the plays in the sample (the anomaly is *The Wasp*, discussed above).

What light then can this analysis shed on Q2 *Hamlet* and the entrances of Osric and the Messenger? To start, these are the only two examples in the entire sample of a character interrupting or potentially interrupting, upon entry, a speaking onstage character mid-sentence. Characters who enter and hail the stage always have to be alert to their moment of entrance; sometimes tight timing, as some of my earlier examples suggest, is simply a feature of this particular stage arrangement. But even Heywood, whose dramaturgy shows a preference for this entrance type, offers no instances of mid-sentence interruptions by an entering character. He instead shapes the action to avoid a small timing fluctuation around the moment of entrance leaving spectators with the impression that the speaking onstage actor has somehow run out of words mid-thought. Shakespeare, for his part, elsewhere suggests that characters are surprised by an entrance by cuing an onstage, rather than entering, actor to interrupt the speaker. Barnardo, for example, is interrupted mid-line and mid-thought by Marcellus, who warns of the Ghost's entrance with 'Peace, breake thee of, looke where it comes againe'.[63] The potential risk of a mis-timed interruption by an entering character is lessened, of course, if he enters early. In the case of the Messenger in *Hamlet*, an entrance up to four lines before his speaking cue would afford him opportunity to time his moment of interruption. It would also make sense of deictic phrasing – '*These* to your Maiestie, *this* to the Queene'[64] – that implies a reasonably close physical proximity to the King as he hands over his letters. The Messenger, however, might be expected to hear anything said while he was on stage. Although the dialogue here only indirectly touches on Laertes's revenge, the unannounced entrance would imply that the privacy of a scene in which the King and Laertes plot Hamlet's murder does not extend to include servants.

This issue of privacy is even more acute in the later scene since Hamlet's intention to murder the King, as John Jowett notes, is implicit in the lines immediately preceding Osric's intrusion.[65] His entrance is thus analogous to Laverdure and Lapoop's intrusion on Dubois in the *Honest Man's Fortune*, in which they arrive on stage just in time to hear their cue. The timing of Osric's entrance, if one is to understand it as an interruption, is thus doubly constrained – he must not enter late, since he has to interrupt a speaking character mid-sentence, but, no less importantly, he cannot enter early. This combination of conditions, as far as I am aware, is unique. If one instead understands Osric entering into the pregnant silence left by Hamlet's unspoken intention to murder the King, then the courtier, entering on or near his speaking cue, still has to hail the Prince from the back of the stage. His greeting is not inconsistent with examples elsewhere of characters who announce themselves immediately upon entry, but such informality and even assertion of ownership of the space might seem inconsistent with a subordinate courtier whose extreme self-consciousness about being in the presence of the Prince will subsequently make him the butt, in both Q2 and F, of Hamlet's gag about his hat (the passage is variant in Q1).

Each of these Q2 entrances strains in its way against mid-scene entrance conventions as they can be discerned elsewhere in the sample. The Messenger's entrance, on the one hand, requires some extra, albeit not extraordinary, consideration from the bookkeeper, and perhaps challenges

---

[63] Q2 *Hamlet*, sig. B1v, F *Hamlet*, TLN 51–2; see also Q1 *Hamlet*, sig. B1v.
[64] Q2 *Hamlet*, sig. L3v, emphasis mine.
[65] *Hamlet*, ed. John Jowett, in *William Shakespeare: The Complete Works: Critical Reference Edition*, ed. Gary Taylor, John Jowett, Terri Bourus and Gabriel Egan, 2 vols. (Oxford, 2017), vol. 1, p. 19, n. 67.

assumptions about privacy. Osric's entrance, on the other hand, traps the courtier near the back of the stage for delivery of his first line, and leaves Hamlet with a speech whose implicit thrust some commentators have found awkward. Each of them, moreover, is variant in F, which instead offers conventionally regular mid-scene entrances. In the first, the King interrupts himself to warn of the Messenger's entrance; in the other, not only does Hamlet finish his thought, but Horatio later warns of the entry, silencing his friend. The Messenger and Osric are both given ready opportunity in F to approach onstage characters who have been made aware of their presence in advance of their first line, and scenes of court intrigue and revenge remain entirely private without, from a practical staging perspective, any need of added effort or consideration on the part of either actor or bookkeeper.

These Q2–F alterations could have come about in a number of ways. Harold Jenkins considers the Messenger's entrance as warned from the stage in F an example of what he calls 'playhouse interpolations'. He argues that actors, misunderstanding the structure of the plot as devised by Shakespeare, improvised the King's part-line along with a half-line reply. According to Jenkins, the Messenger destroys the impact of the moment in which the King learns of Hamlet's return and 'robs [Hamlet's] bomb of the full force of its explosion'.[66] It seems not impossible that this entrance might have been restructured in the playhouse (albeit more probably by a bookkeeper than by the actors, since he held a copy of the play in its entirety and had opportunity to annotate it). Jenkins's claim, however, that F steals Hamlet's thunder feels overly inventive, as perhaps not many spectators (or even close readers) would notice at this point in the action that the Messenger has no way to know the identity of the letters' sender. Where Jenkins infers artistic liberties, one might instead find evidence of theatre professionals who understand their business revising a somewhat difficult entrance. Another possibility is that Shakespeare himself revised these entrances, presumably in response to the same staging considerations. Osric's entrance, in particular, is already caught up in foundational arguments that have shaped perceptions of *Hamlet* as a revised play, and one might suppose that Shakespeare took occasion to build in two warnings from the stage as part of a larger restructuring process.

Each of these hypotheses presumes that two Q2 stage arrangements that are at once unconventional and in certain respects strikingly similar were subsequently altered through forms of textual revision that resulted in the addition of a warning from the stage. As already indicated, however, editors have long wondered about the passage associated with Osric's entrance, asking instead whether something has not been omitted from Q2, rather than (or not only) added to F. And, certainly, one might wonder why an experienced company dramatist would craft similarly problematic mid-scene entrances, twice in the same play, both of which had to be – or, at least, were – subsequently revised. The more straightforward hypothesis might be that Shakespeare, as attuned as anyone in his company to the conventions that served to guide actors through scenes with which they might lack close familiarity, both times warned of the entrance from the stage, but these warnings were subsequently corrupted through inadvertent omission of a part-line, either by the Q2 compositor or, if the printing-house copy was scribal, by a copyist at an earlier stage of textual transmission.[67] To return

---

[66] Harold Jenkins, 'Playhouse interpolations in the Folio text of "Hamlet"', *Studies in Bibliography* 13 (1960), 31–47; p. 36.

[67] Twice elsewhere, the Q2 compositors fail to include a part-line that is essential to a passage's sense, and scholars have argued that both oversights were likely occasioned by marks of cancellation in the manuscript behind Q2. Osric's entrance in 5.2, as already noted, coincides with substantial textual variance between Q2 and F, a staging irregularity that might point to a third site in Q2 where an imperfectly executed manuscript cancellation led to the inadvertent omission in the printed text of a necessary part-line (Horatio's warning of Osric's entrance). For a discussion of cancellations and textual variance between Q2 and F *Hamlet*, see Margaret Jane Kidnie, 'Playhouse markings and the revision of *Hamlet*', *Shakespeare Quarterly* 71 (2020), 69–103.

then to the perceived crux with which this article opened, there is indeed cause to suspect Q2's reading. If there is a fault in Q2, however, staging conventions would suggest it lies not (or, at least, not solely) with Hamlet's implicit phrasing, but with Osric's irregular entrance – not with what Hamlet says, but with what Horatio *fails* to say. Osric's intrusion into the scene, not warned from the stage in Q2 as it is in F ('Peace, who comes heere?'), would occasion practical theatrical challenges that an interrupted thought, left 'hanging in the air', never would.

The implications of this study of mid-scene entrance patterns extend, however, beyond a single local reading. They contribute to existing research into the theatrical labour that guided early modern staging practices, in terms of both scripting and performance, especially as shaped by (potentially evolving) company rehearsal arrangements. Consideration of these conventions also sheds light on some entrances that critics have either disagreed about or found theatrically difficult. Romeo, for example, enters Friar Lawrence's cell in 2.3, eight lines in advance of his speaking cue and in time to overhear the Friar talking about the deadly properties of plants.[68] Dessen comments that this early entrance lays the ground for Romeo's later decision to commit suicide by poison, a suggestion on which Gurr and Ichikawa cast doubt since they consider it 'at least questionable' that Romeo would hear these lines.[69] My analysis suggests that Romeo, who eventually hails the stage and enters with the explicit purpose of engaging the Friar in dialogue, might indeed be thought to hear everything said while he was on stage. The Friar, on the other hand, would pay no attention to his visitor until Romeo announced his presence, and the moment would likely play in performance as the youth waiting for an opportunity to catch the attention of a preoccupied figure of some authority. There would be no particular need for the actor playing Romeo to lurk by the stage doors or even to invent business with which to busy himself. Since both actors know the entrance is as yet unannounced, the Romeo actor would realize he can be anywhere on stage (and his character, as eager to interrupt as he pleases) so long as his positioning avoids making his presence manifestly obvious to the Friar. When his cue finally arrives, he speaks, hailing the Friar and so initiating the scene's dialogue.

One might likewise question Beckerman's characterization of Polonius's intrusion on Hamlet and his schoolfriends to announce the arrival of the players as highly stylized.[70] In this scene, Polonius hails the stage upon entry, so warning the others of his entrance. Hamlet's response, however, is to turn his back on the counsellor – figuratively, and perhaps literally – in order to conspire with Rosencrantz and Guildenstern. Not given his cue to speak, the actor playing Polonius is left at a loose end. The effect is of an announced character, ignored by the stage, awkwardly trying to find a second opportunity to gain the others' attention. In the ordinary course of things, he would hear everything said by the others – the entrance type in and of itself would not preclude Polonius potentially catching their words. This particular staging, however, is shaped by an invitation to guarded speech that is built into the dialogue ('at each eare a hearer', Hamlet instructs his friends). This implied stage arrangement likely suggests that the friends banter out of earshot, but Hamlet's barely concealed mockery of Polonius earlier in the same scene might leave at least some spectators uncertain just quite what Polonius hears.

These two entrances achieve distinctively textured stage effects by conventional means. They require minimal scripting of stage directions, and minimal knowledge, on the part of the actors, of the scene in which they perform. For the actors playing Romeo and Polonius in their respective scenes, the set-up is comparable: they enter and wait for their cue. Setting aside *The Wasp* as perhaps indicative of company-specific staging practices that evolved towards the end of the period under study, analysis of this sample indicates that it

---

[68] *Romeo and Juliet*, TLN 1028–36; Q2 *Romeo and Juliet* (1599), sig. E1. Romeo lacks a cue to enter in Q1 *Romeo and Juliet* (1597, sig. D4).
[69] Gurr and Ichikawa, *Staging*, p. 86.
[70] Beckerman, *Shakespeare*, p. 181; Q2 *Hamlet*, sig. F2v; F *Hamlet*, TLN 1427. The scene is variant in Q1.

is not necessary to invoke group rehearsal to explain how early modern actors working from parts managed to shape mid-scene entrances during live performance. Such conventions as those outlined here would not, of course, preclude small-group or ensemble rehearsal of any scene, and actors undoubtedly took the opportunity to add nuance to their performance if and as they gained confidence with the larger shape of individual scenes and their characters' place within them. In situations, however, in which one or more actors were unable to remember, or perhaps never knew, a scene's fictional structure, the playwright's crafting of the script, sometimes in collaboration with a bookkeeper or other theatre practitioner, allowed players to ground their performance of mid-scene entrances in a system of shared theatrical conventions.

LOOKING FOR PERDITA IN ALI SMITH'S *SUMMER*

BAILEY SINCOX

'A sad tale's best for winter. I have one / Of sprites and goblins' (2.1.27–8), says Mamillius, the young prince in *The Winter's Tale*. In a sense, the whole play is the fairy story that he whispers in his mother's ear, though the forces of evil are more banal than he imagines. As the story goes, his father, Leontes – a man prone to conspiracy theories and violence – accuses his wife, Hermione, of cheating on him with his best friend, Polixenes. He prosecutes her in a public trial that apparently results in her death and Mamillius's. He abandons their newborn daughter, Perdita, to die on the shores of a foreign country.

At first glance, *The Winter's Tale* is not the most obvious Shakespearian inspiration for a novel called *Summer*. Ali Smith's *Seasonal Quartet* – the celebrated meditation on Brexit and other national as well as global crises which begins with *Autumn* (2016) – might be presumed to end on an optimistic note, one of sunlight and greenery rather than 'sprites and goblins'. The novels' titles suggest a schematization in line with Northrop Frye's archetypal criticism, where characters and symbols belong to certain seasons, each confined to its own quadrant in a great graph of human meaning-making.[1] However, Smith is more interested in messiness, in a kind of seasonal confusion: we find a 'time-lapse of a million billion flowers opening their heads' in *Autumn*, and the earth threatening to 'block up your front door in April with snow' in *Spring*.[2] Immediate, dissonant chords sound through each instalment (winter/summer, sad/happy, goblins/not-goblins). *Summer* is no different.

This mixed modality is something Smith's Quartet shares with Shakespeare's late plays, inter-texts which, while noted by critics, have not received their due attention either as bearers of meaning or as tentpoles of novelistic purpose.[3] As Smith is well aware, *The Winter's Tale* changes tack from tragedy to comedy two-thirds of the way through. Perdita survives. She grows up to be a smart, sassy young woman in the country ruled by Polixenes, and she catches the eye of his son. When Polixenes frowns upon Florizel's relationship with Perdita, the pair flee to Leontes's court. The king recognizes his daughter, no longer lost (her name means 'the lost one'), and miraculously his wife turns out to be alive, too. Smith's Shakespearian epigraph for the novel evokes these elements of surprise, reversal – and, yes, dissonance – from her source: 'Oh, she's warm!'[4] This is the very

---

[1] Northrop Frye, *Anatomy of Criticism: Four Essays* (Princeton, NJ, 1957).
[2] Ali Smith, *Autumn* (London, 2016), p. 123; Ali Smith, *Spring* (London, 2019), p. 8. Further references appear in parentheses.
[3] Sara Collins, 'Summer by Ali Smith review – clear-sighted finale to a dazzling quartet', *Guardian*, 8 August 2020; Dwight Garner, 'Ali Smith's "Summer" ends a funny, political, very up-to date quartet', *New York Times*, 17 August 2020; Matt Hartman, 'Novel times: on Ali Smith's "Summer"', *Los Angeles Review of Books*, 7 October 2020; Heller McAlpin, 'Ali Smith brings her seasonal quartet to a close with "Summer"', *National Public Radio*, 25 August 2020.
[4] Ali Smith, *Summer* (London, 2020), n.p. Further references appear in parentheses. Cf. *Winter's Tale*, 5.3.109.

moment when Leontes touches Hermione, supposed to be a statue unveiled for Perdita's homecoming. In this Shakespearian nugget, Smith with her characteristic economy gives us both a manifesto and a pun. A warm winter is an alarming (if familiar) phenomenon these days. But it is precisely the symbolic summer in winter and its inverse, the sad winter's tale in *Summer*, that are this novel's jumping-off points. Smith is interested in forgiveness and in the wake-up call, in the 'gap of time' between Leontes's disintegration and the rebuilding of his family (5.3.155). Importantly, these concepts – return, revelation, interval – converge in Perdita.

Perdita puts the summer in *Summer*; she is the reason *The Winter's Tale* works as a conversation partner for the conclusion of Smith's *Seasonal Quartet*. The improbable reconciliation at the end of *The Winter's Tale* is powered by the pagan orgy of act 4 – the long, seemingly digressive 'sheep-shearing' scene often cut in performances. This burst of music and song in a festival of which Perdita is the 'queen' (4.4.5), likened to the nature goddesses Flora and Proserpina (4.4.2; 116), imbues the girl with an ancient force strong enough to counteract the juggernaut of her father's destruction. Smith is interested in Perdita, in the effect she has on others and on the world of the play. Looking back at the earlier novels in the series, it becomes clear that her versions of Shakespeare's similarly transformative daughters Miranda, Innogen, and Marina are what push the series towards the comic, towards a tentatively hopeful futurity. Yet doubled, inverted, and rotated 90 degrees, Smith's daughters are more than copies; what's more, the new arrangements they create reveal the novels' prospects.

The question facing a reader of *Summer* is this: who – or what – will be Perdita? From where will the power of forgiveness emerge to remake the broken winter-world of Smith's post-Brexit UK? By identifying the daughters of Shakespeare's late plays in each novel, I show just how much the *Seasonal Quartet* depends on Shakespeare – particularly on tessellations of these female characters. *Summer*, with four Perditas, offers the most (and most varied) versions of tragicomic potentiality. However, neither forgiveness nor resolution quite arrive. Instead, Smith ends her series with a series, her last move to conflate the lost girl of nature with her radioactive father, fitting Leontes into the pattern.

FOUR ROMANCES, FOUR MAGIC DAUGHTERS

Each of Smith's *Seasonal Quartet* novels engages one of Shakespeare's late plays: *Autumn* touches on *The Tempest*, *Winter* on *Cymbeline*, and *Spring* on *Pericles*. This sequence is not, of course, chronological (nor is it complete; one wonders what a novelization of *Coriolanus*, *The Two Noble Kinsmen* or *Henry VIII* would look like). While the most obvious explanation for this choice of plays might be that they are the most famous, most often performed, or indeed the most 'Shakespearian', it is also true that the four intertexts share another defining feature: each of these plays has a remarkable daughter. Like Perdita, these female characters are notable for their embodiment of what we might call the plays' 'themes', or, drawing on Sarah Beckwith, the plays' 'grammar[s]', ensuring progression from loss to recuperation, error to forgiveness.[5] In other words, Miranda, Innogen and Marina are intimately tied up with what makes the plays tragicomedies. Avoiding tokenization or essentialism, in each of the installments before *Summer* Smith tessellates Shakespeare's daughters, dispersing their symbolic power throughout the narrative.

In the novel following most closely on Brexit's heels, Smith focuses on Miranda, the daughter who watches a shipwreck. Saying, 'I have suffered / With those that I saw suffer' (*Tempest*, 1.2.5–6), Miranda broadcasts her empathy as well as her insistence on bearing witness. These are qualities Elisabeth Demand, *Autumn*'s protagonist, emulates – and Smith often tags Shakespeare as she does. In the novel's first section, Elisabeth, whose 'ears had undergone a sea-change ... or

---

[5] Sarah Beckwith, *Shakespeare and the Grammar of Forgiveness* (Ithaca, NY, 2011).

the world had' after Brexit (p. 198, cf. *Tempest*, 1.2.403), reads *Brave New World* while waiting in the post office, her eyes taking in a 'Shakespeare 400' commemorative coin display just as she reads '*O brave new world! Miranda was proclaiming the possibility of loveliness, the possibility of transforming even the nightmare into something fine and noble. "O brave new world!" It was a challenge, a command*' (pp. 17–18).[6] Miranda's (and, in Huxley, John's) 'challenge' is Elisabeth's, too: to 'transform' her world – in this case, a Britain without Europe, as well as a Britain that, as Elisabeth wryly observes, is keen to monetize everything, including Shakespeare's death. Thus, Smith simultaneously articulates and ironizes what will become a guiding principle for the *Quartet*: pluck that perfect prism of youthful femininity out of the plays and see what it looks like when you rotate it, reflect it over an axis, or put it somewhere else entirely.

Elisabeth answers the challenge by returning to Suffolk after the referendum to visit her 'neighbour' (p. 43), 101-year-old Daniel Gluck. Elisabeth's affection for English-German-Jewish Daniel, which implicitly rebukes isolationism, is rooted in the aesthetic education she received from Daniel as a child. In the novel's 1990s sections (besides 2016, there are also sections in the 1940s and 1960s), Daniel teaches the young Elisabeth to tell stories and imagine 'pictures' that turn out to be lost collages by the British Pop artist Pauline Boty (pp. 69–74). Daniel animates Elisabeth's life as Prospero does Miranda's. In one dream, she imagines that Daniel 'pulls, straight out of his chest, of his collarbone, like a magician, a free-floating mass of the colour orange' (p. 39), pigmenting a void landscape. In another, she imagines that 'Miranda from The Tempest' arrives 'reading Brave New World' and bearing her a present from '[their] father': a bag of onions and potatoes. 'Never mind, she thinks, When Daniel comes, he'll know a way of making something with these' (pp. 204–5). In this way, though she does not grow up on a remote island without other human contact, it is nonetheless her formative relationship with a Prospero-like man of art that places her where she is: in the British Isles critiquing insularity, making something of nothing. It is thanks to Daniel that Elisabeth is a lecturer in the history of art, documenting xenophobic graffiti and the construction of an SA4A immigrant-detention facility for her work (pp. 138, 132). Whereas, in 2016, 'all across the country, the country was divided' (p. 61), Elisabeth is in the business of unifying – thinking of Daniel, once her 'neighbour', as her 'grandfather', saying simply 'I love him' (p. 216).

Just as Miranda's words are refracted through the dystopian lens of *Brave New World*, Smith's Miranda-function takes on levels of complexity. Because Prospero uses his art not just for Miranda's education but also to destroy his enemies, it is striking that Elisabeth experiences Daniel as wholly benevolent. In a way, Daniel is also her Ferdinand. And so she chips away at her mother's bitterness as Miranda does Prospero's, allowing her to see past his alleged foreignness and queerness. Wendy Demand learns, like Shakespeare's magician, that '[t]he rarer action is / In virtue than in vengeance' (*Tempest*, 5.1.27–8), unexpectedly (to Elisabeth's mind) voting 'Remain' and even protesting SA4A. In Daniel's memories, his younger sister Hannah is a second Miranda, tempering his bubbling hatred at the 'summer-jovial' Berlin that seems to him 'a kind of open threat' with the joy of film, literature and music (p. 184). Of Hannah, then (before the Nazis murdered her), he thinks: 'he now knows for sure that when she grows up she's going to be a great force in the world, an important thinker, a changer of things' (p. 189). Twinned in youth and in adulthood, Elisabeth and Hannah pair witness with action, much like the historical women with whose stories they mingle.[7] Doubling Miranda and orienting her towards two different Prosperos in this

---

[6] Cf. Aldous Huxley, *Brave New World* (New York, 1998), p. 210.
[7] Besides Boty, Smith also includes an interlude in which Daniel, trapped in a tree (Ariel-like) watches scenes from the life of Christine Keeler, centre of a 1960s British political scandal (pp. 89–103).

way, Smith uses *The Tempest* – which Elisabeth understands to be a play 'about a girl whose father, a magician, was sorting out her future for her' (p. 208) – to suggest the generational give-and-take required to turn revenge to love and enmity to kinship.

Smith's Shakespearian adaptation, if we can call it that, eschews A-to-B correspondences. *Autumn* is quite different from, say, Margaret Atwood's novelization of *The Tempest* in the same year, *Hag-Seed*.[8] Like all the Hogarth Shakespeares, Atwood's essentially transposes the plot and characters to a modern setting. The novel's Prospero is a washed-up former festival director, luring the Antonio-like rival who replaced him to his new home in a prison theatre programme. With some twists (for example, Miranda only exists as a voice in Prospero's head), Atwood is faithful to Shakespeare. This *Tempest* novel is in line with Hogarth's mission for the series, which cites the ways in which Shakespeare's plays 'have been reinterpreted for each new generation', explaining that 'The Hogarth Shakespeare project sees Shakespeare's works retold by acclaimed and bestselling novelists of today.'[9] In this formulation, the plays maintain their agential status in novels imagined as conduits between Shakespeare and modernity. Jeanette Winterson prefers to call her Hogarth novel, *The Gap of Time*, a 'cover version' of *The Winter's Tale*.[10] The term is apt, implying a rendition of Shakespeare that, though differing in medium and style, if overlaid would match the original almost exactly. To try the same with the *Seasonal Quartet* would be like placing all forty-five of Picasso's takes on *Las Meninas* over Velázquez's at once – multiple iterations of the same structure which, combined, produce sharp corners and chaotic scribbles, puncturing and obscuring the original.[11] Smith uses the plays to produce a kaleidoscope of divergent, convergent, endlessly tessellated meanings.[12] With Hogarth as counterpoint, it becomes easier to see Smith's Shakespearian tessellation in the *Seasonal Quartet* – a programme that grows more elaborate with each instalment.

Winter stands out as the most allegorical of the *Quartet* novels (Wisdom, Art, Light and Nature walk into a bar, or a great house in Cornwall), as well as the one with the most oblique engagement with Shakespeare. Even so, the novel riffs on *Cymbeline*, making Light and Nature – Lux and Iris, whose nickname is 'Ire' – Innogen-inspired, willing to don disguises and go behind enemy lines in pursuit of justice. Lux pretends to be Art's girlfriend, Charlotte, as well as English and heterosexual, though she is neither. In reality, she is one of the immigrants that Art's mother, 'Philo' Sophia, voted to ban. Sophia inherits her father's 'hatred of people from particular other countries, from his time in the war',[13] a prejudice which precluded her building a life with Art's father, none other than Daniel Gluck ('I didn't want his history to be his son's inheritance', she says) (p. 254). While Sophia considers herself 'more open-minded' in that she believes Lux (as 'Charlotte') 'every bit as English as myself' (113), Lux shows her that, although she is non-English, they are not at war, either. At the same time, Sophia thinks Ire/Iris, angry flower and 'great mythologizer' (p. 156), too militant for her willingness to occupy a nuclear testing site (p. 147), among other rebellions. Ire reinforces Lux's gentle theme of fellow-feeling with more entrenched logic, asserting that there's not 'a them and an us', but just an 'us', combatting her sister's view that the referendum was 'a vote to free our country from inheriting the troubles of other countries' (p. 206), and her nephew's that immigrants, having 'made their choice', are not Britain's 'responsibility' (pp. 54–5).

Thus, though Smith's Innogens are not British princesses but a Croatian refugee and an aging

---

[8] Margaret Atwood, *Hag-Seed* (New York, 2016).
[9] 'About', Hogarth Shakespeare (2020): hogarthshakespeare.com.
[10] Jeanette Winterson, *The Gap of Time* (New York, 2017).
[11] Velázquez's painting may be seen in the Prado in Madrid; Picasso's iterations may be seen in the Picasso Museum in Barcelona.
[12] This is true, too, of Smith's plays on *Oliver Twist* and *Orlando* in her earlier novels *Artful* (New York, 2012), and *How to Be Both* (London, 2014).
[13] Ali Smith, *Winter* (London, 2017), p. 113. Further references appear in parentheses.

hippie, respectively, they nonetheless hold a mirror to Britain's self-conception – or self-estrangement, as when Innogen says of Posthumus, 'My lord, I fear, / Has forgot Britain' (*Cymbeline*, 1.6.113–14). In this vein, Lux channels Innogen and spouts off a *Seasonal Quartet* manifesto when she recounts the plot of *Cymbeline*, her favourite play (pp. 197–201). Art is embarrassed to hear her 'making up a terrible bland fairytale plot that's nothing like Shakespeare and pretending it's Shakespeare' (p. 198), but Sophia recognizes the play, quotes it and muses, 'A play about a kingdom subsumed in chaos, lies, power-mongering, division and a great deal of poisoning and self-poisoning' (p. 200). Lux continues:

I read it and I thought, if this writer from this place can make this mad and bitter mess into this graceful thing it is at the end, where the balance comes back and all the lies are revealed and all the losses are compensated, and that's the place that made him, then that's the place I'm going, I'll go there, I'll live there. (p. 200)

Undercover, like Innogen as Fidele, Lux reintroduces her English interlocutors to their native tragicomedy. Conflating country and poet, she immigrates out of reverence for the kind of Shakespearian reversal she herself embodies. What's more, Lux's spot-on recollection of *Cymbeline* defamiliarizes everything Art believes he belongs to, bringing him home, Posthumus-like. As 'Charlotte' on Cornish shores, not unlike 'Fidele' in Milford Haven, Lux erodes the 'coastline' between Iris and Sophia and advocates the return of the severed head haunting Sophia – really half of Daniel's Barbara Hepworth statue, not to mention a version of Posthumus's presumed decapitation – to its rightful place (p. 284). When Cymbeline, reintroduced to his sons, exclaims, 'O Innogen, / Thou hast lost by this a kingdom', meaning her right to inherit the throne, she responds, 'No, my lord, / I have got two worlds by't' (5.6.374–5). Innogen's image flipped over the x-axis, Lux gains a surrogate family for Christmas, then is forced to Leave. In her afterglow, Iris and Art open the house and the blog, compensating what losses they can.

Pericles, the catalyst for *Spring*, follows a wandering man whose life appears to be over until he recovers his daughter Marina. *Spring*'s chief Marina figure is Florence, a 12-year-old refugee whose mother is detained by SA4A. As placeless as the baby born at sea, Florence jokes of her name, 'I'm a place, too ... City in Italy' (p. 189), poking fun at her Marina-esque association with renaissance, or rebirth. True to form, she exhibits otherworldly powers, walking into detention facilities undeterred ('age of miracles isn't past') (p. 129), successfully petitioning for the detainees' bathrooms to be cleaned, on one occasion ('Shit's all gone ... like magic') (p. 130), and for her mother to be freed on another (p. 138). Like Marina, Florence also breaks up a brothel, freeing underage girls who had been sexually trafficked to the UK. Convincing 'clients out of doing what they were in the middle of the doing' (p. 137), she recalls Marina 'preaching divinity' to a brothel patron who remarks, 'I'll do anything now that is virtuous, but I am out of the road of rutting forever' (*Pericles*, 19.4–9). Florence seeks conversions not of faith but of policy, imagining a world where 'instead of having to prove who you are with a paper booklet or by showing a screen your eye or the print in your finger or the information about your face', a person could show what they '*see*' and '*make*' (p. 196). Though this is not the first time *Pericles* has been connected to the refugee crisis,[14] it is perhaps the first time a novel has fitted Marina's powers of salvation into a mosaic of such wide-reaching political–aesthetic provocation.

Florence saves one Pericles, a washed-up film director named Richard, from throwing himself under a train (pp. 110–12). Richard is wandering, having lost his wife and daughter (who turn out to be Wendy and Elisabeth Demand of *Autumn*) to divorce, if not death. But the Thaisa Richard longs for is not his wife; she is his former screenwriter and best friend, Paddy. (In one memory, she asks him

---

[14] See Ewan Fernie and Katharine Craik, '*The Marina Project*' (Birmingham, 2017). See also Adam Smyth, 'Play for today', *London Review of Books*, 24 October 2019.

'who do you think you are, bloody Pericles of Tyre?' and he quips, 'Pericles of Tired') (p. 31). Furthermore, it is not his daughter whom he searches for, per se, though Richard converses with an imaginary Elisabeth in his head. Instead, Richard mourns a different sort of child, the perfect film he and Paddy would have made together if not for her untimely death (a biopic about Rainer Maria Rilke and Katherine Mansfield living in the same Swiss town in the 1920s). Like Marina, whom Pericles calls 'Thou that begett'st him that did thee beget' (21.183), Florence rebirths Richard as the artist he was with Paddy, the artist who could make the film Smith cheekily titles *April* (p. 45). The girl ferries Richard to the Scottish highlands, where they meet a Harriet-Tubman-type, Alda Lyons, who leads them to the safe harbour where Florence's mother has taken refuge. Revitalized, Richard kickstarts his dying career with a documentary about this underground railroad.

However, despite her efforts with another Pericles, a detention officer named Brittany (called 'Britannia', linking her to the nation and nationalism) (p. 134), Florence does not succeed in saving twice. In contrast to Richard, it is unclear what Brit searches for. Florence awakens her to just how aimless she is, as if 'the machine's' (as in 'Florence and') surveillance of those crossing the sea were even more misguided than Pericles's peregrinations around the Mediterranean (pp. 170–1). Where Richard changes his life's course, Brittany calls the authorities. She exposes the Auld Alliance, undoing years of work; several individuals, including a mother and toddler, are arrested. Though Brittany can imagine that even London pimps 'have been changed by it, and by her – properly changed, changed at life level' (p. 313), she herself is incontrovertible. She is curious about but cannot understand Florence's 'Book of Hot Air' (p. 323), scribblings that turn out to be the lyric interludes in the book we are reading. Florence's voice, like Lux's recounting *Cymbeline* and Elisabeth's reading *Brave New World*, is literalized as the novel's structural, aesthetic and political core. Yet, although Florence reiterates Elisabeth's and Lux's tragicomic concepts of transformation and homecoming, even in a story, stories are not a substitute for policy. The miracle that Florence brings about is not in 'the machine', but in the arts.

Making Shakespeare's daughters characters rather than symbols, Smith reconfigures and recombines Miranda, Innogen and Marina into narratives that include failure, relapse and apostasy as well as progress. The girls push the series forward towards a never-quite-realized vision of equitable community, meeting stiffer rejection in each iteration. Nevertheless, forming a beautiful pattern within her own work and across the *Quartet*, Elisabeth and Hannah, Lux and Iris, Florence and *April* seem to be paving the way for tragicomic resolution. When *Summer* was released in August 2020, one could not help but wonder if Perdita, the lost one, would be found – and whether she would rise to the mounting challenges of global crises.

'IMAGINE YOU ARE A FLOWER': *SUMMER*'S PERDITAS

In *Summer*, Smith's Shakespearian kaleidoscope puts on its most dazzling show yet. There is not just one lost girl, but many – and almost none of them is a girl.

First, there is 16-year-old Sacha Greenlaw, daughter of the recently separated Grace and Jeff (Hermione and Leontes?). Their adjacent homes jokingly recall the 'removed house' where Paulina visits Hermione 'twice or thrice a day' for exactly the length of Perdita/Sacha's life (*Winter's Tale*, 5.2.103–6). Pendant to Elisabeth Demand, over whose shoulder we watch the referendum, Sacha sees the 'Leave' vote put into practice and is tasked with imagining a remedy for the break: 'To mark one week since Brexit, they've all been made to write an essay on the subject of "Forgiveness". Sacha is deeply suspicious of forgiveness. The act of saying *I forgive you*, it's like saying *you are less than me and I have the moral or superior upper hand*' (p. 8). Sacha is positioned as victim, witness and judge. Brexit marks her life much as Leontes's wrath upends Perdita's: Sacha will come of age without EU citizenship, while Perdita is exiled from Sicilia before she even knows what a homeland is. Like Elisabeth, she is issued a challenge, too, though she scorns its very premise.

Sacha has been entrusted with the future; in a sense, she embodies the futurity towards which the previous novels' daughters have only gestured. Perdita bears a similar burden. According to the Delphic oracle, 'the King shall live without an heir if that which is lost be not found' (3.2.134–5). Repatriated, Perdita is as '[w]elcome hither, / As is the spring to th'earth' (5.1.150–1), regenerating the winter-worn Sicilia. Strikingly, however, Sacha's own predictions are dark; she doubts that she will reach her mother's age, 'given what's happening planetarily'. With all Generation Z's rejection of 'cruel optimism',[15] she watches the news of the wildfires in Australia; gives money to a homeless man, Steve, outside Tesco; criticizes the exploitation of bats and pangolins that may have caused COVID-19; and quotes Greta Thunberg. Others find her outspokenness annoying: Robert calls her his 'environ/mental sister'; Grace, her 'revolutionary daughter' (p. 67). While Sacha's admonitions have led many reviewers to call her a 'Cassandra', in fact they are what make her most Perdita. Sacha insists on acknowledging the past, hoping that 'now maybe we will realize that we have to stop being poisonous to each other and the world ... human beings will have to decide whether to be poisonous to others or not, whether we are in a pandemic or not' (pp. 247–8). Leontes might as well be speaking of her when he says, 'The blessèd gods / Purge all infection from our air whilst you / Do climate here' (5.1.167–9). Of course, Sacha no more has the power to cure COVID than Shakespeare had the power to predict it. But, like the 'inner summer' that she accesses while contemplating a (dubious) Hannah Arendt quotation for her essay assignment ('Forgiveness is the only way to reverse the irreversible flow of history') (p. 14), Sacha stands for historical responsibility, environmental stewardship and family bonds – all that she believes the world lacks. Facing the apocalypse, Sacha suggests that the only way forward is backward.

Sacha's 'inner summer' is 'that which is lost' to the *Quartet*'s characters, now united in one quest. When Robert glues an hourglass (really an hourglass-shaped egg timer) to Sacha's hand, which he calls her 'Present ... For the future' (p. 44), a process begins whereby the Greenlaws link up with Art and Charlotte in returning the marble 'child' to Daniel, who is now at Elisabeth's house in Suffolk. With this device, Smith burlesques Time, the Chorus who 'turn[s] [his] glass' at the beginning of act 4, making Shakespeare's restorative art an act of art restoration (4.1.16).[16] Theatre is in need of a pick-me-up, too, as manifest in Sacha's mother, Grace. In one extended sequence inside Sacha's mind, she ventriloquizes Grace, a former actor, saying: '*Imagine you are a flower in water but that your time of taking in water as a plant is over because you're naturally starting to dry up, and the water – though you can't understand it, being a flower and everything – no longer goes up your stem in the same old way*' (p. 27). Envisioning her mother as a desiccated flower, Sacha recalls that moment in *The Winter's Tale* when Perdita disputes whether 'gillyvors', 'nature's bastards' (4.4.82–3), are products of art or of nature. Using reverse psychology, Perdita convinces stodgy old Polixenes that breeding hybrids can make a garden more beautiful, much as inter-marriage between, say, a prince and a shepherdess (which Perdita at that point thinks she is) might be the most natural thing in the world. Sacha and Perdita share the task of renewal through return to ancient truths: nourishment, growth, the nature of things. Where Perdita begins their conversation by offering him 'flowers of winter' that, as Polixenes observes, '[w]ell ... fit our ages' (4.4.78–9), she rewards him at the end with a new bouquet of 'flowers / Of middle summer', more often given 'to men of middle age' (4.4.106–8). Perdita is thus closely aligned with what Polixenes confidently calls 'an art / Which

---

[15] Lauren Berlant, *Cruel Optimism* (Durham, NC, 2011).
[16] And who likely appeared throughout the play if, as Tiffany Stern has argued, other choruses were lost: Tiffany Stern, *Documents of Performance in Early Modern England* (Cambridge, 2009).

does mend nature – change it rather' (4.4.95–6). Smith plays on this moment when Arthur ('Art'), who has helped Sacha to remove the hourglass, says Sacha reminds him of his Aunt Iris and goes on to describe his blog, 'Art in nature', 'which provides thoughtful analysis of the shapes things take in art and nature, and, yeah, things like language too, and the structures of the ways we live, and so on' (pp. 95–6). Recalling *Winter*'s old radical, named for a flower, Smith (tongue-in-cheek as always) signals that the art of *Summer* lies neither in youth's power to transform age nor in forgiveness, but in the movement towards rootedness that Sacha represents.

Hannah returns from *Autumn* as Perdita reflected over the y-axis; like the prophecy bridging the 'gap of time' in *The Winter's Tale*, she spans the first and last novels as well as the temporal reaches of the action. Hannah dominates the second of the novel's two parts, which is made up of facing accounts of Daniel's and Hannah's lives in the summer of 1940. Now 104, Daniel, 'history personified' (p. 270), is warmed by memories of his 'autumn sister' as he drifts in and out of consciousness (p. 192). He thinks of her during his wartime internment on the Isle of Man ('Hannah may still be in Paris. There's no way of knowing') (p. 130). It is Hannah who would know Heine's poetry, Hannah who is 'sometimes a painter' and a 'lover of art' (pp. 170–4), Hannah who recognizes, as he did not, that Charlie Chaplin is 'evergreen' (p. 182). He writes to her *'we have been here behind the wire all through the bright open door of summer'* (p. 186), imaginatively enlisting a bird that might be a swift to wing his words to the fugitive abroad (p. 193). He reaches for her, too, in 2020, as Elisabeth, the Greenlaws, and his nurse – named Paulina, of course – come and go. This Hannah exists only for him, a figment or principle of moral certitude and aesthetic insight. The force that makes him live up to her nickname for him, 'summer brother' (p. 182), she is an absent presence, a missing link.

Hannah – in the darkness of World War II, ferrying Jewish refugees over the Swiss border, months away from execution – recovers the Perditan futurity at which Sacha scoffs. She spins a tale for her infant daughter in which the gods punish a summer day's pride, sending a frost to blight its flowers. But when the frost melts, the flowers 'dr[i]nk all the melted snow', and the townspeople '[a]re glad to have the flowers back, even for the short time a flower lasts. The townspeople knew that the flowers only last a summer, that summer is soon over' (p. 232). Asking her daughter, 'What will we make of this?', she instructs her in the art of memory, or the memory of art: make perfume, preserve the scent of summer flowers to tide you through the next winter (pp. 232–3). In a letter to Daniel, Hannah prays to the gods she does not believe in: '*if you're there can you please make that sunlit summer day longer and these dark days shorter*', begging '*that my girl will grow up / and that time will be kind to her*' (pp. 237–8). Despite the fact that Daniel never sees his sister again and never meets her baby girl, their lives are miraculously recovered when Sacha remembers her grandmother, the orphaned refugee for whom she is named (p. 271). The future that Hannah prays for is Sacha's present. This fulfilment, this continuity, gives Sacha a forward momentum and implicit, hopeful promise, even amid her own apocalypse.

However, Sacha and Hannah are not the only tessellations of Perdita. Grace, bitter about her divorce and her failed acting career, acts as the generational stepping stone between them when she returns to her 'immortal summer' in Suffolk. Remembering 'cornfields high', '[b]lue sky above, sea beyond' and 'the smell of cut grass' surrounding the 'Winter's Tale, summer 89' when she 'was Hermione', Grace recalls nothing short of the Arcadian world of Bohemia (p. 271). But when she abandons her children to retrace her steps of all those years ago, she realizes that it was a 'summer of discontent' after all (p. 276, cf. *Richard III*, 1.1.1–2). Rediscovering this ambivalence, she suddenly doubts the integrity of the seasons – and of Smith's chosen intertext. After a cast debate about why Shakespeare 'infects the play with winter' (pp. 282–4), Grace thinks: 'The Summer's Tale. There's no such play, Grace. Don't be fooled. The briefest and slipperiest of the seasons, the one that won't be held to account – because summer won't be held *at all*, except in bits, fragments, moments, flashes of memory of so-called or imagined perfect summers, summers that never existed' (p. 290). Grace's nostalgia now acts as literary criticism, exposing her conjured images of natural plenitude – images associated with Perdita – as hollow fiction, incompatible with the reality of *The Winter's Tale* or of *Summer*. Remembering her ungraciousness on a day in 1989, Grace asserts that her season, her daughter, herself cannot be held; they may not exist. *The Winter's Tale* might really be a tragedy after all, troubling the efficacy of summer, Perdita, hope and forgiveness all in one.

Reaching for her own Perdita-ness, Grace theorizes Perdita as less a person than a form or design. The problem – the source of her 'discontent', as it were, and the alleged reason Grace was not picked up by a West End casting agent at that point in her career – was that she missed her cue, '*turn good lady our Perdita is found*', failing to say 'You gods, look down, / And from your sacred vials pour your graces / Upon my daughter's head' (p. 279; cf. *Winter's Tale*, 5.3.121–4). As Hermione, she fails to bless Perdita; as herself, she resists the 'inner summer' of her own daughter, Sacha. Yet she gives herself an implicit injunction to pick up that cue as she relives the 'lovely, uncomplicated afternoon' spent with a joiner who taught her that a church lintel is also called a 'summer'. 'The most important beam, structurally', the summer can 'take a great weight', he instructs (pp. 295–6). This lesson metamorphoses her opinion of Shakespeare's play: '*The Winter's Tale*'s all about summer, really. It's like it says, don't worry, another world is possible. When you're stuck in the world at its worst, that's important. To be able to say that. At least to tend towards comedy' (p. 300). Summer might not be real, but it is strong. With Perdita as the lintel of *The Winter's Tale*, of *Summer* and of the *Seasonal Quartet*, we see the symmetry of Shakespeare's daughters from Miranda and Elisabeth to Sacha, Hannah and Grace. Helping the joiner to restore a pew 'good as old', Grace recalls the wrinkled Hermione, revealed to be 'warm' (p. 316), as well as her new willingness to join her daughter in looking the past in the eye.

There is one final Perdita, though – perhaps the most important one for Smith's *Seasonal Quartet*. For, as Grace journeys back to her 'immortal summer', as the memory of Hannah returns to Daniel, and as Sacha has '*brought back the child*' (p. 274), something remarkable happens. Daniel sees Hannah – the child Hannah, his autumn sister – in Robert Greenlaw.

'IT MAKES US US': THE LOST LEONTES

Considering the 'present for the future' that Robert gives Sacha (pp. 44–5), it seems counterintuitive that he should be Perdita, too. Indeed, as he superglues the hourglass to Sacha's hand, he channels no one so much as Leontes, who threatens to burn his newborn daughter or to dash out her 'bastard brains' with his own hands before abandoning her to crows (2.3.140–1). Such violence is entertainment to Robert, who plays a videogame called 'ABUSEHEAP' involving 'Perps' who torture 'Victims' with a repertoire that rivals Leontes's own 'wheels, racks, fires . . . flaying, boiling, / In leads or oils' (p. 65; *Winter's Tale* 3.2.175–6). A bigot who tells his father's Welsh girlfriend to leave 'his' country and gets kicked out of school for making racist remarks about Black people (pp. 17, 34), Robert believes he should be able to say anything, and that the words of others have no value. Waving his banner of 'freedom of speech', Robert says: 'I also explained to them why people hate women for being girly swots and only useful for having sex and having children, especially children that you don't admit to having, because being a man is all about spreading our seed' (p. 34). Robert's misogynistic vitriol echoes Leontes's vision of a 'bawdy planet' where wives are ponds 'sluiced' in the absence of their husband-owners, not to mention his obsession with whether Perdita and Mamillius are his 'issue' (1.2.191–208). Similarly, Robert's imperviousness to the interventions of others parrots Leontes's willingness to declare all the world 'nothing' without the 'just censure' and 'true opinion' only he (according to his mounting conspiracy theory) can access

(1.2.286–98; 2.1.38–55). Clicking through porn and ABUSEHEAP, the refrain of '*Bored*' resounding through his brain, 'Robert sighs the sigh of an ancient tyrant who's seen it all' (p. 65). Robert's behaviour, in Shakespeare's words, 'something savours / Of tyranny', as he seeks to penetrate the private hopes and dreams of those around him (2.3.119–20), exposing what he sees as either a fallacy to be ridiculed or a commodity to be stolen.

However, beneath Robert's cruelty is vulnerability owing to a genuine lack of discernment. The 13-year-old's initial grasp for power involves hiding the television remote, forcing others to abide the ear-splitting volume (p. 16). This juvenile prank reveals the flaw in Robert's thinking, though: while Robert declares absurdly 'I am The Remote' (p. 75), he has in fact posted the remote, so that his claim to absolute power is synonymous with an admission of irreversible chaos (control, according to Smith's pun, is now itself remote). Robert's problem is just this: an inability or unwillingness to distinguish between the speciously similar. Thus, to Robert, his heroes Albert Einstein and Boris Johnson are interchangeable, for where Einstein 'rewrite[s] the universal truths to make them truer', Johnson is skilled in 'the brilliant application of lies' (pp. 54–5). Seeing patterns where there are none, Robert is in danger of becoming what Charlotte describes in *Winter*: 'like beings who'd been birthed not by real historical time and people' but by 'plastic carrier bags', '[t]hat unhistoried', '[t]hat inhuman' (*Winter*, pp. 56–7). But through his love of Einstein, who, as Robert tells Charlotte, 'says the future is an illusion . . . *And* the past. *And* the present' (*Summer*, p. 82), Robert nearly grasps the truth of interconnectedness, of filiation. What is required is that he see the 'illusion' as evidence of his duty to the future, rather than as a reason for repudiating it. The hourglass physicalizes both his particular error and Smith's diagnosis of the post-Brexit situation: a twisted futurity that looks like summer but is really a scorched earth.

Surprisingly, Robert as Leontes shares edges with Sacha and Grace as Perdita. Smith picks up on the commonality of these characters in *The Winter's Tale*, where Perdita is 'the whole matter / And copy of [her] father' (2.3.99–100). Leontes and Perdita are made of the same stuff. Likewise, in *Summer*, though Robert thinks that 'summer can fuck off, it's never as good as you think it'll be' (p. 100), he has just as much 'inner summer' as his sister. Creative and intelligent, he makes short films in his spare time. For a school project he connects the data points of facial recognition technology, forming constellations on the faces of people he loves (he calls it '[F]ART') (pp. 365–7). He possesses the transforming powers of Elisabeth, Lux and Florence, Miranda, Innogen and Marina: he can change people's minds, he can join hands, he can find what others are looking for. The catch is that this summer-quality lies dormant. Sacha, echoing Daniel's appraisal of Hannah in *Autumn*, 'knows [Robert] is brilliant', lamenting that he 'has attached a dimmer switch to his own brilliance and like he is randomly turning it down as low and dark as it can go' (pp. 37–8). This light metaphor continues when Robert is 'sunstruck' by Charlotte (p. 75). He muses: 'It is the first time Robert has ever thought of the world in terms of there being more than himself in it. So how do you find the person you found if you lose the person after finding them and then there are a lot of long dark years between you?' (p. 102). Robert thinks he is thinking about a trick of space–time whereby he and Charlotte would be the same age, but he is in fact demonstrating the ways in which he folds attributes of Leontes (the one who must find that which was lost, according to the prophecy) and Perdita (the lost one) into himself. This literal and metaphorical kinship between the two characters in Shakespeare is what Smith expands and, again, tessellates. This is the insight of *Summer*: that Perdita and Leontes can be the same person. In a Smithian twist, Robert – an internet troll who loves xenophobia, austerity and exploitation – is the missing princess, too.

As Perdita, Robert – who nearly shares a name with the author of *The Winter's Tale*'s Renaissance source, *Pandosto, The Triumph of Time*[17] – brings us back to the *Quartet*'s origin point. Of course, the

---

[17] Robert Greene, *Pandosto, The Triumph of Time* (London, 1588).

Greenlaws only journey to Suffolk because of Robert – both because of the hourglass, which brought Art and Charlotte into their lives, and because of Einstein, whose brief sojourn in Cromer leads Robert to ask the bloggers if he can join them on their trip to see Elisabeth and Daniel (p. 111). Because of him, the four novels meet as they all behold a marble sphere, 'the child' which is Art (secret son of Daniel), Elisabeth (estranged daughter of Richard), Sacha and Robert (great-grandchildren of Hannah). Lightly recalling Shakespeare's oracle, Robert intuits that 'there was some forcefield involved whereby nobody could leave the house until the curse was solved or the destiny was met or the whatever was fulfilled' (p. 108). The fulfilment comes. Robert is substituted for Sacha in the Hannah lineage when Daniel sees Robert as his own long-dead sister, thinking: 'It's her. It's her young self. It's the copy of her young self ... it's Hannah, God help him, there in the room, aged twelve, in the shape of a boy' (p. 195). As the 'summer brother' beholds his 'autumn sister', 'the child' that returns is more than Hannah, for in this grandson of the prayed-for first Sacha, the gap between *Autumn* and *Summer* is filled. Appropriately, when Daniel jokes, 'I thought time had quite undone us' (p. 195), Robert explains some elaborate Einsteinian propositions, asking, in a version of Hannah's bedtime-story call-and-response, 'What does it all make?' (p. 197). When Daniel repeats the question, we watch Robert answer through his eyes: 'It makes you and I more than just you or I, Hannah says. It makes us us' (p. 197). No longer a plastic carrier bag, Robert is reintegrated into his family, into humanity. (What's more, we learn that Jeff chose Sacha's name, and Grace Robert's (after 'Sweet Robert', a foul-smelling herb with healing properties) (p. 304), making him the legacy of her 'immortal summer'.) Robert has been found. Daniel sees him as the Miranda who helped him to help Elisabeth, so that Elisabeth could love Art, so that Art could free Charlotte, so that Charlotte could do a work of kindness for Robert. Read rightly, Robert completes the pattern.

This interweaving of generations, relations, actions and consequences is difficult to trace, but what it says (or doesn't say) becomes more legible through viewing what Ali Smith has made against the Shakespearian plays from which she draws inspiration. Smith not only makes Shakespeare's tyrant into a pubescent boy torn by opposite forces – a victim of bullying, a child of divorce, an undernourished genius. She makes the tyrant into the one who is lost. Robert is a 13-year-old English boy in 2020 whom Daniel mistakes for his German Jewish sister in 1945. The future that Ali Smith's *Seasonal Quartet* imagines lies not so much in an age of summer as in realizing that the years are cyclical; that after summer comes autumn, and that summer only has meaning if we keep an eye trained on the winter behind us. Where *The Winter's Tale* ends with Leontes asking his restored wife and daughter to tell him what happened to them in the years they were apart, *Summer* pivots on the moment when friendly strangers say to Robert: 'And you ... can tell us all at last the story of the hourglass and the glue' (pp. 113–14). As it converses with and elaborates on *The Winter's Tale*, *Summer* reinforces the idea that with time – and the right stories – we will move on.

GRAFTED TO THE MOOR: ANGLO-SPANISH DYNASTIC MARRIAGE AND MISCEGENATED WHITENESS IN *THE WINTER'S TALE*

ZAINAB S. CHEEMA

Shakespeare's late romances engage with the dynastic politics of Jacobean England, particularly through the theme of achieving redemption through royal children and their politically advantageous marriages. In the narrative trajectory of *The Winter's Tale*, the interruption and restoration of Leontes's and Polixenes' relations over the arc of the dramatic plot are entangled with the international order as defined by the bilateral relations of Bohemia and Sicilia. By the play's end, the cross-border marriage of Perdita and Florizel forges the integration of the two kingdoms.[1] In this article, I suggest that *The Winter's Tale* represents the anxieties and potentialities of Anglo-Spanish peace through the Spanish match. I ground this reading upon the racialized associations of Sicilia, which have hitherto not sufficiently been considered in analyses of Leontes and his family. At the time the play was written and first performed, Sicilia was a part of Habsburg Spanish territory, having been incorporated in the sovereignty of the kingdom of Aragon following Frederick III's 1296 coronation in Palermo.[2] James I's pursuit of peace with Continental Europe was initially welcomed by a war-weary England whose economy had been devastated by prolonged naval war with Spain. The Treaty of London was signed in 1604 and ratified in 1605 through the embassy to Valladolid headed by Lord Admiral Charles Howard, the Earl of Nottingham. This embassy was a watershed event: it re-established trade with the Habsburg Empire, established cultural exchange, and suspended Anglo-Spanish naval war, thus paving the way for England's colonial settlement in the Americas. During the period in which Shakespeare's play is estimated to have been composed – from 1608 to 1611, but especially 1610–11 – the political ideology of cross-border grafting would have centred around a dynastic marriage between Prince Henry and a Catholic Habsburg princess, the Infanta Ana, until her 1612 betrothal to the dauphin of France.[3] While the Spanish match came to represent an existential threat to English sovereignty by the 1618 outbreak of the Bohemian Crown crisis, Shakespeare's meditation on bilateral relations in *The Winter's Tale* reflects a more celebratory mood surrounding re-established Anglo-Spanish diplomatic relations following the 1605 ratification of the Treaty of London. Nevertheless, anxieties regarding dynastic incorporation with Habsburg Spain can still be traced in this late romance, given the racialized tropes of Spaniards disseminated in English culture from the Elizabethan period onwards.

---

[1] Christopher Warren and Donna Hamilton read the two kingdoms as a topical representation of England and Scotland. See Christopher Warren, *Literature and the Law of Nations, 1580–1680* (Oxford, 2015); Donna Hamilton, 'The Winter's Tale and the language of Union, 1604–1610', *Shakespeare Studies* 21 (1993), 228–52.

[2] See Clifford Backman, *The Decline and Fall of Medieval Sicily: Politics, Religion, and Economy in the Reign of Frederick III, 1296–1337* (Cambridge, 1995), pp. 29–84.

[3] Glyn Redworth notes that, on his ascension to the throne of England, James pursued the Spanish match as a sign that his newly minted dynasty was worthy to be allied with the Habsburgs. In 1611, James sent John Digby on his first embassy to Spain to request the hand of the Infanta Ana for Prince Henry. Until Ana's 1612 betrothal to the French dauphin, an Anglo-Spanish dynastic match appeared likely. See Glyn Redworth, *The Prince and the Infanta: The Cultural Politics of the Spanish Match* (New Haven and London, 2003), pp. 7–11.

GRAFTED TO THE MOOR: ANGLO-SPANISH DYNASTIC MARRIAGE

David Sterling Brown has stressed the need to talk about race broadly and consistently throughout Shakespeare's oeuvre, thus broadening the canon of the 'race plays'.[4] *The Winter's Tale* is not conventionally numbered amongst Shakespeare's race plays. However, reading Anglo-Spanish relations through the play's Bohemian–Sicilian relations illustrates how Shakespeare might have thought about formations of power, pleasure and gendered property through which early modern England was re-imagining whiteness vis-à-vis its imperial competitor Spain. The subtext of Sicilia's Iberian racialization is pertinent to this article's analysis of Perdita as a border figure who is associated with the wealth of Spain's colonial possessions in the Americas, and who becomes incorporated in England by marrying Florizel. Scholars addressing the matter of Spain in early modern England have discussed England's competition with and emulation of the Iberian pan-Atlantic Empire, even as the English press continued to circulate the Black Legend as a way of racially othering Spain and countering its monopolistic claim to the New World.[5] While these studies discuss the coexistence of imperial emulation and racial othering in English attitudes towards the Spanish, they have not sufficiently addressed how renewed Anglo-Spanish negotiations for cross-border marriage influenced racial imaginaries[6] in the early period of James I's reign. If racial imaginaries can be defined as structures of feeling that reproduce power relations,[7] what does the hypervisibility of Perdita's white beauty in the play tell us about the mobile and unstable formations of whiteness during the period of England's transatlantic expansion and diplomacy for Anglo-Spanish dynastic marriage?

In this article, I examine this question by firstly showing how the bilateral political world of *The Winter's Tale* allegorizes Anglo-Spanish relations of the early Jacobean period, and how Perdita encapsulates the fantasy of England consolidating pan-Atlantic imperial power through the cross-racial romance of the Spanish match. This analysis rests upon the recognition of the racial miscegenation embodied by the Spanish, who were characterized by the Black Legend as mixed with the blood of Moors and Jews. Francesca Royster has analysed hyperwhiteness in early modern English as a racialized marker variously associated with groups such as Goths, Scythians or Spaniards, while Noémie Ndiaye has discussed early modern English culture's anxieties of hybridity resulting from incorporating with racially mixed Iberians and their social practices.[8] Critical race theory has also illustrated that whiteness not only is enforced by property relations – whiteness is itself a form of property that alienates to the claimant reserves of power, pleasure and capital.[9] Unlike colonial propaganda in the Elizabethan period, which was shaped by the overdetermined tropes of purity and geography organized around the Virgin Queen's body, early Jacobean discourse worked through the material praxis of hybrid Atlantics, whereby English notions of colonial property were influenced by the imaginary of the Spanish Americas. I argue that Perdita's racialized beauty in the play embodies the transcolonial property desired by Jacobean England in ways that foreground the pleasures and anxieties of miscegenated whiteness.

Scholars have pointed out the flux and variability in early modern paradigms of race. In early modern England, emergent notions of race as biological

---

[4] See David Sterling Brown, 'Code Black: whiteness and unmanliness in Hamlet', in *Hamlet: State of the Play*, ed. Sonia Massai and Lucy Munro (London, 2021), pp. 101–27, esp. pp. 101–2 and 126–7.

[5] For example, see Eric Griffin, *English Renaissance Drama and the Specter of Spain: Ethnopoetics and Empire* (Philadelphia, 2009), and a number of the essays in *Representing Imperial Rivalry in the Early Modern Mediterranean*, ed. Barbara Fuchs and Emily Weissbourd (Toronto, 2015).

[6] I use the phrase 'racial imaginaries' in reference to Claudia Rankine and Beth Loffreda's essay, 'On whiteness and the racial imaginary', *Literary Hub*, 9 April 2015: https://lithub.com/on-whiteness-and-the-racial-imaginary.

[7] Rankine and Loffreda, 'On whiteness'.

[8] Francesca Royster, 'White-limed walls: whiteness and Gothic extremism in Shakespeare's *Titus Andronicus*', *Shakespeare Quarterly* 51 (2000), 432–55; Noémie Ndiaye, 'Aaron's roots: Spaniards, Englishmen, and Blackamoors in *Titus Andronicus*', *Early Theatre* 19 (2016), 59–80.

[9] See Cheryl I. Harris, 'Whiteness as property', *Harvard Law Review* 106 (June 1993), 1709–91.

essence interacted with other racialized categories of difference such as gender, class, religion, lineage, climate and geohumoral states.[10] While the term 'miscegenation' entered English in the nineteenth century, the concept of racial mixing could often be discussed in the early modern period through terms associated with horticulture and husbandry.[11] In this article, I nevertheless use the term 'miscegenation' when analysing the play's representation of grafting, horticulture and domesticated bodies as racial imaginaries. While early modern racial ideologies are different from nineteenth-century ones, 'miscegenation' captures the dynamic of inscribing and performatively crossing racial boundaries that is integral to the materialization of race as a hierarchical system of domination. In *The Winter's Tale*, the fantasy of domesticating and appropriating Spain's colonial wealth generated considerable anxiety around whiteness as a privileged identity category in early modern England. On the one hand, Perdita's domestication in the Bohemian countryside signifies the transfer of colonial wealth to England, to be consolidated through her marriage with Florizel. However, Perdita's racial passing as Bohemian, Sicilian and North African in various scenes of the play foregrounds the epistemic problem of *both* Iberian and English whiteness being racially mixed with Blackness; she enables this by activating historical memories of Anglo-Spanish dynastic marriages, and also by disclosing race in early Jacobean contexts as a performative repertoire whose logic is to enable the desires and pleasures of transcolonial power. Within the context of the flux in racial ideologies during this period, I argue that whiteness in Shakespeare's late romance can at times emulate Renaissance discourses of Blackness to facilitate political hegemony and transatlantic empire. As Patricia Akhimie has observed of *The Comedy of Errors*, moments of tension in Shakespeare's plays often pressurize the logic of racialism in ways 'suggesting that social differentiation is not a biological but an ideological process'.[12] In this article, I hope to show the anti-racist implications of examining the variable, shifting, often circuitous processes by which whiteness came to be reified in the racial imagination of England's coloniality of power.[13] That is, Shakespeare's play captures how,

in charged moments such as England's negotiation of increased access to transatlantic power via peace with Spain and a possible Anglo-Spanish match, a double move occurs: whiteness's ideological welding to Atlantic colonialization is strengthened, even as whiteness is pressurized in exposing itself as a myriad and fragmentary set of formations.[14] Undoing whiteness at a critical moment in its trajectory towards the hegemonic universalism that it assumed in the eighteenth century is an exercise in allyship that clears space for stories showing how Black lives mattered in the early Renaissance.[15] As Toni Morrison has shown, the construction of Blackness as other has been necessary to the production and performance of whiteness.[16] In addition, showing the extent to which whiteness mimetically borrowed from its own myriad constructions of

---

[10] See Kim Hall, *Things of Darkness: Economies of Race and Gender in Early Modern England* (Ithaca, 1995), pp. 1–24; Sujata Iyengar, *Shades of Difference: Mythologies of Skin Color in Early Modern England* (Philadelphia, 2005), pp. 1–18; Mary Floyd-Wilson, *English Ethnicity and Race in Early Modern Drama* (Cambridge, 2003), pp. 1–5; Jean Feerick, *Strangers in Blood: Relocating Race in the Renaissance* (Toronto, 2010), p. 14.

[11] Jean Feerick, 'The imperial graft: horticulture, hybridity, and the art of mingling races in *Henry V* and *Cymbeline*', in *The Oxford Handbook of Shakespeare and Embodiment: Gender, Sexuality, and Race*, ed. Valerie Traub (Oxford, 2016), pp. 211–27; p. 213.

[12] Patricia Akhimie, *Shakespeare and the Cultivation of Difference: Race and Conduct in the Early Modern World* (New York and London, 2018), p. 86.

[13] The phrase 'coloniality of power' is a reference to Aníbal Quijano's seminal theory. See Aníbal Quijano, 'Coloniality of power, Eurocentrism, and Latin America', *Nepantla: Views from South* 1 (2000), 533–80.

[14] As Ruth Frankenberg has noted, whiteness is not singular: it is a set of socially constructed locations fluidly modulated by local and translocal matrices. See ' Introduction: local whitenesses, localizing whiteness', in *Displacing Whiteness: Essays in Social and Cultural Criticism*, ed. Frankenberg (Durham, NC, 1997), p. 20.

[15] Cassander L. Smith, Nicholas R. Jones and Miles P. Grier, 'Introduction: the contours of a field', in *Early Modern Black Diaspora Studies: A Critical Anthology* (Cham, Switzerland, 2018), p. 2.

[16] Toni Morrison, *Playing in the Dark: Whiteness and the Literary Imagination* (New York, 1993), p. 6.

Blackness as other helps to uncover Blackness at the very centre – not just the margins or fringes – of white power.

A question emerges in the context of the play's repeated description of Perdita as 'white'. If Shakespeare codes Perdita as Spanish, why would the play identify her with miscegenation? While the Black Legend ethno-racialized Spanish as of mixed blood, the English also rhetorically blackened other groups such as Jews, Italians and Irish (not to mention marginalized demographics such as women and the lower classes). If Perdita is a white European Spaniard, how is she miscegenated? In Stephen Knadler's discussion of the term, 'miscegenated whiteness' defines the self-realization of those identifying as white that their whiteness is in fact variegated and fragmented along fluid hierarchies modulated by regional, national, ethnic, gender and class differences. In those identifying as white, this self-realization of one's position in a 'genealogy of white racial variations' awakens the awareness that the white individual could be both white and non-white/other/barbarian.[17] This is pertinent to the early Atlantic context of colonialism and racial formation informing *The Winter's Tale*. While early modern Spanish constructions of race are beyond the scope of this article, the formations of *limpieza de sangre* (blood purity) driving Spanish inquisitorial surveillance and transatlantic colonization are as fluid and anxiety-fuelled as the racial structures of feeling emerging in England.[18] Reading Perdita through the lens of miscegenated whiteness shows the pervasiveness of racialized understandings of difference even where we might least expect them, in Shakespearian texts whose characters appear to be all 'white'.

SITUATING SICILIA AND BOHEMIA IN THE CONTEXT OF ANGLO-SPANISH RELATIONS

In one of his changes to the main source text for *The Winter's Tale*, Robert Greene's 1588 prose romance *Pandosto: The Triumph of Time*, Shakespeare switches the kingdoms of the two boyhood friends, Leontes and Polixenes. Whereas Greene depicts Pandosto (Leontes) as the King of Bohemia, and Erastus (Polixenes) as King of Sicilia, Shakespeare makes Leontes the King of Sicilia and Polixenes the King of Bohemia. The links between Spain and Sicily were established in Renaissance *belles lettres*. For instance, Thomas Elyot's 1533 *Dictionary* defines the Sicani as 'a people in Spayne' and Sicania as 'a country in the Ile of Sicilie', referencing classical ethnographies by historians such as Thucydides who described the Sicani as the first people to inhabit Sicily by emigrating from the Iberian peninsula.[19] After Peter III of Aragón was crowned king of Sicily in 1282 and the Castilian and Aragonese crowns were united in 1479, the king of Aragón's full regnal title officially incorporated the honorific 'King of the Two Sicilies'. As the Habsburg dynasty increasingly moved towards centralized monarchy over the course of the sixteenth and early seventeenth centuries, 'King of the Two Sicilies' became part of the official titles of the king of Spain. References to Spain's dominion over Sicily circulated in early modern English print. George Abbot's *A Briefe Description of the Whole Worlde* (1599) describes the island as 'now also under the king of Spaine: who among his other titles, calleth himselfe king of both the Cicilies'.[20] *The Present State of Spain* (1594),

---

[17] Stephen Knadler, 'Miscegenated whiteness: Rebecca Harding Davis, the "civil-izing" war, and female racism', *Nineteenth-Century Literature* 57 (2002), 64–99; p. 71.

[18] While many literary examples of racial anxiety in Spain abound, scholars often cite Miguel de Cervantes Saavedra's *entremés* 'El retablo de las maravillas' ('The Puppet Show of Wonders'), in which a pair of tricksters con an entire village into believing an imaginary puppet show is real by telling them that only those with blood purity will be able to see the show. See, e.g., Carine Herzig, 'La cuestión de la limpieza de sangre y la disimulación religiosa en algunos entremeses del siglo XVII: de la burla a la sátira social', *Les Cahiers de Framespa* 34 (2020): https://doi.org/10.4000/framespa.8903.

[19] Roberto Nicolai, 'Κατ' ἔθνη καὶ κατὰ πόλεις: from catalogues to archaeology', in *Thucydides between History and Literature*, ed. Antonis Tsakmakis and Melina Tamiolaki (Berlin, 2013), pp. 139–52; pp. 148–50.

[20] George Abbot, *A Briefe Description of the Whole Worlde Wherein is Particularly Described all the Monarchies, Empires, and Kingdomes of the Same* (1599): STC 24.5, *EEBO*.

a translation from a French text, taunted Philip II for claiming Sicily through the bastard Henry II of Castile. 'And by this king, albeit a bastard, commeth all the title that king *Phillip* at this presente raygning hath in Spaine: as in like manner from the side of Bastardes commeth all the rights and titles which he pretendeth to *Milan, Naples, Sicilia*.'[21] Moreover, early modern histories and geographies also cite Sicily's Moorish past to signify the otherness of its hybrid cartography, presenting it as a counterpart to Spain's own history of Moorish rule for early modern English audiences. For instance, *The Mahumetane or Turkish Historie* (1600) described 'the Sarazins of Affrick' as having 'pilled and sacked the Isles of Candia and Sicilia, and so held them more than two hundred yeeres'.[22] Similarly, post-Reconquista Spain was portrayed in French and other European accounts as a space of otherness, marked with material, racial and cultural mixture deriving from the 800 or so years of Moorish rule in Iberia.[23] The essentializing Blackness of this mythology inflects Spain as 'consistently associated with Islam, with Africa, with dark peoples' – its cruel excesses in the New World colonies so desired by rival European kingdoms were attributed to 'its intrinsic Moorishness'.[24] I argue that, as dominion of and historical analogue to Habsburg Spain, Sicilia in *The Winter's Tale* operates as an allegory for England's imagination of a racially miscegenated Spain.

Allegory can be topical, but it is not necessarily synchronic; rather, it enfolds complex constellations of time and place in the relationalities that it imaginatively charts. This applies to the geographic allegories of the two kingdoms in *The Winter's Tale*. Even as the topos of Sicilia in *The Winter's Tale* figures Spain through complex associations of time and space, the play's construction of a coastal Bohemia stands in for England. Early modern geographies describe the lush forests, rivers and verdant beauty of Bohemia, which offers an ekphrastic analogue to the pastoral landscapes of the festive green world in Shakespeare's plays.[25] In its description of Germania, *An Epitome of Ortelius His Theater of the World* observes that 'within it lieth the Kingdome of Bohemia' and that '[it] is a country mightely replenished with goodly cities townes and villages, & exceeding populus, hauing therein many goodly riuers'. It describes Bohemia as 'compassed about with hilles & woods'.[26] Robert Stafford's *A geographicall and anthologicall description of all the empires and kingdoms* similarly calls Bohemia 'a very pleasant kingdom, compast about with a wood called *Sylua Hyrcinia*'.[27] The green world bears a close relationship with the emergent nationhood of England's self-imagination; geographical descriptions of Bohemia are evocative of the English green world. Reading Bohemia as an allegory for England also addresses the geographic implausibility of Antigonus and Perdita arriving at landlocked Bohemia by ship on the open sea.

ANGLO-SPANISH MARRIAGE AND THE BRITISH UNION

As one of Shakespeare's late romances, *The Winter's Tale* is shaped by the genre's impulses towards hybridity and colonial expansion. The paradigm of inter-racial marriage in early modern English romance often unfolds in a unidirectional and gender-specific manner to facilitate the colonization of foreign territories.[28] *The Winter's Tale* sets up

---

[21] Abraham Ortelius, *An Epitome of Ortelius His Theater of the Vvorld, Vvherein the Principal Regions of the Earth are Descrived in Smalle Mappes* (1601): STC 18857, EEBO.
[22] *The Mahumetane or Turkish Historie containing three bookes* (1600): STC 17997, EEBO.
[23] Barbara Fuchs, *Exotic Nation: Maurophilia and the Construction of Early Modern Spain* (Philadelphia, 2009), pp. 3–6.
[24] Fuchs, *Exotic Nation*, p. 117.
[25] See C. L. Barber, *Shakespeare's Festive Comedy: A Study of Dramatic Form and Its Relation to Social Custom* (Princeton, 2011); Mary Floyd-Wilson, *Geographies of Embodiment in Early Modern England* (Oxford, 2020), p. 135.
[26] Ortelius, *An Epitome of Ortelius His Theater of the Vvorld*.
[27] Robert Stafford, *A geographicall and anthologicall description of all the empires and kingdomes, both of the continent and ilands in this terrestrial globe* (1607): STC 23135, EEBO.
[28] Carmen Nocentelli, 'The erotics of mercantile imperialism: cross-cultural requitedness in the early modern period', *The Journal for Early Modern Cultural Studies* 8 (2008), 134–52; pp. 134–40.

a comparison between wealthy, magnificent Sicilia and a pastoral Bohemia whose regenerative green world offers a favourable contrast to the artificiality of the Sicilian court world, but which is likewise governed by an absolutist monarch.[29] By the end of the play, the harmonization effected by the romance plot enables restoration of bilateral relations in a way that advances Bohemia's power – Perdita's marriage to Florizel grafts the wealthy kingdom whose entertainments had so astonished the Bohemian delegation to Bohemia itself. The play demonstrates the proper conditions under which the Spanish match is beneficial rather than harmful to England. In effect, the Spanish match as embodied by Florizel and Perdita's marriage imaginatively achieves Bohemia's national consolidation and imperial expansion, amplifying the wealth and upward mobility of even the low-class subjects of the kingdom – by the end of the play, the Bohemian commoners of Perdita's adopted family, such as the Shepherd and Clown, are notably made gentlemen (5.2.133–42). The colonial logic driving the tragicomic plot of *The Winter's Tale* necessitates the tragic death of Mamillius, one of the unredeemed losses in the play. The utopic possibilities of the cross-border marriage between Florizel and Perdita offer a vision of trans-imperial incorporation that is predicated upon a reformable Sicilia that becomes marital real estate through the daughter's marriage following the death of the male heir.

I read the political and racial desires and anxieties provoked by the romance plot's trajectory towards Florizel and Perdita's marriage as channelling the discourse surrounding Prince Henry's Spanish match. *The Winter's Tale* has a distinct association with Prince Henry given its incorporation of the dance of satyrs from the 1611 Masque of Oberon, which Ben Jonson composed for Henry's investiture ceremonies as Prince of Wales.[30] By 1611, Prince Henry became the centre of a cult of propaganda that fashioned him as the future king who would fulfil England's mandate to gain transatlantic power to rival Spain and Portugal's. In particular, Prince Henry's cult was associated with the expansion of England's transatlantic dominions at the expense of Spain's. Influenced by the mentorship of Sir Walter Raleigh, Henry became a champion for English colonialism, spearheading efforts to compete with Spain for naval power and overseas territories. He took an active interest in the Virginia Company, investing part of his own revenue to become an official shareholder in the Company, and was thereafter called the Patron of the Virginia Plantation.[31] He also became patron of the Northwest Passage Company in order to find a sea-route across the top of America and open up the lucrative oriental trade to British merchants, choosing as his motto the expansionist *Fas est aliorum quaerere regna*: 'It is right to ask for the kingdoms of others.'[32]

Additionally, Henry was associated with amorous Catholic liaisons: in 1611–1612, he was reputed to have had an affair with the Catholic Frances Howard, daughter of Thomas Howard, the Earl of Suffolk, a member of the Spanish faction at the Jacobean court.[33] Moreover, in 1611, James I sent John Digby, the future Earl of Bristol, to Madrid to request the Infanta Ana's hand in matrimony for Prince Henry.[34] As Philip III was concurrently entertaining proposals for Ana from the French court, other Habsburg matches suggested for Prince Henry included the daughter of Charles Emmanuel of Savoy. Despite his Protestant scruples, Henry tepidly assented in October 1612 to plans to wed him to a Catholic Habsburg princess, writing to James that it was 'for your Majesty to

---

[29] Carol Thomas Neely, 'The Winter's Tale: the triumph of speech', *Studies in English Literature 1500–1900* 15 (1975), 321–38; p. 331.

[30] Glynne Wickham, 'Romance and emblem: a study in the dramatic structure of *The Winter's Tale*', in *The Elizabethan Theatre III*, ed. David Galloway (Toronto and London, 1973), pp. 82–99.

[31] J. W. Williamson, *The Myth of the Conqueror, Prince Henry Stuart: A Study of 17th Century Personation* (New York, 1978), p. 51.

[32] Sarah Fraser, *The Prince Who Would Be King: The Life and Death of Henry Stuart* (London, 2017), p. xx.

[33] Roy Strong, *Henry, Prince of Wales and England's Lost Renaissance* (London, 1986), p. 56.

[34] Williamson, *The Myth of the Conqueror*, p. 51.

resolve what course is most convenient to be taken by the rules of State ... [and] my part to play, which is to be in love with any of them, is not yet at hand'.[35] In the 1610–1611 period, a Habsburg match for Prince Henry had appeared all too likely, which generated considerable racial tension. However, royal propaganda under James revisited historic Anglo-Spanish dynastic alliances to make a case for kingdoms becoming dynastically grafted to one another once again. As I argue in the following section, these racial tensions are reflected in *The Winter's Tale*'s adaptation of the romance trope of cross-border marriage through the relationship of Florizel and Perdita. While Shakespeare's late play embraces romance's generic impulses towards recuperation, it also articulates racial anxieties respecting the alterity of Spaniards as kin and other.

PERDITA'S RACIAL PASSING AND WHITENESS AS MISCEGENATION

As Peter Erickson has observed, Shakespeare's early Jacobean plays represent the shift in racial logics of whiteness, influenced by the re-gendering of sovereignty around the persona of the patriarchal king and his family, away from the archetype of the Virgin Queen.[36] Channelling the promise of reproductive futurity embodied by his thriving family, James's sponsorship of the Spanish match re-activated narratives of consolidating dynastic power through cross-border marriage. Nevertheless, cross-border marriage as represented by the Spanish match also troubled conceptions of whiteness as representing genealogical purity of blood, foregrounding the fluid and shifting conceptions of race in this period. *The Winter's Tale* foregrounds this shift in racial ideologies through the figure of the racially mixed Iberian princess staging the performativity of not just Iberian whiteness, but English whiteness as well. In this section of the article, I analyse Perdita's cross-dressing as Bohemian and Libyan in acts 4 and 5 before an erotic male gaze that finds pleasure in, but also registers the performativity of, her racial passing. I argue that Perdita's almost too competent performativity foregrounds the anxieties and pleasures of whiteness as miscegenation by drawing equivalences between English, Iberian and North African registers of phenotypic race.

In act 4.4, we are introduced to the adult Perdita's racially marked beauty through her performance of rural English identity. Clad in her costume for the sheep-shearing feast, she is praised by Camillo as 'queen of curds and cream' (4.4.161) and by Florizel as 'Flora / Peering in April's front' (4.4.2–3). Perdita's close identification with the pastoral flora and fauna surrounding her highlights her domestication in her adopted country, and the competence of her racial passing in the English festive green world. Yet admiring men drawn to her spectacular beauty are on some level able to recognize the artifice in the seeming naturalness of her performativity. The admiring men surrounding Perdita are able to penetrate through her country weeds to read the noble blood through which 'Nothing she does or seems / But smacks of something greater than herself' (4.4.157–8), and which heralds her as '[t]oo noble for this place' (4.4.159). Not only does Perdita's royal blood speak through the class boundaries traversed in the disguise of her adopted identity, but the language of singularity and excess used to describe her beauty attempts to signal the legibility of her racial mixture. Descriptions of the 'rarest' quality (5.1.112) of her beauty and the 'peerless' and 'precious' qualities of her appearance, by Florizel, Polixenes, Camillo and, later, the Sicilian court, foreground her beauty in relation to racially charged, somatic correspondences between her and her parents. The language of corporeal similitude with her parents highlights her embodiment of racialized whiteness through her natal affiliation with barbarous territories of passional extremes. For instance, the play's emphatic references to her visually arresting beauty and her white hand operate as a visual signifier that somatically references her mother. Hermione, the

---

[35] Redworth, *The Prince and the Infanta*, pp. 10–11.
[36] Peter Erickson, 'Can we talk about race in *Hamlet*?' in *Hamlet: New Critical Essays*, ed. Arthur F. Kinney (London and New York, 2002), pp. 207–13.

daughter of the Emperor of Russia, is also described earlier in the play as 'rare' and 'precious' (1.2.448), epithets that mirror the white beauty of mother and daughter.[37] Arthur Little has discussed the charged whiteness of women's hands in early modern English texts as the overdetermined sign of racial and sexual purity that doubles as an emblematic threat of the racial contamination that could leak into the family and body politic through her sexuality.[38] Moreover, Perdita's hand is also described in the play as a synecdoche of her physical resemblance to Leontes. When Paulina brings the newborn Perdita to her father, she describes the baby as a 'print' and 'copy' (2.3.97–8) of the father, describing '[t]he very mould and frame of hand, nail, finger' (2.3.101) as being modelled on Leontes's form. Perdita's racialization through her perfect resemblance to *both* mother and father materializes the types of frozen Muscovite and Black Legend Spaniard which circulated in early modern English drama as mirroring analogues of barbaric excess. Transplanted into the Bohemian green world, these signifiers of Perdita's superlative white beauty offer reminders of the presence of threatening otherness that is nevertheless associated with the pleasures of property through marital enclosure. While there is a degree of inquietude regarding Perdita's domestication in the Bohemian green world, these anxieties are stabilized through her status as (intended) marital property: when we meet the adult Perdita, she is already claimed as Florizel's beloved.

The aesthetic excess of Perdita's racialized whiteness is articulated through metaphors of Blackness. As Kim Hall has noted, white beauty in early modern English discourse required the visual contrast of Blackness to render itself visible and semantically stable; this is reflected in the binary pairings of Black and white, or fair and dark, in Renaissance literature.[39] However, miscegenated whiteness such as Perdita's is itself invoked by metaphors of Blackness. *The Winter's Tale*'s use of Blackness to represent Perdita's white colour signals the problem of Iberian fairness embodying the mixed racial stocks anathemized by the Black Legend. As Florizel says to Perdita:

... I take thy hand, this hand
As soft as dove's down and as white as it,
Or Ethiopian's tooth, or the fanned snow that's bolted
By th' northern blasts twice o'er

(4.4.367–70)

In her lover's praise, the racialization of Perdita's body becomes discernable by her white skin's embodiment of the visual contrast between the proverbial Blackness of an Ethiopian's skin and the white enamel of his tooth; this frames the 'rareness' of her phenotypical whiteness through her embeddedness in darkened racial lineages and stocks that are evoked by her skin even when they don't imprint upon her colour or features. Erupting through the Petrarchan praise of Perdita's white hand as soft as dove's down, or Camillo's earlier pastoral associations of her with 'curds and cream' (4.4.161), the startling image of Perdita as an enamelled appendage of an Ethiopian's body unsettles the conscripted boundaries of the pastoral world by invoking racialized discourses around the popular Renaissance proverb, 'To wash an Ethiop white'. Polixenes obliquely references this proverb when he comments upon Florizel's seizing Perdita's hand: 'How prettily th' young swain seems to wash / The hand was fair before!' (4.4.371–2). The metaphors of genealogical Blackness attached to Perdita's 'fair before' body underscore the flux and ambivalence of racialized whiteness during early Jacobean negotiations for the Spanish match. Perdita is aristocratic

---

[37] In 1.2.103, Leontes refers to Hermione's 'white hand' in referencing the difficulty he had in gaining her consent to his marriage proposal. Florizel compares Perdita's hand to a white dove in 4.4.368. Shakespeare frequently references the extraordinary beauty shared by the mother (1.2.447–9, 5.1.95–103, 5.1.224–7) and daughter (4.4.156–9, 5.1.105–12, 5.1.130).

[38] Arthur L. Little, Jr, *Shakespeare Jungle Fever: National-Imperial Re-Visions of Race, Rape, and Sacrifice* (Palo Alto, 2000), p. 48. Little's reading white hands as racialized signifiers was revisited by David Sterling Brown during his speech at the Plenary Session of the 47th Annual Meeting of the Shakespeare Association of America, 'White hands: gesturing towards Shakespeare's "other race plays"'.

[39] Hall, *Things of Darkness*, pp. 62–122.

and phenotypically fair, all idealized markers for whiteness. Yet she embodies the unwashable Ethiop through her Iberian roots. This underscores the anxieties of distinguishing miscegenated whiteness that might potentially hide its mixed genealogies. The comparison of Perdita's hand to an Ethiopian's tooth signals that her beauty resists visual apprehension through the conventional somatic signifiers for race. The play attempts to salve this anxiety through the trope of miscegenation distinguished through the hypervisibility of its aesthetic surplus indexed through binaries of Black and white. Still, her 'fair before' body is only to become truly fair by legitimation from patriarchal authority. In other words, the unstable racial coordinates of her body can only be stabilized and disciplined by her enclosure in marital bonds with Florizel. While incorporable in the reproductive futurity of the English state, the intemperate and excessive nature of Perdita's beauty illustrates a degree of ambivalence towards 'the stranger within', who nevertheless simulates her adopted country's identity so effectively as to be imagined as embodying the natural energies of the English green world.

However, the connotations of excess and intemperance in Perdita's beauty signal that her whiteness remains problematic. Royster has noted that Shakespeare's explorations of racialized whiteness shift attention away from 'black/white dichotomies to white/white relations', particularly in relation to the 'stranger or foreigner from within'.[40] In an early Jacobean England relieved at the dynastic stability represented by James I's family, the figure of the royal consort was one such stranger within the kingdom: the foreign-born wives of English royalty embodied the fascination and ambivalence provoked by racialized queenship. How these gradients of whiteness would have been represented on stage is an open question. For instance, Royster speculates on the kind of make-up that would have been used to convey "the degrees of separation between Lavinia and Tamora in terms of their skin' – both identified in *Titus Andronicus* as of white hue.[41] The otherness of Perdita's 'white' beauty points to the lingering subtext of the Black Legend, even as the court-sponsored propaganda revived earlier discourses of the Anglo-Spanish complementarity and inter-marriage. Eric Griffin has observed that the Black Legend's circulation in English print culture rendered Spain's 'proximity to and relationship with Africa ... an index of Hispanicity [where] "Africa" begins to signify in such a way as to play into the conjuncture's growing obsession with miscegenation'.[42] In English and Dutch propaganda against the Habsburg Empire, the Black Legend traced a causal link between Spaniards' 'exceptional' violence and cruelty towards indigenous communities of the Americas and their racial intermixture with African blood over the *longue durée* of Moorish rule in the Iberian peninsula. In his 1590 *A Brief Discourse of the Spanish State*, Edward Daunce references the 'eight hundred years' of Moorish rule in Iberia, adding that 'during which time, we must not think that the Negros sent for women out of Aphrick, or that Spaniards were in those days very martiall', portraying Spain 'as a mongrel, miscegenated nation physically tainted by the 800 years of Moorish occupation'.[43] While early modern English travel literature variably describes Moors as 'white', 'tawny' or 'black' depending on their geographic origin and other parameters of difference, Daunce and other anti-Spanish propagandists trope Moors as phenotypically Black to imply that the miscegenation of Spaniards' Gothic blood with African stocks is visibly marked through their being less white than northern Europeans. The Black Legend functioned as a racial imaginary of biological difference that cross-pollinated with concurrent mythologies of racial alterity, including geohumoralism, which attributed conjoined bodily and moral differences to environmental influences.

---

[40] Royster, 'White-limed walls', p. 434.
[41] Royster, 'White-limed walls', p. 434.
[42] Griffin, *English Renaissance Drama*, p. 10.
[43] Barbara Fuchs, 'Sketches of Spain: early modern England's "orientalizing" of Iberia', in *Material and Symbolic Circulation between Spain and England, 1554–1604*, ed. Anne J. Cruz (Aldershot and Burlington, 2008), pp. 63–70; p. 65.

GRAFTED TO THE MOOR: ANGLO-SPANISH DYNASTIC MARRIAGE

The racial ambivalence resulting from Perdita's miscegenated whiteness is foregrounded again when she impersonates a Libyan princess when escaping with Florizel to Sicilia to evade Polixenes's wrath. In mediating the global scope of the racial multiplicity implicit in Perdita's hyperwhiteness, Shakespeare turns to the schematic framework of Moorish performativity, which functions in the play as an act of self-disclosure of the Black Legend roots of her white beauty. Perdita's Libyan guise would presumably implicate dressing *a la moresca*, assuming orientalized clothing and accoutrements that materialize the Moorish miscegenation of her Iberian genealogy. The Libyan role-playing ethnographically surfaces the African/Moorish connotations of Iberian identity that had been foregrounded in the histrionics of Leontes's domestic tyranny, a dark joke elaborated in Leontes's question on her assumed father: '[Libya] [w]here the warlike Smalus, / That noble honoured lord, is feared and loved?' (5.1.156–7). In this scene, Perdita's disguise ironically corresponds to her true identity for the play's early seventeenth-century audience, but it also problematizes the very category of whiteness itself. The Bohemian–Sicilian–Libyan mobility of Perdita's whiteness foregrounds the problem of racialized whiteness as a tint that occludes rather than discloses its genealogies. In other words, if whiteness is what allows Perdita to pass as an English shepherdess and Libyan royalty, then white hue by no means functions as a stable signifier of genealogy; rather, it can potentially dissemble and disguise intermixtures with African blood. In the context of the thematic linkages between her Libyan disguise and her equally competent performance as a Bohemian pastoral shepherdess, Perdita's white beauty not only illustrates the troubling category of Spanish whiteness but also sheds an ironic light upon constructions of English whiteness as genealogical purity. If Perdita can so easily simulate these multiple identities, then the lurking question is: what exactly is English whiteness and how does one distinguish it?

Not only does *The Winter's Tale* stress the problem of distinguishing Spanish and English kinds of whiteness, it also represents whiteness as epistemically behaving *like* Blackness. As Ian Smith has cautioned, filtering the early modern context's fluid and shifting racial imaginaries through a static colourist binary can be misleading, as it can retroactively import epistemologies of Blackness that developed from the Anglo-Atlantic slave trade, which would not come to define England's relation to Africa till the second half of the seventeenth century.[44] The shifting and fluid discourse of whiteness in the early Jacobean period can be observed in *The Winter's Tale*'s portrayal of whiteness as well as Blackness as racialized spectrums of embodiment that encompass a variety of shades and tints. Perdita's embodiment of racialized Spanish whiteness disrupts the normativities of humoral temperance and biological purity through her associations with pleasure and property, illustrating the point that different *kinds* of whiteness might be grafted within the English body politic through emigration and inter-marriage. Through Perdita's Libyan disguise, Shakespeare mobilizes geography as a metaphor for whiteness as variegated bodily embodiment: just as Libya geographically mediated between the geographies of sub-Saharan Africans and Ethiopians and the coastal regions of the white Moors, so too does Perdita's Spanish whiteness mediate a repository of other tints not readily visible to the eye but which are nonetheless associated with excess of beauty and pleasure. In classical and Renaissance geographic chronicles, the place name 'Libya' ambivalently mediated between the racial and geographic topographies of the North African territories on the Mediterranean coastline inhabited by 'white' or 'tawny' Moors and the 'blackamores' of sub-Saharan regions in the western-central area of the continent. However, at times, 'Libya' could also stand in metaphorically for the entire African continent. For instance, in Heinrich Petri's 1540 edition of Ptolemy's *Tabvla Africae III*, the deserts of Libya are located below the Mediterranean coastal zone of 'Mauritania' (roughly corresponding to present-day Morocco) and above 'Aethiopia interior', the

---

[44] Ian Smith, 'Those "slippery customers": rethinking race in *Titus Andronicus*', *Journal of Theatre and Drama* 3 (1997), 45–58; p. 46.

249

imagined western-southern zone of the continent. However, in John Pory's 1600 translation of Leo Africanus's *Description of Africa*, he cites Greco-Roman etymologies for Libya that evoke Libya as a metonym for the entire African continent: he writes that 'Africa' is possibly derived from 'Afer sonne to Hercules of Libya', and that the ancient Greeks once called Africa 'Libya' 'because [the whole continent] was in old time conquered by Libs, the king of Mauritania'.[45] Like Ptolemy, Pory sees Libya as a geographic and ethnographic transition zone dividing the Mediterranean realms of Africa from its dark-complected interior kingdoms. Other Renaissance writers explicitly associated Libya with Islamicate North Africa, highlighting the dimension of religious heterogeneity in the topos. Thomas Elyot's *The Boke Named The Gouernour* identifies Libya with the Barbary Coast, enfolding the Roman locus upon the contemporaneous geographies of Mediterranean Islam: 'Noble Romanes, whan they were in Numidia, Libia, & suche other countrayes, which nowe be called Barbary & Morisco'.[46]

Through the metaphoric connotations of Perdita's Libyan disguise, Shakespeare suggests that Spanish whiteness functions in some ways similar to early modern discourses of Blackness. Just as classical and Renaissance geography positioned Libya both as a topos within Africa and as a synecdoche for the entire African continent, Perdita's whiteness functions in the play as both a specific bodily index of her Iberian origins and a signifier for bodily variegation through the metaphor of the African continent's plural, teeming diversity of geographies, bodies, religions, climates and horticultures as it emerged on global maps. While Jacobean productions such as *The Masque of Blackness* explicitly invoked bodily and geographic alterity that England was beginning to compass imaginatively through imperial fantasies of 'whitening' the constructed Blackness of gendered African bodies entering the body politic, Perdita's Libyan disguise *a la moresca* reframes whiteness by metaphorically mobilizing the diverse geography and ethnography of the African continent to evoke the colourist ambivalences that Renaissance Europe encoded in the figure of the Moor. Variously appellated as 'white', 'tawny' or 'blackamoor' in Renaissance texts, the full colour spectrum embodied by Moors in early modern English texts parallels the geographic–geohumoral ambivalence of locating Libya on the map. In Renaissance discourse, 'black' was often used to denote tints from this broad colourist spectrum, as an effort to limn the fluid, shifting and uncertain ideal of 'normative' whiteness.[47] As with Elizabethan dark ladies who physically sport 'milk hands', 'ivory cheeks' and 'snowy brows', and who are yet branded as 'beamy black' or 'black, but in brightness bright' for some physical or moral departure from this shifting ideal of whiteness,[48] blackness often stands in *as a sign for physical variegation and diversity* as a by-product of this ceaseless labour and toil in defining whiteness.[49] However, in an England contemplating cross-border Anglo-Spanish marriage and the expansion of its own transatlantic colonization as the cornerstone of its emergent globalization, *The Winter's Tale* demonstrates the contingencies where whiteness can also come to appropriate the paradigms of heterogeneity and diversity that it had hitherto shunted off to the colourist scale of Blackness. In other words, not only does whiteness construct myriad exempla of diversity and multiplicity as Blackness in order to define itself as an exceptional singularity in contingent, fluid and shifting contexts, *it can also turn around and emulate these forms of Blackness when wishing to reimagine its relation to the globe*. While Perdita's miscegenated beauty is phenotypically white, the racialized dimensions of its pleasurable excess also

---

[45] Leo Africanus, *A geographical historie of Africa*, trans. John Pory (London, 1600), p. 1.
[46] Thomas Elyot, *The Boke Named The Gouernour* (New York, 1907), vol. I, p. xviii.
[47] As Kim Hall observes, '[w]hiteness ... is as much about a desire for a stable, linguistic order as it is about physical beauty'. See *Things of Darkness*, p. 66.
[48] Hall, *Things of Darkness*, p. 69.
[49] The colourist spectrum of Blackness at times included attendant shades such as 'browne' or 'tawny' as signs of one's bodily marking from humoral-climactic effects, or biological mixtures with phenotypically darker racial, ethnic and religious groups.

ripple out into associations with geographic, ethnographic, colourist and religious multiplicity in ways that contrast the other coexisting constructions of whiteness as the hue of genealogical purity.

Moreover, Perdita's racial passing as Libyan on her return to Sicilia calls attention to how her global, transcolonial whiteness can only be imagined through the forms of Blackness. By 'forms of Blackness', I refer to visual, textual and sonic representations of embodied differences as mapped onto materially and socially situated hierarchies of power.[50] For example, the image of Perdita dressed as African royalty both materializes Black Legend constructions of the biological mixture of Moorish blood in her natal Spanish identity, and marshals the metaphoric associations with Blackness of the global alterity and diversity with which England was re-negotiating its relations, through the political possibilities being opened up by Anglo-Spanish peace and the Spanish match. While I have earlier discussed Shakespeare negotiating with the category of Spanish whiteness, as distinguished from northern European whiteness, I have also discussed how this Spanish whiteness cannot be easily separated or distinguished from the emergent English forms of whiteness that were being normativized through humoral temperance or other discourses. Perdita's desirable beauty thus exposes the function of whiteness in early Jacobean England. Her representations in the play reveal whiteness to be a desiring racial imaginary that constructs the forms of Blackness in the attempt to limn itself, but which also emulates and appropriates those forms in order to reimagine and reorder its own relations of hegemonic power and consumption in the world. Departing from Elizabethan models of racialization, the Spanish context of *The Winter's Tale* illustrates how embodied forms of whiteness in early modern English racial imaginaries imitate and emulate Blackness to access the pleasures of global variegation.

TRANSCOLONIAL RACE: WHITENESS AS BLACKNESS

Early modern whiteness and Blackness are fluid racial imaginaries that shift alongside changing modalities of power transacted through trade, diplomacy and colonial expansion. Numerous scholars have demonstrated how constructions of Blackness proliferating on stage and in print are strategically fictional, shaped by the exigencies, fears and desires associated with the project of fashioning whiteness as a privileged locus of identity. Nevertheless, in the section above, I have argued that Blackness can also be associated with pleasure, and that whiteness as a desiring imaginary can at times be impelled to emulate and incorporate the very qualities associated with the visual, textual and sonic forms of Blackness that it constructs. In *The Winter's Tale*'s investments in the celebratory comic outcome of Florizel and Perdita's inter-racial marriage, the emulation and incorporation of Spanish Blackness is associated with the imaginative pleasures of the Spanish match in the early part of James's reign as promising England's consolidation of transatlantic wealth and property. One of the incentives of the Spanish match was establishing diplomatic acceptance from Spain for the English colonial footprint in the New World. The successful establishment of Jamestown in 1607 was partly due to the Treaty of London putting an end to naval 'cold' and 'hot' wars between England and Spain; partisans of the Spanish match imagined that dynastic marriage would strengthen this colonial footprint, as well as transfer New World gold into English coffers through the wealthy dowry brought by the Spanish bride.

The Winter's Tale has long been associated with the Mediterranean and classical worlds and is very seldom referenced in discussions of Shakespeare's engagements with the Americas. Some notable exceptions to this oversight include Walter Cohen, who locates *The Winter's Tale* within 'the widening spatial, temporal, and religious vistas' of the global mercantile economy; and Lisa Hopkins, who views the world of *The Winter's Tale* as an axis where 'the discourse of the classical world …

---

[50] I am partially influenced in my understanding of 'form' by Caroline Levine, *Forms: Whole, Rhythm, Hierarchy, Network* (Princeton and Oxford, 2015), p. 21.

mingles powerfully with that of the trade and exploration which drove the quest for the New World'.[51] In the Anglo-Spanish context that I have been tracking in the play, Perdita's positioning in Bohemia also speaks to the grafting and hybridization of English spaces and domestic economies to what Jorge Cañizares-Esguerra and Benjamin Breen have called the 'hybrid Atlantics' of the early modern world.[52] That is, the frameworks through which early seventeenth-century England conceptualized, desired and consumed the Americas – navigational, geographic, horticultural, metallurgical, ethnographic – were often Iberian.[53] Transcolonial race describes the way early modern racial imaginaries were shaped by racial, cultural, material and ecological transfers across the hybrid Atlantic worlds, notably between Spanish and Portuguese spheres of transatlantic colonization and emergent English ones.

The metaphors of horticulture through which the play meditates upon race should also be read in relation to references to the hybrid Atlantic worlds mentioned in the play. As numerous critics have observed, Perdita's dialogue with Polixenes on grafting in act 4.1 is evocative of Montaigne's discourse on savagery and bastardization in 'Of the Caniballes'. The Montaigne intertext illustrates how the transatlantic context frames the racial and ecological imaginaries of the play. Through John Florio's 1603 translation, Montaigne's essay as a reflection upon the 'savagery' of New World Amerindians is deconstructed by comparing them to the naturalness of horticulture found growing wild in nature. The Montaigne intertext of Perdita and Polixenes's dialogue grafts the hybrid Atlantic context of the Americas on to the Bohemian pastoral world. Perdita's position is identifiable with Montaigne's championing of the 'naturalness' of wild flora and fauna, contrasted with the luxury and corruption implicit in European techniques of hybridization and grafting, while Polixenes champions the intermingling of kinds that Perdita will herself represent through her marriage with Florizel. As William Steffen observes, their debate on grafting implicates early English writings on Virginia, where early modern horticultural writers promoted the practice of grafting and the movement of a plant from one soil to another as a gesture of potential biological enhancement.[54] More than the other European colonial powers in the Americas, the English cited their use of the land, their engagement in agricultural or pastoral activities, and their improvement of it – which could refer to both grazing (domestic animals) and planting – as the primary means by which they claimed possession of their colonies.[55] While constructing a 'purity' versus 'hybridity' binary, Montaigne also acknowledges that the polarity of ecological–geographic difference between Europe and the Americas has already eroded through the networks of settlement, cultivation and trade with pan-Atlantic empires, such as those of Spain and Portugal, whereby New World produce and foodstuffs had been incorporated in northern European ways of life.[56] In the context of the anxieties attached to Perdita's racialized genealogies, Montaigne's intertext to her ethics of consumption destabilizes the contrast between 'natural' English purity and 'savage' and 'wild' importation. In fact, Perdita's presence in the Bohemian green world and the close identification of her intemperate beauty with the Bohemian pastoral landscape illustrates how England is already

---

[51] Walter Cohen, 'The undiscovered country: Shakespeare and mercantile geography', in *Marxist Shakespeares*, ed. Jean Howard and Scott Cutler Shershow (London and New York, 2001), pp. 128–58; Lisa Hopkins, 'Pocahontas and *The Winter's Tale*', *Shakespeare* 1 (2005), 121–35; p. 128.

[52] Jorge Cañizares-Esguerra and Benjamin Breen, 'Hybrid Atlantics: future directions for the history of the Atlantic world', *History Compass* 11 (2013), 597–609; p. 597.

[53] Cañizares-Esguerra and Breen, 'Hybrid Atlantics', p. 597.

[54] William Steffen, 'Grafting and ecological imperialism in John Fletcher's Bonduca', *Journal for Early Modern Cultural Studies* 17 (2017), 68–96; pp. 71–2. On the subject of *The Winter's Tale*'s link with Virginia, also see Hopkins, 'Pocahontas', pp. 121–35.

[55] Steffen, 'Grafting', pp. 71–2.

[56] Edward Fuller's catalogue of seeds and plants sold near Maypole, London, illustrates the extent to which seventeenth-century English horticulture and agriculture included items identified as incorporable forms of exotic produce associated with Spain and the Spanish Americas. See *A catalogue of plants seeds, &c* (London, 16??).

embedded in the Iberian colonial trade networks and foodways that colonizers were seeking to transplant to Virginia.

Earlier, I discussed Perdita's representation as marital property to be grafted to England through her embodiment of the English green world. The transatlantic associations of the horticultural imagery that Perdita is associated with bring into focus the scope and nature of the desires that she represents: she can be said to embody *transcolonial property* – namely, the racial and material hybridities resulting from importing, appropriating and domesticating Spain's transatlantic wealth and colonial power into an emulous England. In *The Winter's Tale*, the horticultural imagery of grafting opens the imaginative space for Perdita and Florizel's cross-racial marriage and a way for England selectively to incorporate desired Iberian, North African and transatlantic ecological bounty into English spaces. For instance, the grocery list that Perdita hands to her adopted brother, the Shepherd's son, in preparation for the sheep-shearing feast maps on to global foodstuffs that England sought to domesticate into its own economy through its colonial plantations in Virginia. The shopping list includes sugar, currants, rice, mace, dates, nutmeg, ginger, prunes and 'raisins o'th' sun' (4.3.37–48). David Berkeley and Zahra Karimipour have observed that '[t]he foods bought for the sheep-shearing feast in Act IV, Scene iii ... were not ordinary peasant fare' (p. 91).[57] Hopkins agrees, while also making the point that raisins at this time were mostly imported from the Spanish Americas, particularly Mexico.[58] Some notable foodstuffs on Perdita's list are produce sourced from North Africa, the Iberian peninsula and the Spanish Atlantic colonies, which the English sought to reproduce in the warm, temperate climes of Virginia. Sugar, the first luxury item on the list, was still mostly exported from the south of Spain and Morocco at this time; the warm climate of Virginia fuelled English colonial ambitions of replicating this Iberian and North African cash crop in the Americas. In his 1590 pamphlet, *A briefe and true report of the new found land of Virginia of the commodities and of the nature and manners of the naturall inhabitants*, Thomas Hariot hoped that Virginia would prove hospitable to sugar canes, as 'they grow in the same climate, in the South part of Spaine and in Bar|bary'. This project of colonial domestication was influenced by texts such as Bartolomé de las Casas, *Brevísima relación de la destrucción de las Indias* (through English translations such as William Brome's 1583 *The Spanish colonie*), which described Spanish domestication of sugar in the Caribbean. The synergy between the pleasures of consumption promised by Perdita's global shopping list and the visual delight of her own beauty to the spectators surrounding her illustrates how the ecologies and economies of the Bohemian green world are already integrated with hybrid Atlantic worlds. Perdita may defend English garden herbs such as marjoram, thyme and lavender, but she is also associated with the normative consumption of exotic foodstuffs which the English imagined domesticating in the plantations of Jamestown and consuming in England.

If Perdita represents the way whiteness can embody and metaphorically emulate the global associations of Blackness, it is the transatlantic context of *The Winter's Tale* that illustrates the desiring motive for whiteness to take upon itself the variegation and multiplicity of Blackness. Framed within transatlantic global ecologies, Perdita's whiteness provokes intemperate visual delights in the English patriarchal order, because it is enlaced with the pleasures of transatlantic consumption and power that Shakespeare imagines England to be able to consolidate through the Spanish match. The horticultural imagery she is associated with unmoors fairness and whiteness from genealogical purity in favour of the hybridities of grafting a 'gentler scion to the wildest stock' (4.4.93). Within the geo-political context mediated by the play, Perdita's Moorish performativity as a Libyan princess harnesses the topos of Africa to invoke

---

[57] David S. Berkeley and Zahra Karimipour, 'Blood-consciousness as a theme in *The Winter's Tale*', *Explorations in Renaissance Culture* 11 (1985), 89–98.
[58] Hopkins, 'Pocahontas', p. 133.

metaphorically the cosmopolitan globalities of racial, geographic and ecological heterogeneity represented by Jamestown at the beginning of England's colonial transplantation of the Americas. The 1603 Treaty of London established a closer entanglement in Anglo-Spanish relations, restoring bilateral trade and facilitating greater circulation of transatlantic goods and foodstuffs into England. Restored trade with Spain and its dominions whetted English appetites for the transatlantic expansion, while diplomatic negotiations for an Anglo-Spanish marriage for the Stuart heir of England facilitated the shift of imperial competition into the assimilative mode of romance. In this context, whiteness also undergoes a shift: as an emergent hierarchy of power, it desiringly leans towards globality, approaching it through the fantasy of marital incorporation of a racialized Spanish whiteness that signifies difference and heterogeneity through its embodiment of forms of Blackness. While constructions of Blackness are fluid and shifting in the early modern period as a means of defining whiteness, the context of Anglo-Spanish entangled relations and dynastic marriage influencing the play lays open the contingencies in which whiteness can emulate the forms of Blackness that it constructs as a signifier for global alterity, in order to assimilate, domesticate and appropriate the capacious pleasures of New World and global mercantile consumption. Class facilitates this shift away from the Elizabethan period's imperialism through gendered insularity; Perdita's revealed status as a royal wins Polixenes over to the marriage between her and Florizel. In Shakespeare's late romance, the restoration of bilateral relations between two estranged kingdoms is to the distinct advantage of one of them: Perdita grafts the wealth and transcolonial property of Sicilia on to Bohemia.

In this article, I have argued that *The Winter's Tale* cautiously celebrates 'Anglo-Spanish marriage whereby dynastic grafting with Spain can advance the utopic vision of incorporating Spain's imperial territories into an England emerging as a pan-Atlantic empire. While the Spanish match's globalizing possibilities are foregrounded through Perdita's associations with racial and ecological hybridities, there is nevertheless considerable ambivalence attached to the miscegenated nature of her whiteness. *The Winter's Tale*'s racial imaginaries of Perdita's white beauty are charged ones, given the play's composition at a time when the prospect of a Spanish match for Prince Henry was all too tangible. Early modern paradigms of race could encompass markers of biology, religion, gender, class, climate and geography. The proliferation of the Black Legend in the northern European press is often taken as a signpost of the emergent notion of biological race – namely, the notion of Spaniards' difference as essentialized genealogical contamination resulting from the African and European, Moorish and Jewish, intermixtures of blood. However, *The Winter's Tale* makes it clear that whiteness is as plural and racialized as blackness in the early modern period. Through its representation of Perdita's Spanish whiteness, the play reflects upon the significance of different kinds of whiteness that are nonetheless inter-related through Anglo-Spanish kinship and political relations. Perdita's competence in passing as Bohemian and Libyan foregrounds the hyper-visibility of her racialized whiteness and the impossibility of its localization to any one particular region. The context of England's competition with Spain for transatlantic empire also influences the play's representation of whiteness, raising the question of whether the power and pleasure afforded by miscegenated whiteness might not be preferable to the homogeneities of other racial formations of whiteness as temperance and genealogical purity. The globalism of Perdita's miscegenated whiteness emulates Blackness, evoking the metaphoric associations of Africa with racial, religious and geographic heterogeneities to imagine England's own hegemony over the Americas via the assimilative medium of romance and inter-racial marriage. The racial imaginary of acquiring transatlantic power through Spain (rather than despite Spain, as it was in the Elizabethan period) shapes Perdita's status as transcolonial marital property grafted to England through her marriage with Florizel. The power and pleasurable consumption that she enables pressurizes whiteness to mimic and emulate shifting and fluid constructions of Blackness as a signifier of genealogical/geographic heterogeneity. The racial imaginary of this form of whiteness's beauty, and desirable intemperate excess reinforces the problem of interpreting race through a visual logic; if Spanish whiteness is kin to English whiteness, how does one appropriately decipher this tint when (in Perdita's case) it can also connote mixed genealogies not readily visible to the eye, as opposed to homogenous genealogies and stable hierarchies? Additionally, Shakespeare asks whether, if miscegenated whiteness facilitates the power and pleasure of hybrid Atlantics for 'the patriarchal order, does one ultimately wish to distinguish between these different forms of whiteness? Written shortly after the settlement of Jamestown, *The Winter's Tale* reveals how the early Jacobean project of emulating Spain's transatlantic empire contributes to the instability and flux of early modern English racial imaginaries. With the restoration of bilateral peace and the pursuit of dynastic marriage under James I, the hypervisibility of Perdita's racialized white beauty evokes transatlantic England's conflicted desires and anxiety regarding a racialized Spanish monarchy, briefly imagined as once and future kin incorporated in England's global transatlantic futurity.

RHYME, HISTORY AND MEMORY IN *A MIRROR FOR MAGISTRATES* AND *HENRY VI*

MOLLY CLARK

What, is it treason in a riming frame
To clypp, to stretche, to adde, or chaunge a name?

This question is posed by the authors of *A Mirror for Magistrates*, the enormously popular verse history collection that came out in increasingly expanded editions from the 1550s onwards. In the collection, guilty or unfortunate historical figures make didactic orations to the poets who transcribe them, in short poems interspersed with practical and theoretical prose discussions between the poets themselves (Baldwin, Ferrers, Sackville and others). The question quoted above appears in the poem ventriloquizing Collingbourne, a citizen in the time of Richard III 'cruelly executed for making a foolishe rime'.[1] The poem emotively illustrates the risks of satirizing authority figures in verse. The foolish rhyme itself appears to have been merely a couplet: 'The Cat, the Rat, and Lovel our Dog, / Do rule al England, under a Hog' (fol. C.xliii). As the reanimated Collingbourne explains, the cat is Catesby, the rat is Ratcliffe, and the dog is Lovell. Richard III himself is the hog, partly because it is the animal depicted on his device or badge, and partly – as the speaker somewhat disappointingly admits – 'to ryme' (fol. C.xliiv). Overall, the poem reads as a manifesto for freedom of ideas in verse, and a lament for the loss of satirical licence since the ancients. It also raises some questions about rhyme and historical truth. In Collingbourne's couplet, the desire to rhyme (stemming from the desire to 'shewe my wyt, howe wel I could invent') serves as a prompt for the creative and emblematic depiction of the political players. In this sense, rhyme spawns historical portrayal. At the same time, however, the necessity to rhyme is in some sense a check on political or historical accuracy. If Collingbourne had seen himself as a teacher of history rather than a political satirist, and if he had wished to create a statement about the ruling powers that would convey their faults to future generations, would he have used a couplet? Or would he have wished instead to search for the aptest possible epithets? The documentary and the stylistic have a complicated relationship.

There is plenty of evidence in the *Mirror* to suggest that early modern readers thought about history and verse form in a more joined-up manner than most of us would today. In this article, I will argue that this connection is one of the key elements that Shakespeare imbibed from verse chronicles and manipulated in *Henry VI*. One striking feature of the *Mirror* is that almost every poem is in rhyme royal (ABABBCC), generally iambic pentameter, apart from those voicing kings. (This rule is maintained consistently throughout Part 1, the first half, though it is broken on a couple of occasions in Part 2, one of which I will discuss shortly.) We see the first deviation from rhyme royal in Richard II's poem, the first in the collection to ventriloquize a monarch: his rhyme scheme is the ambitious ABABBCCBCB. This challenging

---

[1] Various authors, *A Myrrour for Magistrates* (London, 1563 ed.), fol. C.xxxviii. Further references appear in parentheses.

interlocking pattern seems to suggest that a king's voice requires more poetic effort than that of a commoner; it also sets the monarch apart in the eyes and ears of the reader. Henry VI, too, is distinguished through verse form: his voice is rendered in stanzas of two couplets each, in poulter's measure. With Edward IV, again the poet sets himself a challenge: a twelve-line interlocking stanza, rhyming ABABBCBCCDCD. Towards the end of Part 2, Richard III appears as the only king to speak in the same rhyme royal as the rest of the ghosts. Even here, though, verse form is imbricated with history. Following Richard III's poem, the prose conversation among the poets centres on form. The discussion starts with style more generally: 'it was thought not vehement ynough for so violent a man as kyng Rychard had bene'. It then moves on to more technical points: 'The matter was wel ynough lyked of sum, but the meeter was mysliked almost of all.' The poet's submission is about to be rejected, it seems, before another voice speaks up:

You knowe not whereupon you sticke: elles you would not so much mislike this because of the uncertayne Meter. The cumlynes called by the Rhetoricians *decorum*, is specially to be observed in al things. Seying than that kyng Rychard never kept measure in any of his doings, seing also he speaketh in Hel, whereas is no order: it were agaynst the *decorum* of his personage, to use eyther good Meter or order. And therfore, if his oracion were far wurse, in my opinion it were more fyt for him.

(fol. c.livv)

This defence of stylistic character enactment wins the day, and the poem is included in the collection. In a work that seeks to portray history through ventriloquizing its characters, and to draw moral lessons from that portrayal, verse style is as important as the presentation of facts.

I have begun this article on historical drama with a collection of poems for several reasons. First, and perhaps most obviously, the *Mirror* is widely considered a source for Shakespeare's histories, featuring figures that would go on to appear in *Henry VI*. Second, recent criticism on the *Mirror* has emphasized its own dramatic qualities: Paul Budra argues that it should be read as a collection of soliloquies.[2] Similarly, Jennifer Richards draws out the performative vocality of the poems.[3] As a primary means through which early modern people consumed history, the *Mirror* established some of the paradigms of stylizing the documentary that Shakespeare worked with and manipulated.[4] Finally, the *Mirror*'s enormous and enduring popularity during Shakespeare's time tells us a good deal about the formal associations that theatregoers had. And this was a time when history plays were under intense and deep scrutiny, scoured for subtext and slants of meaning. The request that the Earl of Essex's supporters made for a performance of *Richard II* on the eve of their rebellion against Elizabeth – with deposition scene included – testifies that the stage was expected to call to mind contemporary affairs while representing the past. Audiences were coming to the theatre with widespread knowledge of the *Mirror*, and also a sense of the ways in which the history that it contained might become politically current. And, as a collection of rhymed verse, the *Mirror* directs us towards some of the specific points of conjunction – and disjunction – between history and rhyme.

My article will situate the three *Henry VI* plays in this *Mirror* culture: a culture that sees history not only as legible in a highly crafted verse form, but as intrinsically appropriate for presentation in that patterned structure. I will consider the ways in which *Henry VI*'s couplets invoke the register of the *Mirror* in order to historicize and memorialize

---

[2] Paul Budra, '*A Mirror for Magistrates*' and the '*De Casibus*' Tradition (Toronto, 2000).

[3] Jennifer Richards, 'Reading and listening to William Baldwin', in '*A Mirror for Magistrates*' in Context, ed. Harriet Archer and Andrew Hadfield (Cambridge, 2016), pp. 71–88.

[4] There was also some degree of overlap between historical poets and playwrights in this period. Thomas Sackville, author of one section of the *Mirror*, also co-wrote *Gorboduc*; the prolific playwright Thomas Heywood produced both history plays and the verse chronicle *Troia Britannica* (1609); and Samuel Daniel was a historical poet, a prose historian and a playwright.

dramatic speech; and I will think about the ways in which rhyme conditions a stylized depiction of history, a macro-cosmic tonal principle that governs the dramatic world Shakespeare creates. This broad, universalizing use of rhyme is in part attributable to the time at which *Henry VI* was written. Shakespeare's rhyming trajectory was by no means straightforward, but it does nevertheless fall into broadly articulable stages: generally speaking, couplets amidst the blank verse and prose were relatively frequent in his early years (into which time the first *Henriad* falls), minimal in his middle plays, and resurgent in the late romances.[5] The value of rhyme, not only in drama but in poetry, was under continual renegotiation during Shakespeare's lifetime.[6] In the first years of his career, he uses the couplet form extensively and with great variety: to create a specific brand of metatheatrical humour in the comedies; to lend a stately fatality to the tragedies; and, in the early histories, to achieve effects that I will endeavour to evoke in this article. When describing the rhyming texture of these histories, it is also important to note that, like the *Mirror*, the *Henry VI* plays were written to some extent according to a collaborative model of authorship: other hands worked alongside Shakespeare's to create a schematic and comprehensive dramatic language.[7] It is through this dramatic language that the *Henriad* memorializes itself.

To rehearse the question that the *Mirror* poets put in the mouth of Collingbourne: 'What, is it treason in a riming frame / To clypp, to stretche, to adde, or chaunge a name?' My article will consider this question in a new context: not one of satirical commentary, but one of historical representation. How does the formal nature of rhyme, and the way it necessitates clipping, stretching, adding and changing of historicized speech, manifest in Shakespeare's *Henry VI*? What does rhyme specifically have to contribute to a dramatic portrayal of the past? And what can such a fictionalized form have to do with historical memory?

*

'Dramatic Poesy is as History made visible', wrote Francis Bacon.[8] And it is also, by definition, history made audible. My central arguments are, first, that the couplets of *Henry VI* invoke the register of the *Mirror* to engage in a form of memorializing; and, second, that the intense frequency of couplets in these three plays creates an overarching tonal principle of repetition. This principle of repetition is key to the way in which these plays depict history: as cyclical, as providential, as symbolic. Like the *Mirror*, they present a series of political actors ebbing and flowing like waves of the sea. These early plays come from a time in the development of the early modern historical imagination before the anecdotal and providential took second place to the political: symbolism often trumps fact.[9] Arthur Ferguson has discussed the early modern cultural struggle with the contradiction that history was at the same time a record of change over time, and a timeless record of repeated cycles: 'the paradox of change within a changeless natural order'.[10]

---

[5] For a thorough discussion of Shakespeare's changing rhyme usage and its features, see Frederic Ness, *The Use of Rhyme in Shakespeare's Plays* (New Haven, 1941).

[6] The rhyme controversy, which has been extensively discussed elsewhere, featured Samuel Daniel as rhyme's main defender, against the likes of Thomas Campion in opposition.

[7] It is thought likely that several other authors may have had a hand in the *Henry VI* plays alongside Shakespeare; fellow playwrights may have included Marlowe and Nashe. See, for example, *The New Oxford Shakespeare*, ed. Gary John Jowett, Terri Bourus and Gabriel Egan (Oxford, 2016). For the purposes of this article, I refer to them as part of 'Shakespeare's first tetralogy', both because I find the methods to be consistent with the rest of his oeuvre and because the rhyming intentions of the plays are widespread and integral, regardless of who wrote which scenes and in what order.

[8] Francis Bacon, *De augmentis scientiarum*, in *The Philosophical Works of Francis Bacon*, ed. John M. Robertson (London, 2011), pp. 439–40.

[9] See Richard Helgerson, 'Murder in Faversham: Holinshed's impertinent history', in *The Historical Imagination in Early Modern Britain*, ed. Donald R. Kelley and David Harris Sacks (Cambridge, 1997), pp. 133–58.

[10] Arthur B. Ferguson, *Clio Unbound: Perception of the Social and Cultural Past in Renaissance England* (Durham, NC, 1979), p. 60. Compare also F. J. Levy's remarks about *A Mirror for Magistrates*: 'Inevitably, there was a notion that history is repetitive, for this could not be avoided in any history resting on a moral base' – F. J. Levy, *Tudor Historical Thought* (San Marino: Huntington Library, 1967), p. 214.

I think that we see this paradox played out formally in the couplet rhetoric of *Henry VI*: a series of microcosmic repetitions form the building blocks for a larger cyclical mood. As reigns, governance structures, foreign policies, wars and peacetimes succeed each other, rhyme is a constant sonic reminder of the principle of repetition, offering a touchstone for understanding the world of these three plays. And it is a bleak world. Like the haunted voices of *A Mirror for Magistrates*, forces of resentment and guilt pull the characters of *Henry VI* back and forth; prophecy and miracle, both true and false, hold sway in political machinations; and death is continually hovering. Parallelisms and tragic repetitions in character and plot structure, as David Womersley describes, take an apocalyptic mode of historical representation to its logical conclusion.[11] In achieving this, the playwrights reach for poetic logic over documentary narrative.[12] Rhyme is a crucial part of this governing poetic logic, establishing a representational mode all of its own.

In the *Mirror*, rhymed verse serves as a memorializing record: history's ghosts give warnings to the future. The very first poem, for example, spoken by Robert Tresilian, the corrupt Chief Justice, ends: 'Let them that cum hereafter both that and this compare, / And waying well the ende, they will I trust beware' (fol. iiiv). Later on, the shade of Henry VI himself sets down ample lessons for the living, such as: 'Our kyngdomes are but cares, our state devoyd of staye, / Our ryches redy snares, to hasten our decay' (fol. lxxxiii); and 'God grant my woful haps to grievous to rehearse, / May teach all states to know how deeply dangers pearce' (fol. lxxxiiiiv). Rhyme enshrines the lessons of history. The couplets of the *Henry VI* plays, despite being spoken by living characters, often produce a similar effect. They appear almost to historicize the present. In *1 Henry VI*, Warwick prophesies that the brawl in the Temple garden '[s]hall send, between the red rose and the white, / A thousand souls to death and deadly night' (*1 Henry VI*, 2.4.126–7). He describes the War of the Roses before it has even begun. Similarly, Duke Humphrey of Gloucester's parting lines to the King following his disgrace are spoken with one foot in the grave: 'Farewell, good King. When I am dead and gone, / May honourable peace attend thy throne' (*2 Henry VI*, 2.3.37–8). The couplet form sets a seal on the words, lending to Gloucester's utterance the unapproachable sanctity of a dead man's. The King himself utters a benediction towards the end of the *Henriad*, this one with a more prophetic edge than Gloucester's. Speaking of the child who would go on to be Henry VII, the King urges: 'Make much of him, my lords, for this is he / Must help you more than you are hurt by me' (*3 Henry VI*, 4.7.75–6). The speakers in the *Mirror* have the benefit of hindsight. In *Henry VI*, rhyme seems not only to stand for but to *replace* hindsight, smoothing the plane of utterance into timelessness, freezing the characters' words into auditory tableaux of history. Where, in the *Mirror*, rhyme is a symptom of memorialization, in the *Henriad* it is its cause. And where the speakers in the *Mirror* reflect on history in retrospect, Shakespeare's characters must *make* history before our eyes. Writing for a dramatic medium in which events take place in the 'present' of the stage, Shakespeare invokes the tone and formal character of the *Mirror* to give the sense that we are not only watching the past happen, but also simultaneously looking back on it.

For history is in a sense an act of committing to memory. And here it finds an important connection to poetic form. The *Mirror* authors chose rhymed verse for the voices of the ghosts they ventriloquized. Rhyme's usefulness to the mechanisms of

---

[11] David Womersley, *Divinity and State* (Oxford, 2010).

[12] Levy similarly observes that Shakespeare in the first tetralogy uses a method of 'construction' rather than 'plot', organizing the bitty, episodic historical narrative into spans that deal with particular themes, rather than into beginning-middle-and-end trajectories; Levy, *Thought*, pp. 226–7. I believe that rhyme – a microcosmic device with a macrocosmic effect – serves this particular kind of dramatic unity well.

memorization was – and is – a commonplace. Philip Sidney comments on this in his *Defence of Poesy*:

> that verse far exceedeth prose in the knitting up of memory, the reason is manifest: the words (besides their delight, which hath a great affinity to memory) being so set as one cannot be lost but the whole work fails; which accusing itself, calleth the remembrance back to itself, and so most strongly confirmeth it. Besides, one word so, as it were, begetting another, as, be it in rhyme or measured verse, by the former a man shall have a near guess to the follower.[13]

Samuel Daniel argues similarly in his 'Defence of Ryme' that the device gives 'to the Eare an Eccho of a delightfull report & to the Memorie a deeper impression of what is delivered therein'.[14] Sidney and Daniel might almost be describing not only the experience of a reader learning history through the *Mirror*, but also the experience of an underprepared actor trying to remember his lines. And if rhyme helps words to lodge in the memory of an actor, then it can do the same for an audience member. Throughout the Shakespeare corpus, and early modern drama generally, we hear couplets marking key plot points, moments when the *language* of the play fixes itself to the *story* of the play: we might think of Hamlet's 'The play's the thing', for example. According to Frederic Ness, 'the scene-end couplet is used primarily to indicate the completion of the action'.[15] He goes on to elaborate that this incorporates summary of previous action, plan for future action, and moral or emotional justification of said action. It is instinctively known to anyone who has spent time with Shakespeare that the couplet is often a vehicle for decision and resolve: it is a marker of something important happening. But in the history plays, these calls to attention take on a deeper significance. In depicting the events and decisions of the past, Shakespeare, like the *Mirror* poets, uses rhyme to memorialize. The aural tenacity of rhyme becomes an act of inscription, of setting in stone. Towards the end of Part 1, for example, Joan la Pucelle gives instruction to the Dauphin: 'Command the conquest, Charles, it shall be thine; / Let Henry fret and all the world repine' (*1 Henry VI*, 5.2.19–20). This rhyme does not merely narrate action – it engenders it. It highlights the moment of command, freeze-framing a key juncture in the conflict. Similarly, the end of Part 2's first scene captures York at a historically freighted moment of resolve: 'And force perforce I'll make him yield the crown; / Whose bookish rule hath pulled fair England down' (*2 Henry VI*, 1.1.258–9). This couplet makes an important claim on the memory: it illustrates the character of the claimant; it sketches the reign of Henry VI and its discontents; and it sets up the contest that will go on to change the course of history. A couplet does not always have to mark a moment of active resolve; it can sometimes memorialize a historical moment in a more reflective manner. After the judgement has been made on Gloucester and his Duchess Eleanor, and the former has resigned his staff, Suffolk remarks (almost, it seems, to himself): 'Thus droops this lofty pine and hangs his sprays; / Thus Eleanor's pride dies in her youngest days' (*2 Henry VI*, 2.3.45–6). The *Mirror* resonances are important here, I think: on the one hand, Suffolk perhaps uses the moralizing tone of the historicizing couplet, tinted as it is with this association, to crow over his defeated rival; on the other hand, in isolation from its context, the couplet stands as a *Mirror*-like epigram against hubris.[16] In both layers of register and appropriation, the rhyme acts as a memorializing force.

Acts of memory in the violent world of *Henry VI* are by necessity documents of wrongdoing. Where, in the *Mirror*, guilt is a positive force, a tool for learning, in these three plays it is

---

[13] Philip Sidney, *The Major Works*, ed. Katherine Duncan-Jones (Oxford, 1989; 2002), pp. 233–4.

[14] Samuel Daniel, 'A Defence of Ryme', in *Samuel Daniel: Poems and A Defence of Ryme*, ed. Arthur Colby Sprague (Chicago, 1965), p. 132.

[15] Ness, *Use of Rhyme*, p. 74.

[16] As well as making the connection between verse form and memory, Sidney's *Defence* also speaks to an early modern association between verse form, history and morality. In his view, poetry (with its recourse to artistic licence) can derive moral lessons from the past more effectively than rigorous documentary history can. The moral didacticism of the *Mirror* is a register that Shakespeare plays with in the memorializing couplets of *Henry VI*.

a corrosive poison. The insistent quality of rhyme serves both. In the *Mirror*, for example, Suffolk reflects on his part in Humphrey Duke of Gloucester's death: 'Was never prynce that other dyd oppresse / Unryghteously, but dyed in distresse' (fol. xliii). In *Henry VI*, Shakespeare invokes this register not for a simple didactic purpose, but to create the atmosphere of pervasive shame and error in which his characters live. In this way, he holds history to account. We feel the power of the 'guilty couplet' especially strongly towards the end of Part 1's act 4, when the English nobles lament Somerset's delay in coming to offer succour to the valiant Talbots in France. It is a pair of blank verse scenes with frequent couplets: and every single couplet harps on the fact that they have let Talbot and his son down, and on who is to blame for it.

YORK Mad ire and wrathful fury makes me weep,
      That thus we die while remiss traitors sleep.
LUCY O send some succour to the distressed lord.
YORK He dies, we lose; I break my warlike word;
      We mourn, France smiles; we lose, they daily get,
      All 'long of this vile traitor Somerset.
                                    (4.3.28–33)
LUCY This seven years did not Talbot see his son,
      And now they meet where both their lives are done.
YORK Alas, what joy shall noble Talbot have,
      To bid his young son welcome to his grave?
      Away – vexation almost stops my breath,
      That sundered friends greet in the hour of death.
      Lucy, farewell. No more my fortune can
      But curse the cause I cannot aid the man.
      Maine, Blois, Poitiers, and Tours are won away
      'Long all of Somerset and his delay.
                                    (37–46)
LUCY Whiles they each other cross,
      Lives, honours, lands, and all hurry to loss.
                                    (52–3)
SOMERSET York set him on to fight and die in shame,
          That, Talbot dead, great York might bear the name.
                                    (4.4.8–9)

LUCY Alençon, René, compass him about,
      And Talbot perisheth by your default.
                                    (26–7)
LUCY Never to England shall he bear his life,
      But dies betrayed to fortune by your strife.
                                    (38–9)
SOMERSET If he be dead, brave Talbot, then adieu.
LUCY   His fame lives in the world, his shame in you.
                                    (45–6)

The rhyme is painful here, like a kind of tinnitus. The line endings frequently accentuate error and broken faith: weep, word, grave, death, delay, loss, shame, default, strife, adieu. York states early on that he can do no more than 'curse the cause I cannot aid the man', and yet the couplets carry on relentlessly, casting blame and gnawing at guilty consciences. York repeatedly accuses Somerset, who in his turn attempts with one couplet (4.4.8–9) to lay the blame at his accuser's door; but ultimately everyone recognizes their own part in the disaster. Lucy's couplets are unstoppable, hammering guilt into his hearers beyond the bounds of either poetry or necessity. Throughout the three plays, the unhushable nature of the couplet renders shame inescapable. As in the *Mirror*'s lamentations, history's misdeeds are enshrined in rhyme, proclaimed at a brutal pitch, impossible to ignore. The couplet form, to appropriate a phrase from the second tetralogy's *2 Henry IV*, '[s]ounds ever after as a sullen bell / Remembered knolling a departing friend' (1.1.102–3). Shakespeare emulates the *Mirror* in this regard, using rhyme as an immemorial recorder of wrongdoing. Where the *Mirror*'s speakers look back on their mistakes from the complacency of the grave, however, Shakespeare's historical figures welter in their own guilt: both characters and audience watch the sickening progression of events taking place before their eyes. Shakespeare's use of couplets would evolve by the time he wrote the later history plays. As well as lessening drastically in number, they would become more focused and more aware of themselves as a specific kind of voice. But this work would be built on the foundations laid in this first *Henriad*, in which the couplet's resonance was widely and emotively established. As I have demonstrated in this section, the couplets of *Henry VI* invoke the style of the widely familiar *Mirror* to perform a sort of auto-historicization. It is ironic that it is rhyme – such a self-consciously literary form – that Shakespeare uses to anchor his plays' language most firmly in the portrayal of history. The *Mirror* offers a mode of historical writing that does not so much narrate the past as *look back* on it – and an appropriation of this mode allows Shakespeare to explore historical memory with painful poignancy.

*

Shakespeare uses *Mirror*-resonant couplets in *Henry VI* to memorialize, then; to invoke the concept of memory within a dramatic medium that portrays events as happening in the present. And rhyme's effects in these three plays go beyond the local. It becomes a governing logic, an ominous music to which the characters dance. In this world, the deeds and utterances of the past are never forgotten, and the cycle of destruction repeats itself with rhythmical inevitability. This formal incorporation of the cyclical connects the plays thematically with the *Mirror*, which chooses to frame in rhyme such sentiments as, 'There is no trust in rebelles, raskall knaves, / In Fortune lesse, which wurketh as the waves'; but the blank verse mode in which Shakespeare primarily works calls for more subtle gestures towards repetition – specific choices for specific moments, rather than default rhyme.[17] There are several examples of scenes and speeches that use other repetitive linguistic devices alongside couplets to create a dreamlike (or nightmarish) sense of this worldview. I will now focus on one such scene: act 2 scene 5 of Part 3. We are in the midst of battle, and yet the scene offers a reflective pause, built around symbolism rather than action. It begins with a long soliloquy from the King, who deplores his royal state and wishes for anonymity. We then witness two tragedies of war: a son who has killed his father, and a father who has killed his son, both mistakenly. The son and father are unnamed, simply standing as emblems of the internal destruction that England is waging on its own people. The incident itself offers a sort of visual or symbolic 'rhyme'.[18] This gestural rhetoric of doubling feels consistent with the monologue we have just heard from the King. It begins:

> This battle fares like to the morning's war,
>   When dying clouds contend with growing light,
> What time the shepherd, blowing of his nails,
>   Can neither call it perfect day nor night.
> Now sways it this way like a mighty sea
>   Forced by the tide to combat with the wind,
> Now sways it that way like the selfsame sea
>   Forced to retire by fury of the wind.
> Sometime the flood prevails, and then the wind;
> Now one the better, then another best –
> Both tugging to be victors, breast to breast,
> Yet neither conqueror nor conquerèd:
> So is the equal poise of this fell war.
>
> (2.5.1–13)

The governing conceit is that of a balance tipping in 'equal poise' between two extremes: duality is inherent in the imagery and the argument. This is enacted rhetorically through obsessive doubling. In addition to the significant memorializing couplet at lines 10–11 ('Now one the better, then another best – / Both tugging to be victors, breast to breast'), we see a more unusual ABCB rhyme structure in the opening four lines, twinning 'light' with 'night'. The intensely epistrophic lines 5–9 similarly pit 'sea' and 'wind' against each other again and again, in the same way as the opposing armies fighting 'breast to breast' are 'neither conqueror nor conquerèd'. The speech sets the tone for a scene that transcends the literal, and instead presents the symbolic: rhyme becomes a keynote that reverberates beyond its own instances, enacting the war's push and pull. Its own essential characteristic of repetition, re-hearing,

---

[17] The quotation is from Jack Cade's poem: *Mirror*, fol. xlii.
[18] See John Kerrigan's discussion of repeated visual symbols as gestural rhyme in *Titus Andronicus* (in that instance, the sexual and digestive reiteration of objects entering holes): John Kerrigan, *Revenge Tragedy: Aeschylus to Armageddon* (Oxford, 1996).

mimics the reiterated patterns of history, and their own reiteration upon the stage.

A few lines later in this speech, the King begins to consider the happy state of the commoner, and wishes he could exchange his life with that of a shepherd.[19] His vision of the common man's life is based entirely around the cycles of the clock: he longs '[t]o carve out dials quaintly, point by point, / Thereby to see the minutes how they run' (lines 24–5). He then wistfully imagines calculating time in an anaphoric series of 'how many': '[h]ow many' minutes, '[h]ow many hours', '[h]ow many days', '[h]ow many years' divide up a life (26–9)? The repetition within the language itself echoes the repetition that the King associates with common life, its cyclical nature. When he imagines assigning tasks to those chunks of time, in another anaphoric series ('So many hours must I . . . '), Henry dwells again on the cyclical: sleeping and waking, resting and working, and the repeating stages of sheep-rearing (31–7). While the swain's life is a comfortably repetitious cycle, his own royal existence is an unpredictable series of isolated shocks in the form of 'care, mistrust, and treason' (54). The King's perception perhaps goes further towards engaging with 'the paradox of change within a changeless natural order' than Ferguson gives the majority of early modern thinkers credit for: in Henry's view, the daily life of the common folk develops gradually and smoothly, following its own natural cycles, while political life evolves in a series of linear jumps and jolts. This is the King's perception, at any rate. The play itself seems to take a more universalizing view. Later in the scene, the final highly repetitious speech from the distraught son-murdering father ends with a couplet as he exits: 'I'll bear thee hence, and let them fight that will – / For I have murdered where I should not kill' (121–2). Still hidden, King Henry speaks into nothingness with an answering couplet: 'Sad-hearted man, much overgone with care, / Here sits a king more woeful than you are' (123–4). The magnitude of his sadness is (in Henry's opinion) greater – he is mourning not a single son but a whole self-murdering nation – but the rhyming voice in which he expresses it is the same. Political life cannot be divided from personal life, or royal from common: in the world of this play, both are governed by the cyclical churning of a symbolic mechanism, a higher power that deals in poetic symbols rather than isolated incidents. Like the *Mirror*, this scene establishes rhyme as an apposite vehicle for the historical worldview being posited. Its own repetition echoes the repetition of human life and its wrongs.

*

Couplets in the first *Henriad* are an ever-present keynote, creating a permeating poetics of resonance (or 're-sonance') that enacts a view of history as cyclical and repeating. While rhyme is in itself a memory of a sound – and, moreover, known for its memorability – its connection with the *Mirror* situates it in these plays within a specifically historical mode of remembering. The plays perform an act of historical recall, and also depict a world characterized by memory: repeating cycles of error, ever-present guilt.

When Bacon wrote that historical drama 'represents actions as if they were present, whereas History represents them as past', he got to the heart of an issue of portrayal: plays have no pretensions to the documentary, and therefore have the liberty to conjure up the past with greater liveliness and invention.[20] But this liberty to stray from reality also encourages a free use of reality's own trappings: visible actors performing tangible deeds and speaking audible words. Literary devices such as rhyme straddle this boundary between the real and the depicted. On the one hand, rhyme – as I hope I have proved – plays an important role in the construction of historical worldviews; on the other, it is an open signal of that construction, drawing attention to the process of depiction even while it so vividly depicts. This is a widespread feature of rhyme in Shakespeare's work, but feels particularly significant when it comes to the dramatic representation of the historical past.

---

[19] We might compare this with the moment in the *Mirror* in which Henry VI wishes he had died at his coronation: 'So had I not ben washt in waves of worldly woe, / My mind to quyet bent, had not ben tossed so' (fol. Lxiiii[v]).

[20] Bacon, *Augmentis*, pp. 439–40.

When the highly patterned poetry and Senecan rhetoric of the earlier histories (the first tetralogy and *Richard II*) gave way to the more naturalistic blank verse and prose of the second *Henriad*, new forms of literary self-awareness set in to take their place, culminating in the overtly metatheatrical choruses of *Henry V*. The final words of the second *Henriad* – the last chorus or epilogue to *Henry V* – are spoken in the form of a Shakespearian sonnet. They hark back to the first *Henriad*, in content as well as in their highly patterned style:

> Henry the Sixth, in infant bands crowned king
>   Of France and England, did this king succeed,
> Whose state so many had the managing
>   That they lost France and made his England bleed,
> Which oft our stage hath shown – and, for their sake,
> In your fair minds let this acceptance take.
>   (Epilogue, 9–14)

The rhyme, as well as the allusion to the first tetralogy performed on 'our stage', looks backward in terms of theatre history even while it looks forward in terms of national history. In a repertory theatre, different chunks of history were continually played in parallel and out of order, allowing the audience to compare and contrast the stylistic choices playwrights made when constructing their portrayals. As with all the choruses in this play, the epilogue insistently reminds the audience that what they have witnessed is merely a representation of history and not history itself. By using the sonnet form, Shakespeare restates the connection between rhyme and historical portrayal, a connection established in the audience's mind by verse chronicles such as the *Mirror*, and brought to visceral, tangible life by dramatists. Rhyme becomes, in a sense, the hallmark of artistic licence: though we see and hear real people enacting history in front of us, what we are getting is a dramatic re-envisioning. By harking back in this way, Shakespeare traces a line of continuity back through his earlier histories, and to the influence that stands behind them; he again performs an act of memory through rhyme.

He also displays an awareness of his audience, and the experiences that they bring to bear when watching his plays. Where some may have been reading classical and humanist historiography, and keeping current with the debates and ideas that they spawned, large numbers of others would have come to the theatre familiar with a range of previous plays they had seen there in past months and years. To a performance of *Henry V*, many may have brought along a familiarity not only with the *Henry IV* plays, but with Shakespeare's earlier work, with *The Famous Victories*, and with the morality-influenced histories of the Queen's Men more generally. One text that permeated large swathes of the audience's consciousness, across various sectors of society, was the *Mirror*. Just as Shakespeare made use of dramatic literary forebears and contemporary intellectual views of history in his portrayals of the past and its speech, he also exploited the widespread fame of this crucial text. The *Mirror* established a paradigm for rhyming history and for historicized rhyming. It primed Shakespeare's audiences to extract their sense of what happened in the past not merely from fact, but from style. It made them ready for a kind of understanding, a kind of learning, that was based on impressions and aesthetic response rather than on information intake. It also created an association between rhyme and a recursive look at the past. Shakespeare uses *Mirror* resonances to give his historical enactments a memorializing force: the sense that the characters are speaking from beyond the grave even while they are still alive contributes to the sense of doom that pervades the first *Henriad*. The *Mirror* also stands behind the plays' fateful, cyclical language. But by invoking this register as part of a blank verse medium, Shakespeare went further than his rhyming antecedent in unsettling the boundaries of historical portrayal. History is no longer totally displaced from reality by rhyme, its utterances encased in a translucent box of self-announcing artificiality. Instead, rhyme shimmers in and out of focus, making jarringly concrete utterances in uncertain worlds. Moments of memorialization stand out like eerie clarion calls in the midst of action. Like the decisions and errors of history, rhyme sets itself in stone and cannot be erased.

'BAD' LOVE LYRICS AND POETIC HYPOCRISY FROM GASCOIGNE TO BENSON'S SHAKESPEARE

KATIE MENNIS

Hypocrite auteur – mon semblable – mon frère!
(Adapted from Baudelaire)

In *Edward III* (performed *c*.1592 and printed anonymously in 1596), King Edward attempts to seduce the married Countess of Salisbury by employing Lodwick, his secretary, to compose a love lyric for her. We see Lodwick writing this poem with 'pen, ink and paper' on stage.[1] This ghost-writing arrangement replicates a practice that occurred off stage at this time: in 1596, Thomas Nashe admitted that he similarly 'prostitute[d] [his] pen in hope of gaine' by writing 'amorous *Villanellas* and *Quipassas*' for various '*Galiardos*, and *Senior Fantasticos*'.[2] In the play, however, Lodwick is not a very obliging poet (intentionally, we suspect). He composes only two lines, reconstructed here from his interrupted delivery: '*More fair and chaste than is the queen of shades, / More bold in constancy … than Judith was …* ' (2.333–5). Edward is unimpressed: 'I thank thee then thou hast done little ill, / But what is done is passing, passing ill' (2.340–1). His criticism of Lodwick's lines is twofold. He takes issue with their content, which encourages the Countess's resistance rather than surrender. But he also objects to their poetic quality and weak comparisons: 'Compar'st thou her to the pale queen of night, / Who being set in dark seems therefore light?' (2.309–10). Both Edward's dangerous intent, to 'Beguile and ravish' (2.245), and superior poetry are on show in his recommendations to Lodwick:

> Bid her be free and general as the sun,
> Who smiles upon the basest weed that grows
> As lovingly as on the fragrant rose.
> (2.329–31)

Edward's wish that the Countess be 'general', appropriating the Sermon on the Mount, (Matthew 5.45: 'he maketh his sun to rise on the evil and on the good'), elucidates his earlier response to Lodwick's requests for details of the poem's addressee: '[Her] body is an abstract or a brief / Contains each *general* virtue in the world' (2.248–9). Edward hopes the generality of the poem's tropes will breed the 'virtue' of sexual generality in its reader.

The irony of this scene is that the dramatist supplies Edward with reams of effective lines for the Sidneyan lover whose verse is as much about writing love as praising his mistress, if only he could write them down on paper himself: 'for sighs set down true sighs indeed / Talking of grief, to make thee ready groan' (2.233–4); 'To music every summer-leaping swain / Compares his sunburnt lover when she speaks' (2.273–4). A surprising density of fragmented quotations from Shakespeare's sonnets (not yet printed), including the 'basest weed' and 'fragrant rose' from Edward's lines above and, later, the last line of sonnet 94 ('Lilies that fester … '),[3] crops up in the dialogue surrounding Lodwick's composition. Critics draw diverse conclusions about

---

[1] *King Edward III*, ed. Richard Proudfoot and Nicola Bennett (London, 2017), 2.225. Further references appear in parentheses.
[2] Thomas Nashe, *Have with you to Saffron-walden* (London, 1596), sig. E3v.
[3] *Shakespeare's Sonnets*, ed. Katherine Duncan-Jones (London, 2010), 94.12; 95.5; 94.14 = *Edward III*, 2.617. Further references to this edition appear in parentheses.

whether these fragments originate in the play or the sonnets and, connectedly, about Shakespeare's probable authorship of this scene.[4] Why would the playwright scatter quotations from a 'good' sonnet sequence – likely his own – around a scene of 'bad' poetic composition?

I read *Edward III* as an early instance of Shakespeare's, staging of 'bad' written love lyric in a way that playfully engages with his own, his precursors' and his contemporaries' poetic practice. Several of Shakespeare's plays feature characters who are poets.[5] These poets tend to be love lyricists or sonneteers – often 'bad' ones.[6] The sonnet-writing scene in *Edward III* problematizes characteristics of written love lyrics that Shakespeare will later explore in a more sustained way: their textual or material status and stylistic quality relative to their settings; the felt but implicit presence of the playwright as ghost-writer of the characters' lines; the potential for extraction, misattribution or re-appropriation across genres and media. *Edward III* brings the audience into a fiction of composition in which the target of persuasion is only the mistress, not an external reader, as it is in the reality of sonneting. Because no reconstructed lyric is supplied in full, the external reader and their (perhaps different) assessment of the value of the poem do not interfere in this fiction. But plays like *Love's Labour's Lost* and *As You Like It* that do supply complete 'bad' lyrics on stage and in playtexts allow for – perhaps even covet – assessments of value that differ from their receptions on stage, allowing them to function as 'bad' poems on stage and as good poems outside their dramatic contexts.

In this, I argue, Shakespeare is unusual as a dramatist. The best texts to compare with Shakespeare's practice are prose narratives that contain lyrics written by poet-characters. The narratives that form the context for Shakespeare's staging of 'bad' love lyrics are roughly divisible into two groups. The first kind contains pastoral narratives that are sources of varying importance for *As You Like It*, such as Thomas Lodge's *Rosalynde* (1590) and Montemayor's *Diana* in Bartholomew Yong's 1598 translation.[7] These narratives take a 'good in everything' approach to their characters' lyrics:[8] they are assumed to be good and are not stylistically differentiated from the rest of the narrative. The second group of narratives, including George Gascoigne's *Adventures of Master F. J.* (1573) and Thomas Nashe's *Unfortunate Traveller* (1594), are not Shakespearian sources in the same way,[9] are less pastoral than Petrarchan, and playfully employ 'badness' in the composition of their lyrics and the stances that they adopt towards them. The lyrics in the former group may sometimes be read as 'bad', although they are not intended to be so, especially in light of texts like Gascoigne's and Nashe's. The presentation of poet-characters and their love lyrics, particularly by Nashe and Shakespeare, is more complicated than parody.[10] I would like to suggest that it might be better thought of as 'hypocrisy', a word used by Katherine in *Love's Labour's Lost* to describe the lords' lyrics (a 'huge

---

[4] See Claes Schaar, *Elizabethan Sonnet Themes and the Dating of Shakespeare's 'Sonnets'* (Lund, 1962), pp. 117–35; and Giorgio Melchiori, *Shakespeare's Dramatic Meditations: An Experiment in Criticism* (Oxford, 1976), pp. 42–58.

[5] See B. J. Sokol, 'Poets in Shakespeare's plays', in Sokol, *Shakespeare's Artists: The Painters, Sculptors, Poets and Musicians in his Plays and Poems* (London, 2018), pp. 93–116.

[6] In his Ph.D. dissertation, Matthew Harrison also discusses the poems in *As You Like It* and *Love's Labour's Lost* as 'bad'. See Matthew P. Harrison, 'Tear him for his bad verses: poetic value and literary history in early modern England' (unpublished Ph.D. dissertation, Princeton University, 2015): https://dataspace.princeton.edu/handle/88435/dsp0105741v01w.

[7] On Montemayor, see T. P. Harrison, 'Shakespeare and Montemayor's *Diana*', *Studies in English* 6 (1926), 72–120; pp. 118–19.

[8] I take this phrase from William Shakespeare, *As You Like It*, ed. Juliet Dusinberre (London, 2006), 2.1.17. Further references to this edition appear in parentheses.

[9] Maurice Hunt argues for the influence of *The Unfortunate Traveller* on *Love's Labour's Lost* in 'Thomas Nashe, *The Vnfortvnate Traveller*, and *Love's Labour's Lost*', *Studies in English Literature, 1500–1900* 54 (2014), 297–314.

[10] As Inga-Stina Ewbank puts it, 'Deliberately "bad" Shakespearean poetry is sometimes functional rather than parodic': 'Shakespeare's poetry', in *A New Companion to Shakespeare Studies*, ed. Kenneth Muir and S. Schoenbaum (Cambridge, 1971), pp. 99–115; p. 101.

translation of hypocrisy', 5.2.51). I borrow this word's several meanings to describe a mode of framing love lyric in the period that thrives on, but criticizes and disowns, its own 'badness', ineffectiveness or profitlessness.

By hypocrisy, I mean primarily the act of criticizing someone for something that one is guilty of oneself, as expressed by Christ in the Sermon on the Mount: 'why beholdest thou the mote that is in thy brother's eye, but considerest not the beam that is in thine own eye? ... Thou hypocrite ... ' (Matthew 7.1–5). In *Love's Labour's Lost* in particular, Shakespeare translates allusions to the kind of hypocrisy set out in the Sermon on the Mount to a literary-critical context: criticizing a love poem as 'bad' when that poetic badness is, in fact, one's own. Hypocrisy also means insincerity more broadly, a quality that is even more difficult to attribute to a love lyric than it is to declarations of love in general. 'Given almost any protestation of love by a "good" character in Shakespeare one could transfer it without indecorum to a hypocrite.'[11] Philip Edwards's statement is equally true of the quality of a love lyric taken out of context: given any love lyric by a 'good' poet, one could transfer it without indecorum to a 'bad' poet, and it could become laughable; likewise, any 'bad' sonnet may be redeemed by our awareness of the poet's insincerity. For Aristotle, *hypocrisis* meant 'performance' or 'delivery'; he worried that it could make an undeserving text beautiful, an anxiety that arose from the recent phenomenon of writers composing verse to be performed by others rather than by the poet himself.[12] Performance and personae are variables that make (e)valuation of love lyric by words and images alone impossible. A lyric becomes ridiculous if performed 'ill-favouredly' (*As You Like It*, 3.2.255), but almost any fault can be forgiven if we imagine the author to be dramatizing a lover-persona – a distance that can arise from without as well as within a lyric. The meanings of *hypocrisis* in classical rhetoric collapse distinctions between imitation and parody – even, I will show, between writing, ghost-writing and false attribution.

I argue that Shakespeare's 'poetics of hypocrisy' is latent in certain non-dramatic texts of the period.

This article will provide a series of case studies of love lyrics in prose narratives before discussing the examples from Shakespeare's plays. Finally, I will show that those who extract these lyrics engage playfully with the narratives and playtexts, acting upon the flexibility of lyric value and poetic hypocrisy that they inscribe.

LOVE LYRICS IN PROSE NARRATIVES

... contention for trifles can get but a trifling victory ... Alexander and Darius, when they strave who should be cock of this world's dunghill, the benefit they got was that the after-livers may say:

> Haec memini, et victum frustra contendere Thyrsim.
> ex illo Corydon, Corydon est tempore nobis[13]

It will be helpful briefly to trace the roots of early modern love lyric and its potential 'badness'. *Eclogue* 7 has raised one persistent question throughout its reception history: why does Thyrsis lose the poetic contest to Corydon? It is framed as thoroughly balanced, each poet singing in turn, until the final two lines (quoted above by Sidney in *The Defence of Poesy*): 'I remember this, and that Thyrsis competed in vain and was defeated. From that time it has been Corydon, Corydon for us.' Two defences of Virgil's pastoral perfection come into conflict: that he would not assert Thyrsis' inferiority arbitrarily, and that he would not compose inferior poetry for one of his shepherds. Sidney's take here is lightly dismissive: the triviality of the pastoral genre makes qualitative differentiation between poets trivial. Another commentator, Juan Luis de la Cerda, circumvents the embarrassment of Thyrsis' inferiority by taking the

---

[11] Philip Edwards, 'The declaration of love', in *Shakespeare's Styles: Essays in Honour of Kenneth Muir*, ed. Philip Edwards, Inga-Stina Ewbank and G. K. Hunter (Cambridge, 1980), pp. 39–50; p. 46.
[12] See Aristotle, *The 'Art of Rhetoric'*, trans. John Henry Freese (Cambridge, MA, 1926), 3.1.
[13] *Sidney's 'The Defence of Poesy' and Selected Renaissance Literary Criticism*, ed. Gavin Alexander (London, 2004), pp. 1–54; p. 26.

eclogue as an allegory of imitation, rather than a literally representative contest: Corydon stands for Virgil, Thyrsis for Theocritus and other Greek poets – not Virgil's Roman contemporaries, as other commentators have thought. La Cerda writes, 'What does the king of poets care for Bavius and Maevius, the most terrible poets?'[14] There is no space for Bavius and Maevius, paradigmatic bad poets, in Virgilian pastoral.

Let us take *Eclogue* 7 as a generic microcosm. Paul Alpers reads pastoral romance as 'transformed eclogues',[15] but the format of *Eclogue* 7 – lyric performance with a narrative frame – evolved in more than one direction. Pastoral romance made the frame more prominent, while in Mantuan's fully dramatized eclogues and, later, in pastoral anthologies, it receded. This evolution is concurrent with a tradition originating later, in Dante's *Vita nuova* – love lyric with a narrative and critical frame – via Petrarch, that gave rise to the sonnet sequence on the one hand and a text like Gascoigne's *Adventures* on the other. The status of love lyric is being negotiated in both traditions concurrently in early modernity, on a pastoral–Petrarchan continuum. Sidney's summation of *Eclogue* 7 is symptomatic of an early modern critical blind spot: the *overall* badness of this kind of lyric obscures the question of qualitative differentiation within the genre, in poetics and in practice. Sidney does introduce some mild 'badness' into his pastoral, as Virgil apparently would not, writing 'ruder' verse for clownish characters such as Dametas in the *Arcadia*.[16] In general, however, pastoral narratives take a non-critical approach to their characters' lyrics. The Shakespearian love lyrics that I will discuss are 'bad' in a way that is not technically faulty, does not map onto rusticity, and is specific to written compositions. 'Bavius and Maevius' – inferior but not technically defective poets, whose practice is not remote from the author's – enter the pastoral via a context of lyric and narrative that contains Gascoigne's and Nashe's hypocritical postures towards their lyrics, as well as Lodge's and Montemayor's lack of qualitative interrogation.[17]

The first lyric in Lodge's *Rosalynde* is not a love lyric but the versified will of Sir John of Bordeaux (forebear of Sir Rowland de Bois).[18] The '*salem ingenii*' ('salt of wit'; p. 1) that Sir John possessed in life manifests itself in this lyric's aphoristic fatherly advice. In response, his malevolent son Saladyne introduces the idea of the *authentic axiom* to the narrative: 'shall his words be axioms, and his talk be so authentical, that thou wilt, to observe them, prejudice thyself? No, no, Saladyne, sick men's wills … are like the laws of a city written in dust' (p. 10). Saladyne's refusal to authenticate his father's axioms in action undermines the lyric's status as a textual object, reducing it from a 'scroll' (p. 6) to dust. The love lyrics in *Rosalynde* show the same emphasis on the authenticated axiom, and how it authorizes and is authorized by the lyric as object or song. Saladyne later falls in love with 'Aliena'. On conversing with him, she comments, 'you are a great philosopher in Venus' principles, else could you not discover her secret aphorisms' (p. 126). She spots a 'paper in his bosom', a sonnet that contrasts the lover's fixity with *sententiae* on the world's changefulness:

> If it be true that heaven's eternal course
> With restless sway and ceaseless turning glides;
> If air inconstant be, and swelling source
> Turn and returns with many fluent tides …
> (pp. 126–7)

---

[14] Virgil, *Bucolica et Georgica*, ed. Juan Luis de la Cerda (Frankfurt, 1608), p. 127 (my translation).
[15] Paul Alpers, *What Is Pastoral?* (Chicago, 1996), p. 67.
[16] Dametas's 'rural poesy' contains gently parodic rustic elements – 'Eyes fair and great, like fair great ox's eyes: | O breast in which two white sheep swell in pride' – but the qualitative differentiation is not great: Philip Sidney, *The Old Arcadia*, ed. Katherine Duncan-Jones (Oxford, 1999), pp. 167–8.
[17] With the kind of 'bad' poetry that 'Bavius and Maevius' represent in this argument, contrast that of Crispinus and Demetrius in Ben Jonson's *Poetaster* (1601), which is more 'technical'; their verse is indeed 'faulty' and 'a parody of poetry which has no meaning': Alice Leonard, *Error in Shakespeare, Shakespeare in Error* (London, 2020), pp. 26–8.
[18] Lodge's '*Rosalynde*' Being the Original of Shakespeare's 'As You Like It', ed. W. W. Greg (Freeport, NY, 1970), pp. 7–8. Further references appear in parentheses.

This sonnet's narrative reception is characteristic of *Rosalynde*. For Aliena, Saladyne's sonnet proves that 'Ovid's axiom', which she supplies in Latin (that love relies on leisure), 'is not authentical'. It provides new axioms in its place, authenticated by Saladyne's actions and the paper in his bosom: 'even labour hath her loves' (p. 128). The fact of a lyric's existence, whether written or sung, 'discovers' its author's love to those who encounter it in *Rosalynde* – not an interrogation of its quality or style. Phoebe's sonnet, 'My boat doth pass the straits' (p. 137), for example, sets Ganymede and Aliena to 'great laughter', not because it is bad, but because it proves that proud Phoebe is in love (p. 138). This poem, a translation of Petrarch's 'Passa la nave mia', is in fact one of the least laughable in the narrative, containing subtle intertexts with Wyatt's popular translation:[19]

> My boat doth pass the straits
>   of seas incensed with fire,
> Filled with forgetfulness;
>   amidst the winter's night
> A blind and careless boy,
>   brought up by fond desire,
> Doth guide me in the sea
>   of sorrow and despite
>
> (p. 137)

Phoebe implicitly acknowledges the self-infliction of her suffering by altering Wyatt's line, 'The stars be hid *that led me to this pain*', to 'No star for safety shines, / no *Phoebe* from aloft' (emphasis mine). Shakespeare's take on this moment will play with *Rosalynde*'s lack of critical engagement with its lyrics.

Only one love lyric in Montemayor's *Diana* is composed as a written poem, rather than spontaneously sung.[20] Belisa, its love-object, recounts receiving the poem, titled 'Arsenius *his letter*', to an internal audience in the narrative. She received it 'much against [her] will' (p. 114), but the lyric was highly persuasive, launching a tragic love-plot. It becomes clear that the version of the poem in Yong's text is not a verbatim transcription of Belisa's reading, during which she 'stay[ed] betweene many verses, and repeat[ed] some of them twise' (p. 118), but a reproduction of the imagined textual object that she received, under a narratorial title. This title misattributes the lyric's fictional authorship: 'Arsenius *his letter*' is in fact ghost-written by Arsileus, his son, 'an excellent Poet' (p. 113). Arsileus supplies it to his amorous father unwittingly, via a middle-man, Argastus. So far, so confusing – but Belisa surmises that the lyric 'savoured more of the sonne his quicke wit, then of the father his blunt affection' (p. 119). Unfortunately, Belisa's sharp taste did not prevent the poem from causing her to love 'not onely … *Arsileus*, but also his father' (p. 119). 'Arsenius *his letter*' both betrays its true author's voice as clearly as a sung lyric and elevates its ascribed author; it is personal and characterful, but its value is partially extractable and transferrable. Unlike the lyrics in *Rosalynde*, the letter causes narrative fallouts unique to its status as written text rather than song. Stepping outside the narrative, its false attribution self-reflexively signals the felt presence of Montemayor, and Yong the translator, as 'ghost-writers' behind characters' lyrics – an awareness that often led to such lyrics being attributed directly to Yong in anthologies such as *England's Helicon*.

Neither *Rosalynde* nor *Diana* frame any of their narratives' lyrics as 'bad', although Montemayor problematizes the authorship of 'Arsenius *his letter*' and introduces the possibility of poetry of varying quality (if Arsenius were to compose a lyric himself, it would presumably be 'bad'). As in *Edward III*, Shakespeare's Sonnets offer a slippery counterpoint. T. P. Harrison's comparison of stanzas from 'Arsenius *his letter*' to certain of the sonnets suggests that Shakespeare's interest in the poem might corroborate narratorial claims of Arsileus's poetic excellence:

---

[19] *Tottel's Miscellany (1557–1587)*, ed. Hyder Edward Rollins, 2 vols. (Cambridge, MA, 1965), vol. 1, p. 38.
[20] *A Critical Edition of Yong's Translation of George of Montemayor's Diana and Gil Polo's Enamoured Diana*, ed. Judith M. Kennedy (Oxford, 1968), p. 19. Further references appear in parentheses.

A change a thousand times I see,
And nouels euery day doe raine:
Minds change from that they wont to bee,
Obliuions doe reuiue againe.
In euery thing there is great change,
The which I neuer saw in thee[21]

As a written lyric, 'Arsenius *his letter*' has a multiplicity and flexibility (of authorship and medium) that differentiates it from the singularity and sufficiency of sung lyric in the *Diana*, or any kind of lyric in *Rosalynde*. In other kinds of narrative, the fundamental value and quality of the lines no longer transcends this multiplicity.

In the *Adventures*, Gascoigne is more than a destabilizing felt presence, as Montemayor and Yong become in 'Arsenius *his letter*'. His later admission in the *Posies* (1575) that he had written all the lyrics in the novella is hardly necessary to note Gascoigne's hypocritical game of criticizing his own poems in the *Adventures*. The editor G. T. justifies his publication of F. J.'s lyrics by saying, 'I found none of them, so barreyne, but that ... had in it *Aliquid Salis*.'[22] He commends some of them particularly, sometimes agreeing with F. J. or defending the poems against F. J.'s judgements; however, he finds many of F. J.'s lyrics relatively bad without proper qualifications and context. Of F. J.'s ninth poem, he says, 'were it not a little to much prayse ... I could the more commend it' (p. 178); of his tenth, 'let it passe amongst the rest, and he that liketh it not, turn over the leaf to another' (p. 180). The latter is an adaptation of the same Petrarchan sonnet that Phoebe 'translates' in *Rosalynde*:

> A cloud of care hath covred all my coste,
> And stormes of stryfe doo threaten to appeare:
> The waves of woo, which I mistrusted moste,
> Have broke the bankes wherein my lyfe lay cleere
> (p. 161)

G. T. makes excuses for this poem – 'a rough meeter ... devised in great disquiet of mynd, and written in rage' – and apparently 'F. J. himselfe had so slender liking thereof ... that he never presented it' (p. 162). Like Lodge, Gascoigne does not acknowledge that this lyric is a translation or imitation here, but elsewhere G. T. calls F. J.'s lyrics translations haphazardly to excuse their quality, often where no source is apparent. Gascoigne later evades assumptions that the narrative is veiled autobiography with the same excuse: 'translated out of the Italian' (p. 141, nn.1–2). The whole narrative is a 'huge translation of hypocrisy' in which Gascoigne criticizes and disowns the literary motes in F. J.'s poetry through the unreliable judge G. T.

Gascoigne's narrative inscribes the lyrics with a flexibility of quality by revealing how a lyric's fictional efficacy can differ from its (re)contextualized value across media and genres of lyric compilation, even under different names. Take F. J.'s '*Beautie shut up thy shop*' (pp. 175–6), an extremely long poetic 'challenge to beautie' in Poulter's measure. M. R. Rohr Philmus reads this poem as 'an amused (if coarse) satire on the fantastic excesses of Petrarchism', full of 'absurdity' and 'unusually heavy alliteration'.[23] The love behind this lyric is expressed too covertly for Elinor, a reader who struggles to read even the simplest 'intent' in F. J.'s 'darke letters' (pp. 146–7). Exemplification and pseudonyms go disastrously wrong when the manuscript is published 'without [F. J.'s] consent' by Elinor, jealous 'because hir name was *Elynor* and not *Hellen*' (pp. 176–7):

> Beautie shut up thy shop, and trusse up all thy trash,
> My Nell hath stolen thy finest stuff, and left thee in the lash:
> ... my Hellen is more fayre then Paris wife,
> And doth deserve more famous praise, then Venus for hir life.

G. T. does not rule out Elinor's jealous reading, since, by an incriminating coincidence, F. J. did in

---

[21] Harrison, 'Shakespeare and Montemayor', pp. 118–19. Harrison compares Sonnets 73, 64, 12 and 15.
[22] George Gascoigne, *A Hundreth Sundrie Flowres*, ed. G. W. Pigman (Oxford, 2000), pp. 144–5. Further references appear in parentheses.
[23] M. R. Rohr Philmus, 'Gascoigne's fable of the artist as a young man', *The Journal of English and Germanic Philology* 73 (1974), 13–31; p. 19.

fact have an affair with a '*Hellene*' – 'sixe or seven yeres' later (p. 177)! So, even if it was not intended for her, he 'might adapt it to [*Hellene*'s] name, and so make it serve both their turnes, as elder lovers have done before and ... will do worlde without end. *Amen*' (p. 177). G. T.'s admission of the poem's adaptability rubbishes his own biographical criticism of F. J.'s poems, which is the method of the narrative: G. T. apparently received all the poems in *A Hundreth Sundrie Flowres* 'confusedly gathered together', then 'guess[ed]' which ones were F. J.'s, and put them in a 'good order' or sequence (143), composing the narrative around them. Narrative 'occasions', it is revealed by the Hellene/Elinor substitution, can be changed – or fictionalized. G. T. adapts liturgical language to send up the sanctified yet adaptable and communal language of lovers, whose lyrics are all variations on the same scripture.

This framing of inset lyrics with adapted sacred language to send up and forgive 'bad' love poetry simultaneously is also found in *The Unfortunate Traveller*, in which Nashe 'ghost-writes' three lyrics for his fictionalized Earl of Surrey. Surrey is not only a real poet, unlike F. J., but his poems were printed in *Tottel's Miscellany* and thus were part of the canon of love lyric. Surrey's lyrics, although grouped together, are ordered arbitrarily in *Tottel*, each with an occasional title; only one addresses a Geraldine.[24] Even so, readers tended to cast Surrey and Geraldine as an English Petrarch and Laura,[25] reading Surrey's lyrics sequentially, as G. T. does F. J.'s. The absurdity of the incidents that lead to the composition of the love lyrics in Nashe's narrative, including the substitution of a 'Diamante' for Geraldine, undercuts the apparent logic of the occasional titles and sequential readings of Surrey's poems in *Tottel*. Jack's comments on Surrey's third lyric show that Surrey valorizes the authentic Ovidian axiom as much as Lodge's characters, but they are less valuable poetic currency here: 'With [diamonds] on [the glass] did he anatomize these body-wanting mots: *Dulce puella malum est; Quod fugit ipse sequor* ... '.[26] The lyric itself is not a versified gathering of *sententiae*, however, but a coherent sonnet written '[i]n praise of [Geraldine's] chamber'. It plays on the word *stanza*, neatly glorifies its own poetic space, and christens itself 'Our Ladies chapel':

> Fair room, the presence of sweet beauty's pride,
> The place the sun upon the earth did hold
> When Phaeton his chariot did misguide,
> The tower where Jove rained down himself in gold.
> Prostrate as holy ground I'll worship thee,
> Our Lady's chapel henceforth be thou named
>
> (p. 261)

Surrey's lyrics are not so much hypocritically criticized as ironized in the narrative: 'Who would have learned to write an excellent passion might have been a perfect tragic poet had he but attended half the extremity of his lament' (p. 254). Whether or not they are 'excellent passions', Surrey's wooing of Geraldine via the substitute Diamante renders them 'huge translation[s] of hypocrisy'. Jack comments immediately after the first poems that 'Italy', where Surrey composes the next two, 'stuck as a great mote in my master's eye' (p. 248): this mote hints at not only Surrey's, but also Nashe's own, hypocrisy, in ironizing poems that he has composed himself.

Dorothy Jones reads the three lyrics as clear 'anti-Petrarchan satire' in their essential nature,[27] but Jonathan Crewe finds them 'as authentic (nonparodic) as any of their kind', even suggesting that Nashe composed them sincerely and later gained critical perspective.[28] The truth is probably somewhere in the middle. While there are some clear wrong notes – we might have to discount the second lyric entirely ('Let our tongues meet and strive as they would sting, / Crush out my wind with one straight girting grasp', p. 254) – it seems that Nashe intended them to be passable.

---

[24] *Tottel*, ed. Rollins, vol. 1, pp. 3–31; p. 9.
[25] *Tottel*, ed. Rollins, vol. 2, p. 72.
[26] Thomas Nashe, *The Unfortunate Traveller*, in *An Anthology of Elizabethan Prose Fiction*, ed. Paul Salzman (Oxford, 2008), pp. 205–309, p. 261. Further references appear in parentheses.
[27] Dorothy Jones, 'An example of anti-Petrarchan satire in Nashe's *The Unfortunate Traveller*', *The Yearbook of English Studies* 1 (1971), 48–54.
[28] Jonathan V. Crewe, *Unredeemed Rhetoric: Thomas Nashe and the Scandal of Authorship* (London, 1982), p. 82.

Rollins finds the credulity with which Nashe's Surrey love-plot was accepted as fact for 'two hundred years' astonishing, but he does not emphasize that Nashe's lyrics were also accepted as authentic, as I will later reveal.[29] No critic connects Nashe's 'ghost-writing' of lyrics for the fictional Surrey with his *real* ghost-writing practice, from which he assumes an ironic distance, but for which the production of clear 'anti-Petrarchan satire' surely would not do. Nashe's Surrey poems collapse distinctions between writing, ghost-writing and parodying amorous verse. The third poem succeeds because it is all three.

Whether the lyrics are satirical or authentic, the liturgical cadences with which Jack sends up Surrey's passion are potentially redemptive: 'Not a little was I delighted with this unexpected love story ... Now I beseech God love me so well as I love a plain dealing man. Earth is earth, flesh is flesh; earth will to earth and flesh unto flesh; frail earth, frail flesh, who can keep you from the work of your creation?' (pp. 239–40). Crewe reads this passage as going some way towards 'saving' poetry and resolving *The Unfortunate Traveller*'s superficially antagonistic relationship between antistyle and style.[30] Crewe writes, '[Jack] elicits the truth of Surrey's narrative ... reinscrib[ing] idealism in an inverted form', with 'an informal prose poem' that 'draw[s] humorously but gracefully on liturgical cadences' – not unlike G. T.'s '*Amen*'.[31] Before Surrey's third poem, Jack's prose forms a quatrain that slips seamlessly into the lyric itself: 'The alchemy of his eloquence, out of the incomprehensible drossy matter of clouds and air, distilled no more quintessence than would make his Geraldine complete fair' (p. 260). This elasticity of what Crewe calls antistyle and style chimes with a comment by A. D. Nuttall, who observes that style 'expands to embrace the very rejection of style until that rejection is at last – a style'.[32] Nuttall's example, tellingly, is from *Love's Labour's Lost*: '*Sans "sans"*, I pray you'.[33] Lorna Hutson observes that, in *The Unfortunate Traveller*, Nashe's 'page' – Jack the page being an inescapable figure for the printed page and its value throughout the narrative – reveals the 'moral hypocrisy' of narratives obliged to sacrifice 'everything and everyone' in the interests of profit.[34] This profit is not only monetary, but also that demanded by early modern poetics, the literary hypocrisy of which Nashe reveals. Shakespeare will reveal and claim this literary hypocrisy for love lyric. In *Love's Labour's Lost*, Shakespeare takes up where he left off in *Edward III*, later revisiting love lyric and its badness in light of his reading of *Rosalynde* in *As You Like It*.

'BAD' LOVE LYRICS IN SHAKESPEARE'S PLAYS

In *Much Ado about Nothing,* the fact of a love lyric's existence simply 'discovers' its author's love to those who encounter it, as in *Rosalynde*, except the text of the lyric itself is not supplied. Although Benedick says he 'was not born under a rhyming planet' (5.2.38–9), when 'A halting sonnet of his own pure brain' is produced (5.4.87), it acts as evidentiary without being read aloud or qualitatively interrogated. This is not the case in *Love's Labour's Lost* or *As You Like It*.[35] The badness of the inset written love lyrics in these plays is underdetermined, but the reception of their quality on stage is overdetermined and negative. Critics have followed this negative reception, particularly with regard to Orlando's efforts: Jonathan Lamb, for example, finds Orlando's poems 'admittedly bad'.[36] Although Berowne and the other lords'

---

[29] *Tottel*, ed. Rollins, vol. 2, p. 71.
[30] Crewe, *Unredeemed*, pp. 48, 51.
[31] Crewe, *Unredeemed*, p. 84.
[32] A. D. Nuttall, *Overheard by God: Fiction and Prayer in Herbert, Milton, Dante, and St. John* (London, 1980), p. 16.
[33] William Shakespeare, *Love's Labour's Lost*, ed. H. R. Woudhuysen (London, 2014), 5.2.416. Further references to this edition appear in parentheses.
[34] Lorna Hutson, *Thomas Nashe in Context* (Oxford, 1989), p. 217.
[35] The dramatic sonnet in *Romeo and Juliet* (1.5.92–105) offers a further contrast: being 'composed' spontaneously, collaboratively and without comment, it acts as an effective negotiation of love between the characters.
[36] Jonathan P. Lamb, *Shakespeare in the Marketplace of Words* (Cambridge, 2017), p. 118.

lyrics also go down badly on stage, for G. K. Hunter they are middling:

> They are certainly not the greatest sonnets ever written.... Had we known these poems only in the context of *Love's Labour's Lost* we would, I suspect, regard them as parodic in their essential nature ... But within a narrower range of effects, from neutral to excellent ... poetic sufficiency is absorbed into its dramatic context and takes the particular colour that the context allows.... The energy of the poem does not simply drain away into the context of the play; it remains obvious enough to challenge us, as it were, to remember its anthology potential.[37]

The phrase 'poetic sufficiency' is more telling in the context of the two plays and their sources than Hunter notes here. I will show that they are not only poetically sufficient, but hypocritical.

> If love make me forsworn, how shall I swear to love?
>   Ah, never faith could hold, if not to beauty vowed.
> Though to myself forsworn, to thee I'll faithful prove.
>   Those thoughts to me were oaks, to thee like osiers bowed.
> Study his bias leaves, and makes his books thine eyes,
>   Where all those pleasures live, that art would comprehend.
> If knowledge be the mark, to know thee shall suffice
>   (*Love's Labour's Lost*, 4.2.105–11)

Berowne's sonnet gets into the hands of Nathaniel and Holofernes rather than those of its intended reader, Rosaline. On Nathaniel's reading of the sonnet, Holofernes comments, 'Here are only numbers ratified, but for the ... golden cadence of poesy, *caret*. ... *Imitari* is nothing' (4.2.121–5), invoking a maxim from Quintilian, 'imitatio per se ipsa non sufficit' ('imitation is not sufficient on its own'),[38] which Holofernes splits up and mangles across the play. He later enters with the pronouncement 'Satis quid sufficit' (5.1.1) – not only misquoting the proverbial 'Satis [est] quod sufficit' ('that which suffices is enough' or 'enough is as good as a feast'), but also 'mis-completing' his fragmentation of Quintilian ('Imitari [non] sufficit'). This fragment's summation of nothing at the beginning of a scene reveals the critic's lack of solutions to fill the holes that he picks in others' poetic attempts, preferring to say what they lack, rather than, more positively, 'quid sufficit'. We may well wonder what sufficiency in love lyric sounds like. Berowne's sonnet offers a simple answer – 'to know thee shall suffice' – but better readers than Holofernes think the poem misses its mark. Katherine calls the lords' poems a 'translation' (5.2.51), and the idealized text for translation that Berowne's poem proposes is silent: he will 'make his books [Rosaline's] eyes'. Love lyric must always fall short – or, rather, be too much – as a translation of an ideal, silent text.

Whereas, in the more Petrarchan world of *Love's Labour's Lost*, 'eyes' are the new 'books', in *As You Like It*, as Matthew Harrison also notes,[39] 'running brooks' are the idealized silent text for the quiet style of translation that Duke Senior exemplifies:

> DUKE SENIOR ... this our life, exempt from public haunt,
>   Finds tongues in trees, books in the running brooks,
>   Sermons in stones, and good in everything.
> AMIENS   I would not change it. Happy is your grace
>   That can translate the stubbornness of fortune
>   Into so quiet and so sweet a style.
>   (2.1.15–20)

Although Orlando's poetic aims are closer to Berowne's, the language of his lyrics and their reception opposes his poetic style to the Duke's pastoral standards of sufficiency. The Duke and Amiens 'would not change' their 'desert city' (23). Orlando's second poem loudly violates this principle: '*Why should this a desert be, / For it is unpeopled? No!*' (3.2.122–3). Rather than the Duke's 'Sermons in stones', Rosalind reads a 'tedious homily of love' in Orlando's writing (3.2.152–3). The phrase 'Satis [est] quod sufficit' that Holofernes butchers is used flawlessly by the shepherd Corydon in *Rosalynde*, closing an account

---

[37] G. K. Hunter, 'Poem and context in *Love's Labour's Lost*', in *Shakespeare's Styles*, ed. Edwards, Ewbank and Hunter, pp. 25–38; pp. 32–3.
[38] Quintilian, *The Orator's Education*, trans. Donald A. Russell, 5 vols. (Cambridge, MA, 2001), vol. 4, 10.2.4.
[39] See Harrison, 'Tear him', pp. 154–5.

of the pastoral life: 'we have enough to satisfy: and, mistress, I have so much Latin, *Satis est quod sufficit*' (p. 47). Corydon's usage contrasts Holofernes's in not only its accuracy, but also its enactment of its own sufficiency (which Alpers observes).[40] The way in which Corydon's experience authenticates this axiom in an authorial style is consistent with *Rosalynde*'s love lyrics. Contrastingly, the equivalent passage in *As You Like It*, which directly precedes Orlando's poems, translates the Latin with an absolute sufficiency that reinforces the pastoral standards by which Orlando's verses fail. Corin replies to Touchstone's inquiry as to whether he has 'any philosophy', 'No more but that I know ... the property of rain is to wet and fire to burn ... good pasture makes fat sheep' (3.2.22–9). Orlando's verses, in which 'Rosalind' completes '*every* sentence' and is compiled of '*many* parts' (3.2.133, 146), are now overkill: when the bar of sufficiency is set so low, *satis* sounds like satire.

Lamb notes that *As You Like It* 'fits perfectly into the tradition of ... "florilegia"'.[41] This is also true of *Rosalynde*. Shakespeare revises Lodge, however, not only by introducing badness into some characters' lyrics and their reception, but also by differentiating song from written lyric: the play's two written love lyricists, Orlando and Phoebe, are subjected to harsh criticism. Sung lyric sustains the fiction of the anthology as a forest of songs, but the written lyrics draw attention to this fiction and to themselves as extractable 'anthology pieces'. Of the three written lyrics in *As You Like It*, only Orlando's second lyric ('*Why should this a desert be ... ?*' 3.2.122–51) is a complete, competent written love lyric. Phoebe and Orlando both use trochaic tetrameter, a metre onto which Touchstone easily 'graft[s]' his parodic imitation of Orlando's first poem (3.2.114). The badness of this first eight-line lyric (3.2.85–92) is not underdetermined and could be described as 'technical': every line rhymes with 'Rosalind' with varying degrees of contortion, including a rhyme of 'lined' with '-lind'. Phoebe's epistolary poem to 'Ganymede' is not performed (so not printed) as a complete lyric: Silvius and Rosalind repeatedly interrupt its reading. Accordingly, it is Orlando's second lyric that points to its own 'anthology potential' most clearly.

Phoebe's lyric nonetheless acts as a counterpart to Orlando's earlier endeavour that shows that the quality of a written lyric is in the eye of the beholder and the performance of the reader, as Orlando suggests when he tells Jaques to 'mar no more of my verses with reading them ill-favouredly' (3.2.254–5). Phoebe's poem to 'Ganymede' is not a version of Petrarch; instead, it 'translates' into verse the plainer letter that accompanied that sonnet in *Rosalynde*:

> *Art thou god to shepherd turned,*
> *That a maiden's heart hath burned? ...*
> *Why, the godhead laid apart,*
> *Warr'st thou with a woman's heart?*
>
> (4.3.40–1, 44–5)

Rosalind takes issue with this lyric's 'giant-rude' style (34), which seems ungenerous, as it is not 'rude' in a Sidneyan sense. Shakespeare's choice not to supply a showier lyric product like Lodge's version of Petrarch might seem to align with Rosalind's reading; but this choice is consistent with his replacement of Corydon's '*Satis est quod sufficit*' with Corin's plain sufficiency, which made Orlando's verses seem ridiculous. Orlando's anthological verses are too much; now Phoebe's plainer verses are 'rude' – can any written love lyric suffice?

Rosalind is strongly motivated to spurn these poetic advances, given that she is not who Phoebe thinks she is. She projects her own gendered performance onto Phoebe's lyric hypocritically when she argues that it is ghost-written by Silvius, saying, 'This is a man's invention and his hand' (4.3.29). Rosalind's unwarranted addition of another gender-inverted proxy to the quadrangle – Silvius as ghost-writer for Phoebe, in addition to Rosalind acting as 'Ganymede' – is a self-reflexive gesture like that of 'Arsenius *his letter*', with the added complication of gendered performance. Juliet Dusinberre justifies Rosalind's misreading

---

[40] Alpers, *Pastoral*, p. 198. [41] Lamb, *Marketplace*, p. 120.

in this way: Phoebe's lyric 'betokens masculinity' because it is 'penned by the boy who acts her and composed by the male dramatist'. Dusinberre makes a similar comment about the relation of Orlando's second lyric to the dramatist, reading its description of Rosalind as devised by '*Nature*' as 'a bold statement from the poet Shakespeare'.[42] It is a stretch to take Orlando's poem as a boast in Shakespeare's own voice. But a quotation from sonnet 53 ('*Helen's cheek*', l. 7) and a nod to *Lucrece* make its second half read like a pastiche of Shakespeare's own poetry:

But upon the fairest boughs,
  Or at every sentence' end,
Will I 'Rosalinda' write,
  Teaching all that read to know
The quintessence of every sprite
  Heaven would in little show . . .
Nature presently distilled
  Helen's cheek, but not her heart,
Cleopatra's majesty,
  Atalanta's better part,
Sad Lucretia's modesty.

(3.2.132–7, 141–5)

The poem's admission and suppression of the heroines' less desirable qualities – 'but not her heart', 'better part' – and fates – 'Sad Lucretia' – tends towards the ridiculous. But comparison with F. J.'s boastful patchwork of mythological figures, '*Beautie shut up thy shop*', reveals the gentleness of this poem's burlesque. Shakespeare indicates that this poem, for all its badness, is not unlike – in fact, it *is* – his own.

If the poems in *As You Like It* are anthological, the lords' lyrics in *Love's Labour's Lost* play with the dynamics of the miscellany and sequence, like Gascoigne's and Nashe's narratives. The 'sequence' that the lords' lyrics form resembles *Astrophil and Stella*, as H. R. Woudhuysen observes,[43] more than *Tottel*. Berowne's sonnet is read first, in his absence, just before the 'sonnet scene' (4.3); it shares its programmatic statements, rejection of 'study', and alexandrines with Astrophil's first.[44] In the sonnet scene, none of the lords hears the lyric preceding his own, but they take up each other's imagery with fluctuating progression and stasis. They are sundry similar gentlemen whose lyrics become sequential under the watch of Berowne, who almost directs the sonnet scene ('Proceed, sweet Cupid . . . !' 4.3.20). So, for example, the King continues Berowne's focus on his mistress's eyes' 'lightning' (4.2.114; now 'beams', 4.3.25) and his struggle to praise a goddess with 'an earthly tongue' (4.2.118; 'tongue of mortal', 4.3.38). Dumaine's poem is an apparent departure:

On a day – alack the day! –
Love, whose month is ever May,
Spied a blossom passing fair
Playing in the wanton air.

(4.3.98–101)

Dumaine's trochaic tetrameter (like Orlando's and Phoebe's), invocation of a springtime, pastoral setting, and third person voice differentiates this lyric from its antecedents – but this departure, too, aligns with *Astrophil and Stella*, resembling one of its songs (particularly the eighth, Woudhuysen observes, which opens in a flowery grove in May).[45] William Drummond's annotations in his *Love's Labour's Lost* quarto reveal that he read the lords' lyrics as a sequence in this way. Drummond marks Berowne's, the King's and Longaville's poems with asterisks and numbers (1, 2, 3) and Dumaine's with a cross only.[46] In Drummond's manuscript of *Astrophil*, the sonnets are numbered with cardinal figures and the songs are distributed throughout with a separate numbering system of ordinal roman numerals.[47] Drummond seems to identify Dumaine's lyric as a 'song' that participates in the sequence yet sits at a distance from the preceding sonnets.

Whereas Astrophil's awareness of his poems' 'bad' features is an internal struggle that forms the substance of many of his lines, the badness of the

---

[42] Dusinberre, in *As You Like It*, n. to 4.3.29, n. to 3.2.142.
[43] Woudhuysen, in *Love's Labour's Lost*, pp. 12–13.
[44] Philip Sidney, *Astrophil and Stella* 1, in *The Poems of Sir Philip Sidney*, ed. William A. Ringler, Jr (Oxford, 1962), pp. 163–238; p. 165.
[45] Sidney, *Astrophil*, p. 218.
[46] Edinburgh University Library De.3.74.
[47] Edinburgh University Library De.5.96.

lords' lyrics is criticized from without in *Love's Labour's Lost*, in different voices, in the manner of the *Adventures*. None of the critics is reliable or objective. The lords themselves express frustration with their verse, Longaville saying, 'I fear these stubborn lines lack power to move' (4.3.52). The ladies receive the lords' love lyrics and mock them as a group, valuing them quite differently to Drummond; their readings align more closely with G. T.'s stances in the *Adventures* than with Elinor's. While Elinor would rather F. J.'s poetic praise 'were much more, than any thing lesse' (178), in *Love's Labour's Lost* Maria finds the verses 'too long by half a mile' (5.2.54). The ladies are invested in each other's 'dark meaning[s]' (19), but they refuse to read past the darkness of the lords' ink: 'Beauteous as ink: a good conclusion'; 'Fair as a text B in a copy book' (41–2).

This last comment is a multivalent critique. Katherine suggests that the lyrics are servile reproductions, via Quintilian on imitation again.[48] She hints that the self-involved lyrics are a better portrait of their author, B, than their object, R. Katherine's textual imagery recalls Boyet's reading of the King's expression after his first encounter with the Princess:

> His heart, like an agate with your print impressed,
> Proud with his form, in his eye pride expressed...
> Methought all his senses were locked in his eye,
> As jewels in crystal for some prince to buy;
> Who, tendering their own worth from where they were glassed,
> Did point you to buy them along as you passed.
> His face's own margin did quote such amazes
> That all eyes saw his eyes enchanted with gazes.
>
> (2.1.235–6, 241–6)

Boyet's imagery of eyes as jewels 'tendering their own worth' evolves via the verb 'point' into imagery of textual apparatus: the King's face acts as marginal note to the 'amazes' of the imagined text of his eye, itself a translation of his heart. Boyet's and Katherine's language chimes with Nashe's presentation of his preface to *Astrophil* as 'a margent note of presumption' for pointing out the amazes of 'so excellent a Poet (the least sillable of whose name ... giue[s] the meanest line he writes a dowry of immortality)', but a necessary one, since 'iewels oftentimes com to their hands that know not their value'.[49] As Katherine's critique and Nashe's preface reveal, it is not the mistress's eye but the 'I', not her name but the 'least sillable' of the author's name, that gives a sonnet a 'dowry of immortality'. Just as G. T. transforms F. J.'s lyrics from loose manuscripts into a print product, inscribing them with flexible value while sending up their badness, Katherine's and Boyet's textual language looks to a translation of context that the lyrics will undergo – into print. The letters in a 'copy-book' could be either manuscript or print, but the idea of mass reproduction suggests the latter. The text of the King's face slips into a print product signalling its worth to buyers via Boyet's fast-moving imagery; Nashe's 'margent note' advertises *Astrophil* as a print product for the first time. Shakespeare's characters thoroughly mock the lords' poems, but we can see how their worth might be tendered or quoted differently on the printed page; the crucial name might slip from Rosaline, to Berowne, to Shakespeare, as Drummond's 'margent note[s]' suggest he 'quotes' the sonnets.

Katherine's diagnosis of the lords' poems as 'A huge translation of hypocrisy' picks up language from the Sermon on the Mount used by Berowne in the sonnet scene. Until his own lyric is discovered, Berowne plays the literary critic, mocking the absurdity of his friends' comparisons and describing their style as 'the liver vein' or 'pure idolatry' (4.3.71–2). He reveals himself to them when he still holds the moral and poetic high ground:

> Now step I forth to whip hypocrisy...
> You found his mote, the King your mote did see;
> But I a beam do find in each of three.
>
> (4.3.148, 158–9)

---

[48] Quintilian, *Orator's Education*, 10.2.2: 'Children follow the outlines of letters to become accustomed to writing.'

[49] Thomas Nashe, preface to Philip Sidney, *Astrophel and Stella* (London, 1591), sigs. A3r–A4v; sig. A3r.

Berowne's own hypocrisy is immediately revealed by the arrival of his lyric. He has been a 'critic' of love and its poetry (3.1.171); that critical stance is now shown to be hypocritical.

'Mote' imagery also occurs around the composition of sonnets in *Edward III* and *The Unfortunate Traveller*. Edward traps the Countess's father, Warwick, into interceding for him, making him swear an oath to do so before revealing the task; like Berowne, Warwick will be 'foresworn' if he honours his natural love. Hypocritically, he makes one argument to his daughter to uphold his oath, and another contrary case when she refuses:

> The King will in his glory hide thy shame,
> And those that gaze on him to find out thee
> Will lose their eyesight looking in the sun.
> (2.564–6)

> The greater man, the greater is the thing . . .
> An unreputed mote flying in the sun
> Presents a greater substance than it is . . .
> (2.600–3)

The biblical mote in the eye slips into a mote in the sun via the word 'beam'. The same effect lets us hear the 'mote' of hypocrisy in the King's lyric in *Love's Labour's Lost*: 'So sweet a kiss the golden sun gives not . . . As thy eye-beams when their fresh rays have *smote*' (4.3.23–5). Shakespeare is thinking about love lyrics and hypocrisy across *Edward III* and *Love's Labour's Lost*, although the precise relationship between the scene of poetic composition, the sonnet fragments, the theme of hypocrisy and the doubtful authorship of *Edward III* is elusive. In *Love's Labour's Lost*, the 'mote' is more closely associated with the composition of love lyric, and the hypocrisy it denotes is literary rather than moral.

The mote in Surrey's eye is one of the elements that, Maurice Hunt argues, reveal the influence of *The Unfortunate Traveller* on *Love's Labour's Lost*.[50] Nashe's and Shakespeare's shared reference surely owes more to its biblical origins than to a borrowing on Shakespeare's part, but both writers similarly link love lyric to literary hypocrisy. The mote in Surrey's eye, Jack's imitation of the liturgy to send up and forgive 'bad' love poetry, and the flexible relationship of style to antistyle in Nashe's narrative have much in common with Berowne's 'mote' and his use of biblical cadences to convey a flexible relationship of style to antistyle at the end of *Love's Labour's Lost*:

> BEROWNE Henceforth my wooing mind shall be expressed
> In russet yeas and honest kersey noes . . .
> My love to thee is sound, *sans* crack or flaw.
> ROSALINE Sans 'sans', I pray you.
> (5.2.412–16)

Berowne's resolution alludes to the Sermon again: 'let your communication be, Yea, yea; Nay, nay' (Matthew 5.33–7). This final denunciation of sonneting in sonnet form hypocritically maintains the play's impossible standards of poetic sufficiency to the last; Rosaline's response encapsulates the hypocritical way in which 'style expands to embrace the very rejection of style'.

When characters send up Orlando's performance of a Lodgean anatomization of 'body-wanting mots', these motes expose the beam of Shakespeare's own practice, and of love lyric more generally. Our sense of Shakespeare as ghost-writer in these scenes allows him to distance himself from the verbal formulations that he uses readily elsewhere, but exposes the use of this device for what it is: an excuse. Shakespeare is not above breaking Rosaline's injunction against '*sans*' elsewhere – memorably, at the end of Jaques's 'All the world's a stage' speech in *As You Like It*: '*Sans* teeth, *sans* eyes, *sans* taste, *sans* everything' (2.7.167). Dusinberre suggests that a 1598 audience's recent memory of Berowne may lie behind this affectation, particularly if Jaques was also played by Richard Burbage.[51] Jaques is also a critic of love lyric – he mocks the lover's 'woeful ballad / Made to his mistress' eyebrow' (2.7.149–50) – and of Orlando's style. But Orlando's '*civil sayings*' distil sentiments that Jaques himself values in his famous speech and Amiens's songs. Jaques shares affectations with Holofernes, too: theirs are the only two instances of

---

[50] Hunt, 'Thomas Nashe', pp. 310, 303, *passim*, 301.
[51] Dusinberre, in *As You Like It*, n. to 2.7.32.

the fashionable word 'stanza/o' in Shakespeare (*Love's Labour's Lost*, 4.2.103; *As You Like It*, 2.5.15). Jaques's hypocritical stance towards Orlando's affectations re-performs the hypo-criticism contained within Berowne the poet–critic and helps to reveal Shakespeare's hypocritical attitude to Orlando's verses. 'Hypo-criticism' becomes a flexible median between Lodge's 'good in everything' approach to inset love lyrics and the 'nothing' or '*sans* everything' of the critic.

In his 'Gullinge sonnets' (*c.*1594), John Davies asserts the foolishness of those who cannot tell the difference between good and bad love lyric, daring an unsuspecting reader to 'commend' his sonnets, perhaps by extracting one without recognizing the parody.[52] But, far from wild exaggeration, his fifth sonnet, for example, is a credible specimen of correlative verse hardly distinguishable from others of its kind. As the *Adventures* reveals, a system of re-appropriation, recontextualization and reading for 'occasion' makes the value of a single lyric unit endlessly contingent and indeterminable. In *Love's Labour's Lost* and *As You Like It*, Shakespeare's practice of writing just-sufficient love lyrics is similar to Davies's, but his tone is different – optimistic, permissive – making a flexible virtue, rather than a challenge, of our inability to tell the difference. Gascoigne's text is hypocritical in the Aristotelian sense, detaching its lyrics from an authorial voice with personae, as well as the literary–biblical sense, of criticizing a love poem as 'bad' when that poetic badness is one's own. By merging the roles of F. J. the poet and G. T. the critic in the person of Berowne, Shakespeare reveals the latent hypocrisy of Gascoigne's text; by aligning Berowne's orchestrations in the sonnet scene to the role of the dramatist, he reclaims this hypocrisy for his own practice.

The meanings of *hypocrisis* in classical rhetoric collapse distinctions between imitation and parody, as Davies's sonnets do, and between writing, ghost-writing and false attribution, like Nashe's lyrics. The 'Vita Vergili', for example, quotes an anecdote in which a poet says he could purloin some of Virgil's lines (*inviolare*, meaning anything from plagiarism to imitation), if only he could borrow his *hypocrisis* ('delivery').[53] Shakespeare's sonnet 96 links Boyet's description of the King and Nashe's preface to *Astrophil* to Katherine's 'translation of hypocrisy': 'The basest jewel will be well-esteemed ... To truths *translated*, and for true things deemed' (lines 6–8). Love lyrics' jewels are very easily translated from 'base' to 'well-esteemed' by a sense of authorship, intent or performance; but extraction, ghostwriting and the fictionalization or dramatization of the sonnet sequence reveal the contingency of those tenets of (e)valuation. Performance is not just a variable of the stage: in the print marketplace, the performative text can take on such a function, tendering the worth of its jewels with marginal notes or an author's name. 'Translation' signals slippage from performance to text and back, from text to new context, signifying the flexible value of a love lyric.

'BAD' LOVE LYRICS EXTRACTED

Early in their reception histories, love lyrics are extracted and recontextualized from the texts discussed in ways that their authors did not sanction. Lyrics from *Diana* and *Rosalynde* supply anthologizers with whole forests of stylistically uniform lyrics. The love lyrics of 'Surrey', Orlando and Berowne *et al.* have more adventurous lives of their own.

Nashe's 'Surrey' lyrics are given all conceivable attributions, to their 'true' author, fictional author and a third party, within a century of their composition. Extracts from Surrey's first and third lyrics are attributed to Nashe in *England's Parnassus* (1600).[54] In accordance with the general credulity with which Nashe's story was received, the first and third also appear under Surrey's name in William Winstanley's *Lives of the most famous English poets* (1687); Winstanley evidently extracts these lyrics directly from *The Unfortunate Traveller*,

---

[52] John Davies, 'Gullinge sonnets', in *The Poems of Sir John Davies*, ed. Robert Krueger and Ruby Nemser (Oxford, 1975), pp. 161–8.
[53] 'Vita Vergili', in *Suetonius*, trans. J. C. Rolfe, 2 vols (Cambridge, MA, 1997), vol. 2, pp. 442–59; p. 450.
[54] Robert Allot, ed., *Englands Parnassus* (London, 1600), pp. 397, 469.

given that he borrows some of Jack's contextualizing remarks.[55] Bafflingly, however, Winstanley attributes Nashe's second 'Surrey' lyric, 'If I must die, O let me choose my death' (the more outrageous of the three) not to Surrey, nor to Nashe, but to Thomas Lodge, alongside one of Rosader's sonnets from *Rosalynde*.[56] It is impossible to trace the source of this misattribution. It is striking, however, that Jones considers the scene of poetic wooing from which this lyric is taken, in which Diamante substitutes for Geraldine, to be a parody of Rosader's wooing of Ganymede.[57] The lyrics' collective textual history bears out my claim that Nashe's 'Surrey' poems hypocritically collapse distinctions between writing, ghost-writing and parody.

When Shakespeare's bad love lyrics are extracted, they are attributed, less surprisingly, to Shakespeare himself, alongside his sonnets. William Jaggard includes Berowne's, Longaville's and Dumaine's poems in *The Passionate Pilgrim* (1599). Nicholas Ling assimilates Dumaine's into *England's Helicon* (with some tweaks). John Benson follows Jaggard and adds Orlando's second lyric ('Why should this a desert be . . . ?') to his edition of Shakespeare's *Poems* (1640). Ling and Benson both consulted Jaggard's text, so the lyrics' route from stage to page to successive page seems clear. Jaggard's and Benson's inclusion of these 'bad' poems has been held to be consistent with their generally parsimonious and unauthorized practice, although their volumes have been rehabilitated.[58] Francis X. Connor, Sophie Chiari and Colin Burrow discuss the appearance of the *Love's Labour's Lost* sonnets in *The Passionate Pilgrim*.[59] To support my claims about Shakespeare's hypocritically 'bad' love lyrics and flexible lyric value, I look to Ling's and Benson's volumes. Ling and Benson do not simply lift the lyrics uncritically from Jaggard; both engage with *As You Like It* to some degree, and Benson emerges as a thorough, unexpected, even humorous reader of *Love's Labour's Lost*. Benson's main copy-texts were the 1609 *Sonnets* and the 1612 *Passionate Pilgrim*, as Cathy Shrank notes. Shrank reads Benson's edition as a 'critical, and often sensitive, reading of Shakespeare's Sonnets, which reacts to an ambiguity . . . as to whether it is a sonnet sequence or a miscellany'.[60] This ambiguity is familiar from my reading of Gascoigne, Nashe and *Love's Labour's Lost*. I make two additions to Shrank's argument: first, that Benson engages with a text of *Love's Labour's Lost* (likely a folio, given that he also extracted Orlando's lyric), despite following Jaggard's copy for the poems; and, second, that he reacts to the same 'sequence versus miscellany' slippage, as well as Shakespeare's 'poetics of hypocrisy', in the play.

Ling's and Benson's differing appropriations show that, of the lords' poems, it is Dumaine's lyric that best accommodates both anthological and sequential readings, as Drummond's annotation suggested. James Bednarz suggests that Ling was inspired by the recent theatrical success of *As You Like It* to reprint one of Shakespeare's 'available pastoral poems'.[61] Ling's preface conflates the practice of anthologizing with commonplacing, saying that his appropriation of whole lyrics is no different to 'gather[ing] any saying [or] sentence' and putting one's own name to it.[62] The affinity of this outlook with Orlando's Lodgean poetic

---

[55] William Winstanley, *The Lives of the most famous English poets* (London, 1687), pp. 49–56.
[56] Winstanley, *Lives*, pp. 72–4.
[57] Jones, 'Anti-Petrarchan satire', p. 48.
[58] See James P. Bednarz, 'Canonizing Shakespeare: *The Passionate Pilgrim*, *England's Helicon* and the question of authenticity', *Shakespeare Survey* 60 (Cambridge, 2007), 252–67; and Cathy Shrank, 'Reading Shakespeare's *Sonnets*: John Benson and the 1640 *Poems*', *Shakespeare* 5 (2009), 271–91.
[59] See Francis X. Connor, 'Shakespeare, poetic collaboration and *The Passionate Pilgrim*', *Shakespeare Survey* 67 (Cambridge, 2014), 119–30; Sophie Chiari, 'In and out: Shakespeare's shifting sonnets from *Love's Labour's Lost* to *Passionate Pilgrim*', in *The Early Modern English Sonnet: Ever in Motion*, ed. Laetitia Sansonetti, Rémi Vuillemin and Enrica Zanin (Manchester, 2020), pp. 78–94; Colin Burrow, 'Lyric in its settings: multiple narratives and lyric voices in *Love's Labour's Lost*', unpublished paper delivered at Shakespeare Association of America, 2006.
[60] Shrank, 'Shakespeare's Sonnets', p. 271.
[61] Bednarz, 'Canonizing', p. 263.
[62] Nicholas Ling, ed. *Englands Helicon* (London, 1600), sig. A4r.

practice, in conjunction with Dumaine's and Orlando's shared metre, suggests that not only the play's pastoralism but also, specifically, its self-reflexive scene of anthological composition might have inspired Ling. Dumaine's poem, here titled '*The passionate Sheepheards Song*',[63] is a good substitute for Orlando's, of which there was no published text yet. When Orlando's lyric appears in Benson's collection, it is untitled, in a more 'anthological' section separated from the sonnets, following Marlowe's 'Passionate shepheard to his Love' and several of that poem's replies.[64] Benson's treatment of Dumaine's lyric, however, contrasts Ling's more anthological assimilation by placing it in what Shrank calls one of his 'mini sequences' of Shakespearian sonnets.[65] He titles it 'Love-sicke', then follows it with a pastoral lyric, the title of which is none other than 'Loves labour lost'. Benson recreates the lost labour of the lords' 'sequence' in the play in miniature.[66]

The first of the lords' lyrics in Benson's edition is Longaville's, titled 'Fast and Loose'.[67] This phrase occurs most memorably in *Love's Labour's Lost* when Costard's is riffing on 'l'envoy':

The boy hath sold him a bargain, a goose, that's flat.
Sir, your pennyworth is good, an your goose be fat.
To sell a bargain well is as cunning as fast and loose.
Let me see: a fat l'envoy – ay, that's a fat goose.

(3.1.98–101)

It is hard to take Benson's use of a quotation from the play as the title of Longaville's lyric as anything less than a joke at the expense of Benson himself getting his 'pennyworth' from Shakespeare's play. Given this playfulness, the title of Berowne's sonnet in Benson's volume, 'A constant vow',[68] reads as an ironic comment on Berowne's hypocrisy when he calls his friends 'men of inconstancy', saying 'When shall you see me write a thing in rhyme?' (4.3.177–8). Benson runs with Shakespeare's poetics of hypocrisy, not only by reading the lords' sonnets as 'hypocritically' assimilable to Shakespeare's own 'good' practice by placing them alongside the 'authentic' sonnets (as in *Edward III*), but also by revealing how his own volume plays fast and loose with Shakespeare's texts.

The poetics of hypocrisy that Shakespeare develops across *Love's Labour's Lost* and *As You Like It* reveals that reading, writing, criticizing and extracting 'fast and loose' love lyrics makes hypocrites of us all, due to the impossibility of distinguishing good from bad. Shakespeare's 'hypocrisy' revises the framing of the lyrics in sources like *Rosalynde* and *Diana* and looks back to his earlier treatment of 'bad' love poetry in *Edward III*. Allusions to the Sermon on the Mount in *Love's Labour's Lost* make Shakespeare's play with literary hypocrisy more explicit than Gascoigne's and Nashe's, but those narratives share the plays' flexible, hypocritical approach to lyric value. The same hypocrisy plays out in the reception and extraction of these lyrics. The way in which these lyrics' textual histories are prefigured by their narrative or dramatic settings initially seems ironic. A sonnet written by Nashe for the Earl of Surrey in a narrative that has been read as a 'parody' of Lodge is later attributed to Lodge himself. There is a 'delicious irony' in the extraction of Berowne's sonnet, given its purloining on stage.[69] On closer examination, these ironies look like playfully hypocritical strategies.

---

[63] *Helicon*, ed. Ling, sig. Hr.
[64] *Poems: Written by Wil. Shakespeare Gent.*, ed. John Benson (London, 1640), sigs. K4v–K8r.
[65] Shrank, 'Shakespeare's *Sonnets*', *passim*.
[66] *Poems*, ed. Benson, sigs. C7r–v.
[67] *Poems*, ed. Benson, sig. B2r.
[68] *Poems*, ed. Benson, sig. B3v. [69] Burrow, 'Lyric'.

VIOLA'S TELEMACHY

ROBERT B. PIERCE

From the earliest days, the Homeric poems have been read as educative models, and in particular the Telemachy of the *Odyssey* has offered a version of *paideia* (education, learning) in the moral education of Telemachus, as he is prepared, and prepares himself, to aid his father on Odysseus' return and, over all, to be a fitting heir. In varying degrees, that theme of educative growth continued through the romance tradition that descended from the *Odyssey*.[1] We teachers of literature have often thought of ourselves as imitating the pedagogical role of Athene and her mortal disguises in the shapes of Mentes and, especially, Mentor, as she provides an educative guide for Telemachus during his process of maturation. Shakespeare the dramatist in some ways participates in this broadly didactic tradition of literature, and indeed he repeatedly studies youth in the process of maturation, from his extended portrayal of Prince Hal in the history plays through his greatly foreshortened but vivid picture of Miranda in *The Tempest*, although his Mentor figures are perhaps harder to take seriously than his youths. One thinks of such inept pedagogical guides as Holofernes, Falstaff, Polonius and Volumnia. If there is any historicity at all in the legend of Shakespeare as country schoolmaster who turned to playwrighting, that early experience must have left him with considerable scepticism about the pedagogical role of moral guide, to judge from his dramatic portrayals of mentors.

Homer's Telemachy is ancestor to a long tradition in the classical romances and later tales of youths who go on journeys, have extravagant adventures, and end at a place of maturity, as they take on an adult role in society, and Shakespeare tells many such stories, from his early comedies to his late romances. *Twelfth Night*'s Viola is one of the most attractive of the young protagonists who have such adventures. She enters the play after a shipwreck that has separated her from her last surviving family tie, her twin brother, and she arrives in a strange land that is both threatening and curiously hospitable.[2] There, she takes on a disguise with a new name, social rank and gender, falls in love, gets into all sorts of complicated

---

[1] The classic discussion of this topic is Werner Jaeger, *Paideia: The Ideals of Greek Culture*, trans. Gilbert Highet, 2nd ed., 3 vols. (New York, 1939), esp. vol. 1. For the Greek romance as it affects Shakespeare, see Carol Gesner, *Shakespeare & the Greek Romance: A Study of Origins* (Lexington, 1970); and Mark Houlahan, '"Like to th'Egyptian thief": Shakespeare sampling Heliodorus in *Twelfth Night*', in '*Rapt in Secret Studies*': *Emerging Shakespeares*, ed. Darryl Chalk and Laurie Johnson (Newcastle upon Tyne, 2010), pp. 305–15. It is unlikely that Shakespeare knew the *Odyssey* directly (the 'less Greek' that Ben Jonson attributes to him may well have been none at all), since George Chapman's English translation did not appear until 1614. Chapman's *Seven Books of the Iliads of Homer, Prince of Poets* was published in 1598 and was clearly a source for *Troilus and Cressida*. The *Odyssey* was available in Latin, and Shakespeare surely knew its main characters and much of the story from his beloved Ovid and elsewhere, but his response to the broader tradition is what is primary to my argument.

[2] Trevor Nunn vividly pictures the shipwreck as the beginning of his filmed version of the play, with a richly symbolic image of Viola reborn in her brother's image after immersion in the stormy ocean.

tangles, engages in a mortal combat with Sir Andrew (a farcical version with no real peril), and at the end achieves both a restored family bond with her brother and a new husband. Clearly, Shakespeare is having fun with his wild tale and its romance elements, maintaining a tone very different from the tragicomic resonances of a similar story in the late *Pericles*, for example. In addition to telling an extravagant story, is he in his picture of Viola developing the Homeric theme of *paideia*, albeit in a playful way? I think so, and the significance of his handling in *Twelfth Night* lies both in the familiar elements of the tradition that he adopts and in the distinctive twist that he gives to them.

The most obvious difference from the model of the Telemachy is the absence of any Athene figure as moral pedagogue. Shakespeare offers no Mentor whose wisdom and prudence might protect Viola and help her to attain maturity and the fulfilment of her destiny. Indeed, the closest figure to a moral educator in the play is Malvolio, who from the beginning fancies himself a wise counsellor (to Olivia, rather than Viola), but who immediately has to be corrected by his young mistress in the skills of social etiquette – in particular, how to respond to a court fool's gibes – and who ends up utterly humiliated: locked up as a madman and then shamed in front of the whole community.[3] And Viola quickly demonstrates her instinctive superiority in manners over the would-be pedagogue Malvolio when he tries to carry out his task of giving Olivia's ring to her, believing it to be her own. While he fusses self-importantly over his own inconvenience in having to chase her down, she lies by pretending that the ring is indeed hers, mustering a generous and quick-witted tact in order to hide Olivia's indiscretion from her servant.[4]

A character that undergoes initiation into a mature social role can be growing into it and its defining virtues through the experiences that constitute the story, or can be brought by the events of the plot to manifest qualities that are present in him or her from the beginning. Shakespeare's Prince Hal shows something of both possibilities, fitting into two different conventional narrative patterns.

The Prodigal Son story represents the first pattern, in which the protagonist falls from innocence into corruption and then reforms, growing towards maturity; and the Disguised Prince story suggests rather that, in his behaviour, others (and perhaps even he) discover the self that has been there all along.[5] To the extent that, in the *Odyssey*, Athene offers divine guidance and protection to an inexperienced Telemachus, she helps him to grow into maturity, and her disguise as Mentor lets her embody the ways in which an older generation passes its accumulated wisdom on to youth.[6] But Athene is, of course, the goddess of wisdom, and so her interventions can symbolically represent Telemachus' own mental powers at work, as surely is part of her meaning in the teasingly affectionate relationship between her and his father Odysseus. Odysseus' canny intelligence constitutes the divine spark in him, his piece of Athene. (There is a similar double implication to the moment in the *Iliad* when Athene seizes Achilleus by the hair to stop him from killing Agamemnon in his rage (1.194ff.): the divine intervention manifests Achilleus' own prudence at work.)

Viola, however, has no Athene to guide her, and the nature of her disguise deprives her of any purely human counsel as well, since she cannot reveal her

---

[3] One thinks of Humphrey Wasp, the hapless mentor in Ben Jonson's *Bartholomew Fair*, who has no luck tutoring the egregious Bartholomew Cokes and who ends up in the stocks, the object of general mockery.

[4] Thus I agree with Keir Elam's note at 2.2.12, and with J. M. Lothian and T. W. Craik's interpretation of the episode and, like both editions, reject the emendation to 'She took no ring of me.' See the latter's note at *Twelfth Night*, Arden Second Series (London, 1975), 2.2.11. All quotations from the play are from William Shakespeare, *Twelfth Night, Or What You Will*, ed. Keir Elam, Arden Third Series (London, 2008). Lothian and Craik refer to other views, and, further, see John B. Robinson, 'A ring of truth: another look at a crux in *Twelfth Night*', *English Language Notes* 34 (1996), 1–6.

[5] Cf. the discussion of him in Robert B. Pierce, *Shakespeare's History Plays: The Family and the State* (Columbus, 1971), ch. 6, on 'The Henry IV plays'.

[6] François Fénelon illustrates this potentiality of the story at great length in his novel *Télémaque*, and James Joyce works his own complex variants in *Ulysses*.

situation to a confidant. Even in the intimate conversation between her and Orsino as they listen to Feste's song (in 2.4), Orsino's advice, such as it is, comes to the boy he thinks she is, not really to the lovesick Viola. It is the course of events in the play and her response to them, not wise counsel, that bring her to the Viola of the denouement, and despite her wit and determination she is not at all in control of those events and so does not shape herself as Prince Hal does himself. The events happen to her, and she constantly has to improvise in response to them, as when she forms her plan to serve Orsino in disguise only after the captain tells her that Olivia, whom she first plans to serve, is unreachable because of her vow of cloistered mourning for her dead brother. We never learn why Viola and Sebastian have set out on their sea voyage. She reveals no plan parallel to Telemachus' decision, obeying Athene's command, to undertake a quest for information about his father's fate. Viola sounds confident about her purposes, whatever they are, when she describes her intent to serve Olivia in disguise 'Till I had made mine own occasion mellow', and, when she switches to serving Orsino, she refers vaguely to 'The form of my intent', but we never learn what that intent is, and she quickly sounds less clear in her calculations for the future: 'What else may hap to time I will commit' (*Twelfth Night*, 1.2.40–57). We see nothing in her later behaviour to show any plan of hers in operation. She is truly a wanderer rather than one on a defined quest, without even Odysseus' goal of homecoming, though she is a wanderer who arrives in the fairly benign confines of Illyria. The self she manifests in her adventures is thus a rather Odysseus-like improviser, as manifested above all in her quick wit and clever schemes.

Thus, what shapes Viola and creates our understanding of her is neither a divine or human mentor nor a plan of her own that she executes, but rather the people she encounters and the events that, all taken together, constitute Shakespeare's dramatic structure. So what are the distinctive attributes of that dramatic plot and environment, the shaping forces on Viola? The first of them is her isolation. We have already seen how completely she is alone:

she is an orphan in a strange land, seeking a twin brother who may be dead, and she is deprived of any understanding companion. Even the captain, who knows the truth about her and thus could have been her Horatio, quickly disappears from the play. Like Hamlet and Prince Hal, she is the *eiron*, aloof, holding her own counsel, letting others misunderstand her, though in soliloquy allowing the audience to have glimpses inside her (Hal and she allowing such glimpses much more fleetingly than Hamlet).[7] This isolation within herself coincides with the plot's removal of the usual social determinants of role: family, city, rank, duties and other prescribed activities. The inner Viola is quite alone in a strange place, and all this isolation puts her in the liminal state of initiation described in anthropological theory, cut loose from her past and thrown into an experience that will redefine who she is as she comes to a new social role.[8] None of the external mirroring from an established social community that helps us human beings to understand ourselves and our place in the world seems to be available to her during the play, and so both she and the audience have to find out through events exactly who she is.

The second quality of Viola's experience is its painfulness. It is not that, once she escapes the sea, her very life is in danger, like Odysseus' and, in a lesser way, Telemachus' – the latter because of the suitors' plot to murder him. Orsino's threats against Viola and Olivia in 5.1 are largely verbal and theoretical; he admits as much with 'had I the heart to do it' (5.1.113). Of course, the danger of death in combat with the cowardly Sir Andrew is wholly illusory, but the pain of her apparently hopeless love for Orsino while she is forced to court Olivia on his behalf is quite genuine. Having been plunged into the sea by shipwreck, she is then tossed and turned in a series of events utterly

---

[7] For the concept of the *eiron*, based on Aristotle's *Poetics*, see Northrop Frye, *Anatomy of Criticism: Four Essays* (Princeton, 1957).

[8] In the rich literature on liminality, see especially Victor Turner, *The Ritual Process: Structure and Anti-Structure* (Ithaca, 1977).

out of her control, for all her witty competence, thrown into a helplessness well beyond either Rosalind or Helena, who at least can act with some effect to shape their fates. In Viola's description of her predicament, she gives a veiled self-portrait of one who suffers 'like Patience on a monument, / Smiling at grief' (2.4.114–15), fixed in hopeless endurance like a figure made of stone.

The third quality of her situation, and the central fact of her story, as so often in Shakespeare, is that she puts on a disguise, and again the result is to cut her loose from the normal defining structures of role. She abandons her rank to become a servant of Orsino, though very quickly a servant with a special kind of intimacy (like Nerissa to Portia in *The Merchant of Venice*, and like Feste to Olivia in this play). Neither she nor Orsino is ever clear just how much distance and of what kind exists between them.[9] In this sense, her aloneness is not so much isolation as a shifting, undefined kind of immersion, as a stranger, in the varieties of social relationship that Illyria offers. In that way, she is less Telemachus than Odysseus – she and Odysseus the two wanderers who are cryptically fascinating to all those whom they encounter, each a Noman who moves through all sorts of human society without ever settling into place or being transparent to others.[10] By flashes, she takes on roles as gossiping fellow servant with Valentine, confidant and philosopher of love with Orsino, witty courtier with Olivia, verbal sparrer with Sir Toby and Feste, fearer for her physical safety with Sir Andrew, helpless onlooker in Orsino's train: always the baffled plaything of inexplicable events, yet for all that remarkably agile and resolute.

When Viola disguises herself as Cesario, her gender identity is confused – more or less male in the eyes of others, but no one, certainly neither she nor Orsino, can steadily see her as male, can even understand her through the less sharply masculine figure of the boy.[11] In developing this theme, Shakespeare of course makes use of the still-emerging gender identity of the one who plays her part, the boy actor, whose voice is not yet 'cracked within the ring'.[12] Viola has less fun in her male disguise than Portia, and especially Rosalind, but she does find in it the room to get beyond the limitations of conventional femininity, so that she can inhabit the world dominated by masculinity – even see a side of the man she loves that he would not normally show to a woman. Also, she can express the elements of her self that are not stereotypically feminine. As she and her brother Sebastian move towards each other in the plot, they exchange elements of identity and situation: presumably they are even identical in costume and therefore indistinguishable to the other characters. She explains why Antonio is

---

[9] Laurie E. Osborne describes it as an erotically tinged amity in '"The marriage of true minds": amity, twinning, and comic closure in *Twelfth Night*', in *Twelfth Night: New Critical Essays*, ed. James Schiffer (New York, 2011), pp. 99–113.

[10] Cf. Thomas Van Nortwick, *The Unknown Odysseus: Alternate Worlds of Homer's Odyssey* (Ann Arbor, 2009).

[11] This point raises the issue of Viola's age. Of course, in a modern production, our sense of that is much influenced by the age of the actor playing the part, and no doubt modern productions tend to suggest a somewhat older Viola than on Shakespeare's stage, given our tendency to cast such a star part with someone who has already established herself as a lead player. The boy actor as a figure on the stage would have naturally fitted a young heroine – say, a teenager – and most of Shakespeare's early heroines seem to be about that age, though it looks as though both the abilities of the boy actors and Shakespeare's interests were turning towards more varied, often more mature, heroines about this time. Thus, the boy actor in the company that visits Hamlet presumably takes on a part equivalent to Gertrude in the Player Queen. The *paideia* of Viola has a distinctive colouration if she is a teenager, and I usually imagine her in that way (and Olivia as well, unlike the older stage convention of making her more mature than Viola).

[12] *Hamlet*, 2.2.424. In the huge body of recent criticism exploring this element, some of those paying special attention to Viola are Stephen Greenblatt, *Shakespearean Negotiations: The Circulation of Social Energy in Renaissance England* (Oxford, 1988), pp. 66–93; Dympna Callaghan, '"And all is semblative a woman's part": body politics and *Twelfth Night*', in *Twelfth Night*, ed. R. S. White, New Casebooks (New York, 1996), pp. 129–59; Casey Charles, 'Gender trouble in *Twelfth Night*', *Theater Journal* 49 (1997), 121–41.

confused when he sees what he thinks is Sebastian fighting with Sir Andrew:

> I my brother know
> Yet living in my glass. Even such and so
> In favour was my brother, and he went
> Still in this fashion, colour, ornament,
> For him I imitate.
>
> (3.4.376–80)

Their identical costumes represent for us the incomplete separation of identity that is also expressed by their twinship. As they move through these confusions of identity and role, both siblings go beyond gender limitations, and we see them within all the mysterious aura of twinning. Even the long recognition scene in which Viola and Sebastian sort out the confusions and reclaim their former identities leaves Viola still half-Cesario, as Orsino acknowledges in his stunned reaction, and there is no reason to assume that her return to 'other [woman's] habits' (5.1.380) will reconfine her within conventional gender, though her long silence at the end of the play leaves the audience to read into her what it will.[13]

A fourth element of her situation is her repeated connection with music, which is an important element in ideas of education from the Greeks on. *Mousike* is that which reflects harmony in the cosmos and creates it in the soul, evoking a due proportion among the elements of the soul to echo what exists in the music of the spheres.[14] With their songs in the *Odyssey*, Homer and Demodocus, and Odysseus himself enchant and instruct, move to tears and heal; and music plays a similar role in *Twelfth Night*. Viola's very name suggests a musical instrument, and she first considers a plan to become a singer in her disguise, though that detail quickly drops out of the play.[15] She responds sensitively to the music being played for Orsino in 2.4 and to Feste's singing of it, in which she finds artistic expression of her own thwarted love for Orsino. Indeed, there is a curious kind of emulous sympathy between her and Feste, the two vehicles of wit and *mousike* in the play. With a musician's skill in shaping emotions, each of them is adept at catching the mood of his or her interlocutor and then playing a dazzling countermelody against it. Thus, Feste softens Olivia's rather theatrical grief for her brother with gentle mockery almost as soon as he enters in 1.5, and then Viola enters and cuts through Olivia's aristocratic rudeness with a courtesy that skirts impudence; and each interlocutor transforms Olivia's inner state. The two voices of Viola and Feste give a rich and varied harmony to this most musical of plays, with her poetic set pieces the verbal equivalents of his songs. Their melodic strains affect the others in the play as Ariel's songs enchant Ferdinand (and others) in *The Tempest*:

> This music crept by me upon the waters,
> Allaying both their fury and my passion
> With its sweet air.
>
> (*The Tempest*, 1.2.394–6)

In the social encounters of which the *Odyssey* is fashioned, storytelling and riddling are regular features, as they are of Viola in her disguise. Odysseus

---

[13] Of course I allude to the play's subtitle, seeing in it, as in the title of *As You Like It*, the implication that the audience is free to interpret as it pleases the pleasant but somewhat ambiguous spectacle in front of it. We critics have certainly taken up that offer.

[14] For discussion of this topic, see Jaeger, *Paideia*, and John Hollander, *The Untuning of the Sky: Ideas of Music in English Poetry, 1500–1700* (Princeton, 1961). A sensitive and informed discussion can be found in Nancy Lindheim, 'Rethinking sexuality and class in *Twelfth Night*', *University of Toronto Quarterly* 76 (2007), 679–713.

[15] Orsino has to be told to transfer his request that she sing to Feste in 2.4. The likeliest explanation for this tangle in the text is the unromantic one by Richmond Noble that the boy playing Viola could not handle the singing, and so Feste takes over the role of primary musician in the play. Shakespeare often leaves such minor inconsistencies in his plays when he changes his mind, either during composition or in production. See Lothian and Craik's discussion in *Twelfth Night*, p. xxiii and note 2, arguing that the text makes sense as it stands. They refer there to other views, and see also Robinson, 'A ring of truth'. Elam, on the other hand, argues at length for a continuing significance in the idea of Cesario as singer-eunuch, with, I think, strained ingenuity. See Introduction to Elam's edition, pp. 57–63, and his article, 'The fertile eunuch: *Twelfth Night*, early modern intercourse, and the fruits of castration', *Shakespeare Quarterly* 47 (1996), 1–36.

both conceals and reveals who he is in the various tales that he tells, true and false. (And, of course, he would not be revealing his true identity to us if he did not show his skill as a liar and fabulist, though only Athene and we as audience can grasp that paradox, seeing through the lies that deceive others.) As Viola says to the baffled Olivia, who is trying to make sense of this riddling and enchanting interlocutor who has appeared in her world: 'Then think you right: I am not what I am' (3.1.139). Two of Viola's most eloquent revelations of her love for Orsino are hidden in brief riddling tales. The first purports to describe how she would act if she loved Olivia; she would:

> Make me a willow cabin at your gate
> And call upon my soul within the house;
> Write loyal cantons of contemned love
> And sing them loud even in the dead of night;
> Hallow your name to the reverberate hills
> And make the babbling gossip of the air
> Cry out 'Olivia!' O, you should not rest
> Between the elements of air and earth
> But you should pity me.
>
> (1.5.260–8)

All of Viola is hidden in that hypothetical self-sketch: her love for Orsino, her lyrical wit, her quiet contempt for Olivia's stagily shallow feelings ('I can easily outdo you at that game'), and her deep wish that someone would feel pity for her. Thus, the imagined tale of a Cesario wooing Olivia expresses the real Viola's feelings in her plight and, by its eloquence, moves Olivia to love the boy she thinks Viola is. One might say that Viola voices the love speech that her twin Sebastian never has to utter for himself to woo Olivia.

In the second story, already referred to above, which she tells in her intimate conversation with Orsino in 2.4, she describes to the object of her passion her imaginary sister's concealed love and heroic patience. In that fictional lover, she can reveal herself to Orsino (and perhaps even to herself) with total frankness about her feelings, though even then she may somewhat deceive herself as well as her listener with the image of unmoving patience: Viola is the last person in the world to remain fixed in immobility, declining into a fatal melancholy. Yet in that image she does describe her feeling of being trapped by her disguise into a silence that for now seems to her as final as death. Still, for the most part, the Viola we come to know is, above all, resilient; if the tangle is 'too hard a knot for [her] t'untie' (2.2.41), she will briskly entrust it to time and go right on bustling about the world of Illyria.

Dramatic knots are, of course, untied in a play's denouement, and the final characteristic of Viola's story is the elaborate working-out of her fate and the fates of all of them at the end of *Twelfth Night*. In this most naturalistic of the romantic comedies, the encounter with Sebastian is the place where the play most takes on the Odyssean atmosphere of wonder. After Viola is bounced around among the different aspects of her disguise and the confusion with Sebastian, she finally encounters her brother face to face at his entrance in 5.1, and the play comes to a momentary standstill. Knowing more than anyone else (though by no means everything) who is who, and who has done what to whom, she leads them all step by step to the restoration of her identity, her family and her gender, by means of a strangely protracted recognition scene in which the traditional markers of nationality, rank and family are laid out one by one, in order to restore her true name and manifest her to all in her adult selfhood. We watch all the other characters struggling to understand her in that new identity. Climactically, though she never actually dons her woman's clothes, we see Orsino reclothe her in his mind to be his 'mistress and his fancy's queen' (5.1.381). After her open avowal of love for him, she says not a word as the play ends, though no doubt in the stage action she takes his proffered hand in fulfilment of her love. As we see her go off with her love and husband-to-be, it is Feste, her alter ego in this festive and musical play, who has the last word and closing musical notes, his song and he both gently melancholy but ever resilient, like Viola herself. This journey ends with Viola meeting her lover openly and freely, and, as an earlier song in the play tells us, at least the sons of wise men can see in that meeting her joyful self-completion.

NEW ANALOGICAL EVIDENCE FOR *CYMBELINE*'S FOLKLORIC COMPOSITION IN THE MEDIEVAL ICELANDIC *ÁLA FLEKKS SAGA*

JONATHAN Y. H. HUI

Source analysis has long proven a productive tool in Shakespeare studies, given the breadth, abundance and variety of narrative traditions that Shakespeare demonstrably borrowed from and adapted. In addition to the insight that the study of identified sources can provide into the processes of narrative construction and adaptation in his plays, this approach also sheds valuable broader light on the dynamic literary and cultural mosaics of early modern England and Europe more widely. This, in turn, informs scholarly understanding of what types of stories or texts were known, being actively transmitted and reshaped, and resonating with contemporary readerships and audiences. Additionally, identifying and understanding Shakespeare's sources can often usefully illuminate the chronological development and evolution of individual narrative traditions to which those sources belong, traditions which variously extend back to biblical, classical and medieval roots.[1] Source analysis does have clear and obvious limitations, however. For one thing, the scale of influence on any text or author inevitably varies from source to source, meaning that filiation cannot always be posited conclusively. For another, Shakespeare is recognized to have collaborated actively with other playwrights, which complicates questions of direct influence.[2] For a third, not all of Shakespeare's (or his co-authors') literary sources have survived. Then there is also the substantial matter of oral sources and traditions, of which little can be definitively known, barring the fortuitous survival of sufficient auxiliary evidence such as analogues. The murky uncertainties which arise from such issues are evident in the long debate over the nature of *Hamlet*'s relationship with the putative 'ur-*Hamlet*', which serves to exemplify both the accepted value of source identification and the extent of its limits.[3] Useful as it undeniably is,

---

[1] On the influence of the Bible on Shakespeare, see Naseeb Shaheen, *Biblical References in Shakespeare's Plays* (Newark, NJ, 1999), and, more recently, Hannibal Hamlin, *The Bible in Shakespeare* (Oxford, 2013). On Shakespeare's classical influences, see Colin Burrow, *Shakespeare and Classical Antiquity* (Oxford, 2013). Shakespeare's connection to medieval literature and culture has been the subject of numerous studies, for instance Helen Cooper, *The English Romance in Time: Transforming Motifs from Geoffrey of Monmouth to the Death of Shakespeare* (Oxford, 2004); Curtis Perry and John Watkins, eds., *Shakespeare and the Middle Ages* (Oxford, 2009); Martha Driver and Sid Ray, eds., *Shakespeare and the Middle Ages: Essays on the Performance and Adaptation of the Plays with Medieval Sources or Settings* (Jefferson, NC, 2009); Helen Cooper, *Shakespeare and the Medieval World* (London, 2010); and Ruth Morse, Helen Cooper and Peter Holland, eds., *Medieval Shakespeare: Pasts and Presents* (Cambridge, 2013).

[2] For a survey of attribution scholarship on Shakespeare, see Brian Vickers, *Shakespeare, Co-Author: A Historical Study of Five Collaborative Plays* (Oxford, 2002).

[3] A highly useful, though yet unpublished, summary of the history of the 'ur-*Hamlet*' debate can be found in Hardin Aasand and F. Nicholas Clary, 'The sources of *Hamlet*': https://triggs.djvu.org/global-language.com/ENFOLDED/ABOUT/HamletSource-12-11-09.html. This essay is intended to form part of the introduction to their New Variorum edition of *Hamlet*. Stanley Wells and Gary Taylor remark of the putative 'ur-*Hamlet*' that '[its] authorship is unknown; it is usually conjecturally attributed to either

then, Shakespearian source analysis can only illuminate a fraction of the wider picture of the literary mosaics within which Shakespeare operated.

A wider perspective on the state of contemporary literary traditions can be gained through the study of near-contemporary analogues, whose oblique illumination can bring into greater focus the chronological and geographical context of specific narrative traditions from which Shakespeare drew, and which can thereby raise new perspectives through the decentring of his work. Viewing analogues as cousins within a family, some more distant than others, allows for the comparative evaluation of any given member and its particular relation to the family, as well as a clearer view of the nature of the family itself. This is especially productive in situations where the family can be defined according to a shared set of narrative events – in other words, a folktale. Indeed, the widespread presence of folkloric allusions and influences within Shakespeare's work has long been recognized,[4] and the fruitfulness of targeted analogical analysis along folkloric lines can be seen in such seminal studies as Jan Harold Brunvald's comprehensive survey of folkloric analogues of the main plot of *The Taming of the Shrew*,[5] or Valerie Wayne's recent examination of late medieval and early modern European analogues of Posthumous's wager on the chastity of his wife Innogen in *Cymbeline*.[6] Such an approach sheds important light not only on the place of the Shakespearian plays in question within the relevant folkloric traditions, but also more laterally on the folkloric traditions themselves, which can, to borrow Wayne's metaphor, facilitate 'our seeing the forest for the trees'.[7]

Part of the difficulty with assessing the manifestation of folktales in Shakespeare's plays – or, indeed, many pre-modern or early modern European folktale variants – is that, in many cases, a lack of identified ancient or medieval variants makes it unclear what those folktales looked like in European traditions during or preceding the time of Shakespeare. Some prominent cases, with relatively many known, extant variants, offer more certainty. An example of this is 'Griselda', classified under the Aarne–Thompson–Uther folktale index (ATU) as number 887, which was an influence on *The Winter's Tale*,[8] and which is found in a number of late medieval and early modern sources from across Europe, including works by Petrarch, Boccaccio and Chaucer. However, this is much more difficult in the case of folktales for which few literary variants from medieval Europe have been identified. It is difficult to judge the scale of Shakespeare's modifications of the 'Snow White' tale (ATU 709) in *Cymbeline*, for instance, without knowing what literary forms the folktale took at that time, with which motifs it was associated, and which aspects may have been attested in literary traditions accessible to Shakespeare. The relationship between *Cymbeline* and 'Snow White' will form the starting point of this article, but here it suffices to say that the wider picture of the pre-modern state of this particular folktale remains all but unknown, with only a handful of partial variants from the classical and medieval periods identified thus far. Studying this picture inevitably presents several of the same fundamental problems as source analysis – namely, the loss over time of oral and literary variants, as well as the possibility of extant literary variants yet to be identified. Indeed,

---

Thomas Kyd or William Shakespeare', and that 'no clear external evidence exists for either attribution, and we cannot put much faith in internal evidence drawn from a lost text' (Stanley Wells and Gary Taylor, *William Shakespeare: A Textual Companion* (Oxford, 1987), p. 398).

[4] See, for instance, Harold Coote Lake, 'Some folklore incidents in Shakespeare', *Folklore* 39 (1928), 307–28; Kenneth Muir, 'Folklore and Shakespeare', *Folklore* 92 (1981), 231–40; and, for a recent and expansive treatment of the subject, Charlotte Artese, *Shakespeare's Folktale Sources* (Newark, NJ, 2015).

[5] Jan Harold Brunvald, 'The folktale origin of *The Taming of the Shrew*', *Shakespeare Quarterly* 17 (1966), 345–59.

[6] Valerie Wayne, 'Romancing the wager: *Cymbeline*'s intertexts', in *Staging Early Modern Romance: Prose Fiction, Dramatic Romance, and Shakespeare*, ed. Mary Ellen Lamb and Valerie Wayne (New York, 2009), pp. 163–87.

[7] Wayne, 'Romancing the wager', p. 163.

[8] Grace McCarthy, 'The evolution of the patient woman: examining patient Griselda as a source for Shakespeare's *The Winter's Tale*', *Early Modern Literary Studies* 20 (2018), 1–20.

the study of pre-modern folkloric transmission is often reminiscent of an analogy used by F. P. Wilson with regard to the paucity of surviving English plays from the 1580s – namely, that 'the historian of the Elizabethan drama ... often feels himself to be in the position of a man fitting together a jigsaw, most of the pieces of which are missing'.[9]

The purpose of this article is to identify a new and peculiarly illuminating piece of the folkloric jigsaw to which *Cymbeline* belongs. Building on a seminal study on the folkloric composition of *Cymbeline* recently conducted by Charlotte Artese,[10] the present discussion identifies a number of striking narrative parallels between Shakespeare's play and a late medieval Icelandic romance named *Ála flekks saga* ('The Saga of Áli Fleck'), which was probably composed sometime around the turn of the fifteenth century, approximately one and a half centuries before Shakespeare's birth. One qualification must preface the discussion – namely, that *Ála flekks saga* is a text that Shakespeare could not plausibly have known. There is no evidence that any medieval Icelandic text influenced Shakespeare directly.[11] While his vast array of source material does famously include the medieval Scandinavian legend of Amlethus (Hamlet) – possibly ultimately of Icelandic origin, but probably transmitted to Shakespeare via French[12] – *Ála flekks saga* by contrast has never been influential or well known outside of Iceland, and it appears not even to have been translated from the original Icelandic into any other language until the twentieth century.[13] The saga and Shakespeare's play are distant folkloric relatives, and although studying them comparatively inevitably lacks the sharper focus offered by sources or analogues of closer chronological and geographical proximity, the mere fact that they are independent parts of the same, blurred folkloric picture offers some useful definition to that picture. The present discussion does not seek to posit any route of influence or motif transmission from the older text to the younger, a task further rendered impractical by the paucity of relevant analogues. Instead, two intertwined lines of enquiry will form the basis of the discussion. Firstly, examination will be made of the slivers of light that each of the two texts can shed obliquely on the state of the specific folktale traditions from which both texts drew. In particular, some of the noteworthy overlaps between those slivers of illumination will allow for a tentative process of extrapolative back-triangulation, raising new possibilities with significant implications for scholarly understanding of the development of those folktales. The second line of enquiry will consider what implications those new possibilities may have on the literary construction of the two texts, with a greater focus on *Cymbeline* due to the simple fact that significantly more is

---

[9] F. P. Wilson, *Marlowe and the Early Shakespeare* (Oxford, 1953), p. 106.

[10] Artese, *Sources*, pp. 173–209.

[11] Heather O'Donoghue, *Old Norse–Icelandic Literature: A Short Introduction* (Oxford, 2004), p. 147.

[12] For seminal discussions on the Scandinavian source material from which the Hamlet story was ultimately derived, including the transmission of the story through late medieval Europe, see Israel Gollancz, *Hamlet in Iceland* (London, 1898); William F. Hansen, *Saxo Grammaticus and the Life of Hamlet: A Translation, History, and Commentary* (Lincoln, NE, 1983); and Ian Felce, 'In search of *Amlóða saga*: the saga of Hamlet the Icelander', in *Studies in the Transmission and Reception of Old Norse Literature*, ed. Judy Quinn and Adele Cipolla (Turnhout, 2016), pp. 101–22.

[13] The first edition of *Ála flekks saga* was produced by Åke Lagerholm in 1927 (*Drei lygisǫgur*, ed. Åke Lagerholm (Halle (Saale), 1927), pp. 84–120), and the first translation of the saga into any language appears to have been W. Bryant Bachman and Guðmundur Erlingsson's popular English translation in 1993 (W. Bryant Bachman and Guðmundur Erlingsson, trans., *Six Old Icelandic Sagas* (Lanham, MD, 1993), pp. 41–61). Despite the Danish ancestry of *Ála flekks saga*'s hero, the saga was not part of the flurry of seventeenth-century Swedish and Danish translations of medieval Icelandic sagas deemed to be relevant to the kingdoms' respective waves of nationalistic antiquarianism (on which, see Philip Lavender, 'The secret prehistory of the *Fornaldarsögur*', *Journal of English and Germanic Philology* 114 (2015), 526–61). On this striking absence, see Jonathan Y. H. Hui, Caitlin Ellis, James McIntosh, Katherine M. Olley, William Norman and Kimberly Anderson, '*Ála flekks saga*: an introduction, text and translation', *Leeds Studies in English* 49 (2018), 1–43; pp. 3–8.

known about the circumstances of its composition than those of the saga. In uncovering new contextual information concerning the main folktales underpinning *Cymbeline*, the discussion seeks thereby to re-evaluate the nature of Shakespeare's adaptation and combination of those folktales.

ATU 709, 'SNOW WHITE'

One of Shakespeare's late romances, *Cymbeline* is recognized to have drawn on a wide variety of influences. Familiar motifs can be found in several of his earlier works, including the heroine's consumption of a coma-inducing potion in *Romeo and Juliet*, as well as a husband becoming 'murderously jealous' after being manipulated into wagering on his wife's fidelity in *Othello* and *The Winter's Tale*.[14] Discussions of *Cymbeline*'s key external influences often tend to focus on two particular sources.[15] The first is Raphael Holinshed's *Chronicles of England, Scotland, and Ireland* (first published in 1577), which provided Shakespeare with brief historical material on the first-century Brittonic king Cunobelinus ('Kymbelyne' in Holinshed), and his sons Guiderius and Arviragus. The second text is Giovanni Boccaccio's fourteenth-century *Decameron*, in which the ninth tale of the second day, told by Filomena, begins with Bernabò's wager on the fidelity of his wife Zinevra. This tale heavily influenced Giacomo's bedroom intrusion in *Cymbeline*. Both of these sources will be discussed later. However, another prominent influence on *Cymbeline* was some form of the 'Snow White' folktale, ATU 709. The folktale is often understandably omitted from discussions of *Cymbeline*'s sources because no precise, extant variant has been identified as a direct source used by Shakespeare. Indeed, there is currently insufficient analogical evidence to gauge how many ATU 709 variants Shakespeare could have known in some form, or whether the variants he knew were oral or literary (or both), or how widespread ATU 709 variants were in early modern England or Western Europe.

The basic correspondence of *Cymbeline* with the 'Snow White' folktale was first noted by Karl Schenkl in 1864, who outlined obvious resonances in Innogen's wilderness refuge with Belarius and the brothers Guiderius and Arviragus, her death-like state induced by the stepmother-queen's potion, and the ceremonial treatment of her apparent corpse.[16] Scepticism has been expressed over the extent of the folktale's influence on Shakespeare's play, however. Geoffrey Bullough, for instance, remarks in general terms that the folktale was 'probably not known in Elizabethan England; but elements of the story appear in many ballads and romances'.[17] This assertion is problematic in two ways: it appears to overlook the essential role of oral circulation in folktale transmission (and, indeed, in the transmission of ballads and romances); and it rests on the assumption that any putative ATU 709 variants known in sixteenth- and early seventeenth-century England must have been of a hypotextual form widely recognizable by modern conceptions of 'Snow White', which are based exclusively on texts younger than *Cymbeline*.[18] From a folkloristic perspective, Christine Shojaei Kawan also dismissed *Cymbeline*'s correspondences with ATU 709 as 'rather vague',[19] citing a number of allomotific differences, such as the cause of Innogen's false death being a coma-inducing potion instead of a poison (though the latter was in fact the

---

[14] *Cymbeline*, ed. Valerie Wayne, Arden Third Series (London, 2017), p. 1.
[15] See, for instance, *Cymbeline*, ed. Wayne, pp. 94–109. Discussion of further sources and analogues can be found in surveys such as Geoffrey Bullough, *Narrative and Dramatic Sources of Shakespeare*, vol. 8 (London, Henley and New York, 1975), pp. 3–111; and Kenneth Muir, *The Sources of Shakespeare's Plays* (London, 1977), pp. 258–66.
[16] Karl Schenkl, 'Das Märchen von Sneewittchen und Shakespeare's Cymbeline', *Germania* 9 (1864), 458–60.
[17] Bullough, *Sources*, vol. 8, p. 24.
[18] This latter problem is further exacerbated by the global prominence and de facto canonical status of the best-known variant, the Grimm Brothers' 'Sneewittchen', which was first published in their 1812 edition of their *Kinder- und Hausmärchen* but revised several times until the best-known 1857 edition. The 1857 version would form the basis of the popular Disney animated film of 1937, *Snow White and the Seven Dwarfs*.
[19] Christine Shojaei Kawan, 'A brief literary history of *Snow White*', *Fabula* 49 (2008), 325–42; p. 327.

queen's intention).[20] This characterization is similarly problematized by the hypotextual obscurity resulting from the paucity of identified 'Snow White' variants that antedate *Cymbeline*, and arguably understates the extent of Shakespeare's well-known adaptive tendencies. However, a recent study by Charlotte Artese argued convincingly in favour of *Cymbeline*'s close affinity with 'Snow White'. Artese grounded her discussion in Steven Swann Jones's nine-episode typological structure of the tale type, asserting that, irrespective of allomotific variation, most of the functions of the various folktale episodes are clearly fulfilled in the play (see Table 3).

Cymbeline's precise date of composition is not entirely certain, but, as the first attestation of its performance came in 1611,[24] it was probably composed in 1609 or 1610, and it first appeared in

Table 3 Snow White and *Cymbeline*

Snow White episode[21]	Events in *Cymbeline*[22]
1. **Origin:** The heroine's conception, or at least her familial situation, is described.	–
2. **Jealousy:** A persecutor becomes jealous of the heroine, usually because of her beauty.	The stepmother-queen's desire for her son Cloten to take Innogen's status as Cymbeline's heir (3.5.62–5).
3. **Expulsion:** The persecutor causes the heroine's expulsion, sometimes by ordering her death.	Innogen's flight from the British court (3.2).
4. **Adoption:** The heroine finds refuge with strangers.	Innogen taken in by Belarius, Guiderius and Arviragus (3.6).
5. **Renewed Jealousy:** The persecutor learns of the heroine's survival and again becomes jealous, seeking to do her further harm.	Innogen's consumption of the queen's potion (4.2).
6. **Death:** The heroine is apparently killed by the persecutor.	Innogen's coma-like state (4.2).

(continued)

Table 3 (cont.)

Snow White episode	Events in *Cymbeline*
7. **Exhibition:** The heroine's corpse is exhibited by her companions.	Innogen's body remaining unburied and strewn with flowers (4.2).
8. **Resuscitation:** The heroine is revived.	Innogen's waking (4.2).
(**Extra cycle of persecution:** The persecutor hears of the heroine's survival and marriage, and attempts to kill her again.)[23]	–
9. **Resolution:** The heroine is married, and the persecutor punished.	Reunions and Innogen's formal marriage to Posthumous (5.6).

---

[20] As mentioned, this potion is strongly reminiscent of the one knowingly consumed by Juliet in act 4, scene 3 of *Romeo and Juliet*, probably written in 1594 or 1595.

[21] As put forth in Steven Swann Jones, 'The structure of *Snow White*', in *Fairy Tales and Society: Illusion, Allusion, and Paradigm*, ed. Ruth B. Bottigheimer (Philadelphia, 1986), pp. 165–84. The same material is incorporated into a wider discussion in Steven Swann Jones, *The New Comparative Method: Structural and Symbolic Analysis of the Allomotifs of 'Snow White'* (Helsinki, 1990). Jones subdivides the nine episodes into two parts, with the second part beginning at 'Renewed Jealousy' and encompassing 'a repetition of the pattern of rivalry, attack, rescue, and relocation found in part one, but with more serious consequences' (Jones, *New Comparative Method*, p. 23).

[22] Collated from Artese, *Sources*, pp. 173–84.

[23] Jones remarks that '[i]n about 20 percent of the versions that I have examined, a third repetition of hostilities follows the heroine's marriage' (Jones, 'Structure', p. 173), but this third cycle does not form a part of his overall typological structure due to its relative rarity.

[24] The Oxford Shakespeare: The Complete Works, 2nd edn, ed. Stanley Wells, Gary Taylor, John Jowett and William Montgomery (New York and Oxford, 2005), p. 1185. All references to the text of *Cymbeline* are drawn from this edition.

print in the First Folio of 1623.[25] No direct sources have been identified for its 'Snow White' correspondences, and, in the absence of any such identification, it must be assumed that the source(s) through which Shakespeare received the folktale was oral, or perhaps literary but non-extant. Indeed, apart from several loose or partial ancient variants listed in the Snow White chapter of Graham Anderson's *Fairytale in the Ancient World*,[26] and a medieval Breton *lai* earlier identified as a partial variant by Alfred Nutt,[27] no 'Snow White' variant from before the early modern period had been identified, until a recent study on the medieval Icelandic *Ála flekks saga*.[28] The saga's earliest manuscript witness (Reykjavík, Árni Magnússon Institute (AM), 589 e 4to) is dated by Handrit.is, the online manuscript database of the National and University Library of Iceland, to the second half of the fifteenth century,[29] and the saga itself is thought to have been composed around the turn of the fifteenth century.[30] Its plot runs as follows:[31]

Áli, the saga hero and an English prince, is exposed as a child on his father's instruction. After being adopted by a poor couple, he returns to the royal court and is there recognized and reincorporated into the royal family. One night, he is cursed by a trollish bondwoman, Blátönn:

1. He is to leave the royal court and go into the wilderness to marry her sister, Nótt, on account of a bafflingly spurious reason: he had apparently never greeted Blátönn courteously.
2. Áli counter-curses Blátönn to turn into a stone slab in the kitchen, and to be broken if he should escape her curse.

Áli makes his way to Nótt's cave, but resists her advances and later escapes with the help of her half-human daughter Hlaðgerðr. He then wanders to Tartary, where he wins the favour of the Tartarian maiden-king Þornbjörg, through his military defence of her kingdom. They marry. However, Blátönn's brother Glóðarauga intrudes upon their wedding night by entering their bedroom and issuing a curse:

3. (a) As revenge for killing Blátönn, Áli is to transform immediately into a wolf and ravage Tartary's livestock.

4. Áli counter-curses Glóðarauga to remain fixed to the same chest on which he is sitting and shriek non-stop (i.e. to prevent him from issuing further curses),[32] and to be hung on the gallows if Áli should escape his curse.
3. (b) Glóðarauga quickly counters by extending his curse, so that Áli must now continue on to ravage livestock in his home kingdom of England as well.

After some time, Áli is freed from this curse by his foster-mother. He is then cursed for a third time:

5. As revenge for escaping her clutches and killing Glóðarauga, Nótt appears to him in a dream and whips him, causing festering, debilitating wounds on his physical body which cannot be healed except by her unnamed brothers. If left unhealed, he will die in ten years' time.

Þornbjörg travels the world with the incapacitated Áli in tow and discovers that Nótt's brother Jötunoxi rules a kingdom of giants at the end of the world. With both Áli and herself disguised, she infiltrates his court and agrees to marry him, if he has Áli healed and Nótt killed. Jötunoxi agrees,

---

[25] Stanley Wells and Michael Dobson, eds., *The Oxford Companion to Shakespeare*, 2nd edn (Oxford, 2015), p. 244.
[26] Graham Anderson, *Fairytale in the Ancient World* (London, 2000), pp. 43–60.
[27] Alfred Nutt, 'The lai of Eliduc and the Märchen of Little Snow-White', *Folklore* 3 (1892), 26–48.
[28] Jonathan Y. H. Hui, Caitlin Ellis, James McIntosh and Katherine M. Olley, '*Ála flekks saga*: a Snow White variant from late medieval Iceland', *Leeds Studies in English* 49 (2018), 45–64.
[29] 'AM 589e 4to', Handrit.is: https://handrit.is/en/manuscript/view/is/AM04-0589e
[30] Jürg Glauser, 'Ála flekks saga', in *Medieval Scandinavia: An Encyclopedia*, ed. Phillip Pulsiano and Kirsten Wolf (New York, 1993), pp. 6–7; p. 6.
[31] A text and facing English translation can be found at Hui et al., 'Introduction', pp. 18–43.
[32] Within medieval Icelandic saga literature, it is quite common for protagonists to respond to curses by inflicting some form of counter-attack which causes the wicked curser to lose the power of speech permanently, thereby preventing them from cursing the protagonist again. However, no other instance of this involves a chest. For a brief survey of manifestations of cursing and counter-cursing in medieval Icelandic romance, see Hui et al., 'Snow White variant', pp. 49–55.

killing Nótt and sending his two human servants Andan and Mandan to bring Áli to be healed. After this is done, Andan and Mandan reveal to Áli that they had been kidnapped by Jötunoxi as children. Áli swears blood-brotherhood with them, and they reunite with Þornbjörg and burn down Jötunoxi's hall. With his dying breath, Jötunoxi inflicts a final curse on Áli:

6. Áli will never know peace until he finds Nótt's daughter Hlaðgerðr.

Áli eventually finds Hlaðgerðr in Scythia, saves her life and marries her to the Scythian king. Afterwards, he returns to England and lives happily ever after with Þornbjörg.

Ála flekks saga was only recently identified as a 'Snow White' variant, in a study which argued that the saga's narrative was so holistically adherent to the folktale's typological structure that it seemed to have been deliberately constructed around it.[33] Significantly, unlike the ancient variants listed by Anderson, or the Breton *lai* discussed by Nutt, *Ála flekks saga* is a full 'Snow White' variant, preserving the entire typological structure in relatively plain form, and providing strong evidence that a form of the 'Snow White' tale type with a crystallized structure had been transmitted to Iceland – and therefore northwestern Europe – by the time the saga was composed in the late fourteenth or early fifteenth century. On the surface, the saga appears to lack many of the familiar allomotifs found in the Grimm Brothers' 'Sneewittchen', but some of these can be tellingly illuminated by context or by close medieval Icelandic analogues. For instance, the curse issued by Blátönn as soon as she is introduced may seem jarring in the narrative – and unrelated to 'Snow White' given the lack of any prior relationship with Áli – but in close Icelandic analogues such curses are usually issued by step-mother-figures, who are frequently the persecutors in 'Snow White' tales.[34] Similarly, Áli's body is never formally placed on exhibition, but his incapacitation is firmly based on the state of living death suffered by Tristram in *Tristrams saga ok Ísöndar* ('The Saga of Tristram and Ísönd', the thirteenth-century Norse translation of the Tristan legend) – and in that tale Tristram's body is at least placed in a well-decorated room.[35] Although many of the allomotifs in *Ála flekks saga* may not at first glance be reminiscent of more familiar versions of 'Snow White', the structure of the saga adheres remarkably closely to that of the folktale, in that it is so wholly characterized by the repeated cycles of renewed persecution identified by Jones as a defining feature of 'Snow White' that it even contains a rare post-resuscitation cycle of persecution.[36] Its adherence to the folktale's typological structure is broken down in Table 4, with *Cymbeline*'s presented alongside for comparison.

It will be clear from the above structural comparison that the manifestations of ATU 709 in *Ála flekks saga* and *Cymbeline* are substantially different, and that they are not immediate relatives, but rather very distant cousins, within the 'Snow White' folktale tradition. Absent from *Cymbeline* is a notable Origin episode, as well as a structurally striking post-resuscitation cycle of persecution. Absent from *Ála flekks saga* is actual, recognizable jealousy as a motivation in any of its Jealousy episodes, as well as a comatose state during the Death episode. At best, each text provides oblique evidence for the nature of the other's affinity with ATU 709. Together, they demonstrate that the 'Snow White' folktale was being transmitted in two apparently different structural forms in northwestern Europe by the early seventeenth century. In the absence of identification of further medieval or early modern European ATU 709 variants, there might be little more to be definitively gleaned from this particular 'Snow White' connection – if it were indeed the full extent of the connection between the two texts. However, the texts also share two intriguingly distinct narrative parallels which cannot be accounted for by their basic

---

[33] Hui et al., 'Snow White variant', pp. 55–64.
[34] Hui et al., 'Snow White variant', pp. 55–64.
[35] 'Tristrams saga ok Ísöndar', ed. and trans. Peter Jorgensen, in *Norse Romance*, vol. 1: *The Tristan Legend*, ed. Marianne E. Kalinke (Cambridge, 1999), pp. 23–226; pp. 82–3.
[36] Jones, 'Structure', pp. 172–6.

Table 4 Snow White, *Ála flekks saga* and *Cymbeline*

Snow White episode	Event in *Ála flekks saga* (c.1400)[37]	Events in *Cymbeline* (c.1610)
1. Origin	Áli's conception, exposure and return to the English court (chs. 1–3).	-
2. Jealousy	The bondwoman Blátönn's contrived and unsubstantiated claim that Áli never greeted her courteously (ch. 4).	The stepmother-queen's desire for her son Cloten to take Innogen's status as Cymbeline's heir (3.5.62–5).
3. Expulsion	Áli's departure, under Blátönn's curse, from the English court to the wild to find Nótt (ch. 5).	Innogen's flight from the British court (3.2).
4. Adoption	Áli's new identity in Tartary (chs. 6–8).	Innogen taken in by Belarius, Guiderius and Arviragus (3.6).
5. Renewed Jealousy [, Expulsion and Adoption]	Gloðarauga's curse [and Áli's consequent wolf-transformation] (chs. 8–11).	Innogen's consumption of the queen's potion (4.2).
6. [Renewed Jealousy, Expulsion and] Death	[Nótt's curse and] Áli's consequent physical decay (chs. 12–15).	Innogen's coma-like state (4.2).
7. Exhibition	Þornbjörg's travels across the world in search of a cure, with Áli in tow (ch. 14).	Innogen's body remaining unburied and strewn with flowers (4.2).
8. Resuscitation	Áli healed by Jötunoxi's brothers (ch. 15).	Innogen's waking (4.2).
(Extra cycle of persecution)	Jötunoxi's curse and Áli's consequent departure to Scythia to find Hlaðgerðr (chs. 16–17).	-
9. Resolution	Marriages and descendants (chs. 18–19).	Reunions and Innogen's formal marriage to Posthumous (5.6).

ATU 709 affinity, and it is these tantalizing parallels which will form the main focus of this article.

THE KIDNAPPED BROTHERS

The first and most noticeable narrative parallel between the two texts is that they both contain a pair of brothers whose biographies and roles share a curious number of striking correspondences. The opening scene of *Cymbeline* reveals that, some twenty years prior to the play's beginning, the British king's two sons, 'the eld'st of them at three years old, / I'th' swathing clothes the other, from their nursery / Were stol'n' (1.1.58–60). This lays the foundation for the introduction of Guiderius and Arviragus in act 3, scene 3, whose real identities are quickly revealed to the audience in a monologue by Belarius, their kidnapper and assumed father. The appearance of these three characters midway through the play begins the narrative arc of Innogen's exile into the British wilderness and her 'Snow White' Adoption episode. The brothers' biography is as follows: twenty years after having been kidnapped by Belarius as infants to be raised by him, they play host to Innogen – disguised as a man named 'Fidele' – when she stumbles upon their cave (3.6.61–6). They pledge firm friendship with her at their first encounter (3.6.66–72), with Arviragus explicitly treating her as his 'brother' thereafter (3.6.69, 4.2.2–3, 4.2.30). When the men encounter Cloten, Guiderius duels and then decapitates him off stage (4.2). Later on, Guiderius and Arviragus participate in the Britons' battle against the Romans (5.2, 5.3), and their true royal identities

---

[37] Adapted from Hui et al., 'Snow White variant', p. 64.

are revealed at the end of the play, reuniting them with their father and sister (5.6.326–79).

Shakespeare derived the basic pseudo-historical personages of Cymbeline and his sons, Guiderius and Arviragus, from Holinshed's *Chronicles*,[38] and the exile of the nobleman Belarius to a cave in the wilderness seems to have been one of Shakespeare's borrowings from *The Rare Triumphs of Love and Fortune*, a romantic drama of the 1580s.[39] However, the kidnapping of the infant Guiderius and Arviragus from the royal court and their subsequent upbringing away from society do not come from Holinshed or *The Rare Triumphs*; their narrative arc was clearly derived from a separate tale. To my knowledge, no direct source or close analogue has hitherto been identified for this particular arc. Artese has tentatively posited, as a possible folkloric basis, an opening often found in variants of two ATU 709-related folktales: ATU 709A, 'The sister of nine brothers', a subtype of ATU 709; and ATU 451, 'The maiden who seeks her brothers', which is occasionally found in combination with ATU 709.[40] Both tales sometimes open with the departure or banishment of a set of brothers from home (sometimes by a stepmother-figure in ATU 451) following the birth of their sister, and in ATU 709A, as in *Cymbeline*, the heroine often finds her brothers and stays with them a while. This is by no means a definitive identification, however, as both tales involve the female protagonist going out specifically to search for her brothers, which is an entirely different rationale from the journey to the wilderness found in ATU 709 variants. Artese's suggestion will be revisited later in this section, after the presentation of new analogical evidence.

Curiously, *Ála flekks saga* contains an episode with such close parallels to the Guiderius–Arviragus arc outlined above that it can in fact be said to constitute the closest known analogue. Having been cursed to suffer from fatally debilitating wounds, Áli is brought by Queen Þornbjörg to be cured in Jötunoxi's trollish kingdom at the end of the world. Upon securing from her a pledge of marriage, Jötunoxi sends two human servants, Andan and Mandan, to bring Áli to be healed. After this is done, the brothers introduce themselves to Áli on the return journey as the sons of an otherwise unmentioned earl named 'Pollonius' (a name discussed later in this article). Áli offers to swear blood-brotherhood with them, and they accept. Afterwards, they reunite with Þornbjörg's forces and assault Jötunoxi's hall, where, during the battle, Jötunoxi lays the saga's final curse on Áli before being attacked by Mandan, and although Jötunoxi overpowers Mandan, Áli intervenes and decapitates him. The episode ends with the humans' comprehensive victory, and Andan and Mandan are never mentioned again.

The parallels between the episodes in *Ála flekks saga* and *Cymbeline* can be distilled into at least six distinct events (Table 5):

1. Years before the events of the story, two brothers are kidnapped as children and raised in the wilderness, far from human society.
2. Years later, the protagonist encounters them there.
3. The brothers provide vital help to the protagonist to enable him/her to survive.
4. Almost immediately, the protagonist and the brothers formally cement their firm friendship.
5. Soon afterwards, the brothers confront an antagonist related to a stepmother-figure.
6. One of the brothers duels that antagonist, and performs or plays a major role in his decapitation.

---

[38] Raphael Holinshed, 'The history of England', in *Chronicles of England, Scotland and Ireland*, vol. 1 (London, 1577), pp. 46–66. See *Cymbeline*, ed. Wayne, p. 95; Bullough, *Sources*, vol. 8, pp. 43–6; and Muir, *Sources*, pp. 259–62.

[39] R. W. Boodle, 'Original of "Cymbeline" and possibly of "The Tempest"', *Notes and Queries* 7 (1887), 404–5; *Cymbeline*, ed. J. M. Nosworthy, Arden Second Series (London, 1955), pp. xxiv–xxviii; and Muir, *Sources*, pp. 258–9. The exiled nobleman in *The Rare Triumphs*, Bomelio, is also regarded as a source for Prospero in *The Tempest*, on which see Boodle, 'Original'; *Cymbeline*, ed. Roger Warren, The Oxford Shakespeare, ed. Stanley Wells and Gary Taylor (New York and Oxford, 1998), p. 18; and Allyna E. Ward, 'The Rare Triumphs of Love and Fortune, 1582', in *The Oxford Handbook of Tudor Drama*, ed. Thomas Betteridge and Greg Walker (Oxford, 2012), pp. 446–61; p. 460.

[40] Artese, *Sources*, p. 182.

Table 5 Episodes in *Ála flekks saga* and in *Cymbeline*

Event	Manifestation in *Ála flekks saga*	Manifestation in *Cymbeline*
1.	Jötunoxi had kidnapped Andan and Mandan and raised them in his kingdom at the end of the world.	Belarius had kidnapped Guiderius and Arviragus and raised them in a cave in the Welsh wilderness.
2.	In Jötunoxi's kingdom, Andan and Mandan are assigned to bring Áli to be cured.	In disguise, Innogen stumbles across the cave.
3.	Andan and Mandan bring Áli to be cured of his debilitating wounds.	Belarius and the brothers take Innogen in and provide her with shelter and food.
4.	Áli quickly swears blood-brotherhood with Andan and Mandan.	Guiderius and Arviragus immediately befriend Innogen. Arviragus regularly calls her 'brother'.
5.	Áli, Þornbjörg, Andan and Mandan participate in the assault on the hall of Jötunoxi, brother of the saga's initial stepmother-figure, Blátönn.	Belarius and the brothers encounter Cloten, son of the play's stepmother-figure.
6.	Mandan duels Jötunoxi, but is overpowered. Áli intervenes and beheads Jötunoxi.	Guiderius duels and beheads Cloten.

There are, admittedly, important differences between the two sets of episodes. For one thing, Innogen is the long-lost sibling of the brothers, while Áli is not. For another, Innogen clearly assumes the housekeeper role commonly associated with the 'Snow White' heroine during her Adoption, such that she even takes the trouble to prepare an alphabet soup for the men;[41] Áli performs no such role. Furthermore, in *Ála flekks saga* the brothers' kidnapper is a monstrous villain; in *Cymbeline*, he is a slighted nobleman (though this role will be addressed later in this section). Nonetheless, the closeness of the brothers' functions in the two episodes, as seen in the striking specificity of the parallels outlined above, would seem to point to the common influence of some pre-existing, yet-unidentified tale, perhaps oral, perhaps literary but non-extant. Indeed, the likelihood that this putative ur-narrative was borrowed rather than invented in the case of *Ála flekks saga* can be seen in a somewhat disproportionate honour granted to Andan and Mandan: although they appear exclusively within this episode, their swift establishment of blood-brotherhood with the protagonist would seem to afford them greater importance than their role in the narrative should merit. Where then did this particular narrative arc come from? Was it related to 'Snow White', or did it come from an entirely different tale that was independently grafted onto the texts' 'Snow White' structures by their respective composers? The former seems much likelier, for one simple reason presently to be discussed: each of the six events listed above can be accounted for through tangential affinity with well-attested aspects of ATU 709.

The six events can be divided into three broad thematic strands, with Event 1 constituting the brothers' backstory; Events 2, 3 and 4, their encounter with and assistance of the protagonist; and Events 5 and 6 their pivotal role in the defeat of a prominent secondary antagonist. The middle strand will be discussed first, as it corresponds most obviously to the familiar 'Snow White' tale. The presence of brothers whom the protagonist encounters (Event 2 above) is common in 'Snow White' variants, many of which feature a set of brothers or brother-figures (such as outlaws) who host and offer vital assistance to the exiled and imperilled protagonist.[42] The seven dwarfs, of the Grimm Brothers' 'Sneewittchen' and subsequently Disney's animated film, are the best-known allomotif of this function. Guiderius–Arviragus and Andan–Mandan also unquestionably fulfil this role; the former pair provide food and shelter for

---

[41] Artese, *Sources*, p. 181. [42] Artese, *Sources*, pp. 181–2.

the fleeing Innogen, while the latter pair bring Áli to be cured of his fatally debilitating wounds (Event 3). More than this, many 'Snow White' variants involve the establishment of a fraternal bond between the protagonist and the brothers (Event 4), whether through adoption or blood relation. This motif is listed in Stith Thompson's *Motif-Index* as F451.5.1.2, 'Dwarfs adopt girl as sister'.[43] In *Cymbeline*, the brothers immediately feel a natural affinity with 'Fidele', unaware that she is in fact a woman and their sister. Although they do not fully understand this affinity – Arviragus later admits that 'I know not why I love this youth' (4.2.20–1) – they attempt to come to terms with it in real time. Guiderius rues the impossibility of establishing an affinal relationship with 'Fidele' due to the latter's apparent male gender (3.7.66–8), and Arviragus responds by proposing adopted consanguinity instead, remarking that 'I'll love him as my brother' (3.7.69), and referring to 'Fidele' as 'brother' thrice more thereafter. In the case of Andan and Mandan, as aforementioned, their blood-brotherhood with Áli seems somewhat jarring in the context of the whole saga, almost as though it had been shoehorned in. The long tradition of blood-brotherhood in Old Norse literature denotes a significant, ritualized bond with mutual responsibilities (primarily relating to avenging one's death) and implied parity of character.[44] Yet little is ever revealed of Andan's and Mandan's characters, and they are never mentioned again after the death of Jötunoxi, even though they might have been expected at least to feature, if not during Áli's final adventure, in the usual romance denouement of marriage celebrations and progeny. The discrepancy between the esteem of their blood-brotherhood and their dispensability within the Jötunoxi episode and total absence beyond it would seem to suggest the influence of a source in which two such kidnapped brothers were indeed of greater significance to the narrative, and to the protagonist.[45] In Events 2, 3 and 4, therefore, it is possible to identify in the relationship established between the protagonist and the brothers the usual symbolic currency of 'Snow White' brother-figures, or at least traces thereof. Furthermore, as the three events constitute the characters' encounter and the establishment of their relationship, they form the indispensable core of the sexpartite, two-brother narrative arc outlined above, which would suggest that the arc was intrinsically related to the 'Snow White' tale.

The distinctive abduction backstory of the two brothers (Event 1 above) is intriguing. This parallel between *Ála flekks saga* and *Cymbeline* seems to constitute sufficiently specific evidence of influence by a common ancestor, rather than general archetypal affinity of the sort that might have them considered reflexes of the Roman aetiological legend of Romulus and Remus, for instance. The abduction backstory is not a standard ATU 709 feature, though, and no close analogue has been identified. However, it is not a stretch to regard abduction by a third party as a plausible backstory for a set of brothers later found living in the wilderness, which is a space associated with 'Snow White' brother-figures not only as their usual habitat, but also through the symbolism underlying their frequent manifestation as either non-human creatures (such as fairies) or human outcasts (such as robbers or outlaws).[46] That this abduction, in both texts, should occur years before the events of the narrative, in the brothers' infancy, emphasizes its subordinate role in facilitating the now-adult

---

[43] Stith Thompson, *Motif-Index of Folk-Literature*, rev. and enl. ed., vol. 3 (Bloomington, 1956), p. 111.

[44] For an overview, see Pragya Vohra, 'Creating kin, extending authority: blood-brotherhood and power in medieval Iceland', in *The Palgrave Handbook of Masculinity and Political Culture in Europe*, ed. Christopher Fletcher, Sean Brady, Rachel E. Moss and Lucy Riall (London, 2018), pp. 105–31.

[45] *Ála flekks saga* is not the only medieval Icelandic romance to contain a relatively arbitrary manifestation of blood-brotherhood, but it is notable the saga does not portray any particular compatibility – social status, personality similarities, martial prowess – between Áli and the brothers that would invite the establishment of such a relationship.

[46] Steven Swann Jones remarks that the 'Snow White' protagonist's adopters are 'all outsiders; they are outcasts from society or they are living on the fringe of the civilized world' (Jones, *New Comparative Method*, p. 53).

brothers' presence in the wilderness. In other words, it appears highly plausible that the abduction backstory was developed as an extension to the usual wilderness-dwelling brother-figures of 'Snow White', and that this extension formed part of a 'Snow White'-related tradition from which both *Ála flekks saga* and *Cymbeline* independently drew.

Events 5 and 6 above likewise seem to constitute an idiosyncratic extension to another element commonly associated with ATU 709 – namely, the wicked stepmother. In both *Ála flekks saga* and *Cymbeline*, the protagonist had already evaded a forced marriage pushed by a stepmother-figure. In the Icelandic saga, Áli had escaped Blátönn's curse that he must marry her sister Nótt – a curse usually issued by stepmothers in medieval Icelandic romances – while Innogen in *Cymbeline* had refused a marriage to Cloten pushed by his mother the queen, to their chagrin (as well as that of Cymbeline). However, the protagonist later comes under threat from a figure not typical of variants of ATU 709 proper – namely, a malign antagonist related to the stepmother-figure. In *Ála flekks saga*, this is Jötunoxi, whose villainy is apparent not only through the monstrosity of his dominion and his trollish siblings, but also in the malicious curse he issues Áli after realizing his identity. In *Cymbeline*, this is Cloten, who is introduced in the very first scene of *Cymbeline* as 'Too bad for bad report' (1.1.17), a reputation affirmed throughout his involvement in the play, culminating in his vengeful desire to murder Posthumous and rape Innogen at Milford Haven (3.5.130–45).[47] Although this secondary antagonist is not a standard 'Snow White' figure, the role he plays serves to compound the threat initially posed to the protagonist by the stepmother-figure. There is therefore a certain symmetry in the fact that the surrogate of the initial antagonist is only defeated with the help of a surrogate of the protagonist, in the form of one of the wilderness-dwelling brothers. Indeed, in the context of the 'Snow White' tale, it is logical that this assistant function should fall to one of the brothers, given that they are the protagonist's most important allies – and, in some variants, his/her only allies.

It is true that the manifestation of the antagonist's decapitation (Event 6 above) differs noticeably between the two texts in several ways. For one thing, the agency of the killing blow in *Cymbeline* lies with one of the brothers, Guiderius, while in *Ála flekks saga* Mandan fails in his assault, and the agency is transferred to the saga hero, Áli, as is typical of medieval Icelandic romance. Another major difference is that the decapitation itself has greater functional value to the narrative of *Cymbeline* than to *Ála flekks saga*, in that Cloten's headless corpse deceives Innogen into believing Posthumous dead – although, to qualify this point, the depiction of Innogen's grief is rather short-lived in the narrative, given that her soliloquy is followed within the same scene by the appearance of Lucius's troop, whom she immediately joins. However, regardless of the differences, the most significant function of the decapitation must surely be the emphatic removal of the antagonist in question from the narrative. In *Cymbeline*, Cloten's death leaves the 'Wager' misunderstanding as the only remaining obstacle between Innogen and Posthumous. Following his death in act 4, scene 2, even his malevolent mother fails to pose any further threat, or indeed make another appearance, before her convenient and ignominious offstage death in the play's final scene. Similarly, the death of Jötunoxi in *Ála flekks saga* marks the end of the trollish siblings whose consecutive animosity towards Áli had generated the majority of the saga's narrative traction. In both texts, the denouement does not follow immediately, but the death of this particular antagonist concludes the long-standing threat first posed by the stepmother-figure early on, moving the protagonist one step closer to the story's final resolution.

---

[47] Although Cloten does not succeed, his intended actions mirror those of Demetrius and Chiron in act 2, scene 3 of *Titus Andronicus*, which was composed sometime before 1593.

NEW EVIDENCE FOR *CYMBELINE*'S FOLKLORIC COMPOSITION

As mentioned, Artese identified two folktales, ATU 451 or ATU 709A, as possible influences on Guiderius and Arviragus in *Cymbeline*. The new analogical evidence of *Ála flekks saga* provides a second piece of the jigsaw puzzle, and a close one at that – but just how much can now be deduced about the overall picture? Beyond the two-brother arc, *Ála flekks saga* does not appear to have many echoes of ATU 451 or 709A which cannot be attributed to the saga's affinity with ATU 709 or another source. It does contain several parallels with 'The twelve brothers', an ATU 451 variant found in the Grimm Brothers' *Kinder- und Hausmärchen*, but these could be incidental. The order issued at the beginning of *Ála flekks saga* by King Ríkarðr that his pregnant wife should expose their child if male loosely mirrors the opening of 'The twelve brothers', in which the king orders that his twelve sons be killed if the thirteenth child is a girl, so that she may become sole heir.[48] However, Ríkarðr's rationale is one of foresighted compassion,[49] and though this has a whiff of compositional contrivance, any motivation behind killing an only child (only if born male) would seem to have little basis in issues of inheritance. Like *Ála flekks saga*, 'The twelve brothers' also contains a birthmark as a sign of royalty (a motif discussed in the next section), animal transformations, a wicked stepmother-figure and a misunderstood woman saved from imminent burning at the stake. However, the narrative frameworks surrounding these motifs are so different in both texts, and the first three motifs so common in European literature, that it is difficult to view the sum of the similarities as anything more than fortuitous coincidence.[50]

If *Ála flekks saga* as a whole does not contain any obvious echoes of ATU 451 or 709A, then, the question to be asked is whether any of the parallels between *Ála flekks saga* and *Cymbeline* contained within the two-brother arc can be plausibly attributed to either of those folktales as opposed to ATU 709. One notable possibility might be the malign, sometimes monstrous antagonist often found in ATU 451 and 709A wilderness episodes, who is not responsible for the heroine's exile, and who, in some variants of the former folktale, is killed by the wilderness-dwelling brothers.[51] However, this must be qualified by an important difference: in both *Ála flekks saga* and *Cymbeline*, as earlier discussed, the antagonist is strongly defined by his relation to the stepmother-figure, and the threat he poses represents an extension of hers. This familial relation seems not to be a feature of ATU 451 and ATU 709A, meaning that any argument supporting a connection between either folktale and the two-brother arc of *Ála flekks saga* and *Cymbeline* must assume the premise that the familial relation in both texts is coincidental. Indeed, such an argument would likely have to assume coincidence in any of the parallels between the two-brother arcs which do not correspond to ATU 451 or ATU 709A, including the noteworthy detail that the brothers in both texts are abducted from without, rather than exiled from within. There are two fundamental reasons why it seems unlikely, though not impossible, that such parallels might be coincidental. Firstly, the closeness and specificity of the parallels between two independent texts in *Ála flekks saga* and *Cymbeline* are suggestive of common influence from an already-crystallized narrative, rather than coincidental recombination. Secondly, the arbitrary depiction of the brothers' biography in *Ála flekks saga* reinforces the idea of an already-crystallized narrative, because, unlike

---

[48] Jacob L. K. Grimm and Wilhelm C. Grimm, *Kinder- und Hausmärchen*, 7th ed., vol. 1 (Göttingen, 1857), p. 48. I am grateful to Professor Artese for drawing this parallel to my attention.

[49] Hui et al., 'Introduction', pp. 18–19.

[50] The latter three motifs can also be found in the popular Völsung legend of medieval Scandinavia, including Iceland. At least one – Áli's transformation – appears to have been directly influenced by the corresponding episode in *Völsunga saga*, on which see Hui et al., 'Snow White variant', pp. 8–9.

[51] Hans-Jörg Uther, *The Types of International Folktales: A Classification and Bibliography. Based on the System of Antti Aarne and Stith Thompson*, vol. 1 (Helsinki, 2004), p. 267. A variant of ATU 451 which contains just two brothers is 'The ogre', found in *Folktales of France*, ed. Geneviève Massignon, and trans. Jacqueline Hyland (Chicago, 1968), pp. 145–7. I am grateful to Professor Artese for drawing this to my attention.

Guiderius and Arviragus, most of Andan's and Mandan's biographical details are superfluous within the story. Given that the narrative skeleton of the two-brother arc has been shown to contain substantial evidence of shared symbolic currency with ATU 709, it therefore seems probable that, whether or not the arc was originally influenced by ATU 451, it had already coalesced into a crystallized form of ATU 709 before the composition of *Ála flekks saga* around the turn of the fifteenth century.

Previous scholarship had already independently identified *Ála flekks saga* and *Cymbeline* as variants of ATU 709, 'Snow White'. The foregoing discussion has argued that the sexpartite two-brother arc found in both *Ála flekks saga* and *Cymbeline* can more plausibly be read as a natural expansion to the wilderness episode of ATU 709 – with Events 2, 3 and 4 being staple 'Snow White' occurrences, and Events 1, 5 and 6 plausible extensions to common 'Snow White' elements – than as ATU 709–451 or ATU 709–709A hybrids. The arc would appear to form a distinct part of a version of the 'Snow White' tale, but not as we know it. In other words, it seems likely that both Shakespeare and the *Ála flekks saga* composer independently drew from a separate branch or subtype of the ATU 709 tale – perhaps a putative 'ATU 709B'. There can be little doubt that this was indeed done independently, because, in addition to the differences already outlined, there is also the basic fact that the two-brother arc occurs in a different 'Snow White' episode in each text: in *Ála flekks saga*, it forms part of the late Resuscitation episode; in *Cymbeline*, it takes place in the earlier Adoption episode. It is even possible that this putative ATU 709 branch or subtype may have been a Western European oikotype of some sort – Carl Wilhelm von Sydow's term for a regional folktale variant[52] – and though this is impossible to posit from just two extant variants from separate literary cultures, there may potentially be an extremely faint hint to this effect in one last parallel between the two-brother episodes. Shakespeare's portrayal of *Cymbeline*'s ancient Britons (forebears to the Welsh), including Guiderius and Arviragus, is distinctive, being particularly characterized by a 'warlike and independent spirit' throughout the play,[53] and the suggestion has been made that Guiderius's striking appearance with Cloten's headless body could have been intended to be reminiscent of a sixteenth-century engraving of an ancient Pict – that is, another ancient Celtic people.[54] Andan and Mandan are given no nationality in *Ála flekks saga*, but their names, which are not attested elsewhere in Old Norse literature, appear to be Irish-inspired coinages,[55] a relative rarity in late medieval Icelandic romances and unique within this particular saga. This may simply be an allusion to Ireland's role as the location of Tristram's healing in *Tristrams saga ok Ísöndar* – on whose injuries Áli's incapacitation is based. However, is it possible that this faintest of parallels might alternatively betray some sort of Celtic connection underlying the two-brother ATU 709 subtype, recognized independently by medieval Icelanders and Shakespeare? The evidence is tantalizingly insufficient. Oikotype or not, though, it seems probable from the specificity of the discussed parallels between two unrelated texts in *Ála flekks saga* and *Cymbeline* that Shakespeare knew of and drew from an ATU 709 or 'ATU 709B' variant which contained some form of the distinctive two-brother arc, and that this branch of 'Snow White' had existed in Western Europe by the late fourteenth century, with the composition of *Ála flekks saga* serving as the *terminus ante quem* for its existence.

---

[52] Carl W. von Sydow, *Selected Papers on Folklore* (Copenhagen, 1948), pp. 44–59.

[53] Andrew Hadfield, *Shakespeare, Spenser and the Matter of Britain* (Basingstoke, 2004), p. 166.

[54] *Cymbeline*, ed. Martin Butler, The New Cambridge Shakespeare (Cambridge, 2005), pp. 48–9.

[55] Hui et al., 'Introduction', p. 15. Although the names do not directly correspond to any known medieval Irish names, I am grateful to Professor Máire Ní Mhaonaigh for the additional suggestion that 'Mandan' may have been influenced by the name of the Irish sea god, Manannán (or Manandán) mac Lir. There is a lesser chance that it may have been influenced by the Welsh version of the name, 'Manawydan'.

NEW EVIDENCE FOR *CYMBELINE*'S FOLKLORIC COMPOSITION

The hypothesized identification of the two-brother arc as a characteristic of a separate branch of ATU 709 is illuminating not just in its own right, but also with regard to the wider picture of narrative construction in *Cymbeline*. As mentioned, scholars have noted that the backstory of Belarius, an exiled nobleman living in a cave in the wilderness, was probably influenced by the biography of Bomelio in the 1582 play *The Rare Triumphs of Love and Fortune*. Bomelio's story does not involve any abduction, and so the new medieval Icelandic analogue for the two-brother arc may shed important light on the creative impulses behind Shakespeare's combination of the two stories. To that end, it seems highly plausible, between *The Rare Triumphs* and the putative ATU 709 branch, to read the narrative space of the wilderness as a thematically significant point of confluence in the *Cymbeline* episode's construction. In essence, Shakespeare appears to have attached the figure of the wilderness-exiled nobleman from *The Rare Triumphs* to the wilderness-dwelling abductee-brothers of the putative ATU 709 branch, resulting in the former, Belarius, being additionally responsible for the abduction, adoption and upbringing of the latter, Guiderius and Arviragus. Creative adaptation based around such confluences is in fact idiosyncratic of Shakespeare's recombinant initiative, and can also be seen in other motif-level instances, such as his substitution in *The Merchant of Venice* of the casket trial for the bed test in his Italian source,[56] as well as on a wider, narrative-level scale in the combination in *Cymbeline* of ATU 709 and 882, 'The wager on the wife's chastity', which will now be discussed.

THE TRUNK IN THE NOBLEWOMAN'S BEDROOM

ATU 882 is the other folktale identified alongside ATU 709 as a key component of *Cymbeline*'s folkloric composition, and the folktale is clearly visible in Posthumous's wager with Giacomo over Innogen's fidelity.[57] At least two clear ATU 882 variants have been identified as sources for *Cymbeline*. The scene in which Giacomo hides in a trunk inside Innogen's room, in order to gather evidence regarding her room and her body and thus win his wager with Posthumous, was influenced by Boccaccio's *Decameron*, specifically the ninth tale of the second day, told by Filomena.[58] This story tells of the Genovese merchant Bernabò's confident wager over the fidelity and discretion of his wife Zinevra, made against the equally confident Ambrogiuolo of Piacenza, who vows to seduce her. Upon discovering Zinevra's reputation to be more than well founded, Ambrogiuolo resorts to bribing a maidservant to have him carried into Zinevra's bedroom in a custom-made chest, whence he emerges at night to make note of the room and the woman's body (specifically a mole under her left breast), as well as collect various belongings as tokens of proof. Convinced by Ambrogiuolo's knowledge, Bernabò orders a servant to kill Zinevra, but, at her pleas, the servant spares her and instead brings her clothes back as proof of the purported deed. Zinevra then disguises herself as a man and rises through the ranks of the sultan. Upon encountering Ambrogiuolo and recognizing her belongings, she learns of his actions and realizes the reason for Bernabò's sudden hostility towards her. She then sets up an audience for both Ambrogiuolo and Bernabò before the sultan, inducing confessions from both Ambrogiuolo and Bernabò, before finally revealing her identity. The sultan sentences Ambrogiuolo to tortuous execution, and Zinevra and Bernabò live happily ever after. An extremely similar tale, undoubtedly also influenced by Boccaccio, is found in the sixteenth-century *Frederyke of Jennen*, an anonymous English translation of a Dutch play, which has been identified as

---

[56] Artese, *Sources*, pp. 102–5.
[57] Elfriede Moser-Rath, 'Cymbeline', in *Enzyklopädie des Märchens*, ed. Kurt Ranke et al., vol. 3 (Berlin, 1981), pp. 190–7; and Artese, *Sources*, pp. 184–90. On the wager in the context of contemporary social mores, see William Witherle Lawrence, 'The wager in *Cymbeline*', *PMLA* 35 (1920), 391–431.
[58] A translation can be found at Bullough, *Sources*, vol. 8, pp. 50–63.

another, separate source of *Cymbeline*'s wager.[59] The motif of the specific manner of bedroom intrusion found in both texts, as well as in *Cymbeline*, is listed in Thompson's *Motif-Index* as K1342, 'Entrance into woman's (man's) room by hiding in chest', and there it is associated only with ATU 882.[60]

To be clear, Boccaccio's tale and *Frederyke of Jennen* are not 'Snow White' variants as well as 'Wager' variants, and so their direct influence on *Cymbeline* is unrelated to 'Snow White'. It is generally assumed that the combination of ATU 882 and 709 was Shakespeare's own innovation; Artese has written that '*Cymbeline*'s intricate intersection of "The Wager on the Wife's Chastity" and "Snow White" is Shakespeare's most thorough and accomplished combination of folk materials.'[61] Indeed, the deep appreciation shown for the play by John Keats and Alfred Tennyson, as attested by popular anecdotes,[62] is grounded upon the tragic troughs of the relationship between Posthumous and Innogen, which are caused by the emotionally devastating combination of the misunderstanding of the 'Wager' and the persecution of 'Snow White'. The combination of these folktales is thus central to the play's emotional weight.

However, there is a faint but tantalizing suggestion that this combination may have already existed in *Ála flekks saga* over a century earlier, albeit with far less emotional charge. As outlined above, the saga's plot is driven by the sequence of curses directed by four consecutive villains against the protagonist, and it is the second curser, Glóðarauga, who is associated with a suspicious element which may be a heavily muted form of motif K1342, as described in the following passage:

Glóðarauga hét þræll einn er var í borginni; hann var bróðir Nóttar trǫllkonu. Hann kom í skemmu, er meykonungi ok Ála var í fylgt. Áli var þá afklæddr ǫllum klæðum nema línklæðum. Þá mælti þræll með ógurligri raust:

'Gott hyggr þú nú til, Áli!' segir hann, 'at sofa hjá meykonungi; en nú skal ek launa þér þat, er þú lagðir á Blátǫnn, systur mína, ok því legg ek þat á þik, at þú verðir at vargi ok farir á skóg ok drepir bæði menn ok fé, ok á þat fé grimmastr, er meykonungr á, ok at því mest leggjaz.'

Áli tekr þá svá til máls: 'Með því,' segir hann, 'at þú, Glóðarauga! hefir með fullum fjándskap á mik lagt,

þá mæli ek þat um, at þú sitir á þeirri sǫmu kistu sem nú ok œpir upp yfir þik sem mest getr þú, alla þá stund, sem ek er í þessum nauðum, svá at aldri hafir þú ró. En ef ek kemz ór þessi þraut, þá skulu tveir þrælar leiða þik til skógar ok hengja á gálga.'

There was a slave called Glóðarauga in the city; he was the brother of Nótt the troll-woman. He came to the bower to which the maiden-king and Áli had been led. Áli was then completely undressed apart from his linen undergarments. The slave spoke with a terrible voice:

'You're looking forward to sleeping with the maiden-king, Áli!' he says, 'but now I shall repay you for the curse which you laid on Blátǫnn, my sister, and so I lay this on you: that you will turn into a wolf and go into the forest and kill both men and livestock and attack most fiercely the livestock which the maiden-king owns – may you pursue them most of all.'

Áli starts to speak in this way: 'Because you, Glóðarauga,' he says, 'have laid this on me with complete enmity, I pronounce that you will sit on the same chest as now and shriek as loudly as you can, so that you have no rest, for the whole time that I am in this ordeal. And if I should escape from this hardship, then two slaves will bring you to the forest and hang you on the gallows.'[63]

The key detail that stands out in the above passage is the *kista* (chest) that Áli mentions. Firstly, no other furniture in the room is mentioned apart from the bed to which Áli and Þornbjörg are heading. Secondly, this chest had never previously been mentioned, and is never mentioned again – this being the first and only description of Queen Þornbjörg's bedroom apart from the general introductory remark that the room was *vel innan búna*, 'well decorated', or possibly 'well furnished'.[64] More specifically, and perhaps most suspiciously,

---

[59] *Cymbeline*, ed. Nosworthy, pp. xxii–xxv, and Bullough, *Sources*, vol. 8, pp. 63–78.
[60] Stith Thompson, *Motif-Index of Folk-Literature*, rev. and enl. ed., vol. 4 (Bloomington, 1957), p. 388.
[61] Charlotte Artese, ed., *Shakespeare and the Folktale: An Anthology of Stories* (Princeton, 2019), p. 251.
[62] Catherine M. S. Alexander, '*Cymbeline*: the afterlife', in *Shakespeare's Last Plays*, ed. Catherine M. S. Alexander (Cambridge, 2009), pp. 135–54; p. 135.
[63] Hui et al., 'Introduction', pp. 26–9.
[64] Hui et al., 'Introduction', pp. 26–7.

no mention had been made of Glóðarauga actually having interacted with the chest, either in exposition or in dialogue, until Áli's counter-curse. Why, for that matter, should Glóðarauga be sitting at all, if he had just entered the room to issue a curse? The jarring introduction of this chest into the narrative, where it serves no function of significance, seems to bear the hallmark of a functionally dormant remnant of some literary borrowing, but the paucity of details concerning the chest makes positive identification of any underlying motif impossible. Simply put, the chest alone is not sufficiently significant in the narrative of *Ála flekks saga* to constitute a major part of any determinable motif. However, while this prevents a definitive identification of the motif from which it was derived, a muted motif may nonetheless be telling in its own way, through the application of broad, contextual lines of interrogation. Due to the impossibility of positive identification, such an interrogation can only be conducted by addressing head-on the question of whether Glóðarauga's sitting on the chest could constitute a muted remnant of the specific motif of interest to this discussion – namely, K1342, 'Entrance into woman's (man's) room by hiding in chest'.

One interrogative dead-end must first be mentioned: there appears to be no useful analogical evidence from the contemporary Icelandic literature that survives. This is partly due to the functional insignificance of the chest, whereby the only entry relating to it in Inger Boberg's *Motif-Index of Early Icelandic Literature* is Áli's broader curse, which is classified as the highly specific motif M455.3, 'Thrall cursed to sit on chest and yell and never have rest'.[65] However, Boberg's *Motif-Index* contains no entries for K1342 proper, with the closest comparable motifs found in K1342.0.1, 'Man carried into woman's room hidden in basket' (attested in one catalogued instance, in which the man is the woman's lover, in *Flóres saga ok Blankiflur*, an early thirteenth-century Norwegian translation of the Old French romance *Floire et Blanchefleur*), and K1521.2, 'Paramour successfully hidden in chest' (attested in one instance, in the early fourteenth-century *Grettis saga*, 'The Saga of Grettir').[66] It is not impossible that, like Shakespeare, a late medieval Icelander may have known of K1342 through the *Decameron*, but there is no evidence to suggest that the *Ála flekks saga* episode drew in any way on Filomena's tale of Bernabò's wife, or that the *Decameron* was the source for any potential medieval Icelandic manifestation of this particular motif. The search for a definitive identification of the source motif of the chest is therefore greatly inhibited both by its lack of narrative function and by a lack of obvious parallels in contemporary Icelandic literature.

In the apparent absence of useful contemporary Icelandic analogues, it is perhaps more fruitful to explore the notable parallels between the broader bedroom scenes of *Ála flekks saga* and *Cymbeline*, especially with regard to thematic aspects of ATU 882, or at least hints thereof, which might be expected to accompany K1342 in some form. The chest itself finds few obvious parallels, not least because of its all-too-brief appearance in Þornbjörg's bedroom, in which nothing is said of its regular, everyday function, or what it was supposed to contain. Nonetheless, there is perhaps one potential parallel: many of the attestations of the noun *kista* in saga literature as catalogued by the *Dictionary of Old Norse Prose*, including the two references from *Ála flekks saga*'s fellow indigenous romances,[67] refer to chests containing treasure.[68] Such a function would correspond closely to the pretext Giacomo provides for placing his trunk in

---

[65] Inger M. Boberg, *Motif-Index of Early Icelandic Literature* (Copenhagen, 1966), p. 198.
[66] Boberg, *Motif-Index*, p. 178.
[67] These are *Viktors saga ok Blávus* ('The Saga of Viktor and Blávus') and *Bósa saga ok Herrauðs* ('The Saga of Bósi and Herrauðr').
[68] *Dictionary of Old Norse Prose*, s.v. 'kista': https://onp.ku.dk/onp/onp.php?o43677. It should be noted that the *Dictionary* does list two incidental mentions of an individual sitting on a *kista* (that is, using it as a seat): one instance is an unspecified chest in a booth at the Icelandic legislative assembly, in *Sturlunga saga* ('The Saga of the Sturlungs'); the other is a stern-chest on a ship (in a king's saga in the *Hulda* manuscript). However, in neither instance is the chest introduced as jarringly as in *Ála flekks saga*.

Innogen's 'safe stowage' (1.6.193) – namely, the storage of a 'plate of rare device, and jewels / Of rich and exquisite form' (1.6.190–1). However, there is not sufficiently definitive evidence to ascribe such a function to the chest in *Ála flekks saga*, let alone to assert any motive behind its presence in the bedroom. Nor, in any case, are the purported contents of the chest specified in the *Decameron* or *Frederyke of Jennen*, meaning that this aspect should not be taken as indicative of affinity with ATU 882.

More certainty can be gleaned from the narrative function of the respective antagonists' appearances during their scene with the chest, and here a striking similarity between the two texts presents itself. In both cases, one of the main effects of the antagonist's intrusion into the noblewoman's bedroom is to create a significant disruption to her marriage by forcing her to be separated from her husband for a period of time. In *Cymbeline*, this is Giacomo's sole purpose, as he had struck a high-stakes bargain with Posthumous to test Innogen's honour. Although, upon emerging from his trunk, he expresses his own desire for the sleeping Innogen in a monologue beginning with a reference to the classical tale of Tarquin's rape of Lucrece (2.2.13), he soon returns his focus, with an anacoluthonic jolt, to his original purpose: 'But my design – / To note the chamber. I will write all down' (2.2.23–4). Upon taking Posthumous's bracelet from her, he reaffirms his motivation to ensure 'th' madding of her lord' (2.2.37). Finally, even as his discovery of Innogen's bedtime reading – the classical tale of Tereus's rape of Philomel – re-invokes his earlier allusion to rape, he is not tempted beyond his purpose: 'I have enough' (2.2.46). As in the corresponding scene in the *Decameron*, the single-minded focus of Giacomo's purpose – namely, to disrupt the marriage of Innogen and Posthumous indefinitely – is emphasized through the fact that it overrides his sexual desire. In Ruth Nevo's words, 'Iachimo would rather poison Posthumous' mind than possess Imogen's body.'[69]

Glóðarauga's overarching purpose in Þornbjörg's bedroom is different. He is not there to gather any incriminating evidence, but rather to take revenge on Áli, on behalf of his sister, Nótt, whose marital clutches Áli had escaped. Despite this difference in purpose, he nevertheless emphasizes his satisfaction at disrupting their wedding night – and their marriage, indefinitely – with his very first words: 'You're looking forward to sleeping with the maiden-king, Áli!' Although Glóðarauga's is not the only curse to separate Áli from Þornbjörg temporarily – Jötunoxi's later curse does likewise – this curse alone begins with a spiteful taunt over that particular consequence. Glóðarauga is thus shown to be fully mindful of the harm to be caused to Áli's new marriage not only by the nature of the curse, but also by the timing of it. From the perspective of narrative construction, too, there is an air of deliberateness about this. Of the three rounds of antagonistic curses issued to Áli without immediate provocation (that is, excluding Jötunoxi's), Blátönn and Nótt stage their interventions in the most general of time-frames – 'one evening' and 'one night' respectively[70] – as is common in both saga literature and medieval romances. By contrast, Glóðarauga's curse occurs at a specific point in the saga's chronology – a point at which he is able to disrupt the marriage effectively.

It is symbolically momentous that both the Áli–Þornbjörg and Posthumous–Innogen marriages appear to be interrupted before the act of consummation. In addition to the introductory exposition of Glóðarauga's intrusion, which clearly states that Áli was in the act of undressing for his conjugal consummation at the time of the intrusion, Áli's inability to consummate that night is later implicitly reinforced through the occurrence of a rare second set of marital celebrations held at the saga's denouement,[71] suggesting that the first set was considered incomplete due to their failure to consummate it.[72] Like most other marriages in medieval

---

[69] Ruth Nevo, *Shakespeare's Other Language* (London, 1987), p. 77.
[70] Hui et al., 'Introduction', pp. 20–1 and pp. 30–1, respectively.
[71] Hui et al., 'Introduction', pp. 42–3.
[72] Áli in fact experiences each of three major life events twice – birth, marriage and death; see Hui et al., 'Snow White variant', p. 63.

romance, there is never any real doubt that Áli and Þornbjörg will overcome their trials and earn their happy ending, but it is clear from the deliberately specific and symbolic timing of Glóðarauga's intervention that it is intended to place the marriage in a state of heightened risk. Similarly, Posthumous seems to suggest during his post-deception soliloquy that his marriage to Innogen was yet unconsummated, lamenting that:

> Me of my lawful pleasure she restrained,
> And prayed me oft forbearance; did it with
> A pudency so rosy the sweet view on't
> Might well have warmed old Saturn; that I thought her
> As chaste as unsunned snow.
>
> (*Cymbeline* 2.5.9–13)

Though it is not entirely clear whether Posthumous is referring to marital fidelity or complete virginity, numerous scholars have argued for the latter. Both Anne Barton and Constance Jordan, for instance, have separately discussed the Posthumous–Innogen marriage in the context of the contemporary legal status of clandestine marriages, drawing attention to the tensions of legitimacy inherent in the play's apparently unconsummated form of this liminal relationship.[73] As Barton remarks, the anxieties underlying Posthumous's fury over Innogen's purported infidelity take on a different complexion if their marriage had not yet been consummated.[74] Further to this, it might be suggested that the strain on their marriage caused by Giacomo's intervention is compounded by the backdrop of the earlier intervention attempted by the queen on behalf of Cloten. Indeed, although it may appear as though the logical causality between Blátönn and Glóðarauga's curses against Áli is missing between Cloten and Giacomo – each of whom has a separate agenda regarding Innogen – *Cymbeline*'s two male antagonists are in fact thematically connected. Nevo, building on Murray Schwartz's psychoanalytical study of the characters,[75] describes the link as follows:

Cloten and Iachimo are not simply two rival evils laying siege to Imogen's integrity and virtue, but secret sharers in the psyche of the absent Posthumus for whom they substitute, and it is this that gives the two personae and the psychomachia they articulate its particular depth and interest. Both Cloten and his counterpart Iachimo ('Cloten in civilised dress,' as Schwartz puts it, 227) represent isolated and split-off parts of an ambivalent and unintegrated personality, the one 'arrogant piece of flesh,' pure sexual drive, 'the rebellion of a codpiece' (225); the other, pure, aim-inhibited fantasy as exhibited in the exquisite aestheticism of the bedroom scene.[76]

The precedent of the threat posed by Cloten is important to bear in mind, because it serves as a reminder, as mentioned above, that both Áli and Innogen suffer the effective bedroom intrusion after already having avoided a forced marriage pushed by a stepmother-figure. Áli had escaped Nótt's cave despite Blátönn's best efforts, while Innogen had rejected Cloten despite his mother's best efforts. In both *Ála flekks saga* and *Cymbeline*, therefore, the bedroom intrusion generates significant narrative traction by building on an earlier threat of forced marriage in order to create formidable new obstacles between the protagonist and their spouse, which the protagonist must resolve before the possibility of reunion with their spouse and legitimization through consummation at long last. The intrusion is therefore a structurally critical event – a *noyau* ('nucleus') of the plot, to use the Barthesian term – that serves almost exactly the same narrative function in both texts. In other words, the structural, thematic and symbolic context surrounding the unexplained chest in *Ála flekks saga* is precisely the context in which motif K1342 would be expected to be found in an ATU 882 variant.

The delayed consummation is crucial for the question of whether traces of ATU 882 can be

---

[73] Anne Barton, *Essays, Mainly Shakespearean* (Cambridge, 1994), pp. 20–9; and Constance Jordan, *Shakespeare's Monarchies: Ruler and Subject in the Romances* (Ithaca, NY, 1997), pp. 74–6.
[74] Barton, *Essays*, p. 29.
[75] Murray M. Schwartz, 'Between fantasy and imagination: a psychological exploration of *Cymbeline*', in *Psychoanalysis and Literary Process*, ed. Frederick Crews (Cambridge, MA, 1970), pp. 219–83; pp. 221–31.
[76] Nevo, *Language*, p. 75.

identified in the rest of *Ála flekks saga*, because it would be expected to invoke the familiar theme of chastity. In fact, Þornbjörg's chastity never comes into serious question, let alone as the subject of a wager. A possible substitute might be Þornbjörg's steadfast fidelity, which is highlighted as an essential quality in the later trials of the saga, specifically following Nótt's curse. As Áli lies bedridden with his debilitating wounds, Þornbjörg demonstrates her unparalleled devotion by being the only person able to stay in the presence of the Tristram-esque stench of Áli's festering flesh: 'Enginn af mǫnnum dróttningar þolir at þjóna honum fyrir þeim óþef, er af Ála gekk, nema Þornbjǫrg dróttning' ('Apart from Queen Þornbjörg, none of the queen's people could bear to serve Áli on account of the stench which emanated from him').[77] Her determination and capability, both hallmarks of ATU 882 heroines, are proved in the same episode, in which her search for medical help for Áli leads her across the entirety of the known world – the northern hemisphere, Africa and Asia – to Jötunoxi's kingdom at the end of the world, where she offers Jötunoxi a hollow pledge of marriage in exchange for the healing of Áli, while simultaneously arranging for her troops to storm his hall at the opportune moment. Her entry to Jötunoxi's hall, disguised as 'Gunnvör', could perhaps be read as a reflex of the 'high position at a foreign court' that many ATU 882 protagonists gain,[78] and one that Innogen herself briefly attains, as 'Fidele', in the camp of the Roman ambassador, Lucius.

However, despite the thematic correspondence between Þornbjörg's fidelity and the loyalty of the 'Wife' of ATU 882, the lack of a chastity test in *Ála flekks saga* ultimately means a lack of several of the consequent events that form the latter half of that folktale's core narrative, including the husband's rejection of the wife and the unmasking of the slanderer. Indeed, the dangers of reading too much into Þornbjörg's fidelity can be elucidated through a quick mention of perhaps the final potential ATU 882-related parallel to be discussed here, namely the 'recognition by birthmark' motif (H51.1). In *Cymbeline*, there are two instances of this – namely, the cinque-spotted mole that Giacomo spots on Innogen's breast (2.2.37–9) and the 'sanguine star' on Guiderius's neck (5.6.364–9) which generates far less narrative traction; in *Ála flekks saga*, it is Áli's epithetic fleck, which ultimately proves to be a redundant motif when he is instead recognized, in wolf-form, by his eyes.[79] Although this motif is central to ATU 882 variants, it is also commonly found in medieval European romance, often in the context of royal identification, a manifestation which finds close correspondence with Guiderius's birthmark and Áli's functionless fleck.[80] In ATU 882 variants, its purpose is proof of intimacy; in the romance context, its purpose is usually proof of true identity. Indeed, for Áli's fleck to have derived from ATU 882, it would have had to have been transferred from the 'Wife' to the husband, only to serve no narrative function whatsoever. Thus, unlike Innogen's birthmark, the birthmark motif in *Ála flekks saga* was likely not derived from ATU 882, and the presence of the motif in both texts must be considered coincidental. This particular evidence, in combination with the discussion of Þornbjörg's fidelity, highlights the significant paucity of direct correspondences between the saga narrative and the plot of ATU 882 which cannot be plausibly attributed to coincidence.

How then is the tantalizing but inconclusive evidence regarding *Ála flekks saga*'s relationship with ATU 882, 'The wager on the wife's chastity', to be reconciled? Is the chest in Þornbjörg's bedchamber, though a superfluous detail at first glance, a smoking gun? On the one hand, the bedroom intrusion is remarkably similar – structurally, thematically and symbolically – to those of *Cymbeline*, the *Decameron* and *Frederyke of Jennen*. In all cases, an antagonist stages a highly effective intrusion into a noblewoman's bedroom in order to disrupt her marriage. On the other hand, the remainder of the

---

[77] Hui et al., 'Introduction', pp. 34–5.
[78] Uther, *Types*, vol. I, p. 505.
[79] Hui et al., 'Introduction', pp. 28–9.
[80] Hui et al., 'Introduction', pp. 10–12.

saga apparently has no direct correspondences with the plot of the folktale, and therefore cannot be considered a variant itself. The likeliest solution would seem to run as follows: at least one variant or partial variant of ATU 882 was known in late medieval Iceland, and *Ála flekks saga* drew heavily from its bedroom intrusion episode, but made no other significant borrowings. The implications of this hypothesis are of novel significance on several levels. Firstly, it would constitute the first proof that ATU 882, likely containing motif K1342, had been transmitted to Iceland by the early fifteenth century. Secondly, it would constitute the earliest known combination of ATU 709 and elements of ATU 882, having been composed around two centuries before *Cymbeline* was written. Thirdly, given the implausibility of any influence of *Ála flekks saga* on *Cymbeline*, the hypothesis would point firmly to the ATU 709–882 combination having been formulated independently by the saga composer and Shakespeare, essentially ruling out the possibility of the two texts having shared common influence from a lost ATU 709–882-combinant source or tradition.

The existence of a medieval precedent for the combination of 'Snow White' with elements of 'Wager' certainly does not impinge on Shakespeare's originality or ingenuity in crafting the same combination, particularly as he engaged far more closely with the latter folktale than did the saga, to far greater emotive effect. Rather, the new evidence of *Ála flekks saga* raises the question of why both the saga composer and Shakespeare independently saw fit to create such a combination. The answer seems to be that the two tale types naturally lend themselves to mutual combination due to their sharing of several fundamental points of intersection. In her discussion on the combination in *Cymbeline*, Artese notes that 'the plots [of 'Snow White' and 'Wager'] have several points of contact', and she identifies these as the heroine's singular beauty, her exile under threat of death, the motif of the compassionate executioner and the admiration of the unconscious heroine's body.[81] Each of the events – the heroine's exile, the executioner's mercy and the admiration of the heroine's body – is manifested once in *Cymbeline*. By contrast, *Ála flekks saga* contains no admiration scene, but it is perhaps revealing that Áli arguably experiences two versions of the compassionate executioner motif, the first occurring during his childhood exposure, reminiscent of well-known 'Snow White' variants in setting and process, and the second at the hands of the unwitting Jötunoxi, during the episode in which Þornbjörg's fidelity is strongly foregrounded.[82] Áli also experiences numerous expulsions from human society, including the Glóðarauga-imposed exile that provided crucial evidence for this section. These multiplicities seem to indicate an authorial awareness of two of the major narrative confluences between 'Snow White' and 'Wager' identified by Artese.

The independence with which the saga composer and Shakespeare fused ATU 709 and ATU 882 can be seen not only through their adaptations of episodes of confluence between the two folktales, but also through the ways in which they connected shared episodes. For instance, the connection between the forced marriage ('Snow White') and the bedroom intrusion ('Wager') is manifested very differently, with the stepmother-figure and bedroom intruder made relatives in *Ála flekks saga*, but only joined thematically as assailants on the heroine's chastity in *Cymbeline*. Similarly, the links between the bedroom intrusion ('Wager') and exile ('Snow White' and 'Wager'), and exile and false death ('Snow White'), differ greatly, being heavily affected by the respective texts' balance of the two folktales. The folkloric relationship between *Ála flekks saga* and *Cymbeline* can therefore be described not as one of 'derivation' or 'replication', but rather one of 'multiple discovery'. The new evidence of *Ála flekks saga* adds the substantial weight of universality to Artese's argument for the impulses underlying Shakespeare's combination of

---

[81] Artese, *Sources*, pp. 187–90. The cited discussion by Artese focuses on the two latter confluences; the former two were raised with me in personal correspondence.

[82] On Jötunoxi's unconventional fulfilment of the 'compassionate executioner' role, see Hui at al., 'Snow White variant', pp. 60–1.

ATU 709 and ATU 882, in that it demonstrates how the tales' 'points of contact' identified by Artese were independently recognized in a literary culture and time period significantly distanced from Shakespeare's own. For Shakespeare to have recognized the narrative potential of those folkloric confluences speaks to his clear understanding of the essence of both folktales. For an earlier Icelandic composer to have recognized the same confluences additionally reinforces the folktales' fundamental compatibilities most emphatically. In whichever literary culture 'Snow White' and 'The wager on the wife's chastity' existed concurrently, the potential for these particular folktales to intersect in particular ways was consistent. Certainly, it held just as true in early fifteenth-century Iceland as it did in early seventeenth-century England.

POLONIUS

Although unrelated to *Cymbeline*, the presence of a character named 'Pollonius' in a text antedating Shakespeare cannot go unaddressed here. The origin of the name 'Polonius' in *Hamlet*, for which no earlier attestation had hitherto been identified, has remained an open question over the decades.[83] Numerous theories identifying Polonius as an allusive take on various historical personages have been posited, an endeavour somewhat complicated by the much discussed fact that the character's name is 'Corambis' in the 1603 First Quarto version of the play. Not all of these theories ascribe relevance to the name 'Polonius', which means 'the Polish one' in Latin, but those that do have variously argued for identification with the Polish nobleman Wawrzyniec Grzymała Goślicki (author of the political treatise *De optimo senatore*),[84] the Polish-connected Danish ambassador Henrik Ramel (whose diplomatic mission to England is recounted in Holinshed's *Chronicles*)[85] and an anonymous Polish ambassador who famously irked Elizabeth I.[86] None of these suggestions has achieved widespread scholarly acceptance, and there is currently no consensus as to the name's origin.

Where then did the name 'Pollonius' in *Ála flekks saga* come from? The fact that it is mentioned so incidentally in the saga, as the name of a character playing the most minor of roles, strongly suggests that it was not coined for the saga, but rather borrowed from another text. A borrower the saga was likely to have been in this regard, but a lender it almost certainly was not – not to *Hamlet* or any other text. There is simply no plausible line of transmission from this historically little-known saga. Indeed, nothing is said of *Ála flekks saga*'s Pollonius except that he is the father of Andan and Mandan, and an earl of an unspecified earldom. Despite a potential parallel in social status with *Hamlet*'s Polonius, which is likely to be coincidental, such scant evidence provides insufficient grounds upon which to assert a connection. Yet, given the long-standing debate over the origin of Shakespeare's 'Polonius', it is necessary at least to try to puzzle out a likely process by which a similarly named character came to be in *Ála flekks saga*, and to consider what implications it may carry for *Hamlet*.

Because medieval Scandinavian literature contains no extant attestation of the name 'Pollonius' antedating *Ála flekks saga*,[87] and

---

[83] J. Madison Davis and Daniel A. Frankforter, *The Shakespeare Name Dictionary* (New York, 1995), pp. 391–2.

[84] Israel Gollancz, 'Shakespeariana, 1598–1602', *Proceedings of the British Academy* 1 (1903–4), 199–202; Israel Gollancz, 'The name Polonius', *Archiv für das Studium der neueren Sprachen und Literaturen* 68 (1914), 141–4; and Geoffrey Bullough, *Narrative and Dramatic Sources of Shakespeare*, vol. 7 (London, Henley and New York, 1973), pp. 185–7.

[85] Keith Brown, 'Polonius, and Fortinbras (and Hamlet?)', *English Studies* 55 (1974), 218–38; pp. 220–8.

[86] Bernice W. Kliman, 'Three notes on Polonius: position, residence, and name', *Shakespeare Bulletin* 20 (2002), 5–6.

[87] A close but probably unrelated name can be found in the fourteenth-century *Tristrams saga ok Ísoddar* ('The Saga of Tristram and Ísodd'), an indigenous Icelandic reworking of the aforementioned *Tristrams saga ok Ísöndar*, which features a royal page named 'Pollornis'. See 'Saga af Tristram ok Ísodd', ed. Peter Jorgensen, trans. Joyce M. Hill, in *Norse Romance*, vol. 1: *The Tristan Legend*, ed. Kalinke, pp. 241–92; pp. 244–51. The name may have been based on that of Isolde's page Perinis/Paranis in the continental versions of the legend,

because the character is so minor in the saga that he offers no hint of potential literary parallels, the strongest evidence for the name's potential origin comes from textual variation. It is perhaps typical of this saga's tantalizing Shakespearian affinities that its Polloníus, like *Hamlet*'s Polonius, is also differently named in some manuscripts. As with all other evidence previously discussed, this is not straightforward. The saga's oldest extant manuscript witness, AM 589e 4to, reads 'Jotu*n*oxe hertok okkr f*ra* polloniu jarle fedr okkru*m*' ('Jötunoxi captured the two of us from Earl Pollonius, our father'; italics indicate abbreviations expanded from the manuscript).[88] However, a seventeenth-century copy of the saga's other extant medieval witness (the now-fragmentary, early sixteenth-century manuscript AM 571 4to)[89] reads 'h*an*n tók ock*ur* f*ra* Apollonio faudur ockrum*m*' ('he took us from our father, Apollonius'). The readings of the four main manuscript witnesses of the saga — the two medieval witnesses and their respective seventeenth-century copies — are shown in the diagram below (italics indicate expanded abbreviations, and manuscript dates are sourced from Handrit.is).[90]

[Putative ancestor]

AM 589e 4to
(ca. 1450–1500)
"Jotu*n*oxe hertok okkr f*ra* polloniu jarle fedr okkru*m*" (fol. 22ʳ)

AM 571 4to
(ca. 1500–1550)
[Missing; manuscript defective here]

AM 181k fol.
(ca. 1640–1660)
"Jotunøxi hertok ockur frā Pollonïo jalli fedr ockrum" (fol. 3ᵛ)

AM 182 fol.
(ca. 1635–1648)
"h*an*n tók ock*ur* fra Apollonio faudur ockrum*m*" (fol. 47ʳ)

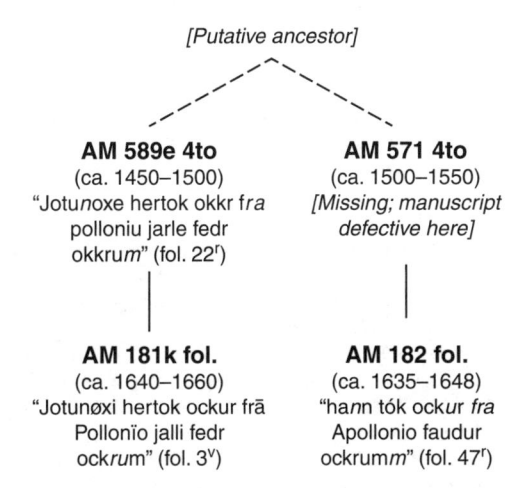

Because AM 571 4to is defective, crucial evidence has been lost as to where in the saga's transmission the divergence occurred. Did a scribe somewhere along the 571-branch hyper-correct 'Polloniu' under the assumption that it was an erroneous reading of 'Apolloniu'? Or is 'Polloniu' a misrendering of 'Apolloniu' as a result of accidental omission? In the absence of further evidence, the latter seems likelier. That 'Apollonius' was the original name is highly plausible given the widespread popularity of the classical story of Apollonius of Tyre in medieval Europe.[91] The story was transmitted to medieval Iceland through its interpolation in the highly influential *Þiðreks saga af Bern* ('The Saga of Þiðrekr of Bern'),[92] a thirteenth-century Norse text thought to have been translated in Norway from a collection of German legends about Dietrich von Bern.[93] Certainly, *Þiðreks saga*'s Apollonius provides a match for the only personal detail that *Ála flekks saga* provides about its 'Pollonius', namely the character's rank of earl.[94] If the hypothesis that 'Apollonius' was the original name in *Ála flekks*

---

and there seems to be little evidence of a connection with 'Pollonius' in terms of phonological variation or palaeographical confusion (such as minim corruption).

[88] A facsimile of this manuscript can be found in *Fornaldarsagas and Late Medieval Romances: AM 586 4to and AM 589 a-f 4to*, ed. Agnete Loth (Copenhagen, 1977), pp. 128–51, with the relevant folio at p. 149.

[89] *Drei lygisǫgur*, ed. Lagerholm, p. lxix.

[90] At the present moment, AM 571 4to (Handrit.is: https://handrit.is/en/manuscript/view/is/AM04-0571) and AM 182 fol. (Handrit.is: https://handrit.is/en/manuscript/view/is/AM02-0182) have been digitized. AM 181k fol. (Handrit.is: https://handrit.is/en/manuscript/view/is/AM02-0181k) has not yet been digitized, nor has AM 589e 4to, which, as mentioned earlier, has been published in facsimile.

[91] On which, see Elizabeth Archibald, *Apollonius of Tyre: Medieval and Renaissance Themes and Variations* (Cambridge, 1991). On yet another tangential note of seemingly coincidental curiosity, the Apollonius legend has also been identified as a partial variant of ATU 709, 'Snow White', in Anderson, *Fairytale*, pp. 147–8.

[92] Archibald, *Apollonius*, pp. 57–8.

[93] R. G. Finch, 'Þiðreks saga af Bern', in *Medieval Scandinavia: An Encyclopedia*, ed. Pulsiano and Wolf, p. 662.

[94] Apollonius's arc can be found in *Þiðriks saga af Bern*, vol. 2, ed. Henrik Bertelsen (Copenhagen, 1905–11), pp. 109–42.

saga is accepted, a plausible explanation for the erroneous 'Pollonius' could be accidental vowel elision, with the adjacent vowels in 'frá Apolloníu' having merged into 'frá Polloníu' in the mind of the copying scribe. Accidental or not, there is one final reason why it seems highly probable that the 'Polloníus' of AM 589 e 4to – written approximately a century before *Hamlet*'s composition – can indeed be considered a rendering of the Latinized Greek name 'Apollonius': there is no evidence for the alternative possibility, namely that it existed in medieval Iceland as a separate name of Latin etymology.

The origin of 'Pollonius' suggested above probably has no direct bearing on *Hamlet*. However, it provides independent corroboration for the possibility that *Hamlet*'s Polonius could also have derived his name from the Apollonius tale, albeit through intentional modification rather than scribal error.[95] Certainly, the chief source for the plot of Shakespeare's *Pericles, Prince of Tyre* was the story of Apollonius found in John Gower's late fourteenth-century *Confessio Amantis* (where the name is spelled 'Appolinus'),[96] which also seems to have influenced the frame narrative of *The Comedy of Errors*.[97] Perhaps a likelier immediate source for Shakespeare, though, would have been the tale of Apolonius and Silla found in Barnaby Riche's *Riche His Farewell to Military Profession* (1581), a tale which heavily influenced *Twelfth Night*,[98] and which was itself influenced to a small degree – including the protagonist's name – by the story of Apollonius of Tyre.[99] Riche's tale is an intriguing possibility for the Polonius question given the closeness of the spelling and the fact that the tale was demonstrably known to Shakespeare. Although such a derivation would appear not to find its basis in any thematic or functional parallels between the two characters – they share no obvious similarities other than their noble stock – it remains entirely possible that the name was bestowed independently of any allusive currency the character may have been intended to hold for contemporary audiences. Thus, while it remains possible that the character of *Hamlet*'s Polonius may have been developed, as has been commonly suggested, as an allusion to Elizabeth I's Lord High Treasurer, Lord Burghley,[100] or perhaps some other noble personage unrelated to Poland, the name itself may have nothing to do with that. As long as this remains a possibility, it cannot be discounted that the 'Polonius' of *Hamlet* may have been derived from a version of the name 'Apollonius', and that both it and the 'Polloníus' of *Ála flekks saga* were independently derived reflexes of that name.

CONCLUSIONS

This discussion has outlined three distinct folkloric correspondences between Shakespeare's *Cymbeline* and the late medieval Icelandic romance *Ála flekks saga*, each of which carries intriguing new implications for both the folktales in question and the processes of folkloric recombination underlying the two texts themselves. The first correspondence is the texts' shared status as variants of ATU 709, 'Snow White'. The two texts attest to the presence of the tale type in separate literary cultures of Western Europe in the late medieval and early

---

[95] The suggestion has been made that Shakespeare derived the name from a reference to the Stoic philosopher Apollonius of Tyre (not to be confused with the fictional character of the same name) – typeset with a drop-capital initial as 'A Pollonius' – in James Sanford's 1576 translation of Lodovico Guicciardini's *L'Hore di Ricreatione*: see John Wardroper, 'By any other name …', *Times Literary Supplement*, 30 May 2003, p. 15.

[96] Albert H. Smyth, 'Shakespeare's Pericles and Apollonius of Tyre', *Proceedings of the American Philosophical Society* 37 (1898), 206–312; and Muir, *Sources*, pp. 252–4.

[97] Muir, *Sources*, pp. 14–15. [98] Muir, *Sources*, pp. 136–7.

[99] Archibald, *Apollonius*, pp. 60–1.

[100] For instance, George Russell French, *Shakespeareana Genealogica* (London, 1869), pp. 301–2; Adolphus William Ward, *A History of English Dramatic Literature to the Death of Queen Anne*, rev. ed., vol. 2 (London, 1899), p. 161; and G. W. Phillips, *Lord Burghley in Shakespeare: Falstaff, Sly and Others* (London, 1936), p. 125. The identification of Polonius with Burghley has also been rejected, for instance in Josephine Waters Bennett, 'Characterization in Polonius' advice to Laertes', *Shakespeare Quarterly* 4 (1953), 3–9; pp. 7–8.

modern periods, and the striking differences in their manifestations of ATU 709 demonstrate the tale's fundamental flexibility. The second correspondence is the presence in both texts of a pair of exiled brothers who possess strikingly similar biographies and fulfil strikingly similar roles, which is a noteworthy correspondence given the lack of prior identification of any source or analogue for the character arcs of Guiderius and Arviragus. The third correspondence is the combination of ATU 709 and elements of ATU 882, 'The wager on the wife's chastity', a combination considered by Charlotte Artese to be 'Shakespeare's most thorough and accomplished combination of folk materials'.

The overarching hypotheses formed on the basis of these parallels are the sums of delicate balances of probabilities formed through abductive inferences. On one hand, the manifestations in the unrelated saga and play of the distinctive two-brother arc in close conjunction with a basic 'Snow White' structure seem too close to reflect parallel, independent processes of combination, and may instead be suggestive of the existence of a separate branch of the 'Snow White' tradition. This putative branch carries highly significant implications for the wider picture of the state of the 'Snow White' tradition in Western Europe during the late Middle Ages, about which virtually nothing is currently known. With regard to the texts themselves, the analogical evidence of *Ála flekks saga* provides a new and plausible possibility for the origin of the character arcs of Guiderius and Arviragus in *Cymbeline*, for which no source had hitherto been identified; and the reverse is also true, though the question of the origin of Andan and Mandan has been far less vexed due to a lack of attention paid to the saga.

On the other hand, the combination in both texts of 'Snow White' and elements of 'Wager' is likely to be an independent coincidence, a hypothesis based not only on the stark differences in the extent and manifestation of the combination in the respective texts – with *Ála flekks saga* apparently borrowing just a single episode commonly found in ATU 882 – but also on the relatively clear view of this particular recombinant process in *Cymbeline* afforded by the prior identification of direct sources in the form of the *Decameron* and *Frederyke of Jennen*. The clear analogical evidence of *Cymbeline* and its 'Wager' sources casts the bedroom intrusion of *Ála flekks saga* into sharp relief, providing a plausible explanation for striking elements that are otherwise curiously specific (such as Áli's near-nakedness) or inexplicable (such as the chest on which Glóðarauga sits), and raising the possibility that a form of ATU 882, or at least an episode thereof, was known in medieval Iceland. The possibility that both texts contain independent combinations of ATU 709 and elements of ATU 882 reinforces the fundamental compatibilities between the two tale types that have previously been raised by Charlotte Artese, and draws attention to one final correspondence between *Ála flekks saga* and *Cymbeline* – namely, that they are both classified as romances. The broad romance genre was an important vehicle of folktale transmission since classical times,[101] and as it grew into the dominant literary genre of the European high and late Middle Ages, the scope for combination and recombination naturally grew. In her study of the development of the romance genre in England, Helen Cooper compared the evolution and transmission of romance motifs and conventions to biologist Richard Dawkins's concept of 'memes', in that they possessed the 'ability to replicate faithfully and abundantly, but also on occasion to adapt, mutate, and therefore survive in different forms and cultures'.[102] The propensity for romances to act as recombinant vessels for motifs and episodes borrowed from elsewhere made them peculiarly suited to the processes of folkloric accretion, adaptation and transmission – processes that facilitated the survival and spread of memetic material across

---

[101] Many of the variants of well-known folktales that Graham Anderson identifies in his *Fairytale in the Ancient World* are romances – see especially pp. 145–57. Northrop Frye regards folktales as the 'direct literary ancestor' of all romances written primarily for entertainment – see *The Secular Scripture: A Study of the Structure of Romance* (Cambridge, MA, 1976), p. 7.

[102] Cooper, *Romance in Time*, p. 3.

time, geographic space and cultural distance. Indeed, it is through multiple sequences of shared memetic material that *Ála flekks saga* and *Cymbeline* – though composed centuries apart and in separate literary cultures – find themselves connected by a complex analogical relationship that is problematized by a paucity of other analogues. Two data points do not a trend make, but, in the case of this discussion, it is clear that what little oblique illumination *Ála flekks saga* and *Cymbeline* can shed on each other provides invaluable context for the larger literary pictures in which they both fit. The striking case of *Ála flekks saga* reinforces the fact that even little-known texts from literary cultures with which Shakespeare did not directly interact can bear indirect but extraordinary witness to the near-contemporary state – or potentially even existence – of folkloric and narrative traditions from which he drew. It also serves as a reminder of the likelihood that further such fringe evidence may well exist, and is waiting to be identified.

'BUT WHEN EXTREMITIES SPEAK': HARLEY GRANVILLE-BARKER, *CORIOLANUS*, THE WORLD WARS AND THE STATE OF EXCEPTION

RICHARD ASHBY

Harley Granville-Barker is widely recognized for his innovative approach to the presentation of Shakespeare on stage. By removing elaborate scenic *décor* in favour of a more open stage, Barker broke with the traditions of Victorian Shakespeare, which had prioritized an aesthetic of scenic realism. His approach allowed for far fewer cuts to the playscript – often needed in past productions of Shakespeare because of the time it took to change the scenery – and a faster pace of delivery and action. His productions of *The Winter's Tale* and *Twelfth Night* (1912) and his *A Midsummer Night's Dream* (1914) at the Savoy Theatre revolutionized the staging of Shakespeare and would come to define 'modern' Shakespeare production, influencing generations of directors, from Peter Brook and Peter Hall to Richard Eyre and Adrian Noble. Barker had been planning on staging *Macbeth*, but his Shakespeare productions were interrupted by the outbreak of World War I, after which he largely turned his back on theatre in favour of academic study.[1] Barker moved from London to the relative isolation of Devon, before emigrating to Paris in 1930. He fled Paris for the US in 1940, shortly before the fall of France, returning to Paris in 1946 and passing away the same year.

Why Barker decided to 'retire' from the theatre after World War I has been a topic of intense debate. Various motives have been proposed. These include his divorce from the actress Lillah McCarthy and his marriage to the American heiress Helen Huntington, whose alleged hatred of the theatre put a strain on his relationship with his former mentor, George Bernard Shaw; his increasing disillusionment with the state of English theatre after World War I and with the scope for reforming its aesthetic; and the possibility, recently mooted by Colin Chambers and Richard Nelson, that Barker was suffering from a consumptive illness (possibly TB) that curtailed his active involvement in theatrical direction and production.[2] It might be that Barker simply wanted to spend more time dedicated to his writing, which, as he revealed to John Gielgud, he wanted to prioritize.[3] Even after his withdrawal from the theatre, Barker continued to make an academic case for Shakespeare as a dramaturg with direct knowledge of stagecraft, most obviously in his celebrated *Prefaces to*

---

[1] For the abortive Barker *Macbeth*, see C. B. Purdom, *Harley Granville Barker: Man of the Theatre, Dramatist and Scholar* (London, 1955), pp. 216–17. Note that Purdom uses the unhyphenated Granville Barker in his title. Barker introduces the hyphen after World War I and his divorce. I use 'Barker' throughout the following for brevity.

[2] Chambers and Nelson posit the consumption theory in the postscript to *Granville Barker on Theatre: Selected Essays*, ed. Colin Chambers and Richard Nelson (London, 2017), pp. 227–51. Chambers and Nelson draw on various archival materials – though not the collection at Senate House – and make the case that Shaw was responsible for the myth that Huntington stole Barker away from the theatre.

[3] John Gielgud, 'Granville-Barker's Shakespeare', *Theatre Arts Monthly* 31 (1947), 48–9.

Shakespeare. These short introductions provided close analyses of individual plays as works of dramatic theatre, as opposed to literature. Barker continued to insist on reading the plays as works of and for performance, but he did not necessarily enact his ideas on stage.

By focusing on the reasons why Barker turned away from the theatre, critics have failed to consider the way in which Barker used Shakespeare to reflect on the nature of war itself – not only the First, but also the Second, World War. Recent years have seen no shortage of criticism devoted to the subject of Shakespeare and war, including *Shakespeare and War*, edited by Ros King and Paul Franssen (2008), *Shakespeare and the Just War Tradition* by Paola Pugliatti (2011), *Shakespeare and the Second World War: Memory, Culture, Identity*, edited by Irena R. Makaryk and Marissa McHugh (2012), and *Shakespeare Between the World Wars: The Anglo-American Sphere* by Robert Sawyer (2019). *Shakespeare Survey* also took for its topic 'Shakespeare and War' in 2019, and in the same year Patrick Gray edited a collection entitled *Shakespeare and The Ethics of War*. Barker is unquestionably one of the foremost Shakespearians of the twentieth century who lived and worked through both world wars. Yet he has rarely featured in criticism intent on bringing Shakespeare and modern war into dialogue. There is only a single mention of him in all the aforementioned critical studies.[4]

Barker does not always refer to contemporary events in his writings about Shakespeare. This is particularly true of his *Prefaces*. These were written with the aim of providing other producers with practical advice about staging the plays, not to analyse parallels between Shakespeare and the present. Some contemporaries criticized Barker for his seemingly myopic approach: L. C. Knights upbraided Barker in 1934 for failing to consider the bearing of Shakespeare on modern life.[5] Barker does, however, address the question of Shakespeare and war in his Arden editions of the plays, which are currently held in the Harley Granville-Barker Collection at Senate House Library, London.[6] Barker sometimes alludes to the events of World Wars I and II in the copious handwritten notes that he made directly in his Arden editions of Shakespeare, usually while he was preparing his *Prefaces*.[7] These annotations have not previously been studied. By drawing on new research that I have completed in the Collection, it is possible to see that Barker used Shakespeare as a way of reflecting on the wars that he lived through and, in the case of World War I, served in.[8]

Most relevant for the present analysis is his 1922 Arden edition of *Coriolanus*, which is very heavily annotated. Up to 95 per cent of the pages are marked; it is rare to find a page that Barker has not written something on.[9] It is a play that Barker obviously felt had urgent contemporary relevance.[10]

---

[4] This is when Robert Sawyer quotes Barker on the writing of Dover Wilson; Sawyer does not consider Barker in relation to Shakespeare and war. See *Shakespeare Between the World Wars: The Anglo-American Sphere* (Basingstoke, 2019), p. 67.

[5] L. C. Knights, 'Review of *A Companion to Shakespeare Studies*', *Scrutiny* 3 (1934), 306–14. See also Christine Dymkowski, *Harley Granville Barker: A Preface to Modern Shakespeare* (London and Toronto, 1986), p. 124.

[6] For the collection, see the Senate House Library website: https://london.ac.uk/senate-house-library/our-collections/special-collections/printed-special-collections/granvillebarker. The Barker Collection consists of his personal library.

[7] The notable exception is the Arden edition of *Hamlet*, in which Barker makes no written notes.

[8] Barker volunteered for (and wrote a wartime history of) the Red Cross, before working for the British Intelligence Corps. See Purdom, *Harley Granville Barker*, pp. 184–5.

[9] The Harley Granville-Barker Collection, Senate House, London, William Shakespeare, *Coriolanus* (London, 1922), [G.-B.C.] 043. When I quote the Arden, I cite the page number where the quote appears. I have incorporated these references in the body of the article. I have done likewise when quoting the notes that Barker makes in *Antony and Cleopatra* (William Shakespeare, *The Tragedy of Antony and Cleopatra* (London, 1920), [G.-B.C.] 061). Because the 1922 Arden edition is not widely used or available, for reference I have used William Shakespeare, *Coriolanus*, ed. R. B. Parker (Oxford, 1994) throughout. For the Collection, see also K. E. Attar, 'Folios in context: collecting Shakespeare at the University of London', *The Library* 19 (2018), 39–62; pp. 60–1.

[10] The specific relevance that Barker felt *Coriolanus* had to wartime is also revealed by his conspicuous failure to make mention of contemporary events in his Arden *Othello*, the *Preface* to which was published in 1945. This partly has to do with the 'public' nature of the action in the play, as opposed

Margery Morgan contends that Barker draws on *Coriolanus* for his 1928 play *His Majesty* – the last original stage play Barker would write – in which he critiques the state of post-World-War-I Europe.[11] Barker depicts an exiled king who attempts to reclaim his throne after the disaster of the Great War and an unfavourable peace. Throughout the action, he uses images of the body and/as the body politic, which Morgan relates to Menenius and his use of the fable of the belly in *Coriolanus* (1.1.84–160).[12] Morgan also contends that the political strategies deployed in the play 'look forward to the tactics of the Reichstag Fire, the mass arrests and rigged plebiscites' – the 'tactics' of emergency and terror – and to the outbreak of World War II.[13] Barker would go on to relate *Coriolanus* to the same events, stating in 1944 that it does not take 'modern costume to make the politics of *Coriolanus* modern enough', and that 'Caius Marcius [*sic*] and Menenius are in politics still.'[14]

This sets Barker apart from some contemporary theatrical interpretations of the play, particularly in the anglophone world. John Ripley has shown that, as late as the 1938 Lewis Casson and 1939 Ben Iden Payne productions of *Coriolanus*, in a period when fascism was rampant in Europe and the onset of war imminent, any notion of 'contemporary relevance' was 'miraculously' missing from the discourse around the play.[15] Until the 1938 Federal Theater Project (FTP) production in New York, *Coriolanus* had also been absent from the American stage since the end of the nineteenth century. The FTP production was inspired by the success of the anti-fascist *Julius Caesar* directed by Orson Welles in 1937, but it 'eschewed both politics and contemporaneity' while 'Mussolini bombed Barcelona and Hitler readied his invasion of Austria'.[16] Barker, however, was living in Paris by the time the riotous Comédie Française production of *Coriolanus* was staged in 1933–4, when right-wing and fascist forces used the play as a weapon against the left-wing governments of Camille Chautemps and Édouard Daladier. The production was ultimately suspended after it provoked serious unrest in the city.[17] Barker, as far as I am aware, does not allude to the 1933–4 *Coriolanus*, though he could hardly have missed its bearing on modern French and European political life. Other stage productions after World War II used *Coriolanus* belatedly to reflect on 'the soldier-hero' as an 'icon of contemporary culture' after the global struggle between fascism and democracy, and to engage with the urgent questions it raised about the subsequent peace and the reintegration of wartime leaders into post-war civil society.[18] Ripley cites the John Houseman production at the Mercury Theatre, New York, in 1954, and the 1959 Peter Hall production at the Old Vic,

---

to the more 'private' action of *Othello*, as viewed by Barker. Though *Othello* depicts the type of race hatred that Barker may have identified with the Nazis, and despite its representation of the abortive Turkish invasion of Cyprus, Barker views the play as a domestic drama. He does make a fleeting allusion to the war in a footnote in his published *Preface* on the play, remarking that the threat of invasion was 'hardly' more present to the Elizabethan mind 'than our own', in Harley Granville Barker, *Preface to Othello* (London, 1993), p. 218, n. 69.

[11] Harley Granville Barker, *Plays: Two* (London, 1994), pp. 237–76. The play anticipates other aspects of pre-World-War-II Europe, including stock-market crashes, hyperinflation and anti-Semitic complaints about the financial influence of 'the international Jew' (p. 255). *Coriolanus* seems spectrally present, too, in the 1922 Barker play *The Secret Life*, not least when the former World War I soldier Oliver exclaims: 'Well, you can't love the mob, surely to goodness! Because that's to be one of them … chattering and scolding and snivelling and cheering … maudlin drunk, if you like! I learned to be a soldier enough to hate a mob' (Harley Granville Barker, *Plays: One* (London, 1993), p. 312).

[12] Margery Morgan, *A Drama of Political Man: A Study of the Plays of Harley Granville Barker* (London, 1961), p. 255.

[13] Morgan, *Drama of Political Man*, p. 254.

[14] Harley Granville-Barker, *The Use of the Drama* (London, 1946), p. 70. Though he cites other Shakespeare plays and characters, *Coriolanus* was clearly on his mind. He makes similar observations about modern dress in his radio address 'Hamlet in plus fours', *Yale Review* 16 (1926), 205.

[15] John Ripley, *Coriolanus on Stage in England and America, 1609–1994* (London, 1998), p. 271.

[16] Ripley, *Coriolanus on Stage*, p. 260.

[17] Ripley, *Coriolanus on Stage*, p. 268. See also Felicia Hardison Londré, '*Coriolanus* and Stravinsky: the interpenetration of art and politics', in *Coriolanus: Critical Essays*, ed. David Wheeler (New York and London, 1995), pp. 159–77.

[18] Ripley, *Coriolanus on Stage*, pp. 278–9.

but he does not consider that Barker may have set an early precedent, criticizing him instead for the 'apolitical' influence of his stage aesthetic.[19]

Though stage productions of the play in the interwar period often shied away from contemporary allusions, *Coriolanus* was used by some to reflect on the fallout of World War I and the impending possibility of future conflict, not least as fascism began to grip the Continent. T. S. Eliot, who famously regarded *Coriolanus* as superior to *Hamlet* as early as 1919, drew on the play for his unfinished *Coriolan* sequence of 1932.[20] 'Triumphal march' and 'Difficulties of a statesman' draw on the play to interrogate the relationship between the 'heroic' individual and the crowd in the tumult of post-World-War-I Europe. Eliot even enumerates the German armaments destroyed under the terms of the Treaty of Versailles in 'Triumphal march'.[21] Eliot was partly inspired by the writings of John Middleton Murry, Wyndham Lewis and G. Wilson Knight on *Coriolanus*. These critics used the play to reflect on the ideological struggles of the interwar period, where questions around the individual and the masses, democracy, totalitarianism, the state at war, and the nature of peace were at the forefront of both politics and culture.[22] These are questions Barker also confronts in his writings on *Coriolanus*, though he does so from the perspective of World War II.

It is not possible to date the notes Barker makes in his Arden *Coriolanus* with complete certainty. Barker gave a talk on the play for the Alexander Lectures, which he delivered at University College, Toronto, in 1942.[23] This talk would form the basis of his *Preface* to the play, which was published in 1947. The question is whether Barker salvaged his copy of the play from his library before fleeing France or whether he purchased his 1922 edition while he was in the US.[24] My hunch is that, while in the US, Barker purchased the other copy of *Coriolanus* in his Collection, the US version of the Arden Shakespeare, published by D. C. Heath and Company. This edition also contains some notes. There are, however, significantly fewer than appear in the 1922 edition of the play. The comments Barker does make in his D. C. Heath edition are limited entirely to the topic of versification in the play.[25] Barker returned to France in the spring of 1946, and died of arteriosclerosis that August. He was certainly working on his *Preface* to the play up to a few months before his death, so he had probably made most of his Arden notes in that short period.[26] It is clearly possible to date the notes after 1941, not least because Barker refers to the attack on Pearl Harbor.

By studying his Arden notes on *Coriolanus* alongside other of his published pieces on Shakespeare and theatre, I want to show that Barker uses the play to reflect on the events of World Wars I and II. I will also consider the contradictions that emerged in his social and political outlook over that crucial period of modern history, and the ideological ambivalence of the ideas that he develops through his interpretation of the tragedy. These have principally to do with states of emergency, the suspension of democratic and legal rights, and the nature of wartime leadership. I will contend that in his interpretation of *Coriolanus*, and particularly the role played by its titular hero, Barker weighs the necessity of an autocratic military leadership that revokes

---

[19] Ripley, *Coriolanus on Stage*, pp. 283–98.
[20] T. S. Eliot, 'Hamlet and his problems', in *The Sacred Wood and Major Early Essays* (New York, 1998), pp. 55–9.
[21] T. S. Eliot, 'Triumphal march' and 'Difficulties of a statesman', in *The Complete Plays and Poems: 1909–1959* (London, 2014), pp. 85–9.
[22] See Steven Matthews, '"You can see some eagles. And hear the trumpets": the literary and political hinterland of T. S. Eliot's *Coriolan*', *Journal of Modern Literature* 36 (2013), 44–60.
[23] See Elmer W. Salenius, *Harley Granville Barker* (Boston, MA, 1982), p. 153.
[24] Purdom, *Harley Granville Barker*, p. 274.
[25] The article 'Verse and speech in *Coriolanus*' was published separately in the *Review of English Studies* in January 1947, appearing later in the 'The Verse' section of the *Preface*. I believe that Barker worked on the verse section while in the US, then completed his *Preface* after his return to Paris. See Harley Granville-Barker, 'Verse and speech in *Coriolanus*', *Review of English Studies* 23 (1947), 1–15.
[26] Purdom, *Harley Granville Barker*, pp. 225, 275.

'BUT WHEN EXTREMITIES SPEAK': GRANVILLE-BARKER

13 Barker cites the strike on Pearl Harbor in *Coriolanus*, 1.2. © Image courtesy of Senate House Library, University of London.

democratic rule in order to prepare for and fight war properly. This is required when democratic society fails to confront threatening enemies.

CORIOLANUS AND PEARL HARBOR

The relationship Barker draws in his Arden edition between the action of *Coriolanus* and the events of World War II is most obvious in his response to act 1, scene 2, when Aufidius laments that 'they of Rome are entered in our counsels' (1.2.2) and have discovered from the use of spies that the Volscians intend to invade Roman soil. Aufidius worries that:

> By the discovery
> We shall be shortened in our aim, which was,
> To take in many towns ere, almost, Rome
> Should know we were afoot.
>
> (1.2.22–5)

Next to the speech, Barker writes simply 'Pearl Harbour' (Figure 13).[27] Barker, who was in the US by the time of Pearl Harbor, clearly sees parallels between the Volscian plan to invade Rome and 'take in many towns ere, almost, Rome / Should know we were afoot' and the surprise 1941 strike by Japan against the US naval base in Hawaii, which took place before an official declaration of war.[28] The attack was intended to catch US forces unawares, while also serving the aim of ensuring that the US would not intervene as Japan sought to 'take in' new territory in the Indian and Pacific Oceans. Winston Churchill, reflecting on the events of Pearl Harbor, wrote 'I never received a more direct shock': 'There were no British or American capital ships in the Indian Ocean or the Pacific except the American survivors of Pearl Harbour who were hastening back to California.'[29] Even so, the night after the strike, Churchill 'slept the sleep of the saved and thankful', knowing the US would have to respond.[30]

Barker may also have slept more soundly. It should certainly not be too surprising to find him alluding to the event that finally brought the neutral US into the war. During his time in the US in

---

[27] The handwriting is uncharacteristically legible. Barker learned to use a typewriter in 1942 and quipped that it was one benefit the war had brought to his friends, who no longer had to struggle with his handwriting. See *Granville Barker and His Correspondents: A Selection of Letters by Him and to Him*, ed. Eric Salmon (Detroit, 1986), p. 295.
[28] For the prelude to the attack, see Steve Twomey, *Countdown to Pearl Harbor: Twelve Days to the Attack* (New York, 2016).
[29] Winston Churchill, *The Second World War* (London, 2013), p. 496.
[30] Churchill, *The Second World War*, p. 493.

World War II, Barker worked for the New York-based British Information Service (BIS). Prior to Pearl Harbor, the BIS had been tasked with providing propaganda against American neutrality. Barker was briefly head of the Speaker Section, arranging lectures and talks to US audiences that promoted British culture and perspectives.[31] Barker often complained that he could not be more actively involved in the war, or 'digging trenches in Norfolk'.[32] But he also stated his belief that in his role at the BIS he could use Shakespeare as a 'war asset'.[33] Barker had found himself in a comparable position at the outset of World War I: over the period 1914–1915, Barker toured Shakespeare and Greek drama in the US, as part of a British propaganda campaign against alleged German war crimes in Belgium and American neutrality.[34] His role at the BIS obviously informs the allusion Barker makes to Pearl Harbor in *Coriolanus*, as does his past history of contesting American neutrality and his status as a British national living in wartime exile in the US. Barker is also concerned with the problem of deficient preparation for war in his reading of *Coriolanus*, perhaps another consideration underpinning his allusion to the strike on Pearl Harbor.

Through the analogy with Pearl Harbor, Barker casts the Romans in the role of the Americans and the Allies, while the Volscians represent the Japanese and the Axis. Barker is wary of simplistic dichotomies and warns in his *Preface* that 'Shakespeare is not painting' in 'ultrapatriotic black and white'; but, nonetheless, 'We are on the Roman side, and they are "foreigners".'[35] This distinction between 'the Romans' and 'foreigners' is also apparent in the way Barker aligns the Roman virtue of stoicism with English wartime endurance. This is in contrast to his less flattering depiction of the Volscians, who for Barker are overly concerned with the 'spoils' of war and driven by a ravening *libido dominandi*, a lust for new territory ('To take in many towns').[36] It is not unusual for Barker to comment on the 'Englishness' of Shakespeare or his characters.[37] But the tendency is particularly marked in *Coriolanus* and its depiction of war. When Martius and Titus lay a 'wager' (1.4.1) on whether Cominius has engaged the Volscian army, Barker observes that the figures might almost be 'Two Englishmen happily betting!' (p. 32). It is a point he returns to in his *Preface*, where he comments that Martius and Titus calmly laying bets before a battle is 'an English trait if not a Roman'.[38] He makes the same observation when Menenius remarks that necessity means recent travails 'must be patched / With cloth of any colour' (3.1.253–4). It is a 'make-do and mend' approach Barker describes as 'very English' (p. 107). Barker also alludes to the 'Englishness' of Coriolanus when he refuses 'to recant' his criticism of the newly democratic system of popular representation in the 'de-election' scene at the Roman Senate, where Coriolanus stands his ground against the far superior forces ranged against him (p. 125). Barker cites Martin Luther and his steadfast 'Here I stand, I can do no other, God help me' and calls it, in his Arden, 'That English insistence' (p. 125). Barker is evidently oblivious to the irony of using a German theologian to characterize the English. He also seems to overlook that Coriolanus is 'standing firm' against the social and political system of democratic rights, which Barker understood as synonymous with

---

[31] For his time at the Speaker Section, see Eric Salmon, *Granville Barker: A Secret Life* (London, 1983), pp. 286–9. See also Nicholas John Cull, *Selling War: The British Propaganda Campaign against American 'Neutrality' in World War II* (New York and Oxford, 1995), pp. 159–60.

[32] Quoted in *Granville Barker and His Correspondents*, ed. Salmon, p. 295.

[33] Quoted in *Granville Barker and His Correspondents*, ed. Salmon, p. 295.

[34] See Niall Slater, 'Touring the Ivies with Iphigenia, 1915', *Comparative Drama* 44/45 (2010/2011), 441–55, and '"The greatest anti-war poem imaginable": Granville Barker's *Trojan Women* in America', *Illinois Classical Studies* 40 (2015), 347–71.

[35] Harley Granville Barker, *Preface to Coriolanus* (London, 1993), pp. 55–6.

[36] Barker, *Preface to Coriolanus*, p. 175.

[37] For instance, in the notes of his Arden *Antony and Cleopatra*, Barker writes 'how English!' (p. 18) when Antony stoically delays telling Enobarbus that Fulvia has died.

[38] Barker, *Preface to Coriolanus*, p. 82.

English culture. The avowed stoicism of the English was an important ideological symbol of resistance to Nazi Germany in the period 1939–1941, prior to the entry of the US into the war, and it is a virtue Barker discerns in the action of *Coriolanus*.[39]

The obvious distinction between Pearl Harbor and the action of *Coriolanus* is that the Romans become aware of the Volscian invasion through the intervention of spies. Barker – perhaps reflecting his time in British military intelligence in both world wars – is drawn to the representation of espionage and subversion in *Coriolanus*, often noting the action involving spies and spying.[40] He remarks that 'much "intelligence" passes between Rome and the Volsces – a point to be made more than once' – and laments that Rome, not unlike wartime France and Britain, 'has her fifth column'.[41] Barker echoes the phrase in his thoughts on the 'curiously diseased scene between the spies' (p. 153) in act 4, scene 3, when he remarks that 'The Roman is a Fifth Column fighter, a Volscian spy, on his way to his masters.'[42] The term, which is thought to have originated in the Spanish Civil War, became common during the late 1930s and the 1940s.[43] The fear of betrayal was deepened by the rapid fall of France in 1940, which was sometimes blamed on the activities of a pro-German Fifth Column, a theory of which Barker was no doubt aware. Churchill insisted in a speech in June 1940 that 'Parliament has given us the powers to put down Fifth Column activities with a strong hand', as he sought to reassure the country about subversion.[44] The phrase was also current in the US: in July 1940, *Time* magazine insisted talk of a Fifth Column was a 'national phenomenon', while *Life* took a more sensationalist approach, running a series of photos supposed to reveal 'Signs of Nazi Fifth Column Everywhere'.[45] The term also has relevance to Pearl Harbor: the US Secretary of the Navy, Frank Knox, stated after the war that 'the most effective Fifth Column work of the entire war was done in Hawaii'.[46] Once again, the interpretation of *Coriolanus* that Barker develops is clearly inflected by the events and discourse of World War II. By alluding to subversive Fifth Columnists in Rome, Barker also continues to identify the Romans as the Allies, while the Volscians represent the Axis.

By drawing out some of the allusions that he makes in his Arden edition, I do not want to contend that Barker reduces the action of *Coriolanus* to the events of World War II. The play is too cynical in tone and ironic in form for any kind of 'tidy allegorizing', not least because the Roman hero Coriolanus will defect to the enemy and not only march against Rome, but also threaten to raze it.[47] It is also important to stress the provisional nature of the notes Barker makes in his Arden editions. These represent his spontaneous reaction to his reading and ideas that are not always developed *in situ* or pursued more fully in his published writings on Shakespeare. Even so, the allusions to contemporary events in his Arden *Coriolanus* do show that Barker perceives parallels between the play and the events of World War II. Barker also uses the play to reflect on the relationship between World Wars I and II, considering the developments that would see 'half to half the world' (1.1.231) again in conflict. This is most

---

[39] See Mark Connelly, *We Can Take It! Britain and the Memory of the Second World War* (London and New York, 2004), esp. pp. 54–94.

[40] See pages 25, 151, 152, 153, 155.

[41] Barker, *Preface to Coriolanus*, p. 80.

[42] Barker, *Preface to Coriolanus*, p. 137.

[43] For the origins of the term, see *OED Online*, 'fifth column, n.': www-oed-com.ezproxy01.rhul.ac.uk/view/Entry/70006?redirectedFrom=fifth+column.

[44] Churchill referred to Fifth Columnists in his famed 'We shall fight them on the beaches' speech to Parliament in 1940. See the digitized editions of Commons and Lords Hansard, the Official Report of debates in Parliament: https://api.parliament.uk/historic-hansard/commons/1940/jun/04/war-situation.

[45] Quotations from *Time* and *Life* are taken from Richard W. Steele, *Free Speech in the Good War* (New York, 1999), pp. 75–6.

[46] Quoted in Robert Loeffel, *The Fifth Column in World War II: Suspected Subversives in the Pacific War and Australia* (Basingstoke, 2015), p. xxvi.

[47] R. B. Parker, 'Introduction' to *Coriolanus*, pp. 1–132; p. 77.

obvious when Barker analyses the peace treaties depicted in the play. These cause him to think about the nature of peace, the perils of appeasement, and the conditions that provoke renewed conflicts between states.

By virtue of the dialogue that he establishes between *Coriolanus* and modern war, Barker develops an interpretation that emphasizes the foresight and military heroism of Coriolanus, while remaining conscious of his obvious personal and political flaws. Through his reading of the play, Barker considers the potential benefits of a strong military leadership and the merits of suspending democratic institutions, especially when the people and democratic society seem unwilling to fight war. His era saw tyrannical regimes on the march throughout Europe and the world; ironically, however, Barker would seem to endorse the autocratic suspension of democracy, to prosecute the war against those very regimes.

Writing towards the end of World War II, Barker anticipates recent critical trends, which – drawing on the writings of Giorgio Agamben – are interested in the way *Coriolanus* dramatizes the suspension of law and the response to 'exceptional' conditions of social and political crisis.[48] Agamben observes that, in England, the state of exception is related historically to martial law and World Wars I and II. He writes that World War I 'played a decisive role in the generalization of exceptional executive [*governamentali*] apparatuses in England', citing the 1914 Defence of the Realm Act (DORA) with its 'serious limitations on the fundamental rights of the citizens'.[49] The Emergency Powers (Defence) Act of 1939 provided for similar limitations in Britain. Agamben points out that the state of exception was also deployed not only by Nazi Germany after the Reichstag fire, but also by France and, after Pearl Harbor, the US, where Barker spent World War II. This made the state of emergency the norm in both the totalitarian and the democratic societies that were at war with each other.[50] Agamben traces the modern state of exception back to ancient Roman law and the so-called *iustitium*, which allows for the complete 'suspension of law' in times of tumult, in order to protect the state from internal unrest or threatening enemies.[51]

Before World War I, Barker was prominent amongst the Fabians, the democratic socialist movement that insisted on a gradualist approach to social and political reform. He often stressed the foundational historical and practical relationship between democracy and drama, which requires the 'democratic' collaboration of individuals for a greater purpose, from the Greek *demos* onward.[52] 'The drama', writes Barker in *The Exemplary Theatre*, 'has always tended to be a democratic art.'[53] Barker understands Shakespeare as a vital part of the ongoing relationship between drama and democracy, not least as the 'unruly life' of his characters emphasizes the rise of the individual and his or her democratic and legal rights over against arbitrary forms of power – again, something Barker describes as characteristically

---

[48] See, in particular, James Kuzner, '"Unbuilding the city": *Coriolanus* and the birth of Republican Rome', *Shakespeare Quarterly* 58 (2007), 174–99; Nichole E. Miller, 'Sacred life and sacrificial economy: *Coriolanus* in No-Man's Land', *Criticism* 51 (2009), 263–310; and Andreas Höfele, 'Of hybrids and hydras: early modern political zoology – and Shakespeare's *Coriolanus*', *Actes des congrès de la Société française Shakespeare* 38 (2020): http://journals.openedition.org/shakespeare/5235. Russel M. Hillier also touches on Agamben in relation to *Coriolanus* in his '"Valour will weep": the ethics of valor, anger and pity in Shakespeare's "*Coriolanus*"', *Studies in Philology* 113 (2016), 358–96, as do Liza Blake and Kathryn Vomero Santos in '"What does the wolf say?": animal language and political noise in *Coriolanus*', in *The Routledge Handbook of Shakespeare and Animals*, ed. Karen Raber and Holly Dugan (New York and London, 2020), pp. 150–62.

[49] Giorgio Agamben, *State of Exception*, trans. Kevin Attell (Chicago and London, 2005), pp. 18–19.

[50] Agamben, *State of Exception*, pp. 12–13, pp. 20–2, and pp. 14–16.

[51] Agamben, *State of Exception*, pp. 41–51.

[52] On Barker and Fabianism, see Philippa Burt, 'Granville Barker's ensemble as a model of Fabian theatre', *New Theatre Quarterly* 28 (2012), 307–24. See also Christopher Innes, 'Granville Barker and Galsworthy: questions of censorship', *Modern Drama* 32 (1989), 331–44.

[53] Harley Granville Barker, *The Exemplary Theatre* (London, 1922), p. 266.

'English'.[54] Barker writes that Shakespeare was writing at 'a time, above all, when in England individual character began to count as never before', so that his plays mark the emergence of individual rights and increasing demands for democratic representation.[55] This is not to claim that Shakespeare can in any way be thought of as a didactic political dramatist. But to 'say Shakespeare was not interested in politics', sniffs Barker in his *Coriolanus*, 'is to say he was not an Englishman' (front cover 2). Barker aligns Shakespeare historically with the rise of the individual and 'English' democratic political culture.

It was a culture that Barker understood to be in mortal danger in World War II. Barker saw World War II as nothing short of a fight for the future of civilization – and democratic civilization above all – against barbaric social and political forces that were obsessed with total power and the cult of personality. Barker observed shortly before the outbreak of war, in his presidential address to the English Association in 1938:

does not the whole march of human history show us the gradual advance of the individual in liberty and dignity of status? With many a set-back doubtless; after wars or political and economic disturbances, or with the bringing of less civilized peoples into the framework of a settled civilization. But these have proved episodes only; the march has been resumed. By which testimony, are not these Fascist, Soviet, and Nazi revolutions of today mere episodes, aberrations – though with much that may be salutary in them – from the main line of the march? The liberal tradition ... by which the ultimate test of any social policy is that it advances the individual in liberty and dignity, has ancient and sacred sanction.[56]

Barker contends that liberal democracy and individual dignity will always prevail over other forms of society, an argument that reveals his Fabian belief in 'gradual advance', rather than revolutionary movements, in history. He even conscripts the history of colonialism and 'less civilized peoples' to bolster his case, an observation that conflicts with his more critical insights into English colonialism.[57] By 1944–1945, Barker could use the end of the war to ratify his faith in the progress of history, insisting in *The Use of the Drama* that the war 'was bound to be won', even if the English 'had been left to fight it out alone' without the intervention of the US after Pearl Harbor, because 'the world does not go backward in its tracks'.[58] But, after 'the most destructive of wars', Barker is not always quite so sanguine about the future of democratic culture.[59] 'We must be strong in our civilization', he states.[60] Barker observes that 'world history' is at 'a fateful juncture', and that 'we are at this very moment pledging ourselves – we democratic nations in particular – to be more prudent shepherds of its future than we have proved of its past'.[61] Barker also seemed more conscious not only of the 'gradual advance' of democratic freedom, but also of 'an ever-encroaching industrial, mechanical, scientific civilization', culminating in 'two world wars', 'catastrophe' and the development of the atomic bomb.[62] The future of democratic culture was not, it seemed, quite as historically inevitable as Barker had thought before World War II, raising questions about the type of 'strong' emergency actions that might be necessary in a period of wartime tumult and the rise of 'barbaric' totalitarian political systems.

These thoughts on World War II and the future of democratic society contrast with his more

---

[54] Harley Granville-Barker, *From Henry V to Hamlet* (London, 1925), p. 11.
[55] Harley Granville-Barker, 'The perennial Shakespeare', in *Broadcast National Lectures* (London, 1937), p. 8.
[56] 'Quality', in *Granville Barker on Theatre*, ed. Chambers and Nelson, p. 130.
[57] Christopher Wixson makes the case that, in his 1923 play *The Secret Life*, Barker draws parallels between the oppression of women (Barker was a supporter of the Suffragette movement) and the evils of English colonialism. See his 'Doing the usual things: gender, race, and inwardness in Harley Granville Barker's *The Marrying of Ann Leete* and *The Secret Life*', *Comparative Drama* 43 (2009), 497–519.
[58] Granville-Barker, *The Use of the Drama*, p. 75.
[59] Granville-Barker, *The Use of the Drama*, p. 74.
[60] Granville-Barker, *The Use of the Drama*, p. 27.
[61] Granville-Barker, *The Use of the Drama*, p. 47.
[62] Granville-Barker, *The Use of the Drama*, p. 71. For the added footnote about the bomb, see *Granville Barker on Theatre*, ed. Chambers and Nelson, p. 223. In *The Secret Life*, Evan Strowde voices his concerns about 'the break up of the atom' (Barker, *Plays: One*, p. 295).

critical view of World War I. Barker hoped that if 'The Great War' was not 'the war to end war', it might at least prove to be an end to war 'of the stupidest sort'.[63] He also remarked in private correspondence that many of his closest friends were 'enemy aliens' – by which he meant foreign nationals resident in England who were compelled to register with the police, and who were at risk of being interned or deported under the Aliens Restriction Act (ARA) of 1914, the emergency law passed by Parliament the day after war was declared on Germany.[64] As a personal friend of the Prime Minister, Asquith, however, Barker supported the war publicly, and was one of the signatories of the 'Author's Declaration', a 'manifesto' signed by various prominent authors and intellectuals, with Thomas Hardy, Sir Arthur Conan Doyle, H. G. Wells, Arnold Bennett, J. M. Barrie, G. K. Chesterton and A. C. Bradley among them. Prompted by the newly established War Propaganda Bureau in 1914, the Declaration stated that 'Great Britain could not without dishonour have refused to take part in the present war', and that it was necessary to uphold 'common justice between civilized peoples, to defend the rights of small nations, and to maintain the free and law-abiding ideals of Western Europe against the rule of "Blood and Iron" and the domination of the whole Continent by a military case' – namely 'the iron military bureaucracy of Prussia'.[65] The 'Author's Declaration' provided implicit support for the actions of the British government in its prosecution of the war. This included DORA and its state of emergency, as well as the ARA that, at least in private, Barker had lamented – acts that do not necessarily square with 'the free and law-abiding ideals of Western Europe'.

THE 'GOOD PEACE' AND APPEASEMENT

These questions about democracy, authoritarianism, war and peace also inform the notes that Barker makes in his Arden edition of *Coriolanus*, which reveal some politically equivocal interpretations of the action of the play. One phrase that Barker uses in both these notes and in his *Preface* to the play is 'the good peace'. What he means by the phrase is the ability of rival states to achieve a mutually advantageous peace after a period of war, which is intended to prevent fresh outbreaks of violence in the future. Barker takes his cue from the terms and aims of peace treaties depicted in the play. After the Romans – or, rather, Martius: 'Alone I did it' (5.6.117) – conquer Corioles and put down the rest of the Volscian forces led by Aufidius, Cominius immediately sets about establishing the basis for a peace treaty between the warring nations. Wisely overlooking the warlike Coriolanus, Cominius declares:

> You, Titus Lartius,
> Must to Corioles back. Send us to Rome
> The best, with whom we may articulate
> For their own good and ours.
> (1.10.75–8)

'W.S. [William Shakespeare] [is] making the "good peace"' writes Barker (p. 54). Cominius is seeking an equitable peace on equitable terms: he not only stipulates that 'The best' of the Volscian nation be sent to Rome to parley, avoiding a peace secured on a socially unequal footing, but insists that the peace terms should be 'For their own good and ours' – the Volscian 'good' even taking precedence over Rome. Though not stated explicitly in the play, Barker is by no means wrong to believe that the 'good peace' in *Coriolanus* is one that prevents future war by ensuring that the defeated side is not treated too harshly or unjustly by the victors. What

---

[63] Harley Granville Barker, *The Red Cross in France* (London, New York and Toronto, 1916), p. 166. Barker does not refer to *Coriolanus* in his history, though he does allude to *King Lear* (p. 24) and *Hamlet* (pp. 76–91).

[64] Quoted in *Granville Barker and His Correspondents*, ed. Salmon, p. 287. For more on enemy aliens, see J. C. Bird, *Control of Enemy Alien Civilians in Great Britain, 1914–1918* (London, 2015).

[65] I have quoted the 'Author's Declaration' from the Project Gutenberg website: http://www.gutenberg.org/files/13635/13635-h/13635-h.htm#page82. The 'Author's Declaration' appeared in the *New York Times* in 1915: once again, Barker found himself in the position of contesting American neutrality.

is to be avoided at all costs is the sort of peace that 'makes men hate one another' (4.5.234–5).

The precise terms of the peace treaty brokered by Titus are never established in the play, though those brokered by Coriolanus are. After he reneges on his plan to destroy 'ungrateful' (4.5.131) Rome, Coriolanus characteristically complies with the demands of his mother, Volumnia, who tells him that his fame (5.3.144–9) can be ensured by securing peace between the rival states, and not by wreaking personal vengeance so dishonourably on the city of his birth. She insists that 'our suit / Is that you reconcile' Rome and Volsce (5.3.136–7), so that

> the Volsces
> May say, 'This mercy we have showed', the Romans
> 'This we received', and each to either side
> Give the all-hail to thee and cry, 'Be blest
> For making up this peace!'
> (5.3.137–40)

What Volumnia wants, writes Barker, is 'a "good peace"' (p. 219), though it is clear that Martius does not achieve it, despite his claim that he will 'frame convenient peace' (5.3.192). Martius asks Aufidius to 'advise' (5.3.198) him about the peace he should make with Rome, but Aufidius never replies. Later, Aufidius will criticize Martius for 'making a treaty where / There was a yielding' (5.6.68–9) and complain that the terms of the peace are not as favourable as might have been exacted. He and some of the other Volscians do not consider the return of 'a full third part' (5.6.78) of the cost of the invasion of Rome a fair reparation, but a slight that fuels an almost immediate desire for vengeance against Martius. This is despite some of the Volscian nobility stating that Aufidius 'should trouble not the peace' (5.6.128) – a call for peace that, as I will show, is also heard in Rome in act 3, scene 3.

Barker had a full copy of the Versailles Peace Treaty in his library collection and reveals in correspondence written at the end of World War II that he had read the treaty in its entirety.[66] The phrase 'the good peace' was certainly current at the end of World War I. The controversial British delegate and Labour politician Harold Nicolson – whom Barker names in the notes in his Arden edition of *Antony and Cleopatra* – wondered 'Are we making a good peace?'[67] Nicolson was concerned, as were many other British and American observers, that France wanted to exact reparations from Germany that were far too damaging. There were fears that the more conciliatory approach advocated by the US President Woodrow Wilson, with the aim of instituting a new international order under the auspices of the League of Nations, was being imperilled. John Maynard Keynes also used the phrase in *The Economic Consequences of the Peace*, in which he lamented that the brutally 'Carthaginian' peace treaty may lead to German resentment and renewed conflict. Keynes insisted that 'disinterestedness' and 'magnanimity' would have 'given us the Good Peace'.[68] For his own part, Churchill reflected on the paradoxical truth that those 'who can win a war well can rarely make a good peace, and those who could make a good peace would never have won the war'.[69] When he uses the phrase 'good peace', Barker is invoking the end of World War I and the Treaty of Versailles, which – as he knew by the time he came to engage with *Coriolanus* – had failed to establish a lasting peace. If his reflections on the play can be dated to 1945–1946, it may also be that Barker is alluding to the type of peace to be negotiated at the end of World War II, and that mistakes about the nature of a post-war settlement should not be

---

[66] *Granville Barker and His Correspondents*, ed. Salmon, p. 585.
[67] Quoted in Antony Lentin, 'Germany: a new Carthage?' *History Today* 62 (2012), 20–7; p. 26. Nicolson would go on to challenge the policy of appeasement prior to World War II. Barker compares the upstart Thidias to Nicolson in his Arden *Antony and Cleopatra*. He states that Thidias is 'a gay cocksure prig of a diplomatist' and that his whipping is akin to 'Harold Nicolson whipped!' (p. 131).
[68] John Maynard Keynes, *The Economic Consequences of the Peace* (New York, 1920), p. 274.
[69] Churchill is quoted in James W. Muller, ed., *Churchill as Peacemaker* (Cambridge, 1997), p. 25. In the notes in his Arden edition of *Antony and Cleopatra*, Barker remarks that Caesar deals directly in the peace treaty 'as a General should' (145). It would seem that Barker approves of a military presence in the negotiation of peace, which should not be an entirely civilian affair.

repeated, if future war was to be averted. Barker states in *The Use of the Drama* that, with the end of the war in sight, the question of peace was paramount:

> But what of the peace? ... Its utility depends on the worth of the men who are to work it, upon *our* worth, if we mean to continue in our democratic way of life ... Certainly we have high ideals, and, in providing for the world's peace, the very best intentions. But these can make hell's pavement, as we know ... The victors in a war are not as a rule very apt at self-examination. For ten years after the last war I lived in France, a county I love much. The French custom was to speak of November 11, not as armistice day ... but as *le jour de la victoire*. There was nemesis in the very words. Victory this time is to lay on us an even greater responsibility than that we shouldered and let slip twenty-five years ago. Shall we be equal to it? There is a grim question.[70]

With the spectre of the end of World War I still haunting him, Barker recognizes the 'responsibility' of producing a lasting peace after World War II. Once again, though, his tone is not always sanguine, concluding as he does that whether the victorious nations are equal to it is 'a grim question'.

While he relates the action of *Coriolanus* to peace, Barker is also concerned that a desire for concord can slide all too quickly into appeasement. This becomes apparent in his Arden edition in the notes on the action of act 3, scene 1. Enquiring into the rearmament of the Volscians and the rushed peace terms that a new show of force requires, Coriolanus asks:

CORIOLANUS: Tullus Aufidius then had made new head?
LARTIUS: He had, my lord, and that it was which caused
Our swifter composition.
CORIOLANUS: So then the Volsces stand but as at first,
Ready when time shall prompt them to make road
Upon's again.
COMINIUS: They are worn, lord consul, so,
That we shall hardly in our ages see
Their banners wave again.

(3.1.1–8)

Barker, in his *Preface*, describes Cominius as the 'pacific Cominius'.[71] But in his Arden edition he is blunter. With a dash pointing to his speech beginning 'They are worn', Barker inscribes the word 'appeaser!' (p. 101; Figure 14). Once again, Barker alludes to the events of World War II. This time, however, it is the policy of appeasement, as pursued by the British government over 1937–1939.[72] Barker implicitly casts the Volscians in the role of the rearmed Germans – ready to 'make road' into Europe again – while the Romans, or at least Lartius and Cominius, are cast as appeasers, attempting to bring peace by 'swiftly' 'composing' the terms of peace and consenting to new demands, or by simply denying that the Volscians are able to make war again. Far from a lasting and mutually beneficial peace, the peace treaty between Romans and Volscians begins, as Barker sees it, to resemble the infamous Munich Agreement of 1938 – it is a hastily patched-up treaty designed to prevent or postpone aggression from the newly armed Volscian nation.[73] Perhaps with World War I in mind, Barker writes that the threat posed to the Romans by a previously defeated but newly armed enemy is 'The usual result of victory!' (pp. 101, 100), and that 'the Volsces having been soundly beaten want more war' (p. 167). Barker is conscious that failed or inequitable peace treaties can lead to more war, insisting on the necessity of reaching a 'good peace' that does not impose too strict conditions on the defeated. But, from the perspective of World War II, he also seems suspicious of simply appeasing enemies that intend to return to all-out war, when the time 'shall prompt them'. Cominius appears to believe that the Volscians have been so 'worn' – both by the war and, perhaps, by the conditions of the peace settlement – that they will not be able to make future

---

[70] Granville-Barker, *The Use of the Drama*, pp. 75–6.
[71] Barker, *Preface to Coriolanus*, p. 112.
[72] See Robert J. Caputi, *Neville Chamberlain and Appeasement* (London, 2000).
[73] While Labour and some Conservative MPs – including most famously Churchill – opposed appeasement, many contemporary historians have argued that the policy 'bought' crucial time for Britain to prepare economically and militarily for war. See, in particular, James P. Levy, *Appeasement and Rearmament: Britain, 1936–1939* (London and New York, 2006).

'BUT WHEN EXTREMITIES SPEAK': GRANVILLE-BARKER

14 Barker calls Cominius an appeaser in *Coriolanus*, 3.1. © Image courtesy of Senate House Library, University of London.

war, which quickly turns out to be wrong. The spy Adrian confirms in act 4 that the Volscians 'are in a most warlike preparation' (4.3.16) even before Martius arrives in Antium, as he seeks his erstwhile enemy Aufidius. Barker has similar reservations about the peace brokered between Caesar and Pompey in act 3, scene 7 of *Antony and Cleopatra*, wondering if a pact 'made under such conditions' of clear imbalance between the parties 'could last' (p. 86).

If, for Barker, Cominius appears in the guise of a Neville Chamberlain, appeasing rearmed enemies and gullibly declaring 'Peace for our time!', Coriolanus begins to appear as Churchillian in his anticipation of conflict between Rome and the Volsci. This leads Barker, both in his notes on the play and in his *Preface*, to develop a relatively supportive interpretation of the hero and his actions over the play, as he analyses the value of a strong military regime as opposed to the democratic demands of the people and a popular desire for continued peace.

CORIOLANUS AND THE STATE OF EMERGENCY

Barker writes in his Arden notes that Coriolanus is the 'least sympathetic' (p. 23) tragic protagonist Shakespeare produces, and that Shakespeare also seems to have little 'natural' feeling for the warrior figure or the 'man of action' *per se* (front cover 1).[74] This partly reflects the way Barker conceived of drama and the way Shakespeare developed as a playwright.[75] Barker writes in *From Henry V to Hamlet* that, in *Henry V*, Henry is so committed to military action that he is left wanting a more developed sense of interior life, and insists that Shakespeare probably found the play 'a disappointment'.[76] With *Julius Caesar* and Brutus, however, Shakespeare moves the proper place of dramatic action from the 'outside' to the 'inside', a movement that reaches its apex with *Hamlet*. Shakespeare increasingly places his emphasis on internal rather than outward action, from 'plot to characterization and the emotional and moral content of the situation'.[77] The rule does not hold for Coriolanus, however. Barker insists that, unlike previous tragic heroes in Shakespeare, Coriolanus is not necessarily

---

[74] W. H. Auden goes further and insists that, apart from the largely 'mute' Virgilia, there is 'no really sympathetic character in the play (*Lectures on Shakespeare*, ed. Arthur Kirsch (Princeton and Oxford, 2019), p. 243).
[75] Granville-Barker, *From Henry V to Hamlet*, p. 14.
[76] Granville-Barker, *From Henry V to Hamlet*, p. 10.
[77] Salenius, *Harley Granville Barker*, p. 13.

'poetic'. He speaks verse, but he is not chiefly concerned 'with that which is beneath the surface of things', which is the way Barker understands 'the poet' and poetry, whether in verse or prose.[78] Barker comments in his Arden notes on the relative absence of soliloquies in *Coriolanus*, which he takes to be indicative of a play whose titular hero is far more concerned with mere doing than with the conundrums of being – with the outer, as opposed to inner, world (pp. 154, 182).[79]

But, although Martius may not be an entirely 'poetic' or indeed sympathetic character, he does possess qualities which, as Barker sees it, qualify him as the most obvious leader of Rome at a time of conflict, and which should be weighed by a properly discerning audience against the less endearing aspects of his personality. Barker makes a defence of Coriolanus:

Wrong-headed, intolerant and intolerable in his dealings with the citizens he may be, but upon the actual issues between them is he so wrong? He foresaw the first Volscian attack when the Senators – 'our best elders' – did not, and the hungry populace could think of nothing but their hunger. Victory won and a 'good' peace granted the enemy (a little to his impatience), himself made Consul, he foresees another attack.[80]

Barker is more than alive to the profound irony that it is Coriolanus who will ultimately lead the very 'attack' he warns against, in revenge for his banishment from Rome. But the important point for Barker is that Coriolanus – however lacking he may be in 'poetic' insight into his own inner life, or indeed in his recognition of the needs of others, and however unlikely he is to arouse sympathy in the audience – is 'right' about the 'actual issues' of the war with the Volscians, when others are not. When the quarrel between Coriolanus and the citizenry is interrupted by the 'best elders' (1.1.224) of Rome in the opening scene, the First Senator tells Martius ''tis true that you have lately told us. / The Volsces are in arms' (1.1.225–6). It would seem that Martius has been warning of the Volscian threat but has not been heeded.

The way Barker interprets the play, it is his anticipation of impending war with the Volscians that makes Martius so intolerant of self-indulgent civil unrest – 'Being i'th' war, / Their mutinies and revolts, wherein they showed / Most valour, spoke not for them' (3.1.127–9) – and that underpins his desire to revoke the newly won system of democratic representation. *Coriolanus* is set shortly after the expulsion of the Tarquins – 'When Tarquin made a head for Rome, he fought / Beyond the mark of others' (2.2.86–7), Menenius reminds the citizenry when defending Martius – and the supposed end of absolute rule in Rome. It also depicts the creation of the Tribunate, which introduced plebeian representation in the Roman Senate. Martius tells Menenius that the 'rabble' (1.1.215) have been granted Tribunes – something that Martius clearly resents as 'chief enemy to the people' (1.1.6–7). Barker is sympathetic to the citizens represented in the play, remarking in his notes on act 1 that, 'unlike other (J.C.) [*Julius Caesar*] citizens more reasonable, surely' (p. 3). This is a point echoed by Annabel Patterson, who comments that the citizens of the play are not the unruly and irrational mass Martius imagines, but are individualized by Shakespeare and are 'clearly ... capable of reasoning'.[81] What he is more critical of is the way the people are manipulated by the scheming Tribunes, so that Shakespeare turns his ire not against the people, but against the demagogic 'politicians who exploit them!' (p. 8) – a critique of the Tribunes I will return to.

Though he supports the 'reasonable' claims of the citizens, however, Barker clearly believes that Coriolanus is foresighted in his prediction of a coming war and possibly right to want to suspend or revoke democracy in a moment of crisis, where the 'yea and no / of general ignorance' may 'omit /

---

[78] Salenius, *Harley Granville Barker*, p. 124.
[79] Agnes Heller puts the point succinctly when she writes that Coriolanus 'cannot talk to himself', in *The Time Is Out of Joint: Shakespeare as Philosopher of History* (New York and Oxford, 2002), p. 286.
[80] Barker, *Preface to Coriolanus*, p. 44.
[81] Annabel Patterson, *Shakespeare and the Popular Voice* (Oxford, 1989), p. 143.

Real necessities' so that 'Nothing is done to purpose' (3.147–51). When Coriolanus learns that the Volscians have rearmed, the news 'makes C. [Coriolanus] immediately more dictatorial' (p. 102) – indicating that his authoritarian tendencies are, for Barker, related not only to his unregenerate anti-plebeian bias, but also to his knowledge of a coming conflict. It is straight after Coriolanus learns of the possibility of a fresh Volscian invasion of 'Roman ground' (p. 102) that the Tribunes appear (3.1.20), sharpening the sense that the imminent military needs of the state are going to be undermined by democratic institutions. The same dynamic is apparent for Barker in act 1, when Martius initially confronts the rioting citizenry. Barker writes that Martius is so peremptory with the citizens because he 'knows of approaching war' and so is 'only military in his appeal to them' (p. 15). With his knowledge that war is imminent, Martius has no time for empty stomachs. This conflict reaches a crescendo in act 3, scene 1, where Martius implies that, as consul, he would use his power to 'at once pluck out / The multitudinous tongue' (3.1.157–8) of representative democracy and restore to the state 'that integrity which should become't' (3.1.161) – a threat that earns him the charge of 'traitor' (3.1.164) and even 'innovator' (3.1.176). Coriolanus may seek absolute, 'Tyrannical power' (3.3.2) for himself; but, for Barker, that desire is born partly of his belief that war will return and that an autocratic military – as opposed to democratic – leadership is required to see off the Volscian threat.

It is an interpretation Martius would seem to support after he is banished from Rome by the Tribunes and the commons. He mockingly tells the citizens that they are welcome to

> Have the power still
> To banish your defenders, till at length
> Your ignorance – which finds not till it feels –
> Making but reservation of yourselves –
> Still your own foes – deliver you
> As most abated captives to some nation
> That won you without blows!
>   (3.3.128–34)

Martius once again ties his critique of democratic 'power' to the imminent danger of invasion by a rival nation. His animus against democracy is partially driven by the threat of impending war, and Barker is not necessarily critical about the way Martius aims to rescind democratic rule in a period of wartime crisis. He writes that, as the system of plebeian representation 'is so recent a concession when C. wants to go back on it his "treason" is not so grave' (18). The quotation marks around treason suggest that Barker questions whether suspending democracy in the name of national defence truly constitutes treason. Barker may have been a democratic socialist; but, in *Coriolanus*, 'when extremities speak' (3.2.43) in a time of war, democratic society may no longer be practicable and could even result in national ruination.

Despite his warnings, the state of emergency that Martius attempts to institute is resisted by the commons. The commons are not necessarily unwise to do so: Martius never gives any indication that his revocation of democratic norms would be temporary, reflecting his fundamental mistrust of any form of popular representation and his hatred of the masses. The *iustitium* that he intends would clearly not be provisional, but permanent. Agamben warns that the state of emergency, where both democratic and legal rights are postponed, often becomes the rule, not an exception which only holds till the ostensible 'emergency' is over and normality returned. What may take place in the space '*that opens up when the state of exception starts to become the rule*' is, as Agamben contends, a reign of complete terror, where the life and body of the citizen are at the mercy of untrammelled social and political power.[82] Emergency turns the state into 'an unnatural dam' that eats up 'her own' (3.1.295–6).

---

[82] Giorgio Agamben, *Homo Sacer: Sovereign Power and Bare Life*, trans. Daniel Heller Roazen (Stanford, 1998), pp. 168–9 (emphasis in original). The space that Agamben refers to is the concentration camp. Barker does not appear to have mentioned the Holocaust or the camps. For his 1940 production of *King Lear*, in relation to the Holocaust, however, see my *King Lear 'After' Auschwitz: Shakespeare, Appropriation and Theatres of Catastrophe in Post-War British Drama* (Edinburgh, 2021), pp. 103–4.

Even so, it is worth pausing over the way Martius is resisted in act 3 and the language the citizens use, which, as Maurice Hunt has observed, involves repeated calls for peace.[83] 'Why are the commoners not pacificists?' (p. 21) wonders Barker in his Arden edition – but the commoners are perhaps more pacific than he realizes. During the tumult preceding the exiling of Martius from the city, the cry for peace is heard no less than nine times: 'Peace! – Peace! – Peace!' (3.1.189). There is an overwhelming democratic clamour for 'Peace' (3.1.194) in act 3, which drowns out the dark warnings of war voiced by Martius. When Menenius attempts to address Sicinius, the Tribune responds with 'peace' (3.1.193) and the word is repeated over and again as the citizens shout down Martius and his supporters. It would seem that part of the motivation for removing Martius from the consulship and eventually from the Roman body politic is that there is a popular desire for peace, of precisely the type the warlike Martius is clearly liable to undermine. For the people, it may even be that the constant threats of war proceeding from Martius are devised only to rationalize the suspension of democratic institutions. What the citizens offer in response is a cry for peace and the continuation of the democratic representation that Martius threatens. This desire for peace is no doubt laudable. But, for Barker, Martius is right to insist on the pressing Volscian threat. The argument could even be made that, in marching on Rome himself, Martius aims to demonstrate that Rome is unprepared for war and unable to defend itself from its antagonists, while the state is undermined from within by the newly enfranchised citizens and the wavering 'yea and no' of a more democratic system.[84] Martius is contemptuous of the mere 'shows of peace' (3.3.36) when war still threatens the nation.

This is not to say that Barker embraces without qualification the suspension of democratic and legal rights. When Menenius attempts to gain access to Martius, to try and convince him not to march on Rome, he is stopped by an unnamed guard. The guard is utterly dismissive and tells him that his 'name' is not 'passable' (5.2.13–14). Barker writes that the dialogue is typical of 'the tussle, familiar to any wartime, between soldier and civilian, the Somebody in peace and Nobody in war'.[85] Barker refers to the reduction of the individual – even the prominent individual, the 'Somebody' – to a complete nonentity, a 'Nobody' without prestige or any obvious status, legal or otherwise. This is possibly an allusion to his own travails in France and Portugal during the war, when he attempted to secure his transit to America, where he did eventually find that his own name was 'passable'.[86] There was certainly some worried confusion over the precise whereabouts of Barker in 1940 amongst his friends and collaborators: Hallam Fordham, in his observations on the 1940 production of *King Lear* at the Old Vic, could say only that Barker 'was believed to be in the United States'.[87] Barker is writing in the same vein when he criticizes Martius for his statement – however ironic – that he wishes the nobility would lay aside its 'ruthful' granting of democratic representation so that he may use his sword to 'make a quarry' of the common people as high as he can pitch his lance (1.1.195–7). It is a threat Menenius takes seriously enough to insist that the citizens are already 'all most thoroughly persuaded' (1.1.198). 'This sort of talk is always attractive', writes Barker, 'to the average weakling!' (16). There is also the irony that the Tribunes themselves seek to suspend individual rights and the process of legal representation in order to kill or exile Martius:

---

[83] Maurice Hunt, 'The physiology of peace and *Coriolanus*', *Ben Jonson Journal* 26 (2019), 78–96.
[84] Stanley Cavell writes that Coriolanus wants Rome to 'understand what it had done to itself', in '"Who does the wolf love?", reading *Coriolanus*', *Representations* 3 (1983), 1–20; p. 7.
[85] Barker, *Preface to Coriolanus*, p. 67.
[86] See Purdom, *Harley Granville Barker*, pp. 264–6.
[87] Hallam Fordham, 'Player in action' (unpublished MS, Folger MSS collection Tb17: www.shakespeareinperformance.amdigital.co.uk/Documents/Details/FSL_MISC_PROMPT_BOOKS_Tb_17.

> He hath resisted law
> And therefore law shall scorn him further trial
> Than the severity of the public power,
> Which he so sets at naught.
>
> (3.1.269–72)

Sicinius argues that, as Martius intends to violate the law, he should not be under its protection. The state of emergency Martius wants to bring about, whatever his motivations, rebounds on him, as the individual, democratic rights of legal representation are waived, with the ostensible purpose of protecting the survival of those very rights from the authoritarian threat he poses: 'He is a disease that must be cut away' (3.1.297). This means reducing Martius to a form of 'bare life', or life that, being devoid of any form of right or rights whatsoever, can be summarily destroyed without recourse to the usual processes of lawful representation or trial.[88] What the Tribunes enact is 'the separation of force of law from the law', to quote Agamben.[89] It is in that sense the Tribunes may, as Barker insists, be considered 'dictatorial' (p. 122). For the 'extra'-legal death-sentence pronounced against Martius represents the 'incorporation of the state of exception and anomie directly into the person of the sovereign, who begins to free himself from all subordination to the law and asserts himself as *legibus solutus* ("unbound by the laws")'.[90] The Tribunes appear as 'living law' ('in him the life of the law coincides with a total anomie'): as the very embodiment of the 'voices' (3.3.9) of the people, the words of the Tribunes carry 'the "force of law"', without requiring that standing legal practice is necessarily followed.[91] 'I' th' people's name', proclaims Sicinius, 'I say it shall be so' (3.3.105–6). Menenius will insist that the Tribunes should still agree to 'Proceed by process' (3.1.316). But, more than once, Barker in his Arden will refer to the Tribunes as 'lawyers' (pp. 98, 133). The Tribunes are obviously aware of the legal (or extra-legal) conditions of emergency or exception under which Roman law can be suspended.

Barker uses the word 'dictatorial' (Tribunes, p. 122; Martius, p. 102) to describe the Tribunes and Martius, as both parties attempt to achieve some form of 'power tyrannical' (3.3.65) via states of emergency. Barker is, however, far more critical of the Tribunes than of Martius, calling the pair villainously 'subtle', with 'twisted minds' and 'demagogic' tendencies (pp. 99, 75, 58). He also writes that the Tribunes 'have as real a contempt for the people' as Martius (p. 99), though that contempt is shown less in simple abuse than it is by constant political manipulation. The distinction for Barker is that the Tribunes use the commons to pursue and retain personal power, for self-aggrandizement – 'Then our office may / During his power go sleep' (2.1.218–19) – whereas Martius is more concerned with the safety of Rome in a period of war: 'Keep Rome in safety' (3.3.34). 'The blood he hath lost', states Menenius, 'he dropped it for his country' (3.1.301, 303). Both Martius and the Tribunes may seek to suspend or contravene the law. But, for Barker, Martius would seem to do it for 'nobler' (front cover 1) reasons. This means that Martius, as Barker writes in his *Preface*, is for Rome 'just such a leader as she may most need, with war, as is hinted, likely to threaten her again'.[92] So when, in *The Frontiers of Drama*, Una Ellis-Fermor critiques Coriolanus for being so completely identified with his public role of soldier that it 'suppresses' his character, Barker writes in his notes that Ellis-Fermor 'much underrates' Coriolanus as a leader: his unwavering dedication to martial values is timely in a period of war.[93]

---

[88] Kuzner, '"Unbuilding the city"', p. 174.
[89] Agamben, *State of Exception*, p. 38.
[90] Agamben, *State of Exception*, p. 69.
[91] Agamben, *State of Exception*, p. 69 and p. 39.
[92] Barker, *Preface to Coriolanus*, p. 113. By contrast, Paul A. Jorgensen argues that Coriolanus is, by Jacobean standards, both a recklessly wayward soldier and an unwise peacetime statesman. Writing in 1949, Jorgensen perhaps has in mind those wartime leaders who, like Coriolanus, failed to make the transition from 'th' casque to th' cushion, but commanding peace / Even with the same austerity and garb / As he controlled the war' (4.7.43–5), as to a certain extent Churchill did. See Jorgensen, 'Shakespeare's *Coriolanus*: Elizabethan soldier', *PMLA* 64 (1949), 221–35.
[93] The Harley Granville-Barker Collection, Senate House, London: Una Ellis-Fermor, *The Frontiers of Drama*, [G.-B. C.] 042, p. 51.

The question of leadership is vital for Barker. Throughout his critical writings, Barker stresses the educational role of the theatre in society, and insists that theatre should not be only for the cultured few but should work to improve the capabilities of all citizens, who, by watching a play, can become more imaginative and empathetic.[94] This is a theme that Barker develops in *The Use of the Drama*, where he brings a new dimension to the question of drama and education. Barker contends that art – and particularly drama – not only enriches the imaginative and empathetic capacities of audiences, but also has value insofar as it empowers citizens to make more discriminating choices about the type of people who may be most suited to positions of leadership.[95] Drama has a vital role to play in democratic society, because it enables audiences to think about the sort of individuals that would make the most capable leaders of society. Published in 1946, *The Use of the Drama* is partly a response to the rise of totalitarian personality cults, where swathes of people supported the most reprehensible leaders imaginable, something Barker may have put down to the absence of proper educative development of the type he imagined his ideal theatre providing. This poses a problem, however, when it comes to wartime society. What sort of leader does *Coriolanus* endorse, as Barker interprets the play? Barker has no time for the Tribunes or for most of the ruling class of Rome, whom he generally views as too passive. He is also critical of Coriolanus and various aspects of his character, while also being conscious that his is a personality unlikely to invite audience sympathy. Nevertheless, only Coriolanus appears as a capable leader for the war-torn times the play depicts. Paradoxically, the education in democracy that Barker believes is part of the social and cultural role of theatre may mean promoting the type of leader who would, in a situation of impending crisis, suspend the democratic process.

The dangers of the wrong type of leadership at the wrong time emerge in the course of *Coriolanus*. Barker contends that, after the banishment of Coriolanus, the Tribunes – with the support of the commons – have risen to dominance, with the result that, by act 4, 'the Tribunes now govern Rome' (p. 171). This seems to usher in a period of peace. The Tribunes Sicinius and Brutus talk of 'the present peace' (4.6.2): 'This is a happier and more comely time' (4.6.29). They mock Menenius, saying that 'Your Coriolanus is not now much missed' (4.6.14) because his portents about social dysfunction and the threat posed by rival states have not come to pass. But, in his *Preface*, Barker worries that the Tribunes have formed a 'pacifist government': 'It is implied in more than one passage that the Tribunes now rule Rome, and Aufidius has just remarked of them that they are "no soldiers". Theirs is, in fact, what would be called today a pacificist government, quite unprepared for war.'[96] What is so problematic about the 'pacifist' leadership instituted by the Tribunes is that it is unprepared for war and seems to believe that its democratic peace will last forever. There is an obvious dramatic irony at work in the play: when the Tribunes celebrate newfound peaceful times, the audience is already aware that Martius is marching on Rome with the Volscians. 'It cannot be', insists Brutus on hearing of the invasion, 'The Volsces dare break with us' (4.6.49–50).

The need for a strong individual, as opposed to democratic, authority in a period of war is an idea Barker returns to when he considers the speech in which Martius declaims that:

> when two authorities are up,
> Neither supreme, how soon confusion
> May enter 'twixt the gap of both and take
> The one by th'other.
> (3.1.111–14)

'Keynote of W. S. thought' (p. 108) in the play, writes Barker in his Arden. Barker does not necessarily mean that Shakespeare is generally supportive of authoritarian rulers, not least

---

[94] See, in particular, the chapter, 'The educational basis', in Barker, *The Exemplary Theatre*, pp. 36–95.
[95] Granville-Barker, *The Use of the Drama*, pp. 28–9; see also Salenius, *Harley Granville Barker*, p. 117.
[96] Barker, *Preface to Coriolanus*, p. 221 (n. 48).

because he aligns Shakespeare historically with the rise of individual rights and democracy. The point for Barker is that, in *Coriolanus*, internal division disables the state and undermines its ability to prepare for and conduct war properly. This is reinforced by another allusion Barker makes in his Arden notes. Next to the speech, Barker writes 'c.f. Fortescue *History of the B. Army*' (p. 108) – by which he means *A History of the British Army*, by the military historian Sir John William Fortescue. This monumental work was produced over the period 1899–1930 and covered the history of the British army, from its very earliest beginnings to 1870.

A History of the British Army is composed of no less than thirteen volumes, and Fortescue does on occasion refer to Shakespeare (the Histories, not the Roman plays) for evidence of military life and conduct in the early modern period. Although he does not provide a specific reference, I believe that Barker is most probably alluding to the Epilogue of the final volume, volume XIII. This volume was finished in 1929 and published in 1930. The Epilogue is notable in that it refers to *Coriolanus*-like civil strife – namely the General Strike of 1926. Fortescue critiques the food shortages the strike created, 'a kind of civil war, though many who abetted it were loudest in denunciation of war in the abstract'.[97] He also denounces new demands for representation, peace and 'talk of a universal brotherhood'.[98] This has caused only unpreparedness for war, due to a lack of rearmament after World War I.

These anxieties have some startling resonances with the action of *Coriolanus*, particularly as read by Barker – with the obvious distinction that the food scarcity of *Coriolanus* is the cause of popular upheaval, as opposed to being a result of it. Fortescue worries that civil unrest and appeals for 'universal' brotherhood and peace on the part of the commons could hinder readiness for war, so that rivalry between social and political authorities, the democratic and the military, may undermine the nation from within. He states that 'there is a pathetic effort to make an end of war by making an end of armaments', and that if 'unreadiness for hostility be any furtherance of the cause of peace, then assuredly the English cannot be blamed for leaving the experiment untried'.[99] Under conditions where 'split' authorities undermine the ability of the nation to prepare for and make war, the apparent necessity of quelling popular democratic and pacificist movements becomes more urgent, instituting a single abiding 'authority' that promotes the martial and patriotic ideals of 'obedience, service, sacrifice'.[100] Fortescue is concerned about the ability of a divided state to prepare for and conduct war. He even begins to sound like Coriolanus in his denunciation of the commons, whom he thinks 'like nor peace nor war ... The one affrights you, / The other makes you proud' (1.1.166–7). He denounces the people as nothing but 'shirkers' who have abandoned the duty 'to make adequate preparation for war'.[101] Barker would probably have baulked at the patronizing tone. But his allusion to Fortescue reveals his apparent endorsement of emergency intervention to ensure that the state is ready to fight war, even if that means suspending democracy and stymying popular movements.

CONCLUSION

Barker does not always develop his preliminary thoughts and notes in his published writings on Shakespeare. But the allusions to be found in his copy of *Coriolanus* do reveal that he used

---

[97] John William Fortescue, *A History of the British Army*, vol. XIII (London, 1930), p. 580. For more on *Coriolanus* and the General Strike, see Terence Hawkes, *Meaning by Shakespeare* (London, 1992), pp. 43–61. Hawkes reminds us that 'the General Strike was ... the major public political demonstration of the century in Britain' (p. 51).
[98] Fortescue, *A History of the British Army*, p. 580.
[99] Fortescue, *A History of the British Army*, p. 580.
[100] Fortescue, *A History of the British Army*, p. 582.
[101] Fortescue, *A History of the British Army*, p. 580.

Shakespeare to reflect on the wars that had such a momentous impact on his life and times. Writing in a period of total war, Barker confronts the questions *Coriolanus* raises about war, democracy, military leadership and peace. His response to the play reveals some of the profound ideological ambivalences that the state of emergency entailed. It also prefigures important developments in contemporary criticism on *Coriolanus* and situates Barker as an important, unduly neglected voice in critical debates about Shakespeare and modern war.

SHAKESPEARE PERFORMANCES IN ENGLAND, 2021

LOIS POTTER, London Productions

THE GLOBE'S SUMMER SEASON

A crucial feature of Sean Holmes's *A Midsummer Night's Dream*, first performed in 2019, was the recruitment at each performance of a different audience member to play Starveling, with the sympathy and encouragement of the rest of the cast. He had very few actual words to speak, but, during the *Pyramus and Thisbe* performance, his job was to keep pumping the organ that (supposedly) kept the lights functioning on the amateur stage; at the end, sent back to his seat, he was generously applauded. Though in the 2021 revival this part of the play was somewhat diluted by the need to keep him at a safe distance from the actors, it still produced some enjoyable moments and a final round of applause. In retrospect, it also strikes me as emblematic of 2021: it was a year in which plenty of amateurs got to play Shakespeare (in numerous online Zoom reading groups) and in which, even when theatres reopened, focus was as much on the audience as on the play. Theatre, never considered a particularly safe medium, suddenly had to think of safety at all costs (and the costs were often horrendous).

So how were 'we', the audience, to be 'kept safe'? In some cases, by arriving 45 minutes early, entering by a specified door, and staying in our seats, or on our feet, without intervals and without refreshments. A production had to be good to leave an audience with any memories apart from these. At the Globe and the big West End theatres, the spectators in the highest and cheapest seats were those who had to arrive earliest, so there was also a subtle reinstatement of the class distinctions that were the original reason for separate entrances for different social groups. And, of course, there were the last-minute cancellations because someone in the production had tested positive; in one case, the announcement came only 5 minutes before the play was due to start (fortunately, not one that I was reviewing).

Our mental health was also looked after, perhaps excessively. The website for the Young Vic *Hamlet* warned that the play contained 'themes of death and bereavement, as well as acts of violence, self-harm, and death on stage'. The Almeida gave a similar warning about *Macbeth*, referring us to the Samaritans if we felt disturbed by the play's content. At the end of the curtain call for the Globe *Romeo and Juliet*, as recorded in the live performance on Globe Player, you can hear Adam Gillen (Mercutio) tell the audience that there are places to get help if they have been affected by this play. Some might think that anyone not affected by it needs even more help, but I know what he meant.

Were we also being 'kept safe' from uncomfortable interpretations? Some reviewers thought so when the Globe's revival of *A Midsummer Night's Dream* opened in May 2021. The first production in that popular space for a year and a half, it was colourful to the point of garishness, vaguely Mexican-themed, and determined to get laughs even before it began, with the onstage band members trying to exchange repartee with the audience. In the socially distanced space, with 'groundlings' seated in widely spaced chairs around the yard, much of this fell flat. Even so, a theatre-starved audience greeted the production enthusiastically and I doubt that most of them wanted to see any emphasis on the darker side of the play. A few minor cuts (such as 'the lunatic, the lover and the poet') kept the production short enough to perform without an interval. The splitting of Puck's role among several actors allowed him to pop in and out of different parts of the theatre with amazing speed. Sophie Russell, as Bottom, showed that it was possible to play a comic male character in a very feminine style. Within its parameters, the production's handling of tone seemed to me sure-footed. On the night I saw it, there was an audible audience reaction when Lysander's wild rejection of Hermia (a black actress) culminated in his calling her an 'Ethiop'. Interpretations of audience behaviour differ even more than interpretations of a play, but I thought it registered both a desire to express shocked disapproval and a sense of the absurdity of Lysander's extreme language, which belonged to Elizabethan Athens rather than pandemic London.

Because productions and performances changed so much in tandem with changes in government regulations, I shall review them in the order in which I saw them, rather than looking for thematic groupings. The Globe could open early because it is an outdoor theatre, but, in normal times, its spectators are closely packed in. When I saw *Romeo and Juliet* in July, the theatre still had staggered arrival times and designated entrances, and only a few (seated!) groundlings. *Twelfth Night*, in August, had a larger seating capacity and a limited number of standing groundlings on its opening night, but on my second visit there seemed to be as many groundlings as ever. The result was an enormous difference in the level of laughter and other signs of audience involvement (like the mock-sympathetic 'aww's when Sir Andrew said, 'I was adored once too'). Michelle Terry has argued, rightly, that intervals often break the momentum of a production, but an unbroken 2 hours and 40 minutes is a ridiculous time to ask spectators to stand or sit on backless benches. Even though we were told that we were welcome to come and go freely, at the Globe this is easy only for the groundlings; it's difficult to move from the benches without disrupting a whole row.

No one could say that the remarkable *Romeo and Juliet* (dir. Ola Ince), clearly aimed at young audiences, was playing safe or overlooking the play's dark side. This small-cast, heavily cut interpretation largely dispensed with lyricism, treating the story instead as an illustration of the awfulness of being young in a patriarchal society. Surtitles gave us statistics on youth poverty, violence and suicide (Figure 15). Possibly to deter anyone thinking a love-suicide might be romantic, Romeo's death from poison was protracted and agonizing, while Juliet shot herself with the gun that Paris had brought, and the play ended almost immediately afterwards. What kept the whole thing from being unbearably grim, at least for a young audience, was its extensive use of pop music. Here is a passage from Arifa Akbar's *Guardian* review (9 July 2021), that meant nothing to me, but clearly explained many audience reactions that I had not understood: 'There are witty trombones and trumpets played alongside punkishly performed numbers (from Arctic Monkeys, Jill Scott, the Streets). Max Perryment's music raises the drama in fight scenes, while the Capulet ball is a cabaret (at which Dwane Walcott's Paris woefully missteps by singing Lionel Richie's Hello to a cringing Juliet).' Reading this, I realized that somebody else should be writing this review.

However, there were some elements of the production that even I could appreciate: Alfred Enoch's energetic Romeo was often delightfully comic, as when, listening to Juliet while perched on a ladder at the edge of the yard, he asked the audience, 'Shall I hear more, or shall I speak at this?', or when, running through the groundlings in the yard, he thoughtfully pulled up his scarf to serve as a mask. Juliet (the equally vital Rebekah Murrell) was first seen kickboxing with her cousin Tybalt, with whom she also performed during the Capulet's party; this emphasis on the closeness of her relationship with the man her lover will kill is a potentially interesting strand of the play, though it was not developed further. Sirine Saba's nurse was also something of

15 *Romeo and Juliet*, Shakespeare's Globe. Alfred Enoch as Romeo. © Marc Brenner.

a revelation. Much younger than usual, she clearly had not yet got over the death of her daughter: we first saw her cuddling one of Juliet's stuffed animals. A surtitle announcing that many women are afraid to go out alone illustrated the scene in which Mercutio and Benvolio not only tease and insult her (there was no servant with her in this version) but run off with two of her shopping bags. Bernard Shaw wrote long ago that he found nothing funny in Mercutio's behaviour, and this production obviously agreed. Within its own terms, the production was consistent if hardly lovable. Friar Lawrence, before marrying Romeo and Juliet, spoke an interpolated prayer saying how much he loved these young people, but in the final scene he went completely to pieces, then planted his crowbar by Romeo's body, apparently to cover up his own action in breaking into the tomb. Perhaps the point was simply that one should never trust anyone over 30, but it left me wondering whether something had been lost from the original concept when it was cut down to even less than 2 hours' traffic.

Twelfth Night, directed by Sean Holmes, had the same cast as *A Midsummer Night's Dream*, and some of its pleasure, for those who saw both productions, came from its revelation of the resemblances between characters in the two plays (with possible implications for the original casting). For instance, Shona Babayemi, constantly in pursuit of an apparently unattainable object, grew from the rather breathless Helena of the *Dream* into the more complex Olivia; she ended up with Sebastian, played by the same actor (Ciarán O'Brien) who had played Demetrius. Bryan Dick, as Lysander, had felt a temporary and irrational passion for her; when he played Orsino, his obsession with Olivia looked like the temporary aberration of an otherwise competent ruler. George Fouracres, delightful as Flute, had much more scope as Sir Andrew Aguecheek. Peter Bourke, whose excellent verse speaking had stood out in his Theseus/Oberon double, turned up in yet another awful wig as Antonio, doubling with the Sea Captain. As in the *Dream*, there were a number of gender-swappings: Jacoba Williams (Snout) was Fabian; Nadine Higgins (Peter Quince) was a splendidly loutish Sir Toby Belch, and Sophie Russell moved from Bottom to Malvolio. Both these characters were played as male. On the other hand, Victoria Elliott, who had played Titania, became an ambiguous Feste, first seen as a sexy woman singing a touching folksong, and later as a cross between a Pierrot and a baseball player.

The one new element in the cast, Michelle Terry's Viola, was a catalyst both as character and as actor. In a surprisingly realistic touch, she entered clutching her brother's doublet, apparently saved from the waves, and when she decided to impersonate a man she undressed in front of the sea captain and gave him her clothes. The business thus explained both why she stresses that she is taking a chance on his character and why she says later that he has her women's garments. (The colours worn by the twins inspire Viola's image of 'green and yellow melancholy': Figure 16). Playing a man was a struggle for her: any word with 'man' in it became embarrassing ('I am a gentleman' came out first as 'gentle *man*' and she had to try it again, with a different stress). When Orsino slapped her on the back, she did the same thing, clumsily, a few moments later. While, as a character, she was often bemused by events, as an actor she was able to hear and react to audience noises without breaking the spell. Whereas most productions make Sebastian an amiable if rather characterless young man, Ciarán O'Brien oozed entitlement and was so patronizing to Antonio that it was impossible to imagine an erotic subtext in their relationship. Only the suggestion that he might be growing out of his obvious immaturity kept me from thinking that Olivia might have done better to marry Orsino.

As in *The Dream*, the setting was both recognizable and fantastic: Illyria was a place built on discarded junk, where, as in a Las Vegas hotel, everyone was perpetually dressed for a costume party. Some of the onstage paraphernalia, like the dead deer hanging overhead and the juke box, seemed irrelevances until they were used for a single startling effect. There were very few cuts: Sir Andrew did not read his letter of challenge aloud; the duel scene and Feste's comic turn in dialogue with himself as Sir Thopas, both of which are often stretched out for minutes with comic business, were kept very brief. The mood was varied by music – folksong and ballad rather than pop – and dancing. Maria initially tries to stop the singers of 'Hold thy peace', who keep shushing each other, but she ends up playing the guitar for them. Of course, the volume becomes thunderous

16 *Twelfth Night*, Shakespeare's Globe. Michelle Terry as Viola and Ciarán O'Brien as Sebastian. © Marc Brenner.

and the audience is encouraged to join in, so that Malvolio can address his indignation to them as well as to the onstage characters.

Though the production was full of clever touches that derived from thorough knowledge of the text, these were mostly incidental rather than thematic, since Holmes was obviously not looking for a novelistic through-line. He reserved many of his best surprises for the end – or, rather, the endings, since the production recognized that, like the *Dream* (and several other comedies), *Twelfth Night* has more than one apparent stopping-point. The first climax, at Sebastian's entrance in 5.1, was comically deferred: Sebastian entered through the audience and Viola, seeing him from the stage, hurried towards him, expecting an immediate rapturous recognition. Instead, assuming her to be a servant, he handed her his walking stick while he addressed first Olivia and then Antonio. When we finally saw the elaborately protracted recognition of brother and sister, it got the applause of deferred gratification.

The second false ending occurred when Viola's identity had been revealed and Olivia issued a general invitation to a double wedding. Orsino burst into song, which developed into what seemed like a closing number, and everyone started to pack up the stage. Malvolio came through the audience, a walking afterthought at first unnoticed, completely out of tune with what had gone before. Fabian's explanation of the plot against Malvolio led to another false ending. While some productions (notably John Barton's at the RSC in 1970) make the most of every opportunity to prepare for Maria's marriage to Sir Toby, it was clear in the Globe production that Fabian was trying to save Maria from being punished, first by insisting that Sir Toby was the main mover and, with a sudden inspiration, adding that the two were married, an idea that clearly startled both of them. A sense of improvisation seems right both for this play and for the Globe, where the outside world constantly impinges on the acting space and actors must be ready to deal with the unexpected.

MACBETH AT THE ALMEIDA

Indoor theatres, on the other hand, allow a more unified visual and aural experience, and Yaël Farber's *Macbeth* at the Almeida showed directorial control at its best. This is a play that I usually find unsatisfactory on stage: the greyness of Macbeth's life after the murder seems to transfer itself to the theatrical experience. Farber made it consistently gripping, by turning it into the kind of play everyone wishes it were. The Almeida's publicity described the production's setting as 'A little later than now, in the ruins of a theatre'. Though the minimalist set did not look theatrical to me, it could be called elemental, with the sure and firm-set earth supporting a fire; there was a water pipe at which characters washed their hands and which eventually flooded the stage; at the beginning there was also a supply of air on which the elderly, wheezing Duncan appeared dependent. It seems to have disappeared with his death, leaving a suffocating atmosphere.

Unlike the other productions of this year, with their gender-swapping and gender ambiguity, this *Macbeth* strongly emphasized gender difference. The men, including James McArdle's Macbeth, were mainly large and muscular, and the Scots speech gave a meaty quality to their lines. In the first part of the play, McArdle was a commanding figure and when, at the start of the banquet scene, he danced with his wife to the sound of Vera Lynn singing 'We'll meet again', there was a brief glimpse of the dream that they had worked together to fulfil.

Yet the women were almost a different species: Saoise Ronan's blonde Lady Macbeth, Akiya Henry's dark Lady Macduff, and the onstage cellist, Aiofe Burke, who also played the Gentlewoman. Lady Macduff was present, with her children (older than usual), almost from the beginning. At a banquet table presided over by Duncan, she sang 'Come away', a song from Middleton's *The Witch*, though with haunting new music by Tom Lane; it seems to be referenced in *Macbeth* (hence the argument that the latter was revised by him between Shakespeare's death and its publication in the 1623 Folio). Farber also created a new relationship when Lady Macduff, again with her children, gently comforted their sobbing hostess after the discovery of Duncan's murder. The Macbeths' loss of a child was hinted at only subtly, in the way that Lady Macbeth looked at Fleance and at the Macduff children.

There were no sinister female figures. Rebecca Tomas's programme note argues that James I's misogynistic fear of witchcraft had led Shakespeare to give the three impersonal fates the characteristics of witches as the popular imagination saw them. Restoring what she considered their real nature, Farber called them Wyrd Sisters; the three women in men's suits who appeared at the beginning of this play were sexless rather than bisexual. They were often silent presences in the scenes of other characters.

Farber rarely changed Shakespeare's words; rather, she redistributed them, particularly to show the mutual dependence of Macbeth and his wife. Although Lady Macbeth's first soliloquy is addressed to Macbeth, he is not usually on stage at the time; here, he entered immediately after her reading of the letter, and she advised him directly. Again, when his admission that he had killed the grooms was followed by a silence heavy with suspicion, it was she who leaped in to defend him in words that belong to him in the text. He talked to her, also, in scenes where she is not usually present, and even after her death.

He also told her of his intention to kill Macduff's whole family, and she was given the lines and role of the anonymous character who unsuccessfully urges Lady Macduff to flee just before the murderers arrive. She remained on stage throughout these protracted and vicious murders, seeing everything, yet the murderers seemed not to see her; I wondered whether the scene might be happening only in her mind. After the sleepwalking scene, she was visible on her bed at the back of the stage, from which she (and only she) heard Lady Macduff's song, 'Come away'. At the words, 'We lack but you', she rose from her bed and went to join the dead. In the rest of the play, McArdle's fine performance as the crumbling and increasingly brutalized king of the play was set against an all-male world. The final image, with the entire cast on stage, repeated the opening one, as well as the opening line, 'When shall we all meet again?' The replacement of 'three' by 'all' was the one significant change to the play's language. Fleance, whose father had showed him how to use a gun and who had fled the murder scene only because he heard 'Thou may'st revenge', stood, fully armed, in a spotlight.

The undercutting of any sense of a happy ending is not unusual these days, and the most successful productions of the last fifty years have been those that emphasized, like this one, the relationship of the central couple. On reflection, I was struck by the resemblance beween Farber's 21st-century adaptation and William Davenant's Restoration one: he too developed the relationship between Macbeth and his wife, created an important role for Lady Macduff, and, possibly influenced by Middleton before him, extended the musical part of the play, since music controls audience response more effectively than the spoken word. He even offered an implicit condemnation of a male world of war and brutality, since his Lady Macduff is a pacifist who says that 'The world mistakes the glories gain'd in war.' I am not suggesting that Farber was influenced by Davenant. Davenant rewrote extensively; Farber changed almost nothing verbally; both, however, reflect a common dissatisfaction with the play as it exists, and it will be interesting to see whether other directors follow some of the textual transpositions that made this such an interesting production.

HAMLET AT THE YOUNG VIC

By contrast with the mainly chiaroscuro world of *Macbeth*, Greg Hersov's *Hamlet* at the Young Vic dressed the characters for the most part in bright colours and lit them brightly too, with no attempt at atmosphere or a sense of the supernatural. The performance was long, despite heavy cutting, but never dragged. However, perhaps because it was not a 'concept production', no one seemed to know quite what to make of it. Cush Jumbo played

Hamlet as male, and looked convincingly male. Some reviewers found her sympathetic, while others assumed that the character was being portrayed negatively; no one seemed sure whether he was really mad.

Like the First Quarto (which it followed in placing 'To be or not to be' early in the play), Hersov's version seemed primarily interested in the characters' relationships. Our sense of Hamlet's character came primarily through the kinds of people he chose as his friends. He seemed to have liked the company of trendy students (the female Rosencrantz and male Guildenstern), but what Ophelia and Horatio had in common was a sort of unpretentious, almost klutzy, goodness. Horatio (Jonathan Livingstone) was comic in his confusion about how to address a ghost and his reluctance to take the oath in blood for which Hamlet asks. He looked as poor as Hamlet says he is (I wondered if he was a university dropout that Hamlet had found on the streets), but he was a totally devoted friend. For the very young Ophelia (Norah Lopez Holden), he was obviously a first love; she might have been his first too. Like other young relationships, it seemed to have developed largely through music. We were given a brief glimpse of her dancing with him, a dance which might have been happening in the present, in her memory or even in her fantasy. After *The Mousetrap*, he went wild and, to raucous music, tried to drag her into another dance.

Nearly all the reviews were negative about Adrian Dunbar and Tara Fitzgerald, the Claudius and Gertrude, but it was hard for them to project authority with so little context. It might have been easier for them to play their roles in the corporation setting that has become something of a cliché of modern-dress productions. We were not in Denmark or anywhere in particular, there wasn't much of a court, and the time was the present or something like it. What was clear was that, for the young people, the older generation were irrelevances, and the latter were puzzled by their own inability to understand the young – something that came out most clearly in the carefully detailed Polonius of Joseph Marcell. This highly experienced actor succeeded in showing both the pompous father that his children ridiculed and the father that he saw himself as being, concerned for his children's welfare. It was possible to believe in 'the poison of deep grief' (4.5.74) that his death inflicted on both Ophelia and Laertes. I also enjoyed Leo Wringer as the Gravedigger (there was only one). But there was something so low-key about much of the production that, like other reviewers, I was left with little real impression of it. Perhaps the mirrored sides which the stage pillars sometimes turned to the audience were a way of telling us that the play's characters were not larger-than-life beings but ordinary people in which we could see ourselves.

Even the livestream of the production, which extended its audience exponentially, allowed for multiple interpretations. Viewers could choose which camera's view to share, or, for a more conventionally edited film version, see the 'director's cut'. Like the *Hamlet* with Ian McKellen, which had ended its run at the Theatre Royal in Windsor immediately before the Old Vic one opened, this production ended with Horatio's 'Goodnight, sweet prince'. In both cases, it felt unfinished.

MEASURE FOR MEASURE AT THE WANAMAKER

As the start of the Globe's winter season (to be joined in 2022 by *Hamlet* and *The Merchant of Venice*), *Measure for Measure* was billed as a study of the individual's search for justice in a corrupt society. In her previous Globe production, *Bartholomew Fair*, Blanche McIntyre had changed the configuration of the theatre and kept the lights on, but on her return she found ways of making effective use of the theatre's famous candlelight. Those who paid attention to the advance publicity would have known that the play had been set in the 1970s, the era of the three-day week and frequent power cuts, so, after about 5 minutes of electric lighting, the stage was plunged into darkness, servants rushed on to light the chandeliers, and the rest of the play took place by candlelight, which aided the plot of disguise, mistaken identity and moral dilemmas.

When Angelo made his blackmailing proposal to Isabella, she held a candelabra up to his face as she tried to blackmail him in return, and he blew out the candles as he replied, 'Who will believe thee, Isabel?' Even when the Duke returned to Vienna, the lights did not come back on. The reason may have been purely technical, but, in the context of this production, it may have been making a point about the character's lack of power.

Casting Hattie Ladbury as the Duke (Figure 17, played as female, with female pronouns) was obviously going to create problems for an already problematic character, especially at the end; Lucio refers to the Duke as 'a shy fellow' and Ladbury created a shy lady (a spinster rather than a widow) prone to nervous giggles, as when she was explaining her disguise plans to Friar Thomas and when, having told Juliet that her sin was 'heavier' than her lover's, she realized that the adjective had a double meaning in the context of the young woman's advanced pregnancy. Having got off to a bad start in her Friar impersonation, she made matters worse by her insensitivity in telling Juliet that Claudio was about to be executed, something that the Provost was trying to keep secret. Looking variously like a member of the royal family or a fusion of Margaret Thatcher and Theresa May, she might have been illustrating women's difficulty in being accepted as authority figures. Or, indeed, their difficulty in accepting themselves in such roles: in her singsong delivery of the final rhyming couplets of her soliloquy at the end of 3.1, she seemed to be sending up her own creaky plot.

How this neurotic woman developed into the competent authority figure of the final scene was not easy to understand: she did not show any erotic attraction to Isabella. The macho Lucio, Gyuri Sarossi, was obviously making his claims of inside knowledge about her sex life on the assumption that any unmarried woman must, of course, be a lesbian. So did the Duke decide to avoid media speculation by giving herself a recognizable partner? Did she simply decide that she would benefit from seeing more of a person with such an uncompromising moral sense? McIntyre cut the explicit proposal of marriage that the Duke makes to Isabella immediately after Claudio's appearance, so that the only indication of her wishes was the ambiguous statement:

17 Hattie Ladbury as the Duke, in *Measure for Measure*, Sam Wanamaker Playhouse © Helen Murray.

> I have a motion much imports your good,
> Whereto, if you'll a willing ear incline,
> What's mine is yours, and what is yours is mine.
>
> (5.1.533–5)

After sending everyone else off to 'our palace', she remained on stage with Isabella and leaned towards her, waiting for a reply. What exactly was Isabella being asked to do? This might in fact be what she herself was about to ask: she too was leaning forward as the lights went down. The company then performed one of the best final jigs I have ever seen at either the Globe or Wanamaker, as if to say that we could now forget all the problems thrown up by the play.

Hattie Ladbury died from cancer only a few weeks after the play's run ended, a fact that inevitably cast her performance in a retrospective light, or shadow, and perhaps explained why the Duke's role dominated the play, and the characters of Isabella and Angelo, more than it usually does. When Isabella (Georgia Landers) chose to support Mariana at the end, her decision was firmly logical ('His act did not o'ertake his bad intent': 5.1.448), not an indication of a change in her view of life; Angelo (Ashley Zhangazha) was a harsh authoritarian who became an uncomplicated villain when his appetite was awakened. The production made up for the relative simplification of some of the characters by giving everyone except the already doubled Duke an opportunity to display versatility in playing another part. There were particularly fine examples of virtuoso doubling from Eloise Secker (Pompey and Mariana) and Ishia Bennison, who got applause after her initial turn as Barnardine because spectators recognized that she had just given her *fourth* performance; her other roles were Escalus, Francisca and Mistress Overdone. (They also noticed with pleasure that Barnardine's brief appearance in the final scene was made possible by a dummy.) There were obvious financial reasons for the smallness of the cast but, thematically, the doubling was in keeping with the play's occasional implication that identity can shift in shifting circumstances.

So vulnerability – ours and the actors' – has dominated even this period of recovery. There was a time when I went to a Shakespeare production expecting to get new insights into the play; now, almost always, I find that I am learning about the current state of the theatre, which, at the moment, means a practical emphasis on spectators' safety and the company's lack of money, alongside an ideological commitment to diversity of all kinds in the production's personnel. Successful productions can treat these imperatives as opportunities. But they are also distractions.

A final note: all the productions that I have been describing are, or will be, available to watch at some point, which means that those who read my review can check its accuracy. Of course, I can always claim that things happened slightly differently at the performance I saw; nevertheless, I am becoming aware that some of what I always thought a review should do – describe and interpret a performance for those who were not able to see it – has probably become unnecessary. I may have to do some serious rethinking about this job.

PETER KIRWAN, *Productions Outside London*

Advertising the company's 2021 tour of its three-person *Romeo and Juliet*, The Handlebards cheekily embraced the comical–tragical paradoxes of performing Shakespeare during an ongoing pandemic. Artwork featuring a masked Juliet (Lucy Green) and Romeo (Paul Moss) snogging passionately through two layers of fabric (Figure 18) acted as a neat encapsulation of a theatre returning to business, but not yet to business as usual. It also, to indulge in an over-reading, visualized the sense of being so near yet so far, a gratification muted by the necessary compromises that allowed in-person Shakespeare to take place in a limited capacity. But this photograph is also a reminder of the creative and self-reflexive ways in which companies worked to make Shakespeare happen around the country, complementing the rich vein of born-digital Shakespeare productions that continued throughout the year.

While physical theatres remained dark for the most of the first half of 2021, Shakespeare persisted. *Romeo and Juliet* dominated in almost every format: the live choose-your-own-adventure Zoom-based production of Creation Theatre; a film shot by the National Theatre in its rehearsal spaces; and an intriguing but disastrously realized theatre–film hybrid by Metcalfe Gordon Productions that filmed actors separately in a theatre space and superimposed them onto the same image. The proliferation of *Romeo and Juliet*s was perhaps inevitable in an ongoing time of separation of loved ones, interrupted deliveries (not least as the impacts of Brexit made themselves increasingly felt) and anxieties over public health. Yet the affordances of Zoom and other communications technology also allowed for a rich online offering of staged readings, archival releases and live digital productions. Physical theatres in England, though, remained dark.

By the end of 2021, London theatres had largely reopened their doors, with major new productions of *Hamlet* at the Young Vic and *Macbeth* at the Almeida, as well as a full season of new productions at Shakespeare's Globe. But for in-person Shakespeare in the rest of England, it was a different story. Monologues, staged readings and short new plays for small casts were preferred as regional theatres tested the waters to see whether audiences would feel safe returning to their buildings, and there appeared to be little appetite for assembling companies of the scale needed for full-length Shakespeare productions. The London-adjacent Theatre Royal Windsor bucked the trend with a heavily promoted and starrily cast *Hamlet*, but the watchword elsewhere was caution. The Royal Shakespeare Company abandoned a planned *Pericles*, but eventually put together a striking programme of work that never put audiences and actors in the same building, but which showed welcome innovation and investment in new ways of producing Shakespeare. And if it took a lot of work to see a Shakespeare show outside of London under a roof, public parks and town squares provided welcome venues for the network of touring open-air Shakespeare companies that continued undaunted through the summer months, providing a safer alternative for those longing to be part of a physical audience.

OLD HAMLET

From the moment that Theatre Royal Windsor's recently appointed artistic director, Sean Mathias, announced that he would be producing *Hamlet* with Ian McKellen in the title role, the production was able to coast on its own publicity. As a programming move, this was canny, drawing global attention to the theatre's new creative vision (though, as of December 2021, the website no

18 The Handlebards, *Romeo and Juliet*, publicity art. Photography by Rah Petherbridge.

longer advertises an association with Mathias) and ensuring enviable ticket sales. Further, the production generated no end of media discussion. Much of this was regrettable, as backstage tensions led to the last-minute replacement of Steven Berkoff with Frances Barber as Polonius (and Barber herself then immediately becoming embroiled in social media feuds when she was called out for transphobic and Islamophobic remarks she had previously made), casting something of a cloud over early performances. But, more obviously, the production fuelled debates about casting in the theatre's appropriation of what it called an 'age, colour and gender-blind' approach. Even in its dated language to try and explain its choices, the production felt out of step with the times even before it opened.

Strategies of non-traditional casting are, fundamentally, designed to rebalance onstage representation and address historical exclusions. Here, the pledge to disregard age, race and gender served as justification for allowing traditionally privileged groups to dominate the stage. With the exception of Laertes (Ashley D. Gayle), all of the major parts were played by white actors, and predominantly ones in late-middle or old age. While there was more diversity in supporting roles, the Theatre Royal's approach of using language designed to redress power imbalances felt disingenuous at best. While the production can lay a claim to history in the casting of the oldest actor known to have played Hamlet, the attempt to give an artistic rationale for the casting felt like retrospective special pleading. The theatre wanted a bankable name playing a bankable part, and it got it. For the first time in a British theatre in years, I found myself part of an audience that gave an ovation to the cast when they entered at the start of the first scene; no further work was required of the production.

Disappointingly, the production had few ideas beyond its casting, and no coherent vision. One casting choice seems emblematic of the production's issues: Francesca Annis as the Ghost. Annis had played Juliet to McKellen's Romeo for the RSC back in 1976, and their onstage reunion was picked up by much of the advance commentary. Yet, having cast Annis, the production than decimated the Ghost's role. Act 1, scene 1 was cut in its entirety, and the Ghost remained off stage during McKellen's confrontation with Gertrude in her closet, with only one pre-recorded line evoking the Ghost's presence. While the Ghost was given a spectacular entrance via trapdoor for its sole scene with Hamlet, the actual scene itself was performed with the two actors standing still at opposite ends of an overhead gantry, Annis barely visible to the audience. There may be any number of reasons why the production chose to limit Annis's onstage visibility, but the overwhelming impression was of someone having had a cool idea for a headline but no idea what to do with it, of a casting and rehearsal process with little thought for the consequences of its choices.

In December 2021, Lyn Gardner published a piece asking what was wrong with Shakespeare productions in the UK. Contributing to her article, my answer was the tendency of both productions and critics to focus on 'the delivery of individual actors and how they performed their part, rather than examining what the production is doing as a cohesive whole'.[1] What I did not speculate on further within that piece is whether this tendency in some (not all) Shakespeare productions may be, or may have been in the case of *Hamlet*, exaggerated by rehearsal conditions during the pandemic. I cannot know what happened during the development of *Hamlet*, but the overwhelming impression at the performance I attended was of performers working in isolation, at least in the lead roles. The production opened with the whole ensemble walking on stage together in a line, dressed for an outdoor funeral and raising umbrellas. But as they went their separate ways at the end of this opening scene (1.2), the characters' various journeys trapped them in self-contained set-pieces with their own aesthetic and tone. The generic set – a series of gantries and stairways, with two banks of onstage seats for audiences who wished to pay extra for an intimate encounter with the cast – lacked even a spatial coherence, with actors entering and exiting from all directions in ways that left this Elsinore feeling like an open plan barn, and at times implied that Jonathan Hyde's Claudius held court in a tiny basement. The onstage audience, too, were ill-served by a gimmick that left them unable to see any of the action – including most of McKellen's big soliloquies – that took place on the gantries directly above their seats.

The chief affordance of casting an older man as Hamlet was the authority that he carried. Combining McKellen's age and star quality meant that McKellen's Hamlet was treated with unusual deference by those around him. Hamlet was measured, thoughtful, restrained. The effect was extended further by breaking up key speeches; his first soliloquy, for example, was interrupted after a few lines for a scene change, continuing as he arrived back in his own quarters to begin training on an exercise as he mused 'Frailty, thy name is woman'. Similarly, 'To be or not to be' was played as a single-scene speech, as Hamlet sat in a chair while Ben Allen's Horatio shaved his head. Excerpting the soliloquies in this way might perhaps be an after-effect of McKellen's 2019 one-man national tour, during which he celebrated his eightieth birthday by performing selections of speeches interspersed with anecdote. Within the context of the production, the choice placed even more emphasis than usual on Hamlet's thought process, the soliloquies acting as heavily marked punctuation that slowed down the flow of the play and emphasized the planning that went into this Hamlet's decisions. Hamlet's violence towards those he targeted, in this light, became colder. He did not touch Alis Wyn Davies's Ophelia

---

[1] Lyn Gardner, 'Staging Shakespeare: is too much reverence holding UK theatremakers back?' *The Stage*, 2 December 2021: www.thestage.co.uk/long-reads/long-reads/staging-shakespeare-is-too-much-reverence-holding-uk-theatre makers-back.

during the nunnery scene, but instead devastated her verbally from a distance. Conversely, when Rosencrantz pleaded with Hamlet following 'The Mousetrap' to remember the love they once shared, Hamlet grabbed his friend's crotch, a possessive and entitled gesture of control that was genuinely shocking.

However, while the slowness and deliberation of McKellen's Hamlet allowed for some indulgently resonant readings of key speeches, it also arrested any forward momentum the production managed to build up. It was unclear what any of the characters were trying to achieve. Hyde worked hard as Claudius to show the new King trying to consolidate his power while also wrestling with his own guilt, and when he was alone on stage – as in the excellent praying scene, in which Hyde expertly demonstrated the torment that Claudius feels before swallowing and committing to his present gain – the production sang. But in a production deprived of the Ghost or any sense of the court of Denmark, Hyde's performance felt like it was taking place in a vacuum. Similarly, there was clearly an idea behind the presentation of Wyn Davies's Ophelia as a wannabe folk singer, but such a distinctive identity felt anomalous against a stark and undifferentiated cultural backdrop. Wyn Davies performed the mad scenes as a short concert, her speeches turned into planned songs that projected anger and sorrow at the King and Queen; but the choice to make her madness into something so planned and articulate was unsupported by anything in her surrounding scenes.

The production felt, in fact, like it was awaiting Gayle's return. When Laertes entered and marched across the stage to confront Claudius, the production suddenly found its sense of purpose, and Laertes's anger became the directional force around which the remainder of the production coalesced. Perversely, for all the production was advertised around McKellen, the dramatic centre made this Laertes's tragedy more than Hamlet's, a choice which seemed to be as much of a surprise to the company as it was to me. Gayle's confident performance was one of the few among the main cast that was targeted towards the other performers, that demanded direct response and interaction, rather than turning outwards towards the audience and excerption. This was mirrored in the supporting performances; the Players and Gravediggers, for example, felt like miniature, gelled ensembles with a physical interplay and collaborative approach that rendered moments like the dumbshow before 'The Mousetrap' or the dialogue between the Gravediggers far more interesting than the rest of the production.

This was not without its ideas. A recurrent motif focused on hair: Hamlet had his head partly shaved in order to play mad, and Ophelia shaved her own head in her madness. Gertrude (played by Jenny Seagrove with the only Scandinavian accent in the play) had her wig torn off during the nunnery scene, and she threw it down at Claudius's feet at the end of the scene rather than replacing it. With hair as a marker of transforming identity, the production gestured towards the possibility of a bodily reading of distress and trauma, though this possibility never developed beyond a gesture. More frustrating was the directorial incompetence throughout. Polonius, Claudius and Gertrude were all pushed into extreme downstage corners for their deaths in ways that crowded crucial action in areas that were largely obscured from the audience; in the case of Polonius, the decision seemed to be driven by a lack of confidence in how to get Frances Barber off stage following Polonius's murder. Once more, this felt emblematic of larger problems with a production that had made its choices without forethought, and then was left trying to work out how, literally and figuratively, to get itself out of the corners it had trapped itself in. In the rush to get a production back on stage so soon after theatres were allowed to open their doors, we perhaps got not the *Hamlet* we wanted, but the one we deserved.

OPEN THEATRE AT THE RSC

The RSC did not rush its return to live performance, but instead used the hiatus of lockdown to experiment with different means of bringing

Shakespeare to audiences. One of the most ambitious of these, if not entirely successful, was *Dream*, a virtual reality (VR) motion-captured production. Performed live by actors in a VR studio, the sparse narrative imagined Puck (EM Williams) as a floating group of animated stones who roamed a CGI forest landscape, searching for the other fairies as the forest descended into ecological catastrophe. Little other than the names of the fairies connected this 30-minute production to Shakespeare, but it acted as a fascinating proof-of-concept for digital performance. The surrealistic forest and inspired character designs (Cobweb was a single, terrifying eye staring out at Puck from a cranny in a tree), and the climactic storm that saw the spirits gathered together and then destroyed in a bleak depiction of the consequences of deforestation and climate change, all showed the potential for future development in this area. As a piece of theatre, though, it was dull, playing more like a demo screen for a computer game than something entertaining in its own right. A much-trumpeted interactive element – which allowed viewers to touch their screens to guide Puck with lights – was an abject failure, with no connection apparent between viewers' actions and what was seen on screen, and the script was sparse and gnomic (though given gravitas by the coup of casting Nick Cave as The Voice of the Forest). Developing the company's experiments in live performance capture, *Dream* was a curio, and at least allowed for audiences to begin gathering together again in synchronous time.

The company's output during 2021 could be seen as a series of experiments in identifying what the RSC's value actually is. Erica Whyman's *Winter's Tale* was a full-scale production mounted in the Royal Shakespeare Theatre, and was the production that looked most like a traditional RSC offering, but was performed without any live audience and released on television as a pre-recorded theatrical film. Phillip Breen's *The Comedy of Errors* had the distinction of having a brand-new theatre built for it, the impressive Lydia & Manfred Gorvy Garden Theatre in the gardens immediately outside the Swan Theatre, allowing for actors and audiences to share a space under the sun and stars, before the production went on tour to more traditional indoor spaces. And, in an especially bold move, Gregory Doran and Owen Horsley reimagined the first part of their planned *Henry VI* sequence as an open rehearsal process, resulting in what I argue is the company's most interesting work in years.

The screen director for *The Winter's Tale* was Bridget Caldwell, who is the first female broadcast director I am aware of who has been hired by a major British theatre to remediate its stage productions. Caldwell's background is mainly in large-scale television capture of public events, from the Proms to Margaret Thatcher's funeral and the reinternment of Richard III, and she was a canny decision for a production that showed marked interest in the circumstances of its own remediation. Set in 1953 and 1969, the production recalled the remediation technologies of that period. Hermione's trial (Figure 19), with the Queen placed on a high podium in front of a wall of bars, was set up as a piece of state theatre. Onstage cameras gave Leontes a captive audience, and the production shifted to the grainy black-and-white point of view of those cameras throughout the trial. Leontes, showing a Prince Philip-like interest in the potential of this new remediating technology, interposed himself between Hermione and the cameras; whenever Hermione's powerful, sincere, self-possessed pleas threatened to become too persuasive, he approached the camera directly, obscuring her from view, and spoke into it, ensuring that his gloss on events was privileged over her oratory. Later, in a North East-accented Bohemia, revellers at the sheep-shearing captured their festivities on an early home video camera, with a confident Perdita, in the flush of sixties flower power, flirting with the camera as she leaned into her role as mistress of the feast. Across the production, the characters of *The Winter's Tale* showed a mid-twentieth-century awareness of themselves as mediated subjects, exploring their relationship to the technologies that would preserve them for all time, and perhaps raising the stakes for those who

19 Hermione (Kemi-Bo Jacobs) on trial in *The Winter's Tale*, dir. Erica Whyman. Photograph by Topher McGrillis, © RSC.

knew they may one day be held accountable for their present choices.

While Lucy Bailey directed a touring production for the RSC in 2013, *The Winter's Tale* has had relatively few productions by female directors, and Whyman's take on the play felt like a corrective in parts in its evisceration of the play's patriarchal power structures. At the production's heart was a reinvention of the Bear as an explicitly feminist revenge fantasy. As the action shifted to Bohemia, Antigonus (Colin Gormley) found himself standing at the centre of a ring of fans, cradling Perdita in his arms while five women approached him from upstage, walking backwards towards him in an ominous and threatening gesture. As they turned to face him, the women slashed their arms towards him, sending Antigonus reeling. As he was killed, a large sheet descended and hovered in mid-air, floating in the wind of the fans, until Hermione stepped forward, pulled the sheet down, and deftly reconstructed it as a bundle that became Perdita. This second birth for Perdita, remade in Bohemia, acted as a reclamation of the child from the violence of Sicilia and the actions of weak men, and suggested a providential historical force that would seek to protect Perdita and, by extension, work against a failing patriarchy.

The weakness of men was epitomized in Joseph Kloska's Leontes. Kloska had one of the most difficult jobs in the context of this production's circumstances, given that Leontes spends so much of his first few scenes in soliloquy/self-reverie, and that Kloska did not have a live audience to play to. This resulted in an awkwardly compromised performance. At times Kloska simply bellowed to the auditorium, giving a performance that felt too large too soon for the camera and flattened out the nuances of his exploration of Leontes's jealousy. At other times, Kloska played directly to the camera, inviting the audience in as confidant. Here, though, the camera became too complicit. At one point, the camera even went for a close-up to show Hermione (Kemi-Bo Jacobs) and Polixenes (Andrew French) holding hands, a gesture that Leontes himself was unable to see, as if the camera had decided to help Leontes to make his case and offer independent verification. But all this Leontes was able to do was gesture impotently. Nobody seemed cowed by him: Hermione stared him directly in the face when denying his accusations, Paulina talked rings around him, and even Camillo talked back to his master without apparent fear. All that Leontes had was the respect accorded him as king, which seemed unquestionable, but Whyman and Kloska pushed as far as possible the inadequacy and ineffectiveness of this Leontes. His awareness of this ineffectiveness was what pushed him towards more abhorrent actions; in an especially shocking moment, when Perdita's crib was placed on the stage, Leontes kicked it hard and sent it flying; fortunately, Perdita herself was by this point being cradled by one of the gentlemen.

This Leontes should have been easily dissuaded from his actions, but in Whyman's reading, the only people strong enough to do so were women, and women could be ignored. The men around Leontes were unable to stop him, for instance, from grabbing Perdita's head in a vice-like grip, and even as Antigonus attempted to speak reasonably to Leontes, he himself indulged in sighing at the outspokenness of his wife, Paulina (Amanda Hadingue). Women had no problems speaking out. Paulina strode with confidence across the stage to confront Leontes, and showed no patience towards her husband. Hermione, too, showed none of the insecurity of her husband. From her podium during the trial, she ignored the camera and addressed those present, relying on her authority to persuade the people she could. Leontes's appeals to the camera betrayed his loss of confidence in his ability to command authority in his own person. Following the gap of time, too, the production returned to a much more peaceful Sicilia dominated by women (Cleomenes and Dion were both played by and as women), with a subdued Leontes now looking to the women around him for guidance and assurance. Yet the women were not reduced to simplistic paragons of strength; one of the most affecting moments came as Paulina, following Hermione's 'death', spent herself in castigating Leontes and then crumpled to quietly cry.

The Bohemian scenes struggled a little to create a festival atmosphere without an audience in the room, though a lively onstage band certainly worked to create energy. Bohemia – or at least the area of it we saw – was itself dominated by women, including Zoe Lambert as a regendered Shepherdess, and enlarged roles for Mopsa and Dorcas at the start of the Clown's encounter with Autolycus (Anne Odeke). Odeke took over Leontes's privilege with the camera, making jokey asides and acting as a kind of live documentarian of the festival. The festive camaraderie of this women-led festival was disrupted by the intrusion of Polixenes. Andrew French had played the character quietly in the Sicilia scenes, developing a gentlemanly affection with both Leontes and Hermione. But, in the context of his own kingdom, he showed his true colours, erupting into the festivities with a sudden roar of rage against his son for falling in love with Perdita that suggested that patriarchal entitlement was alive and well in Bohemia, even if it only revealed itself when men in authority felt threatened.

The contrast between a space of authoritarian male oppression and liberated female expressiveness, coded onto the starkness of 1950s England and the freedom of 60s free love, is a classic juxtaposition for *The Winter's Tale*. Within such a specific historical setting, though, the force of its critique of institutional misogyny for the present felt muted, as if second-wave feminism had successfully resolved these issues half a century ago. The more abstracted moments of feminist expression, such as the

20 The Lydia & Manfred Gorvy Garden Theatre. Photograph by Pete Le May, © RSC.

Bear, lacked the necessary context to extend their implications beyond the aesthetic, and the unusual prominence given to the engagement of Camillo and Paulina in the closing scene – for which the production slowed down and marked significance in a way that even Hermione's awakening did not quite manage – reinforced a conventional heteronormativity that Perdita's free sexual expression in Bohemia had suggested might not be the direction in which this production would pursue resolution. Notwithstanding, Whyman's production turned the empty auditorium of the RST at least momentarily into a crucible for examining the emptiness of fragile masculine authority, and offered a welcome feminist reading of the play.

Outside the RSC's buildings, on the banks of the Avon, the newly constructed Lydia & Manfred Gorvy Garden Theatre exchanged an empty theatre building for a closely gathered audience (Figure 20). The RSC's riverside spaces have regularly served as a venue for outdoor Shakespeare during the summer, with the cast of *The Comedy of Errors* performing Shakespeare-related skits during summer 2020 when rehearsals for the original run were cancelled. However, the Garden Theatre allowed for something on a much more impressive scale. Modelled after Greek auditoria, with a raked audience stand curving around a raised circular stage, the theatre allowed 500 spectators to gather for each performance in the open air, and created a much-needed focal space for Stratford-upon-Avon during the summer of 2021.

Where the Windsor *Hamlet* had professed 'blindness' to its cast, Breen capitalized on the distinctive qualities of his diverse cast. Perhaps most notably, and in a much needed gesture towards more equitable working practices, the production featured a pregnant actor, Hedydd Dylan, in the role of Adrianna. Rather than try to hide Dylan's pregnancy – or, worse, recast the role – Breen and Dylan instead built the role around Dylan's pregnancy, allowing the actor's body to create meaning within the production; then, as the production later toured around the country, the RSC enabled Dylan to continue performing for as long as possible by turning the role into a job-share with another actor, Naomi Sheldon, until she went

21 Adrianna (Hedydd Dylan) in *The Comedy of Errors*, dir. Phillip Breen. Photograph by Pete Le May, © RSC.

on maternity leave.[2] Having Adrianna visibly pregnant was transformative on the play, making Antipholus of Ephesus's philandering seem even more cruel. Antipholus was abandoning his family responsibilities and his imminent fatherhood, while a neglected and physically uncomfortable Adrianna stewed at home. As such, Adrianna's extraordinarily explosive outbursts at her husband evoked not the nagging wife, but the terrified mother-to-be, furious at her husband but also desperate not to lose him, cradling her belly as she asked if age had made her ugly (Figure 21). While this at times seemed to play too far into tropes of the Hysterical Pregnant Woman, with gathered crowds backing away fearfully as she raged at Antipholus of Syracuse in a restaurant, the pregnancy meant that the comedy of the relationship was escalated by the sense of a family in jeopardy.

The Comedy of Errors was set in the 1980s in an unnamed Arab state, at the meeting point of East and West. The ethnicity of actors was key to interpreting characters' roles within this cosmopolitan, oil-rich Ephesus. The military uniforms and rich trappings of Solinus and his guards established that the city was run by a quasi-dictatorship, but one with aims of wooing the West. Most of the action was set in and around an enormous new hotel, with celebrities and the world's media gathering for a grand ribbon-cutting. Russian mafiosi mixed with Western tourists heading for the mall, while the locals served dinner in fancy restaurants or arranged deals for hard-to-obtain goods with new arrivals. There were instances in which the production felt indulgent in its stereotypes; the idea that Solinus would be trying to court the West while also ordering for Egeon to be executed in public by a man with a machete pointed to inconsistencies in the politics of this imagined state, with choices instead seeming to draw on white-centred assumptions about the Middle East. But the main affordance of the setting was its sending-up of ideas of white privilege.

---

[2] Vanessa Thorpe, 'It's a family show: actors with new babies job-share leading role', *Observer*, 12 December 2021: www.theguardian.com/stage/2021/dec/12/its-a-family-show-actors-with-new-babies-job-share-leading-roles.

A doo-wop chorus of four singers created the aural environment for the show, moving about the stage and singing during scene changes. At one point, they named the core thematic interest of the show, as they sang together the word 'Capitalism!' The Westernization of this state was most obvious in the shopping bags being carried by almost everyone, back and forth, translating the mercantilism and object exchange of the play into a consumer culture that threatened homogeneity. In this world, the white Antipholus of Ephesus (Rowan Polanski) and Adrianna played as privileged ex-pats. Antipholus had a position of some authority within the state, his whiteness perhaps useful to Nicholas Prasad's Solinus, with Antipholus particularly prominent as a host and speaker at the ribbon-cutting ceremony for the new hotel that opened the play's second half. But this privileged status, the couple living in a protected bubble of wealth, also fuelled disrespect for the local population, used by Antipholus for procuring goods and sex. Antipholus swiped his hotel key confidently to try and get into his own apartment; and when he could not get access, his revenge was to go and buy gifts for the Courtesan; the power and influence he wielded was inseparable from his purchasing ability, and his ostentatious display of wealth was coupled with his privileged access to the spaces of the city. When the two (apparently frequently) had their public bust-ups, treating public spaces as their own, the dignified locals exchanged glances, waited for the fight to end, and then got on with their business. This dignity contrasted, of course, with the image of the locals expounded by Antipholus of Syracuse – of their being sorcerers and witches. Any evil here was that which white tourists and settlers had brought with them, along with their money.

The centring of a farce on the relatively few white characters neatly reversed stereotypes about faces of people of colour being interchangeable with one another; for the people of Ephesus, in many ways, it did not really matter which Antipholus or which Dromio they were encountering, as what they were engaging with was white entitlement and the tourist dollar. But the two sets of twins here led to the breaking of two inviolable laws of capitalism. Firstly, it meant that transactions went incomplete. Two economies were overlaid, one on top of the other, here: the instant purchases of the malls and hotels, in which wealth and goods immediately changed hands; and the more informal barter economy of the marketplace, complicated further by the black market of the Russians. Every time a promise of payment was accepted in lieu of actual payment, the production added another failed economic exchange to its tally, and the consequences of these failed exchanges ranged from the bringing out of guns and knuckle dusters by the Russian Second Merchant and his intimidating bodyguard (William Grint and Dyfrig Morris) to the appeal to marketplace constables, to the shutting down of electronic access to the private spaces protected by capital interests. The second law of capitalism that the twins challenged was the notion of individual wealth. Mistaken identity here became identity theft, and it was this that particularly threatened Antipholus of Ephesus, whose identity was so wrapped up in his money. From the moment he could not access his own flat, his dissociation from his economic privilege began, and over the course of the production he became an increasingly unhinged exemplar of failed capitalism, his wealth doing nothing to protect him when he could no longer access his purchasing power. By the final scene, with bloodied face, bitter snarl and bound hands, he was the voice of an upturned system of values, and found himself in the position of not-having that his wealth normally necessitated in others. But his pleas for redress were drowned out by the cacophony of other victims of failed capitalism also appealing to Solinus; the dissolution of individual capital owing to thwarted exchanges meant that only collective redress could be offered.

This is to read the production seriously, but this *Comedy of Errors* succeeded predominantly by being very funny. The ineffectiveness of capitalism was perhaps most beautifully realized when Antipholus and Dromio of Syracuse struggled to unwrap a gift knife block among their acquisitions in order to defend themselves. Dr Pinch (Alfred Clay) was a yoga teacher to the wealthy, leading Adrianna and Luciana through exercises while the two women gossiped with one another; later, though, when he tried to make a peaceful intervention in respect of Antipholus and was punched in the face for his efforts, Pinch threw aside all façade of enlightenment and launched himself bodily at his aggressor. The physical ensemble comedy was tight throughout, from silly sketches (a waiter whose toupee kept flopping down from his head, to the hilarity of the Syracusan twins who found ways to crowbar references to hair into their dialogue), to confused diners, to the international footballer who had been flown in to cut the ribbon for the hotel with an enormous pair of gold scissors, who was very unhappy to be there. The production offered a fourth-wall-breaking apology for the fatphobia of the Nell sequence, delivered as a set-piece stand-up routine into microphones, but this rather spoke of the production's failure to find a way of integrating this sequence; this was a sour note, though, in a production whose hard work with physical comedy created deep environments with richly populated scenes, and visual jokes that always paid off.

As in the best productions of this play, though, the comedy also led back to the play's thematic interests in togetherness and separation. The two Dromios, Jonathan Broadbent (Syracuse) and Greg Haiste (Ephesus), were unusually distinct from one another. Dromio of Syracuse was a confident, happy man with an amiable relationship with his master. Dromio of Ephesus, however, was worse for wear. He wore clothes slightly too big for him and shambled around; he also bore the marks of years of being beaten. Where the Syracusan Dromio was a witty observer of the world, the Ephesian Dromio spat his jokes out with anger and frustration, culminating when he grabbed a microphone to set out the historical abuses he had received at the hands of his master. This is not to suggest that Antipholus of Syracuse was a saint; indeed, when he finally raised his hand to both Dromios in turn, the production paused for a moment to show Antipholus's horror at what he had done, while also making clear how easy it was for a master–servant relationship to slip into violence, in a way that had clearly become normal for his Ephesian twin many years ago. The bringing together of the two very different Dromios allowed the production to end on a note of beauty. Antipholus of Ephesus was allowed a reconciliation with Adrianna, the two standing together and Antipholus lowering his hand to touch the belly containing his future child, returning to his family. But more powerful was Dromio of Syracuse gently removing a piece of rope from around his brother's hand before the two embraced, suggesting that their solidarity might allow one to help the other heal. In the only production in Stratford to bring audiences and actors together, the choice to end on a moment of physical, healing intimacy, an embrace between two long-lost family members, gestured towards a broader collective set of hopes about the end of lockdown.

In the RSC's circular, well-lit rehearsal room above the Swan Theatre, a very different kind of connection was formed in the *Henry VI, Part One Open Rehearsal Project* (Figure 22). Over a three-week period, an ensemble of actors rehearsed a cut-down version of the play, while a camera crew captured the process. Online audiences were invited to watch along in real time three times a day: the daily warm-up, a 90-minute lunchtime rehearsal, and a half-hour 6 p.m. 'green room chat' about the day's work. At the end of the three weeks, the company gave a live stagger-through of the whole play. The end result was one of the best events I saw all year.

The emphasis was on process. The talk throughout of the 'bravery' of the company exposing themselves in this way was, perhaps, a little overstated; after all, with no plans to go forward to a full production of *1 Henry VI*, the rehearsal *was* the end product, performed in large part specifically for the cameras. But the company did effectively manage to capture something of the realities of rehearsal. The warm-ups, in particular, often led to the oddly voyeuristic and faintly ridiculous situation of tuning in in order to watch actors lying on the floor

22 The ensemble in *Henry VI, Part One Open Rehearsal Project*, dir. Gregory Doran and Owen Horsley. Photograph by Ellie Kurtz, © RSC.

breathing quietly; there was not an attempt to make this especially camera-friendly or even entertaining, but for those of us rejoining the rehearsals day after day, it began introducing the actors and creative team, with sessions on movement or voice showing off the RSC's resources. The evening events, meanwhile, ranged from lectures by Stephen Greenblatt and Stuart Hampton-Reeves to talkbacks with actors. One event drew together five of the younger members of the ensemble to talk to the RSC's partner schools about their first experiences with Shakespeare and what they had been learning through this process, allowing actors in minor parts to talk movingly about their educational backgrounds (in one case, an actor reflecting on his homelessness) and also the sense of generational difference from other actors. I was particularly struck by this event, which not only felt surprisingly frank in its diagnosis of some of the issues of the weight of expectations that 'Shakespeare' carries with it, but also contained some rare exploration of minor roles, as in Liyah Summer's insights into the relative silence of the Bastard of Orleans and what that silence might mean in the character's scenes.

The real pleasure of this experiment, though, lay in the main rehearsals. Here, over three weeks, the play gradually took shape through close text work, exercises, conversations and stagger-throughs. Getting to see the play in the rehearsal room, moreover, without the usual polish of a finished production, drew attention to the core spatial principles of the production, resulting in an unusually coherent end product. The circular rehearsal room was set up with musicians and offstage actors around the edges and a few fixed points: a balcony structure for scenes above, a large heavy throne. As the cast performed, they approached the centre of the circle, which read as the centre of power; and *Part One* coalesced around a structural principle of fighting for the central position, with characters moving towards and away from that position as their fortunes wavered.

Objects shifted to the centre of the circle to create a clear focal point. The final run-through began with Henry V's coffin as the central point; later, the rose bush and the equipment case that served as the scaffold for Joan's execution took their turn in that spot. Proximity to that central point marked a character's relationship to it; Minnie Gale's Bedford, for instance, stood immediately next to her brother's coffin, while Winchester (Mark Hadfield) kept his distance. While this seemed immediately to suggest a straightforward hierarchy of power, Hadfield's distance from the coffin brilliantly exploited the other core locus of power in the rehearsal room: the camera. With the cameras positioned around the edges of the room, the play itself offered a different structural principle for establishing power through asides. In order to address the camera directly, actors moved away from the centre of the circle to the edges of the room, standing in between the camera and the main point of dramatic focus (as Leontes had done in Whyman's *Winter's Tale* during Hermione's trial) and assuming the privilege of direct address. The complication this offered was profound. While characters such as Talbot and Joan moved to the centre of the circle to draw attention to themselves and rally their troops, schemers like Winchester and Suffolk kept more to the edges, sharing their insights with the audience, and literally plotting from the sidelines. The push-and-pull of this structuring principle offered a simple but revelatory interpretation of the play, in which it was those who most effectively navigated these two power points, rather than simply those who went for the most powerful position, who ultimately came out on top. This is why Henry VI (Mark Quartley), dwarfed by the enormous throne he curled up in, felt so ineffective and boyish; and this is why Joan (Lily Nichol), so confident as she strode into the centre of the Dauphin's court and took possession of the circle, found herself caught out: her exposure in the circle's centre throughout the production made her a spectacle, and it was in the centre of the circle that she was placed on an equipment case and sentenced to be burned.

The privileging of direct address brought characters such as Amanda Harris's Exeter to the fore; Exeter became a Chorus, interpreting action for viewers with whom she claimed allegiance. Oliver Johnstone's Suffolk, meanwhile, was slyer with his addresses, and even coyly pushed the camera away when preparing to kiss Gale's Margaret. The pull of these characters towards the sidelines helped to foreground the fundamental power vacuum at the play's centre. The ease with which power could be renegotiated was best demonstrated by Talbot's encounter with the Countess of Auvergne (also Harris). The Countess took the centre of the stage to exult over Jamie Ballard's world-weary Talbot, displacing him and asserting her own dominance over the circle. But as Talbot gestured and his soldiers entered, suddenly the Countess's position of power became one of vulnerability, Talbot's men easily able to surround an indefensible position (Figure 23). This moment, though, also brought out the beauty of Ballard's rendition of Talbot. Ballard is not a physically imposing man, and indeed conducted himself throughout as someone tired, even sad, overtaken by younger and hungrier warriors. The ease with which Joan bested him in their combat informed a quiet resignation throughout, making the moment in which he lamented the death of his son before quietly dying all the more affecting.

The project showed off the RSC at its best as an ensemble company, using a rarely staged play as a vehicle for exploring process. *Henry VI, Part One* is ideal for this because of the relatively egalitarian distribution of its parts, and because it is a play that repeatedly cedes space for other characters to take temporary control. During the rose-plucking scene, characters walked forward to the rose bush in the centre before immediately retreating again, no one staking their claim to the power centre at this point, and this work of negotiation offered a powerful gloss on the start of the Wars of the Roses, with Henry's own decentred throne failing to exert sufficient influence to stop others from making their own claims. And by opening up the rehearsal process, the company offered an extensive and multivocal interpretive framework for the choices made. Far more than *Dream Online*, which privileged technology at the expense of the features more usually associated with the company, the *Open Rehearsal Project* made a powerful renewed case for the effectiveness of the RSC's particular

SHAKESPEARE PERFORMANCES IN ENGLAND, 2021

23 Talbot and his men capture the Countess of Auvergne in *Henry VI, Part One Open Rehearsal Project*, dir. Gregory Doran and Owen Horsley. Photograph by Ellie Kurtz, © RSC.

expertise in text-based, ensemble exploration, and I hope this is the first in many such experiments.

REDUCED SHAKESPEARE

Of course, Shakespeare does not need an enormous ensemble, and the low-budget touring companies who bring Shakespeare to community audiences all year round thrived during the summer. I missed tours by the Lord Chamberlain's Men (*Macbeth*) and The Pantaloons (*The Tempest*), but I finish this year's review with two tiny and very funny productions that aimed for joy and a little bit of DIY theatrical magic.

Nottingham Playhouse and Lakeside Arts Centre collaborated on a four-person, 80-minute *Tempest* that played in locations around Nottingham in July 2021. Bemoaning the lack of an actual thunderstorm (though one was conveniently scheduled for the afternoon on which I saw the show), children gathered in the carpark at Lakeside Arts Centre were given rainmakers and ratchets in order to collaborate in creating the tempest, conducted by Charlotte East's Prospero, who kept time on a cajon. The four-person ensemble split the roles between them, with even East doubling as Stephano, and Ariel manifesting as a pair of sunglasses that was passed between the members of the cast.

The Handlebards, meanwhile, toured several productions around the country, including their three-person *Romeo and Juliet*. In keeping with the Handlebards ethos of cycling to every production, the set itself was constructed out of cycling materials, with reassembled bicycle frames creating a frame for a simple drape, pumps acting as swords, and a bicycle bell serving as a ring (get it?). As with *The Tempest*, characters were signified by single items of clothing, allowing – in one of the most frenetic scenes – Tom Dixon to carry out a dialogue between the Nurse and Friar Laurence by himself, one moment standing under a bald headpiece held up by one of his colleagues to be Laurence, the next flipping round an enormous false bosom to become the Nurse. The dizzying costume changes were built into the production's comedic timing, with Romeo's run to Friar

Laurence's cell extending to several laps of the stage as the cast waited for someone to complete a change.

Coming off the back of a year of predominantly Zoom-based Shakespeare performance, both productions emphasized the joy of creative physical play over attempts at psychological realism. The Handlebards, especially, were content to laugh at Romeo and Juliet, the former played as a moony teenager, the latter as a brat with a tendency to fly into tempers. The first kiss between the two was an abject disaster as they tried to work out where to put their tongues. But leaning into the hilarity and incongruity of children trying to be in a grown-up relationship ended up serving the production well, with Friar Laurence barely able to keep the two hormonal teenagers from groping one another long enough to marry them. Their impulsiveness and exaggerated feelings also meant that their death scene played out with all the seriousness of *Pyramus and Thisbe*, and yet still managed to find flashes of sincere empathy for young people who should have been served much better by the adults nominally responsible for them.

Part of the fun of these two productions was that, in aiming for laughs, minor characters found rare prominence. *The Tempest* heavily cut all of the scenes featuring the nobles and Miranda, while Trinculo (Peter Watts) had his role expanded to be the main interlocutor with the audience and indulged in metatheatrical creativity, such as taking off his clown's fake nose and placing it under Caliban's sheet in order to sniff out his bedfellow remotely, or using a COVID mask as a makeshift umbrella as the rains began. In *Romeo and Juliet*, Friar John (played by two different actors) stole every scene he appeared in, wielding a spray bottle of holy water with which he doused every expression of extreme emotion from those who visited Friar Laurence's cell; his ethereal, detached hilarity took on more serious import later when his failure to deliver Laurence's letter sealed Romeo's fate. For both productions, the miming of violent actions turned the play's darker edges into scatological comedy, as Juliet went through a performance of dry-excreting from every orifice in the wake of taking Laurence's potion, while *The Tempest*'s Antonio gave up on trying to explain his murderous plans to Sebastian and instead resorted to a full-bodied dumbshow of a particularly gory butchery of the sleeping nobles. In moments such as these, theatre itself felt much more important than Shakespeare, text abandoned in favour of the corporeality of actors' bodies in relation to one another and to an audience. In their acts of parodic playfulness, Shakespeare became a vehicle to celebrate togetherness – an ethos shared by all productions this year, whether or not they took themselves seriously.

PROFESSIONAL SHAKESPEARE PRODUCTIONS IN THE BRITISH ISLES, JANUARY–DECEMBER 2020

JAMES SHAW

The information is taken from *Touchstone* (www.touchstone.bham.ac.uk), a Shakespeare resource maintained by the Shakespeare Institute Library. Touchstone includes a monthly list of current and forthcoming UK Shakespeare productions from listings information.

On 11 March 2020, a global pandemic was declared. Five days later, on 16 March the UK went into lockdown and the theatres closed, resulting in a smaller than usual number of productions this year. Most of the productions listed are by professional companies, but some amateur productions are included, notably for the latter half of 2020 when, despite being able to open, social distance restrictions meant it was not profitable for most professional theatres to stage productions.

ANTONY AND CLEOPATRA

Acting Gymnasium. Theatro Technis, Camden, London, 28 September–4 October.
www.actinggymnasium.co.uk
Director: Gavin McAlinden

THE COMEDY OF ERRORS

Grosvenor Park Open Air Theatre and Storyhouse. Grosvenor Park, Chester, 8–30 August.
www.grosvenorparkopenairtheatre.co.uk
Director: Alex Clifton
Played with two sets of identical twin actors.

CORIOLANUS

Sheffield Theatres. Crucible Theatre, Sheffield, 6–17 March.
Director: Robert Hastie
Virgilia used sign language with surtitles. The main cast of fourteen supported by nearly twenty members of Sheffield People's Theatre.

HAMLET

Adaptations

Hamlet: Rotten States
6Footstories Theatre Company. The Hope Theatre, London, 14 January–1 February.
www.6footstories.co.uk
75-minute version with a cast of three.

Ophelia
Old Red Lion, London, 12–15 February.
www.oldredliontheatre.co.uk
Playwright: Emma White
Director: Jake Leonard
One-woman show exploring love, mental health and suicide.

HENRY V

Maltings Open Air Theatre and OVO Theatre. Maltings Open Air Theatre Festival, St Albans, 19–31 August.
Director: Matthew Parker
Henry V: Mara Allen
http://maltingstheatre.co.uk

JAMES SHAW

Framed as a school production with a teacher giving instructions about social distancing measures to be observed.

HENRY VI, PART 2

Shakespeare's Globe. Sam Wanamaker Playhouse, London, 5 November 2019–26 January.
www.shakespearesglobe.com
Conflation of Henry VI, Parts 2 and 3.

HENRY VI, PART 3

Shakespeare's Globe. Sam Wanamaker Playhouse, London, 5 November 2019–26 January.
www.shakespearesglobe.com
Conflation of Henry VI, Parts 2 and 3.

JULIUS CAESAR

The UnDisposables Theatre Company. The Space Arts Centre, London, 10–16 March.
www.undisposables.co.uk
Director: Kate Bauer

Adaptation

I, Cinna (the Poet) – Write a Revolution
The Unicorn Theatre, London, 5–29 February.
www.unicorntheatre.com/ICinna
Playwright and performer: Tim Crouch
Solo show about Shakespeare's unluckiest character.

KING JOHN

Royal Shakespeare Company. The Swan Theatre, Stratford-upon-Avon, 19 September 2019–16 March.
www.rsc.org.uk
Director: Eleanor Rhode
King John: Rosy Sheedy

KING LEAR

Adaptation

Kunene and the King
Royal Shakespeare Company. Ambassador's Theatre, London, 24 January–16 March, transfer from Swan Theatre 2019.
Playwright: John Kani
Director: Janice Honeyman
Jack Morris: Antony Sher
Lunga Kunene: John Kani
A Black South African nurses a terminally ill white classical actor.

MACBETH

The Watermill Ensemble. Wilton's Music Hall, London, 22 January–8 February.
www.watermill.org.uk
Director: Paul Hart
Playing in rep with *A Midsummer Night's Dream*.

A Queen's Theatre Hornchurch and Derby Theatre production. Queen's Theatre, Hornchurch, 7–29 February; Derby Theatre, Derby, 3–14 March.
Director: Douglas Rintoul

Guildford Shakespeare Company. Holy Trinity Church, Guildford, 8–29 February.
www.guildford-shakespeare-company.co.uk
Director: Charlotte Conquest

Lazarus Theatre Company. Greenwich Theatre, London, 26 February–7 March.
https://lazarustheatre.com
Director: Ricky Dukes

Adaptations

The Old Rep Theatre, Birmingham, 5–7 February.
www.oldreptheatre.co.uk
Cast of three.

Macbeth: Playing Shakespeare with Deutsche Bank
Shakespeare's Globe Theatre, London, 26 February–16 March.
www.shakespearesglobe.com
90-minute version created for young people.

Queer Lady M
1623 Theatre Company. Century Theatre, Coalville, Leicestershire, 13 March and tour.
Performer: Shane Gabriel
www.1623theatre.co.uk
Solo performance from drag artist Lady M.

PROFESSIONAL SHAKESPEARE PRODUCTIONS 2020

Opera

Opera in a Box Theatre Company. The Loco Klub, Bristol, 23 February–1 March.
www.operainabox.com
Director: Marianne Vivash
Composer: Giuseppe Verdi
A promenade production underneath Temple Meads railway station.

THE MERRY WIVES OF WINDSOR

Maltings Open Air Theatre and OVO Theatre. Maltings Open Air Theatre Festival, St Albans, 19–31 August 2020.
www.ovotheatre.org.uk
Director: Adam Nichols

A MIDSUMMER NIGHT'S DREAM

The Watermill Ensemble. Wilton's Music Hall, London, 28 January–15 February; Watermill Theatre, Newbury, 19 February–7 March.
www.watermill.org.uk
Director: Paul Hart
Playing in rep with *Macbeth*.

Scoot Theatre and River Barn Arts Centre. Shepperton Cricket Club, Shepperton, 26 August 2020.
www.scoottheatre.com
Director: Joseph O'Malley

RICHARD III

Shakespeare's Globe. Sam Wanamaker Playhouse, London, 21 November 2019–26 January.
www.shakespearesglobe.com
Director: Sean Holmes and Ilinca Radulian
Richard III: Sophie Russell

ROMEO AND JULIET

Adaptations

& Juliet
Shaftesbury Theatre, London, 2 November 2019– March.
Director: Luke Sheppard
Book: David West Read
Jukebox musical.

West Side Story
Curve Theatre, Leicester, 23 November 2019–11 January.
www.curveonline.co.uk

THE TAMING OF THE SHREW

Royal Shakespeare Company. The Barbican Centre, West End, 5 November 2019–18 January and tour to 16 March.
www.rsc.org.uk
Director: Justin Audibert
Reverse gender production. Touring in rep with *As You Like It* and *Measure for Measure*.

Shakespeare's Globe. Sam Wanamaker Playhouse, London, 1 February–16 March.
www.shakespearesglobe.com
Director: Maria Gaitanidi

Adaptation

Kiss Me Kate
Northern Ireland Opera and the Lyric Theatre Belfast. Lyric Theatre, Belfast, 1–22 February.
Director: Walter Sutcliffe

THE TEMPEST

Jermyn Street Theatre, London, 11–16 March.
www.jermynstreettheatre.co.uk
Director: Tom Littler
Prospero: Michael Pennington

TWELFTH NIGHT

Yard Players Theatre Company. Jack Studio Theatre, London, 14 January–1 February.

Pantaloons Theatre Company. Sheffield Botanical Gardens, 21 August and tour of outdoor venues to 13 September.
https://thepantaloons.co.uk

DIY Theatre, Hogacre Common, Oxford, 17–19 September.
Director: Mike Wroe

Toby Belch: Ben Shaw
Amateur production. Outdoor production with socially distanced audience.

MISCELLANEOUS

The Second Best Bed

Victoria Hall, Settle, 5 March.
Playwright: Avril Rowland
Anne Hathaway on the night of Shakespeare's funeral.

Shake It Up Shakespeare

Hen and Chickens Theatre Bar, London, 10 February and 9 March.
William Shakespeare writes a new play with suggestions from the audience.

Upstart Crow

Gielgud Theatre, London, 7 February–20 March.
Playwright: Ben Elton
Director: Sean Foley

THE YEAR'S CONTRIBUTION TO SHAKESPEARE STUDIES

1. CRITICAL STUDIES

REVIEWED BY JANE KINGSLEY-SMITH

Following the pulling down of the statue of slave-trader, Edward Colston, in Bristol in the summer of 2020, in response to the Black Lives Matter movement, the historian David Olusoga observed, 'the problem isn't the statue; it's the pedestal'. At a similar moment, the question of Shakespeare's function as a potential symbol of racial oppression encouraged Ayanna Thompson to ask the question, 'Is Shakespeare a statue?' Some of the most valuable scholarship in Shakespeare produced this year asks directly or obliquely what kind of oppressive function Shakespeare-as-statue serves, and interrogates the kind of pedestals which have placed him there.

In Arthur L. Little's essay, 'Is it possible to read Shakespeare through Critical White Studies?', he attempts to reassure white scholars that our conversations about Shakespeare and race are not in themselves an act of iconoclasm: 'Shakespeare scholars of color do not typically call for the plays to be hidden, burned or otherwise erased. We do call for them to be approached differently: with less reverence and more attention to their encoding and spreading of white supremacist and patriarchal relationships.' One answer to this call is the collection in which Little's essay is published: *The Cambridge Companion to Shakespeare and Race*, edited by Ayanna Thompson, which poses two central questions: how did early modern drama, and Shakespeare's plays in particular, engage in acts of 'racecraft' and of 'white-world-making', and how should we respond through the performance and critical interpretation of those plays 400 years later? The urgency of such questions, and the genuinely interrogatory nature of the material, is reflected in titles which are a departure from the usual, unassuming *Companion* style: 'Are Shakespeare's plays racially progressive?', 'Was sexuality racialized for Shakespeare?' and so on. The tone for the collection is set by Thompson's no-holds-barred introductory essay, 'Did the concept of race exist for Shakespeare and his contemporaries?', which will immediately make you want to read (or re-read) everything Thompson has ever written on Shakespeare and race.

She begins with her own experience of studying Shakespeare at university, when it was assumed that race was an anachronism which could not be applied to Shakespeare's plays, or that references to slavery had nothing to do with the European slave trade – an experience that will resonate with many readers. More striking still is the conspiracy of silence among editors that has so long surrounded racist and racialist allusions in the text, so that references to the 'Ethiope' against whom Hero's or Juliet's beauty is measured, but also created, often go without a gloss. Thompson's introduction allows the reader a brief sense of progress: 'The book that you are holding and reading ... would have been nearly impossible to create – and, sadly, even impossible to conceive – when I was in university', and she acknowledges the methodological impact of 'post-colonial studies, African American studies, critical race studies, and queer studies', in enabling us to re-examine archives and read documentary evidence in new ways. Nevertheless, the meaning of 'race' needs to be repeatedly emptied out, with reference to seminal work by Geraldine Heng ('race is a structural relationship for the articulation and management of human differences'), and Karen E. Fields and Barbara J. Fields: 'Race is constructed by a social process that one might call race-making or "racecraft" ... Race does not exist, but racism does.'

The first section of the book explores the ways in which early modern drama constructed race on the stage, and the political, nationalist and economic interests which those constructions most obviously served. The collection gets off to a terrific start with Farah Karim-Cooper's chapter on the materiality of Black and white identities, through the different technologies of cosmetics and costume, and she also offers an important overview of the binary of Black and white, and its origins in Christianity. The need to revisit the archive is frequently apparent. Karim-Cooper draws on the work of Imtiaz Habib and Robert Hornback, in particular, to demonstrate the presence of Black people in Shakespeare's audience, not least Reasonable Blakemore, a silk-weaver who lived in Southwark and may have supplied the theatre companies. Ambereen Dadabhoy returns to the famous 1601 Elizabethan proclamation against 'divers blackamoores' to argue that it is specifically inflected through English hostility towards the Spanish, but also that its expectations about deportation allude to the Spanish enslavement of Black Africans. Her subsequent reading of George Peele's *The Battle of Alcazar* (1594) shows the influence of these 'technologies of empire that facilitate the plunder of Africa and naturalise the bondage and enslavement of black bodies'.

The second section focuses on the performance of Shakespeare on historical and contemporary stages. Here, Ira Aldridge makes a number of appearances, not least in Scott Newstok's thought-provoking chapter, 'How to think like Ira Aldridge', but also important is Joyce Green MacDonald's work on early actresses of colour who were prevented from performing in full-length Shakespeare productions but turned to elocution and the 'art of dramatic reading' to create their own alternative public performances.

Perhaps the most important work that this collection does is to bring these critical and theoretical discussions, predominantly by scholars of colour, to a broad audience, and to enable readers to follow up on these brief discussions in their extended critical monographs. I was grateful to be directed to Patricia Akhimie's *Shakespeare and the Cultivation of Difference* (2018), for example. But perhaps the most lasting emotional impression is one of electrifying honesty, from Adrian Lester's 'I don't particularly like [*Othello*]. If it is done very well and I have to watch it, I find it deeply upsetting and I come away angry' to Akhimie's more restrained, but no less devastating: 'I do not find it necessary or effective to attempt to soften the hard edges of Shakespeare's racist humour.' The emotional cost to these actors and scholars of engaging with Shakespeare is clear, as is the generosity with which they attempt to excavate something of personal and cultural value from the work.

This question of value is also the subject of Todd Landon Barnes's book *Shakespearean Charity and the Perils of Redemptive Performance*, which examines the phenomenon of the TV-documentary-about-underprivileged-students-being-transformed-by-their-experience-of-Shakespeare. This emerged in the USA and UK *c.*2004–2017, including films such as *Why Shakespeare?* (2005), *Shakespeare High* (2011) and *Kings of Baxter: Can Twelve Teenage Offenders Conquer Macbeth?* (2017). Whilst his field of enquiry is comparatively narrow, Landon's work resonates with much larger questions. When we, as Shakespeare scholars, teachers, readers and theatregoers, think about Shakespeare as being 'good for you', for whom do we mean exactly? What does it mean to give Shakespeare as a 'gift' to students, and what do we expect in return? In his overview of the teaching-Shakespeare documentaries, Barnes focuses more on the effect that these narratives are intended to have on the audience than what they achieve for the students. We do not really find out whether these formative experiences with Shakespeare have longer-term consequences for students, who have clearly learned what their teachers want them to feel. Barnes notes:

All of these films, to varying degrees, and in very different ways, argue for Shakespeare's power to transform or redeem poor students, most of whom are students of colour. In fact, watching these films feels in many ways like watching the same film over and over, a repetition that must index an urgent social anxiety around the intersections of class, race, education and documentary.

Barnes's central argument is that embracing a transcendental Shakespeare allows these films to erase cultural and racial difference. 'Shakespeare' serves to deflect attention away from the social injustices that create difference, on to the individual's responsibility to 'redeem' themselves. Underpinning this experience, Barnes argues, are the discourses of neoliberalism, which 'individualises social inequality' and undermines the welfare system, and 'emotional capitalism', through which social antagonisms 'are couched in the "benign language of emotion and personality"'. This is not, however, a modern phenomenon. Barnes identifies the 'White Christian Shakespeare Complex ... rooted in the big emotional payoff white saviors – and viewers – feel', as indebted to evangelical conversion narratives dating as far back as the seventeenth century. The analysis of the documentaries identifies key tropes which recur across them. For example, the notion of 'the underdog' is a term that students use about themselves, and that teachers often apply to their students, particularly in the context of competition where, for example, a student triumphs in a Shakespeare festival. But Theodor Adorno reminds us that 'In the end, glorification of splendid underdogs is nothing other than glorification of the splendid system that makes them so', and, as Barnes notes, 'if these films show us "underdogs" who become emotionally healthy and are culturally rich, they do not challenge or depict the structures that made them unhealthy or poor to begin with'.

Barnes's analysis is particularly astute when it comes to the racial fantasies at play. He draws on Sharon Willis's work on the career of Sidney Poitier, who appeared in a number of films set in an educational environment. These films, Willis notes, offered 'a fantasy of racial understanding and "assimilation" that requires no effort on the part of white people'. Although these Shakespeare documentaries appear to take on social issues, like Poitier's movies, they 'unfold in isolated environments, where cultural and social conflicts and contradictions become displaced onto the individualised, private negotiations'.

The question of how documentaries about Shakespeare teaching might do better is explored in the conclusion, but the answer is at least partly to change the focus group. The students in the documentary *A Touch of Greatness: A Portrait of a Maverick Teacher* come from affluent, middle-class backgrounds, and are not required to suffer and emote in the same way. Barnes praises the playfulness of their encounter with the text and sees this as the way forward:

Because the arts and humanities, like other forms of social welfare, are under siege, one might therefore argue that now is not the time to critique their power to transform lives. However, I would argue that now more than ever we should resist representations in which the arts and humanities are wielded as cudgels to better shape future workers or as a spiritual force sent to redeem a pathologized and sinful underclass. We might instead try to imagine the arts and humanities' power to invent new ways of being and performing together, ways in which difference or particularity need not be erased in the name of some homogeneous culture of excellence.

Part of the challenge of the book is that one is left, on the one hand, wanting to believe that the experience of Shakespeare has potentially changed these students' lives for the better, and, on the other, with the sense that the 'gift' of Shakespeare remains fundamentally flawed no matter the good intentions of the giver. Barnes writes powerfully about the emotions of sympathy and empathy which the films produce. He quotes Susan Sontag: 'So far as we feel sympathy, we feel we are not accomplices to what caused the suffering. Our sympathy proclaims our innocence as well as our impotence', so that it actually enables us to 'disavow our connection to others'.

Katharine A. Craik's introduction to her essay collection, *Shakespeare and Emotion,* begins from a similar position of needing to defend the continued attention given to Shakespeare's works. Craik finds this in Shakespeare's interest in the 'emotional lives of others', even if we have to do more as critics to acknowledge the differences that we bring to this experience: 'The continuing life of the plays indeed surely depends on our willingness to acknowledge the imbalances of power, privilege and gender which make accessing the emotional lives of others so difficult, and so important.' The subsequent twenty-three chapters are arranged into two parts. 'Contexts' ranges from sixteenth-century rhetoric and medicine to early 21st-century Bollywood. 'Emotions' dedicates a chapter to 'Fear', 'Grief' and 'Love', but also digresses winningly into 'Nostalgia', 'Wonder' and 'Confusion'. Nevertheless, there are themes that cut across this organization. For example, Craik's introduction acknowledges the relationship between emotion and movement, based on the origins of *emovere* (Latin, 'to move out'), and a number of chapters acknowledge the dynamic nature of emotion in the plays. This is literal in Bridget Escolme's suggestive chapter 'Acting', which makes the point that 'in early modern drama, emotion moves one around the world and the stage, in an act of feeling'. The physical movement of actors creates the effect and the affect of emotion, as explored by Evelyn Tribble's work on 'kinesic intelligence'. Relating this assumption to modern theatre practice, Escolme explores how the technique of 'actioning' – 'which involves attaching verbs to actors' lines to describe what each line is doing to another character, in order to give purpose, direction and focus to performance' – might be sharpened by thinking about emotion as motion.

The attempt to control the emotion created within the playhouse is another important theme of the collection. Elizabeth Williamson's essay on martyrdom explores this ambivalent spectacle which was intended by one faith to inspire heightened devotion and empathy, and by the other to prompt fear and purgation. But, as Williamson observes, 'it continually generated feelings that overflowed the punitive structures designed to contain them', and this might explain Shakespeare's reticence to stage the martyrdom of Joan La Pucelle or of Sir John Oldcastle. Tanya Pollard's fine essay on 'Audiences' also picks up the threat of intense emotion as a metatheatrical theme. In *Much Ado about Nothing* and *Measure for Measure*, both Claudio and the Duke avoid emotional experience through substitution: 'Like the audiences who watch them in playhouses, both plays' spectators enter their performances through investments in surrogate figures who resemble themselves, generating emotions that are simultaneously foreign and native, authorised and illicit, genuine and artificial.'

This over-laying of emotions also emerges as a recurring theme. If, Robert White argues, Shakespeare was influenced by Marlowe 'to depict passion-driven figures in tragedy and even in comedy', he 'wrote with more inclusive "multiconsciousness" than Marlowe, attributing to such figures ambivalent and multiple motivations and emotional states'. In his essay on 'Love', David Schalkwyk observes that it 'is not an emotion, even if it necessarily involves emotions', and that these emotions 'cannot be reduced to a single feeling, they may even contradict each other as well as the supposed affect we want to think of as love, namely the warm feeling of companionate closeness and desire'. Similarly, in Timothy M. Harrison's work on 'Confusion', understood in the early modern sense of 'lacking distinction', he too reiterates the idea that emotion in Shakespeare is always plural, but explores the complex interplay of emotion and reason, and those moments when characters (futilely) try to rationalize and thereby impose order on their emotions. This is particularly the case in *Cymbeline*, where 'confusion' as indistinction underpins key moments, as when the image of Posthumous seems to melt away in the distance, or when Cloten's body is mistaken for that of Posthumous. For Harrison, confusion is the natural state for all of us and his conclusion is worth pausing over: that confusion is the 'one constant factor in the history of human emotional life, a steady presence that binds the passions of Shakespeare's characters to the affect of twenty-first century readers and theatregoers'.

According to Ludwig Wittgenstein, emotion is shaped and defined by social convention. Developed out of his theory of language as a social activity, he speaks of the 'grammar' of emotion. For Ross Knecht, there are clear analogies between the work of the twentieth-century philosopher and the way that early modern people thought about emotion, as echoed in the title of his work which comes from Sidney's *Arcadia*: *The Grammar Rules of Affection: Passion and Pedagogy in Sidney, Shakespeare and Jonson*. This book brings together the recent 'affective' and 'pedagogical' turns in early modern studies, as represented by Lynn Enterline's *Shakespeare's Schoolroom* and Jeff Dolven's *Scenes of Instruction*, which have demonstrated early modern male writers' compulsive return to the schoolroom and its psycho-sexual allure. Whilst Knecht is also interested in the schoolroom setting as a site for 'disciplinary and amatory experience', particularly in Sidney, his interest in grammar is broader. He reminds us of the range of meanings it held in the period, encompassing 'the study of languages, eloquence in writing and speaking, textual interpretation, scholarly practices like translation and commentary, and the theory of language in general'. Drawing on Wittgenstein, but also on Monique Scheer's work in practice theory, which 'considers people as embodied actors deeply enmeshed within their environments and operating in accordance with both inculcated habit and conscious intention', he sets out to explore the linguistic basis of early modern passion, reminding us that Aristotelian *pathos* is both emotion and grammatical term, a state of suffering and the passive voice, linking affection and language thereafter in Western culture.

Knecht's stated aims are both historical and theoretical. He intends to show that grammar school education affected the perception of emotions, which came to be seen as 'patterns of action and expression rendered coherent by a set of conventional standards, just as the speaking of a language is made intelligible by the rules of grammar'. This argument is placed at a particular historical juncture between the medieval discourse around grammar as reflecting 'the ideal structures of the mind and the world' and the Renaissance humanist emphasis on language 'as an activity and a practice bound up with our worldly existence'. Knecht's theoretical aim is to advocate for the value of Wittgenstein's writings as a way of understanding early modern literature, and his larger investment in the concept of emotion as an 'extended process rather than an isolated object or condition'.

The readings that follow focus on Sidney's *Astrophil and Stella* and *The Defense of Poesie*, Shakespeare's *Love's Labour's Lost* and *Hamlet*, and Jonson's Humours plays. A major part of this discussion is the 'grammar of love', and Wittgenstein's discussion of the difference between pain and love certainly resonates here, as summarized by Knecht:

We identify a feeling as love only when it endures, when it persists in spite of obstacles, when it is borne out by devotion and fidelity. If it fails to do these things, we say that it is false, or a different thing altogether: a passing fancy or an adolescent infatuation. We have tacitly agreed to call that love which abides by certain conventions, rules and standards that Wittgenstein calls 'grammar'.

This definition is obviously a gift for *Love's Labour's Lost*, and that chapter persuasively examines how the men of Navarre's wooing exposes the set of conventions and interactions by which love is performed. In his discussion of *Hamlet*, Knecht writes compellingly of the ways in which the play undermines Hamlet's desire to escape language, or to identify an interiority that exists beyond language:

'ineffability is paradoxically enabled by the structure of language'. Moreover, the distinction between 'action' and 'passion' falls apart, with Knecht reminding us that the verbs 'to passion', or 'passionate', include just those gestures that Hamlet rejects.

Knecht's attack on interiority elsewhere in the book is perhaps less persuasive. He argues that the opening sonnet of *Astrophil and Stella*, with its insistence that Astrophil 'Look in [his] heart and write', is an expression of the humanist requirement that one learn 'by heart' rather than by rote: 'what appears to be an appeal to an inward passion distinct from the traditions of erotic lyric is in fact evidence that love is enabled by and manifest in a set of linguistic and pedagogical practices'. It is at such moments that a tension emerges between the historical and theoretical ambitions of the book. The pendulum swings more towards *Astrophil* being used to support a theoretical belief based on Wittgenstein than as a historical excavation of a lost layer of meaning in the text of *Astrophil*. But this may not trouble all readers, depending on the assumptions that they bring about that vexed question of Renaissance interiority. What the book consistently achieves is a sense that there are significant benefits to be gained from reading early modern literature 'alongside' the writings of Wittgenstein, and that Renaissance passion is both more rich and more strange than we might have thought.

Faith D. Acker's book *First Readers of Shakespeare's Sonnets, 1590–1790* allows us to look over her shoulder as she handles some of the earliest editions of Shakespeare's Sonnets in print and manuscript – a vicarious thrill when many of us have been debarred from archives for so long. The early modern book, often interleaved with other texts, annotated with random initials and Latin aphorisms, adorned with love notes and angry scrawls, emerges viscerally through Acker's descriptions and illustrations.

Acker's central thesis is that the Sonnets have a broader range of meanings than has previously been thought, a narrowing partly created by modern critics' 'exclusive focus on the sonnets' biographical interpretations, [...] which] limits the versatility and flexibility that the sonnets' earliest readers imagined in and around these poems'. Acker posits a distinction between two groups: private readers, who copied and annotated the poems for their own use, as Francis Meres attested to in 1598, and '"specialist readers"', including editors, anthologists and stationers, 'who not only read the sonnets, but evaluated them against cultural and literary trends within their larger societies and mediated their presentation to the wider community of readers at large'. This approach is sometimes less convincing in the case of early 'editors' such as Bernard Lintott, whose summary of the Sonnets as '154 poems addressed to his mistress' may be because he had not read them, but it works very well in the case of someone like Edward Capell, who seemed to fall into editing the Sonnets in the process of his engaged reading.

The main disadvantage to Acker's book is that its overall argument – that the Sonnets are more versatile than we think, and that pre-nineteenth-century readers found in them a range of meanings beyond the biographical interpretation – is not new. This argument has been made a number of times over the last few years, guided by Katherine Duncan-Jones's still superlative work in her Arden edition, and by Sasha Roberts's ground-breaking *Reading Shakespeare's Poems in Early Modern England*, and there is a general feeling of time lag between what may have been the conception of Acker's argument and its publication. This is particularly notable in the early chapters, where the discussion of Jaggard's brand-awareness in putting *The Passionate Pilgrim* together under Shakespeare's name would have benefitted from James P. Bednarz's important essay on this topic, just as the discussion of Michael Drayton's sequence compared to Shakespeare's could have been enriched by Meghan C. Andrew's recent work on their mutual influence. The sense that the book is not quite up to date is perhaps most apparent in Acker's breezy assertion that 'Shakespeare probably wrote his sonnets in the late sixteenth century, but fifteen or twenty years passed before most of them reached print.' This ignores the recent argument, largely indebted to the work of

MacDonald P. Jackson, that the Sonnets were written across a period of approximately twenty-seven years, with six distinct groupings, and were most likely revised in 1609. Acker's misconception about their dating encourages a misreading of some of the Sonnets themselves. Sonnet 107, for example, with its elliptical line 'The mortal moon hath her eclipse endur'd', seems very likely to acknowledge the peaceful transition from Elizabeth I to James I's rule. Acker acknowledges the political appropriation of the Sonnet later in the seventeenth century to reflect the execution of Charles I, but she skews our sense of what the Sonnets may have meant for their first readers by insisting that the 1609 Quarto was an 'Elizabethan' collection.

The book's strength really emerges in chapters on the late seventeenth and eighteenth centuries. Acker's analysis of a miscellany owned by a Cambridge student in the 1650s demonstrates how Shakespeare's Sonnets might bend to a moral and religious will: the procreation sonnets are reshaped in a way that suppresses their amorous context but retains the warning against selfishness. We can also benefit from Acker's assiduous reading of a whole manuscript miscellany in order to weigh up the status of the Shakespeare sonnet as compared with the work of other poets. The Cambridge compiler, for example, saw no distinction between the 'authorial capital' of Shakespeare and of the Cambridge poet, Nicholas Hookes, though few people would be able to quote the latter's love lyrics now. Acker's work is also valuable in extending our sense of how the Sonnets were being understood and informally edited in the late eighteenth century. She is particularly good on Edward Capell's long entanglement with the Sonnets and the inconsistencies which emerge within his treatment of them, and, though she may not acknowledge the debt that Edmond Malone owed to Capell's work, she does demand that we approach with greater caution Malone's 'definitive' edition of 1780 and the process of interpretive narrowing through the temptations of biography which it initiated. As the book draws to a close, Acker notes that 'It is time to expand scholarship on the sonnets and to celebrate the versatile interpretations and contexts they were afforded by their earliest readers.' This work may be further on than Acker is aware of, but it is nonetheless valuable to have *First Readers* as a resource for the further exploration of the Sonnets' afterlife.

One important recent manifestation of this afterlife will be Paul Edmondson's and Stanley Wells's *All the Sonnets of Shakespeare* (2020). This is a deceptively radical volume, which conceals its transgressive ambitions beneath a cover illustration of lilies and curlicues, and a quote from Dame Judi Dench on what a 'fresh and lovely idea' it represents. The volume dispenses with the 1609 Quarto sequence by reordering the Sonnets according to their supposed date of composition, by pushing the familiar numbering system to the footnotes, and by interspersing sonnets from the plays among the 'Sonnets' to create a poetic miscellany of 182 lyrics. The consequences of these decisions are bold and exciting.

For one thing, we are more strongly aware than ever that Shakespeare was a sonneteer for nearly the whole of his career, and by adding sonnets from the plays the period of his working in this form is extended to 1582–1613. In fact, although Edmondson and Wells do not explicitly state this, by arguing that the Cupid poems, Sonnets 153 and 154, are schoolboy translations of Marianus (the only argument I have encountered that makes sense of these poems, with one a draft and one a revised version) actually pushes these dates even earlier into the 1570s.

Another consequence of the abandonment of the Quarto sequence is the disruption of any straightforward attempt to read them biographically, at least in the bipartite arrangement of Shakespeare-to-Fair-Youth, Shakespeare-to-Dark-Lady, that originated with Malone. Edmondson and Wells do not avoid a biographical component entirely, making a distinction between 'an historical, autobiographical narrative and an emotional, psychological and spiritual memoir, in part made up of [Shakespeare's] addresses to other people, in part his soliloquies played out primarily for himself'.

In terms of the sonnets (or foreshortened sonnets) that Edmondson and Wells dig out from the plays, there is some sense of Shakespeare's expanded repertoire, though it is still nothing like the variety afforded by John Milton. Nevertheless, the editors argue persuasively that 'Shakespeare includes sonnets in his plays at many points in his career to change, vary, and heighten the dramatic mood ... Sonnets alter the verbal and aural textures of the drama. In hearing them, his audiences may be set momentarily at a critical distance from the action, character, and story.' The otherworldliness of Diana and Jupiter in the later plays seems appropriately conveyed by their speaking in sonnet form.

In terms of what this new arrangement tells us about the Sonnets we already know, there are at least two intriguing effects. One is a renewed sense of Shakespearian bawdy in the pairing of sonnets written praising Venus from *The Passionate Pilgrim* with the 'Dark Lady' sonnets. The latter look less misogynistically anatomical as a result. The other effect is a renewed sense of the Sonnets' freshness (Dame Judi was right) in the lack of extensive notes, glosses and collations at the bottom of the page. These can too often crowd out the voices of the sonnet itself. But this is not the case here, and one innovation, the use of single- or two-sentence paraphrases, has a particularly revivifying effect. These are certainly a bold choice, given the proliferation of meanings usually attributed to single words in the sonnet, but their remarkable reductiveness is partly the point, stimulating the reader's creative and interpretive faculties in a way that being in a sensory deprivation chamber makes one's remaining senses much more distinct. Take, for example, Sonnet 93, 'So shall I live supposing thou art true', for which the paraphrase is 'Since you always appear beautiful and loving, I always assume you are being faithful to me, though you may not be.' To go back to the original sonnet is to be reminded afresh of its deliberate acts of self-deception and layers of irony. Similarly, Sonnet 87, 'Farewell, thou art too dear for my possessing' is paraphrased: 'Farewell, you are too precious for me to keep, and I was mistaken in your love.' In the face of the paraphrase's pathos and dejection, the sonnet vibrates with irony, bitterness and even malice, the feminine endings signifying the inability to contain the rage that the speaker feels, as well as potentially invoking the master–mistress of the poems.

There are paraphrases which will exercise the readerly eyebrow: 'If thy soul check thee that I come so near', with its multiple puns on 'Will', is glossed: 'My name, my desire, and my penis want to fill you entirely.' But some of these one-line summaries, in laying bare some aspect of the sonnet, also make them more contemporary. Eschewing obfuscations about dark ladies, the gloss to Sonnet 131, 'Thou art as tyrannous, so as thou art', produces an arguably more honest account of what the sonnet is doing: 'You are proud and cruel and, although some say you are not that sexy, I know you to be utterly so. Your physical blackness does not make you unattractive, but your black deeds do.' It feels important that blackness be allowed to signify in these sonnets. In the same way, the openness to addressees being either male or female is not only important to allow readers to engage with them, but also acknowledges the bisexuality of the sonnets in a more open and accepting way than the binary division has allowed.

There is no doubt that readers who want a scholarly edition of the Sonnets already enjoy an embarrassment of riches, and our understanding of the Quarto sequence and its historical and cultural context is well served by these editors. But very few people can enjoy the experience of reading the sonnets in the Quarto sequence, whereas this is a volume into which one can dip suggestively, creatively and repeatedly to find things new. It is, frankly, the most exciting reconception of the Sonnets since John Benson's *Poems* in 1640, and the same motive of making them 'serene, clear and elegantly plain' serves to intensify their drama, their diversity and their brilliance.

It seems highly unlikely that we do indeed possess 'all' of the sonnets of Shakespeare, though the absence of any trace of these missing lyrics makes conjecture about their contents impossible. This is not so with Shakespeare's lost plays, which may leave sufficient material trace as to be entirely reconstituted, as in the case of *Cardenio*. More generally, attempts to incorporate early modern lost plays within our notions of the repertory of a particular theatre company (the Queen's Men, the King's Men), or the career of a particular writer (*Early Shakespeare*), or a particular theatrical period (the *Before Shakespeare* project) or a particular cultural theme ('Brutan histories', see Gilchrist below), have proliferated in the last two decades, and this is attributable to the ground-breaking scholarship of David McInnis and Matthew Steggle, who have equipped us with the theoretical and digital tools to do this valuable work. In *Shakespeare and Lost Plays*, McInnis offers a rigorous, passionate and game-changing argument in defence of lost plays and the reasons why none of us can afford to overlook them. He begins with a number of analogies for the way in which lost plays define canons of extant plays, using the psychologist Edgar Rubin's vase, which figures a vase and two faces in profile at the same time, demonstrating how 'when "two fields have a common border", there exists the potential for the "figure"' and the 'ground' in an image to interrelate in unstable ways, such that '[a] field which had previously been experienced as ground can function in a surprising way when experienced as figure'. I was also struck by the analogy of the white spaces in the early modern printed text: 'What the reader perceives as a gap or a blank is in fact structured by the presence of a piece of physical type.'

McInnis proceeds to set out some of the damaging assumptions about lost plays, which have still not gone away – most obviously, that they would have survived if they were either aesthetically or commercially successful. His work on Henslowe's diary demonstrates that this is not the case: of the eight plays that made 60s or more for the Admiral's Men between April 1596 and January 1597, seven out of the eight are now lost. An early warning that the Shakespeare canon will look significantly different after McInnis has finished with it is suggested by his comparison of the extant repertory of the Chamberlain's Men, compared with the much fuller records we have for the Admiral's Men. Using Martin Wiggins's *Catalogue* to flesh out the possible missing plays, documented elsewhere and potentially attributable to the company, McInnis suggests that a further 270 Chamberlain's Men plays are unaccounted for, and that the notion that the company's repertory was primarily dedicated to, and shaped by, Shakespeare is misguided. One of McInnis's broad conclusions is:

how closely related the plays of early modern London were in terms of recurring subject matter, popular genres and forms, plot devices, and other dramatic features that might otherwise be assumed to have been unusual or distinctive if our attention were restricted to the extant drama alone. Every extant play is deeply embedded in its repertorial moment, influencing and reacting to the other commercial offerings available on the London stages.

The ensuing chapters trace the Shakespearian canon across four periods – 1594–1598, 1599–1603, 1604–1608, 1609–1613 – and post-1616 with the lost apocryphal plays. Within these chapters, McInnis pays meticulous attention to changes of theatrical playing space, the repertory of rival playing companies, even the stage properties that might shed light on the subject matter of the lost plays in each period. Throughout the book, McInnis is to be admired not only for the depth of his research, and his elegant and engaging writing style, but for the restraint that he shows in his speculations: 'Remaining vigilant about questioning assumptions and showing our working is vital if we are to avoid reproducing received narratives without interrogation and allowing theories to ossify into facts.' But one suspects he also has a lot of fun in speculating about some of the most canonical Shakespeare plays from the perspective of the lost plays, and achieves some fairly jaw-dropping conclusions.

Perhaps the most captivating example relates to *Hamlet*. McInnis argues that critics have not paid enough attention to a seam of plays about Denmark, which acted as a kind of shadow to the political fortunes of England, as evidenced by the lost plays *the taner of Denmarke* (1592) and *A Danish Tragedy* (1602). Some work on the meaning of 'tanner' produces the revelation that it was proverbial, 'those that are of hautie behaviour, and vaunt of their doings'. McInnis, brilliantly, makes the connection with Marlowe's reference in *Edward II* to '[t]he haughty Dane [who] commands the narrow seas'. Hence, one of the possibilities is that this lost play might actually have been about Hamlet's father, Horvendile. Equally exhilarating is the discussion of what exactly might be meant by the title of another lost play, *felmelanco* (1602), which McInnis tentatively suggests might be a contraction of 'Philip Melanchthon', the Protestant scholar, 'considered one of the founders of Protestantism', and therefore an apt response by the Admiral's Men to the Wittenberg graduate, Hamlet. As McInnis concludes, 'It is tempting to think that *Hamlet* has been approached from every conceivable scholarly angle, but here I have attempted to show how attention to lost plays might produce new intertextual connections or contexts for consideration.' The book does much more than this, not only for Shakespeare scholars but for anyone interested in early modern drama.

One of the reasons for the loss of plays was their vulnerability (and versatility) as paper objects. McInnis cites the case of John Warburton, who claimed that his library of manuscript plays fell foul of his cook Betsy, by whom 'they were unluckily burnd or put under Pye bottoms'. In her monograph *Boxes and Books in Early Modern England: Materiality, Metaphor, Containment*, Lucy Razzall tells a similar story of how the library of John Dee, hidden in a chest, was discovered, but the owners 'made no great matter of these Books &c.: because they understood them not; wch occasioned their Servant Maide to wast about one halfe of them under pyes and other like uses, wch when they discovered they kept the rest more safe.' The chest that was supposed to keep these books and papers safe betrays them; it fails as a container. One conclusion that this analogy suggests is that the relationship between books and boxes is more intimate than we might otherwise have thought.

Razzall begins with the heightened visibility of boxes in early modern households as a result of increased international trade and consumerism: 'almost everyone would have owned at least one box of some kind for the storage of personal possessions, including anything from papers and books to tools, jewels, spices, medicine, linen, plate or money'. Particular kinds of box will come in for detailed analysis, including chests, caskets, coffins and reliquaries. Of the latter, Razzall observes that 'For iconoclastic reformers, the murky box of the reliquary (like the frequently invoked "box" containing the bread of the Eucharist) epitomised the inherent falseness of the Roman Catholic faith. These boxes had to be emptied out in rhetorical as well as literal terms, and ultimately destroyed.' But a broader anti-Catholic perspective also explains the ways in which books become like boxes in the threatening disparity between their outsides and their insides.

Razzall notes how the terms 'box' and 'book' share an etymological origin in kinds of wood (respectively, 'buxus' or boxwood, and 'beech'). They also look particularly similar in early modern culture, being constructed many times of wood, with visible bands/bindings, and an elaborately decorated 'lid'. They open with a similar hinge to reveal their secrets, as reflected in numerous book titles, which refer to them as 'cabinets', 'store-houses', 'closets' or 'caskets' in which things might be 'opened', 'displayed', 'revealed', 'unlocked' or 'disclosed'. Razzall identifies two key tropes for thinking inside the box when it comes to books: Plato's discussion of Silenus' statue in the *Symposium*, which appears to be rough and ugly on the outside but opens to reveal a beautiful interior; and the apothecary's box which was synonymous with a beautiful exterior that revealed deadly poison. Razzall demonstrates the prevalence of these two tropes in thinking about 'the various ways in which books might operate as similarly deceptive and potentially dangerous receptacles'.

Having pursued the association of box and book, Razzall moves on to the relationship between the body and the box, and the recurrent imagining of the body as 'a receptacle ... which encloses complex systems within a bounded surface punctuated by various openings and orifices, and with which we interact in and with many other comparable receptacles'. This results in a striking new reading of Shakespeare's *Cymbeline*. The play features an apothecary's box, which the Queen believes to contain poison, the Doctor fills with a sleeping draught, and Pisanio believes to contain life-saving medicine. This transformation, Razzall argues, foreshadows the disturbing transformations of the 'trunk' later in the play. This is the chest (reminiscent of the marriage chest or *cassoni*) which Imogen agrees to store in her chamber, but from which Giacomo secretly emerges in the night in order to reveal private details about Imogen to persuade Posthumous that she is unfaithful. As Razzall points out, the language of the chest eerily shapes Giacomo's perception of what he is doing: 'This secret / Will force him think I have picked the lock and ta'en / The treasure of her honour' (2.2.40–2). The presence of the book, which has previously been opened at the story of a rape, resonates with the trunk, so that 'body, book, and box all work in a synchronised way in this scene, each furnishing the stage as sites of tension to be manipulated by various intrusive acts of folding and unfolding, opening and shutting'. What we might call the horror of the chest is finally encapsulated in the image of Cloten's headless 'trunk'.

This brings us to some of the book's strongest material on early modern thinking about death. The conceptualization of death as a breaking open of a precious box to lose or spill the precious contents is surprisingly ubiquitous, from the description of Arthur's death in *King John* – 'They found him dead and cast into the streets, / An empty casket, where the jewel of life / By some damned hand was robbed and ta'en away' (5.1.39–41) – to this extraordinary description of man's 'injurie and despite' against Christ: 'as to have broken the christall box of his humanitie, receptacle of the divine'. Part of the increase in boxes in early modern experience was due to the relatively recent practice of burying the dead in a coffin, as opposed to a shroud or winding sheet. This was intended to emphasize the individuality of the corpse contained therein, but also – with an eye to Judgement Day – to keep the body parts together. One of the consequences of this practice was that 'Although the coffin was only required after death, it permeated the ways in which the writers thought about the living body as well, in a sort of anachronous recolouring of corporeality from the grave.' It emphasized the perception of the body as a box containing the soul. This brings us inevitably to John Donne, with his perception of death-in-life, imaginatively and rhetorically shaped by boxes within boxes.

In this manner, Razzall moves from the material to the metaphysical, developing a sense of the box both as a solid, material, domestic object, and as something much more labile and insubstantial: 'For early modern writers, the box offered a concrete way to think about the opportunities, challenges and mysteries of embodiment, but at the same time it offered a versatile metaphor with which to figure out the almost unimaginable aspects of that embodiment – the relationships between the body and the soul, the challenges of interiority, and the distinction between life and death.' Razzall's book offers a unique and illuminating perspective into early modern culture, through its attitude to boxes and to books. Like a *wunderkabinet*, it preserves some truly fascinating physical objects and creative and intellectual tropes, to persuade even the most sceptical reader of the value of thinking inside the box.

Two monographs have recently encouraged us to rethink the 'Britishness' of Shakespeare's Jacobean plays, and, given the embattled status of the British archipelago at the current time, it is an invitation many will want to take up. In *The Subject of Britain, 1603–25*, Christopher Ivic offers a densely packed but open-minded account of the debate over the Union following James VI of Scotland's accession to the English throne in 1603, at which time his subjects were required 'to repute, hold, and esteeme both the two Realmes as presently united ... and the Subjects of both the Realmes as one people, brethren and members of one body'. By limiting his time period to the twenty-two years of James's rule, Ivic is able to offer a comprehensive analysis of how the relationships between the realms of England, Wales, Scotland and Ireland were contested through a number of different 'imagined geographies'.

A deliberate elision of those troubling elements of the identities of both king and kingdom is a central feature of Ivic's discovery. He demonstrates the creative ways in which James's new English subjects refashioned his foreignness, by appropriating the imagery of his Elizabethan predecessor; by emphasizing his Tudor heritage through his descent from Margaret Tudor; and by obscuring his Scottishness, so that, in a tract called *Englands Wedding Garment*, he is called an 'English lion'. Titles prove equally obscurantist, as when a proclamation of 24 March 1603 refers to him as 'King of England, France and Ireland', ignoring/absorbing his Scottish title entirely. Moreover, what one might have thought were relatively stable entities – the definition of a land-mass as an island, for example – become surreally unclear. As Ivic notes, 'Shakespeare's plays often present not Britain but England in a continent-like manner, detached from neighbouring Scotland and Wales.' But Shakespeare was not alone in this; Spenser dedicates *The Faerie Queene* to Elizabeth, 'Great Ladie of the greatest Isle': 'Britain could designate the entire island of Great Britain, or England and Wales only, or England only.'

How a range of early modern writers negotiated the conflicting demands of a Scottish monarch on an English throne, and the different geopolitical spaces which emerged, is a central part of the book. In Chapter 2, Ivic explores how Michael Drayton, Samuel Daniel and Ben Jonson all wrote panegyrics celebrating the accession, but inflected in different ways and with varying degrees of success: Jonson lacks the 'deep-seated English patriotism' of Drayton and Daniel and therefore seems to have appealed more. In the chapter on Shakespeare, Ivic traces a longer trajectory, from the Elizabethan history plays, which refer overwhelmingly to England as an island, to the British plays which largely reject that insular image and refer to 'Albion' or 'Britain'. Ivic offers a detailed discussion of critical debates around this transition in Shakespeare's work, and in the process deepens our understanding of the anomalous nature of *Macbeth*. Indebted to chronicle history, and resembling perhaps most obviously an Elizabethan play like *Richard III*, *Macbeth* is revealed to be far more ambiguous in its response to Jacobean union politics and discourse than it might have seemed.

Part of the book's strength is Ivic's meticulous attention to shifts in language across his time period – and within the Shakespearian canon particularly – from 'English' to 'British', or from 'kingdom' to nation'. The word 'British' doesn't appear in *Macbeth*, though 'English' does repeatedly, as does a Shakespearian coinage which appears nowhere else in the canon: 'birthdom', as a term Macduff uses about Scotland. Ivic asks a series of searching questions through these disputed terms: how Scottish is the play? To what extent is Macbeth deliberately gaelicized, in opposition to the anglicization at work in and through Malcolm, who renames his followers Earls rather than Thanes at the end of the play? Is Macbeth 'a Scottish patriot'? Or does the play seem to justify the anglicization of Scotland as a means of rescuing it from itself, through 'a vision of a broken, treacherous kingdom crying out for English oversight' (Robert Crawford)? Or does it expose the threat represented by such a mingling of kingdoms, on behalf of English and Scottish historians? I am not wholly convinced by the argument that *Macbeth* acts as a kind of negative stereotype of nationalism, 'a kind of nationalism that underpinned anti-union and anti-naturalisation discourse', but Ivic certainly puts *Macbeth*'s euphemistic title 'the Scottish play' in a new light.

'The myth of Britain's Trojan origins ... surfaces again and again in the succession literature of 1603.' Though there is little space for a thorough investigation in Ivic's book, happily we also have Kim Gilchrist's *Staging Britain's Past: Pre-Roman Britain in Early Modern Drama*. This highly original study explores how early modern culture articulated its own ancient, pre-Roman origins, from the arrival of Brute in 1180 BCE to the Roman invasion in 52 BCE, a period of 'Brutan' history originally set down by Geoffrey of Monmouth in the *Historia regum Britanniae* (*c.*1135). Where Ivic deals with selective amnesia and deliberate elision in the naming of nations and kingdoms, Gilchrist is confronted by a history whose credibility was fraying, following the disavowal of Polydore Vergil in the *Anglica historia*, wherein he questioned the veracity of the Galfridian account, declaring instead that 'There is nothing more hidden, nothing more uncertain, nothing more unknown than early deeds of the Britons.' This fear of nothing resonates powerfully throughout the book, and explicitly so as Gilchrist develops a series of intriguing allusions between, for example, the interweaving of Brutan history into the play *Nobody and Somebody*, and the nothingness which afflicts that Brutan protagonist King Lear. But this is to get ahead of ourselves.

Part of the book's achievement is its ability to navigate a landscape characterized by gaps and absences. Two of the plays Gilchrist wants to talk about, *King Lude* (1594) and *The Conquest of Brute* (1598), are lost, and understanding how those who did not have access to Folio history books (and, indeed, in most cases could not read) still gained access to this Brutan heritage and made sense of it is fraught with gaps. That said, part of the strength of Gilchrist's meticulous research is its ability to weave a persuasive reception history out of these materials, through analysis of what else was being performed in a particular theatrical season; the textual differences between different print editions of particular works; and his attention to a range of popular cultural forms including civic pageants and ballads. The lived experience of these origin stories comes through particularly strongly. So King Lud is commemorated in Ludgate and the name of the capital city; Inns of Court students were studying English laws attributed to Mulmutius Dunwallo or Queen Marcia; Leir was supposed to have founded Leicester, and so on. The physical landscape had been shaped by Brute and his ancestors, and these figures would occasionally rise up from the dead in order to represent their local descendants in a specific political cause. This is evident in the 1486 pageants planned to welcome the new King Henry VII, following the Wars of the Roses: 'At a time of profound national transformation both York and Bristol initiated and negotiated their relationships with the new monarch via the public performance of Brutan founders. These were local figures of origin and foundation whose status as ancient rulers of Britain integrated the local into a larger national story, thereby asserting regional autonomy and dignity.'

At the same time, Gilchrist explores the appropriation of the Brutan histories as part of the pro-Union rhetoric deployed by James I, and staged in Anthony Munday's *The Triumphs of Reunited Britannia*, wherein James is repeatedly identified as a second Brute. Less familiar is the fact that earlier monarchs (Edward I, Henry VIII) had also reached for the Brutan history books in order to defend their violent invasions of Scotland, on the basis that, according to Brutan history, these territories had once belonged to Brute, in a romanticized past when the island was 'whole'. Gilchrist's point about how the legends 'bolster[ed] English interests ... competing with a rival, and amusingly different, Scottish account of ancient Britain' ties in with Ivic's argument about the tendency to equate 'a material representation of the landmass comprising England, Scotland and Wales ... as the "isle of England" alone'.

What is most compelling about Gilchrist's book is the way in which it testifies to 'both a culture's deep-seated need to embody and encounter its origins and the disorientating energies released when those origins begin to erode'. This is not to say that disbelief happened steadily or consistently, with law courts and livery companies seeming to be particularly unwilling to renege on their commitment to this ancient history. But the contradictions and wavering beliefs prove to be fertile territory for drama, and Gilchrist offers two original readings of *King Lear* and *Cymbeline* through his conjoined notions of 'etiological erosion' and 'historical dissonance'. The discussion of *King Lear* includes a defence of the now-edited Q reading, '*Historica passio*', as exemplifying 'the kind of historiographic rejection the Brutan histories were undergoing'. *King Lear*'s cancelling out of dynasties and future hopes registers the destruction of the myth, most notably in his awareness of himself as his own shadow. Also suggestive is Gilchrist's argument that the play responds to the death of not one, but two, infant princesses, Mary and Sophia, in 1607: 'a sense of tragically lost British futurity may have been mirrored in the play's savage depiction of filial death and parental grief'.

In the case of *Cymbeline*, the book offers support for its deliberate positioning at the end of the First Folio (1623), not only through the play's incorporation of multiple genres and narrative endings, but also through its sense of a Brutan historicity coming to an end. Imogen, named after Brute's wife Innogen, is revealed as peculiarly sensitive to gaps in both distance and time, and is herself identified with the insubstantiality of air. Her speech on Posthumous disappearing into the distance, 'melt[ing] to ayre', draws on both the *Aeneid* and the *Historia* and represents a conflation of the beginning and the end of Brutan history. It also serves as an appropriate conclusion to this review of the year's critical works. In some ways, the distances created by our lost access to the past have been overcome. Through scholarly research and new digital technologies, the lost repertory of Shakespeare and his contemporaries can be partially rediscovered, and can reshape what we already see and know. At the same time, 'Shakespeare' loses some of his monumentality, as we take ownership of the kinds of pedestals we have created for him, and anticipate what future Shakespeare studies might look like.

WORKS REVIEWED

Acker, Faith D., *First Readers of Shakespeare's Sonnets, 1590–1790* (New York and London, 2021)

Barnes, Todd Landon, *Shakespearean Charity and the Perils of Redemptive Performance* (Cambridge, 2020)

Craik, Katharine, ed., *Shakespeare and Emotion* (Cambridge, 2020)

Edmondson, Paul, and Stanley Wells, eds., *All the Sonnets of Shakespeare* (Cambridge, 2020)

Gilchrist, Kim, *Staging Britain's Past: Pre-Roman Britain in Early Modern Drama* (London and New York, 2021)

Ivic, Christopher, *The Subject of Britain, 1603–25* (Manchester, 2020)

Knecht, Ross, *The Grammar Rules of Affection: Passion and Pedagogy in Sidney, Shakespeare and Jonson* (Toronto, Buffalo, London, 2021)

McInnis, David, *Shakespeare and Lost Plays* (Cambridge, 2021)

Razzall, Lucy, *Boxes and Books in Early Modern England: Materiality, Metaphor, Containment* (Cambridge, 2021)

Thompson, Ayanna ed., *The Cambridge Companion to Shakespeare and Race* (Cambridge, 2021)

2. STUDIES IN SHAKESPEARE IN PERFORMANCE, 2020–2021
reviewed by RUSSELL JACKSON

When Pascale Aebischer's *Shakespeare, Spectatorship and the Technologies of Performance* was published in 2020, the first lockdown in response to the COVID-19 pandemic was already in place in the UK. In the light of these circumstances, in *Viral Shakespeare* in the Cambridge Elements series (2021), she reflects on her 'responses to some of the unique spectatorial configurations, novel experiences and creative innovations that emerged in the time of the pandemic' (8). The result is a remarkable personal account of the 'fleeting insights and experiences garnered from watching Shakespeare in lockdown', which are 'worth preserving because they speak to a moment of unprecedented intensity and emotional rawness that is profoundly marked by Shakespeare' (11). 'Viral' is, of course, a metaphorical adjective in the digital world that has acquired a distinctive resonance since the beginning of 2020. Aebischer describes an important consequence of the sudden abundance of Shakespeare performances available online: 'The broadcasts intersect and impact one another so that precursors turn into successors, what follows after can change the meaning of what comes before, and dialogues between productions defy the laws of chronology. The linearity of succession makes way for viral interpenetration, as contagion travels freely between any broadcasts that come into contact' (25). A notable instance of the challenge to the laws of chronology was the Berliner Ensemble's (re)production of Dimiter Gotscheff's 2007 version of Heiner Müller's *Hamlet Machine*, in which the play had been reconceived 'as a monologue that could be segmented, repeated, and shared between himself and his fellow actors, with the roles of Hamlet and Ophelia distributed across several bodies', uncoupling the text 'from affect and subjectivity' (35). With a recording made in 2013 by Gotscheff, who was terminally ill, to take his place in a tour to Cuba, the company has revived *Hamlet Machine* annually on his birthday. Consequently, 'while the living actors seemed able, for the duration of the ritual, to pull Gotscheff back into the space of the theatre as if in a seance, the medium of the broadcast juxtaposed their liveness with his recordedness in such a manner as to make them all feel equally alive and dead, present and absent' (38). Accessing the production remotely thus added a further element of the uncanny: one senses from Aebischer's account that this doubly remediated performance was at once enriched and rendered more disturbing by the circumstances in which she watched it.

Viral Shakespeare complements the essays in *Shakespeare and the 'Live' Theatre Broadcast Experience* (2018), which Aebischer co-edited with Susan Greenhalgh and Laurie E. Osborne. It also adds a new dimension to *Shakespeare, Spectatorship and the Technologies of Performance*. Among the subjects this addresses are the early modern technologies of the Sam Wanamaker Playhouse (SWP), the experience of watching camera operators during the live streaming of the RSC's 2016 *Hamlet* (directed by Simon Godwin) and the place of digital technology within Greg Doran's *Tempest* in the same year. The book's juxtaposition of the different modes of spectatorship on offer is both informed by historical and technical scholarship and infused with her sensitive personal responses. The description of the experience of spectators in the SWP's upper gallery hardly amounts to an advertisement for the theatre, where, for those who cannot afford better accommodation, '[w]atching demands physical investment and is charged with affect born out of a combination of frustration, distance and physical effort in a sensually charged atmosphere'. These unfortunates are 'coaxed into taking greater, and more individual, responsibility for choosing where to look and for using their imagination to fill the obstructions to their gaze' (47). This is an important observation on the relative nature of the theatrical experience: like Rob Conkie's *Writing Performative Shakespeares: New Forms for Performance*

Criticism (2016), it serves as a reminder that the communal experience of Shakespeare's audiences was fragmented, rather than unified, by their playing spaces. Aebischer is persuasive in her account of the SWP's other affordances, and of the manner in which, for the soliloquies in the 'live broadcast' of the RSC *Hamlet*, camera close-ups replaced the potential effect of direct address with a different kind of intimacy. Here, the analysis is informed by her adoption of Hans-Thies Lehmann's dual concept of a theatre audience's 'responsibility' and 'respons-ability', as well as the observation that the filmed performance has the potential to elide the private *locus* with the more public *platea* identified by Robert Weimann's *Shakespeare and the Popular Tradition in the Theatre* (1967; published in English translation in 1978). There are moments when the medium may have become the message at the expense of some necessary question of the play. The most notable is the claim, regarding the use in the RSC *Tempest* of projections and the digital capture of Ariel's body movements, that '[i]n its confrontation between Beale's human Prospero and Mark Quigley's posthuman Ariel, it cast a spotlight on the perceived threat digital media pose to empathy and the capacity for politic-ethical response-ability/responsibility in technologically enhanced theatre' (88). In the book's terms, this is an incontestably valid point, but it fails to acknowledge the less sophisticated response that this was simply a clever new way of delivering an Ariel 'live' with some of the advantages of film or video technology. It should also be noted that the illusion was imperfectly available to audience members at the side of the thrust stage: it seemed to be fully effective only from seats facing the centre of the stage, and in the streamed version. (There, however, it was arguably part of the familiar repertoire of film and video special effects.)

In an essay in *Shakespeare and the Live Broadcast Theatre Experience*, Susan Greenhalgh remarks that 'Live broadcast is turning what was once a single-medium space – the stage – into a hybrid space accommodating multiple media' (35). A recurring topic in discussions of such productions is the potential for the performance to become an archival document, supplementing if not supplanting in-house archive videos, which are often created with a single fixed camera. M. J. Kidnie observes of the Stratford Festival of Canada's recordings that 'the achievement of liveness – when and if it is achieved – is fleeting, and live transmission will inevitably, eventually, transform into recorded live theatre' (141). As well as addressing the specifics of the recording and transmission process, the collection encompasses the range of audience reactions, from Julie Raby writing as spectator present in the theatre during a broadcast, to Kitamura Sae's account of the reception of NTLive broadcasts in Japanese fan culture and Keir Elam's report on 'Hamlet Bolognese' in two very different cinemas in Bologna. *Broadcast Your Shakespeare: Continuity and Change across Media*, edited by Stephen O'Neill, offers a comparable range of topics, each essay adding a fresh insight into what might be (to coin the title of J. L. Styan's 1970 book) another 'Shakespeare Revolution'. Diana Henderson describes her experience of work on the MIT Global Shakespeare project in a 'SWOT' analysis of strengths, weaknesses, opportunities and threats. This is indeed, as she describes it, 'a case study that may assist others wrestling with the challenging, changing digital/Shakespeare studies landscape' (70). Christy Desmet evaluates 'emo Shakespeare', in which 'videos scattered through Facebook mimic ironically the ethos of their subject matter. Disaffected, disconnected, disenchanted, emo Hamlet reflects the state of social media in the age of platform proliferation, random videos distributed across the communicative landscape, with no ability to forge connections or propagate.' As a social media phenomenon, this 'points us towards the transformation of emotion (as the possession of an individual) into affect (feeling distributed socially along webs and networks) in the new media' (114). The Internet has also accelerated and redefined celebrity: Anna Blackwell examines the way Tom Hiddleston's 'Shakespearean' status has been established 'in the multimedia exchange spaces of digital culture' (245).

Shakespeare in the Theatre: The King's Men by Lucy Munro draws on a wealth of textual and archival evidence to demonstrate how the King's Men, 'as theatre-makers in their own right, exercised a generative and transformative influence on Shakespeare's plays', with practices that 'over four decades shaped traditions that would define Shakespearean performance' (xiv). This historical study's approach is informed but not dominated by theoretical awareness. In a series of case studies, with 'interludes' on specific performance occasions, Munro explores the significance of the theatre's repertory system, and what would now be called its business model, in the work of actors as well as playwrights, A 'double sense of "service"' is posited as 'crucial to the operations of the King's Men' (xv) and the situation of the actor himself, who (as David Schalkwyk has suggested) 'embodies his enabling relationship to the master by whose grace his personations are permitted; as a member of a commercial theatre dependent on a paying audience, he enacts service in a more modern, market sense'.[1] Munro illustrates the audiences' role in 'helping to shape and sustain' the repertory, and 'the impact of both individual players and the broader structures of the playing company on the performance and reception of plays' (7). This is a wide-ranging study, attentive to the challenges of the work of the boy players, 'generally required to move between different roles and styles of performance' (38), as well as to '[t]he performance tactics that made Burbage appear natural onstage: controlling his vocal delivery, working gesture and speech in tandem and maintaining his performance when he was not speaking' (25). Munro identifies ways in which these 'company-focused readings of Shakespeare's plays' offer 'new critical perspectives on their narrative and dramaturgical structures' (54). Discussion of *Othello* and *The Alchemist* 'suggests something more complex' than the idea of clearly defined 'lines' of characters 'inherited wholesale' by the actors' younger colleagues (66). She reads backwards and forwards between the actors, the specifics of the venues and the scripted roles. For instance, in the case of Othello, Munro identifies a character who 'epitomizes the techniques of the leading actor, drawing power from his position at the centre of the Globe audience's attention and from his very status within the playing company' (68). As well as being a model of historical procedure, attentive to the material circumstances and dynamics of performance and playing spaces, this study of the King's Men is an invaluable contribution to the interpretation of the plays in its repertoire.

David Wiles, in *The Players' Advice to Hamlet: The Rhetorical Acting Method from the Renaissance to the Enlightenment* (Cambridge, 2020), takes Elizabethan acting as its starting-point, but his scope is more comprehensive than the explication of the prince's rather presumptuous notes session. (In many productions I have seen, the seasoned professional actor's response has been deferential but with a degree of amused tolerance.) Wiles surveys the theory and practice of rhetoric from its Greco-Roman origins to the point when, in his estimation, it began to suffer at the hands of Diderot and other enthusiasts for the expression of the individual character's state of mind. Wiles sees 'the history of pre-modern acting' as having been 'bedevilled by a polarization of "rhetoric" and "naturalness", with rhetoric forced to stand as the negative moral and aesthetic term' (174). Stanislavski figures as a source of the continuing error among the players, and the commercial theatre as a siren whose blandishments caused Bertram Joseph to stray from the right path in his studies of Elizabethan acting. As for the prince himself, Wiles opens up a new line of approach: 'Hamlet resorts to violence after failing to master the instruments of verbal combat. He lacks the skill to be a rhetorical actor because his performance training has been deficient' (334). This formidably documented and forcefully argued study makes a strong case that perhaps may not carry conviction with all its readers, but which raises familiar questions in a fresh and invigorating manner.

Alisa Grant Ferguson's *The Shakespeare Hut: A Source of Memory, Performance and Identity, 1916–1923* deals with a very different set of circumstances,

---

[1] David Schalkwyk, *Shakespeare, Love and Service* (Cambridge 2008), p. 10.

300 years on from the heyday of Shakespeare's company, in which a temporary (but quite substantial) 'Tudor' building on the site of the present London School of Hygiene and Tropical Medicine 'occupied a liminal space between "timelessness" and "timeliness". In the same way, perhaps, as Shakespeare has done, at least as a cultural icon' (5). The real estate had been earmarked first for a national Shakespeare memorial to Shakespeare, then for the National Theatre, but became a centre for the recreation and accommodation of New Zealanders on leave from the Western Front. The main hall offered 'an austere wartime stage on which there was no room for spectacle or pedantry' (40), and the entertainments constituted 'a female-led version of Shakespearean production that effortlessly crossed the boundaries of cultural forms' (165). This cultural radicalism benefitted from 'the strange and powerful maelstrom of a new, militarized imperial bardolatry during which the Tercentenary would fall'. It also shared one of the purposes of the YMCA's work in London, protecting soldiers from the less respectable opportunities afforded by their leave, described by an Australian newspaper as 'the woman-peril of the streets' (133). Ferguson documents the hut's career in detail, emphasizing its links with the feminist movement in the theatre as well as its avoidance of the antiquarianism that characterized much of the reaction against the lavishness of mainstream Shakespearian performance. Its final function, as a centre for Indian students, meant that, 'in all its guises', it was also 'permeated by the radical politics and dynamic national identity formation of its very specific temporary moment, 1916–23' (184).

Gemma Miller, in *Childhood in Contemporary Performance of Shakespeare*, examines 'the affective power of the child in performance, whose stage presence (and absence) invariably exceeds his/her textual significance'. It may be possible that this is 'increasingly evident in contemporary productions' (6) because audiences – including Miller herself – have become increasingly likely to look for it, but the identification of the child as 'a site of conflicting hopes, desires, fears and doubts' (20) is supported by thoughtful and meticulous examination of four plays in performance: *Richard III*, *Macbeth*, *Titus Andronicus* and *The Winter's Tale*. Miller's critiques are invariably stimulating and insightful, deriving much of their strength from the sharp focus on specific scenes, as well as the more general effect of the child's participation in productions. The chapter on *Titus Andronicus* draws on the staging by Deborah Warner (RSC, 1987), Jane Howell's BBC Shakespeare production and Juliet Taymor's film *Titus*. The 'Fly' scene (4.1) is shown to have become 'an important moment of revelation in performance, displaying in microcosm the play's precarious balance of pity and cruelty, terror and humour, madness and clear-headed sanity' (101), and Taymor's child, first seen playing a violent war game on a kitchen table, provides 'a fascinating case study in the interconnected worlds of the child and the moving image and a key figure in terms of understanding how to interpret the overall message of this film' (118).

Bridget Escolme's *Shakespeare and Costume in Practice* addresses the contribution of costume in productions of *Hamlet*, *Much Ado about Nothing* and *The Tempest* to the ways in which a modern audience 'potentially experiences an early modern drama dually, as both familiar and historically alien at different points of a performance' (161). In 1600, Hamlet's 'inky cloak and suits of solemn black' were 'a personal choice, a visual symbol, and a political statement' (26). Now, though, 'the barely noticeable black Hamlet costume of the modern dress production helps to foreground *Hamlet* as a play about the central character's psyche rather than about his social world' (56). An exception that proves the rule was Paapa Essiedu's defiance of convention in the RSC's 2016 *Hamlet* set in a fictional African state, where his clothing choices were signs of his struggle 'for a mode of expression that was outside of the ways in which both his uncle's corrupted court made visual sense of the world, and outside of the visual traditions of his father and nation' (67).

Costume also figures in a chapter of *About Shakespeare: Bodies, Space and Time*, a contribution by Robert Shaughnessy to the Cambridge Essentials series. The book's overall purpose is to address 'how performances are "about" Shakespeare in other ways than being explicative of or determined by their scripts' (2), and Shaughnessy writes out of the conviction that 'Shakespeare's works continue to matter as much for the conversations, connections and arguments that they catalyse as for themselves' (4). The meanings attached to (or, perhaps, embraced by) Falstaff's belly and the prosthetic devices used to realize it are situated in the context of 'a world where rotundity is more generally perceived as an index of ill health, self-abuse and low self-esteem' and 'is more associated with poverty, underachievement and failure' (20). As with the other elements of *About Shakespeare*, like a successful seminar paper, this raises questions – 'Yes, but' – that readers will wish to pursue for themselves. The genial and generous dimensions of other illustrious fat men heave into view: Oliver Hardy, Sidney Greenstreet's characters in *The Maltese Falcon* and *Casablanca*, the immensity of the later Orson Welles (especially in *Chimes at Midnight*) and, of course, the conventional representations of Santa Claus. Contemporary anxieties about 'fat shaming' have to vie for the same mental space as celebrations of the intellectual, and frequent physical, nimbleness of fiction's fat men. Another discussion broached by Shaughnessy with a characteristic combination of intellectual rigour and historical acumen concerns the audiences at the recreated Globe on London's Bankside: 'To what extent is Globe performance a mutually supportive, shared game, and to what degree is it a site of antagonism, a power struggle, a context for control?' (29). Paradoxically, the critics' characterization of yard denizens as 'an appetite-driven, taste-deficient and self-indulgent underclass' is at odds with the reports of actors that – perhaps understandably in view of their professional loyalty – seem to present these 'understanders' as 'a discriminating, participative, popular audience' (32). These two sections can be read, in terms of the longer historical and social view, as relevant to understanding of the 'original' Shakespearian audience and its imaginary. Less easily enlisted in this manner is Shaughnessy's account of Thomas Ostermeier's *Richard III* at the Berlin Schaubühne. As in Aebischer's reflections in *Viral Shakespeare* on viewing a video of the same director's *The Taming of the Shrew*, the emphasis is on 'a changing media landscape in which the relations between text and image are being rapidly reconfigured' (58).

Other Cambridge Elements that address issues in contemporary theatrical performance include Regina Buccola's *Haunting History on Stage: Shakespeare in the USA and Canada*. With specific reference to history-play cycles staged in Chicago and at the Stratford Festival of Canada, Buccola asks what attracts audiences in these former colonies 'to sign up for three hours or seven hours of theatrical medieval violence, particularly when directorial choices link "medieval" violence to millennial violence?' (7). (Although she suggests that, in the United Kingdom, 'audiences might be expected to have a working familiarity with British history' (1), arguably, this knowledge derives mainly from the plays themselves.) Buccola's account of the productions, and of the experience of attending the 'marathons', is detailed and discerning, and the answer to her question would seem to be – as one might expect – that the adapted texts work as pretexts for addressing political and social questions of the present day. She observes, for example, that, although 'Shakespeare's Yorkist men hate Joan and Margaret; increasingly, women directors love them, and stage them as loci of a reclaimed power emanating from the sexuality socially constructed as a liability, as a reason to deny them power' (32). *Shakespearean Futures: Casting the Bodies of Tomorrow on Shakespeare's Stages Today*, by Amy Cook, addresses the opportunities of diversity in casting – notably what she terms counter casting, 'where bodies are used by the director against type to change our minds, to stretch and alter our categories' (2). A familiar but important distinction is drawn between casting that is supposedly blind to race or gender, and that which 'specifically uses the bodies of the actors to respond to the play and to stage the future' (16). *King Lear* is identified as one of the plays that might speak to 'this particular moment of heightened chaos' (43), and there is a note of optimism as well as alarm in Cook's insistence that theatre offers 'new metaphors to think our way out of trouble', and that 'At this moment, we need a new story about who we are in relation to the planet and its other inhabitants' (62). With its account of the cultural and politics of *Othello* productions in Holland, Coen Heijes's *Shakespeare, Blackface and Race: Different Perspectives* provides 'a different perspective on blackface and race in a supposedly tolerant, Western country' (73). The cultural background includes the controversy over 'Black Peter', Saint Nicholas's traditional exotic companion, whose duties notionally include the chastisement of children judged naughty rather than nice, and consequently ineligible for Christmas presents. A prime exhibit in Heijes's compelling exposition of Holland's version of so-called 'culture wars', and the legacy of its colonialist past, is the *Othello* first seen at Het Nationale Toneel, the National Theatre, in 2018, and revived in 2020. This was the first time a black actor had appeared in a main-house production of the play: 'Opposite the black Othello in this production, all the other actors were whitened up even further to highlight the extreme whiteness of the ruling elite' (6). Its 'highly enthusiastic yet also problematic reception', summed up in the headline of one of its reviews, is telling: 'Othello is Black and that matters' (52).

In the same series, *Robert Lepage's Intercultural Encounters* by Christie Carson challenges the acceptance of the director's 'credentials as an intercultural director' (4). Situating his non-Shakespearian as well as Shakespearian work in the context of Quebec's diverse regional and ethnic cultures, in 'two different languages and at least four different theatre traditions' (2), Carson identifies some of the contradictions and controversies in his engagement with Canadian history and the varied identities of its communities. The rhetoric of multiculturalism is identified as 'a continuation of colonial ideals, taking ethnicity and formulating it into manageable representative packages, which can be demonstrated and displayed as folkloric spectacle' (67–8). The coincidence across the world of the pandemic and protests about racism has provided 'an extraordinary moment of clarity about current and possible future directions for the study of Shakespeare and performance in general and Lepage's work in particular' (5).

Like Lepage, Yukio Ninagawa has often figured in discussions of 'intercultural' and 'international' Shakespeare, at the expense of attention to his dedication to the specifics of his engagement with his own culture. Conor Hanratty's account of his career, in the Arden series *Shakespeare in the Theatre*, redresses the balance, demonstrating that 'his primary artistic focus was on telling stories to his own people'. The interpretation of his productions as being 'conceived specifically (or worse, exclusively) for foreign consumption' has taken no account of a 'lifetime commitment to his Japanese audience' (27). The small proportion of his Shakespeare productions seen outside Japan – about a third of the total – serves as a reminder that one of his principal aims was 'sophisticated, deliberate manipulation of Japanese images for *Japanese* viewers' (31). Framing devices and other metatheatrical strategies were designed to 'explain the rules of a given production' (23), and for Japanese audiences his deployment of their traditions of representation and performance was the reverse of Brechtian alienation, being, rather, the helpful familiarization of foreign plays. Hanratty's account of the circumstances of Ninagawa's Shakespeare – for example, his eight separate productions of *Hamlet* – reveals an artist of extraordinary energy, whose focus was 'always on forward motion and improvement, on addressing problems that he had not quite solved' (6). With its layering of devices and effects, his 2006 *Comedy of Errors* was 'an intricately constructed *millefeuille* of perspectives' (145). Hanratty has convincingly identified Ninagawa as a man for all (theatrical) seasons, for whom 'appropriation', far from being suspect, is a way of life: 'There was such a breadth of imagination in his work that it could simultaneously be described as intercultural or intertextual, global or local, Victorian or postmodern, cinematic or immediate, nostalgic or contemporary' (196). One detail suggests the instinct for simple effects that lay behind the grander gestures and seemingly exotic elements of performance for which he was celebrated internationally. On a research trip to Italy before directing *Romeo and Juliet*, he was surprised to see young people running in the street, 'still a comparatively rare sight in Japan'. This became 'a major element' of all his productions of the play after 1974. Hanratty's expert and comprehensive study is a valuable corrective to simplistic evaluations of the widely toured productions that treat their aesthetic as the imposition of *Japonaiserie*.

'Intercultural' gives way to an arguably more accommodating term in the title of Sudhaseel Sen's *Shakespeare in the World: Cross-cultural Adaptation in Europe and Colonial India, 1850–1900*. After a closely argued introduction, Sen addresses the significance of adaptive strategies in Verdi's *Otello*, and responses to *The Tempest* in the novel *Kapālakuṇḍalā* (1866), with its fusion of Caliban and Miranda, and the essay 'Śakuntalā, Miranda, and Desdemona' (1875) by Bankimchandra Chatterjee, 'one of the first and most influential among writers from colonial India to cultivate the novel as a genre' (21). Sen emphasizes the benefits of appropriation in the Indian adaptations, which 'provided the opportunity for adapters to not just have Shakespearean influences transform their own cultural values but also to transform Shakespeare's texts when they deemed fit. One could write back to Shakespeare, as it were, and still consider him to be a writer of towering significance' (11). Verdi emerges from Sen's expert musicological and cultural study as a subversive innovator, with *Otello* 'offering a palimpsest of different approaches towards race, religion, and gender, its subversive element predominating as a result of the greater expressive weight carried by music and because of Verdi's unexpected stylistic choices with regard to the music and staging' (60). *Aida*, Verdi's last completed opera before *Otello*, might have suggested an orientalizing approach to Cyprus and the drama unfolding there. But the composer's musical subversion lies in his positing the 'self/other binary' in terms not of 'the European vis-à-vis the exotic (or oriental)', but of the Germanic (and Wagnerian) 'valorisation of the systematic development of motifs, of orchestral complexity, and of increasing chromaticism' versus the traditional 'Italian Self' represented by the 'importance attached to melody, to the expressive supremacy of the human voice, and to harmonic simplicity' (86). This is a richly rewarding book, suggesting important adjustments to the manner in which adaptations, in reaction against discourses of fidelity, have served diverse cultural formations. Sen insists eloquently on attention to individuals and specific circumstances and goals, rather than vague pigeonholing of artists and audiences in accordance with (admittedly) well-intentioned liberal consensus:

> In both the European and the Indian contexts of Shakespeare reception, we need to move away from the tendency to pigeonhole Shakespeare's adapters into larger essentialist categories, such as the racist European or the culturally colonised 'native,' without forgetting that such people also existed. Instead, we need to consider the methodological implications of the fact that individuals within a group are still individuals, and that it is the duty of the scholar to examine the extent to which the ideological coordinates of any adapter were consonant with those of his/her larger community *as well as to what extent they were not*. (100)

By focusing on European as well as Indian re-visioning of Shakespeare, Sen challenges some of the assumptions behind commentary on adaptations, in terms that resonate widely in the field of Shakespeare studies.

The successful appropriation of Shakespeare in Indian popular culture is also addressed in a groundbreaking collection, *Shakespeare and Indian Cinemas: Local Habitations*, edited by Poonam Trivedi and Paromita Chakravarti. With its fifteen critical essays, three interviews and a chronological filmography of 115 titles, this provides a welcome and long overdue account of a subject hitherto treated only piecemeal in English-language scholarship. The plural 'cinemas' is important, because the currency of the term 'Bollywood' has, Trivedi points out, led to the erasure and scholarly neglect of the thirteen full-fledged regional-language cinemas in India: 'Since Hindi is the largest spoken language ... and a designated national language (along with English), its cinematic dominance is numerically accountable. But, though the regional film industries also cater primarily to their own language constituencies, each has a distinct cultural identity and historical trajectory, and independent modes of financing and production' (3). In her own essay, Trivedi, who has contributed an overview of the director's work to the recent *Cambridge Companion to Shakespeare on Screen* (2020), focuses on the figure of the female avenger in the films of Vishal Bhardwaj. This is representative of the combination of range and depth in *Shakespeare and Indian Cinemas*, qualities that should contribute to wider engagement in Shakespeare studies with the creative vitality of an impressive body of cinematic achievement. The acknowledgements page of *Asian Interventions in Global Shakespeare: 'All the World's His Stage'*, edited by Trivedi, Chakravarti and Ted Motohashi (2021) notes that its twelve essays 'emerge largely out of presentations made at the second biennial conference of the Asian Shakespeare Association in Delhi, 1–3 December 2016'. The volume offers a complementary perspective to that of the salutary local emphasis of *Shakespeare and Indian Cinemas*, taking in literary and digital media, manga and anime, as well as cinema across the continent.

After dealing in an impressively concise manner with the theories of adaptation, *Studying Shakespeare Adaptation* is a wide-ranging introductory text that will be rewarding for seasoned specialists as well as a student audience. The examples chosen by Pamela Bickley and Jenny Stevens range across media, time and place of origin to break the monopoly of the usual suspects. The Dryden/Davenant version of *The Tempest* is in the company of W. H. Auden and Derek Jarman, while, for *The Winter's Tale*, Mary Cowden Clarke's *The Girlhood of Shakespeare's Heroines* finds a place alongside the ballet by Christopher Wheeldon, and Greg Doran's 1999 RSC production. The writing is often witty, as well as incisive: in the Reinhardt/Dieterle film of *A Midsummer Night's Dream*, the little Indian boy, appropriated successfully by Oberon in 'an opportunistic kidnapping', is equipped with a miniature version of his new protector's headdress, 'antler-like branches fitting for a regal male spirit of the forest', and his 'inscription into the male symbolic order' is thus 'managed without any trace of lasting trauma' (59).

Another work designed primarily for student use, *Studying Shakespeare on Film* by Rebekah Owens, manages a comparable combination of coverage and fresh thinking, exemplified by the sympathetic consideration given to the positive qualities of Keanu Reeves's much-criticized Don John in Kenneth Branagh's *Much Ado about Nothing*: 'This is not a diminution of Shakespeare's creation, nor a performance that showcases Reeves's supposed shortcomings as a classical actor', but an appropriate response to the characterization in the dialogue of someone who is 'not able or willing – to be subtle'. With such lines as 'I cannot hide what I am', Owens asks, 'what else could Reeves do but scowl a lot, wear black and throw out the occasional maniacal laugh?' (36). Michael Keaton's unabashedly over-the-top Dogberry in the same film is treated to a similar revaluation. Many readers will still find the actors and the film guilty as charged, but the verdict may have been edged closer to the useful 'not proven' available in Scottish law. Addressed primarily to a student readership, both *Studying Shakespeare Adaptation* and *Studying Shakespeare on Film* take their place among the other works reviewed in reflecting the maturity and continuing appeal of the study of Shakespeare adaptations and of performance in particular.

A few lines of valediction seem in order. Over the ten years during which I have been writing these annual reviews, the field has become increasingly sophisticated in response to the rise of new ways – sometimes challenging and surprising – in which the plays can be interpreted, performed and enjoyed. At the time of writing, when circumstances have militated against live theatrical presentation in the presence of audiences, innovative responses to performances in the newer media have proved to be more than merely a stopgap. The scholarly writing exemplified in the works discussed here has risen to the opportunities and challenges of the present. At the same time, stimulating revisions of the earlier history of Shakespearian performance have enriched understanding of the past, and, at a time of global upheaval and threatened or imminent division, 'global' perspectives have challenged the primacy of the anglophone and European sphere. Attention has been paid increasingly to the priorities and values of artists and audiences across the globe, and the study of Shakespeare in Performance has been enriched to a commensurate extent. On a personal level, I am grateful to the authors whose work has made writing these reviews a pleasurable task.

WORKS REVIEWED

Note: As well as books issued in 2021, this review takes into account books that appeared in 2020, and – in some cases – work published earlier but not available in paperback until then.

Aebischer, Pascale, *Shakespeare, Spectatorship and the Technologies of Performance* (Cambridge, 2020)

Viral Shakespeare (Cambridge, 2021)

Bickley, Pamela, and Jenny Stevens, *Studying Shakespeare Adaptation* (London, 2021)

Buccola, Regina, *Haunting History on Stage: Shakespeare in the USA and Canada* (Cambridge, 2019)

Carson, Christie, *Robert Lepage's Intercultural Encounters* (Cambridge, 2021)

Cook, Amy, *Shakespearean Futures: Casting the Bodies of Tomorrow on Shakespeare's Stages Today* (Cambridge, 2020)

Escolme, Bridget, *Shakespeare and Costume in Practice* (London, 2021)

Ferguson, Alisa Grant, *The Shakespeare Hut: A Story of Memory, Performance and Identity, 1916–1923* (London, 2018)

Hanratty, Conor, *Shakespeare in the Theatre: Yukio Ninagawa* (London, 2020)

Heijes, Coen, *Shakespeare, Blackface and Race: Different Perspectives* (Cambridge, 2020)

Miller, Gemma, *Childhood in Contemporary Performance of Shakespeare* (London, 2020)

Munro, Lucy, *Shakespeare in the Theatre: The King's Men* (London, 2020)

O'Neill, **S**tephen, ed., *Broadcast Your Shakespeare: Continuity and Change across Media* (London, 2018)

Owens, Rebekah, *Studying Shakespeare on Film* (Liverpool, 2021)

Sen, Sudhaseel, *Shakespeare in the World: Cross-cultural Adaptation in Europe and Colonial India, 1850–1900* (London, 2021)

Shaughnessy, Robert, *About Shakespeare: Bodies, Space and Time* (Cambridge, 2020)

Trivedi, Poonam, and Paromita Chakravarti, eds., *Shakespeare and Indian Cinemas: Local Habitations* (London and Abingdon, 2019)

Trivedi, Poonam, Paromita Chakravarti and Ted Motohashi, eds., *Asian Interventions in Global Shakespeare: 'All the World's His Stage'* (London and Abingdon, 2021)

Wiles, David, *The Players' Advice to Hamlet: The Rhetorical Acting Method from the Renaissance to the Enlightenment* (Cambridge, 2020)

3. EDITIONS AND TEXTUAL STUDIES
reviewed by EMMA DEPLEDGE

The year 2020–2021 witnessed the publication of important titles that invite us to reflect on the history of editing and textual studies, their specific relationship to earlier approaches such as New Bibliography, the responsibilities we bear when presenting new or revisionist narratives, and ways in which the field can do more to embrace diversity. A landmark resource was released in the form of the two-volume New Variorum Edition of *King Lear*, with Richard Knowles's breath-taking textual notes recording all variants in seventy-seven editions from the period 1619 to 2000. *The Arden Shakespeare Third Series Complete Works* was released, as was the much anticipated second edition of Andrew Murphy's *Shakespeare in Print*, complete with an updated chronological appendix that now takes us to the year 2017. The first scholarly edition of the commonplace book *Bel-vedére or the Garden of the Muses* was also published, and exciting new monographs by Faith Acker, Zachary Lesser and Molly G. Yarn were joined by edited collections entitled *Shakespeare / Text* and the *Arden Research Handbook of Shakespeare and Textual Studies*.

EDITIONS

Richard Knowles's colossal edition of *King Lear*, which consists of two volumes of around 1,000 pages each, diligently upholds the New Variorum series's reputation as the foremost reference source detailing centuries of emendation history and textual scholarship. Knowles does not simply update Horace Howard Furness's 1880 edition; with the help of student assistants – John C. Hill, Becky Bohan, Vivian Foss and Elizabeth Reinwald – he has redone the work of collating seventy-seven editions, including Furness's. The first volume contains the text of the 1608 First Quarto, the first printed edition of the play, and includes 110 additional lines taken from the First Folio. Knowles states that it must include both Q-only and F-only lines 'because all of those lines have been subject to commentary and theatrical use' (xv). Q1 was selected, he writes, because it 'reflects the general belief today that it not only is the earliest edition but also offers the earliest version of the play, one close to Shakespeare's original drafts, and that the Folio represents a later version incorporating changes made for various theatrical and artistic purposes' (xv). Textual issues are analysed in detail in the second volume, where Knowles sets out what is known about the printing history of Q1, Q2 and F before surveying the multifarious opinions about both the texts' relationship to one another and what, if anything, they might tell us about 'Shakespeare's intentions' (1042). Ultimately, he finds in favour of a hypothesis that 'allows for the possibility that some of the revisions in F might be authorial but recognizes also that numerous other hands could have intervened, and in all probability did' (1205).

Each page of text records collations from Q2 of 1619 through to Stanley Wells's 2000 Oxford edition, in addition to hundreds of years' worth of critical and editorial commentary on individual words. It is, of course, not a text for reading – one seldom gets more than six lines of the play-text to a page – but it is one from which a great deal can be learned about the play's editorial and critical history. It might be surprising, for example, to discover that A. C. Bradley speculated at length about the reasons why Lear may have addressed Burgundy before France in the play's first act; Bradley suggested that 'the apparent choice in public here is a mere fiction because Cordelia's marriage has been prearranged', as opposed to simply seeing the exchange with Burgundy as a delay deliberately designed for dramatic effect, with 'Burgundy's backpedaling', as Knowles sensibly suggests, winning sympathy for France and Cordelia (100-1). Sagacious and accurate throughout, Knowles's editing is of the highest quality.

A much appreciated material feature that greatly adds to the volume's utility and convenience is the inclusion of the sigla for editions in both volumes' end-paper paste-ins, where they are arranged both chronologically and alphabetically. The sigla, of vital importance to anyone wishing to follow the condensed formulae used to record textual collations, are also included in Knowles's 'Plan of the work', but it is much easier to refer back to the opening of the volume, or else to consult the paste-downs of the second volume, whilst reading from the first volume, than it is to find the correct page in the plan. The edition's appendix, contained in Volume II, is also worthy of strong praise. The play's stage history, produced by Paula Glatzer, includes seventeenth-century performances, a survey of significant performances of the play from 1681 to 2000, and an overview of changes to the text as recorded in adaptations and prompt books from 1681 to 2000. A further three pages are dedicated to 'Films, adaptations, and offshoots', from silent films to novels, and there is also a section on the play's use of music, complete with 'possible contemporary musical settings for some of its lines, and of later music inspired by the play' (1864). The incredible survey of interpretive criticism, written by Kevin Donovan, who is listed as Associate Editor of the edition, is also joined by detailed discussion of the play's sources.

Knowles's *Lear* is the last New Variorum Shakespeare edition to be published by the Modern Language Association. It was completed long before its release date suggests, with publication initially delayed due to financial issues. It is therefore a relief to note that the series now has a new home; according to the series's website, in 2019, 'Laura Mandell, Director of the Center of Digital Humanities Research (CoDHR) at Texas A&M University, generously offered to publish the NVS and contracted with Anne Burdick to build a site for the series in order to bring it to the WWW and thereby to a broad audience.' New editions of this vitally important series, aptly described as an 'edition as archive' in Murphy's *Shakespeare in Print* (358), will thus continue to be produced, and editions previously published in print will be available online.

Another volume that marks a milestone in Shakespeare editing, though with a very different kind of readership in mind than Knowles's *Lear*, is *The Arden Shakespeare Complete Works*, edited by Richard Proudfoot, Ann Thompson, David Scott Kastan and H. R. Woudhuysen. This represents the first collected edition of a full set of Arden texts, given that the last Arden *Complete Works* featured a mixture of Arden 2 and Arden 3 texts. The individual playbooks of the Arden Third Series have been extensively reviewed by my predecessors, and the series as a whole was analysed in Jennifer Young's excellent review essay in the previous issue of *Shakespeare Survey* (74 (2021)), but it is nonetheless worth reflecting on what changes most when a series of individual poetry and play editions becomes a complete works edition. For example, the order in which one receives individual editions depends on their release date; here, instead, the sonnets and poems are followed by the plays, arranged not in the order in which their editing was completed, nor in their most likely original chronological order of printing or performance, or even according to genre, but rather in alphabetical order. In stark contrast with the pages of individual Arden 3 editions, where annotations and collation notes at times take up more space than the text of the plays, the pages of texts here presented are void of marginal glosses, footnotes or detailed notes on collation (with the exception of *King Lear*, *Titus* and *Thomas More*, discussed below). The work aims to create 'clarity and consistency' through the application of what the general editors define as 'conservative' editing: by silently 'modernizing the spelling and punctuation ... regularizing (and not abbreviating) the names of characters, and rationalizing entrances and exits' (vii). The effect is that the individual texts resemble each other typographically and the reading process is seldom interrupted. The *Complete Works*' bibliography and glossary also link the texts by offering coverage of the plays and poems together at the end.

The series's most novel content features – the inclusion of *Double Falsehood*, *Sir Thomas More*, *King Edward III* and the three-text *Hamlet*, i.e., the First and Second Quarto texts of 1603 and 1604–1605, and the 1623 First Folio text – are accounted for in the 'General Editors' Preface'. The introductions preceding *Falsehood*, *More* and *Edward III* also argue (albeit here in much briefer form than in the individual editions) the case for their plays' inclusion in the *Works*. Of *Hamlet*, the general editors insist that 'the text of Shakespeare's most complex play cannot adequately be presented singularly' (vi); briefly summarize the key theories surrounding the relationships between Q1, Q2 and F; and suggest that 'most editors ... offer a "conflated" text', before concluding that 'in the absence of a consensus about the precise relationship between the texts it seems preferable to treat each as if it were an independent entity' (vi). Applied to *Hamlet* alone, and made at the start of the volume, might cause some readers to assume (mistakenly) that there *is* a consensus about 'the precise relationship between the texts' of Shakespeare's other plays and poems.

That said, the introductions to individual plays do offer brief accounts of, for example, 'anomalies and dislocations in the text', and ways in which scholars have explained them (*Measure for Measure*, 919). The introductions and texts of *Lear*, *Titus* and *Thomas More* go further by alerting readers to conventions the editors have used to signal significant variants between different early printed versions of the texts, and, in the case of *Thomas More*, between 'the manuscript sections and the principal hand in each one' (1160). The *King Lear* text, based on the Folio, indicates words and passages present only in the 1608 Quarto by using a superscript Q, and uses a superscript F to mark those unique to the Folio (751). The 1594 First Quarto is used as the base text for *Titus* and this is annotated using the superscript 'Q2' at the beginning and end of passages to alert readers to 'a few corrections from the 1600 Second Quarto'. The 'addition of 3.2 from the 1623 First Folio' is likewise designated by a superscript F; and passages that 'Q1 should probably have deleted' are placed within braces '{ }' (1271). The various hands involved in the manuscript of *Thomas More* are indicated by more detailed typographical conventions, with a font change (to sans serif) used to indicate occasions when a second hand intervenes, superscript initials used to identify hands in the text, marginal lines used to alert readers to longer deleted passages, underlining used to show shorter deleted passages, and subscript letters / initials used when the identity of the hand responsible for a deletion is known (1160).

Another noteworthy material feature is the presentation of six sonnets per page in two columns – which arguably emphasizes links between different groupings – rather than dividing them into the pattern described in the introduction. Sonnets 1–16 are, like in most editions, said to be 'mainly addressed to a man younger and of higher social standing than the poet; sonnets 127–52 to an unfaithful mistress, whose other lovers include the young man', and the final two sonnets 'on the traditional themes of Cupid and Diana' are said to 'stand apart from this pattern' (17). The *mise-en-page* in the *Complete Works* does set 153 and 154 apart in the sense that these two final sonnets appear alone in the right-hand column (with 150–2 in the left-hand column), but it also sees 126 ('O thou my lovely boy') appear alongside the first five 'dark lady sonnets'. This arguably invites echoes between the 'sovereign mistress' (a clear personification of nature) of 126 and the mistress mentioned in 127 (line 9) which sits below it, as well as in 130, which sits adjacent to 127 and below right of 126. The Arden text is based on the 1609 First Quarto, where part of 127 also appears below 126 but, in the Quarto, 127 is divided at line 8, thus pushing the word 'mistress' onto the verso (H3^r). Stripped of the textual gloss and collation found in Katherine Duncan-Jones's stand-alone Arden edition, the mysterious parentheses that famously occupy the place of 126's final couplet also invite ambiguity and confusion for those turning to the *Complete Works* to read the sonnets for the first time. It is thus a perfectly competent *Complete Works* edition that presents very clean texts in which the reading process will seldom be interrupted, but I suspect all will not always appear as clear or 'accessible to modern readers' as the editors intended (vii).

TEXTUAL STUDIES

Readers of the sonnets are considered afresh, away from the kinds of biographical readings which flourished in the wake of Edmond Malone's 1780 biographical commentary on them, in Faith Acker's *First Readers of Shakespeare's Sonnets, 1590–1790*. Her study consists of nine short chapters that address the sonnets' production and circulation in print and manuscript over a 200-year period. Acker brings together a range of early discordant responses to the sonnets that have thus far escaped scholarly attention, and argues for the need to study what she sees as the 'priorities and interpretations' of early readers by recovering 'four lost critical' approaches to the sonnets: 'early readers' interests in Shakespeare's classical adaptations, political applicability, religious themes, and rhetorical skill during the seventeenth and eighteenth centuries' (i). The monograph draws on the methodologies of book history, editorial theory and manuscript studies to investigate the 'sonnets' public and private readers' (47). Her account seeks to highlight 'the versatility and flexibility that the sonnets' earliest readers imagined in and around these poems' (1), something which she claims has been obscured by the persistence of biographical readings.

The study joins a handful of recent monographs that provide reconsiderations of Shakespeare's poetry. Acker's painstaking reading of sonnet collections 1590–1790, annotated printed books, *Sammelbände* and manuscript sources result in numerous original findings, and it is refreshing to see manuscript and print history handled within the same study. For example, chapter 3 makes reference to twenty-one seventeenth-century manuscripts containing Shakespeare sonnets, and Acker observes that Sonnet 2 was the most 'widely transmitted Shakespeare sonnet' in the seventeenth century, with some compilers reading the poem 'in sexual contexts, considering the pleasures of intimacy even as they valued the rhetorical emphasis on the sexual product, with all its benefits to lineage and authority', while others 'seem also to have found the sonnet relevant within the contexts of their own political ambitions' (71).

Chapter 1 provides a clear and coherent overview of the publication history of the sonnets. It is here argued that the '(1599) *Passionate Pilgrim*'s brevity, single-sided printing, careful genre associations, and affiliation with Shakespeare's classical texts were meant to entice a wide range of possible buyers', from those 'who appreciated the courtly ideals of Renaissance sonnet sequences', and those who were keen to purchase more Shakespeare poetry after appreciating earlier publications, to those who appreciated 'Shakespeare's long-standing association with classical texts' (11). Elsewhere, she reads annotations found in print editions to note patterns by which early readers 'corrected the volumes they owned, sometimes updating their own editions to match variations and corrections suggested in other editions, and sometimes relying on their own experiences and intuition' (6). She further notes that transcribers of Shakespeare's poems produced manuscript miscellanies in which the sonnets were frequently 'enjoyed without the benefit of a larger sonnet sequence', or else 'set Shakespeare's sonnets between works by other poets, repeatedly mingling his works with poetry by members of their local communities and often pairing poems thematically rather than authorially' (7). The sparsity of extant evidence does, however, at times lead to a touch of overstatement concerning readers/transcribers. For example, she writes that 'Jaggard's clients, newly elevated to the elite status of Shakespearean sonnet readers, valued the collection's content and themes, and did not seem to notice stylistic discrepancies between the four formal sonnets by Shakespeare and several other poems – some by other poets – that completed the volume', but this claim is supported by reference to only 'a few extant manuscript transcriptions' (12).

Acker's strongest chapters are those which lie at the centre of her monograph. Chapter 4 offers an important reappraisal of John Benson, a stationer who was for a long time written off as a pirate, or else accused of meddling with the sonnets to discourage certain types of biographical readings. Acker provides a convincing reading of Benson as both a commercial stationer and an 'engaged and thoughtful reader' who, 'faced with a diverse array of short poems by a popular author' (97), put much thought into an arrangement that would offer internal coherence by illuminating common themes and accommodating changes in addressee and tone, whilst simultaneously deploying material features that helped to align the collection (visually) with earlier sonnet sequences. Indeed, she presents a case for crediting Benson with providing 'the most thorough textual apparatus for Shakespeare's poems within the first century and a half of their composition' (78). Chapter 6 demonstrates that, contrary to popular critical belief, it was not simply Shakespeare's plays that were altered during the second half of the seventeenth century: 'verses from Thorpe's 1609 sequence and Benson's 1640 collection – both featuring poems of procreation, temporal decay, and tumultuous passion – progressively became a Royalist song, a cross-dresser's dialogue, devotional poetry in praise of a virtuous King, two seductive conflations, and a laudatory preface' (124). Acker thus provides an important corrective for those of us who, by focusing on print alone, wrongly assumed that Shakespeare's poems were overlooked in the post-1650 period.

What is perhaps needed in this study is a clearer overview of how the nine chapters contribute to Acker's overarching thesis. Acker is right to consider stationers and editors as early readers of the sonnets, and I appreciated her insistence that the interventions of these stationers 'reveal the breadth of circumstances in which they imagined the sonnets might be read, as well as the agency they exerted upon other readers' experiences' (3). It would, however, have been helpful to have a clearer idea of how she defines (and distinguishes between) types of readers and transcribers, alongside a statement on the wider conclusions we can draw about the influence and 'agency' different manuscript and print sources had on different readers, and on the afterlife of Shakespeare's sonnets more generally. There is nonetheless much to be discovered in the individual chapters of this learned study, and the overviews of the sonnets' print history in particular will prove a valuable resource for students and scholars alike.

Another source for uncovering ways in which Shakespeare's plays and poems were approached by early readers are commonplace books – collections of excerpts, copied from contemporary texts, that were deemed worthy of extraction for later moral or rhetorical use. One such print collection is *Bel-vedére or The Garden of the Muses,* which we now know to contain at least 240 quotations from Shakespeare's plays and poems, thanks to the publication of the first scholarly edition of the text. *Bel-vedére* was popular during its own time, with two editions published within a decade of each other (1600 and 1610). Although made available in facsimile reprint in 1875, its utility for scholars of early modern literature was for a long time undermined by the fact that its verse quotations were presented without attribution.

Bel-vedére has now been carefully edited for the first time by Lukas Erne and Devani Singh, who have analysed and identified more of the authors and texts behind its approximately 4,500 verse quotations than ever before. Erne and Singh's edition offers clean, easy-to-read text with annotations alerting the reader (where possible) to full records and verbatim quotes from the source texts for comparison. The editors inform us that the sententiae, assorted under headings such as 'Of God', 'Of Hate', 'Of Friendship, &c', and 'Of Fate', are taken from the works of anonymous authors as well as canonical writers such as Shakespeare, Edmund Spenser (*c.*232 quotations), Christopher Marlowe (*c.*51), and others.

The main strength of the edition lies in their extensive work to identify the sources of *Bel-vedére*. Erne and Singh build on the work of a previous owner, Thomas Park (1758/9–1834), whose annotated copy of *Bel-vedére* resides in the Newberry Library, and of Charles Crawford, who published an edition of *England's Parnassus* in 1913 and set out (but ultimately did not manage) to produce an edition of *Bel-vedére* for Oxford's Clarendon Press. According to the current editors, Park 'assigned a total of 193 passages, 186 of them correctly' (xxxvii), and Crawford manged to identify substantially more, as recorded in a 1911 article, in 'interleaved [manuscript] sheets inserted into a copy of Crossley's 1875 facsimile of *Bel-vedére*, now at the British Library' (xliii), and in his personal copy of his edition of *England's Parnassus*, which is now held at the Folger Shakespeare Library.

Further aided by digital resources not available to their predecessors, such as EEBO TCP, but hindered by the fact that so many of the source texts were modified and not cited verbatim, Erne and Singh identified the source texts for all but 926 of *Bel-vedére*'s 4,482 passages before going to press. Their Introduction promises a follow-up website in which they will provide 'a searchable database of quotations that enables users to view material in the edition and to refine their queries by author, text, genre, year of publication and keyword' (lii). The database, which is not yet available (though the website shows an additional 177 newly identified passages, reducing the number of unidentified sources to 749, only 0.16 per cent of the passages in the text), will offer scholars a unique opportunity to mine this commonplace book in ways that are most relevant to their own research projects.

Erne and Singh's detailed Introduction includes analysis of *Bel-vedére*'s position in the history of early modern commonplacing, detailed discussion of the structure and contents of *Bel-vedére*, a textual introduction that covers the context for the text's original publication, as well as its bibliographical afterlife. Four impressive appendices also provide users with an 'Index of authors or texts quoted or adapted in *Bel-vedére*', 'The paratexts of the first edition of *Bel-vedére* (1600)', the 'Origins of the source identification of the passages in *Bel-vedére*', and an overview of the overlap between passages quoted in both *Bel-vedére* and *England's Parnassus* (1600), another commonplace book published in the same year, which is further discussed in the Introduction (xxvii–xxviii). This new edition of *Bel-vedére* therefore looks set to become a key reference tool for early modern scholars interested in reception histories, authorship studies and the changing status of English literature in the early modern period.

Murphy's *Shakespeare in Print*, already celebrated as a vital resource and reference tool for scholars of Shakespeare and textual studies, has been updated. His extensive revisions include a new Introduction, an entirely new chapter, two radically amended chapters, and a chapter that has been significantly expanded. Chapter 11, previously entitled 'The later twentieth century', is now entitled 'Shakespeare in the modern era', taking Murphy's analysis up to the present day by including important discussion of complete works editions such as *The New Oxford Shakespeare*, the *RSC Shakespeare* and *Norton 3*. The Chronological Appendix has also been updated and extended (by a decade and a half), with minor errors corrected, and the volume's story of Shakespeare in print has been revised to reflect a wealth of new scholarship. One of the most significant ways in which the volume as a whole has been updated is through Murphy's interaction with challenges made to New Bibliography, 'the impact of the New Bibliography on mainstream Shakespeare publishing' (291), and the persistence of its methods.

The entirely new chapter, entitled 'Shakespeare beyond print', addresses the history of digital Shakespeare, from the pioneering contributions to Shakespeare texts in 'Machine Readable Form' (and to computational linguistics more generally) by Sister Dolores Marie Burton, SND (Sisters of Notre Dame) and Sally Yeats Sedelow in the 1960s, to 21st-century Shakespeare apps produced by the likes of Luminary, Heuristic Media and Touch Press. This is no mean feat, given that records concerning digital texts tend, rather ironically (given their temporal proximity to us), to be more difficult to locate than those pertaining to Shakespeare in print. Murphy nonetheless succeeds in detailing landmark moments such as the advent of the CD-ROM in the late 1980s, Michael Hart's 'Project Gutenberg' and its free-to-access Shakespeare, and the mapping of variants in digital editions of series such as the New Variorum.

Included in this chronological overview of digital Shakespeare are biographical accounts of key figures in this phase of Shakespeare's afterlife, many of which – like that of Hart's family – are truly fascinating.

Murphy remains as alert to issues of access and economics in the new chapter as he was when discussing print editions of Shakespeare. He distinguishes between private research initiatives (such as those of Burton and Sedelow) and those released for public consumption, and outlines how much it cost to acquire the earliest commercial digital Shakespeare publications. For example, the Oxford University Press *William Shakespeare, Electronic Edition*, the Electronic Text Corporation's *WordCruncher Bookshelf Shakespeare*, and the Oxford Text Archive's *Shakespeare's First Folio and Early Quartos* – released in the 1980s – all required a substantial financial investment, with prices in the region of $150 to $299, plus the price of the software needed to read the texts, and not to mention the time investment needed to master 'the intricacies of complex text analysis programs' (327–8). As Murphy rightly notes, although made available to a wider public, these second-wave digital Shakespeare editions were in essence still specialist resources, primarily designed with researchers in mind.

He identifies a key turning point in the late 1980s and early 1990s, with the advent of the CD-ROM and the release of the first internet browser in which text and graphics were integrated: Mosaic. This was, he writes, the moment when 'a fundamental shift in digital Shakespeare' design and distribution took place (329), leading to the creation of digital Shakespeare editions which contained texts that were primarily designed to be read, and which became increasingly affordable and (later) even free-to-access. Key examples include *Shakespeare on Disc!* (containing all the plays, poems and sonnets), which was made available for users of PCs and Macintosh computers. Another important title was *Library of the Future*, which sold Shakespeare's works alongside other Classical and canonical writers, and which was sufficiently successful to go through 'four different editions, being expanded from version to version until it finally ran to more than 5,000 texts' (330). The release in 1994 of the Gutenberg Shakespeare (334), along with other websites drawing on Grady Ward's 'Moby Shakespeare' made Shakespeare texts free to download for the wider public, but most of these early resources were not concerned with textual cruxes. Indeed, as Murphy notes, early Shakespeare sites, important though they were in increasing accessibility to versions of the plays and poems, have 'sometimes given readers the mistaken impression that all texts are more or less equal, with the differences between them being of little more than passing local significance' (337).

Murphy makes important distinctions between texts that were *rendered*, versus those which were *born*, digital. For example, the Internet Shakespeare Editions (ISE) broke new ground as they were not only produced 'specifically in a form native to the Internet', but also, in some cases – cf. the example of David Bevington's ISE *As You Like It* – equipped with the option to show textual variants that are colour-coded according to the edition in which they first appeared (349). Astute points of contrast and comparison are made between the story of Shakespeare in print presented in earlier chapters and the story of Shakespeare beyond print, particularly in terms of the different rates at which the production technology behind the two media developed. Murphy also places digital texts in the context of the wider developments in Shakespeare editing discussed earlier in his volume. He highlights, for example, how the scholarly conventions of the New Variorum Shakespeare, with its extensive recording of textual variants, lent itself to digital delivery (first on CD-ROM and now via the series's online platform), where such variants could be presented free from 'the constraints of the limited space available on the printed page', prompting him to conclude that 'the digital text offers a level of multiplicity that the printed text can never manage fully to accommodate' (359).

Murphy's comparisons and his consistency of approach when discussing print and electronic Shakespeare editions are to be applauded. It is a shame, however, that the two media at times seem pitted as rivals. He summarizes that 'the final trajectory of this chapter may appear ultimately to confirm the narrative of the triumph of the printed book in the face of upstart technologies and theories: the digital text has not fully displaced the printed text', before nuancing this with the statement that 'such a reading would fail to take into account certain important facts', such as technological improvements in terms of 'portability, usability – and, indeed, very simply, in terms of battery life' (362). But the two media need not be placed in competition. As this chapter and the revised volume as a whole demonstrate, Shakespeare texts have enjoyed a rich, multifaceted and often contradictory journey in both printed and digital form.

Murphy is somewhat generous when noting the limitations of facsimile editions, like those provided by the expensive resource Early English Books Online, particularly in light of his discussion of shortcomings associated with free-to-access apps. He cites Bruce R. Smith's observation that his exciting discovery of a printer's hair in a Huntington Library material copy of Scaliger's *Poetics* (1561) would have appeared as a mere scratch on a digitized image as an example of what can be lost with the remediation of printed texts, but there are far more potential issues with resources such as EEBO, as Ian Gadd and others have pointed out, including the fact that one does not always know what they are looking at when consulting EEBO facsimiles. This is an issue that is handled deftly in Claire M. L. Bourne's excellent chapter, 'Shakespeare and "textual studies": evidence, scale, periodization and access', in Erne's edited collection, *The Research Handbook of Shakespeare and Textual Studies* (discussed below). As Bourne insists, EEBO:

does not provide information about the copy (like a shelfmark) beyond the name of the collection where the copy is held (or was at the time it was photographed for the UMI microfilm). Sometimes the repository is not named. Bibliographers and book historians working in the digital age will tell you that EEBO is a good entry point but that it is 'best practice' to consult the object in person if you wish to make any claims about its material features. Without a shelfmark, this can be a challenge. For instance, the EEBO record for the First Folio ... (STC 22273) indicates that the image set of this edition is a '[r]eproduction of an original in the Folger Shakespeare Library'. The Folger ... has eighty-two copies of this edition in its collection, making it impossible to identify which copy we are looking at. This matters because no two copies of the First Folio are identical, not just because of the contingencies of moveable type printing or the fact that *Troilus and Cressida* was added belatedly and thus appears in some copies and not others but also because each copy of the book has its own unique 400-year old history that might affect what it is we are looking at. (39)

Murphy's warning that 'many free-to-access [Shakespeare] apps offer very little information at all about the providence of the standard texts they provide' should thus be extended to resources such as EEBO (359).

Shakespeare in Print remains a breath-taking work of bibliographical scholarship. It has, and will always have, a central place on any Shakespearian's bookshelf (hopefully with a scan of its Chronological Appendix on their desktop too), but *Shakespeare in Print* is much more than a reference work. Murphy's accounts of what he terms 'a set of intertwined textual histories' are a joy to read (9). Citing the work of Zachary Lesser, Adam Hooks, András Kiséry, Tara Lyons and others, he writes of the move towards contextualist approaches to bibliography, and himself provides details of the wider careers and apparent tastes of Shakespeare's early publishers and printers in a lively and engaging manner. As mentioned above, the return to historical debates in the field and the new chapter on Shakespeare beyond print make this second edition an important record documenting key developments in the field over the last two decades. For his monumental contribution, his attention to detail and his willingness to tackle this formidable project not once but twice, Murphy deserves the gratitude of all scholars of Shakespeare and textual studies. His modest tone and respectful engagement with the work of others also provides a model for us all to emulate, particularly in a field that was once – and sometimes still is –

known to be aggressive, pedantic and exclusionary.

Bourne's aforementioned chapter is taken from an impressive Arden resource aimed at those starting out in the field. *The Research Handbook of Shakespeare and Textual Studies*, edited by Erne, consists of seventeen essays, produced by established experts in the field. The chapters are divided into four parts which offer overviews of 'Research Methods and Problems', 'Current Research and Issues', 'New Directions' and 'Material for Further Research', respectively. This structure offers readers a comprehensive grounding in Shakespeare and textual studies, with topics covered including 'The Shakespeare manuscripts', 'The early printed texts of Shakespeare', paratexts, the early modern book trade, the Shakespeare canon and apocrypha.

There are also essays on editing which cover analysis of the approaches and contributions of editors from the eighteenth century to the present day (Murphy), a stimulating overview of the debates and choices (conflation, eclectic, single-text, etc.) that have shaped modern editors' preparation of Shakespeare texts (Margaret Jane Kidnie), and the apparatus of modern editions of Shakespeare, how they vary according to intended readers/consumers, their value, and the extent to which their creation is motivated by scholarship versus commerce, i.e. presses wishing to maximize sales (Suzanne Gossett). Additional resources, which will no doubt be welcomed by general readers, students, and scholars looking to increase or refresh their knowledge, include a chronology detailing landmark moments in the history of Shakespeare and textual criticism – from the publication of *Venus and Adonis* in 1593, through the field-reshaping work of Henrietta Bartlett, A. W. Pollard and W. W. Greg (plus that of 21st-century scholars), to the completion of the Arden Third Series and the release of the New Oxford Shakespeare. There is also an A–Z of key terms and concepts – from Accidentals to Watermarks – for quick reference, and a wonderful annotated bibliography (produced by Jean-Christophe Mayer) in which the most relevant scholarship in the field has been arranged in categories such as 'Authorship and the Shakespeare canon', 'Shakespeare's early texts' and 'Beyond Shakespeare: bibliography, book history and the book trade'. The volume thus contains more or less everything someone approaching the field might need or wish to know, and those reading it from cover to cover will certainly be able to hold their own when talking or writing about the field.

The collection will prove a valuable aid for many years to come; indeed, it offers both a stocktaking of the history of the field and its most important developments, and ideas for future projects and ways in which one can gain further training, conduct research of one's own (be it with books in the wild, or through electronic resources), attend annual conferences and apply for funding opportunities. I appreciate the fact that essays are commissioned many years in advance and that few of us expected to still be reeling from the impact of the COVID-19 pandemic, but it is nonetheless a shame that the section entitled 'New directions', which contains only two essays, was not expanded to include more work by emerging scholars, and reflections on the ways in which the pandemic has impacted the way many of us work. The relevant and excellent chapters on 'Shakespeare and authorship attribution methodologies' (by Hugh Craig) and 'Shakespeare and digital editions' (by Sonia Massai) are, however, supplemented by chapters in another Arden collection released almost simultaneously: Bourne's collection, *Shakespeare / Text*.

Bourne's volume encourages authors to 'rethink patterns of influence, both historical and scholarly' by focusing on single binaries that have 'long defined how "the Shakespearean text" has been treated in scholarship, editing, performance and criticism' (2). The twenty chapters are organized into four sections entitled 'Inclusive / Exclusive', 'Before / After', 'Authorized / Unauthorised' and 'Present / Absent'. Many chapters feature established scholars returning to their fields of expertise from the fresh perspective of their assigned binary, but there is also new work on show from emerging scholars. Highlights include Aleida Auld's piece on 'Canon / Apocrypha', which identifies the release of varying configurations of the poems in the early eighteenth century as the watershed moment in the formation of the Shakespeare canon; Hannah August's 'Text / Paratext', though it might have been more accurately named 'Title Page / Playbook'; and Miles P. Grier's 'Black / White', where he offers a thought-provoking combination of textual analysis, performance studies and material considerations in his discussion of Aaron and Tamora's inter-racial relationship in *Titus*. Grier argues that 'the page' is the only means by which Tamora can 'conceive (of) a child with Aaron' as there simply is not time in the play (326), adding that Aaron and Tamora's union is seen to lead not to the birth of a human child, but instead to the delivery of texts carrying 'a moorish parent's black "stamp" and "seal"' (320). He also builds on the work of Philip Kolin to demonstrate how such notions are literalized in performance, with the '*blackamoore childe*' wrapped and carried in the nurses' arms being 'not merely *like* the books [Lucius carries onstage] but [instead] made *of* (and made *into*) reading material' (331). 'Bundled rages', the primary ingredient used to make early modern paper, were, he explains, 'often used to represent infants in early modern performance' (331).

In one of the collection's other stand-out essays, B. K. Adams discusses the legacy of New Bibliography from the angle of race. Adams's chapter focuses on 'Fair / Foul', terms Greg and others used to talk about textual legitimacy, with foul used to describe draft – as opposed to polished ('fair') – copies behind editions. Her chapter traces the ways in which binaries such as 'fair/foul' and 'Shakespeare/Text' have been used and reworked across time, to demonstrate 'how they are used within book historical and bibliographical contexts to reproduce ideologies of race and gender (often imbricated) in early modern England', with Shakespeare presented as fair and his perceived status as white and pure upheld by the efforts of New Bibliographers working in the early twentieth century (30). Adams makes important points about the need to reconsider 'and dismantle the kinds of binaries intrinsic to foundational scholarship in the field of bibliography and textual scholarship', whilst urging us to recognize the 'political power of the archive' and *unfair* structures that continue to prevent equal access (30). As she insists, '"foul" papers, or the technical aptitude needed to edit Shakespeare's plays, have always been held in decidedly "fair" spaces', such as research libraries and universities that for a long time 'were not particularly welcoming to white women and certainly not hospitable or open to Black, Indigenous or other People of Colour interested in the field' (42–3). If discussions about 'whiteness, fairness and race are just beginning to happen in bibliography and book history despite over fifty years of concentrated study on the history of race in early modern England', then it is, she poignantly concludes, precisely because 'fair spaces' and conversations 'were never quite accessible to the *unfair*' (43). Adams's call to welcome new voices in the field echoes that made by Young at the end of her review of the Arden Shakespeare Third Series, where she noted both the progress that series made in its inclusion of female editors and the 'urgent need for further diversity in scholarly editing' (*Shakespeare Survey* 74 (2021), 371).

The work and theories of New Bibliographers – which, Adams rightly notes, went 'unquestioned' for a disproportionate amount of time – are reassessed in great detail in Zachary Lesser's *Ghosts, Holes, Rips, and Scrapes: Shakespeare in 1619, Bibliography in the Longue Durée*, a remarkable work of analytical bibliography that will become this generation's go-to study for anyone wishing to read about or examine the so-called 'Pavier Quartos' for themselves. Lesser's book – which he describes as an extended case study – addresses the infamous collection of ten plays (nine playbooks as *The Whole Contention* contains versions of 2 and 3 *Henry VI*), known since the early twentieth century as the 'Pavier Quartos' (by Lesser labelled the 'Jaggard Quartos'), which are or were once connected to Shakespeare. These quartos can frequently be found bound together in libraries.

Much mystery has surrounded the quartos, some of which are undated (*Whole Contention*), whilst others are dated 1600, 1608 or 1619. Many 20th-

and 21st-century scholars have proposed their own theories in response to the hypotheses of Pollard and Greg, but Lesser is the first to return to examine the material evidence in detail. In a remarkable feat of solo and collaborative analysis, he was able to consult an impressive 92 per cent of the 372 extant copies of these quartos, 289 himself and 53 with the help of others. Indeed, whilst research on the quartos will forever be associated with Greg and Pollard, it must be noted that Lesser has consulted far more copies than the two men put together, and that, whilst Greg's work on the so-called 'Pavier Quartos' first helped to establish analytic bibliography as an important method of enquiry, Lesser's study both reaffirms the value of material bibliography and showcases the ways in which techniques and tools of analysis – such as multispectral imaging – have developed over the course of the last hundred years.

Having come across two volumes in which the quartos were bound together as sets, Pollard initially suspected that the collection consisted of remaindered copies; in other words, left-over copies of editions that had not sold well. In 1908, Greg famously undermined Pollard's suggestion when he analysed the watermarks within the paper on which the quartos were printed and found that playbooks with different purported title-page dates contained the same mixed paper stocks. This did not add up because one simply does not find the same paper stocks in books printed so many years apart, as paper was an expensive and perishable commodity that Stationers sought to utilize soon after it was purchased. As Lesser remarks, when coupled with his analysis of printer's devices and typographical features of the title pages, Greg's evidence demonstrated that 'the plays dated earlier than 1619 were deliberately falsified. In fact, they were all printed at the same time in the shop of William and Isaac Jaggard, the same printers who would soon be involved in the First Folio' (9). William Neidig then added to these findings, exploiting developments in composite photography to demonstrate that the title pages of the different quartos had been printed 'from standing type within days of each other' (12). These quartos have had important implications for the story of Shakespeare's rise to cultural prominence because the idea of remaindered copies suggested that his plays did not sell well, whilst a publishing venture designed to release a collected edition of his plays (four years prior to the 1623 First Folio) implied that the opposite was true.

Lesser's Introduction sets out the views of Pollard and Greg, noting what they did and did not suggest, as well as the ways in which their thinking about the quartos developed, and the various responses of revisionist scholars such as Gerald Johnson, Peter Blayney, Andrew Murphy, David Scott Kastan, Lukas Erne, Sonia Massai, James J. Marino and Cyndia Clegg. The important questions at the heart of the mystery surrounding these quartos are then rehearsed – Who was behind the project? What were the aims of the publishing venture? Why were dates falsified and was this to conceal evidence from other Stationers, the King's Men, the Lord Chamberlain? – before Lesser proceeds to present new evidence that sometimes supports 'the revisionists, sometimes the New Bibliographers, sometimes neither', and which often leaves him with more questions than answers (32).

The study's three main chapters are organized around evidence provided by ghosts, holes, and rips and scrapes. In other words, around the material features of copies of the quartos that have enabled Lesser to draw new conclusions. Chapter 1, 'Ghosts', builds on the work of Jeffrey Todd Knight and a form of bibliographical evidence whereby one is able to identify copies of books once bound and/or pressed together by observing how the rich oils within printers' ink have transferred between adjacent leaves after reacting with the acidity levels in paper. Ghostly images, usually showing images of title-page text, do not always appear as their development depends on the levels of acidity within a given sheet of paper. Such transferred images thus enable Lesser to make observations about the plays included and the order in which they were bound, whilst other forms of 'ghostly evidence' – including old library catalogue entries and annotations made by previous owners – are said to draw attention to more volumes of the Pavier Quartos that are now lost (47).

He surmises that quarto collections were less uniform than New Bibliographic narratives of their production would have us believe, that they were sold as a set more often than was first suspected, that their order of binding varied, and that the venture was not designed as a single-author collection. Indeed, he plausibly argues that *A Woman Killed with Kindness*, a Thomas Heywood play that was clearly attributed to Heywood on its title page, was not added to the series later by an owner (as Knights suggested in 2010), but instead 'formed part of it from the start, offered for sale with the 1619 Shakespeare quartos and possibly with other plays altogether' (55). Heywood's inclusion in the collection is also a key reason why Lesser refers to the quartos as Jaggard's Quartos, since Isaac Jaggard printed and published Heywood's play 'in the same shop where the 1619 quartos were printed' (77).

'Holes' adds to Aaron Pratt's impressive work on stab-stitching, with Lesser focusing on the absence of stab holes in the majority of copies of the quartos to deduce that approximately half of the surviving copies 'seem to have initially been sold as part of a bound volume' (74). When sold individually, most playbooks were sold stab-stitched – i.e., they were held together by a single piece of thread that passed through the assembled quires. Lesser reports that evidence of stab-stitching was found in only 39 per cent of the 265 copies he examined. This chapter also makes inferences based on the disproportionately high survival rate of the quartos when compared with other Shakespeare quartos as 'another indication that many Pavier Quartos were offered from bookshops specifically as bound collections, not merely left up to individual book buyers to purchase as a group or not' (75–6) – the logic here being that playbooks bound within *Sammelbände* are statistically more likely to survive than more ephemeral publications – before addressing his theories as to why Jaggard may have chosen to include Heywood's play in the collection.

Chapter 3, 'Rips and scrapes', is arguably the most novel and exciting section of Lesser's project. Here, he turns his attention to copies of quartos that demonstrate how easy it is 'to turn an accurate imprint into a less-than-truthful-one', by observing how, after printing, the paper of some title pages has been 'torn and extremely skilfully repaired', with pen facsimile used to modify the date (87, 89), whilst others have had their paper scraped thin to remove original print before being inked. These acts of modification, often invisible to the naked eye, can be detected through the application of transmitted light, even though 'great care was taken to disguise the repair, going so far as to match the chain lines and wires lines of the papers' (87), and by observing the lack of impression on the verso of the date where printed numbers would have bitten into the paper. Lesser provides a convincing case for thinking that 'these title pages were altered early in the life of these copies', but ultimately, and understandably, comes up short when trying to find a satisfactory explanation as to precisely why this may have occurred (123).

In addition to the fascinating new 'facts revealed by a return to primary bibliographical analysis of the Jaggard Quartos' (134), Lesser's study is to be praised for its emphasis on the importance of adhering to the evidence contained within individual copies of a given edition. He stresses the importance of observing what he terms the 'multiple temporalities' of copies, and the need to consider both the '*before*' and the '*after*' (22–3), particularly as it was the New Bibliographers' focus on print production that blinded them to the evidence provided by 'the circulation of books after the sheets left the press' and ultimately limited the narratives they proposed about the quartos (46). Put differently, Lesser astutely argues that 'thinking bibliographically must involve not merely *seeing behind* the later historical accretions that intervene between us and the "finished book," although that remains important, but also *thinking through* this long history', because 'the book is a palimpsest: we can use sophisticated tools to read what is written underneath, but if we fail to grapple with how what has been overlaid can rewrite the substrate, we may misread both texts' (23).

Lesser ends his study – as all responsible bibliographers ought – not with the forceful assertion of a new Sherlock-Holmesesque revelation, but instead with clear questions, reflections, and invitations for future scholars to build on the field-reshaping evidence presented. A key aim of *Ghosts, Holes, Rips and Scrapes* is to highlight the extent to which an unquestioning acceptance of the narratives that New Bibliographers attached to their material analysis has 'shaped the material existence [of the quartos] in the Shakespeare archive and obscured the evidence of their earlier form, both from the New Bibliographers themselves and from us, their inheritors' (146). It thus seems apt for Lesser to end with a series of provocative questions and insights.

His prose is clear and engaging throughout and he makes a constant effort to convey complex bibliographical evidence to non-experts. (That said, I think even hardcore book nerds may need a shot of espresso before they can fully get to grips with the wonderful example of the 'ghostly palimpsest' presented in his conclusion.) Lesser's study is, moreover, furnished with two excellent appendices to assist those willing to take on the mantle and tackle the remaining mysteries for themselves: 'a census of known sets of the 1619 quartos' and 'the order of plays in known bindings of the 1619 quartos' (147–8 and 149–50). He also lists the different copies of each quarto consulted in his study and illustrates his analyses with a wealth of colour images – many taken with the aid of different light sources (ultraviolet light, raking light, etc.) – which offer a sumptuous showcase of the beautiful, complex topography of handmade laid paper, showing variously: the small ridges created by the wire and chain lines of the paper mould, the bite of type and tacky printers' ink, the transfer of oils and pressure from leaves once bound together, and increased transparency where small sections have been scraped thinner than the remainder of the leaf. It is like being transported to the numerous libraries where Lesser conducted his meticulously researched study as he guides us through his interpretation of the evidence without ever concealing it from us.

Molly G. Yarn's *Shakespeare's Lady Editors: A History of the Shakespearean Text* is another important contribution that leaves the door open for future scholars to build on its author's exciting discoveries and find more 'undiscovered treasures' (203). It is a timely contribution and a much-needed study, the usefulness and interest of which is so immediately apparent that it is hard to believe that it has not previously been attempted. Yarn's work details the ways in which the history of Shakespeare editing has been constructed, and why it is important to recognize its biases. She presents a unique body of original documentary evidence, diligently gathered from libraries across the US and UK, in order to make connections that help to write women back into the history of Shakespeare editing, 1800–1950, whilst also questioning how and why the received history of Shakespeare editing incorrectly presented the field as being male dominated until the late twentieth century.

As she demonstrates, the 'story is far more complex, and far more consequential, than it has seemed'; the number of editions prepared by women decreased during the later twentieth century, with eighty-one appearing between 1910 and 1940 and only thirteen between 1940 and 1970, but at least sixty-nine female editors working in the period 1800 to 1950 have nonetheless been 'excluded from the editorial record' (15). She suggests that the drop in editions by women – and the failure of modern critics to appreciate fully the contributions of those working in earlier periods – may in part be explained by the rise in influence of New Bibliography. She is by no means suggesting that Greg, R. B. McKerrow, Pollard, Fredson Bowers, Charlton Hinman, John Dover Wilson et al. were 'consciously hostile to female-scholars' (171). Rather, she suggests that their work had important implications for the ways in which 'true' editorial labour came to be defined as 'hard science' and saw the ranks of those deemed qualified to edit largely restricted to research universities, a kind of monopoly that she likens to the Tonson house's control of editorial authority in the eighteenth century (201). This situation changed when 'the merging of the textual and the critical, spearheaded by critics such as Jerome McGann and D. F. McKenzie' opened scholarly editing up to '"non-specialist" editors, whose alternative viewpoints were seen as both intellectually viable and increasingly marketable' (201). Like Sonia Massai, who alerted us to the need to avoid the teleological narratives of editing that have seen the work of sixteenth- and seventeenth-century print houses overshadowed by the advent of so-called 'modern' editing in the eighteenth century (see Sonia Massai, *Shakespeare and the Rise of the Editor* (Cambridge, 2007)), Yarn highlights the problems of judging nineteenth-century editorial labour by twentieth-century standards: 'demanding proleptic modernity from nineteenth-century editors results in an unjustified elision of a large span of editorial activity' (16).

Previous studies have considered individual figures, such as Mary Cowden Clarke and Charlotte Porter, but Yarn's is the first to study women editors as a collective group. Her monograph is divided into chapters that address 'Recovering women editors of Shakespeare'; 'Female collaborators and ambiguous literary labour', which focuses on issues of gendered editorial labour by considering male–female collaborations within the network of the New Shakespeare Society; 'Women editors and scholarly networks in America', in which she analyses communities of female editors found in American women's colleges; 'Women and the New Bibliography', discussing the idea of bio-bibliography, which focuses on the value of studying editors and their contributions through the lens of their own biography. She also includes two short chapters, referred to as 'Sidenotes'. The first, on 'Women editing not-Shakespeare (or not editing)' takes her field of enquiry beyond Shakespeare studies to recognize women editing early modern texts by other writers for scholarly societies, such as the Malone Society and the Early English Text Society, under the general editorship of Greg and Frederick Furnivall, respectively (sometimes after her cut-off date of 1950), and women who carried out textual work beyond editing, such as transcription and the creation of concordances. The second is entitled 'Early student editions of Shakespeare', an important inclusion given that we are told that, up until the 1940s, women edited a significant number of Shakespeare texts for school children.

Yarn covers more than 160 editions, predominantly produced by female editors, and introduces readers to the work of almost 70 female editors. The study opens with the story of Laura Valentine and her involvement with the Chandos Classics series's *Works of William Shakespeare*, an affordable home library series, which was for a long time advertised without naming an author, before finally naming Valentine as the text's editor in 1894. As Yarn rightly argues, the story of Valentine demonstrates how 'the Shakespearean editorial tradition, as it is currently known, remains fundamentally incomplete'; indeed, the evidence to connect Valentine with the Shakespeare editorial tradition was there, 'the connection simply has not been made before now' (7). In reading Yarn's work, we discover that women produced a range of different types of Shakespeare texts for a number of series, and that the Shakespeare plays most frequently edited by women – alone or in collaboration with men – between 1800 and the present day are: *As You Like It* (37 editions), *Twelfth Night* (32), *A Midsummer Night's Dream* (32), *The Merchant of Venice* (30), *Julius Caesar* (30), *Macbeth* (30), *Hamlet* (29), *The Taming of the Shrew* (28), *Othello* (28), *The Tempest* (28) and *King Lear* (27). Yarn also draws on 'material from letters, diaries, ledgers, contracts, census documents, published reports, reviews, advertisements, wills, life records, and even novels' to give readers 'as detailed an account as possible' of these important nineteenth- and twentieth-century women editors (7).

As with Lesser's invitation for scholars to build on his work, Yarn too aids her successors by providing helpful appendices. There is a table of all known 'Shakespeare editions prepared by women, 1800–2021', organized chronologically by play and including – importantly – volumes that were commissioned but never completed, but (due to space limitations) not including editions abridged, marked up or adapted for performance (Appendix B). There is also a quick reference guide to women involved in the preparation of editions between

1800 and 1950 (Appendix A: 'Women editors of Shakespeare, 1800–1950'), though readers will find more detailed accounts of most of these women in the main body of the monograph. Where relevant, readers are also guided to existing biographies for more extensive coverage. The study also contains wonderful illustrations that help to bring Yarn's revisionist history to life.

In sum, Yarn has produced a study that many of us have been longing to read, and her exploration of the important contributions women made to the history of Shakespeare editing does not disappoint. In addressing the topic of women editors, Yarn simultaneously offers a lucid account of how Shakespeare editing as a field has developed between the eighteenth century and the present day and redefines what being a Shakespeare editor has meant at different points in time. Looking to the future, her epilogue notes how more women editors have been commissioned for series such as The Norton 3 (21 women editors to 19 male editors) and Arden4 (a 50/50 breakdown is expected), before rightly stressing the need for the field of Shakespeare and textual studies to 'continue to actively engage with expanding diversity beyond binary gender to engage with questions of race, sexual orientation, gender identity, gender expression, nationality, and institutional affiliation' (203).

WORKS REVIEWED

Acker, Faith, *First Readers of Shakespeare's Sonnets, 1590–1790* (New York, 2020)

Bourne, Claire M. L., ed., *Shakespeare / Text: Contemporary Readings in Textual Studies, Editing and Performance* (London, 2021)

Erne, Lukas, ed., *The Arden Research Handbook of Shakespeare and Textual Studies* (London, 2021)

Erne, Lukas, and Devani Singh, eds., *Bel-vedére or the Garden of the Muses: An Early Modern Printed Commonplace Book* (Cambridge, 2020).

Knowles, Richard, ed., *A New Variorum Edition of Shakespeare's King Lear* (New York, 2020)

Lesser, Zachary, *Ghosts, Holes, Rips, and Scrapes: Shakespeare in 1619, Bibliography in the Longue Durée* (Cambridge, 2021)

Murphy, Andrew, *Shakespeare in Print: A History and Chronology of Shakespeare Publishing*, 2nd ed. (Cambridge, 2021)

Proudfoot, Richard, Ann Thompson, David Scott Kastan and H. R. Woudhuysen, eds., *William Shakespeare: Complete Works* (London, 2020)

Yarn, Molly G., *Shakespeare's Lady Editors: A History of the Shakespearean Text* (Cambridge, 2021)

ABSTRACTS OF ARTICLES IN *SHAKESPEARE SURVEY 75*

RICHARD ASHBY

'But When Extremities Speak': Harley Granville-Barker, *Coriolanus*, the World Wars and the State of Exception
This article analyses the handwritten notes that director Harley Granville-Barker (1877–1946) made in his 1922 Arden copy of *Coriolanus*, which include allusions to World Wars I and II, and considers his ideologically and politically ambivalent response to war, democracy, military leadership, peace and, above all, the state of exception.

LISA M. BARKSDALE-SHAW

'The Moor's Abused by Some Most Villainous Knave, Some Base Notorious Knave, Some Scurvy Fellow': Legal Spaces, Racial Trauma and Shakespeare's *The Tragedy of Othello, the Moor of Venice*
This article submits that the socio-psychological and the clinical psychiatric effects of racial trauma on Moors not only emerge on the early modern stage, but also manifest themselves in both legal and cultural consequences for the Moor, and reap identifiable behaviours characterized by the larger society.

MARK THORNTON BURNETT

Understanding *Iago*, an Italian Film Adaptation of *Othello*: Clientelism, Corruption, Politics
Iago (dir. Volfango di Biasi, 2009), an Italian film adaptation of *Othello*, controversially offers us Iago's backstory rather than Othello's, envisioning the 'honest' lieutenant as a wronged hero. This article argues for a reading that explores representations of race and difference inside intersecting representations of corruption, clientelism and class.

PATRICIA A. CAHILL

Othello's Kin: Legacy, Belonging and *The Fortunes of the Moor*
This article argues that *Fortunes of the Moor* – a 1990s Afrocentric drama co-authored by Barbara Molette and Carlton Molette and centring on a custody battle over the infant son who is Othello's heir – offers both a radical critique of Shakespeare's tragedy and a provocation to today's predominantly white Shakespeare industry.

ZAINAB S. CHEEMA

Grafted to the Moor: Anglo-Spanish Dynastic Marriage and Miscegenated Whiteness in *The Winter's Tale*
This article interprets the political geography of Shakespeare's *The Winter's Tale* as allegorizing Anglo-Spanish relations, where Perdita's marriage to Florizel represents the Spanish match pursued by James I. It argues that

ABSTRACTS OF ARTICLES

Perdita's beauty embodies a racial whiteness that is associated with Iberian ethnic otherness and transatlantic wealth.

MOLLY CLARK

Rhyme, History and Memory in *A Mirror for Magistrates* and *Henry VI*
The enormously popular rhyming poetry collection *A Mirror for Magistrates* encourages its readers to connect verse form with the depiction of history. This article reads Shakespeare's *Henry VI* plays in this light, thinking about the ways in which their *Mirror*-marked rhyming couplets evoke memory and fate.

JENNIFER J. EDWARDS

Suffering Ecstasy: *Othello* and the Drama of Displacement
This article argues that representations of ecstatic experience in *Othello* contribute to the tragedy's dramatization of fractured subjectivity. First examining Cassio's drunkenness, it moves to consider Othello's trance as an epileptic ecstasy, exploring how these altered states of consciousness intersect with issues of identity, emotion, race and affect.

JOSHUA R. HELD

Pitying Desdemona in Folio *Othello*: Race, Gender and the Willow Song
The Folio-only Willow Song of Desdemona deepens at once her premonition of death and her commitment to face it. By confirming her love for Othello and following the model of her mother's maid Barbary, Desdemona in the Folio obtains a double portion of pity – as a Black woman.

JONATHAN Y. H. HUI

New Analogical Evidence for *Cymbeline*'s Folkloric Composition in the Medieval Icelandic *Ála flekks saga*
This article explores several curious correspondences between *Cymbeline* and a medieval Icelandic romance, *Ála flekks saga*, examining the oblique illumination shed by each text not only on the folkloric composition of the other, but also on the folktale traditions from which both of them drew.

MARGARET JANE KIDNIE

Warning the Stage: Shakespeare's Mid-Scene Entrance Conventions
This article argues that the writing and performance of mid-scene entrances in early modern drama were guided by theatrical convention and enabled a working method premised on minimal group rehearsal. Analysis of a sample of twenty-six plays suggests corruption, rather than revision, of two mid-scene entrances in *Hamlet*.

JEREMY LOPEZ

Desdemona's Honest Friend
Focusing on Emilia's role as Desdemona's servant, I reject the possibility – pervasively endorsed by criticism and performance – that the women share an affective bond that constitutes a form of resistance to the homosocial (and, indeed, the *social*) tensions that drive this tragedy so explicitly concerned with the 'curse of service'.

ABSTRACTS OF ARTICLES

ABHIRUP MASCHARAK

Circumventing Marginality: The Curious Case of India's *Othello* Screen Adaptations
This article discusses four Indian *Othello* films – *Saptapadi*, *Izzat*, *Kaliyattam* and *Omkara* – and their circumvention of the theme of marginality and difference in the play.

RICHARD MEEK

Othello's Sympathies: Emotion, Agency and Identification
This article explores the representation of sympathy within *Othello* – not merely as a contagious or magical phenomenon, but as a form of intersubjectivity. Rather than simply subscribing to a humoral or physiological model of the passions, *Othello* proposes that individuals have considerably more emotional agency than such concepts might suggest.

KATIE MENNIS

'Bad' Love Lyrics and Poetic Hypocrisy from Gascoigne to Benson's Shakespeare
This article discusses 'bad' love lyrics in *Edward III*, *Love's Labour's Lost* and *As You Like It*. It coins the term 'poetic hypocrisy' to describe a mode of framing love lyric that is latent in prose narratives of the 1570s–1590s and becomes explicit in these plays.

JOHN-MARK PHILO

Ben Jonson's *Sejanus* and Shakespeare's *Othello*: Two Plays Performed by the King's Men in *c.*1603
Othello and *Sejanus* are complexly interwoven, with Shakespeare even taking a starring role in the latter. This article examines multiple points of overlap between the two plays in text and performance, highlighting the shared creative and social spaces which Jonson and Shakespeare inhabited at the turn of the seventeenth century.

ROBERT B. PIERCE

Viola's Telemachy
Though Shakespeare frequently adapts the Odyssean story of extravagant adventures – voyaging on a quest for home, restoration and renewal – he is no Fénelon moralizing the tale of Homer's Telemachy. However, we can still read *Twelfth Night* as Viola's *paideia* and note the similarities and differences between her adventure and Telemachus'.

IMAN SHEEHA

'[A] Maid Called Barbary': *Othello*, Moorish Maidservants and the Black Presence in Early Modern England
Othello's depiction of Barbary subverts contemporary theatrical and pictorial traditions of representing African women in service. In her African origins and position in service, Barbary resonates with many members of the early modern audience, including Black female servants, a playgoing demographic of whom recent scholarship is increasingly making us aware. The article argues that, seen from the perspective of a Black servant, *Othello* has more to say about race than has hitherto been acknowledged.

NICOLE SHERIKO

Iago and the Clown: Disassembling the Vice in *Othello*
This article uses *Othello* as a case study for examining the Vice's influence on the development of stage character. It argues that what critics isolate as

ABSTRACTS OF ARTICLES

clownishness is an older theatricality more widely dispersed across diverse kinds of characters beyond just clowns and villains, which shapes inter-character dynamics in performance.

BAILEY SINCOX

Looking for Perdita in Ali Smith's *Summer*
This article sketches how Ali Smith's *Seasonal Quartet* tessellates the daughters of each novel's Shakespearian intertext (*The Tempest*, *Cymbeline*, *Pericles* and *The Winter's Tale*). It argues that *Summer* (2020) provides a tragicomic ending to the series by multiplying Perditas, ultimately transforming its Leontes figure into a Perdita, too.

ANDREA SMITH

'More Fair than Black': Othellos on British Radio
BBC radio has been broadcasting productions of *Othello* for nearly a century. Yet for the majority of its history, the actors portraying the titular character were white. This article charts the changing attitudes as to who plays Othello on BBC radio by looking at key productions of the play.

YIK LING YONG

***Othello*: A Dialogue with the Built Environment**
Clustered around this article are created impressions of specific built forms in *Othello*: urban streets, coastal structures, temporary lodgings and houses of the elite. My argument about these built forms focuses on the way they have been used to shape the sense of space, constructing identities. By analysing the use and functions of building forms that articulate social differentiation, I explore created spatial dynamics, connecting generated tensions to Othello's developing states of mind.

AGNIESZKA ŻUKOWSKA

'This Fair Paper': *Othello* **and the Artists' Book**
Othello-inspired artists' books respond to the play's recurring imagery and dramatic design, with special attention to the blending of the textual and the textile, the poetics of animality and the silencing of women. Echoing Shakespeare's interest in artifice and objectification, they also position themselves against the conventions of book production.

INDEX

Aarne-Thompson-Uther folktale index (ATU), 288
Aasand, Hardin, 287
Abbot, George, 243
Abd el-Ouahed ben Messaoud ben Mohammed Anoun, 92
Abdalla, Khalid, 57, 58, 59
Acker, Faith D., 366, 374, 387–388, 398
Adams, B. K., 393
Adams, Thomas, 190
Adamson, Jane, 149
Adamson, W. D., 149
Adelman, Janet, 149, 152, 181, 193
Adler, Doris, 66
Adorno, Theodor, 363
Aebischer, Pascale, 29
   Shakespeare, Spectatorship and the Technologies of Performance, 375–376, 383
   Shakespeare and the 'Live' Theatre Broadcast Experience, 375, 376
   Viral Shakespeare, 375, 383
Agamben, Giorgio, 320, 327, 329
Aguilera Linde, Mauricio D., 189
Ahmed, Sara, 184
Ainley, Henry, 49–50, 54, 56
Akbar, Arifa, 334
Akhimie, Patricia, 242, 362
Ála flekks saga, 287–312, 400
Albertazzi, Daniele, 2
Aldridge, Ira, 362
Alexander, Catherine M. S., 302
Alexander, Gavin, 267
Alexander, Michelle, 121
Alford, Stephen, 119, 121
Allen, Ben, 344
Allen, Mara, 357–358
Allen, Michael J. B., 152, 211
Allot, Robert, 278
Alpers, Paul, 268, 274
Alter, Stephen, 19
Altman, Joel B., 156, 167, 171
Ames, William, 183
Anand, Chetan, 24

Anderson, Carol, 115, 121
Anderson, Graham, 292, 309, 311
Anderson, Jane, 56–57
Anderson, Judith H., 71
Anderson, Kimberly, 289
Anderson, Linda, 166
Andrew, Meghan C., 366
Aneesh (Keralan victim of honour killing), 21
Annan, Noel, 50
Annis, Francesca, 343–344
anonymous works, 343
   Charlemagne, 213, 214, 215
   Edmund Ironside, 213, 214, 217
   Englands Wedding Garment (tract), 372
   The Famous Victories of Henry V, 264
   Frederyke of Jennen, 301–302, 304, 306, 311
   The Mahametane or Turkish Historie containing three bookes (trans. R. Carr, 1600), 244
   Mankind, 144, 145–146
   Notes for my Perambulation in and round the Cityw of London, 128
   The Present State of Spain (1594), 243–244
   The Rare Triumphs of Love and Fortune, 301
   Tarlton's Jests, 143
   Thomas of Woodstock, 213, 214
   The Two Noble Ladies, 213, 214, 217
   The Wasp, 212–213, 214, 223–224, 225, 227
   A Whip for an Ape: Or Martin displaied, 214
   see also sagas, Icelandic, 140
Antor, Heinz, 148
Arber, Edward, 125
Archer, Harriet, 257
Archibald, Elizabeth, 309, 310
Aristotle, 267, 278, 365
Armin, Robert, 143, 146
Artese, Charlotte, 146
   Shakespeare and the Folktale: An Anthology of Stories, 302
   Shakespeare's Folktale Sources, 288, 289, 291, 295, 296, 299, 301, 307–308, 311

Asante, Molefi Kete, 36, 37
Ashby, Richard, 313–332, 399
Ashcroft, Peggy, 49
Asiedu, Awo Mana, 42
Assaf, Sharon, 63
Astington, John H., 212, 222
Attar, K. E., 314
Attiah, Karen, 115, 121
Atwood, Margaret, 232
Aubrey, John, 126, 129
Auden, W. H., 140, 165, 325, 382
Audibert, Justin, 359
August, Hannah, 393
Auld, Aleida, 392–393
Ayres, Philip J., 122

Babayemi, Shona, 335
Babington, Gervase, 203
Bachman, W. Bryant, 289
Backman, Clifford, 240
Bacon, Francis, Baron Verulam and Viscount St Albans, 193, 258, 263
Bailey, Lucy, 347
Baker, J. H., 114, 118, 121
Balachander, K., 27
Balakrishnan, Sarah, 33, 38
Baldwin, James, 48, 116
Ballard, Jamie, 354, 355
Bandopadhyay, Tarashankar, 30
Barber, C. L., 137, 244
Barber, Frances, 343, 345
Barker, Hannah, 149
Barksdale-Shaw, Lisa R., 103–121, 399
Barnard, Peter, 55
Barnes, Todd Landon, 362–364, 374
Barnett, Douglas Q., 34
Barrie, J. M., 322
Barrough, Philip, 183
Bartels, Emily C., 32, 89, 90, 149, 152, 201
Barthelemy, Anthony Gerard, 90, 149
Barthes, Roland, 185
Barton, Anne, 129, 305
Barton, John, 337

403

INDEX

Basumatary, Kenny, 31
Bates, Catherine, 63
Bauer, Kate, 358
Bayman, Louis, 14
Beadle, Richard, 143
Beaumont, Francis, 128–129
Beckerman, Bernard, 211, 212, 227
Beckert, Sven, 107
Beckwith, Sarah, 230
Bednarz, James P., 279, 366
Bell, Derrick, 107–108, 111, 121
Bene, Carmelo, 1–2
Bennett, Arnold, 322
Bennett, Josephine Waters, 310
Bennett, Kate, 126
Bennett, Nicola, 265
Bennison, Ishia, 341
Benson, John, 279, 368, 388
Benson, Sean, 73–74, 75, 79, 82
Berger, Thomas L., 135, 151, 171, 172, 174
Berkeley, David, 253
Berkoff, Steven, 343
Berlant, Lauren, 235
Berlusconi, Silvio, 2, 5–6, 10
Berman, Mitchell N., 107, 121
Bernstein, Leonard, 359
Berry, Ralph, 170
Bertelsen, Henrik, 309
Betteridge, Thomas, 295
Bever, Linsey, 120, 121
Bevington, David, 122, 139–140, 141, 186, 390
Bhardwaj, Vishal: *Omkara*, 15–20, 23, 27, 31, 381–382
Bible: Gospel of Matthew, 267
Bickley, Pamela, 382, 383
Bigliazzi, Silvia, 2
Bijleveld, Celine, 57
Billen, Stephanie, 57
Billington, Michael, 55, 56
Billington, Sandra, 138
Binns, J. W., 191
Bird, J. C., 322
Bittel, Carla, 61
Blackwell, Anna, 376
Blain, Keisha N., 111, 121
Blake, Liza, 320
Blakemore, Reasonable, 362
Blank, Dan, 127
Blanke, John, 92
Blayney, Peter, 394
Blinder, Alan, 33
Bloom, Gina, 71
Bloom, Harold, 115, 166, 175
Blount, Thomas, 192–193
Boberg, Inger, 303
Boccaccio, Giovanni, 303
    and *Cymbeline*, 290, 301–302, 303, 304, 306, 311
    and 'Griselda', 288
Bohan, Becky, 384

Boodle, R. W., 295
Boose, Lynda E., 12, 35, 99, 150, 167
Booth, Edwin, 171
Borbonesa (artists' collective), 64–69
Boswell, Eleanore, 217
Bottigheimer, Ruth B., 291
Boty, Pauline, 231
Boulton, Susie, 8
Bourke, Peter, 335
Bourne, Claire M. L., 154, 391
    Shakespeare / Text: Contemporary Readings in Textual Studies, Editing and Performance, 392–393, 398
Bourus, Terri, 123, 258
Bovilsky, Lara, 149, 157–158
Bowman, Thomas D., 166
Bradley, A. C., 59, 166, 167, 175, 322, 384
Bradley, David, 212, 221
Bradwell, Stephen, 183
Brady, Sean, 297
Branagh, Kenneth, 382
Braunmuller, A. R., 167
Bray, Alan, 93
Breen, Benjamin, 252
Breen, Phillip, 346, 349–352
Brennecke, Ernest, 160
Britton, Dennis Austin, 149, 150, 152
Broadbent, Jonathan, 352
Brook, Clodagh, 2
Brook, Peter, 313
Brown, Arthur, 217
Brown, David Sterling, 241, 247
Brown, John Russell, 95, 167
Brown, Keith, 308
Brunvald, Jan Harold, 288
Bruster, Douglas, 95
Buccola, Regina, 379, 383
Buckworth, Everard, 122, 125
Budra, Paul, 257
Bullough, Geoffrey, 122, 125, 290, 295, 301, 302, 308
Bump, Philip, 33
Burbage, Richard, 126–127, 128, 133–134, 135, 277, 377
Burbank, Carol, 48
Burghley, 1st Baron (William Cecil), 310
Burke, Aiofe, 337
Burke, Kenneth, 149
Burnett, Mark Thornton, 1–14, 399
Burns, Timothy, 168
Burrow, Colin, 198, 199, 279, 280, 287
Burt, Philippa, 320
Burt, Richard, 35
Burton, Sister Dolores Marie, SND, 389
Burton, Nefertiti, 46
Busby, Olive, 138
Butler, Judith, 180, 189, 193
Butler, Martin, 2, 122, 186, 300
Butts, Hugh, 106

Byrd, James, Jr, 114
Byrne, Muriel St Clare, 218

Cabiddu, Gianfranco, 1–2
Cahill, Patricia A., 32–48, 399
Cain, Tom, 122, 124–125
Calbi, Maurizio, 2, 14
Caldwell, Bridget, 346
Callaghan, Dympna, 62, 63, 89, 148, 154, 165, 284
Campbell, Lily B., 60
Campion, Thomas, 258
Cañizares-Esguerra, Jorge, 252
Capell, Edward, 366, 367
Capp, Bernard, 93, 101
Caputi, Robert J., 324
Carey, Henry, 1st Baron Hunsdon, 92
Carlin, Claire L., 190
Carlin, Martha, 128
Carnegie, David, 222
Carr, Amber, 104
Carr, Yolanda, 104
Carrol, Monica, 64
Carson, Christie, 380, 383
Carter, Matt, 115
Cartwright, Kent, 151
Caruth, Cathy, 109, 121
Casaubon, Meric, 189, 190, 191, 193
Casellas, Jesús López-Peláez, 189
Cassius Dio, 122
Casson, Lewis, 315
Castaldo, Annalisa, 188
Catling, Christopher, 8
Cave, Nick, 346
Cavell, Stanley, 328
Cecil, William, 1st Baron Burghley, 310
Celli, Carlo, 5
Celsius, Olof, 190–191
Centerwall, Brandon, 125
Cerda, Juan Luis de la, 267–268
Cervantes Saavedra, Miguel de, 243
Chakravarti, Paromita, 22, 29–30, 381–382, 383
Chalk, Darryl, 32, 195, 281
Chamberlain, Neville, 325
Chambers, Colin, 313, 321
Chambers, E. K., 124, 125, 150
Champagne, L., 47
Chapman, George, 129, 281
Chapman, Matthieu, 38
Charles I, King of Great Britain, 367
Charles, Casey, 284
Charney, Maurice, 137
Charron, Pierre, 191
Chatterjee, Bankimchandra, 381
Chatterjee, Koel, 22
Chaucer, Geoffrey, 95, 288
Chautemps, Camille, 315
Cheema, Zainab S., 240–255, 399–400
Chernaik, Warren, 123
Chester, Robert, 129

INDEX

Chesterton, G. K., 322
Chiari, Sophie, 151, 279
Chiatti, Laura, 1, *13*
Childress, Alice, 34
Chioneso, Nkechinyelum A., 105
Chopra, B. R., 15
Churchill, Winston, 317, 319, 323, 324, 325, 329
Cinthio, Giraldi: *Hecatommithi*, 90, 106, 107, 122, 135, 166, 168
Cipolla, Adele, 289
Clark, Molly, 256–264, 400
Clarke, Mary Cowden, 382, 397
Clary, F. Nicholas, 287
Clavell, John: *The Soddered Citizen*, 213, 214, 215, 219
Clay, Alfred, 352
Clayton, Thomas, 208
Clegg, Cyndia, 394
Clifford, Lady Anne, 92
Clifton, Alex, 357
Coates, Ta-Nehesi, 48
Cobb, Keith Hamilton, 48, 106, 108–109, 121
Coghill, Nevill, 150, 157
Cohen, Stephen, 201
Cohen, Walter, 57, 251
Cole, Susan G., 138
Coleridge, Samuel, 115
Collingbourne, William, 256, 258
Collins, Patricia Hill, 33
Collins, Sara, 229
Colston, Edward, 361
Conkie, Rob, 375–376
Connelly, Mark, 319
Connor, Francis X., 279
Conquest, Charlotte, 358
Cook, Amy, 379–380, 383
Cook, Ann Jennalie, 149
Cooke, Alexander, 126–127
Cookman, Anthony, 52
Cooper, Helen, 287, 311
Coppola, Francis, 19–20
Corballis, R. P., 129
Corporaal, Marguérite, 166
Cottino-Jones, Marga, 5
Cotton, Jeff, 3
Coveney, Michael, 55
Cowhig, Ruth, 149
Cox, John D., 140, 212
Craig, Hardin, 208
Craig, Hugh, 392
Craik, Katharine A., 192, 233
  Shakespeare and Emotion, 199–200, 364–365, 374
Craik, T. W., 282, 285
Crane, Ralph, 187, 215
Crawford, Charles, 388–389
Crawford, Robert, 372
Creaser, John, 126
Cressy, David, 100–101

Crewe, Jonathan, 271, 272
Crews, Frederick, 305
Cronin, Kate, 60–65
Crooke, Helkiah, 189, 192
Crouch, Tim, 358
Cruz, Anne J., 248
Cull, Nicholas John, 318
Culpeper, Nicholas, 192
Cummings, Brian, 196
Cunningham, Karen, 121
Curio, Augustine, 190
Cushman, L. W., 138

Daborne, Robert: *The Honest Man's Fortune*, 213, 214, 215, 217, 219, 220–221
Dabydeen, David, 149
Dadabhoy, Ambereen, 89, 91, 362
Daileader, Celia R., 89
Daladier, Édouard, 315
D'Amico, Jack, 89, 149
D'Angelo, Bob, 104, 121
Daniel, Samuel, 257, 258, 260, 372
Daniels, Guy, 145
Dante Alighieri, 268
Daunce, Edward, 248
Davenant, William, 338, 382
Davies, John: *Gullinge Sonnets*, 278
Davies, John, of Kidwelly, 190
Davis, C. H., 154
Davis, J. Madison, 308
Davoine, Françoise, 112, 120, 121
Dawkins, Richard, 311
Dawson, Giles E., 151
De Francisci, Enza, 2
de Grazia, Margreta, 140
de la Torre Moreno, Maria Jose, 189
De Silva, Pietro, 5
Dean, Aaron, 103–104
DeGruy, Joy, 108, 111, 121
Dekker, Thomas, 121
  The Bachelers Banquet, 196–197
  The Welsh Ambassador, 213, 214
Delgado, Richard, 121
Dench, Judi, 367, 368
Dent, R. W., 205
Depledge, Emma, 384–398
Despinois, John, 92
Dessen, Alan C., 186, 211, 215, 219, 227
Dethick, Henry, 191
Deutermann, Allison K., 192
Devgn, Ajay, 16
DeVries, David N., 138
Dharmendra, 24–25
di Biasi, Volfango, 1–14
DiAngelo, Robin, 115, 121
Dick, Bryan, 335
Dickerson, Adam, 64
Dickson, Andrew, 56
Diderot, Denis, 377

Dieterle, William, 382
Digby, John, 1st Earl of Bristol, 240, 245
Digges, Leonard, 130, 136
Dimmock, Matthew, 189
Dioume, Mamadou, 1
Disney, Walt, 290, 296
Dixon, Thomas, 200, 355
Dobson, Michael, 145, 292
Dodd, William, 143
Dolven, Jeff, 365
Donaldson, Ian, 122, 123, 124, 128, 186
Donawerth, Jane, 150
Donne, John, 186, 192, 371
Donno, Elizabeth, 223
Donovan, Kevin, 385
Doran, Gregory, 385
  Henry VI, Part One Open Rehearsal Project, 346, 352–355
  The Tempest (2016, with digital effects), 375, 376
  The Winter's Tale (1999), 382
Douglass, Frederick, 111
Downing, David, 42
Doyle, Sir Arthur Conan, 322
Drakakis, John, 49, 148
Drake, Alfred, 52–53
Drayton, Michael, 366, 372
Drifyeld, Stephen, 92
Driver, Martha, 287
Drucker, Johanna, 61–62
Drummond, William, 275, 276
Dryden, John, 382
Du Bois, W.E.B., 37, 111
du Chesne, Joseph, 192
Duffin, Ross W., 160
Dugan, Holly, 320
Dukes, Ricky, 358
Dunbar, Adrian, 339
Duncan-Jones, Katherine, 260, 265, 366, 386
Dusinberre, Juliet, 266, 274, 277
Dutt, Michael Madhusudan, 30
Dutton, Richard, 123, 150–151, 186
Dyall, Valentine, 52
Dylan, Hedydd, 349–350
Dymkowski, Christine, 314

Earle, T. F., 107
East, Charlotte, 355
Eden, Richard, 189
Edmondson, Paul, 367–368, 374
Edward I, King of England, 373
Edwards, Jennifer J., 180–193, 400
Edwards, John, 101
Edwards, Philip, 208, 267, 273
Egan, Gabriel, 123, 129, 258
Ejiofor, Chiwetel, 56–57, 59
El Hamel, Chouki, 115
Elam, Keir, 282, 285, 376
Eligon, John, 33
Eliot, T. S., 316

INDEX

Elizabeth I, Queen of England, 367
Elliott, Victoria, 335–336
Ellis, Caitlin, 289, 292
Ellis-Fermor, Una, 329
Ellison, Katherine, 114, 121
Ellison, Ralph, 116
Elton, Ben, 360
Elton, W. R., 218
Elyot, Thomas, 360
    The Book Named the Gouernour, 250
    Dictionary, 243
Emmott, Bill, 5
Empson, William, 143, 170
Engler, Balz, 150
Enoch, Alfred, 334, *335*
Enterline, Lynn, 91, 198, 365
Erickson, Peter, 63, 64, 89, 98, 99, 158, 246
Erlingsson, Guðmundur, 289
Erne, Lukas, 112, 151, 394
    The Arden Research Handbook of Shakespeare and Textual Studies, 391, 392, 398
    Bel-vedére, or the Garden of the Muses: An Early Modern Printed Commonplace Book (ed.), 384, 388–389, 398
Esche, Edward, 29
Escolme, Bridget, 148, 364, 378, 383
Espinosa, Ruben, 158
Essiedu, Paapa, 378
Evans, Robert C., 12, 89, 90
Ewbank, Inga-Stina, 266, 267, 273
Eyre, Richard, 313

Fagotto, Matteo, 46
Faircloth, Nicki, 199, 205
Fanon, Frantz, 111, 121
Farber, Yaël, 337–338
Farjeon, Herbert, 49, 51, 59
Farley-Hills, David, 124, 135
Farman, Nola, 67
Fausset, Richard, 33
Fazel, Valerie M., 3
Fearon, Ray, 54–56, 59
Feerick, Jean, 242
Felce, Ian, 289
Felton, Felix, 59
Fénelon, François, 282
Fennor, William, 125
Ferguson, Alisa Grant, 377, 383
Ferguson, Arthur B., 258–259, 263
Fernie, Ewan, 233
Fewster, Anna, 64
Ficino, Marsilio, 191
Field, Nathan, 191
    The Honest Man's Fortune, 213, 214, 215, 217, 219, 220–221
    The Knight of Malta, 94–95, 99–100
Fields, Barbara J., 107, 362
Fields, Karen E., 107, 362

Finch, R. G., 309
Fiorato, Sidia, 148
Fishburne, Laurence, 35
Fitzgerald, Tara, 339
Fitzpatrick, Peter, 115
Fitzpatrick, Tim, 219, 222
Flather, Amanda, 101
Fleay, Fredrick Gard, 129
Fleming, Matt, 64–69
Fletcher, Christopher, 297
Fletcher, John, 67
    The Honest Man's Fortune, 213, 214, 215, 217, 219, 220–221
    The Knight of Malta, 94–95, 99–100
    Sir John van Olden Barnavelt, 213, 214, 215
Florio, John, 94, 252
Floyd-Wilson, Mary, 32, 195, 201, 242, 244
Foakes, R. A., 124
Foley, Sean, 360
Foot, John, 2, 6
Ford, John, 94
Fordham, Hallam, 328
Forgacs, David, 10
Forman, Simon, 92–93
Fortescue, Sir John William, 331
Foss, Vivian, 384
Fouracres, George, 335
Fox, Cora, 196
Francis, Jacques, 92
Frankenberg, Ruth, 242
Frankforter, Daniel A., 308
Franssen, Paul, 314
Fraser, Sarah, 245
Fredrickson, George M., 89
Freehafer, John, 130
Freeman, Morgan, 46
French, Andrew, 348
French, George Russell, 310
Freud, Sigmund, 86
Frobisher, Sir Martin, 78
Frost, Gary, 62, 63
Frye, Northrop, 229, 283, 311
Fryer, Peter, 90, 92
Fuchs, Barbara, 241, 244, 248
Fuller, Edward, 252
Fuller, Thomas, 127
Fumerton, Patricia, 88
Furness, Horace Howard, 171, 384
Furnivall, Frederick, 397

Gabriel, Shane (Lady M), 358
Gadd, Ian, 391
Gaitanidi, Maria, 359
Gajowski, Evelyn, 157, 167
Gale, Mariah, 354
Galen, 183, 194, 195, 196
Galloway, David, 245
Galt, Rosalind, 6
Gambon, Michael, 55

Garber, Marjorie, 73
Gardner, Lyn, 344
Garner, Dwight, 229
Garner, Shirley Nelson, 80, 149, 159
Garzoni, Tomaso, 183
Gascoigne, George: *The Adventures of Master F. J.*, 266, 268, 270–271, 275–276, 278, 279, 280
Gaudillière, Jean-Max, 112, 120, 121
Gaya, Aurélien, 1
Gayle, Ashley D., 343, 345
Geddes, Louise, 3
Gerrard, Nicci, 56
Gesner, Carol, 281
Ghazoul, Ferial J., 57
Ghidoni, Fabio, 3
Gielgud, John, 49, 313
Gielgud, Val, 49–50
Gil, Daniel Juan, 203
Gilbert, Felix, 75
Gilchrist, Kim, 372–374
Gillen, Adam, 333
Ginsborg, Paul, 1, 5, 7
Girouard, Mark, 77
Glapthorne, Henry: *The Lady Mother*, 213, 214, 219
Glatzer, Paula, 385
Glauser, Jürg, 292
Gleijeses, Lorenzo, 3
Godwin, Simon, 375
Gold, Barbara K., 150
Goldie, Grace Wyndham, 50
Golding, Arthur, 182
Gollancz, Israel, 289, 308
Gopi, Suresh, 20
Gore-Langton, Robert, 54, 55
Gormley, Colin, 347
Gossett, Suzanne, 392
Gotscheff, Dimiter, 375
Gouge, William, 97
Gower, John: *Confessio amantis*, 309, 310
Gowing, Laura, 101
Grady, Kyle, 4, 115
Graham, Lindsey, 115
Grandage, Michael, 56–57
Granville-Barker, Harley, 59, 313–332, 399
Gray, Patrick, 314
Green, James, 54
Green, Lucy, 342, *343*
Greenblatt, Stephen, 57, 148, 284, 353
    Renaissance Self-Fashioning, 153, 180, 195
Greene, Robert, 195
    [*John of Bordeaux*], 213, 214
    Orlando Furioso, 221
    Pandosto, The Triumph of Time, 238, 243
Greenhalgh, Susan, 375, 376
Greg, W. W., 150, 215, 217, 221, 268, 397
    on Pavier Quartos, 393

406

INDEX

Grennan, Eamon, 93–94, 96, 97, 149, 156
Grier, Miles P., 242, 393
Griffin, Andrew, 186
Griffin, Eric, 241, 248
Griffiths, Paul, 92
Grimm, Jacob and Wilhelm, 290, 296, 299
Grint, William, 351
Gross, Kenneth, 153
Guevara, Antonio de, 183
Guicciardini, Lodovico, 310
Gulzar (Sampooran Singh Kalza), 27
Gurr, Andrew, 93, 123, 137, 146, 209, 222, 227
Gussow, Mel, 33

Habermas, Jürgen, 135
Habib, Imtiaz, 33
   Black Lives in the English Archives 1500–1677, 92, 101, 158
   'Hel's Perfect Character', 98, 99
   '*Othello*: the state of the art', 89
   '*Othello*, Sir Peter Negro, and the Blacks of early modern England', 90
   'Racial impersonation on the Elizabethan stage', 106, 121
   'The Resonables of Boroughside, Southwark', 89, 91, 92, 93, 99, 102, 362
Habib, Khalil M., 168
Hacket, Thomas, 194, 195
Hadfield, Andrew, 257, 300
Hadfield, Mark, 354
Hadingue, Amanda, 348
Haiste, Greg, 352
Halasz, Alexandra, 137
Hall, Kim F., 48, 89–90
   'Object into object?', 98
   Othello: Texts and Contexts, 106, 107, 205
   '*Othello* and the problem of Blackness', 150, 152
   'Reading what isn't there', 89
   Things of Darkness, 89, 99, 121, 148, 242, 247, 250
Hall, Peter, 313, 315–316
Hamilton, Donna, 240
Hamlin, Hannibal, 287
Hamlin, Larry Leon, 46
Hampton-Reeves, Stuart, 353
Hannen, Hermione, 51
Hanratty, Conor, 380–381, 383
Hansberry, Lorraine, 34
Hansen, William F., 289
Happé, Peter, 139, 140, 141, 143
Harding, Emma, 57–59
Hardy, Thomas, 322
Harewood, David, 60
Hariot, Thomas, 253
Harper, Robert Francis, 121
Harris, Amanda, 354
Harris, Bernard, 167
Harris, Cheryl I., 241

Harrison, Matthew P., 266, 273
Harrison, T. P., 266, 269–270
Harrison, Timothy M., 200, 364–365
Harry, Berger, Jr, 167
Hart, H. C., 171
Hart, Michael, 389–390
Hart, Paul, 358, 359
Hartman, Matt, 229
Hartman, Saidiya V., 118
Hastie, Robert, 357
Hatch, James, 35–36, 45
Havers, George, 190
Hawkes, Terence, 331
Hawkins, Jack, 52, 53
Hazlitt, William, 164–165
Hebert, L. Joseph, Jr, 168
Hecquet, Philippe, 191
Hegerty, Stephanie, 103, 121
Heijes, Coen, 380, 383
Held, Joshua R., 148–165, 400
Helgerson, Richard, 91, 258
Heller, Agnes, 326
Henderson, Diana, 376
Hendricks, Margo, 91, 99, 148
Heng, Geraldine, 149, 362
Henry VII, King of England, 373
Henry VIII, King of England, 373
Henry, Prince of Wales, 240, 245–246, 254
Henry, Akiya, 337–338
Henry, Lenny, 56, 57, 58, 59
Henslowe, Philip, 123, 369
Henze, Catherine, 144
Hersov, Greg, 338–339
Herzig, Carine, 243
Heywood, Thomas, 182
   The Captives, 213, 214, 217, 222
   Troia Britannica, 257
   A Woman Killed with Kindness, 212, 213, 214, 215, 219, 224, 395
Hibbard, G. R., 208
Hiddleston, Tom, 376
Higgins, Nadine, 335
Hill, Anthony D., 34, 46
Hill, John C., 384
Hillman, David, 148
Hinman, Charlton, 151, 152
Hitchcock, Tim, 101
Hobgood, Allison P., 148, 190
Hodgdon, Barbara, 22, 35
Hodgson, John, 86
Hoeniger, David, 188
Hoenselaars, Tom, 123
Höfele, Andreas, 320
Holden, Norah Lopez, 339
Holinshed, Raphael, 290, 295
Holland, Peter, 137, 140, 141, 150, 201, 212, 279, 287
Holland, Philemon, 196
Hollander, John, 285
Holme, Randle, 190
Holmer, Joan Ozark, 164, 206

Holmes, Sean, 333–334, 335–337, 359
Holmes, Steven A., 33
Homer, 281–286, 401
Honeyman, Janice, 358
Honigmann, E. A. J., 124, 150
   Othello, Arden Third Series, 36, 58, 81, 92, 95, 112, 121, 125, 144, 150, 166, 167, 171, 197, 199
   The Texts of Othello and Shakespearean Revision, 94, 96, 150
Hookes, Nicholas, 367
Hooks, Adam, 391
Hopkins, Anthony, 54
Hopkins, Lisa, 251–252, 253
Hornback, Robert, 143, 145, 362
Horsley, Owen, 346, 352–355
Hoskins, John, 183
Houlahan, Mark, 196, 281
Houseman, John, 315–316
Howard, Charles, 1st Earl of Nottingham, 240
Howard, Henry, Earl of Surrey, 271
Howard, Jean E., 62, 91, 148, 150, 252
Howard-Hill, T. H., 215
Howe, Ruth-Arlene W., 47–48
Howell, Jane, 378
Hui, Jonathan Y. H., 287–312, 400
Hulse, Clark, 89
Hunt, Martita, 50–51
Hunt, Maurice, 266, 277, 328
Hunt, Simon, 88
Hunter, G. K., 91, 92, 149, 267, 272–273
Huntington, Helen, 313
Hutson, Lorna, 130, 272
Huxley, Aldous, 231
Hyde, Jonathan, 344, 345
Hyland, Jacqueline, 299

Ichikawa, Mariko, 209, 210, 215, 220, 222, 227
Igweonu, Kenechukwu, 42
Ince, Ola, 334–335
Innes, Christopher, 320
Inoue, Naomi, 104
Ioppolo, Grace, 124
Irish, Bradley J., 196
Issa, Islam, 57
Ivic, Christopher, 371–372, 373, 374
Iweala, Uzodinma, 110
Iyengar, Sujata, 3, 9, 145, 188, 242

Jackson, C. Bernard, 35, 48
Jackson, Henry, 128, 136, 148, 164
Jackson, Macdonald P., 366–367
Jackson, Russell, 18, 375–383
Jacobs, Kemi-Bo, *347*, 348
Jaeger, Werner, 281, 285
Jager, Eric, 62
Jaggard, Isaac, 394, 395
Jaggard, William, 394
   The Passionate Pilgrim, 279, 366, 368, 387

407

INDEX

Jahi, Runako, 46
James VI and I, King of Scotland and of Great Britain, 240, 245–246, 367, 371–372, 373
James, Susan, 200
James, William, 203
Janik, Vicki, 138
Jardine, Lisa, 154
Jarman, Derek, 382
Jayalalitha, 24–25
Jayaraj, 15–16, 20–23, 31
Jefferson, Atatiana, 103–104, 120–121
Jefferson, Marquis, 104
Jenkins, Harold, 226
Jensen, Bo Søndergaard, 121
Johnson, Gerald, 394
Johnson, Harvey, 46
Johnson, James Weldon, 47
Johnson, Laurie, 64, 281
Johnson, Lyndon B., 116
Johnson, Nora, 137
Johnson, R. C., 143
Johnson, Samuel, 159, 164
Johnson-Haddad, Miranda, 220
Johnstone, Oliver, 354
Jones, Dorothy, 268, 271
Jones, Eldred, 149
Jones, John, 150
Jones, Nicholas R., 242
Jones, Reginald, 105
Jones, Robert C., 143
Jones, Steven Swann, 291, 297
Jonson, Ben, 372
   The Alchemist, 126, 128
   Bartholomew Fair, 126, 282, 339
   Catiline, 130
   The Devil is an Ass, 186–187
   Discoveries, 130
   Every Man In His Humour, 124, 126, 127, 128, 135, 365
   Every Man Out Of His Humour, 126, 128, 365
   The Masque of Blackness, 250
   The Masque of Oberon, 245
   Poetaster, 127
   Sejanus, 122–136, 401
   The Seven Deadly Sins, 126–127
   Volpone, 123, 124, 126, 127, 186
Jordan, Constance, 121, 305
Jorgensen, Paul A., 329
Jorgensen, Peter, 293, 308
Joseph, Bertram, 377
Joseph, Kevin P., 21
Joubin, Alexa Alice, 8
Jowett, John, 8
   The New Oxford Shakespeare (2016), 123, 258
   The Oxford Shakespeare: The Complete Works (2005), 125, 291, 295
   William Shakespeare: A Textual Companion, 209

Joyce, James, 282
Jumbo, Cush, 338–339

Kalinke, Marianne E., 293, 308
Kamaralli, Anna, 166
Kani, John, 358
Kar, Ajoy, 15–16, 23, 28–30, 31
Karim-Cooper, Farah, 145, 362
Karimipour, Zahra, 253
Kashyap, Anurag, 19
Kastan, David Scott, 212, 385–387, 394, 398
Kataria, Vandana, 31
Katariya, Sharat, 27
Kathman, David, 126–127
Kaufmann, Miranda, 90, 92, 93, 101
Kawan, Christine Shojaei, 290–291
Kean, Edmund, 55
Keaton, Michael, 382
Keats, John, 302
Kellet, Edward, 189
Kelley, Donald R., 258
Kemp, Will, 102, 127, 133–134, 140, 146, 224
Kendi, Ibram X., 111, 121
Kennedy, Judith M., 269
Kernan, Alvin, 171
Kerrigan, John, 262
Keynes, John Maynard, 323
Khan, Mansoor, 27
Kidnie, Margaret Jane, 112, 151, 208–214, 376, 392, 400
Kim, Susan, 114, 121
King, Peter, 101
King, Rosalind, 142, 158, 314
Kingsley-Smith, Jane, 361–374
Kinney, Arthur F., 246
Kirsch, Arthur, 325
Kirwan, Peter, 342–356
Kiséry, András, 391
Kitamura Sae, 376
Kliman, Bernice W., 308
Kline, Karen, 16, 31
Kloska, Joseph, 347–348
Knadler, Steven, 243
Knecht, Ross, 365–366, 374
Knight, Edward, 215
Knight, G. Wilson, 50, 153, 316
Knight, Jeffrey Todd, 394
Knight, Rhonda, 188
Knights, L. C., 314
Knolles, Richard, 125
Knowles, Richard, 384–385, 398
Knox, Frank, 319
Knutson, Roslyn L., 139, 212
Kolin, Philip C., 35, 63, 94, 150, 166, 393
Korda, Natasha, 91
Krueger, Robert, 278
Kumar, Mohan, 24
Kumar, Tarun, 30
Kumar, Uttam, 28, 29, 30

Kussmaul, Ann, 93
Kuzner, James, 155, 320

la Boétie, Étienne de, 180
la Primaudaye, Pierre de, 183
Lacy, John, 129
Ladbury, Hattie, 340–341
Lagerholm, Åke, 289, 309
Lake, David, 150
Lake, Harold Coote, 288
Lamb, Jonathan, 272, 274
Lamb, Mary Ellen, 288
Lambert, Zoe, 348
Lancashire, Anne, 222
Landers, Georgia, 341
Lane, Christopher, 104
Lane, Tom, 337
Langley, Eric, 185, 193, 195
Lanier, Douglas M., 3
LaPerle, Carol Mejia, 12, 201
Laroque, François, 137
las Casas, Bartolomé de, 253
Laslett, Peter, 93, 101
Lateiner, Donald, 150
Latham, Robert, 164
Lavagnino, John, 95
Lavender, Philip, 289
Lavers, Annette, 185
Lavia, Gabriele, 1
Lawrence, Friedrich, 135
Lawrence, Jason, 151
Lawrence, William Witherle, 301
Layton, Cassie, 58
Lee, John, 195
Lefebvre, Henri, 73
Lehmann, Courtney, 2
Lehmann, Hans-Thies, 376
Lemnius, Levinus, 199
Lemon, Rebecca, 183
Lennam, Trevor N. S., 145
Lentin, Antony, 323
Lenz, Carolyn, 166
Leo Africanus, 201, 250
Leonard, Alice, 268
Leonard, Jake, 357
Leonard, Nancy S., 123
Leong, Elaine, 61
Lesser, Zachary, 391, 393–396, 398
Lester, Adrian, 106, 362
Lever, J. W., 223
Levesy, Gabriell, 93
Levin, Richard, 137, 141, 143, 164
Levine, Caroline, 251
Levy, F. J., 258, 259
Levy, James P., 324
Lewis, Wyndham, 316
Lindheim, Nancy, 285
Lindmark, Daniel, 190–191
Lindqvist, Sven, 110
Ling, Nicholas, 279–280
Lintott, Bernard, 366

INDEX

Little, Arthur L., Jr, 42, 247, 361
Littler, Tom, 359
Livingstone, Jo, 111, 121
Livingstone, Jonathan, 339
Lloyd, Janet, 137
Lodge, Thomas: *Rosalynde*, 266, 268–270,
    273–274, 278, 280
Loeffel, Robert, 319
Loffreda, Beth, 241
Londré, Felicia Hardison, 315
Long, William B., 219
Longinus, 191
Loomba, Ania, 22, 90, 148, 149, 201
Lopez, Jeremy, 166–179, 400
Loth, Agnete, 309
Lothian, J. M., 282, 285
Loughnane, Rory, 129–130
Lowe, K. J. P., 107
Loxley, James, 123
Luckyj, Christina, 96
Luhrmann, Baz, 3, 7
Lumley, Robert, 10
Lupton, Julia Reinhard, 150
Lussana, Sergio, 40
Luther, Martin, 318–319
Lyons, Tara, 391

McAlinden, Gavin, 357
McAlindon, Tom, 175
McAlpin, Heller, 229
McArdle, James, 337, 338
McCarthy, Grace, 288
McCarthy, Lilah, 313
McDaniels, Pellom, III, 46
McDermott, Jennifer Rae, 63–64
MacDonald, Ann-Marie, 47, 165
MacDonald, Joyce Green, 148, 362
MacDonald, L., 105
McDonald, Russ, 123, 167
McEachern, Claire, 372
McFarlane, Brian, 49, 51
McFarlane, Colin, 55
McGann, Jerome, 396
McHugh, Marissa, 314
McInnis, David, 369–370, 374
McIntosh, James, 289, 292
McIntyre, Blanche, 339–341
Mack, Maynard, 167
McKellen, Ian, 339, 342–345
McKenzie, D. F., 396
MacLean, Sally-Beth, 139
McManaway, James G., 151
McManus, Clare, 157, 205
McMillin, Scott, 94, 139, 150, 151, 158, 212
McMullan, Gordon, 153
Macnair, Michael R. T., 118, 121
McNeill, T. E., 81, 82
Macready, Henry, 53
Macready, William, 49
McVeigh, Karen, 120, 121
Maguire, Laurie, 92, 100

Maher, Vanessa, 10
Majidi, Majid, 20
Makaryk, Irene Rima, 314
Malone, Edmond, 367
Malone, Karen, 75
Mamdani, Mahmood, 115, 121
Mammone, Andrea, 5, 10
Manjrekar, Mahesh, 19
Manjule, Nagraj, 31
Mann, Roderick, 51
Mannoni, Octave, 110
Marcell, Joseph, 339
Marcus, Leah S., 106, 112, 151–153
Marianus Scholasticus, 367
Marino, James J., 394
Marlowe, Christopher, 123, 258, 364, 388
    Edward II, 370
    The Jew of Malta, 123, 140, 145
Marsden, Jean, 34
Marston, John, 94–95, 102
Martin, Emily, 69–72
Martin, Randall, 126
Mascharak, Abhirup, 15–31, 401
Massagli, M., 105
Massai, Sonia, 2, 392, 394, 397
Massignon, Geneviève, 299
Massinger, Philip, 397
    Believe As You List, 213, 214, 216
    The Honest Man's Fortune, 213, 214, 215,
        217, 219, 220–221
    The Knight of Malta, 94–95, 99–100
    The Parliament of Love, 213, 214
    Sir John van Olden Barnavelt, 213, 214, 215
Masten, Jeffrey, 152
Matar, Nabil, 90, 99
Mathias, Sean, 342–345
Matteo, Sante, 10
Matthew, Gospel of, 267, 276, 277, 280
Matthews, Steven, 316
Maus, Katharine Eisaman, 106, 111, 121,
    155
Mayer, Jean-Christophe, 392
Medici, Marie de', 68
Meek, Richard, 194–207, 401
Melchiori, Giorgio, 143, 266
Meldrum, Tim, 101
Mennis, Kate, 265–280, 401
Merbury, Frances, 145
Meres, Francis, 366
Middleton, Thomas, 366
    The Changeling, 95, 96
    The Second Maiden's/Lady's Tragedy,
        213, 214, 215, 222
    The Witch, 337–338
Miller, Gemma, 378, 383
Miller, Gordon S., 138
Miller, Hayley, 103, 121
Miller, Nichole E., 320
Millier, Russel H., 320
Mills, Charles W., 40
Milton, John, 368

Minear, Erin, 164
A Mirror for Magistrates, 256, 400
Mishra, Sudhir, 19
Mitra, Trisha, 21
Miura, Cassie, 196
Mohamed ben Abdallah, 42
Molette, Barbara J. and Carlton W.,
    32–48, 399
Mollica, R., 105
Montaigne, Michel Eyquem de, 180–181,
    182, 252–253, 279
Montemayor, Jorge de, 266, 268,
    269–270, 278, 280
Montgomery, William, 125, 209, 291, 295
Montironi, Maria Elisa, 2, 5, 10
More, Henry, 190, 192
Morgan, Margery, 315
Morockoe, John, 92
Morris, Clara, 177
Morris, Dyfrig, 351
Morrison, Toni, 111, 113, 242
    Desdemona, 48, 89, 106, 108, 110, 111,
        121, 165
Morse, Ruth, 287
Mortimer, Jeremy, 54–55, 57
Moser-Rath, Elfriede, 301
Mosley, Della, 113
Moss, Paul, 342, *343*
Moss, Rachel E., 297
Moss, Stephanie, 188
Motohashi, Ted, 382, 383
Mountfort, Walter: *The Launching of the
    Mary*, 213, 214, 216
Moyer, Ann E., 195
Moyers, Bill, 116
Mucciolo, John, 151
Mudimbe, V. Y., 106, 107
Muir, Kenneth, 140, 266
    'Folklore and Shakespeare', 288
    Othello, Penguin edition, 66–67, 84
    Shakespeare's Plays in Quarto, 152, 211
    The Sources of Shakespeare's Plays, 122,
        290, 295, 310
Mukherjee, Sudhir, 28
Mukherji, Subha, 167
Müller, Heiner, 375
Muller, James W., 323
Munday, Anthony, 375
    John a Kent and John a Cumber, 212–213,
        214, 218–219
    The Triumphs of Reunited Britannia, 373
Munich, Adrienne, 3
Munro, Lucy, 126, 139, 376–377, 383
Münster, Sebastian, 189
Murphy, Andrew, 392, 394
    *Shakespeare in Print: A History and
    Chronology of Shakespeare
    Publishing*, 384, 389–392, 398
Murrell, Rebekah, 334
Murry, John Middleton, 316
Musgrove, Sidney, 123–124

INDEX

Myers, Linda James, 105
Mzezewa, Tariro, 114

Nagy, Phyllis, 47
Nashe, Thomas, 140, 258, 265, 268, 279
  preface to Sidney's *Astrophel and Stella*, 276
  The Unfortunate Traveller, 266, 271–272, 277, 278–279, 280
Ndiaye, Noémie, 241
Neely, Carol Thomas, 97, 149, 166, 245
Neidig, William, 394
Neill, Michael, 148, 152, 166, 181
  Othello, Oxford edition, 89, 94, 106, 196, 198, 201, 202
Nelson, Richard, 313, 321
Nemser, Ruby, 278
Ness, Frederic, 258, 260
Nestruck, J. Kelly, 138
Nevo, Ruth, 304, 305
Newman, Karen, 90, 148, 152, 171
Newstok, Scott, 362
Newton, Thomas, 190
Nichol, Lily, 354
Nichols, Adam, 359
Nicolai, Roberto, 243
Nicoll, Allardyce, 91, 151
Nicolson, Harold, 323
Ninagawa, Yukio, 380–381
Noble, Adrian, 313
Noble, Richmond, 285
Nocentelli, Carmen, 244
Norman, William, 289
Norridge, Zoe, 104
North, Sir Thomas, 183
Nosworthy, J. M., 295, 302
Novy, Marianne, 180, 204
Nunn, Trevor, 96, 167, 281
Nutt, Alfred, 292
Nuttall, A. D., 272

O'Brien, Ciarán, 335, 336
O'Connor, Marion F., 148
Odeke, Anne, 348
O'Donoghue, Heather, 289
Oertzen, Christine von, 61
Okri, Ben, 106
O'Leary, Niamh J., 96
Olivier, Laurence, 25, 55
Olley, Katherine M., 289, 292
O'Loughlin, Katrina, 196
Olusoga, David, 361
Om, J., 24
O'Malley, Joseph, 359
O'Neill, Fionnuala, 123
O'Neill, Stephen, 3, 376, 383
Oosterveen, K., 101
O'Rawe, Catherine, 3, 14
Orgel, Stephen, 140, 167, 212
Orkin, Martin, 8, 91, 152
Orlin, Lena Cowen, 12, 33, 88, 167, 220

'Desdemona's disposition', 80, 149
Locating Privacy in Tudor London, 76, 78
Othello: The State of Play, 89, 90, 91, 92, 97, 100, 150, 167, 198
Ortelius, Abraham, 244
Osborne, Francis, 122
Osborne, Laurie E., 284, 375, 376
Ostermeier, Thomas, 379
Ostovich, Helen, 186
Ottaway, Robert, 53
Ovid, 182
Owens, Rebekah, 382, 383

Pafford, J. H. P., 215
Pagitt, Ephraim, 190
Palfrey, Simon, 139, 211
Panja, Sharmistha, 21
Pao, Angela C., 37
Paracelsus, 185–186
Paré, Ambrose, 186
Park, Thomas, 388–389
Parker, Matthew, 357–358
Parker, Oliver, 2, 35
Parker, Patricia, 39, 91, 99, 148
Parker, R. B., 314, 319
Parnassus Plays, 127, 133–134
Parr, Anthony, 186
Parrott, Thomas Marc, 137, 208
Partlicius, Simeon, 192
Pasolini, Pier Paulo, 1–2
Paster, Gail Kern, 148, 195, 196, 199, 201, 202
Patra, Augustina, 92
Patterson, Annabel, 326
Paul, R. F., 181
Payne, Ben Iden, 315
Pearce, Emery, 52
Pechter, Edward, 124, 150, 151
  Othello, editions, 106, 171
  Othello and Interpretative Traditions, 100, 149, 166, 167
Peck, Raoul, 107, 110–111, 115
Peele, George, 362
Peiris, Suzanna, 92
Pender, Stephen, 202
Pennington, Michael, 359
Pepys, Samuel, 100, 122, 164
Perkins, Judith, 150
Perry, Curtis, 287
Perry, Imami, 48
Perry, Twila, 47
Perryment, Max, 334
Pertile, Giulio J., 188
Peterson, Kaara L., 188
Petrarch, 110, 268, 269, 270, 288
Petri, Heinrich, 249–250
Pettway, Erica, 104, 121
Phillips, G. W., 310
Philmus, M. R. Rohr, 270
Philo, John-Mark, 122–136, 401
Philpott, Maryam, 58

Picasso, Pablo, 232
Pierce, Robert B., 281–286, 401
Pieterse, Alex, 104, 121
Pigott, Michael, 2, 3
Plato, 370
Pliny the Elder, 122, 196, 199, 206
Plouviez, Peter, 54
Plutarch, 196, 199
Poitier, Sidney, 363
Polanski, Rowan, 351
Pollard, A. W., 393
Pollard, Tanya, 192, 364
Popescu, Lucy, 57
Porter, Charlotte, 397
Pory, John, 201, 250
Potter, Lois, 90, 122, 153, 177, 333–341
Prager, Carolyn, 102
Prager, Leonard, 141, 142
Prasad, Nicholas, 351
Pratt, Aaron, 395
Preiss, Richard, 137, 143
Prince, Lucy Terry, 111
Prokop, Andrew, 33
Proudfoot, Richard, 265, 385–387, 398
Psarra, Sophia, 74
Ptolemy (Claudius Ptolemaeus), 249–250
Pugliatti, Paola, 314
Pulsiano, Phillip, 292, 309
Purdom, C. B., 313, 314, 316, 328

Quarshie, Hugh, 36
Quartley, Mark, 354
Quayle, Antony, 53
Quijano, Anibal, 242
Quinn, Judy, 289
Quintilian, 273, 276
Quiros, Laura, 116

Raber, Karen, 320
Raby, Julie, 376
Radford, Michael, 2
Radulian, Ilinca, 359
Raffel, Burton, 118
Raleigh, Sir Walter, 245
Ralhan, O. P., 24
Ranald, Margaret Loftus, 149
Ranke, Kurt, 301
Rankine, Claudia, 241
Rao, T. Prakash, 15–16, 23–28, 31
Ravera, Oscar, 80
Ray, Sid, 188, 287
Razzall, Lucy, 370–371, 374
Read, David West, 359
Rebecca, Lemon, 115
Redworth, Glyn, 240, 246
Reeves, Keanu, 382
Reinhardt, Max, 382
Reinwald, Elizabeth, 384
Renwick, W. L., 216
Resonable family, 91, 93, 99
Reynolds, Gillian, 54

410

INDEX

Rhoads, Rebecca G., 217
Rhode, Eleanor, 358
Riall, Lucy, 297
Rice, Emma, 147
Rice, Julian C., 156
Richards, Jennifer, 257
Richardson, Catherine, 73
Riche, Barnaby, 310
Richie, Lionel, 334
Ridley, M. R., 95, 144, 166, 171
Riley, Clayton, 34
Ringler, William A., Jr, 275
Rintoul, Douglas, 358
Ripley, John, 315–316
Rippy, Marguerite, 2
Rizvi, Pervez, 150
Rizzo, Michael, 117
Roazen, Daniel Heller, 327
Roberts, Sasha, 366
Roberts, Steven, 117
Robertson, John M., 258
Robeson, Paul, 53
Robinson, Cedric J., 114, 121
Robinson, Grace, 92
Robinson, John B., 282, 285
Robson, Mark, 123
Rolfe, J. C., 278
Rollins, Hyder Edward, 269, 271–272
Ronan, Saoise, 337
Ronk, Martha, 158, 205
Roper, Derek, 94
Rosenberg, Marvin, 166
Rosenfeld, Colleen Ruth, 90, 97, 167
Ross, Charlotte, 2
Ross, L. J., 142
Rothenburg, Nina, 2
Rouse, W. H. D., 182
Rowe, Nicholas, 171
Rowland, Avril, 360
Rowlands, Samuel, 94
Roy, Bimal, 24
Royster, Francesca, 241, 248
Rubens, Peter Paul, 98
Rubin, Edgar, 369
Rubinstein, Nicolai, 75
Ruiter, David, 158
Russell, Donald A., 273
Russell, Sophie, 334, 335, 359
Rutter, Barrie, 57
Rutter, Carol Chillington, 90, 95, 96–97, 157, 167
Ryan, Kiernan, 193
Rymer, Thomas, 120, 166

Saba, Sirine, 334–335
Sacks, David Harris, 258
Sackville, Thomas, 1st Earl of Dorset, 257
sagas, Icelandic, 27
   Ála flekks saga, 287–312, 400
   Tristrams saga ok Ísoddar, 308
   Völsunga saga, 299

Sahu, Kishore, 27
Saigal, Ramesh, 24
Salenius, Elmer W., 316, 325, 326
Salgado, Gamini, 100
Salkeld, Duncan, 89, 91, 92, 99, 102
Salmon, Eric, 317, 318, 322, 323
Sanchez, Melissa E., 149
Sanders, Julie, 47, 73, 123
Sanders, Norman O., 125, 166, 199
Sanford, James, 310
Sansonetti, Laetitia, 279
Santos, Kathryn Vomero, 320
Saraf, Babli Moitra, 21
Sarossi, Gyuri, 340
Sawant, Vishram, 19
Sawyer, Robert, 314
Schaar, Claes, 266
Schalkwyk, David, 148, 166, 364, 377
Scheer, Monique, 365
Schenkl, Karl, 290
Schiffer, James, 166, 284
Schliesser, Erik, 195
Schoenbaum, S., 266
Schwartz, Murray M., 305
Scofield, Paul, 53–54, 55
Scolnicov, Hanna, 212
Scott, Charlotte, 199
Scott, Harold, 37
Scragg, Leah, 140, 141
Seagrove, Jenny, 345
Sears, Djanet, 45, 48
Secker, Eloise, 341
Sedelow, Sally Yeats, 389
Seeff, Adele F., 90
Selleck, Nancy, 198
Sen, Aveek, 167, 170, 177
Sen, Debu, 27
Sen, Suchitra, 28
Sen, Sudhaseel, 381, 383
Shaffer, Elinor S., 115, 120, 121
Shaheen, Naseeb, 287
Shakespeare, William, 121
  career, 121
    as actor, 126, 127, 135–136
    as possible schoolmaster, 281
  editions, 281
    Arden 1, *Coriolanus*; Granville-Barker's annotations, 314, 316
    Arden 3, 316
      Arden Shakespeare Complete Works, 384, 385–387, 398
      Sonnets, 366, 386
    Benson, Poems (1640), 368, 388
    Chandos Classics, 397
    Edmondson and Wells, *Sonnets*, 367–368
    Folio, 367
      As You Like It, 212
      Hamlet, 208–210, 211, 222
      Henry V, 212
      Julius Caesar, 212

      King Lear, 384
      mid-scene entrances, 208–210, 211, 212, 214, 222
      Othello, 96, 125, 148–165, 187, 400
      Twelfth Night, 212
    New Variorum, *King Lear* (Knowles), 384–385, 398
    Penguin, *Othello* (Muir, 1968), 66–67, 84
    quartos, 66
      Hamlet, 308
      mid-scene entrances, 208–210, 211, 213, 214, 222, 225–227
      King Lear, 384
      Othello, 96, 125, 150–153, 154–155, 158–159, 160, 161–162, 163, 164, 187
    Pavier, 393–396
    Thorpe, *Sonnets* (1609), 388
    by women editors, 396–398
  plays, 396
    Antony and Cleopatra, 182, 357
    As You Like It, 284, 397
      'bad' love lyrics, 266, 267, 272, 273–275, 277–278, 279–280, 401
      mid-scene entrances, 212, 214
    The Comedy of Errors, 310, 346, 349–352, 357, 380
    Coriolanus, 281, 357
      Granville-Barker and, 313–332, 399
    Cymbeline, 365, 374
      and Ali Smith's *Seasonal Quartet*, 230, 232–233, 234, 402
      Boccaccio and, 290, 301–302, 303, 304, 311
      boxes, chests and trunks in, 301–308, 370–371
      folkloric composition, and *Ála flekks saga*, 287–312, 400
    Edward III, 386
      'bad' love lyrics, 265–266, 267, 272, 277, 280, 401
    Hamlet, 201, 260, 284
      antecedents, sources and connections, 123–124, 287, 289, 308–310, 369–370
      Hamlet's character, 283, 325
      emotions in, 191, 365–366
      mid-scene entrances, 208–210, 211, 213, 214, 218, 220, 222, 225–227, 400
      performance studies, 377, 378
      Polonius's role, 281, 308–310
      productions, 333, 338–339, 342–345, 375, 376, 380
      three-text, in *Arden Shakespeare Complete Works*, 386
      women editors, 397
    Henry IV, 140, 261, 281, 282, 283, 364

INDEX

Shakespeare, William (cont.)
   Henry V, 123–124, 128, 143, 264, 325, 357–358
      mid-scene entrances, 212, 213, 214, 217, 218, 219–220
   Henry VI, 358, 379
      and *A Mirror for Magistrates*, 256–264, 400
   Henry VIII, 200
   Julius Caesar, 315, 325, 358, 397
      Caesar's epilepsy, 187, 191–192
      Cassius' role, 114, 117
      and Jonson's plays, 124, 130
      mid-scene entrances, 212, 214, 215, 217, 218
   King John, 358, 371
   King Lear, 124, 137, 327, 373–374, 397
      mid-scene entrance, 211, 219
   Love's Labour's Lost, 60, 143, 146–147, 192, 281, 365
      'bad' love lyrics, 266–267, 272–273, 275–278, 279, 280, 401
   Macbeth, 4–5, 95, 124, 372, 397
      productions, 313, 333, 337–338, 358
   Measure for Measure, 124, 339–341, 364
   The Merchant of Venice, 77, 123, 284, 301, 397
      Moorish maidservant, 99, 101–102
   The Merry Wives of Windsor, 359
   A Midsummer Night's Dream, 95, 313, 333–334, 359, 397
   Much Ado about Nothing, 77, 94, 96, 140, 146, 272, 364
   Othello, 1–207, 290, 377, 380, 397
      and the artists' book, 60–72, 402
      British radio productions, 49–59, 402
      and the built environment, 73–88, 402
      di Biasi's *Iago* and, 1–14, 399
      ecstasy and displacement in, 180–193, 400
      Emilia's role, 166–179, 400
      Indian screen adaptations, 15–31, 401
      and Jonson's *Sejanus*, 122–136, 401
      legal spaces and racial trauma in, 103–121, 399
      maidservant Barbary and Black presence in England, 89–102, 401
      and Molettes' *The Fortunes of the Moor*, 32–48, 399
      representation of sympathy, 194–207, 401
      the Vice's influence, 137–147, 401–402

      the Willow Song, race and gender, 148–165, 400
   Pericles, 282, 309
      and Ali Smith's *Seasonal Quartet*, 230, 233–234, 402
   Richard II, 257
   Richard III, 123, 140, 359, 378
   Romeo and Juliet, 141, 147, 227, 272, 290, 291
      productions, 333, 334–335, 342, 380–381
   Sir Thomas More, 213, 214, 217, 386
   The Taming of the Shrew, 288, 359, 397
   The Tempest, 110–111, 121, 123–124, 140, 281, 285, 397
      and Ali Smith's *Seasonal Quartet*, 230–232, 234, 402
      productions, 359, 375, 376
   Titus Andronicus, 121, 145, 298, 378, 393
      Aaron's role, 110, 123, 140
   Troilus and Cressida, 281
   Twelfth Night, 146–147, 182, 310, 397
      mid-scene entrances, 213, 214, 215, 222–223
      productions, 313, 334, 335–337, 359–360
      as Viola's Telemachy, 281–286, 401
   The Winter's Tale, 288, 290, 378
      and Ali Smith's *Seasonal Quartet*, 229–239, 402
      and Anglo-Spanish relations, 240–255, 399–400
      productions, 313, 346–349, 354
play, apocryphal: *Cardenio*, 368–369
poems, 368
   The Rape of Lucrece, 275
   Sonnets, 275
      'bad' lyrics and, 265–266, 269–270, 278, 279
      editions, 279
         Benson (1640), 368, 388
         Duncan-Jones, 366, 386
         Edmondson and Wells, 367–368
         in *The Passionate Pilgrim*, 279, 366, 368, 387
         Thorpe (1609), 388
      First Readers of Shakespeare's Sonnets, 1590–1790 (F. Ackers): reviews, 366, 387–388
adaptations, 387
   The Comedy of Errors, 387
      Angoor (Indian film, Gulzar), 27
      Do Dooni Char (Indian film, Sen), 27
      Local Kung Fu (Indian film, Basumatary), 31
   Hamlet, 31

      Haider (Indian film, Bhardwaj), 27, 31
      Hamlet (Indian film, Sahu), 27
      Hamlet: Rotten States (75-minute, cast of three; 6Footstories Theatre Company), 357
      Hamlet Machine (Müller, dir. Gotscheff), 375
      Ophelia (one-woman show; White, dir. Leonard), 357
      Un Ameleto di meno (film, Bene), 1–2
   1 Henry VI, 1
      Henry VI, Part One Open Rehearsal Project (dir. Doran and Horsley), 346, 352–355
   Julius Caesar, 355
      Cesare Deve Morire (film, Taviani), 1–2
      I, Cinna (the Poet) – Write a Revolution (solo show, Crouch), 358
   King Lear, 358
      Kunene and the King (Kani, dir. Honeyman), 358
   Macbeth, 358
      Macbeth (cast of three, The Old Rep Theatre, Birmingham), 358
      Macbeth (opera, Verdi; promenade performance, dir. Vivash), 359
      Macbeth: Playing Shakespeare with Deutsche Bank (90-minute version for young people), 358
      Maqbool (Indian film, Bhardwaj), 19, 20, 27
      Omkara (Indian film, Bhardwaj), 27
      Queer Lady M (solo performance from drag artist Lady M), 358
   The Merchant of Venice, 358
      Noblemen (Indian film, Kataria), 31
      William Shakespeare's 'The Merchant of Venice' (film, Radford), 2
   A Midsummer Night's Dream, 2
      10 ml Love (Indian film, Katariya), 27
      Dream (virtual reality motion-captured production, RSC), 346
      A Midsummer Night's Dream (film, Reinhardt/Dieterle), 382
   Much Ado about Nothing, 27
      Much Ado about Nothing (film, Branagh), 382
   Othello, 382
      American Moor (Cobb), 48

INDEX

British radio productions, 49–59, 402
Che cosa sonole le nuvole? (film, Pasolini), 1–2
Desdemona (Morrison), 48, 89, 106, 108, 110, 111, 121, 165
Desdemona: A Play about a Handkerchief (Vogel), 165
Desdemona in Her Own Words (artists' book, Martin), 69–72
The Fortunes of the Moor (B. J. and C. W. Molette), 32–48, 399
Goodnight Desdemona (Good Morning Juliet) (MacDonald), 47, 165
Hamraaz (Indian film, Chopra), 15
Harlem Duet (Sears), 48
Iago (Italian film, di Biasi), 1–14, 399
Iago (Jackson), 48
Indian screen adaptations, 15–31, 401
Izzat (Indian film, Prakash Rao), 15–16, 23–28, 31, 401
A Jealousy So Strong, that Judgement Cannot Cure (artist's book, Cronin), 60–65
Kaliyattam (Indian film, Jayaraj), 15–16, 20–23, 31, 401
Mirch (Indian film, Shukla), 15
Omkara (Indian film, Bhardwaj), 15–20, 23, 31, 401
Othello (film, Parker), 2, 35
Othello (opera, Verdi), 381
Othello: A Bestiary – with Floral Additions (artists' book, Borbonesa), 64–69
Saptapadi (Indian film, Kar), 15–16, 23, 28–30, 31, 401
Romeo and Juliet, 401
  & Juliet (jukebox musical, Read, dir. Sheppard), 359
  Ek Duuje Ke Liye (Indian film, Balachander), 27
  Qayamat Se Qayamat Tak (Indian film, Khan), 27
  Romeo and Juliet (choose-your-own-adventure Zoom-based, Creation Theatre), 342
  Romeo and Juliet (film, National Theatre), 342
  Romeo and Juliet (film, Zeffirelli), 2
  Romeo and Juliet (theatre–film hybrid, Metcalfe Gordon Productions), 342
  Romeo and Juliet (three-person, Handlebards), 342, *343*, 355–356
Sairat (Indian film, Manjule), 31
Sud Side Stori (Italian film, Torre), 1–2, 14

West Side Story (musical, Bernstein), 359
William Shakespeare's 'Romeo + Juliet' (film, Luhrmann), 3, 7
The Taming of the Shrew, 7
  Kiss Me Kate, 359
  The Taming of the Shrew (film, Zeffirelli), 2
The Tempest, 2
  Hag-Seed (novel, Atwood), 232
  Kapālakuṇḍalā (novel, Chatterjee), 381
  'The Sea and the Mirror' (poem, Auden), 382
  La stoffa dei sogni (film, Cabiddu), 1–2
  The Tempest (Dryden/Davenant adaptation), 382
  The Tempest (film, Jarman), 382
  The Tempest (four-person, 80-minute, Nottingham Playhouse and Lakeside Arts Centre), 355, 356
Titus Andronicus, 356
  Titus (film, Taymor), 378
Twelfth Night, 378
Twelfth Night (film, Nunn), 281
The Winter's Tale, 378
  The Girlhood of Shakespeare's Heroines (Clarke), 382
  The Winter's Tale (ballet, Wheeldon), 382
miscellaneous, 382
  Hogarth Shakespeare series, 232
  The Second Best Bed (Rowland), 360
  Shake It Up Shakespeare (Shakespeare writes new play with suggestions from audience), 360
  TV documentary films on teaching Shakespeare to underprivileged students, 362–364
  Upstart Crow (play, Elton, dir. Foley), 360
Shankar, Dilip, 19
Sharda, Saksham, 18
Sharpe, Christina, 39, 112, 121
Sharpe, Pamela, 101
Shaughnessy, Robert, 378–379, 383
Shaw, Ben, 360
Shaw, George Bernard, 52, 313, 335
Shaw, James, 357–360
Shaw, Justin, 188
Shearman, Lee, 64–69
Sheedy, Rosy, 358
Sheeha, Iman, 89–102, 401
Sheffey, Ruthe T., 47
Sheldon, Naomi, 349–350
Shepard, Matthew, 114
Sheppard, Luke, 359

Sher, Antony, 145, 358
Sheriko, Nicole, 137–147, 401–402
Shershow, Scott Cutler, 62, 252
Shrank, Cathy, 279, 280
Shukla, Vinay, 15, 19
Sidney, Philip, 19
  An Apology for Poetry, 120, 191
  Astrophil and Stella, 275, 276, 365
  The Defence of Poesy, 260, 267, 365
  emotions in, 365, 366
  The Old Arcadia, 268
Sierhuis, Freya, 196
Sigona, Nando, 10
Silove, D., 105
Simpson, O. J., 35
Simpson, Robert Ritchie, 185
Sincox, Bailey, 229–239, 402
Sinden, Donald, 55
Singh, Devani, 388–389, 398
Singh, Jyotsna G, 39
Sisson, Charles J., 216
Slater, Ann Pasternak, 120
Slater, Niall, 318
Slights, Camille Wells, 38
Slights, Jessica, 143
Sloan, Anna, 2
Smith, Ali, 229–239, 402
Smith, Andrea, 49–59, 402
Smith, Bruce R., 391
Smith, Cassander L., 242
Smith, Emma, 151, 181
  Othello, 76, 78–80, 86, 87, 88, 204
Smith, Ian, 88
  'Othello's black handkerchief', 69, 150
  'Those "slippery customers": rethinking race in *Titus Andronicus*', 249
  'We are Othello: speaking of race in early modern studies', 12, 41, 106, 149, 188
Smith, Richard M., 101
Smith, Rochelle, 159
Smith, Shawn, 149
Smith, Warren D., 211
Smyth, Adam, 233
Smyth, Albert H., 310
Sokol, B. J., 266
Solomon, Julie R., 202
Somoygi, Nick de, 171
Sontag, Susan, 364
Soto, Isabel, 121
Speed, Samuel, 182
Spencer, T. J. B., 84
Spenser, Edmund, 372, 388
Spicer, Joaneath, 101
Spillers, Hortense, 110, 121
Spivack, Bernard, 138, 140
Spivak, Gayatri Chakravorty, 111
Sprague, Arthur Colby, 137, 260
Sprengnether, Madelon, 80, 149
Stafford, Robert, 244

413

INDEX

Stamatakis, Chris, 2
Stanislavski, Konstantin, 377
Stanton, Kay, 154
Steele, Richard W., 319
Stefancic, Jean, 121
Steffen, Willem, 252
Steggle, Matthew, 90, 91, 92, 369
Steigerwalt, Giulia, 3
Stendhal, 100, 145
Stengle, Jamie, 103, 121
Stern, Tiffany, 139, 211, 212, 221, 235
Stevens, Jenny, 382, 383
Stewart, Alan, 119, 120, 121
Stinney, George, Jr, 120–121
Stockton, Will, 149
Strier, Richard, 153, 198
Strong, Roy, 245
Strowde, Evan, 321
Struever, Nancy S., 202
Stuart, Esmé, 3rd Duke of Lennox, 125
Stubbs, Imogen, 96, 167
Stutesman, Drake, 3
Suetonius, 110, 122, 278
Sullivan, Erin, 196
Sullivan, Garrett A., Jr, 181
Summer, Liyah, 353
Sundberg, Martin, 68
Surrey, Earl of (Henry Howard), 271
Sutcliffe, Walter, 359
Sutton, John, 64
Swarthye, Edward, alias Nigro, 92
Sweeney, Maxwell, 53
Sydow, Carl Wilhelm von, 300
Syme, Holger Schott, 186

Tacitus, 122, 125
Tamiolaki, Melina, 243
Tarleton, Richard, 140, 146
  Tarlton's Jests, 143
Tate, R. Candy, 33
Taviani, Paolo and Vittoria, 1–2
Taylor, Gary, 1
  'The canon and chronology of Shakespeare's works', 129–130
  The New Oxford Shakespeare (2016), 123, 258
  The Oxford Shakespeare: The Complete Works (2005), 125, 291
  Shakespeare: A Textual Companion, 151, 209, 287
  Thomas Middleton: The Collected Works, 95
Taymor, Juliet, 378
Teague, Frances N., 69
Tearle, Godfrey, 51–52
Temkin, Owsei, 186
Tempera, Mariangela, 2
Tennyson, Alfred, 1st Baron Tennyson, 302
Teramura, Misha, 110, 121

Terence, 110, 116
Teresa of Avila, St, 181
Terry, Michelle, 334, 336
Terry-Morgan, Elmo, 46
Theobald, Lewis: *Double Falsehood*, 386
Theocritus, 267–268
Thevet, André, 194–195, 197, 200, 201
Thomas, Vivian, 199, 205
Thomasen (Black maid at court), 92
Thompson, Ann, 153, 385–387, 398
Thompson, Ayanna, 398
  Blackface, 25
  The Cambridge Companion to Shakespeare and Race, 10, 12, 149, 361–362, 374
  '*Desdemona*: Toni Morrison's response to *Othello*', 165
  'Introduction', *Othello*, Arden third edition revised, 36, 58, 106, 112, 121, 144, 145
  Passing Strange: Shakespeare, Race and Contemporary America, 201
  Performing Race and Torture on the Early Modern Stage, 121
Thompson, Garland Lee, Sr, 46
Thompson, Stith, 297, 302
Thompson-Spires, Nafissa, 111, 121
Thomson, Leslie, 211–212, 220
Thomson, Peter, 211, 217
Thorpe, Vanessa, 350
Thucydides, 243
Thurman, Howard, 107
Tietz, Ward, 60
Tilley, Morris Palmer, 99, 202
Tillotson, Geoffrey, 148
Tilmouth, Christopher, 200
Tilney, Edmund, 128
Titian, 98
Tomas, Rebecca, 338
Topsell, Edward, 66
Torre, Roberta, 1–2, 14
Tottel's Miscellany, 269, 271
Trainor, Genevieve, 70
Traoré, Rokia, 111, 121, 165
Traub, Valerie, 148, 242
Travitsky, Betty S., 90
Tribble, Evelyn B., 64, 212, 364
Trivedi, Poonam, 18, 22, 381–382, 383
Tronch-Pérez, Jesús, 208
Trouillot, Michel-Roph, 106, 109, 121
Trump, Donald J., 32–33
Tsakmakis, Antonis, 243
Turner, Edna Godfrey, 49
Turner, Henry S., 139
Turner, Victor, 283
Twomey, Steve, 317
Tyard, Pontus de, 191
Tydeman, John, 53–54
Tylney, Edmund, 128
Tyson, Brian, 124

Ungerer, Gustav, 93
Urkowitz, Steven, 123
Uther, Hans-Jörg, 299, 306

Valencia, Symon, 92
Valentine, Laura, 397
Van Nortwick, Thomas, 284
Vanita, Ruth, 159
Vaporidis, Nicolas, 1, *13*
Varma, Ram Gopal, 19
Vaughan, Alden T., 89, 90, 91, 99, 101, 195
Vaughan, Virginia Mason, 99
  'Before *Othello*: Elizabethan Representations of sub-Saharan Africans', 89, 90, 91, 99, 101, 195
  Othello: A Contextual History, 102
  '*Othello*': New Perspectives, 151
  Performing Blackness on English Stages 1500–1800, 89, 90, 91, 94–95, 98, 99, 106
Velázquez, Diego, 232
Veltri, Giuseppe A., 5, 10
Venkiteswaran, C. S., 22
Verdi, Giuseppe, 359, 381
Vergil, Polydore, 373
Vickers, Brian, 150, 287
Videbaek, Bente A., 137, 140
Virgil, 37, 267–268
Vitkus, Daniel J., 150, 189
Vivash, Marianne, 359
Vives, Luis, 200
Vogel, Paula, 165
Vohra, Pragya, 297
Vuillemin, Rémi, 279

Wade, David, 54
Walcott, Dwane, 334
Wale, Thomas, 370
Walen, Denise A., 94, 96, 157, 160
Walker, Alice, 151
Walker, Greg, 295
Walker, Lynne, 57
Walter, J. H., 215, 216
Walter, Melissa, 149
Wanamaker, Zoe, 96, 167
Ward, Adolphus William, 310
Ward, Allyna E., 295
Ward, Grady, 390
Wardroper, John, 310
Warner, Deborah, 378
Warren, Christopher, 240
Warren, Roger, 295
Washington, Von H., Sr, 46
Wasserman, Krystyna, 62
Waterson, Lambert, 93
Watkins, John, 287
Watts, Peter, 356
Watts, Robert A., 141, 144
Wayne, Valerie, 288, 290, 295

INDEX

Webster, John, 95, 96, 99, 117
Webster, Margaret, 145
Weimann, Robert, 137, 143, 376
Weiss, Hedy, 44
Weissbourd, Emily, 32, 38, 195, 241
Welles, Orson, 25, 315
Wells, H. G., 322
Wells, Stanley, 322
    All the Sonnets of Shakespeare, 367–368, 374
    The Cambridge Companion to Shakespeare Studies, 211
    Othello (Oxford edition, 1986), 171
    The Oxford Companion to Shakespeare, 292
    The Oxford Shakespeare: The Complete Works (2005), 125, 291
    Shakespeare Surveys, 63, 137, 142, 143, 158, 222
    William Shakespeare: A Textual Companion, 151, 209, 287
Welsford, Enid, 138
Welsing, Frances Cress, 105, 121
Werstine, Paul, 209, 212, 221, 224
West, Cornel, 33
West, William N., 139
Wheale, Nigel, 29
Wheeldon, Christopher, 382
Wheeler, David, 315
Whipday, Emma, 77
White, Emma, 357
White, Joseph L., 105
White, R. S., 196, 284
White, Robert, 364
White, Willard, 55
Whitmore, Ian, 64–69
Whittington, Leah, 156
Whyman, Erica, 346–349, 354
Wickham, Glynne, 245
Wieland, Christoph Martin, 191
Wiggins, Martin, 369
Wiles, David, 138, 144, 224, 377, 383
William, George Walton, 94
Williams, Chancellor, 106, 121
Williams, E. M., 346
Williams, Jacoba, 335
Williamson, Elizabeth, 364
Williamson, J. W., 245
Williamson, Nicol, 53
Willis, Deborah, 110, 121
Willis, Sharon, 363
Willoughby, Edwin Eliott, 151
Wilson, Derek, 121
Wilson, F. P., 288–289
Wilson, John Dover, 151
Wilson, Woodrow, 323
Winstanley, William, 278–279
Winterson, Jeanette, 232
Wintour, Patrick, 111
Wise, Charles E., 46
Wittgenstein, Ludwig, 365, 366
Wixson, Christopher, 321
Wolf, Kirsten, 292, 309
Wolfe, Heather, 61, 63
Womersley, David, 259
Wood, David Houston, 203
Woods, Allie, Jr, 46
Worthen, W. B., 22
Woudhuysen, H. R., 272, 385–387, 398
Wray, Ramona, 2
Wright, Charles, 111
Wrightson, Keith, 101
Wringer, Leo, 339
Wroe, Mike, 359
Wurmsser von Vendenheym, Hans Jacob, 126
Wyatt, Sir Thomas, 269
Wyn Davies, Alis, 344, 345

Yachnin, Paul, 143, 164
Yankowitz, Susan, 47
Yarn, Molly G., 396–398
Yong, Bartholomew, 266
Yong, Yik Ling, 73–88, 402
Young, Cynthia, 121
Young, Jennifer, 385, 393
Young, Richard, 183, 184, 185

Zanin, Enrica, 279
Zeffirelli, Franco, 2
Zhangazha, Ashley, 341
Żukowska, Agnieszka, 60–72, 402
Zúñiga, Laura Torres, 189